Florence King

STET, Damnit!

The Misanthrope's Corner
1991 to 2002

To obtain more information, or to order bulk copies for educational
or business uses, please contact:

National Review Books
215 Lexington Avenue
4th Floor
New York, NY 10016

www.nationalreview.com

ISBN: 0-9627841-6-8

Jacket and book design by Luba Myts

PRINTED IN THE UNITED STATES OF AMERICA

To the memory of my aunt,
Ellen Beetham Sprague

STET—Latin for "let stand," a proofreading term that means "Don't change the author's wording."

Damnit—One of Miss King's milder expressions when dealing with proofreaders.

CONTENTS

AUTHOR'S NOTE

WHENEVER people ask me how long I've written "The Misanthrope's Corner" for *National Review*, I am always tempted to reply, "Forever." That's how long it feels, but the correct answer is ten years plus a few months.

I can't remember the exact launch date without looking it up, but I know how it all started. One day in 1990, John O'Sullivan, then *NR*'s editor, called me and said he had just read my second book, *Wasp, Where Is Thy Sting?* which he happened to see in Peter Brimelow's apartment while waiting to go out to dinner.

He said he liked my style and asked me to write "something" for *NR*. The anti-smoking campaign was in the news at the time so I suggested an article in defense of my favorite bad habit. The result was "I'd Rather Smoke Than Kiss," which John loved and turned into a cover story.

Sometime after that, he called again to say that Keith Mano, author of *NR*'s long-running column, "The Gimlet Eye," was leaving, and would I like to take it over? It wasn't on the last page then, just tucked away in the back of the magazine. The length was flexible: anything from a page and a half to two pages of grouchy wit. That was right up my alley so I wrote a couple, but then John decided to turn it into a backpage column using two alternating writers. I became one of them, writing one "Gimlet Eye" a month.

Old-timers will recall that at this time, *NR* did not use bylines. Pieces were signed at the end with a dash, followed by the author's name in a small, discreet typeface. As I told John, this might be tasteful, but when you have two tiny columnists both identified as "The Gimlet Eye," readers would have a hard time telling one writer from another, or even realizing that there were two.

Having just published my eighth book, *With Charity Toward None: A Fond Look at Misanthropy*, I asked John if we could call my half of the column "The Misanthrope's Corner." When he agreed to that, I next asked if I could have a real byline up at the top, instead of lurking in cryptic good taste at the bottom. He agreed to that too, and so the column as you know it today was born.

For the first couple of years I alternated with "The Gimlet Eye." I had several "roommates," as I called the other columnists (all men), but they kept leaving to go on to other things. We ended up with a turnover problem, so in mid-1995 John decided to abandon the dual-column arrangement and asked me if I would be interested in having the back page all to myself. I said yes, and thereafter "MC" appeared in every issue.

Writing a backpage column turned out to be the best thing that ever happened to me as a writer. Before, when I wrote for other magazines or newspapers, I had to meet an approximate word length, give or take a couple of hundred words either way. If I came up short they could stick in an ad or some filler copy; if I spilled over they could use a "jumpline" (i.e., "continued on page 86"). But a backpage column has nowhere to jump; it must fit exactly on one page, and there can't be anything else on the page with it.

To see how this stricture benefited me as a writer, look at the preceding paragraph: I initially wrote "if I went a little bit over," then saw that I could save four words by changing it to "if I spilled over." This is called "tightening" and it does a lot more than save space: It's the key to the clarity, simplicity, and economy that define the classical style. The great masters of classicism were obsessed with tightening, none more than Nicolas Boileau, whose 17th-century how-to guide for writers, *L'Art Poétique*, advises: "Polish, repolish, every color lay; sometimes add, but oftener take away."

Gradually I developed a tightening technique. If I found myself running long, the first thing I did was read through to see if I could find any instances of the word *very*. It's the most useless word in the English language and can always come out. More than useless, it is treacherous because it invariably weakens what it is intended to strengthen. For example, would you rather hear the mincing shallowness of "I love you very much" or the heart-slamming intensity of "I love you"?

Once I got rid of the *verys* I hunted down words ending in *-ly* because they violate the literary fashion sense. Good writing is Coco Chanel's little black dress, but -*ly* adverbs are women who wear too much jewelry and pin flowers in their hair. I like to rip them, tear them, strip them off until there's nothing left but sleek, chic verbs.

Tightening helped me measure my "hemlines" just right. I found that a perfect column fit came to 109 lines on my computer, so if I ended up with 110, deleting a *very* or an -*ly* here and there could pull up a whole line and get me back to the magic 109. (So can using "found" instead of "discovered," as in the second sentence of this paragraph.) Every little bit helps; I don't know whether "one person can make a difference" and I don't much care, but I do know that one word can, and writing a backpage column has trained me to find it.

The everpresent need to make the most of a limited space has also helped me express myself better than I ever did before. I was never prolix or sprawly, but the open-ended format of books inculcated some bad habits, such as compound adjectives. A book ends where it ends, but a column ends at the bottom of the page, so I had to learn that "hit-or-miss" and "catch-as-catch-can" are best rendered as "uncertain," or better yet, "iffy."

Columns like mine are sometimes called "think pieces," but that heralds a fatal level of relaxation. The backpage is no arena for cosying up to a subject with a view toward leisurely cogitation. I take my cue from Horace's *Ars Poetica*: "Capture your reader, let him not depart, from dull beginnings that refuse to start." In other words, write a good lead, the shorter and snappier the better. Ideally, it should be no more than three lines long, and must state what the column is about, or as Boileau decreed: "Assure that from the opening of the scenes, the first will tell us what the author means." It's not unusual for me to spend several hours on an opening paragraph before I get it exactly right, but that is as it should be. A writer's first duty is to be easy to read, and that means taking time and going over and over your work until you get all the kinks out—what Samuel Johnson meant when he said: "What is written without effort is read without pleasure."

These and other self-editing techniques were not perfected overnight, which is why this collection, when read consecutively as a book, is what reviewers call "uneven." That's the lit. crit. way of saying that the later columns are far superior to the earlier ones. No one knows this better than I. When I first discussed this project with *NR* I thought about revising the earlier columns, but then I decided to leave them alone because they showed how I've "grown." That's another lit. crit. term, something like "growing in office," except it's bad when politicians do it but good when writers do it. A volume containing ten years of a writer's output fulfills the important purpose of illustrating the development of a long-running column, and the increasing ease, spontaneity, and confidence of its author, so it would be dishonest to revise anything.

To make sure nobody else fiddled with it, I composed a "warts 'n' all clause" and asked *NR* to insert it in our agreement:

"FIDELITY TO ORIGINAL TEXT: *NR* guarantees that the columns reproduced in the Book shall be reprinted exactly as they appeared originally in the magazine, with no editorial changes whatsoever. This stipulation shall include any factual, grammatical, or spelling errors committed by the Author that were not changed or corrected by the *NR* editorial staff at the time of the original publication."

That should cover the dangling participle I seem to rememember. I finally got tired of looking for it, but I could swear it's in there someplace. See if you can find it.

Florence King

1991

A MERICANS are so emotionally fragile that soon we will have to be carried around in plastic bubbles and fed with an eye-dropper.

Entertainment's time-honored rule, "Always leave 'em laughing," has given way to "Always leave 'em secure." The last segment on news shows now features individuals who do strange things for muzzy reasons.

A man stands on a corner during rush hours to wave at passing motorists. A woman in a state that renews drivers' licenses on the driver's date of birth stands outside the motor-vehicles office singing "Happy Birthday" to everyone who goes in. A man cuts trees on a mountain slope into the shape of a heart visible for miles so that weary travelers can "take heart": Christ of the Andes meets Burma-Shave.

Asked why he does what he does, the subject shrugs, smiles indulgently at the self-evident question and replies, "I love people."

The jumpy, black-and-white commercial featuring a tormented soul wringing his hands because his long-distance phone system has ruined his life is usually a prelude to the "Family Of . . ." solution. Americans work for a Family Of, are insured by a Family Of, get their mufflers and brake jobs from a Family Of, buy and sell homes through a Family Of, get moved cross-country by a Family Of. Buy something from a mail-order house and you will become a member of the Damark Family; return it and you will become a member of the UPS Family. What all these firms really are selling is the perfect security of High Middle Ages feudalism, with the CEO as lord of the manor.

Like medievalists keeping a track of good and evil spirits, we divide people into "threatening" and "non-threatening." The latter, incredibly, is the person who falls upon a total stranger with a bear hug.

We constantly flash hideous smiles involving both rows of teeth. It isn't a smile, it's a rictus; the mouth simply drops open like a crocodile's. The banks of the Wabash have turned into the banks of the Nile.

We meet hostility with salvos of bigger and better niceness and warnings of "There's more niceness where that came from." This is not a virtue. Sunny congeniality and people who can't function without it cause more strain than a fistfight. Moreover, it's completely insincere: these smiling Jacks are simply trying not to get sued by someone even more insecure than they are.

How did we get this way? It began when the first settlers wondered, "Are the natives friendly?" and then found themselves looking at stoic Indians. Unsmiling faces have struck terror in the American heart ever since.

Next we acquired the melting pot. There are so many different kinds of people in America, with so many different boiling points, that we don't know how to fight with each other. The set piece that shapes and contains quarrels in homogeneous countries does not exist here.

The Frenchman is an expert on the precise gradations of *espèce de* and the Italian knows exactly when to introduce the subject of his mother's grave, but no American can be sure how or when another American will react, so we zap each other with friendliness to neutralize potentially dangerous situations.

The heritage of aloof warmth that prevails in countries old enough to have had a hierarchical past is not available to us, so we are forced to leap feet-first into cloying intimacy. The tender formality of "*gnädige Frau*" makes old ladies easy to respect, and stiff Englishmen long ago learned to express intrasex affection with "my dear Smith," but Americans have nothing to call each other except first names.

Insecurity produces a strange form of treason in the American heart. In our desperation to believe we are not hated personally, we relax and bask in relief when terrorists say, "It's the American government we hate, not the American people."

Our insecurity keeps us from solving our most pressing problem: crime. The few unequivocal souls who are willing to unleash the necessary curative measures shun politics because they know they would never even get nominated, much less elected. Captive of maudlin priorities, America instinctively shrinks from the only kind of personality capable of solving the problems we constantly deplore. Instead we vote for candidates with whom we "identify," i.e., those whose eyes plead, "Like me."

Trying to please others emotionally instead of ethically is the basis of insecurity. Buttering people up carries an ever-present threat of sliding on grease, so insecure people tend to be dangerous. The millions who are currently fiddling with self-esteem while America burns would do well to examine an entry in the journals of James Gould Cozzens:

> The seamy side of human nature. You must be careful how you treat people as your equals. The average person has much more respect for you if, even though he resents it, you make it plain to him that you consider him of no great importance. The line may be a thin one, but if you're nice to him beyond what he, perhaps subconsciously, feels are his deserts he will much more often than not despise you for it.

By contrast, the aloof are sturdy oaks with a host of admirable if paradoxical virtues. Good manners build high walls, so those averse to intimacy make exceedingly pleasant "ships that pass in the night." As long as you remain a stranger they will be your friend forever.

They are punctiliously law-abiding, not because they are good people, but because good people are much more likely to be let alone. The aloof don't commit crimes because they know that prison life is communal. Moreover, long before he arrives at the ultimate communality of prison, the criminal must live a gregarious life. Most crimes require a gift of gab and an ability to inspire trust in the victim. Aloof people never become con artists or fences; as for child molestation, in order to molest a child you must first be in the same room with a child, and I don't know how perverts stand it.

The freemasonry of the insecure that surrounds illness in America explains why we are a nation of hypochondriacs. My worst nightmare is being a patient in a hospital and coming to the attention of volunteer strokers who serenade me with "You'll Never Walk Alone." I am sick—of compulsory gregariousness, fevered friendliness, we-never-close compassion, goo-goo humanitarianism, sensitivity that never sleeps, and politicians paralyzed by a hunger to be loved. Therefore this column will be devoted to winning one for the sonofabitch.

August 12, 1991

MERICANS react to wit as Dracula to the Cross. Wit is undemocratic. Its standard modifiers, *rapier* and *stiletto*, were weapons of Renaissance aristocrats. The last witty civilizations, eighteenth-century France and England, were also the last aristocratic civilizations. After them came the deluge of democracy and the rise of the middle class. Both found their natural homes in America, where the double entendres and bons mots of biting wit fell victim to the desire for respectability and the restraint demanded of the socially mobile. Pulling oneself up by one's boot-straps is a good way to choke; living in dread of saying the wrong thing, Americans rejected wit and embraced that favorite of the self-made man, the tall tale.

Next came the melting pot. Diversity may be good for the body politic but it spells disaster for the funny bone. Wit and its handmaidens, satire and parody, require a strong point of view, a common ground, and a ruthless audience—conditions that conflict with the miasmic national squish we call "consensus."

Diversity has truncated American wit by depriving us of a national comic figure that everyone knows in his bones. The French have the miser, the Irish have the biddy, the Italians have the jealous husband, the English have the doggy lady, but what does America have?

Paul Bunyan, Dagwood Bumstead, Babbitt the traveling salesman, the Southern senator, the Jewish mother, the Boston Brahmin, and the good ole boy—to name just a few. It sounds like a rich comedic heritage, but one man's aberration is another man's ethos; what is funny to millions of Americans leaves millions of others bemused.

Our diversity also kills the spontaneity that wit must have. Our worst nightmare is that backbone of wit, the generalization. Samuel Johnson's quip, "If you give a Scot something, he'll either break it or drink it," would cause mass cardiac arrest in the land of the free and the home of Jimmy the Greek. Jesse Jackson and Ted Kennedy would go on *Nightline* and wail, "Some Scots are clumsy drunks but the vast majority of Scottish-Americans are well educated and responsible citizens."

There goes your sprightly discourse. Proper timing is impossible when compassionate liberals keep popping up and saying *some*.

We are so afraid of giving offense that we have turned into oral basket cases. Not daring to trust each other to filter sweeping statements, we clutter up our speech and writing with awkward adverbial easements like "general-ly speaking" and "by and large," dragging in carefully documented excep-tions on the grappling hooks of equivocation, getting so tangled up in what we are trying *not* to say that we commit wit's bugbear, unintentional humor, e.g., "Americans of all nationalities."

Wit goes for the jugular, not the jocular, and it has no "healing power" whatever. It is, said Dorothy Parker, "the humor of the indifferent," so it is bound to be anathema in a nation where headline writers see nothing funny about "HEARTS GO OUT TO BRAINLESS BABY." In our frantic pursuit of sensitivity and compassion, we reject corrosive rejoinders in favor of the bland heartiness and tense jocularity of the toastmaster's gentle dig.

Even on the rare occasion when some American actually gets mad, he instinctively tries to blunt his remarks with broad humor. Asked his opinion of Jerry Falwell, Barry Goldwater replied, "Somebody should kick him in the ass." It was supposed to be harmlessly funny, but as Somerset Maugham observed, "There is not much kick in the milk of human kindness." In a similar exchange, America's last aristocrat produced a witticism that would have won plaudits from Samuel Johnson. Asked his opinion of William Jennings Bryan, the frosty Charles Francis Adams said: "He is in one sense Scripturally formidable, for he is unquestionably armed with the jawbone of an ass." Today such a remark would be a candidate for damage control.

Another enemy of wit is American "pragmatism"—i.e., laziness. The pinnacle of wit is the *jeu d'esprit*—wit for its own sake, with no purpose but sheer joy in words. The *jeu d'esprit* should be popular in a country obsessed with games, but it collides with our preference for the quick 'n' easy. It takes a lot of reading and reflection to come up with puns, maxims, epigrams, and ripostes, but Americans can't be bothered. Our wish to be clever without going to the trouble of being learned is reflected throughout our culture, most notably in *Cosmopolitan* magazine, whose notorious italics are a substitute for archness.

The witty woman especially is a tragic figure in America. Wit destroys eroticism and eroticism destroys wit, so a woman must choose between taking lovers and taking no prisoners.

As with stilettos and rapiers, the problem is one of adjectives. A woman who is "sharp," "cutting," and "surgical" is disturbing to men. Wit also demands attitudes that have been bred out of women for centuries. Taught to say, "I love people" and "sex is beautiful," the average woman finds it impossible to summon the sang-froid, contempt, impatience, sarcasm, pessimism, and bawdiness required to crack ice at thirty paces.

If she is married, total solemnity is but a husband away. America's leading expatriate, Henry James, deplored our Noah's Ark complex, saying: "An amiable bachelor here and there doesn't strike me as at all amiss, and I think he too may forward the cause of civilization."

Wit flourished in the conversational salons of the eighteenth century largely because they were not attended by "couples." But American spouses go everywhere together and spend the evening signaling each other what not to say with daggerish stares, elbows in the ribs, kicks under the table, and hisses of "Shut up!" lest a clever riposte arouse fear and loathing in all the other married couples who go everywhere together.

These are the same people who reply "a good sense of humor" in surveys about the qualities they look for in a mate. They lie. The man who says he wants a wife with a good sense of humor actually is looking for that quality of benumbed resignation found in women known as "good sports"; the woman who says she wants a husband with a good sense of humor actually is looking for someone who won't be mean to the children.

The biggest reason why Americans hate wit is the clouding effect it has on sexual identity. Wit is aggressive and therefore masculine, but it is also waspish and therefore feminine. Therefore, witty people are a little funny.

September 9, 1991

L OGOS has two meanings in Greek: *word* and *reason*. Together they add up to *logic*—except in America, land of post hocky ergo propter hocky, where Occam's Razor wouldn't cut butter.

The professoriat likes to claim, "We teach students *how* to think, not *what* to think." This does not mean studying logic; it means staring at a photograph from *Erskine Caldwell's America* and writing on "what it makes me feel." The average college student's mental rigor is consequently so soft that you can almost hear the squish. He likes Voltaire's "I may not agree with what you say but I will defend to the death your right to say it," but tell him that its premises are masochism and chaos, and he will nod sagely and say, "That's what America's all about."

We have heard so many politicians say, "Let us go forward and put it behind us," that we no longer recognize idiotic statements. The newest bromide, "Whites are no longer prejudiced against blacks as blacks; prejudice is now a matter of class rather than race," ignores the fact that prejudice cannot go from "no longer" to "now" and still be called prejudice. It becomes *post*judice, defined as: "the compliment that common sense pays to experience."

Contesting James J. Kilpatrick's stand that honoring Martin Luther King Jr. with a national holiday puts him on a par with George Washington, an op-ed writer in my local paper argues: "Dr. King has already replaced George Washington on the most widely used individual intelligence test for adults, the Wechsler Revised. There used to be a question on the old test, 'When is

Washington's birthday?' That question has been deleted and a new question has been added, 'Who was Martin Luther King Jr.?'"

This is the fallacy, *petitio principii*, or "begging the question," an argument that fails to prove anything because it merely takes for granted what is to be proved: because King has replaced Washington on an IQ test, he should be honored with a national holiday. It is also an example of *ad verecundiam*, or "to the shameful," an appeal to an unsuitable authority, in this case the authors of the IQ test.

Challenging Kilpatrick's suggestion that we wait fifty years until all the FBI files on King become available, the writer argues: "I don't want to have to wait for the 25th anniversary commemorative march on Washington in order to answer my children's question, 'Who was Martin Luther King Jr.?' And I don't want them to wait for fifty years before they can tell their children who Martin Luther King Jr. was."

This is an *ignoratio elenchi*, or "ignorance of the connection," an argument that overlooks the fact that there is no connection between the premise and the conclusion: no one is stopping this man from telling his children anything he likes whenever he likes. It is also an example of *ad misericordiam*, "an appeal to pity."

Feminism's way around logic is *quod erat demonstrandum*—that which was to be demonstrated has been demonstrated, or: It's true because I said so. *Lear's* combines QED with *ad verecundiam*: "But testosterone, the so-called male hormone that's produced in the testes and adrenal glands of men and in the ovaries and adrenals of women, is for both sexes the most important hormone in sexual desire. In their book *Human Sexuality*, William H. Masters and Virginia E. Johnson point out that although men produce 12 to 16 times as much testosterone as women, there's no evidence to suggest that women in general have a lower sex drive than does the generality of men." They admit testosterone is the aphrodisiacal hormone, yet they insist the trickle of it meandering through women is as powerful as the rivers of it pouring through men.

L OGIC has acquired an elitist reputation, but ordinary people used to have bona-fide debates that drew them quite naturally into moral philosophy. Take the "pencil test," which originated in the days when legless World War I veterans sold pencils on the street.

The question: "Should you take the pencil?" sparked rigorous colloquies between people who had never heard of syllogisms or fallacies. One school of thought held that an honorable person gave the veteran a nickel but refused the pencil. The other held that it was more honorable to take the pencil because that made the veteran a businessman instead of a beggar.

Whichever side people took, the argument followed a straight track from veteran to pencil to nickel to benefactor. Today's incessant "dialogues" on ethics get routed onto the spur line of "bad judgment," where the aura of wrongdoing gets uncoupled from the wrongdoing itself.

"Bad judgment" is now the sin of record, morality's scene stealer, standing alone in all its short-circuited glory, with no before and no after, no cause and no effect, no wheat and no chaff. Suggest that bad judgment leads to a decision that leads to an action, and that it is the *action* that constitutes the moral lapse, and you will be nabbed by the Compassion Police. Was your congressman found *in flagrante* with a Doberman on the steps of the Capitol? He's not guilty of bestiality. Bestiality has nothing to do with bestiality, it was just bad judgment, and if you don't agree, you're judgmental.

QED.

October 7, 1991

L ET US NOW praise insensitivity before it's too late. The old adage that sticks and stones may break our bones but words can never hurt us is not true. Words do hurt, and can therefore help in stanching what the New Euphemists call "a breakdown in the social order."

The Sensitivity Industry started with a 1941 movie, *Blossoms in the Dust*, starring Greer Garson as Edna Gladney, the Texas woman who campaigned to have the word *illegitimate* removed from birth certificates. The movie's message that the word *illegitimate* follows people through life is dramatized in the account of the character who commits suicide rather than produce her bar-sinistered birth certificate when applying for a marriage license with a man who does not know her origins. The climax comes when Miss Garson, before the Texas legislature, delivers her famous clincher line, "There are no illegitimate children, only illegitimate parents!"

I first saw *Blossoms* at age six in Washington's Tivoli theater, then the jewel of a solid middle-class neighborhood and now an abandoned, rat-infested shell in a neighborhood where illegitimate births run rampant. When I saw the movie again recently, I decided Edna Gladney's good intentions had paved a good stretch of the road to hell that we are currently traveling.

What the movie does not show are the unmarried girls of that supposedly unenlightened era who must have thought twice about having sex because they did not want to ruin the life of the child that might result. But because of Edna Gladney and our memories of the glamorous Greer Garson in the movie role, girls of my generation grew up saying earnestly, "I would *never* go all the way before I'm married, but *if* I did, and *if* I got pregnant, I would give the baby up for adoption so it could have a fresh start."

That sounds highly moral in our present age of abortion and "single parenting." But had we known that there was no such thing as a fresh start, and that *illegitimate* would be stamped on that baby's official papers forever, our pseudo-sophisticated earnestness would have died a-borning.

"Social pressure" has lately acquired a bad name and been blamed for the epidemics now plaguing us, but we had better start giving it a good name soon because in an unlimited democracy dominated by mass media, the law of social pressure is the only law that people can be counted on to obey.

Edna Gladney has done her questionable work. *Bastard* now means "Hollywood agent" and there is no going back, but insensitivity is not dead. We can still cramp a few destructive styles with some choice colloquialisms that were mothballed in the compassionate Sixties.

For starters we could make *drunk* a noun again and call drug addicts *dope fiends*. Next, stop talking about "significant others" and "relationships" and start talking about *shacking up*. If we use this richly descriptive phrase often enough, the other-directed will be loath to live together without benefit of clergy. When that happens, we can re-educate them to the mature and sophisticated pleasures of the discreet affair, defined as: "When somebody goes home afterward."

The retraining of silver-haired politicians and CEOs who divorce their life companions to take second or "trophy" wives can be achieved by reviving the kind of jokes that the Sensitivity Industry calls "mean-spirited." Jocular references to "the foolish age" used to discourage many older men from acting out their fantasies lest they end up in a punchline. But now, smarmy compassion has joined forces with pseudo-science to produce solemn pronouncements like "self-realization" and "mid-life crisis" that give such men a perfect excuse to jump the fence. The solution, therefore, is to start telling the one about the old goat and the spring chicken.

"PUTTING people down" is now the deadliest of sins but the practice has always kept society functioning in a reasonably civilized way. For years the traveling-salesman joke protected unescorted women from unwelcome attentions because the traveling salesman was such a famous symbol of crudeness that any woman could get rid of any man merely by calling him one. Nowadays he's a "sales executive," which only encourages him.

The iceman joke saved bored housewives from themselves. The punchline scene of the husband coming home and finding a block of melting ice on the kitchen floor was so firmly embedded in the national psyche that people dreaded getting involved in an afternoon amour: the human spirit recoils from the idea of turning into a cliché. Today such a comedy of errors is given the humorless name of "encounter" and credited with saving marriages.

"Social pressure" itself is a euphemism; its real name is *shame*. Current levels of social chaos suggest that nothing but a revival of merciless mockery will turn the tide. Compassionate liberals who declared war on putdowns should look around at the cesspool that has resulted from our refusal to judge people harshly and reflect on the wise words of George Orwell: "Jokes about nagging wives and tyrannous mothers-in-law . . . do at least imply a stable society in which marriage is indissoluble and family loyalties taken for granted."

November 4, 1991

WELCOME to America the Mealymouthed. The most revealing moment in Anita Hill's Oktoberfest came when her supporter, Judge Susan Hoerchner, said in her mincing, teacher's-pet voice, "I have never known Anita to express anger." It was supposed to be a compliment.

Watching the hearings, it was hard to believe feminists had once urged women to get mad. Learning how to explode was the cornerstone of their early "consciousness-raising." Twenty years ago, when I lived next door to a feminist who conducted assertiveness-training workshops, my walls shook with bellows of "This steak is tough!" and "I demand to speak to the manager!" But feminists fell all over each other in their rush to excuse Anita Hill for not nipping Clarence Thomas's libido in the bud and telling him where to get off the very first time he allegedly talked dirty to her.

Their explanation? Womanly forbearance. Women don't *do* that sort of thing. Women swallow their pride and remain silent for fear of losing their jobs. Women meet aggression with salvos of forbearance and dire threats of "There's more forbearance where that came from," but they never, ever come out swinging.

It was not always thus. The Anita Hill in a popular Gay Nineties ballad was a waitress who could easily have lost her job when she lowered the boom on two traveling salesmen making suggestive remarks to her:

> *My mother was a lady,*
> *Like yours, you will allow,*
> *And you may have a sister*
> *Who needs protection now.*
> *I've come to this great city*
> *To find a brother dear,*
> *And you wouldn't dare insult me, sir,*
> *If Jack were only here!*

That would never play in Mealymouthed America, where even laxatives are gentle. Today the spunky waitress would be called what we call everybody who shows the slightest propensity for lowering the boom: "out of control." It's the newest catchphrase, having sprung up around the same time as that softener for the declarative sentence: "Hey." Few Americans use declarative sentences now, but when they wish to express a strong opinion without appearing to do so, they kick off with "Hey" to achieve a tone of good-natured recalcitrance, as in George Bush's frequent, "Hey, I'm not against that." We also use "Hey" to soften other people's declarative sentences. If certain unequivocating authors, now dead, were to come back to life and tour their books, this is what we would hear:

"Ed, you've been pretty hard on the barbarians, but, hey, don't you think that extending the frontiers of the Empire gave the Romans a chance to meet new people?"

"Oswald, you said a lot of critical things about the West, but, hey, don't you think it's God's country?"

I submit that last month's sexual-harassment World Series was only incidentally about sexual harassment. It was actually about our national dread of getting mad and throwing a fit.

WE DREAD tempers for three reasons. The first has to do with the primacy of psychiatry in our national life, and the insidious potential danger it poses to us all. In a story about the reaction of the people of Utah to Senator Orrin Hatch's part in the Thomas–Hill hearings, *Washington Times* reporter Valerie Richardson quotes an anti-Hatch letter sent to the State Democratic Party by an Anita Hill partisan: "As Mr. Hatch's temper flared, his eyes glared, and his voice rose, he himself demonstrated he was the one mentally and emotionally disturbed."

There you have it. Don't get mad because "out of control" has joined the long list of American euphemisms. It means *crazy*, and if enough armchair psychiatrists pin the rose on you, people will believe it. The blood libel is out and the Rorschach libel is in.

The second reason is more fun than a barrel. Losing one's temper is undemocratic—really, it is. Think of sword fights and dueling oaks, think of the Southern hothead known as the "*beau sabreur*," think of the Southern belle. These people are not peasants because peasants don't have the kind of nostrils that "flare," nor do they carry the riding crops and walking sticks that help get things started.

Getting mad, really mad, is aristocratic, which is elitist, which is verboten. The American object of your un-American explosion will become what is now known as "shaken," because getting mad, really mad, is like using "whom" in an offhand remark in the supermarket. When egalitarian American eyes are not smiling they are flashing inchoate and inarticulate alarm like heat lightning. A nostril-flaring explosion probably wouldn't help a victim of sexual harassment in today's political climate. A Southern-belle tantrum, properly thrown, used to bring a man to his knees, but it was class, not gender, that did the trick. Today, class is more of a damsel in distress than women ever were.

The third reason Americans dread loss of temper is simple. Hey, the country's on the brink of a civil war, and we're trying to delay it as long as possible. The Day the Niceness Stopped is fast approaching, but look on the bright side: At last I shall have been avant garde.

December 3, 1991

1992

I DON'T make New Year's resolutions but I do make lists, e.g., People I'd Shoot If They Weren't Already Dead.

Seeing how much of our social degeneration can be traced back to Jean-Jacques Rousseau is like seeing how many words can be formed from *antidisestablishmentarianism*. In both cases the answer is: a lot.

Rousseau's *Discourse on the Origins of Inequality* praised "natural man" over his civilized counterpart, who, Rousseau believed, had been ruined by knowledge, culture, luxury, and "insincere" polished manners. Civilization, said Rousseau, really ought to be torn down and all laws abolished so that everybody could be happy like the simple peasants who placed heart over head, emotion over logic, nature over culture, soul over all.

He sent a copy to Voltaire, who replied: "I have received, sir, your new book against the human species, and I thank you for it. No one has ever been so witty as you are in trying to turn us into brutes; to read your book makes one long to go on all fours. As, however, it is now some sixty years since I gave up the practice, I feel that it is unfortunately impossible for me to resume it."

Esconced as the man of the hour by bored French arisocrats who considered him the last word in radical chic, Rousseau turned out a plethora of how-to and self-help treatises on subjects ranging from music to hiking to breastfeeding, writing and talking so much about primitive scenes, mother's milk, and peasant warmth that breastfeeding became a national fad, even among women of the nobility who had always used wetnurses.

He had fathered five illegitimate children by a scullery maid, but, having gained entrée into Parisian society, he did not want to advertise this plebeian connection, so he dumped all five little ads in a foundling home and then wrote a book on how to raise children. *Emile,* as it was called, laid out a program of "natural" behavior over rigid discipline and "freedom" from stifling rules.

Rousseau's philosophy can be summed up by the buzzword of his day: *sensibilité*—what our age calls "getting in touch with your feelings." His methodology consisted of crying in the woods. Nature was particularly well-suited to his overwrought vocabulary. The woods were *wild, untamed, primitive, lush.* The woods were full of *nooks, copses, verdant canopies, umbrageous illusions.* They were also full of sobbing Rousseau fans but never mind that, you could be *alone with nature* in the woods, *lose yourself* in their beauty, *let it wash over you,* sleep *naked* in a *bower* and *become as one* with nature's torrents. Afterward, you could write about your sylvan crying jag and claim to be *drunk with emotion,* a cliché that is with us still.

His novel, *La Nouvelle Héloïse,* equates sincerity with manic depression ("I love you as one must love, with excess, madness, rapture, and despair"). His friend Diderot, one of the so-called Enlightenment philosophers, also endorsed coming apart: "Move me, astonish me, unnerve me, make me tremble, weep, shudder, and rage."

If Rousseau's war on rationalism did not actually cause the French Revolution, it certainly set the tone. The neoclassicist Blaise Pascal had penned the famous line. "The heart has its reasons of which reason knows nothing," but he said it and got out, leaving posterity an exquisitely balanced epigram. Rousseau said it and kept on saying it over and over in purple prose until his followers were as conditioned as Pavlov's dogs. His message of *I feel, therefore I am* ushered in a self-indulgent primitivism that spilled over into political anarchy and gave the Jacobins an excuse for the Reign of Terror.

R OUSSEAU destroyed forever man's pride in self-mastery. His glorification of "natural" behavior foretold the Freudian theory of repression, the hippie credos of "Let it all hang out" and "If it feels good, do it," and the coarse sexual honesty called "getting down and dirty."

The self-realization and human-potential movements that have shredded our social fabric in the name of "feeling good about myself" are outgrowths of the oxymoronic mass individualism that Rousseau promoted in his *Confessions,* which contains the Western world's first mantra: "I am not made like anyone I have seen; I dare believe that I am not made like anyone in existence. If I am not better, at least I am different."

"A special type of sincerity," wrote Irving Babbitt, "is itself an outcome of the Rousseauistic movement. It seems to be assumed in certain quarters that almost any opinion is justified provided it be held with sufficient emotional vehemence."

The politicized nervous breakdown is a standard feature of Greenpeace junk mail. "Listening to five hundred dolphins shrieking in panic as they fight and gasp for air . . . standing by helplessly as living dolphins were dragged aloft thrashing and flailing in terror" sounds just like the heroine of *La Nouvelle Héloïse* in full throttle.

Crying in the woods is back, too. The New Man sobs over his tom-tom; female love addicts let it wash over them in that indoor version of the verdant canopy, the confessional talk show. The cheapness and utter lack of class that ooze out of Oprah, Donahue, and Geraldo are the recycled *sensibilité* of Jean-Jacques Rousseau, who dumped human dignity in a foundling home.

January 20, 1992

THANK GOD I'm over the hill. The only heat I have left comes from hot flashes, my promiscuity is confined to the words "one size fits all," and I buy my white cotton unmentionables at Boadicea's Retreat, not Victoria's Secret. Nothing described at the Palm Beach rape trial could possibly happen to me now unless we're invaded by some Slavic republic whose soldiers aren't fussy.

Since it's a dead cert that Private Slobov Slobovovich is not much of a talker, I could concentrate on trying to shoot the sonofabitch without first having to endure what the sexual revolutionists of Palm Beach kept calling "an interesting conversation." The message of the William Kennedy Smith trial was crystal clear: Liberation has replaced the sweet nothings of romance and the feisty wordplay of sexual tension with the boring drone of equal partners.

The most telling moment in the accuser's testimony came when she said she never misses a chance to discuss her daughter's medical problems whenever she meets a doctor socially. She elaborated on this with a snooty, pathetic pride in her ability to meet doctors as equals, leaving no doubt that she actually believed this made her irresistible to Doc Smith.

Is there a doctor alive who doesn't dread such females? They do the same thing when they meet lawyers at parties. Trying frantically to be what women's magazines and self-help books call "interesting," they babble about asthma and torts, sublimely unaware that they are dragging their captive professional men on a busman's holiday.

Nowhere in the reams of testimony given by Smith and his accuser do we find the slightest hint of clever repartee on the night in question. Risqué banter elevates squalid situations, as when the satyrish Napoleon III asked, "What is the way to your heart?" And Eugénie replied, "Through the chapel, Sire."

Scintillating verbal foreplay is the way to a man's mind, the fortress a woman must breach if she wants to make him aware of her "as a person," but Willie Smith's accuser just didn't get it. Stuffed with propaganda about professional equality and sexual freedom, she droned on about acute mycoplasmal tularemia and then started digging in his pants.

This is not Madame Récamier trading *bons mots* with Talleyrand, nor even Hepburn trading *bons mots* with Tracy. It's Messalina with a master's degree.

Palm Beach proved that the English duchess who reputedly said "Sex is too good for the common people" was on to something. It takes more than a trust fund to make a lady. Despite her money, Willie Smith's accuser is an updated version of the put-upon figure of Victorian melodrama, the "little shopgirl."

There are million of them in every age—today's version is That *Cosmopolitan* Girl—and they invariably get enmeshed in sexual tragedies because they lack the personality trait a woman must have if she intends to be a truly liberated, bona-fide hussy: a bandit streak.

Falling somewhere between eccentric and sociopath, the female bandit is tough, but it's not the slutty toughness of Madonna or the desperate, doomed toughness of the protagonists of *Thelma & Louise*. It's the toughness that used to be called "stouthearted." She also has a flair, a style, a whiplash outrageousness found only in natural aristocrats.

Nell Gwynn displayed the bandit streak when she stepped out of her carriage into the howling anti-Catholic mob that had surrounded it and said, "Calm yourselves, my good people. I am the Protestant whore." Edwardian actress Stella Campbell displayed it when George Bernard Shaw snidely asked her what her new husband was like and she came out with the matchless rejoinder: "Six-foot-four and everything in proportion."

FOR FEMALE banditry on the witness stand we can do no better than Caroline of Brunswick, consort of George IV, who was called to testify in the House of Lords when the King, who was secretly married to his mistress, Maria Fitzherbert, tried to divorce her. Asked whether she had ever committed adultery, Caroline shot back: "Only when I slept with Mrs. Fitzherbert's husband." Palm Beach could have used a rapier thrust like that. Caroline also could have punched up the droning seminar on stained intimate garments with her famous boast to Lord Malmsbury: "I change my drawers once a year whether they are dirty or not."

Female banditry is an elite sisterhood but America is entirely capable of making a level playing field out of a bed, so all the little shopgirls think they too can make it to the majors. The democratization of banditry owes much to *Cosmopolitan*, which stands in relation to true seductiveness as Robespierre to the Ancien Régime. You can bet that Willie Smith's accuser and her friend Anne Mercer read it faithfully. Listening to their testimony, we heard not the hiss of the serpent of the Nile, but Helen Gurley Brown's deathless exhortation to the daughters of the Common Man: "If you're a little mouseburger, come with me. I was a mouseburger and I will help you."

February 17, 1992

I N ALL the incessant babble about the suddenly noble "middle class," no one has mentioned the subdivision of it that has done so much to wreck America: the High-Strung Class.

Mind you, I'm "high strung" in the lower-case sense. All writers are, so are all artists and musicians, but we have an excuse: we're *supposed* to have sensitive nerves. If we didn't, we couldn't do what we do. Known as "creativity" or "artistic temperament," it has ever been the despair of those foolish enough to fall in love with us and demand our undivided attention. We may hurt those closest to us, but we don't hurt the whole country, and in the final analysis we give more than we take.

The High-Strung Class is something else altogether. It is composed of thin-skinned pseudointellectuals who make their living second-guessing people completely different from themselves.

America's leading Strungleur was Henry David Thoreau, who took it for granted that "the mass of men lead lives of quiet desperation" because the mere thought of holding down a steady job set his teeth on edge. Our era produced Betty Friedan, an unhappy Smith graduate who polled other unhappy Smith graduates and concluded that the housewives of America were clamoring to leave their "comfortable concentration camps" for careers.

The High-Strung Class crawled out from under the rocks during the

New Deal and never went back. The original Strungleurs often were the first members of their families to go to college; they are now second- and third-generation college graduates, but fear of the lunch bucket and the time clock dies hard. Laboring now as government planners and think-tank philosophers, they have turned "I couldn't stand it" into public policy. By "it" they mean everything they have escaped: factory jobs, housewifery, "overcrowded" homes (i.e., each kid doesn't have his own room), or living, like Dorothy Parker, in shabby residence hotels where even dishes and cutlery are furnished and the management discourages what Strungleurs call "individual touches" and bona-fide intellectuals call "clutter."

Strungleurs are too dense to grasp a simple fact: we who work with our minds could not function without a plodding working class and traditional housewives. These are the people who produce the strong families that make for an orderly society—what Strungleurs call a "productive environment" and I call "peace and quiet."

Because they work in places where "hostile" rivals destroy each other's research notes, Strungleurs are walking spider webs of sensitivity. Unable to conceive of having the kind of job you can forget about after work, they assume that brawny machinists need stress management workshops and transcendental-meditation breaks, too. The "human potential" movement of the Seventies, when companies trained managers to "relate" to employees, placing blissful concepts of selfhood over production schedules, is a typical Strungleur contribution to the economy.

Florence Nightingale had no patience with Victorian England's High-Strung Class, whose passion for improving the lot of the dregs of society she dismissed as "poor-peopling." In this area, our Strungleurs have killed the thing they claim to love by their pursuit of the Pyrrhic victory of social leveling.

High civilization needs seedy poets, artists in garrets, and philosophers who are poor by choice. The intellectual pretensions of the High-Strung Class make them the logical champions of bohemianism, yet the poverty programs they conceive and relentlessly administer have destroyed its natural milieu.

One of life's intriguing paradoxes is that a hierarchical social order makes cheap rents and outré artists' colonies possible. Raffish bohemian neighborhoods flourished in the days of racial segregation; under integration the artistic poor have no safe places in which to create. The urban intellectual enclaves once so hospitable to them are gone with the windy blessings of egalitarian Strungleurs. If America lacks a vigorous culture it is partly because studios and ateliers have become crack houses.

For that matter, we don't even have ivory towers any more. The machinations of the High Strung have turned charming absent-minded professors into politically correct, tenured paranoids with total recall.

T HE MASS of mankind like their lives the way they are and ask only that sensitive thinkers leave them alone. As James Gould Cozzens wrote: "When Thoreau judged that most men lived lives of quiet desperation I think he failed to consider the fact that, by a merciful provision of Providence, most men have little or no more imagination than an animal. Good reasons for despair may be all around the average man, but he won't see them."

That is less cruel than telling women their homes are "comfortable concentration camps" and then "helping" them escape by shredding the social fabric of an entire country in the feminist manner. Less cruel, too, than the incredible statement by labor leader Samuel Gompers, who must have been a closet Strungleur: "The promise of America for the laboring man is the promise of someday no longer having to work with his hands."

March 16, 1992

D URING the 1988 presidential campaign a female reporter produced a unique take on the so-called gender gap. Women did not like George Bush, she said, because "he reminds them of their first husband."

I've never had a husband, so I must look elsewhere for the source of the intense antipathy he rouses in me. He reminds me of a boy I dated in college who wore one black shoe and one brown one and pretended to be surprised when someone noticed. He also trippped on purpose when entering restaurants, slid jauntily onto barstools and deliberately missed, and replied "Where?" when someone said "Hello."

The comparison is accurate as far as it goes, but I sense that America is saddled with someone much worse than my old beau. George Bush is increasingly coming to resemble Czar Alexander I (1801–1825), whose personality mystified the foremost figures of his age.

Napoleon: "I find that there is a piece missing in his character, but I cannot discover what it is."

Chateaubriand: "The Emperor of Russia has a strong soul and a weak character."

Metternich: "He is the Sphinx of the North."

Alexander's father was Catherine the Great's mad son, Paul, a flat-faced sadist who liked to boast, "No one can say I am led around by the nose because I don't have one."

Catherine, the most doting of grandmothers, called Alexander her "deliciousissimus individual," declared that he had a "crystal soul," and hired two tutors to turn him into what she called an "enlightened despot." Frédéric de la Harpe, an idealistic liberal intellectual, was in charge of the enlightenment; a Cossack general with the blood-and-guts name of Saltykov was in charge of the despotism.

After Catherine's death, Paul's brief, brutal reign triggered a palace revolution, but Alexander, who by this time was accustomed to two opposing views of everything, could not make up his mind whether to join it. As the assassins closed in on his screaming father, Alexander sat on the edge of his bed trying to decide what to do.

He spent the rest of his life being all things to all men. Called upon to deal with some of Europe's most macho leaders, Alexander suffered attacks of inferiority in their presence, often displaying what seemed to be compulsive silliness, as when he asked Lord Grey to submit "a plan for the creation of an opposition in Russia." The astonished Grey replied: "If you really want to cause trouble for yourself, all you need do is set up a parliament."

When the question arose of what to do with the defeated Napoleon, Alexander was determined to be nice. Elba, he insisted, was far but not *too* far. When Napoleon subsequently escaped from Elba, a petulant Alexander whined to the Duke of Wellington: "Why did you let him escape?" The Iron Duke, not troubling to hide his contempt, snapped: "Why did you put him there?"

Possessing a handsome face but strangely curvaceous hips, Alexander was that rarity: a male tease. Preferring the chase to the prize, he flirted with the lubricious Queen Louise of Prussia, then panicked on realizing that she expected him to deliver, and locked his bedchamber door in case she came after him.

The most important woman in his life was Baroness Julie de Krudener, the Aimee Semple McPherson of the Bourbon restoration, who held salvation teas for the great in her Paris home. There, amid mystical hijinks and incoherent invocations, Alexander found God and dreamed up a kinder, gentler Realpolitik based on Christian love that he called the "Holy Alliance." Metternich called it "one of the periodic evolutions of the Czar's mind," and Castlereagh dismissed it as "sublime nonsense."

He didn't stay Saved for long. Returning to St. Petersburgh, he fell under the influence of a reactionary nobleman named Arakcheyev and abandoned religion for autocratic repression. Next he decided, out of the blue, to move from the capital to a remote abandoned fort on the Sea of Azov called Taganrog, where he hurled himself into the task of hanging curtains, laying carpets, and turning the bleak redoubt into a home.

T HERE IS NO telling what he would have done next, but soon after moving to Taganrog he died—at least we think he did. Rumors arose that he ran off to Siberia and became a holy man, and that the body of a soldier who resembled him was used in the funeral. It is a tribute to his unquenchable feyness that Alexander the Tease lured three governments into opening his coffin to see if he was in it. His nephew, Alexander II, went first, and allegedly transferred to a common grave the unroyal remains he found. Next, Alexander III took a peek, and finally, the Soviets. Both said the coffin was empty.

Alexander's most recent biographer, Henri Troyat, wrote:

> He smiled at everyone, shared the most contradictory opinions with equal graciousness, flattered people he would have liked to slap in the face. . . . The instability of his mood was almost pathological. He acted only on nervous impulse, passing from enthusiasm to prostration, from openness to trickery, from superficial pleasures to profound meditation.

Except for the last, it's George Bush. Russia and America share the dubious honor of having produced the ultimate anomaly: a nerve-wracking Sphinx.

April 13, 1992

T HE MORE things change the more they remain the same. Hillary Clinton, that little female gnome standing next to Skeezix, that wolfish dominatrix of the Dem's den, that smiling barracuda waving her arms off, is none other than an updated version of my old college nemesis from the Fifties, the "great girl."

In pre-feminist times the Great Girl was the female equivalent of the Big Man on Campus. She got her sobriquet because everybody kept saying what a great girl she was; a *really great* girl, with a *great* sense of humor, meaning she was good at knock-knock jokes.

Striving for healthy averageness, good adjustment, and earnest purpose, the Great Girl made a point of being "well-rounded." She majored in Soc or

Psych because "All you have to do is read," and chose classes with professors who gave nothing but multiple-choice exams. She was a whiz at them; if a homicidal maniac had jumped out of a dark alley yelling "Sartre!" she would have replied "Umm, existentialism" without turning a hair.

Uncerebral but as smart as the proverbial whip, the Great Girl belonged to one of those female honor societies with a name like The Valkyries that required a B average and emphasized "service to the school," meaning you couldn't get in unless you had so many extracurricular activities that the printer had a nervous breakdown trying to get them all on the same yearbook page with your picture. She never met a committee she didn't like, so she had little cuts on her fingers from making pasteboard signs with razor blades, and if you couldn't find her, all you had to do was follow the crepe-paper trail.

Having been told by legions of progressive teachers that she was a "natural leader," the Great Girl was always rushing off to meetings, in winter arriving at her destination with cold teeth from having smiled all the way across campus. Yet despite her surface friendliness there was something of the Thugee about her. She liked to organize group sings and square-dance lessons to "bring people out of their shells," and God help the clams who did not join these agapes. She was president of the Girls' Dorm Council, so you might find yourself hauled up before her cosy little star chamber and being told, "We know you want to do better and we're here to help you."

The Great Girl was always engaged by her senior year—it was on her list of Things To Do—and her fiancé was always a Big Man on Campus: two wrongs make a Mr. Right et Ux. This alliance brought her to the attention of corporate recruiters who checked out the future wives of their potential executives before closing the deal. Two minutes in her presence and they could relax, secure in the knowledge that she would never become the Emma Bovary of Corning Glass. Not that she wasn't "attractive." It was just that she poured all of her ferocious energy into the kind of extracurricular activities that can be listed in a yearbook; she firmly believed that whenever a boy tried to pet, you should distract him by toasting marshmallows, and it showed.

The Great Girl is the type for whom self-help books like *The Sensuous Woman* are written. She is constitutionally incapable of taking the author's advice to have sex in a bathtub filled with Jello, but she would have a grand time making the Jello, running back and forth between stove and tub with bowl after quivering bowl, exclaiming, "Golly, isn't this fun?" It would remind her of the contests and races she organized for Spring Carnival, and the Christmas when she made a hundred pounds of fudge in the housemother's kitchen.

T HE Great Girl of the Fifties became a suburban housewife, baking cook-ies, volunteering, and chairing meetings in an extension of her college days. This was her métier and she enjoyed it, but she was also a conformist, so when feminism came along she ran with the crowd just as she always had, and switched from Feminine Mystique to Tort Mystique. Everybody's going to law school? It must be the *in* thing to do, so the "leader" exchanged her Tupperware for Blackstone and turned into Hillary Clinton.

I tell you, it's the same woman: I'd know that snippy little face anywhere. She gets better grades now, and the crepe-paper trail is now a fax-paper trail, but if you tapped her you would still get an echo. The liberal press claims Hillary Clinton is "defining" the role of future First Ladies, but it's the same old Great Girl trick of "leading" where everybody else is already going. *Newsweek* wondered whether America was ready for such a "self-confident" woman, but it's not true self-confidence. It's the Great Girl kind, in which the confidence resides not in the self but in the feminist model on which the self is based: Ayn Rand would love it.

If Bill Clinton is an adulterer, I don't blame him. As Alice Roosevelt Longworth said of another Democrat: "He deserved some fun—he was mar-ried to Eleanor."

May 11, 1992

W E CAN comprehend the big things that are happening to America by examining the little thing that happen to us. Recently a Georgia literary festival asked me for a pair of my shoes to hang on their Christmas tree, and a North Carolina political campaign wanted "something used by you personally" for a fund-raising auction.

Collectors have always sought the personal artifacts of performing artists, alive or dead. I remember when bobby-soxers ripped buttons off Frank Sinatra's coat, and now their grandchildren do the same to Michael Jackson. Writers, being less exciting, used to have to be very, very famous and very, very dead before the scavengers got interested. Why, then, would anyone want my detritus?

Commenting on Kitty Kelley's celebrity exposés, the scholarly biogra-pher Justin Kaplan said, "I'd guess that a large part of the outrage generated by Kelley's book comes from something we don't like to acknowledge: our dependency on totemic figures." Nowadays mere autographs are for earth-

lings. As religion dies we are replacing the Calendar of Saints with a calendar of celebrities—complete with relics.

In religious centuries, when everyone from the King down to the most
brutish peasant held the same unquestioning belief in the soul's immorality,
fame was unimportant and, indeed, did not really exist as we know it today.
The common people of France were permitted to wander in and out of
Versailles and watch the King at his banquet table. He ate in public so that the
people could see, not the King, but God's representative on earth.

These public displays were in no way comparable to photo ops; they
were quasi-religious rituals. When people said excitedly, "I saw the King!" it
was not the same as "I saw Liz Taylor!" The latter is always followed by *in
person,* but the idea of seeing the King in person would have been a contradiction: It was his spiritual, not his corporeal, presence that mattered.

In today's secular world only celebrities, whose names will "live," can be
certain of attaining the immortality that the humblest medieval serf took for
granted. The ultimate expression of materiality, *in person*, is an ironic
reminder that now only the famous have souls.

It's Calvinism all over again, a hard nut to crack, but nothing is too hard
for the American Dream. Everybody's gotta right to be the Elect, so murder
a famous person and become a famous murderer.

The essence of fame is the approval of others, always desired by
Americans, so become a politically correct camcorder tattletale like George
Holliday, who vidoetaped the Rodney King beating and went on to savor the
joys of giving press conferences and interviews. Of course he acted solely out
of a burning commitment to civil rights, not because the name *Abraham
Zapruder* was burning in his brain, promising a footnote's worth of celebrity
in the history books. The same noble purpose surely motivated all the people
who subsequently sent sales of video cameras soaring nationwide, and the
vigilant citizen in Fort Worth who videotaped Officer E. J. Parnell beating
one Ernest Anderson on July 5, 1991.

I suspect that even our productivity problems and the epidemic of
"human error" plaguing the workplace are caused in part by our obsession
with fame. The worker who misses a cog in the wheel because he's brooding
over being a cog in the wheel produces an American car.

A house of ill fame divided against itself cannot stand. America has
never grasped the difference between celebrity and stature. In his introduction to *The Education of Henry Adams*, James Truslow Adams wrote that
America destroys her best families by withholding, in the name of democracy, the means of preserving them: hereditary titles that create a ruling class.

Thus the superior gene pool that was the Adamses survived for only three generations before being rejected in favor of liberty and stature for all.

Ironically, the three-generation rule has been democratized until it now applies to virtually all Americans. After a family's first college graduates produce the first crop of doctors and lawyers, it probably won't rise any higher unless exceptional physical beauty or creative talent are present. These are the inborn ingredients of fame but that doesn't faze the American Dream. "Everybody's gotta right to be beautiful" is the driving force behind the plastic-surgery fad; "Everybody's gotta right to be talented" has produced the Indiana high school where tone-deaf kids play in the band in the name of self-esteem.

The brutal fact is, fame is all that America has left. Learning is gone, honor is gone, culture is gone, and civilization itself is down and counting, so we cling to spurious, democratized fame like drowning swimmers to a life raft. Telling ourselves that barbaric societies do not produce exalted celebrities, we can kid ourselves into thinking that we are still separating the wheat from the chaff.

T HE NADIR of the fame game was reached on March 5, 1991, during the Gulf War, when CBS News featured the mother of Melissa Rathbun-Nealy, the first female POW, talking on the phone with her daughter. Significantly, the soundbite chosen by the news editors was the mother's excited question, "Do you know how famous you are? The whole world knows you."

Word for word, an almost exact replication of the Black Mass Annunciation scene in *Rosemary's Baby*.

June 8, 1992

I GET the distinct impression that feminists don't like strong, healthy specimens of womanhood. They're forever ransacking history in search of "role models," but they always seem to ignore the fine strapping girls and focus on the kind who fit my grandmother's definition of a good movie: "She dies in the end."

Take, for example, their virtual blackout of Eleanor of Aquitaine (1122–1204), Queen of France and England, who lived to be 82 in the twelfth century, *sans* mammograms, *sans* Pap smears, *sans* everything. You would think such an indestructible old rip would do feminists proud, but they have avoided her like the plagues and poxes she never caught. Their aim is to make women "feel better about themselves," so they obsess over the welts and weals of Fredegund of Thuringia, dead at 17, a victim of medieval diaper rash whose chastity belt killed her.

The same thing has happened in the realm of mental health. The women's studies crowd has snubbed Charlotte Corday, the slip of a girl with nerves of steel who single-handedly conceived and carried out the assassination of Jean-Paul Marat during the French Revolution. What do feminists want? Charlotte stabbed a white male in his bathtub, for God's sake, and was such a brick on the scaffold that the executioner, infuriated by her unfeminine stoicism, slapped the face of her severed head.

But bricks don't sit well with feminists. They much prefer nervous wrecks like Alice James, or those frayed women writers like Jean Stafford, who, in the words of one critic, "read her glowing reviews behind locked doors at Payne Whitney."

Woman as picture of health had a brief day in the sun during the early years of feminism, when Ashley Montagu's *The Natural Superiority of Women* was still in vogue and there was no one else to quote. For a while feminists crowed that women live longer than men, are less susceptible to color-blindness and dyslexia, and withstand cold temperatures better, but they soon began to sound hollow and dispirited, if not downright bored. This was not the stuff of girltalk.

Then came the abortion debate, the crisis over the dangerous side-effects of the Pill, the crisis over the dangers of IUDs, and the crisis over the dangers of synthetic estrogen. This was more like it. Describing their aches and pains at congressional hearings opened up a heretofore unimaginable world of pelvic politics; instead of laying a guilt trip on one man in the privacy of their homes, they could wear down a tableful of men on television.

It took the Los Angeles riots to dislodge silicone implants as the lead story on the evening news. Night after night we watched rubber-gloved hands squeezing liquid beanbags and performing blood-drenched open-breast surgery during what Sam Donaldson calls "the dinner hour." At congressional hearings, as women recited the history of their lumps and described in detail how it feels to be a vessel of leaking, seeping, dripping silicone, the faces of the trapped congressmen left little doubt that they were secretly thinking what Hemingway came right out and said: "It's being sick that makes them act so bloody awful and it's because they're sick that you can't treat them as you should. You can always trade one healthy woman in on another. But start with a sick woman and see where you get."

As a final fillip, Sam's Dinner Hour carried a story that Berengaria of Westphalia and Elfrida of Northumbria would be hard put to match: the Texas woman who was in such silicone agony that she slashed her breasts and threatened to yank out her implants unless her insurance company agreed to pay for the operation.

L.A. burned down the same week this story broke. Remember that, the next time somebody starts talking about "root causes." If South-Central had to be incinerated to get Gundrun of East Anglia off the tube, then so be it.

Female invalidism, real or simulated, has had a much too long and successful history to pick up its chaise longue and go quietly into the feminist night. When the Victorian woman pretended to be sick to avoid sex, illness as female metaphor took root in the male mind. Woman's physical weakness came to imply spiritual strength, as if a compensating Nature had drained all the health from her body and transferred it to her soul, thus making her morally superior to the sturdy male—a dichotomy that came to full flower in the character of Melanie Wilkes: "She never had any strength, she never had anything but heart."

T HIS KIND of quasi-sainthood is looking better and better in today's sexually savage world, where the warning Margaret Mead issued in 1970—"Women's liberation has to be terribly conscious of the danger of provoking men to kill women. You have quite literally driven them mad"—has come true.

Illness is to women what "fear-grinning" is to baboons: a way to disarm dangerous Alpha males. If women are once again instinctively using illness as protective coloration, it is a subconscious way of saying that they want their moral superiority back. That they seem to be placing special emphasis on pelvic and mammary disorders should come as no surprise. After all, when you think about it, there is nothing more feminine than "female trouble."

July 6, 1992

B ASTILLE DAY found me thinking about one of my favorite fictional misanthropes.

"Why do I drink, Mr. Darnay? I am a disappointed drudge, sir. I care for no man on earth, and no man cares for me. So we are not much alike in that particular. Indeed, I begin to think we are not much alike in any particular, you and I."

Sydney Carton and Charles Darnay of *A Tale of Two Cities* look alike, but the resemblance ends there. Sydney is a nihilistic cynic, while Darnay is a

Rousseau-stuffed humanitarian who is so guilty over being the scion of the noble St. Evrémonde family that he gives up his titles, changes his name, and moves to England to earn his living by his own labor.

On the Channel boat Darnay meets Lucie Manette, whose father has just been released from the Bastille, where he was imprisoned by Darnay's evil uncle, the Marquis St. Evrémonde. The sight of the luscious Lucie makes Darnay's guilt rise, so he confesses his passion for the American Revolution. Overheard by his uncle's spy, he is arrested for plotting against George III. Defended by barrister Sydney Carton, he is saved from hanging by Sydney's brilliant cross-examination.

Lucie marries Darnay, and Sydney resigns himself to his unrequited love for her. Some years later, after the French Revolution breaks out, the earnest Darnay blunders again. He receives a letter from his old tutor, who has been arrested as a member of the Evrémonde household and condemned to die on the guillotine for aristocratic sympathies. The tutor has no aristocratic sympathies: it was he who stuffed Darnay's head with Rousseau. Moreover, he's already dead, murdered by the Defarges as soon as he finished writing his summons to Darnay—the letter was a ploy to lure Darnay, the last of the St. Evrémondes, back to France.

Cynical Sydney instantly grasps the danger Darnay will be in if he returns to France in the middle of the Terror, but the idealistic Darnay never gives it a thought. After all, didn't Rousseau say that all men are brothers? Didn't Rousseau say that tearing down society would make everybody nice? Certain that the Jacobins will like him for giving up his titles, changing his aristocratic name, and getting his root causes right, he walks blithely into their trap.

He is promptly arrested for being a St. Evrémonde and sentenced to death despite liberal Dr. Manette's ingenuous efforts to save him. The night before the execution, Sydney, wiser in the ways of human nature, bribes and blackmails his way into Darnay's cell, chloroforms him, assumes his identity, and takes his place on the guillotine.

The question is, why? Ostensibly he did it out of love for Lucie, gladly sacrificing his wastrel's life to save the man who could make her happy. As touching as this interpretation is, it ignores the egoism that fairly oozes out of Sydney's interior monologue as he looks into the future from the steps of the guillotine:

"I see *her* with a child upon her bosom, who bears my name. . . . I see that I hold a sanctuary in their hearts, and in the hearts of their descendants, generations hence. I see her, an old woman, weeping for me on the anniversary of this day. I see her and her husband, their course done, living side by side in their last earthly bed, and I know that each was not more honored and held sacred in the other's soul, than I was in the souls of both.

"I see this child who lay upon her bosom and who bore my name, a man winning his way up in the path of life which once was mine. I see him winning it so well, that my name is made illustrious there by the light of his. I see the blots I threw upon it faded away. I see him, foremost of the just judges and honored men, bringing a boy of my name, with a forehead that I know, and golden hair, to this place—then fair to look upon, with not a trace of this day's disfigurement—and I hear him tell the child my story, with a tender and faltering voice."

But what of Charles Darnay? He is mentioned in Sydney's last thoughts only by implication, as the necessary progenitor of those later generations who will pay their respects at the Place de la Concorde. How did Darnay feel when he found out what Sydney had done?

D ICKENS, as upbeat as George Bush, would undoubtedly say, "I don't want to get into that," but the darkling temperament can't resist rewriting the ending.

Living the rest of his life with the knowledge that Sydney died for him must have finished the job Rousseau started and turned Darnay into Colman McCarthy in knee britches. It's impossible to think that the perverse Sydney did not know this would happen, or that he did not foresee the tensions that would arise between Darnay and Lucie as they lived out their long and honorable lives with his ghost always between them.

Picture Eleanor Clift as Lucie and you've got it. Each time Colman McDarnay proved incapable of raising anything except guilt, the Blessed Decibel would slap herself on the forehead like the candy eater in the V-8 commercial and shriek as only she can: "I coulda married Sydney!"

August 3, 1992

A T THE Japanese war trials of 1946, the defunct empire's former propaganda minister, Shumei Okawa, inadvertently made a good pun. Leaping to his feet, he screamed in his uncertain English: "I hate United States! It is democrazy!"

America can democratize anything. Imagine for a moment that we revived the "natural aristocrat" theory held by the Founding Fathers.

Somebody would go on *Nightline* and say, "Everybody's gotta right to be a natural aristocrat." Then it would start: the Natural Aristocrat Task Force, the Natural Aristocrat Resources Center, the Natural Aristocrat Hotline, the Natural Aristocrat Crisis Team, Natural Aristocrat Head Start, Natural Aristocrat Counseling, Natural Aristocrat Awareness, Natural Aristocrat Month, "Natural Aristocrat Minutes" delivered by Sally Struthers and Nick Nolte, a best-seller called *How to Help Your Child Be a Natural Aristocrat*, and articles in *Cosmopolitan* blurbed "What if He's Not (Sob!) a Natural Aristocrat?"

Or imagine that we came up with a counterrevolutionary measure called "Your Money or Your Vote." Only voters would pay taxes; everyone who gave up his right to vote would be exempt. A good deal, right? Wrong. The vote would become a rich man's toy like the early automobile. Voting would become an activity of the select few, proof that you, unlike the Joneses, can afford to pay taxes.

Here come the ads. A sexy blonde draped across a voting booth. A huge ballot spanning a golf-course lake: "Call this number to apply for The Vote. We'll take your application over the phone. The Vote will show them that you've arrived." A voting booth held under water: "It still works."A voting booth that goes from city councilman to President in eight seconds: "This is not your father's voting booth." A voting booth sitting in the middle of nowhere—in the desert surrounded by mesas, or peeping through a gauzy mist in the Alleghenies—while a voice-over says, "This could be you. Go for it."

Meanwhile, self-sacrificing mothers keep chanting, "I'd scrub floors to send my kids to a voting booth," and Southern good ole boys save their money so they can be half the voter their daddy was. To achieve the American Dream of poll taxes for all, the amount of tax a citizen must pay to qualify as a voter gets lower and lower. This is called a "level voting field." The NAAVP is founded, along with a United Voter Fund whose slogan is: "A vote is a terrible thing not to have to pay for when you can't."

The pressure mounts until Congress passes Votefare, wherein the government gives money to people who can't afford to pay taxes, so they can use it to pay taxes, so they can vote.

If you think the foregoing riffs are exaggerated, let me remind you that several equally unbelievable adventures in "democrazy" have actually occurred and succeeded. The democratization of lesbianism, for instance.

For centuries the traditional or classic lesbian was always a spinster and often a tweedy intellectual, with a stark glamor that intrigued men and women alike. With no left-wing pressure from organized homosexuality, the traditional lesbian tended to be a conservative—or even a red-in-tooth-and-claw Tory like *Well of Loneliness* author Radclyffe Hall—because she was an elitist in the sense that elitism was defined by the Irish writer Frank O'Connor: "Yet contact itself is the principal danger, for to marry is to submit to the standards of the submerged population, and for the married there is no hope but to pass on the dream of escape to their children."

This is the woman feminists destroyed when they pressured the media for positive images of lesbians.

As open enrollment struck the Sapphic elite, we got the lesbian detective, the lesbian ghost, the lesbian vampire, the possessed lesbian, the lesbian next door, the lesbian with a heart of gold, and the lesbian with cancer.

WE ALSO got the Jason's Mommy lesbian. After her divorce, Jason's Mommy discovered not only her own potential but some other woman's as well. Having between them enough children to start a kindergarten, they decided to live together and practice family values. When some member of the big, bad Establishment threatened this happy home with a pink slip or an eviction notice, the whole ménage went on *Donahue* to tell *their* story.

As the loathsome little Jason raced up and down the aisles, the studio audience got the soothing idea that the children of lesbians are seen, heard, nasty, brutish, and short, just like everybody else's. By the end of the show everything seemed so normal that the audience forgot that the guests were lesbians. To leave viewers smiling through their tears, Jason was given the last word, piping the fade-out with, "Mommy and Aunt Betty love each other."

The traditional lesbian is no more. In the name of "democrazy," feminists rolled her up in her tweeds, weighted her with her scholarly tomes, and threw her overboard. The last thing she heard was, "Everybody's gotta right to be a lesbian."

"The Regency," wrote Louis Kronenberger, "was a way of life at the expense of life in general." Nonsense, democracy is. Each time I see President Bush peel down to his shirtsleeves before making a speech, Beau Brummell looks better and better.

August 31, 1992

INDIA's great tradition of immolation is called suttee. America's is called huggee.

Huggee is a lustless lust for flesh-on-flesh popularized by Jimmy

Carter after he was grabbed by Leonid Brezhnev at a treaty signing. Nobody remembers the treaty but everybody remembers the batty, pole-axed grin that came over Mr. Peanut, like an old-maid librarian finally getting a taste of life, as the Russian crushed him in an ursine embrace.

Huggee got an additional boost from the "ethnic awareness" craze of the Carter Seventies, when Americans liberated themselves from what was then known as "our Anglo-Saxon heritage." Sexual restraint had to go, and it did. Now, Anglo-Saxon having metastasized into "white male," the axe has fallen on emotional restraint.

It has just about disappeared. Soon everyone will have hugged everyone else, and then it will be only a matter of time before one of Oprah's guests displays a jar containing a do-it-yourself extrauterine conception, and Oprah hugs the jar.

Huggee is a political form of "*pusillanimata*," or "scrupulosity," the spiritual hypochondria of the Middle Ages in which the sufferer was haunted by doubts about the strength of his piety. Americans are haunted by doubts about the strength of our squish. Are we caring enough? Loving enough? Spontaneous enough? Warm 'n' fuzzy enough?

George Bush is photographed with his arm slung around the shoulders of Illinois Governor Jim Edgar, who is holding hands with Mrs. Edgar as the three stroll through the state fair. A female caller on the Larry King show kicks off with, "I love you, Ross," and Perot replies, "I love you, too." Bill Clinton, remarking that he nearly dislocated his shoulder while shaking hands, suddenly realizes that he has registered a complaint and quickly adds: "I think it's important for us to touch as many of the American people as we can."

Of the two political conventions this summer, the Republican Huggee, I regret to say, was the more revolting. Watching it made me feel as if something hot and wet were crawling all over me. I expect Democrats to fling themselves about and emote like peasants because that's what they are, but the spectacle of maudlin Republicans is unbearable in view of the centuries-long conservative tradition of frostiness. Seneca on health care: "Scorn pain; either it will go away or you will." Talleyrand on family values: "A married man will do anything for money." Ambrose Bierce on children's rights: "Study Herod, madam, study Herod." Not a code word in the lot.

Huggee pyres are everywhere. The Weather Channel features a "Pain Index" illustrated by a "respiratory distress map" with different colors for gasping, coughing, and sneezing, as well as a Heat Index and a Wind-Chill Factor to make conditions worse than they are so we'll have yet another excuse to comfort each other with hugs.

Just as the best-laid fires of suttee sometimes fizzle out, the lustless lust of huggee occasionally ignites, as D.C. Mayor Sharon Pratt Kelly discovered when Jack Kent Cooke patted her on the behind as they were hugging good-bye after a meeting about relocating the Redskins. As Mrs. Kelly later explained at a press conference, the hug was par for the course. "It was, you know, the way people hug each other," she said with a casual shrug. It was the pat she objected to.

If for some reason you can't hug, you can do the next best thing and slap high-fives. This congratulatory fleshly contact, which started as a light tap between athletes who didn't have time for a formal handshake, has become strangely intense lately. Even in once-staid golf, players rear back like dinosaurs and slam their palms together in a horrendous crash, as if compelled to establish their bona fides as red-blooded touchers.

It's even worse in baseball; a few years ago a player sprained a finger this way and ended up on the DL. Slapping high fives is now a tedious, touchy-feely ritual involving the whole dugout—not just for homers, but for routine things like tagging up and scoring from third after a fly. For that matter, the fan in the stands who catches a foul slaps high-fives with every other fan within reach. Should he miss and accidentally slam somebody in the face, as I saw happen once, he can tell himself that an unconscious stranger is a friend you haven't hugged yet, and fall to.

HUGGEE is but one aspect of a larger trend toward unrestrained behavior, which is why the orgasmic grunts of players in televised tennis matches are deliberately amplified: like *"La Donna è mobile"* in *Rigoletto*, it's "the good part."

Familiarity breeds democracy, so the crowning glory of huggee is the indiscriminate *tutoyer* adopted during the French Revolution, when the formal *vous* was banned in favor of *tu*. English has an intimate form of "you," but most Americans are unaware of the grammatical connotations of "thee" and "thou." Let us pray that they don't figure it out.

Meanwhile, you're nobody till somebody hugs you—so I'm worried. Suppose I, a spinster and an only child, decided to go into politics? Who would hug me? Mr. Buckley? Mr. O'Sullivan? Not on your tintype. That's what I like about this magazine: Nobody ever says a word about "the NATIONAL REVIEW family."

October 5, 1992

ELECTION-YEAR twitch is a disease of print commentators who have watched too many talking heads on TV. True, we can take half of our cable bills as a tax deduction, but it's not worth putting up with:

Dan Rather, whose membership in the "cultural elite" proves that America really is a classless society.

PBS shows in praise of the Year of the Woman that lead in and sign off with Renaissance music to soothe the savage beastie in the tote-bag set.

The Bobbsey twins of *Capital Gang*, Mona Charen and Margaret Warner, cavorting in their hotbeds of moderation and sinking deeper and deeper into the Geraldine Fitzgerald part of sympathetic best friend.

Liberal guilt so unfettered and naïve that it resembles that universal tragicomic dilemma of childhood: lying in bed idly peeling off the mattress tag, only to find that it says DO NOT REMOVE UNDER PENALTY OF LAW.

Male liberals with BORN TO FAX tattooed on what passes for a biceps.

The feminist who inadvertently promotes the ne plus ultra of choices: If a man went to bed with her, should he put the bag over her face or her personality?

Worse, several must-watch public-affairs shows have been running the same GE ad for almost three years. In it we see all of Hungary being flooded with light as Liszt's Hungarian Rhapsody mounts to a frenzy and delirious Hungarians exclaim, "Everything is wonderful, I'm so happy. . . . It's like a dream, a beautiful dream."

GE's "new" ad, on for about a year now, is not calculated to soothe the nerves of anyone who writes for a living: "This is the man who turned on the light that lit up the room where he worked on the computer that was linked to . . ." and ad infinitum, a hideous run-on sentence that non-union teachers used to call "The House That Jack Built." I have watched these commercials so many times that I frequently find myself singing, "We Bring Good Things to Life!" I can also sing it in Japanese, thanks to the one about flooding Tokyo with light.

BURNOUT LEADS to nightmares, and I had one—about, of all things, the art-appreciation course I took as a college sophomore in 1954. I was sitting in the classroom taking notes on the slide lecture when suddenly the statue on the slide turned into a real statue. It got bigger and bigger, filling the room with stone until there was no space left. The air grew thin; we were walled in and starting to suffocate—

I woke up. Shaking, I lit a cigarette and tried to analyze the dream, but I had no associations to go on. I have led an art-free existence except for seeing *Moulin Rouge* and *Lust for Life,* and even then I got impatient with the painting montages, wishing they would get on with the story. We dream about things that matter to us, not things that make us shrug. I took the Art Ap course solely to fulfill the humanities requirement; art is the only area of high culture that bores me, so dreaming about it is like dreaming about the only vice that bores me. I've never dreamed about gambling, so why did I dream about art?

I found out the next day while I was watching Bill Clinton on C-SPAN. My memories of sophomore Art Ap sharpened, until it dawned on me that late September 1992 was no different from late September 1954: I was still looking at the same thing.

Art Ap was one of those relentlessly chronological survey courses in which you miss a hundred years if you drop your pencil and lean down to pick it up. By late September we had finished with Egyptian tomb paintings and Assyrian ziggurats and gotten to the sculpture of the Archaic Age, specifically the *kouros* or *kouroi* (??), male statues with bodies still locked in the rigid Egyptian manner, but whose faces contained a hint of the glorious triumph of the human spirit that would reach apogee in the golden age of classicism yet to come.

The hint was a tip-tilted little smile, as if the sculptor had made a vee of his fingers and pushed up the corners of the mouth while it was still wet, or still soft, or whatever, and let it set into the Great Stone Simper of my professor's slides. Or maybe he gave it two final whacks with his chisel, one at each corner, to create a monolithic moue that would last through eternity. However they were made, the simple-minded expression they all bore had a name. It was called, said the professor, the "Etruscan smile."

Clinton's Etruscan smile is everywhere. It's in the picture of the teddy bear on my dentist's ceiling, strategically placed so that patients can see it when the chair is tilted back. It was on the face of the eager-to-please witness in South-Central L.A. who said he saw "four gentlemen throwing rocks through windows." It's the smile of Crown Prince Rudolf, of whom historian Betty Kelen wrote: "That such doubts of himself occurred habitually to him is written plainly on his face, in the quivering, imploring glance of his eye."

I was going to sit out the 1992 election but at last I have found that elusive "reason to vote for Bush" everybody has been looking for: If you can't trust an Etruscan—don't.

November 2, 1992

M Y RECENT remarks on "Huggee" drew so many supportive letters that I shall continue my assault on emotional warmth.

Of the six candidates for national office in the late campaign, five were named Bush, Quayle, Clinton, Gore, and Stockdale. It was a veritable festival of Anglo-Saxons, but you never would have known it. A true Wasp would just as soon break out of an egg or rise from the sea on a shell, but the Gang of Five never shut up about Familee.

"The English," wrote G. M. Trevelyan, "have always been singular for caring little about their cousins and ignoring their distant relatives."

The language of the Anglo-Saxon race has no words to denote the relationship between one in-law and his or her opposite number. In Yiddish the father-in-law is the *machuten* and the mother-in-law the *machetayneste*, and all relatives by marriage are called *machetunim*. In Waspish they're called "Oh, God, here they come!" By forcing us into tongue-twisters like "my daughter-in-law's brother's father-in-law," Waspish discourages us from even talking about them, much less inviting them to visit.

It's a Wasp thing, but Al Gore doesn't understand. Watching the face of little Albert Gore III while his calculatingly smarmy father described his son's injuries in explicit detail at the Democratic Convention, it was obvious the embarrassed child longed to heed the call of his genes and become one of those plucky lads who leave home at 12.

The little Wasp wanderer was immortalized in Thomas Hovenden's painting, *Breaking Home Ties*, and in the nineteenth-century ballad, "Where Is My Wandering Boy Tonight?" Seeking his fortune out West or going to sea as a cabin boy, he never saw his own family again, but he hit it off so well with someone else's that he became the sole heir of a rich stranger for whom he did some minor good turn—like Pip taking food and drink to the escaped convict in *Great Expectations*.

The will reading is full of infuriated blood relatives, as well it might be: "I, Edward Fairfield, having disowned my four sons and declared them legally dead, do hereby give and bequeath all my worldly goods to Thomas Trueheart, who very kindly returned my lost scarf thirty years ago. So that my sisters will not be able to interfere with my wishes in this matter, I leave them each the sum of one dollar."

Waspdom's straggly family ties fascinated the Eastern European immigrants who built the Hollywood movie industry. The remittance man whose family *pays* him to stay in Rangoon, having no parallel in Jewish life, exerted a morbid hold on the Jewish imagination. So did letters marked RETURN TO SENDER remailed from Tasmania, or funerals attended by no one except a dry-eyed housekeeper played by Agnes Moorehead, but what really enthralled the moguls was the Wasp-sister plot.

Two sisters loathe each other. One is plain, the other is pretty; one cleans the house, the other messes it up; one is a virgin, the other is a wanton; one wears glasses, the other can see in the dark. Something has happened to put what Wasps call "bad blood" between them—a redundancy, that: to our way of thinking, bad blood is the only kind of blood there is.

Someone is planning to drown someone. It's an easy death to arrange because the sisters always live on a bleak, blustery, inaccessible coast. They must go to the mainland to pick up their mail, and Mean Sister always rows. Nice Sister can't swim.

If drowning fails, Mean Sister chops at a tree until it falls on Nice Sister's side of the house. Failing that, Mean Sister tries to drive Nice Sister insane. She gets up in the middle of the night and moves the furniture, tampers with the grandfather clock that hasn't lost a second in fifty years, kills squirrels and nails them to the door, and so on. Driving someone insane is hard work, but after all, she's your sister.

Nice Sister obediently loses her mind, but instead of sending her to an asylum, Mean Sister decides to take care of her at home. Why the sudden solicitude? Because 15 years earlier, Mean Sister stole Nice Sister's fiancé. Now her Wasp conscience asserts itself, as Wasp consciences will, and tells her that she must Do the Right Thing for the crazy bitch.

I T SOUNDS like the end, but it isn't. Now comes the second climax, proving that relatives are *twice* as bad as we thought. It's true that Mean Sister married Nice Sister's fiancé, which accounts for Mean Sister's guilt. But now we learn that on the wedding night, Nice Sister sneaked into the lighthouse to murder Mean Sister, and murdered the bridegroom by mistake. This accounts for Nice Sister's greater guilt and explains why she has so graciously submitted to Mean Sister's cruelty all these years. After all, she had to make it up to the slut.

Wasps have disdained the ties that bind because the political institutions we invented relieved us of the need to huddle together. Thanks to the dead white males who gathered at Runnymede, Americans have never heard the knock on the door in the middle of the night. Familee has less to do with "traditional values" than with an unspoken fear that our liberties are imperiled.

November 30, 1992

W E'VE HEARD much about "Bubba" recently, but in the vast sto-
ried realms of Southern antonomasia, Bubba is not terribly
important. What Americans should contemplate is the South's
sobriquet for a certain type of woman.

We call her a "luhvly puhson."

Southerners don't go in much for gender-free language, but the Lovely
Person is the exception that proves the rule. "Lovely Person" and "lovely
woman" are *not* synonymous. The latter has sensual connotations, and the
Lovely Person has finished with that, if she ever started, and acquired a more
rarefied image, so calling her a "person" signifies the complimentary kind of
indeterminate gender associated with awesome mythological figures and
angels.

Nobody ever sat me down and explained what a Lovely Person is, but
somewhere along the line Southern osmosis kicked in and I *just knew*, the
way I *just knew* the difference between a good ole boy and a redneck, or the
subtle social gradations of ordinary, common, and trash. Thus, when I read
Gone with the Wind at the age of eight, I understood that Scarlett O'Hara's
mother was a Lovely Person: "To Ellen, mares never foaled nor cows calved.
In fact, hens almost didn't lay eggs. Ellen ignored these matters completely."

There are nicey-nice women everywhere, but in the South, where fire-
bells in the night ring a little louder, the Lovely Person is Lord Chesterfield
in Depends. To her way of thinking, life is a menopausal bladder that must be
rendered *comme il faut* come hell or high water.

So that ye may know her, the Lovely Person has a signature sentence that
she uses to stop people before they get to the juiciest part of the latest gossip,
or whenever any conversation gets too interesting. Probe a subject that fasci-
nates the vast majority of humankind—Jack the Ripper, Lizzie Borden, the
Donner Party—and the Lovely Person will flutter her fingers delicately as
though fanning an unpleasant odor, and murmur with gentle reproachfulness:
"I don't *want* to know."

She follows that with, "Let's talk about something pleasant," which is
why the Arabs upset her so. Judging from the baroque bloodthirstiness of
their political rhetoric, there isn't a Luhvly Puhson in the entire Middle East.
It was bad enough when they called us the "great Satan" and predicted that
"Everyone who conspired against Iraq is moving toward a black end, to the
hell of oblivion, ruin of present and future," but what really made Arabs non-
puhsons in her eyes was the Iraqi mother's vow: "I would cut off the head of
my baby and swallow it if it would make Bush lose."

The Lovely Person prefers headlines like the one I recently clipped for my files: "The Bonding Power of Andrew: Hurricane's Rampage Added Strength to Family Ties." Chances are a Lovely Person wrote it, because it is no longer necessary to be a rarefied Southern female to qualify for the sobriquet.

A country that calls Andy Rooney a curmudgeon can't take much unpleasantness. Americans are turning into Lovely Persons quicker than you—or even I—can say "son-of-a-bitch." As soon as the election was over, pundits began flagellating themselves over the way they had covered it, and came up with self-assessments that sound just like the Lovely Person tamping down her dinner table.

Fred Barnes was condemned for his "chilling hostility" to Eleanor Clift on *The McLaughlin Group*. Sam Donaldson was "snarlingly rude" to Cokie Roberts on *This Week with David Brinkley*. I found both of these exchanges to be merely vigorous, but other words used to describe the campaign coverage include *flay, icy, savage*, and that stepfather of all television images: *threatening*.

Even speaking in a manner described as "crisp" is cause for alarm in Lovely Person America, where "demanding" means punctual, "cold" means efficient, and "obsessive-compulsive" means neat. Our favorite word is "vulnerable." If I'm vulnerable and you're vulnerable, we're all okay—which is why the words "human error" make any catastrophe acceptable, especially when Dan Rather brings them out in that gulpy voice he uses to make himself sound large of soul.

Lovely Personhood is the driving force of our age. Political correctness is Lovely Personhood. The uproar over negative campaigning is Lovely Personhood. The moral collapse known as "growing in office" is Lovely Personhood. And the quintessence of Lovely Personhood is self-defeating guff about a "kinder, gentler" America.

L OVELY PERSONS are everywhere nowadays. Some merely say nice things as the easiest way out, like the husky young Marine interviewed by CBS after Hurricane Andrew. Asked if he was surprised to find himself helping hurricane victims instead of fighting, he replied that he had joined the Marines "to travel and to be part of humanitarian relief."

Other would-be Lovely Persons are motivated by narcissistic challenge—like Oxford's Bill Clinton, who "befriended the curmudgeonly former sergeant major of artillery who was the British school's porter," according to the *Washington Times*.

Having myself become a target of "threatened" professional extroverts since my misanthrope book came out, I know all about this trick. I can just see First Bubba honing in, extending himself and going out of his way, all the while thinking: "If I can crack *this* nut I must really be a Luhvly Puhson."

December 28, 1992

1993

I T'S NO LONGER fashionable to admit it—it's no longer fashionable to admit anything—but I loved "girltalk." I use the past tense because girltalk is dead.

It died around 1970 when feminists, convinced that women never talked about anything important, established "consciousness-raising" groups based on techniques used in Communist Chinese political re-education camps. Early Women's Lib CR was the granddaddy, so to speak, of the support-group/task-force/problem-solving craze currently filling the land with endless dreary talk, so the wonky din you hear is essentially a product of feminism.

Women no longer need girltalk to gossip privately about men-the-beasts and "the female complaint." Now that the secrets of the bedchamber and the distaff sickroom are aired on TV, we have lost one of the most richly satisfying sentences ever to fall from female lips. I first heard it in 1939 while watching Garbo as Camille, when my grandmother leaned across me and whispered to my mother: "The doctor ought to tell him not to *bother* her."

Girltalk was said to be rambling and repetitive, but it paled beside the speech code concocted by our new HHS Secretary, Donna Shalala, when she was chancellor of the University of Wisconsin. Sounding like a Roget rolling brakeless downhill, she barred insensitive speech about "race, color, national origin, ancestry, religion, creed, sex, sexual orientation, disability, and age." She forgot personal appearance, but then she's such a humanitarian that she never thinks of herself. (Oh, Lord, stop me from being catty, but not yet.)

A woman worried about her teenage daughter said to me, "I know she's sexually active." It sounded cold and detached. The girltalk phrase, "I just know she's having things to do with him," expressed real concern: euphemisms have passion. They also develop the imagination. As a child overhearing gossip of a couple "running around together," I visualized them tearing down the street hand in hand, like François Villon and Catherine de Vaucelles fleeing the Burgundians.

Girltalk had ingratiating rhythms. Inserting that theatrical "*just*" in front of verbs gave female voices a pleasing springiness. The susurrant tones of female speech have flattened out; women now talk in the "caucus voice," metallic, grinding, scourging, the voice that filled the French Foreign Legion.

Feminism creates boring women the way democracy creates bad-tempered artists. Under the patronage of an absolute monarch who could do no wrong, artists were emotionally as well as financially secure, free to be openly elitist instead of covertly elitist in the democratic manner. The system produced charming courtiers like Jean Racine, instead of surly snobs like NEA chief John Frohnmayer.

Many otherwise charming women lapse into feminist Newspeak whenever someone hits the right button. I got a fan letter from an obviously intelligent, well-bred woman who lives in a town I was thinking of moving to, so I asked her to tell me about it. Her letter describing housing and shopping was thorough and helpful, as well as witty and colorful, but suddenly Newspeak squirted out of her like ink from a squid: "I would not stand living here in the provincial, white-male dominant society if it were not for the liberating and liberal influence of the colleges and for the respect I have for what my husband does within this particular setting."

I no longer enjoy talking to women because I know that sooner or later they're going to say, "The operative word is 'choose.'" Some other verbal dental drills are "career move," "glass ceiling," "institute" as a verb, "perception" meaning any non-feminist point of view, and "passive-aggressive." That last is Newspeak for "Patient Griselda, always spinning," a literary allusion now lost in the mudslide of multicultural ignorance. Today's Patient Griseldas are always wonking, especially if they went to law school, where normal, intelligent women without speech defects are turned into rolling balls of tangled wool.

I especially avoid married career women because they want to talk about how boring their husbands are. Flaubert could describe Emma Bovary's boredom without becoming boring himself, but feminist matrons induce the sleep that knits up the ravell'd sleave of dress-for-success suits.

Above all, I avoid lesbians. It's impossible to enjoy a martini when someone keeps saying, "I'm tired of being invisible."

T HE SORRY STATE of female conversation is but one aspect of a larger problem. To explain, let me tell you a story I heard in one of my most interesting girltalks.

Once upon a time, a woman was so hounded and pestered by a man that she nearly went mad. Shrewdly recognizing him as the kind of persistent suitor who, once he gets a woman, loses all interest, she realized that there was only one way out of her problem. "I married him," she explained, "to get rid of him."

Now, a perpetually hoarse new President has taken office in tandem with his lawyer-wife. As The Billary wonk and crunch their way through what remains of the English language, we just might get so glazed and numb that we will let them do anything they want if only they will shut up.

In other words, we will marry them to get rid of them.

February 1, 1993

T HE LATEST New South—the eighth by my count—is coping with another trauma. This time it's the invasion of Damnyuppies, whose lust for "relocating" (they never say "move") is turning our gothic paradise into a homogenized Sunbelt.

If Oakland has no *there*, Damnyuppies have no *from*. Whatever ethnic background they once possessed has faded with the geographical and psychological distance they have put between themselves and their origins. Most of them seem to have no distinctive traits, habits, or accents—just master's degrees. Higher education, which bestows mobility, has made Damnyuppies *fromless*. If anyone wishes to say, "That's what America's all about," now is the time to say it.

Southerners, perhaps the only Americans still capable of homesickness, can now experience it without leaving home. Damnyuppies are why Southern towns now have Neighborhood Watch to stamp out the crime that used to be stamped out by watchful neighbors. Damnyuppies are why "Mall" is now capitalized, like Golgotha, and why it has replaced the bus station as a good-ole-boy hangout: the bus station has been torn down to make room for a brand-new "Old Town."

Perpetually searching for instant traditions and the quick 'n' easy identity they call the "New You," Damnyuppies display a paradoxical urge to feed off Southern uniqueness on the one hand, and reject it on the other. Take, for example, their linguistic voyeurism. If a Southerner makes an idiomatic reference to the subtle regional hierarchies known as "ordinary, common, and trash," the Damnyuppie gets that lean, hungry look and asks him to explain the difference.

Ever polite, the Southerner complies, "If you have a beat-up ole car in yore yard, but it runs, you're ordinary. If you have a beat-up ole car in yore yard and it won't run, you're common. But if you have *pieces* of a beat-up ole car in yore yard, you're trash."

A few days later, expect to see a letter-to-the-editor pleading for more sensitivity to what Damnyuppies call "socio-economic status."

Damnyuppies secretly fear Southern *excess*, as well they might. In *Colonel Effingham's Raid*, Berry Fleming says that this trait is rooted in topology; lacking the breathtaking scenic views of the New England coast or the mountainous West, we atone for our humble red clay and commonplace sand hills by substituting breathtaking characters.

I think Southern excess is rooted in our earliest history. The Pilgrims got good Indians but we got bad Indians. Our ancestors had bleeding heads—not bleeding hearts—from being scalped. They died like flies of famine—not hunger, famine. They fell victim to madness—not neurosis, madness—from living on the edge of a wilderness as sultry as black velvet and not knowing what might happen next. The only way to relieve such tension is to do something outlandish—i.e., *that's* what happened next.

Southerners are no different from anyone else, it's just that we do things that never seem to happen in Nebraska and Connecticut. The only shade of grey we ever produced is the Confederate uniform, and Damnyuppies know it. That is what makes them nervous. They never know what we might do.

"What will the South do?" has ever been the leading question in American political life. What will the South *do* if Lincoln is elected? What will the South *do* if Geraldine Ferraro is nominated? What will the South *do* if Ross Perot runs? The clot of primaries called "Super Tuesday" grew out of the conviction that the South was bound to *do* something, and so, unable to stand the suspense, politicians came up with Super Tuesday to find out what we would *do* before we did it.

Handed the historical role of reacting, we performed it so well, and with such undiluted joy, that the rest of the country is secretly disappointed whenever we seem to settle down. I am convinced that the reason for the current fascination with earthquakes, hurricanes, and meteors is that the South hasn't *done* anything lately.

T HE PRESENCE of Damnyuppies in our midst has given an interesting
   new twist to Southern graciousness and hospitality. Now that our towns
are being swallowed up by interstate highways and metropolitan areas, a new
kind of letter-to-the-editor has been cropping up with suspicious frequency in
local newspapers.

They are lavishly worded paeans from grateful commuters who have
been saved from various fates by native good samaritans. Stalled motorists
get help from farmers and hunters, who stop and fix their cars for them right
on the road. One obviously awestruck motorist wrote in praise of a samaritan
who drove all the way to Napa to buy him a new fan belt, drove back and
installed it, and refused to accept any payment for his labor. These letters
always end with effusions such as, "I didn't think there were people like that
left!" and "It proves how much good there is in human nature!"

Well, maybe. Putting aside the possibility that the samaritan was one of
those good ole boys who will grab any excuse to go to Napa, what it proves
is the strength of the unreconstructed Southern ego. We simply get a kick out
of being gracious when it results in an awestruck non-Southerner. That's why
the South is the only place in the world where even the working class practices noblesse oblige.

March 1, 1993

A FEW WEEKS ago a woman in town noticed I was limping and
   asked what was wrong. When I said I had an ingrown toenail she
   beamed with joy and recommended her podiatrist, singing his praises so fervently that I couldn't get a word in. Finally, when she paused to dig
in her bag for his card, I spoke.

"Stop. I don't care to associate with the sort of person who majors in
feet."

An ingrown toenail is as challenging as a crossword puzzle. I had a
martini to prepare myself for surgery; then, when I felt good and supple, I
sterilized my instruments in boiling water and went to work. I got the little
bugger out, then doused my toe with rubbing alcohol, followed by hydro-
gen peroxide—"Stand the sting and you get to watch the foam," as my
grandmother used to say when she doctored my skinned knees.

Afterward, I had another martini to celebrate my recovery. As I sat
watching my foaming toe, it occurred to me that what I had just done might
well be declared illegal in the not-too-distant future. Now that the Gray

Gelding has put Regina Dentata in charge of national health, I could end up in the Hillary–Billary dock.

The charge would not be anything so forthright as "practicing medicine without a license"; no, they would call it "medical unawareness" or, better yet, "health dissing."

Once they found out my medical history and realized my family invented health dissing—no prenatal care, mother ate and smoked for two, born at home, delivered by grandmother, father stayed in kitchen—I would be sent, like poor Marge Schott, to a re-education camp and given electroshock treatments to clear my brain of an opinion I have held as long as I can remember, which I'd yell at my captors as they dragged me away: "Fussing over your health is low class!"

Nobody ever told me this in so many words, but somehow I imbibed it, just as I imbibed the idea that the more money you have, the less you should appear to have. When I read *The Late George Apley* I instinctively liked the rich protagonist for having darned tablecloths and threadbare rugs, just as I instinctively liked Honoré de Balzac when I read his biographer's calculation that he drank 50,000 cups of coffee so he could write all night in spite of what it did to his heart.

Churchill put it best when he observed, "Most of the world's work is done by people who don't feel very well," but nowadays practitioners of aristocratic stoicism are said to be "in denial." A sterner, nobler America is anathema to New Age philosophes; their ideal is the wailing proletarian who lives by the soap-opera credo, "I'm sick, therefore I am."

Deer-on-velvet sensibility comes through loud and clear in the ubiquitous "Health Watch" segments on television news. These emotion-drenched reports feature scuzzy-looking individuals who hold up their drainage bags or their cross-eyed kids to the camera; unappetizing women with their breasts clamped in mammogram machines; and blank-eyed expectant mothers who allow themselves to be photographed in the stirrups.

Invited to "tell their story in their own words," they slip into the whining nasal tones of trailer-park grievance collectors, explaining that it all started when the medicine that was supposed to cure *this* caused *that*; then another medicine they took for a disease they thought they had but didn't caused the double vision that caused the accident; and then the triplets ate the asbestos.

These sagas of pain and wrecked lives and germ-free plastic bubbles are supposed to be moving, but they move me to expropriate George V's words on hearing that one of his courtiers liked little boys: "I always thought people like that shot themselves."

N EW AGE hypochondria lends itself to the literary exercise feminists call "deconstruction." If we keep peeling the artichoke of "health awareness" we eventually will uncover an unpleasant truth that pollsters cannot reach.

Notwithstanding our worship of perfect bench-pressed bodies, we like them much better if their owners admit to overdosing on steroids and waste away before our very eyes, preferably in public-service commercials about the dangers of steroids. New Age hypochondriacs glorify the lame, the halt, and the defective. Like Bill Clinton compulsively retelling the story of the New Hampshire boy who navigated his wheelchair down an icy winter highway to get to a Clinton rally, they cheer every insane feat the handicapped undertake, from double amputees climbing mountains to blind yachtsmen sailing the Atlantic alone.

New Age hypochondriacs call such foolhardy exploits "courageous," and woe be unto anyone who disagrees with this fashionable rationalization, because something very important is at stake here.

Extolling pointless and unthreatening physical courage helps New Agers forget their own lack of moral courage. They actually hate the healthy and wish to encourage hypochondria because they are "in denial" about America's most serious problem, and Louis-Ferdinand Céline, a French physician-turned-novelist, provided a merciless explanation of why: "When people can stand up, they're thinking of killing you. Whereas when they're ill, there's no doubt about it, they're less dangerous."

Our Great Diversity rides again. Suppose they gave a civil war and nobody was well enough to come?

March 29, 1993

H ILLARY CLINTON's obsession with Eleanor Roosevelt brings back old times.

One afternoon in 1940, our family doctor unwrapped his blood-pressure cuff from my grandmother's arm and took my parents aside for a conference.

"You'll have to stop her from reading that column."

He meant "My Day" by Eleanor Roosevelt. As usual, Granny had snatched up the paper and turned directly to the fatal page. As she read, I saw the faint pink birthmark between her brows darken until it burned like a scarlet brand. In another moment she seemed to be imitating the contents of my

Crayola box, as lethally glorious shades of maroon, magenta, and vermilion suffused her face and spread down her neck and chest, turning her heaving bosom (cup size DAR) into multitudinous waterwings incarnadined. Suddenly, she dropped the paper and emitted a strangled cry.

After the doctor's ultimatum, my father came up with a solution: "Florence likes to cut things out of the paper. Let her cut out the column before your mother sees it."

I couldn't read but I had no trouble finding "My Day" because Mrs. Roosevelt's picture was on it. Even at four I would have known that face anywhere. It worked a couple of weeks, until Granny had another seizure bending over the trash can to retrieve the discarded columns. My parents decided it was safer to let her read, so my career as the Littlest Censor came to an end.

Granny rarely called Mrs. Roosevelt by name. She was "She."

"She made him pack the Supreme Court."

"She made him recognize Russia."

"*She got them all stirred up!*"

When the subject was over her head, like the gold standard, she used her all-purpose accusation: "She drugged him."

Thus, when we saw the movie of H. Rider Haggard's *She*, I thought it was a newsreel about Mrs. Roosevelt. I kept waiting for her to appear; finally, when the withered old woman died in the snows of Tibet, I whispered to Granny: "Is that Mrs. Roosevelt?"

"Would that it were!"

Hillary Clinton can commune with Eleanor's spirit, pray to her, "identify" with her all she wants, but our new First Lady will never be "She," and not only because she clanks around dragging the chains of all three of her names behind her. The differences between the two women are immense.

I never look at Hillary without thinking, "Who *is* this yuppie dreadnought?" At least Eleanor went back to something we knew, if not in our lives, at least in our racial memory: the lady of the manor. Viewed from this angle, her do-gooding came across as part of a reassuring social hierarchy that seemed all the more solid for her efforts to dismantle it.

"These poor gypsies seem to be having a difficult time," she wrote to Harry Hopkins. "Is there any chance of their being put on a homestead in Florida or Arkansas, where they could be warm and where they might carry on their coppersmith work as well as farming?" Thus do left-wing aristocrats use their hereditary privilege of goofiness to maintain class distinctions. The trick is remembering not to call people "human resources."

Eleanor, like Hillary, had repulsive friends. Esther Lape and Elizabeth

Read were rich lesbians whose Greenwich Village socialist salon was ER's favorite hangout in the Twenties when she was First Lady of New York. She also had her own private Three Fates—Rose Schneiderman, Maud Schwartz, and Marion Dickerman. They were such chromos that no one had to be told that they were thick with the Women's Trade Union League—one look and you just knew.

Eleanor's friends were no oil paintings, but they had something Hillary & Co. lack. In their tweed suits and men's ties, with the nicotine-stained fingers of bohemian intellectuals and the grim facial expression that used to be called "intense," they remind us there once was a time when obnoxious women were at least authentic bluestockings, instead of uncultivated, syntax-deprived policy wonks who smile with both rows of teeth.

It's easy to imagine ER's friends at Auntie Mame's soirées, denouncing anti-Dadaists or reciting "Leaves of Grass" after their seventh Singapore Sling, but the Friends of Hillary would never get in the door. They all look like Agnes Gooch, except for Laura Tyson, who looks like a Class Chaplain. As for the alleged lesbians among them, they are less Willa Cather than Dykes on Bikes.

T HE BIGGEST difference between Eleanor and Hillary is the sexual climate of their respective First Ladyships. Men and women did not hate each other when Eleanor entered the White House. The Suffragettes were still fresh in people's minds, but they had gone after the vote and nothing else, and when they got it they faded away. Respectable matrons and virtuous spinsters, they did not rend the social fabric with single motherhood and paranoid harassment charges as modern feminists have done, so Eleanor never became a symbol of destructive female sexuality.

Hillary has come to power at a time when men are roiling with an entirely justified loathing of women, so our First Symbol should not be surprised if they look at her and think: "Her briefcase sucks forth my soul; her capped teeth *are* the towers of Ilium."

April 26, 1993

I WATCHED Helen Gurley Brown on television the other night. If that sentence sounds oddly like "I said goodbye to Mr. Chips the night before he died," it's because I wrote for *Cosmopolitan* two decades ago.

Helen was plugging her new book, *The Late Show: A Semiwild but*

Practical Survival Plan for Women over Fifty, a vade-mecum on how to canoodle without a libido and why you should never, never stop doing it even though you no longer want to. "If you're not having sex you're finished," she claims. "It separates the girls from the old people." As for whom to do it with, she recommends borrowing the husbands of your aging girlfriends, and if you can't afford a facelift, she advises that Preparation H hides wrinkles temporarily. One way or another, she always manages to turn American womanhood upside down.

At 71, her surgically lifted face is stretched so tight that she can't fully open her mouth, the better to speak in a whispery, girlish voice. Thin to the point of emaciation (her favorite accolade is "skinny," which even her editors tried to get her to stop using), she wore a miniskirt that exposed pitiful toothpick legs and a low neckline that revealed knobby collarbones and crêpy flesh despite the massive doses of estrogen she takes, and promotes in her new book.

I first came to Helen's attention via my 1974 *Harper's* article "The Good Ole Boy." She bought the reprint rights and asked me to write original pieces for *Cosmo*. Thus began two years before the masthead that I will never forget.

I will say this for *Cosmo*. They pay with the speed of sound, and they know exactly what they want. Other women's mags call up and say, "We want something . . . not too short, not too long, on . . . oh, you know . . . sex." *Cosmo* calls up and says, "We want 1,200 words on 'Your First Night with a New Man,'" and sends you a tip sheet containing the free-associative thoughts of the entire editorial staff from Helen on down. They not only write to the writer, but back and forth to each other as well, so what you get is slice-of-*Cosmo*.

I saved these tip sheets for what I grandly call my literary papers. The one for "Your First Night with a New Man" says:

"It will really be a *splendid* article if we have any luck—*all* girls start new affairs *all* the time and sexual etiquette (or better known as getting used to the new guy) is always a little harrowing."

"Might include ploys for getting out fast if you realize he is A Mistake, ways to politely introduce *your* favorite fetish, or politely decline *his*."

"Suppose he's a *masochist???* You can't *hit* him, that's like drowning a fish."

In my first draft I ran into the eternal toothbrush question. We had several phone calls about this. If you keep new toothbrushes on hand, he'll think you're the kind of girl who keeps new toothbrushes on hand. On the other hand, if you don't have an extra one, he can't brush his teeth. Note on next tip sheet: "Can't he use finger? Think we covered this in 'How to Behave the Next Morning.'"

For a while I was *Cosmo*'s golden girl, turning out one written-to-order piece after another, but then something happened. God knows how to punish people who contribute to the corruption of a generation of women. For a writer, the tortures of the damned can be defined as having to write the kind of material you don't enjoy reading. I started drinking, and the tip sheets reflected it.

"Well now! Florence's anything is better than most anybody else's and this is no exception, but we must try to make it work. I'm just saying since Florence is *not* a shallow, pippypoo, over-simplified writer let's don't destroy something that's a little more warpy and woofy than we get from most writers." (That's HGB.)

"It just seems a *tiny* bit less succinct and cohesive than her other pieces . . . a little more *spready*."

"Think it needs something more foxy and 1975ish."

Not bloody likely: I was brooding over the mass canoodling I was helping to promote. A few hussies add spice to society's soup, provided they are rich in their own right, like George Sand, or well kept, like Lillie Langtry, but too many hussies bring the house down. Female chastity (or at least the pretense of it) keeps us civilized, but *Cosmo* had aroused in men the ancient dread of the insatiable female. I decided rapists were saying, in effect: "Here's some sex you *won't* enjoy."

M Y CRISIS peaked with "The Sexual You: Why and When Women Want Sex," whose tip sheet said: "How can one determine at 50 what her physical needs will be at 80? No, you don't necessarily slow *down*, you may get *activer*."

Somewhere in my martini-soaked brain a tip sheet of my own took shape: "No! The belle *must* turn into the chaperone or else life is *flux* and nothing *makes sense*." Then I quit.

After Helen, the deluge. *Cosmo* will fade away because no one else can be the magazine, and she has become a curiosity. But she was kind to me, and we did have our moments, and so I say goodbye, Mr. Chips.

May 24, 1993

I F LOVE means never having to say you're sorry, America is on tender hooks. Somebody is always apologizing.

Country-club memberships, baseball "necessities," Confederate flags, water buffalo, Madame Butterfly, boathouses in Kansas (isn't that like "Swiss navy"?), speaking English, being male, roasting people at roasts, belittling the flexed-arm hang, Hiroshima, oil spills, babies without fathers, swimmers without buoyancy, Columbus, You People, Tammy Wynette, and the 1916 song, "Where Did Robinson Crusoe Go with Friday on Saturday Night?"

I threw that last one in just to see if you were paying attention. It hasn't become a *cause célèbre* yet, but only because few people now alive know the words: "Did they dine out with wild mens on cannibal trimmins? / Where there are wild mens there must be wild wimmens." That's a twofer.

The vocabulary of apology grates on the nerves like chalk squeaking across an African-American board. The moment we hear "to any and all" we know an apology is coming, so we bite down hard and wait for "inappropriate," "regrettable," and "perceived," the last being a politically correct hint that white feminists can jump to conclusions. The jaws start to relax at "Let us put it behind us and go forward," a signal that it's over until the next time.

"Never apologize, never explain," said Immanuel Kant. This maxim has so many versions that it qualifies as received truth. From the Frenchman who said, "*Qui s'excuse, s'accuse*," to John Wayne's signature line in *She Wore a Yellow Ribbon*, "Never apologize, mister, it's a sign of weakness," the wisdom of taking one's knocks, thumbing one's nose, and leaving well enough alone was universally acknowledged.

No more. Now we eat our way down a Baskin-Robbins menu of apologies with something to satisfy every craving. "The buck stops here" is the apology of choice for people in the throes of a calm, firm, manly panic. VMI's contention that single-sex schools "celebrate diversity" is the steadfast cave-in sundae: when you defend yourself with the enemy's language, you are apologizing whether you know it or not. Claiming "humanitarian" reasons for your government's actions avoids the need to apologize for having a national interest. And those who believe that cringing actions speak louder than craven words can savor the gesture-as-apology and voluntarily turn in their guns at community drives.

On it goes. The only way to say what you really think is to talk into an open mike and then apologize for not knowing it was open.

Tender Hooks can be laid at the doors of the nursery and the sewing room. Hurt feelings and apologies have always been special concerns of women and children, who conduct interminable, maniacally detailed hearings on the finer points of emotional affronts the instant someone wails, "Johnny talked mean to me!"

Women consequently have developed a third ear for the subtle tones, trenchant pauses, and vocal syncopation that only a connoisseur of bad vibes can catch. She is peerless, as every man who has had this exchange with a woman can attest:

"But what did I say?"

"It was *how* you said it."

WELCOME to the Zeitgeist. America, no longer a man's country, is now rigged for the exquisite sensibilities of women and children—the same people who gave us "If you can't say something nice, don't say anything at all," and "Take that back or I'll never speak to you again as long as I live!"

Tender Hooks has made crisp, concise language an object of fear and loathing. I don't mean just clumsy vagaries like "native American," but the far more serious trend of using words to mean what we wish them to mean, and banishing outright any word whose definition fails to satisfy our emotions.

The distinction between *sympathy* and *empathy* is deliberately ignored, even by people who know better, like the editors of *Time*. Sympathy is the ability to commiserate with someone who is different from ourselves: it always includes the element of pity; empathy is the ability to commiserate with someone like ourselves: the element of identification is always present.

Obviously, sympathy requires more effort and hence is the greater virtue, but we have cast it into outer darkness and "empathize" with everybody under the sun. In our rush to gild the lily of apology we have convinced ourselves that "empathize" sounds more sympathetic, but in truth we are afraid of the implied insult in sympathy. "Pity," wrote Mary McCarthy, "signifies a conquered repugnance."

The word games of Tender Hooks are producing an increasingly ungrounded, insubstantial personality type. How many people can you identify with before giving "you are what you eat" new meaning?

The whole country has a bone in the throat—the real cause of our much-touted "stress." As Boris Pasternak noted in *Dr. Zhivago*: "Health is ruined by the systematic duplicity forced on people if you say the opposite of what you feel, if you grovel before what you dislike and rejoice at what brings you nothing but misfortune."

Tender Hooks will not keep the peace. "Why are you always saying
you're sorry?" is, after all, the signature line of the wife beater.

June 21, 1993

I T IS TYPICAL of America that having invented efficiency apartments,
singles bars, Soup for One, and That *Cosmopolitan* Girl, we have
dropped *spinster* from the language and consider *old maid* a sexist slur.
  I make a point of using both. If I fill out a form that asks for my marital
status I skip the printed selections, write in *spinster*, draw a block beside it,
and check it. When an aluminum-siding telephone salesman asked to speak
to the "man of the house," I said, "There isn't any, I'm an old maid," and
derived enormous satisfaction from his audible gulp.
  Spinsterhood was powerful long before feminism hit the fan. Point to any
area of "sex discrimination" and you will find that old maids have always
sailed through unscathed. Businessmen know all too well that the hand that
rocks the cradle rocks the boat. Most married women with children are no use
to anybody unless the stock exchange is hiring amok runners, but spinsters
give females a good name. We come to work on time with no visions of
babysitters and day-care centers dancing like rancid sugar plums in our
heads; we can work overtime on a moment's notice, and there is never any
spit-up on our paperwork.
  Credit ratings? An old maid and a divorcee with three children to support
are both "single," but the resemblance ends there. Instead of urging women
to conceal their marital status under the muzzy blanket of "Ms.," feminists
should have encouraged the inclusion of *spinster* on applications. It would
have pulled up women's overall credit rating and eliminated the automatic
discrimination against them caused by the bill-paying problems of liberated
divorcees.
  Remember the classic old-maid joke. Before going to bed she spent an
hour locking the doors and windows of the house that she occupied alone.
Sounds like a big house, doesn't it? She also hired lots of "hired men," and
when she begged them to marry her she always reeled off a long list of her
economic assets to sweeten the deal: the "feminization of poverty" was
nowhere in evidence.
  Auto insurance? Old maids look at the road, not at what Jason did to
Debbie's dress. As for life insurance, take a peek at the tombstones in Old
Maid Gardens:

Susan B. Anthony—1821–1906
Anna Dickinson—1842–1932
Elizabeth Blackwell—1821–1910
Clara Barton—1821–1912
Dorothea Dix—1802–1886
Elizabeth Peabody—1804–1894

A certain teacher and reformer little known today is the undisputed star of Old Maid Gardens. Here she is, that perennial unplucked flower of reform politics:

Emily Howland—1827–1929

By God, that's what you call a good set of bowels. Have you ever noticed that there are no old maids in laxative commercials? They beam the message that women are three times more likely to suffer constipation, yet the sufferers portrayed are always matrons and their married daughters, who conclude that the problem comes from "doing so much for others"—an unconscious gem of truth-in-advertising hinting that marriage and motherhood are the ties that bind.

I WISH my fellow conservatives would tone down their plangent testimonials to the Great God Family. I also wish that feminists would try to harden women, as real feminists should, by preaching renunciation, instead of tearing them apart by simultaneously promoting masculine work and condemning masculine work habits, e.g., Adrienne Rich: "I want to make it clear that I am *not* saying that in order to write well, or think well, it is necessary to become unavailable to others, or to become a devouring ego. This has been the myth of the masculine artist and thinker; and I repeat, I do not accept it."

Bull, madam, bull. If you really reject it, why not say so simply and briefly, instead of dragging in defensive preambles and italics?

The "myth" of the masculine artist and thinker—or any worker—is not myth but fact. Its real name is *concentration*, and it is achieved by making oneself unavailable to others. He travels fastest who travels alone, and that goes double for she.

Mendacious pep talks such as Miss Rich's keep married women in a perpetual state of conflict and make them jealous of unencumbered women. The jealousy crops up in a phrase I hear regularly: "If I could do what you do . . ."

Write the same goddamn page twenty times? Write all day Christmas? Get halfway through a book only to realize that you started too late in dramatic time and the whole thing is turning into a flashback? Anybody who chose that moment to ask "When's dinner?" would get *killed*, ladies, and liberal Adrienne Rich knows it. She won't tell you; I just did.

Of all the benefits of spinsterhood, the greatest is carte blanche. Once a woman is called "that crazy old maid" she can get away with anything.

July 19, 1993

H OW DOES a weeping, empathizing President drop bombs? The same way porcupines mate: carefully. Updating this old joke, Colin Powell called the damage Clinton inflicted on Baghdad "collateral"; Al Gore called it "proportionate," but the best rationale came from Pat Schroeder, who whined earnestly, "It shows he's sensitive."

Clinton's sensitivity is usually attributed to the pacifist Sixties, but anti-war protestors yelled and broke things. He's actually a product of the feminist Seventies, when the "humanized" male was ordered to report for duty.

The Seventies buzzword was "unisex," the canard was "Tenderness is strength," and the book was *The Liberated Man*, by Warren Farrell, who advocated the "Human Pronoun"—tis, ter, tes—and worse, used it.

Sporting long hair, bell bottoms, and ties as wide as a woman's scarf, Sensitive Man lived in perpetual suspense: What would feminists demand next, and would he be able to give it to them? He learned to say "I'm into women" without laughing; followed "burning bed" murder cases and came out in favor of equal suttee; and trained himself to be receptive, emotional, tearful, supportive, nurturing, and passive.

Letting women undress him was the latest thing for a while, and I helped it along in one of my *Cosmopolitan* articles, extolling the practice while keeping my real thoughts to myself: When a man undresses a woman he feels like a rogue; when a woman undresses a man she feels like an undertaker. Ergo, he feels like a corpse.

Like the political prisoner he was, the Seventies male made public confessions. "My name is Sensitive Man and I used to be a male chauvinist," he would say, describing the macho sins he committed until the day he saw the light, giving it plenty of schmaltz and piling on the clichés. "I stood there . . . suddenly I realized. . . . It was as if I had become two people."

To show how sexually secure he was, he circulated among the women at parties saying, "I'm impotent." It made him seem soft, as it were. It also helped him acquire new bedmates without going to the trouble of seducing them: with so many newly minted feminists eager to practice their sexual aggression, the impotent man became, incredibly, a real catch.

Along the same line, Sensitive Man confessed that he used Johnson's Baby Shampoo and shaved under his arms. "Deodorant works better that way," he said with a shrug. "Why shouldn't a man shave under his arms? Of course, some men might feel threatened by it, but I don't worry about being 'effeminate.'" To prove it, he cried.

This is the man feminism destroyed. There are millions like him, and one is in the White House.

Clinton supporters who defend his sensitive antics succeed only in bestowing the kiss of death. In a *Washington Post* column, "What's So Bad about Zigzagging?" Judy Mann praised him for "not being John Wayne," credited him with being "secure enough that he can change his mind," thanked him for violating "the Western, male, rationalist code of behavior," and predicted that he will "redefine our expectations of men."

In a syndicated feature headlined "Clinton Takes His Style Cues from the Feminine," National Public Radio commentator Steven D. Stark writes, "It should not be surprising that a Democrat is feminizing the Presidency" because Democrats are the "mommy party." Feminization also explains the Comeback Kid phenomenon; "because women are usually perceived as softer and less powerful than men, negative attacks often end up only creating sympathy for them. The same may be true for Clinton."

Can it get worse? Yes. Stark concludes: "The good news is that we finally have a feminine leader. The bad news, of course, is that she's a man."

These "compliments" are nothing but warmed-over Seventies bromides. *Time*'s Margaret Carlson dredged up the tritest one when she effused that the example of the Billary proves that "it takes a solid, secure man to marry a strong woman."

O H, PLEASE. Clinton is Sensitive Man. He is also one of those peevish, overwrought males that Southerners call an "old maid in britches." Familiar literary portraits of the type include Scarlett O'Hara's jumpy second husband, Frank Kennedy, constantly clawing his beard. Another is Waldo Lydecker in Vera Caspary's *Laura*. Clifton Webb played him as an urbane switchblade in the movie but in the book he's a captious hysteric: Bill Clinton with a porcelain collection.

Sensitive Man has bad nerves because his politics keep him in a perpetual state of guilt and his passivity keeps him in a perpetual state of sexual anxiety. Stir in the temperament of an old maid in britches and you've got double trouble. "Stress, probably," said the *Arkansas Democrat Gazette*'s Paul Greenberg in his assessment of Clinton's "tearful over-reaction" to Brit

Hume's Rose Garden question, adding cryptically: "he betrays signs of a political crack-up of Scott Fitzgerald dimensions."

To hell with Sensitive Man; I'll take Rush Limbaugh. The Vain Brain is male ego personified, a Jove among Apollos, a laughing cavalier, a welcome daily reminder of what real masculinity sounds like. May he thrive.

August 23, 1993

T O LIBERALS he's the "blue-collar, white-male, racist, sexist homophobe." To feminists he's the "unsocialized" male because he continues to elude their gelding shears. I call him the Matchbook Man because he was the target of self-improvement ads in the matchbooks of my childhood.

Having had a mother who smoked four packs a day, I saw a lot of matchbooks and practiced my reading with them. On the inside of the cover were tiny grey coupons and ads that said: "Finish High School at Home in Your Spare Time!" or "Learn Locksmithing" or "Study Radio Repair" or "Be a Private Detective"—always at home in your spare time.

Some of the same ads can still be found in gun magazines or on late-night TV, but today's dwindling supply of matchbooks has been classed up. Now the inside is blank, while the cover contains embossed pictures of exclusive hotels and restaurants that the Matchbook Man never enters.

He frequents places like the pool hall where I have my midday beer after I finish my errands. I like it because there are no talkative waiters named Bruce, just chain-smoking waitresses. The clientele neither know nor care who I am, so no one says to me, "I've always wanted to write."

It was the day of the House budget vote and several young workingmen were watching the news. When the announcer said, "Congressman Timothy Penny has resigned," the T-shirted, tattooed viewers exchanged eager glances, their eyes lighting up with an energizing spark that seemed to bounce from face to face, linking them all in a circuitry of joy. There was something profoundly touching about it, and also something familiar. I had seen this raw masculine pride before.

It was during the 1962 Cuban missile crisis, when Adlai Stevenson cornered the Soviet representative at the UN and demanded the truth, vowing, "I'll stand here till hell freezes over!"

The next day, some tree pruners were working outside my apartment building and I heard one of them say, "Boy, old Stevenson really told 'em, dint he?" His face was lit with the same glow that I saw on the faces of the boys in the pool hall. It's a look that never comes over a woman even though she may share the opinion that brings it on. Epiphanies composed of bellicose swagger and a purity that has nothing to do with sexuality are the exclusive property of the Matchbook Man.

It's just about all he has left. He used to be "the man who found a home in the Army," but now he must look hard to find the Army amid the welter of homemaking missions on which it has embarked. Craving an aura of Spartan hardness in which to prove himself, he gets instead Operation Restore Hope, made glorious by "the interaction we're accustomed to seeing between American troops and people we help," said Dick Cheney; or Operation Provide Comfort on the Iraqi border—where, wrote Mary McGrory, "Americans thrilled to the sight of U.S. soldiers changing babies."

While liberals form task force after task force to cure alienation in their beloved urban underclass, the Matchbook Man is being driven crazy by the growing primacy of warm feeling over cold justice in American life. His own moral center has the bleak, unequivocal beauty of a January dawn, but let him display it and it will be dismissed as an "inappropriate response."

When he watches news reports about "Iron John" manhood-weekend outings, he sees the same whey-faced academics who condemn him during the week, who know nothing about a carburetor except how to spell it. When he changes channels he will very likely find Weekend Man's feminist wife holding forth in a panel discussion about "the myth of masculinity." And should he leaf through a magazine he will find one of those nasty little editorial asides that politically correct journalists take pains to insert in their copy—e.g., *Time*'s Richard Corliss's gratuitous description of Mike Tyson as "an exemplar of all those sad studs who are prisoners of manhood."

When he objects to Betty Boop congresspersons like Pat Schroeder and an attorney general with the mean mouth of a social worker on the rampage, it merely proves that "he just doesn't get it." What he does get all too well are our new definitions: an honorable man is one who doesn't cave until the last minute, and a maverick is one who teases like a belle to get primetime coverage. Every time it happens the Matchbook Man dies a little, but no, he's not alienated.

T O HIM, every week is the Week That Was. He recoiled when California Highway patrolperson Melanie Singer burst into tears on the witness stand and wrecked the defense in the second LAPD trial. Now he has a brand-new crazymaker: the majestically ditzy Marjorie Margolies-Mezvinsky, a dead ringer for Zasu Pitts, who changed her mind at the last minute and put the Clinton budget over the top, then spent the following day on the tube wondering whether she had "fallen on her sword." Another noble Roman concept bites the dust.

Feminists will find my response to the Matchbook Man inappropriate, but I'm sure Mae West would back me up: I like a man who just doesn't get it.

September 20, 1993

ASKED if he would like to live somewhere else besides New York, George M. Cohan replied, "Where else is there?"

I feel the same about Southern men: "What other kind is there?" I've been involved with other kinds, but I always felt oddly off-base, as if matters were somehow incomplete and destined to remain so. I suppose I sensed nothing crazy was going to happen, and that's a bad way to feel in romantic situations.

What I like best about the Southern man is his matchless gift for self-parody. He secretly enjoys being the American other Americans are always trying to understand.

In his new book, *New York Days*, Willie Morris tells of being at Gettysburg College for a speech, when all of a sudden he took a notion to see the battlefield by moonlight. He was stopped by a longsuffering security guard who said, "It happens all the time. And it's always Southerners. Why always you Southerners?"

Such questions are music to the Southern man's ears, which is why he's glad the latest New South has become part of corporate America. Millions of Yankees are moving down here now, and they're all trying to understand him.

Knowing that his reputation precedes him, he likes to move in on a Yankee woman and match her preconceived notions of gallant Southern gentlemen. If his wife gets mad he will reply innocently, "I was just being polite," or "She's our *guest.*" These are unanswerable and he knows it; hospitality being sacred, his Southern woman must keep her mouth shut while his Yankee woman sits there with hers hanging open, so mesmerized by his megachivalry that she looks pole-axed.

He can, in the words of Georgia writer Rosemary Daniell, "make a woman feel as if she is being bathed in melted butter." He can also make her feel shut out as no other man can. He does it whenever he feels his masculinity is threatened.

As much as he enjoys playing the Southern gentleman, he is painfully aware that the image smacks of the drawing room and the dancing master, requiring behavior that makes him feel foppish. One part of him wants to squire the ladies, but another part wants to escape from them entirely, and so he periodically rebels.

His worst episode is the hunting trip that allows him to go a record number of days without a bath. The idea is to smell bad, so if he can't get away he will go out on the porch and sleep with the dogs.

Another is his frat-rat number, when he hangs out with his friends and everybody gets down-and-dirty in the manner of novels blurbed "All the Fine Young Men."

Then there is gun cleaning. Considering the number of guns Southern men own, this can go on for days. It's hard to miss the symbolic rejection in his Smith & Wesson petting parties; the rubbing and caressing he puts into polishing the stocks are bad enough, but wait till he cleans the barrels.

Next he inspects his various collections. He still has the old cigar box containing his boyhood treasures. These include standard little-boy items such as baseball cards, marbles, and penknives; but scattered among the ordinary mementos are things that only a little Southern boy would save: a frog's skull, a cameo watch fob with half the face sliced off, and the skin of the snake that bit him.

Finally, he opens the trunk containing buttons stamped CSA, faded flags full of bullet holes, torn epaulets, and crumbling scraps of blood-stained gray cloth. As he sifts through these talismans, his mood of bittersweet sadness is impenetrable.

All men occasionally shut women out, but Southern men are more unmistakable about it. A man who holes up with paperwork from the office might actually be doing something that must be done right away, but when a man ignores you to polish his great-granddaddy's sword, you know you're *de trop*.

His psychosexual conflicts can be extreme, but they defy psychiatric sophistry. Far from being a "latent" homosexual, he has an unusually strong identity, for he is the South personified: simultaneously a female oasis of gentility and grace, and a male wasteland of taverns and guns, both vying for the accolade of the "real South."

S OUTHERN MEN and psychiatrists are creatures from different planets. They don't even speak the same language. In *Southern Honor: Ethics and Behavior in the Old South*, Bertram Wyatt writes, "Honor, not conscience; shame, not guilt; were the psychological and social underpinnings of Southern culture."

This is why the Southern man feels he has given a thorough accounting of himself when he "explains" a fist fight or a sudden job resignation with: "I had to." Some corner of his heart will always be consecrated to Edmund Ruffin, the South Carolinian who fired the first shot of the Civil War at Fort Sumter—and who, when he received word of Lee's surrender, wrapped himself in a Confederate flag and shot himself.

Why? He had to.

Present Presidents excepted, the Southern man navigates by fixed stars. There's no telling what he might do if he gets riled, but he says grace and he says ma'am and he loves his countries—both of them.

October 18, 1993

L OGIC ought to be sacred. That's why I have been on the alert ever since Yamaha named a motorcycle "Virago" and Shakespeare's symbol of unreliability ("false, false, false Cressid!") inspired a car.

How on earth did it happen? We can't blame it on "cultural differences." The companies are Japanese, but their advertising and PR firms are geared to the Western world. It is impossible to believe that these wildly wrong names could slip past the panoply of research and development, market testing, and "creative" meetings that go into such decisions. We can bet the connotations were known and discussed, but in the end someone probably said it won't hurt sales because the slobs don't know the difference and the eggheads will just write us snotty letters about the Trojan War.

The latest assault on logic is the opera-backed commercial. In the one for a recreational vehicle, we first see the product covered with mud, then a titanic inundation of water comes out of nowhere and washes it clean while a soprano voice sings *"Un bel dì"* from *Madama Butterfly*. The same aria is used in another ad for athletic shoes, sung to visuals of stouthearted runners straining heroically toward a finish line. What is the connection here? The aria is about a girl who has been jilted and is too dumb to realize it.

Another one, for a luxury car or an aftershave, I forget which, shows a woman in a slinky black evening dress running across the lawn of a palatial estate at sunrise while a soprano voice sings *"O mio babbino caro"* from Puccini's *Gianni Schicchi*. This aria has the melting quality of romantic passion but it isn't that at all. The title character of this one-act comic opera is a wily Tuscan peasant; the aria, sung by his daughter, starts, "Oh, my dearest Daddy," and is a plea for him to engage in trickery to get her a dowry.

Don't assume Madison Avenue is full of philistines: it isn't. They knew, all right, but they didn't care. Opera is perceived as classy, therefore products advertised with opera are perceived as classy, so don't worry about which aria you use as long as it "soars."

This might sound like a minor point in a country where millions can't even read, but remember little things mean a lot, or as the logician Aulus Gellius put it: *Ex pede Herculem,* "From the foot alone we may infer Hercules."

Contempt for logic grows daily. Nobody has "ideas" any more, just shattering mental jolts known as "wake-up calls." Books with titles like *You Just Don't Understand* and the daily crowing over people who "don't get it" betray an undeniable pride in flux and chaos. In *Earth in the Balance,* Al Gore condemns "the Cartesian model of the disembodied intellect," and the majority have accepted the feminist canard that logic is masculine (bad) and emotion is feminine (good). The new literary criticism demonstrates, point by unraveling point, that nothing means anything because every book now has a "subtext," and our kneejerk characterization of any utterance that makes no sense whatsoever is "thoughtful."

Americans have gotten the message that life is easier if they don't think straight. Aware that logic demolishes political correctness, they conclude that meaninglessness is the better part of wisdom and eagerly embrace fuzzy thinking as a refuge against charges of -ist, -ite, -phobe. Thus we have letters to the editor like this one in the *Washington Post*: "Mr. Maguire has a right to question the fairness of affirmative action, but his reference to a specific group's test scores was an unwarranted and malicious act."

The only time we even hear the L-word nowadays is when voters lie to exit polls and equally fuzzy pundits sigh, "There's no logic behind it."

Post hocky ergo propter hocky has hit the fan. Need an objection to the law barring HIV-positive persons from entering the country? Just say, as one activist did, "Travel doesn't cause HIV."

Need to make sure the whole world knows there is no connection whatsoever between you and your mind? Just go on *Nightline* and say, as Lani Guinier did: "Most important, I think, is not what I wrote but who I am."

Need to destroy your own argument? Object to the implications of the politically correct language now used in Lamaze classes, where instructors now speak of "partners" or "moms and coaches" instead of "husbands" and "wives," and then write, as Mona Charen did: "Now, I do not disparage the sentiments expressed at all, merely the terminology."

I N AMERICA, when Birnam Wood moves to Dunsinane it brings along its own developers. Is it any wonder we got the Clintons? This gang says military "mission" when they mean up the creek without a paddle, and "moving deadline" for a date that will live in infamy just as soon as they decide what it is.

Significantly, after Billy Boop had his "spirited" bipartisan meeting about Somalia with congressional leaders, an aide describing the fray to reporters took eerie liberties with a name CBS recently bestowed on a regular segment of its evening news show. The meeting, said the aide, was "a good reality check."

Need an operatic aria for Hillary's health-care commercials? How about "*L'ora suonò*" from *Don Carlo*? It means "Down with tyrants."

November 15, 1993

T HEY SAY a drowning person sees his whole life flash before him as he goes down for the third time. The feminization of America is having the same effect on me.

The chain of reasoning in date-rape cases brings back my grandmother's lecture on the proper way for a lady to walk past a barbershop.

"Always look straight ahead. If you look in, the men will think you're looking in."

"But if I looked in, I *would* be looking in."

"Yes, but not really."

Whenever I watch debates about women in combat, I begin hurtling through time the moment a worried general utters the words "male bonding" and "unit cohesion." The brass had better worry; anyone who has ever been in a girls' gym class has heard a snippy little voice say, "I'm not going to throw the ball to *her*."

Dee Dee Myers's disjointed press briefings? I am back once more in a Fifties dorm, listening to a panicky coed as she tries to figure out when her last period started.

"It's my middle, but it isn't really my middle because it's February, and that messes everything up because it's so short. I think it was the day you traded that green sack dress you hated for Flo's blue shrug—no, no, wait a minute, it was *before* that, because Flo wore the shrug to the movies the night I had cramps. What movie did we see? If I knew that, I could call the theater and find out when it played. Oh, I know! It was the one where Deborah Kerr saved the boy from being a sissy—no, no, wait! I take that back. It was the one where Charlton Heston was Andrew Jackson, and Yul Brynner did . . . um, something, I forget what, and there was this big battle."

Just about everything brings back memories of how I got started in writing. The 2,476th feature on mammograms, the 4,728th segment on unwed mothers, the eternal "special" hosted by Connie Chung, Meryl Streep's face as she discusses her "films"—expose me to any one of these and I will start reciting verbatim from the 1958 *Writer's Market*:

> True-confessions stories must be about subjects of interest to women: marital discord, adultery, problem children, alcoholism, insecurity, anxiety, depression, nervous breakdowns, accidents, illness, surgery, and sudden death. Upbeat ending essential. No humor; our readers take life seriously. Length 3,000 to 5,000; payment 5 cents per word. Enclose SASE.

The first story I sold was called, "I Committed Adultery in a Diabetic Coma." I think of it every time a Women's Health Special Supplement falls out of the newspaper.

The feminization of America has progressed so far that sometimes I have a hard time telling whether I'm watching the news on CNN or a three-hankie weeper on American Movie Classics. Barry Goldwater's sudden espousal of gay rights, or Barbara Stanwyck yearning for social approval? George Bush sabotaging himself to preserve his "place in history," or Lana Turner agonizing over What People Will Think? The scandal-tainted politician who decides to retire "to spend more time with my family," or Joan Crawford growling, "I'll do anything for those kids, you hear me, anything"?

It's especially confusing to watch old movies in the era of apologies. A nation so nice-nellied that it sees nothing odd about apologizing for homeless gypsies has only one apology left, and we just used it. In October, the Senate passed a resolution apologizing to Hawaii for overthrowing Queen Liliuokalani in 1893. It finally happened: we apologized to ourselves. Is that Joan Fontaine cringing through *Rebecca* or not?

I FOUND myself aboard another time capsule when the Houston Oilers fined football star David Williams for skipping out on a game in order to attend the birth of his child. The Sensitivity Patrol led by Anna Quindlen flew into the usual hysterical rage, but I flew back to the 1940s and sat on the floor beside our huge Philco console with my ear pressed against the brocaded vent so as not to miss a word of *Abbott & Costello*.

This particular show was as wonderfully wacky as the others. Not once did Lou Costello give any indication that anything was wrong. Not until the next day did we learn that he had gone on the air only hours after receiving word that his son had drowned. No one called him "insensitive" for leaving his wife alone while he made the whole country laugh; in the flood of admiring editorials that followed, one word stood out: "trouper."

The feminization of America has made emotions sacrosanct while condemning as cold and unfeeling rigorous concepts such as duty and honor. Propelled by incessant hosannas to woman's "finer" this and "softer" that, we make emotional decisions instead of ethical ones and congratulate ourselves for having "heart."

We need to get a grip on ourselves while there's still time. A bracing antidote to feminization is Mary Wollstonecraft, the Ur-feminist of the rational eighteenth century, who knew that political correctness is nothing more than female touchiness writ large. Said she: "I wish to persuade women to endeavor to acquire strength, both of mind and body, and to convince them that the soft phrases, susceptibility of heart, delicacy of sentiment, and refinement of taste, are almost synonymous with epithets of weakness."

December 13, 1993

1994

NYONE trying to get to the bottom of a complicated subject is advised, "Follow the money." I don't have a good enough head for figures, and in any case my interests lie elsewhere. I'd rather watch human nature expose its flanks, so my rule is, "Follow the quirk."

The health-care debate leads me down the trail of doctors as the linchpin of America's class system.

Jewish-mother jokes: "Help! My son the doctor is drowning!"

Subtle advice: "It would be nice if you married a doctor" kept several of my female classmates in American Lit from understanding the point of Sinclair Lewis's *Main Street*. "What's she griping about?" asked one. "She caught a doctor, didn't she?"

Unsubtle advice: "Always wear nice underwear in case you get hit by a bus." It was always a bus or a truck, never an ordinary car, the idea being to attract as many doctors as possible when they carried you into the emergency room.

In the Fifties, men trying to pick up girls either claimed to work for the CIA, or else tried to pass themselves off as doctors. The incident that sticks in my mind involved two buddies working in tandem. My masher said nothing about being a doctor, but midway in his pitch, another man strolled up to us, did an exaggerated doubletake, and exclaimed, "Why, Doctor! It certainly is good to see you again, Doctor! How are you, Doctor?"

Whereupon the first man passed a weary hand over his brow and said, "I was up all night in the operating room (*sigh*). Cardiac patient (*sigh*). But I managed to save him."

The way to my heart is through my funny bone; if they had made me laugh I might have let them buy me a drink, but their ineptness insulted my intelligence. I blew up.

"If you two hams want to impress me with titles, why don't you try *real* titles like duke, marquess, earl, viscount, and baron? That's what would make me sit up and take notice—not some little old *doctor!*"

I devoured historical novels in those days. Now, however, in the light of HillaryCare, my outburst takes on new meaning.

America's only title is *Doctor*, the medical profession is our peerage, and Hillary & Co. are the New Jacobins. I suspect that the entire health-care agenda is nothing more than camouflage for a wish—perhaps subconscious, perhaps not—to storm hospitals like so many Bastilles, overthrow the medical profession, and symbolically send doctors to the guillotine.

Remember feminist doctor hatred? One of the first "insensitive" villains was the arrogant gynecologist who kept turning up in the *de rigueur* childbirth scene in sisterhood novels like Marilyn French's *The Women's Room*, prompting intense agitprop about "our bodies, ourselves," do-it-yourself artificial insemination, home birthing, and a movement to bring back the midwife.

The same Far Left mindset drives HillaryCare, whose proponents fully intend to decide who goes to medical school. Two provisions of the plan not included in the abridged paperback, *Report to the American People*, are: a) Set up a new National Council on Graduate Medical Education, appointed by the Secretary of HHS, to certify the number of physicians allowed to enter training programs in specialties; and b) Require 55 per cent of new doctors to practice more generalized "primary care."

Quick, who comes to mind? Remember *Madame Bovary*? Her husband, Dr. Charles Bovary, was an "*officier de santé*"—a "health officer," not a real doctor at all but a kind of medic—who barely scraped through his courses and screwed up a club-foot operation so badly that the patient had to have his leg amputated.

Status symbols, like social stigmas, keep people on their toes. Lower the doctor's rank and you reduce medical expertise. Add affirmative action, which is already law, and we will be overrun with Charles Bovarys. That should end the medical peerage.

B UT turning doctors into commoners is only the beginning. HillaryCare intends to go for the jackpot and turn them into social undesirables. On

page 9 of *Report to the American People* we read: "New criminal penalties
. . . [prohibit] the payment of bribes or gratuities to influence the delivery of
health services and coverage."

Sound familiar? Hint: ". . . the manufacture, sale, or transportation of
intoxicating liquors within, the importation thereof into, or the exportation
thereof from the United States and all territory subject to the jurisdiction
thereof for beverage purposes is hereby prohibited."

Commenting on HillaryCare's proposed criminal penalties, Robert Bork
said, "I can't think of a legal justification for keeping people from using their
own money to get care. That is pure radical egalitarianism. They want to
bring everyone down to their own level."

I can see it now, and it's not what grandmothers call "good husband material." The peephole slides back and the patient says, "Pssst! Joe sent me. I got
a pain in my side." An operating table is hidden in the woods and the doctor
is armed with a shotgun, drawing a bead on intruders like the moonshiner we
ran into when I was at Ole Miss, who said, "Iffn yew-all frum the guvmint,
yew gonna carry yore ass home in a bucket."

January 24, 1994

H AVING a birthday shortly after New Year's is like having the whole
world to yourself. The rest of mankind has just staggered off the drag
strip known as the "holiday season." They rev up their motors at the
first gobble of the Thanksgiving turkey and floor it until the last note of "Auld
Lang Syne." Afterward, they're so worn out that the prospect of another fête
sends them crawling into the nearest cave, leaving you, lucky Capricorn, alone.

My usual version of dinner is running into the kitchen to gnaw on something, anything, so I can get back to work, but I'm a good cook when I take
the time. I was between books and there was no news to grapple with;
Troopergate seemed to have died of its own bad timing and Whitewatergate
was over my head, so having nothing to do, I took the time.

I was in an upbeat mood as I prepared my birthday dinner of veal scalop-
pine, parsleyed potatoes, and candied carrots. When everything was done, I
set the table with real silver instead of my everyday Delta Airlines cache, put
the food in the warmer, and mixed the martinis. Lifting my ice-encrusted,
salt-rimmed glass, I sang, "Happy birthday to me," then picked up the newspaper that I hadn't bothered to read earlier. The headline said: "WOMAN, 59,
GIVES BIRTH."

I think I eventually ate the dinner but I don't remember doing it. The egg-plant story hurled me into a melancholy funk which I proceeded to drown in gin. It had nothing to do with regret over being childless. My hero has always been Good King Herod; children are seen, heard, nasty, brutish, and short, and if I had any eggs left I would turn them in for guns.

Nor did I stew over the "ethical question." To me, that's the simple part. I oppose the "right" of post-menopausal women to create orphans. Furthermore, although I am an Episcopal agnostic, the lost Roman Catholic that lives in every Episcopalian tells me that aborting female fetuses to harvest their eggs is a mortal sin—and that's that. Television's sacred goal of "equal time" is neither sacred nor a goal as far as I'm concerned. My blood may be Anglo-Saxon, but when it comes to impartiality I stand with Father Gilhooly of *Studs Lonigan*—wipe the floor with 'em, knock 'em into the middle of next week, and God bless all in this house.

W HAT I DID stew over was a mélange of things, inchoate emotions and memories that flashed through my brain like heat lightning as I worked my way down to the bottom of the cocktail shaker. Guy de Maupassant defined a writer as one who "looks at the underside of things," and as you know from my last column, my motto is, "Follow the quirk." Combine those with six martinis and you have my disquisition on the egg plant, to wit:

It will destroy that rollicking female imperiousness that has flourished wherever post-menopausal women gather to swap old wives' tales. Be it the Roman gynaecium, the Saxon brydbur, or the Daughters' meeting, without a rousing elegy on "change-of-life babies" none dare call it sisterhood.

A change-of-life baby, as I learned from a childhood spent eavesdropping on my grandmother's unfinished sentences, is always unplanned.

"She thought she was too old, so she didn't bother to . . ."

A change-of-life baby is also an embarrassment.

"She won't set foot out of the house because everybody can just look at her and know that she and her husband still . . ."

Or maybe they don't still.

"They say that last one belongs to . . ."

A change-of-life baby may never get born. By now the Daughters are hitting the sherry bottle, so we hear no-holds-barred stories about "the Woman Who. . .": the woman who was in labor for two weeks, the woman who split in half, and—so help me—the woman who died when the fetus kicked a hole in her aging womb, and when the undertaker opened her up, what do you think he found? Two tiny little footprints on her liver.

If the change-of-life baby does get born, several things will happen.

"The older children will be made to tend it, and they'll resent it so much that they'll never want any children of their own."

"It'll go wrong because the parents will be too tired to raise it right." (A problem alluded to by Rose Kennedy in an unguarded moment after Chappaquiddick.)

"It'll be brilliant but not very bright, like those professors who get run over and stab themselves with letter openers."

It may also be "a little funny." Many communities used to have a homosexual nobody could miss, a mauve-decade throwback complete with ascot, lisp, falsetto, and flapping wrist. Nobody persecuted him, however, because old wives' tales work in mysterious ways, their wonders to perform. As any blue-haired old lady would tell you, "There's nothing really wrong with him, he's just a change-of-life baby."

Bid farewell to my beloved colorful dowagers. We already have had a figurative menopausing of America wherein problems are regarded as something not to think through but to "cope" with, "handle," and "survive." Now here comes the literal kind.

February 21, 1994

LORENA BOBBITT'S surgical strike made me remember a time when I associated edged weaponry with perfect congeniality between the sexes.

It is circa 1940 and I have been posted on the back porch as a look-out. Soon the object of my scrutiny appears and makes his way down the alley. There is a small wheel on his back and every few paces he throws back his head and shouts, "Scissaman!"

My British father called him the "scissors grinder," but such precise diction was rare in the very southern Washington of those days. The rest of us, like the grinder, were generic Virginians or Marylanders with tongues influenced by black English, so we called him, as he called himself, "the scissaman."

He was in his sixties, with thick white hair and rosy cheeks, as Dickensian as all get-out. He sharpened all the knives and scissors in the house for fifty cents, but it was understood that you were supposed to offer him food and drink. Thus did he eat his way through the neighborhood—a sandwich here, a bowl of oyster stew there, pie and coffee somewhere else—

making it possible for him to live cheaply in a single room with virtually no expenses except rent.

In return he was a perfect guest who made the goodwives' day. His working life was peopled exclusively by housebound women, so he felt comfortable with them and could talk the talk. He knew the drill perfectly: ailments, especially the kind that lend themselves to well-timed interjections of "she's wasting away" and "it runs in the family." His innate gentlemanly delicacy allowed him to discuss the finer points of kidney stones without ever crossing the line into coarseness, yet clearly he was no male hen. He had an adventurous jack-of-all-trades past and big scarred hands, but he was nonetheless a "woman's man," and it came so naturally to him that neither he nor his customers ever thought about it.

The scissaman was one of many "man men" in my childhood, and now I find myself remembering them hungrily as I watch the battle of the sexes grow steadily more vicious and sanguinary.

There was the insurance man who came once a month to collect the premiums and lingered to swap Eleanor jokes over coffee and cake. There was the Fuller Brush man who ended up lying prone on our kitchen table while Granny prepared a homemade mustard plaster for his back, which he told her all about over iced tea and cookies when he was able to sit upright. There was the motor-man—as in streetcar—whose virtually total right-of-way allowed him to carry on detailed conversations with bevies of women embarked on leisurely mid-day shopping trips. And then there was the iceman (we had a refrigerator at home but an icebox at the beach cottage). The nature of his product made it impossible for him to tarry, but he cut a dashing figure in his leather shoulder pad, lending credence to the nursery rhyme that goes "the ice man is a nice man."

Scissaman & Co. were part of the fabric of city life that came unraveled with the rise of the suburbs after World War II. The connection between the disappearance of "man men" and the rise of feminism is comically and pitifully obvious.

No pre-war city housewife ever had cause to utter that plaintive cry, "He never talks to me." She enjoyed a parade of garrulous males, all of whom were seasoned students of the female psyche, well able to minister to what are now called "needs." Scissamen may not have felt like talking to their own wives after their gossipy, coffee-drinking rounds, but by talking to everyone else's wife they took the onus off countless husbands, who were not then met at the door by resentful women starved for male conversation.

The postwar suburban housewife sharpened her own knives on one of her many labor-saving appliances, and brooded; when the can-opener attachment fell off the knife sharpener, as it invariably does, she burst into tears. For this she spent four years in college? Stuck in a house with no one to talk to but kids, whose conversational powers lacked something—like syntax. Or other women, who talked about nothing but kids. Her purdah was rarely broken except for the Tidy Didy driver, but he left his truck running to hurry to the next stop, and besides, he was a pimply lout.

G OING TO BED with a man, said Mrs. Patrick Campbell, is the best way to get his undivided attention, so the lonely suburban housewife had affairs. When her lovers treated her badly she went to a psychiatrist, but she did all the talking; the shrink, like her husband, hardly said a word. Then she read *The Feminine Mystique*.

But for a nail . . .

But for a scissaman, the sexes might not now be at each other's throats. Fathers, husbands, professors, and employers may be woman's most important male relationships, but they are also the most tension-ridden. America contains millions of women who hate men in general because they have never met men in general. Invading male preserves like the military could be her twisted way of seeking the chaste intimacy of Scissaman & Co.

March 21, 1994

I NCREDIBLY, many conservatives are still haunted by charges of "mean-spirited rhetoric" at the 1992 Republican convention. Personally, I thought it was great; I haven't had so much fun since the Girl Scouts and the Mormons got a shock from my broken doorbell.

The conservative at war with his own temperament is a curious spectacle that began in the New Deal, when Republicans were shamed into joining the race to compassion. At first a merely fatuous Me Tooism, it grew into the logic-defying desperation of Eisenhower's earnest credo: "I'm a conservative on fiscal issues but a liberal on human issues."

Thirty years ago Barry Goldwater called himself a "cheerful malcontent." Now Bill Kristol calls himself a "cheerful pessimist" and Rush Limbaugh calls himself "a harmless little fuzzball." The Christian Coalition recently advised its members to soften "intemperate rhetoric and show more tolerance"; instead of using metaphors like "religious war," they should substitute sports analogies because they "sound playful."

At the American Cause conference on ending welfare, Charles Sykes took his idioms from the old vaudeville melodrama about the evil landlord and the sweet young mortgagee: "We don't need to be perceived as simply flinthearted about this. We need to re-establish what it means to really care about people and show that conservatives are not simply pennypinchers. There is a conservatism of the heart."

How, pray, is it possible to practice conservatism of the heart and at the same time "bring back the stigma of unwed motherhood"? You can't just say, "The stigma is back." Knowing the words is not enough, we must also know the tune, and as anyone can testify who was in junior high when Ingrid Bergman got caught, it is a heartless chorus involving shunning, smirks behind hands, and smug hubris ("It won't happen to me"), and it is sung chiefly by other women.

These heart-and-caring conservatives sound like transfer students trying to be popular fast. Or like those Nice Women who flutter around saying, "I just want everybody to be happy," whenever a family fight gets interesting. Before getting bogged down in A Place Called Slop they should realize that if they lack the courage of their temperament, it won't be long before they lack the courage of their convictions.

The conservative temperament is masculine-realist; the liberal temperament is feminine-idealist. In literary terms it assays out to classicism versus romanticism. Ours is most assuredly a bleak mindset, but as Dryden scholar John J. Enck pointed out: "Reason, as the seventeenth century regarded it, tends to unearth in even the most personal and intense suffering, ironies whose very recognition furnishes a sardonic strength."

I have found this to be true. Somebody is always calling me "mean-spirited," while my more imaginative enemies have come up with "Fascist Flossie" and "Ku Klux King." I refuse to try to soften myself, however, because I understand the benefits of the conservative temperament.

Conservatives fare better psychologically because we don't expect much of human nature. Our outlook provides an answer to the question that destroys so many idealists: "How can people do such things?" I knew a Jewish woman who read one Holocaust book after another, trying to find the answer in ever more arcane speculations. She thought if she could trace the Holocaust to Wagner's music, German cleanliness—anything—she would understand it and be able to banish her horror. She eventually had a nervous breakdown because she clung to her idealistic belief in the perfectibility of mankind. A conservative, by contrast, readily admits that human nature is inherently bad and people are capable of anything. It's not a pretty thought but it explains the inexplicable, which is some comfort.

The liberal temperament, however, is based on the discomfiting arrangement that Tennessee Williams called "the kindness of strangers." In an egalitarian democracy the only source of respect and dignity is the "niceness" we practice on each other. It's an eerily sinister version of the behavior of royalty, who must be gracious all the time because it makes the common people feel safe. The difference is that being smiled upon by a queen is reassuring, but being smiled upon by a determined humanitarian makes people aware of the arbitrary nature of the humanitarian impulse and leaves them feeling more, not less, insecure.

R EAL humanitarians tend to be curmudgeons because they must deal with bureaucratic blockheads. One of the shortest fuses in history belonged to its foremost angel of mercy, Florence Nightingale, who was also a foremost female misogynist. Admonished by a do-gooder about the dangers of exposing patients to night air, she exploded: "It's the only kind of air there is at night!"

To thine own self be true. If liberals call you mean-spirited, ask: "Don't you ever feel like saying what you really think instead of smiling and saying what you're supposed to think?" They have to agree, else look like one-celled blobs without a nervous system, floating in a Petri dish.

If you really want to destroy them, offer my cure for crime: "The only thing that really works is fear itself." The New Deal rhythms drive them nuts.

April 18, 1994

‘ T O AMERICANS," wrote Randall Jarrell, "English manners are more frightening than none at all." It's true. We hate good manners; they make us feel shut out and held at arm's length. We would much rather be at each other's throats, which at least has the advantage of resembling a hug. Given a choice between the starched collar of respect and the rump-sprung britches of love, the American fashion has never been in doubt.

Manners have always co-existed uneasily with our national purpose. Cherishing the canard that nobody is better than anybody else, we enshrined informality so as to put people at ease instead of in their place, until we concluded that it is impossible to give offense in a democratic society. Then along came the multiculturalists, who said, "Offense is a group thing, and you'd better understand." We understood perfectly: if it's not bigotry, it's not rudeness. Now we are so busy being sensitive that we have become barbaric.

Mouth-slapping cereal commercials give us a view of food inside the actor's mouth, and "Washington apples, they're as good as you've heard," presents crunch after crunch after crunch, until the last cruncher catches the drip with his finger and licks it off with a loud slurp.

Now to the other end. The Odor-Eaters man mourns, "My feet stink!" Macintosh has a file-compressing software called "StuffIt." The "Marvin" comic strip contains regular references to "poopy diapers." A typical Metro headline reads: "Dog Owners Warned to Scoop Poop." A laxative commercial features a constipated construction engineer worried that the little pill he took will "kick in" while he is on top of his half-finished skyscraper, and ABC News ran an interminable segment about odors in the shuttle toilet, which, we were needlessly told, "smelled like a men's room."

Being earthy is like being satirical. The satirist needs a like-minded audience of co-conspirators who are secure enough not to take everything literally; they cannot be incorrigible romantics or nervous status seekers. Successful earthiness likewise demands a unified outlook. A British historian's deadpan description of the Tommy's standard laxative in Victorian India—"a spoonful o' gunpowder in a cuppa 'ot tea"—is funny because everything is all of a piece, but American diversity, with its goal of "inclusion," has no common ground but the lowest common denominator. That we have become the land of the bathroom joke was a foregone conclusion.

Our vocabulary of manners has shrunk. Every review (except mine) of H. L. Mencken's diary contained the sentence, "His racism is inexcusable." But nothing else is inexcusable, and anyone who uses the word about a lapse in etiquette is told to "lighten up." A nurse who does not first-name her ninety-year-old patients is *punctilious*, which now means cold. As for *civility*, it is rarely used in its broadest sense; usually it crops up in arguments about arguments, as in "civil discourse," when pundits fret about the proper way to be rude on *Crossfire*.

We lighten up in the wrong ways, at the wrong times, in the wrong places, with the wrong people, and call it inclusion, when in fact it is a faux pas most grievous. Having a Tomb of the Unknowns insults the Unknown Soldier because more than one destroys the whole concept. Fiddling with holidays to create three-day weekends institutionalizes disrespect. Rush Limbaugh, anxious to prove that conservatives practice inclusion, interrupts a respectful young caller with, "You don't have to call me sir." Why not? A brilliant man and natural leader who is admired by millions certainly should be called sir.

T HE PURPOSE of manners is to make life serene for those about us. The most ignored form of civility nowadays is being clear and concise. Atlanta lawyers used to say that it was impossible to misinterpret a Will written by Eugene Mitchell, Margaret Mitchell's father. "In drawing a Will," he always advised, "just look after the grammar, and the law will look after itself."

So will the manners, but democracy makes Druids of the intelligent. Some of our most intelligent people, at least in terms of raw IQ, are young male technologists known as computer jocks. Having grown up hearing that "everyone is equal" when they know perfectly well everyone is not, they get even by writing User's Manuals that no one can understand. A badly written User's Manual can cause literal accidents, but when it makes people feel stupid it can also cause figurative accidents, harder to define but just as damaging. The contempt that fairly oozes out of these impenetrable oak groves is rudeness incarnate.

The current state of American manners makes me feel as if I were trapped in a Brueghel painting of a rustic kermiss in full swing—peasants, peasants everywhere and much the worse for drink, grabbing food and each other and gnawing on both with untrammeled gusto. God may have loved the common people, but a trip to any shopping mall suggests that He made far too many of them.

When loutishness becomes the rule, the people who suffer the most are women, for whom manners originally were devised. Instead of identifying with the scum of the earth, feminists should reflect that a bold peasantry, their country's pride, when once leashed can never be denied.

May 16, 1994

I KNEW there was something familiar about Bill Clinton. The moment Paula Jones said "hotel" and "convention" my youth came back to me. The Prez reminds me of the Man on the Plane, the ubiquitous middle-aged businessman with *husband* written all over him who lives for out-of-town flings.

Like the laws of the Medes and the Persians, his seduction line altereth not. You can tell how many times he must have said it by the way it all runs together. His "God you're lovely I've got to have you let's go to bed" sounds like the flight attendant's "Please fasten your seatbelts and place your serving tray in the upright position."

Smiles ("Whatcha lookin' so sad about, honey?") are his life's blood. He is convinced that if he can get a woman to talk, he can get her to smile, and if he can get her to smile, he can get her to bed. Any *no* from a woman is a sexual no. If she refuses his little bag of airline cashews, he feels subconsciously that she has refused him sex; his crestfallen look gives him away. Any refusal, no matter how minor, sets off desperate cajolery. Does she want his magazine? No. A pillow? No. Another drink? No. He will press on, burrowing through her refusals like a mole, offering her his earphones, his mints, his crossword puzzle, his pencil—he must get a *yes* out of her, no matter how meaningless.

He also requires lots of laughs. A serious woman is a sexually unresponsive woman, so he must cheer her up, as it were. Proud of his scintillating repartee, he orders a tray of "whore's drawers" to go with cocktails; defines a French breakfast ("a roll in bed with honey"); extols the technique of the author of *She* ("ride 'er haggard"); and deconstructs *The Rape of the Lock* ("Here comes the key!").

Next come his maxims. "Only a man can play the violin because it's like getting a response out of a woman's body, hee-hee" (wink-wink). This is his version of Balzac's comparison between an inept lover and an orangutan with a violin, but don't try to untangle it or he will jab you in the ribs and boom, "Hey, the party's getting serious!" Worse, any mention of Balzac will inspire a vaudeville routine about Zack's balls.

The wise woman will shriek with mirth over his bons mots. Merely smiling politely is a confession that you have experienced mild pleasure but not orgasm. He will keep pumping away, repeating his punch lines and elbowing you in the ribs in a symbolic attempt to send you over the top, so fake the laugh.

When he's ready to steer the conversation into intimate waters, he uses a technique he calls "getting her to open up."

"What do you want out of life?" he asks soulfully, his eyes narrowing to pensive slits. Next: "Don't you ever get lonely?" Then: "What are you so unhappy about?" Finally, he shakes his head, smiles his worldly-wise smile and murmurs, "What are you afraid of?"

This plangent third degree is designed to prove that you are a love-starved waif. Any woman thus grilled finds herself trying very hard to sound active and sophisticated, but watch out when he starts comparing lonely life in the big city to the rich communalism of his home town. If you say, "Small towns are dull," he will retort, "You like excitement, huh? Hee-hee," accompanied by every gleam and wink in his repertoire. His conversational terrain is full of such land mines.

C ASANOVA wrote that for men, "Love is three-quarters curiosity," an observation reiterated by Theodore Reik: "Nothing in the psychology of women can be compared to the sexual inquisitiveness of the male."

The Man on the Plane is a sexual quidnunc. Knowing nothing about women, he has an insatiable need to know everything about them. Every woman is familiar with his speculative gaze across a hotel lobby: it's one of the few times he's quiet and still. Deep in reverie he sits, eyes squinched up and a puckish smile lifting the corners of his mouth, a man in search of she-ness.

He wants to be "a man who understands women," yet he fears that such an understanding would be evidence of a dangerously large feminine component in his own makeup. The fun would be over then; he could no longer go out with the boys and talk about how hard it is to understand women. Worse, the boys might start having trouble understanding *him*. Unwilling to risk this, he puts the lid on his deeper speculations and limits himself to "I wonder what she's like in the sack."

He is a self-proclaimed expert at spotting arcane lubricious distinctions across a crowded room. A woman whose eyes slant is hot. A woman with a cleft chin is hot. A woman who slips off her shoes is hot—not just her feet, but all of her. This is what he heard behind the barn and he still swears by it.

I don't know if the Arkansas troopers propositioned woman after woman until one said yes, but I do know that the Man on the Plane said, "They'll never repeal the law of averages, hee-hee."

June 13, 1994

I AM the opposite of a hypochondriac, whatever that is. I consulted the thesaurus for an antonym but hypochondria has no entry of its own. It is listed under Dejection, along with typical Roget synonyms like "infestivity." The antonyms are listed under Cheerfulness and include "canty."

My vocabulary problem arises from the fact that hypochondriacs have cornered both sides of the neurosis. They are obsessed with being sick, but they are also obsessed with being well, so it is impossible to be the opposite of a hypochondriac. All I can do is state my philosophy: If whisky or salt won't cure it, then to hell with it. I worry about important things. I'll sit up all night nursing an ailing paragraph, but I refuse to bow down before the latest sacred udder. I never had a mammogram and never hope to get one, and far from dreading mastectomy, the subject makes me positively canty: I could get a better fit in a shoulder holster.

American hypochondria has undergone an interesting change in recent years. The classic or "normal" hypochondriac simply wanted to be sick so he could want to get well. He did not want others to be sick lest they steal his thunder, and he did not harbor any hostility to healthy people; indeed, he was very fond of them and liked having them around because they made him seem sicker.

The New Hypochondria throbs with the morbid narcissism of liberalism. New Hypochondriacs don't really want to be either sick or well, but rather "information receptive" and "medically aware"—code words for intelligent and educated and thus a delineator of class, a way of separating the people who read "The Forgotten Spleen" in the *Washington Post* Sunday Health section from the people who don't. To the New Hypochondriacs, the fun lies not in the croup kettles and mustard plasters of times past; they want to skip both illness and health so they can get to prevention and recovery, co-dependency and enabling, and have vanity plates that say SUVIVR.

The hypochondria of education and awareness is why we have commercials for medicines whose purpose is never revealed. These spots invariably sound like snide academics sitting on the floor playing Scrabble.

"Like many people, you're probably curious about Rogaine," the shill begins. He goes on in that vein, with teasers like, "Of course you want to know more about Rogaine," but he never says what Rogaine is or what it's for. "Ask your doctor about Rogaine," he concludes, adding in an offensively high-handed tone: "Go on, what are you waiting for?"

Then there's the colloquy between the pharmacist and the customer. The customer hands over a prescription for "Cardizem SR" and the pharmacist asks, "Have you tried Cardizem CD?"

"No, can you give me Cardizem CD?" asks the customer.

"Only your doctor can prescribe Cardizem CD," chides the pharmacist.

"Cardizem CD? Okay, I'll ask my doctor."

We never find out what Cardizem SR is, much less Cardizem CD, but we don't really want to know. The human spirit needs tantalizing mysteries but our supply has run out. Now that femmes fatales practice total honesty, medicine is the only thing left that keeps us guessing.

As New Hypochondriacs convince themselves that the only thing we have to fear is food itself, a bitter resentment against the French is peeping out of the lucubrations of the politically correct. France, long the nirvana of alienated intellectuals who want to escape crass America, is the land of the pig-out. Butter, lard, goose liver pâté, and two packs of Gauloises a day, and still France lives. Our medically aware elite is hurt by this picture of health, but they are incapable of grasping—or admitting—the reasons for it.

The French are a secure, adult people who are proud of their language and culture and never apologize for being French (quite the contrary). They are also a homogeneous people, and thus never come down with Americanoma Diversititis Democratosis, which kills with kindness. Above all, although they are not religious, they are Catholic, a seeming conflict that they understand perfectly and that gives them a stress-defying spiritual ease that few Americans know. You couldn't clog a French artery if you injected it with silicone.

W E ARE LIVING in ironic times and I relish the coming spectacle. The New Hypochondriacs are all pumped up from exposure to shows like The Learning Channel's week-long series, "The Operation," which features complete surgical procedures, a different one for each day, like a teenage girl's underpants. What happens when they get hit with socialized medicine? Hypochondriacs need complete medical freedom to do their stuff, but the same government that made them medically aware is now promising two bureaucrats in every pot and Hillary in the garage.

The Nanny State soon will need a cautionary tale, so I have written one for them:

When they came for the smokers I kept silent because I don't smoke. When they came for the meat eaters I kept silent because I'm a vegetarian. When they came for the gun owners I kept silent because I'm a pacifist. When they came for the drivers I kept silent because I'm a bicyclist.

They never did come for me. I'm still here because there's nobody left in the secret police except sissies with rickets.

July 11, 1994

I NCREASINGLY, letters to the editor and calls to talk radio are kicking off with: "If this were a sane country . . ." It isn't, of course. People deprived of rational thought always go bonkers.

Our deprivation continues apace. Recently in an electronics store at the mall, I was one of a crowd of shoppers watching a bank of television sets all tuned to the same channel. The news came on and a man-in-the-street interview began. Suddenly, eerily, there were two dozen images of the same earnest citizen saying in unison with himself: "We can't balance the budget on the back of the *Titanic*."

I broke up, but no one else reacted except to give me a dirty look. Our sense of the absurd, that great ballast against neuroticism, is gone. Our civic life is so riddled with banalities and clichés that their precise arrangement no longer matters; we can scoop them up and dump them together like the contents of a spilled handbag. By now "the backs of the poor" sounds almost the same as "the deck chairs on the *Titanic*," so—hey!—it's close enough.

The logical fallacy of *petitio principii* has become our way of life. Confronted by ravines of contradiction, we step over them like so many puddles without stopping to ask the obvious questions. If, as countless elegies to Jacqueline Kennedy Onassis claimed, "she taught us how to behave with taste," how come it didn't take? If "she taught us how to grieve with dignity," why is everyone crying on television?

If genetics is the hot new science with all the answers, why is it racist/classist/elitist to say, "The apple never falls far from the tree"? If a role model disgraces himself, why do we absolve him because we can't afford to lose him as a role model? If "mental illness is no longer a stigma," why do politicians think they can destroy their rivals by digging up proof that they once saw a psychiatrist?

It's getting harder and harder to follow an American discussion. We used to chide worryworts with: "Suppose one thing, suppose another, suppose a jackass was your brother?" Now, however, supposition is the handmaiden of political correctness. I often run into this because of my penchant for voicing unthinkable opinions. "I'm sick of women," I will say, and my opponent retorts, "Suppose you substituted *blacks* for *women* in that sentence?" It goes on. "Bugger the spotted owls." Suppose you substituted *Jews* for *owls*? "Brand criminals on the forehead." Suppose you substituted *gays* for *criminals*? This is not sensitivity but rhetorical tumult.

It's no wonder that the stores are filled with clear cola, clear beer, clear dishwashing liquid, clear deodorant. The clear craze reminds us that there once was a time when ideas were "as clear as a bell," good people were "as transparent as glass," and our heads were on so straight that we could "see right through" a charlatan. Now the only thing we have that's clear is clear itself, so take a sip or a squirt and forget our mental chaos.

America is starting to look a lot like the Middle Ages, when morbid fears and nervous prostration took up a large chunk of everyone's time. Where medieval man saw stigmata we see skin cancer. They were invaded by incubi, we are invaded by aliens. They carved gargoyles with chilling reality, we computerize dinosaurs with Virtual Reality. They dreaded plague, we dread the face-eating virus. They had food tasters, we have the Food and Drug

Administration. They imagined their wells were poisoned, we imagine everything is poisoned.

Medieval eclipses were underexplained and ours are overexplained, but the resultant mood of foreboding is the same. And while our commitment to diversity obviates the hunchbacked gypsies that reduced Cob and Perkin to jelly, the lawsuits growing out of the Americans with Disabilities Act produce just as many nightmares.

T HEN THERE is leadership. We assume that medieval man was emotionally secure despite the uncertainties of daily life because he had godlike rulers called the Lionheart, the Bold, and the Hammer. They, however, were the exceptions. More often than not, Cob and Perkin could trace their worst seizures to the very foot of the throne, for the most unavoidable source of medieval mental strain was, by charming coincidence, the same as ours: the Pious, the Fat, and the Mad.

Bill Clinton entered office to hosannas of "He speaks in complete sentences!" He doesn't now. One moment he is red with rage, pounding the podium and yelling about stolen bathrobes and jumping into tanks. The next he is glassily detached and blankly ethereal, his voice taking on the meandering gauziness of a Debussy tone poem as he calls the dollar's drop "puzzling" and sighs over an economy that is performing "in a funny way."

I would not be surprised if he became the first sitting President to crack up. What better way to acquire the national constituency he so desperately wants? All he has to do is pull his old trick of leading where everybody else is already going.

August 15, 1994

A CORNERSTONE of Western thought that has vanished without a trace is admiration for ancient Sparta.

Essayists of centuries past, secure in their manhood and steeped in classical education, extolled Spartan discipline and self-control. Their commentaries inspired generations of schoolboys to pen compositions in praise of the Spartan lad who flinched not as the fox gnawed his vitals, and shaped the American beau ideal of the "strong silent type." To call a man laconic, from Sparta's formal name, "Lacedaemon," was to crown him with laurels.

Now it would be an insult, if the word even existed, which it doesn't— it's vanished, too. Feminist assaults on male emotional containment and ten

million women's mag articles called "How to Get Him to Open Up" at last
have achieved their fiendish goal. The male's "Y" chromosome has come to
stand for "yap." Men now talk even more than women, and being the bigger,
stronger sex, they are making the non-stop human voice a greater weapon of
torture than it has ever been. If they don't shut up I'm going to run away and
join the ladies' auxiliary of the French Foreign Legion.

I can no longer bear to watch *Crossfire*, a show inspired by Pat
Buchanan's boyhood dinner table. The whole family must have ulcers. Soon
I won't be able to watch anything, because men are slipping into Southern-
belle locutions. "Never, ever, as long as I live!" she trills, to which the guilty
bureaucrat replies, "I'm very, very, very sorry," while O.J. pleads,
"Absolutely one hundred percent not guilty!" and Bill Clinton insists, "No,
no, no, no, no, no, no, no!"

Many men who would rather not yap are forced to by the demands of
positivism and other insidious practices of Nice Guyism, such as the need to
prove their sincerity. Listening to sincere men talk is like trying to get chew-
ing gum off the sole of a shoe.

They also are lured into garrulousness by the kind of questions put to
them. Our therapeutic age is hostile to declarations of action emerging from
clear thought, so we have developed a new verb tense, the Recumbent
Ruminative. Barbara Walters would never ask the Spartan lad, "What did you
do?" but rather, "What went through your mind when you saw the fox dragging your intestines across the field?"

Another cause of the Forced Yap is the proliferation of professions in a
democracy. A craftsman is quiet, e.g., the mechanic grunting softly to himself while he peers under the hood. But the first word in "professional" is
"profess," and it has become a *carte blanche* that goes with white collars.

Betty Friedan wrote that housework expands to fill the time available.
Similarly, yapping expands to fill the widening abyss in our body politic. The
worse things get, the more men heed the internalized command, "Gentlemen,
start your analogies."

The leader of a nation exemplified by "E pluribus unum" is, by definition, a man of few words, but when this ideal is corrupted to "Ex uno plures,"
he must constantly spell out his mission by vowing to be the President [gov-
ernor, mayor] "of all the people," a gaseous cliché guaranteed to turn him into
a compulsive oral list maker.

"Growing in office" means doing the wrong thing for the wrong reason,
which takes a lot more explaining than doing the wrong thing for the right
reason or the right thing for the wrong reason. "Incorporating dissenting

views" takes twice as long as "sending a message," and "sharing thoughts" takes twice as long as incorporating dissenting views. Betraying "a lack of conviction" means yapping harder to prove otherwise, and being "willing to listen" means somebody else is yapping.

"Seeking balance [consensus, accord]" is especially fatal. When people look for something they're usually quiet about it, but when the verb changes to seek you can bet somebody is yapping. Emile Zola became the conscience of mankind when he barked "*J'accuse!*" but U.S. Yap, sworn to be "non-judgmental," becomes the bane of existence when he prattles, "I would like to utilize this opportunity to neutralize the opposition." Listening to his squishy monologues about "conflict resolution" and "the politics of persuasion," I find myself wondering: Whatever happened to keel hauling and trial by ordeal?

T HE PROCESS of emasculation is cumulative; when men take on one female trait, others follow. It is no accident that the yappiest administration in our history is also the one that hides behind women's skirts: Clinton behind Hillary's and Janet Reno's, and now Roger Altman behind Jean Hanson's.

And what of the opposition? Insurrections, civil wars, and revolutions are mounted by angry young men, but if ours are anywhere near the barricades they have a cellular phone in one hand. America is primed for a revolution but we probably won't have one for a while because Jacques is too busy yapping on the phone with Rush Limbaugh.

Yapping is keeping the peace but frustration is building. Eventually, male yappers will feel self-disgust, as men always do when they see themselves behaving like women. It's already begun. Men always find a "real man's" way to do things, and On Line is becoming the real man's way of talking. The messages may be garrulous but at least they are silent.

September 12, 1994

N ORMALLY I score very low in the victimhood stakes. In the discrimination list that begins "without regard to . . ." I can claim only "gender," which makes me a one-fer, not much of a prize in a nation that gives preference to mentally retarded transvestite dwarfs.

But hark! I'm not bona-fides-deprived after all. CNN says I'm a "chronic renter," prone to "compulsive renting" and suffering from "rental addiction." My compadres in Detroit already are enrolled in a workshop, and Atlanta columnist Marilyn Geewax has called for "home-ownership education programs." Soon there will be a self-help book, *Chasing Your Rental Demons*, containing a certain case history: Florence K., chronic renter for 35 years . . .

Not quite. I bought a condo in 1978 and learned to hate the American Dream for screwing up the content of my character. As a renter I was vibrant and whole; when something needed attention, I simply called the landlord and said, "This thingamabob is funny," and returned to my real interests while somebody fixed the thingamabob. As an owner, however, I became a dismal cretin; haunting hardware stores, watching Bob Vila instead of reading Evelyn Waugh, and engaging in moribund conversations with the Pond Scum Committee.

The turning point came when I used a snake to unclog my sink and the Plumbing Committee dropped by for a scintillating discussion about whether my downstairs neighbor owned half of the clog. That did it. Disgusted with picayune concerns, I sold the condo and happily resumed collecting what Americans contemptuously call "a drawerful of rent receipts."

Why does the govenment push ownership so vigorously when mortgage-interest deduction costs them $43 billion a year in lost revenue? Knowing the government as we do, they must have an awfully good reason for passing up $43 billion. What ever could it be?

George F. Babbitt: "When folks own their homes, they ain't starting labor troubles, and they're raising kids instead of raising hell."

William J. Levitt: "No man who owns his own house and lot can be a Communist. He has too much to do."

He won't give the government any kind of trouble, Communist or otherwise, because he has lobotomized himself with his own hoe. His overriding concern is caca—horse, cow, sheep; you name it and he'll talk about it. He even buys processed caca in big slabby bags with green lettering and mixes it with rotting vegetables and fish bones to make his grass grow. Being a home owner transforms him from a thinking reed into a tinkering, puttering, dull, distracted, small-minded bore, and that's just the kind of citizenry the government wants.

Only in America would a crushing thirty-year debt be regarded as a safety valve against civil insurrection. We use mortgages to shove as many people as possible into the middle class—the nervous, self-conscious, pettifogging class that Disraeli despised—to create a bogus squirearchy with "something to lose," so they will live in dread of losing it. Never has domestic tranquillity been courted in quite such an odd way.

Now, echoing Babbitt and Levitt, are the enterprise-zone conservatives with their big, confident EZ Con grins and their booming mantra, "Owning property is the beginning of conservatism." They claim the inner city would wither away if the government gave public-housing residents the money to buy their own units, but underneath their noisy optimism is the same peace-through-distraction mindset that devised Atlanta's panicky slogan, "The City Too Busy to Hate." Subconsciously the EZ Cons hope to stave off an imminent race war by creating poor black "home owners," and then convincing them that their highest priority, their noblest goal, the most important thing in the world is to stay indoors so they won't miss the Johnny B. Quik man.

N OW COMES the "rental addiction" movement, designed to corral the last of the red-hot renters and turn us into Dagwood Bumstead and Herb Woodley arguing over who owns the hedge clippers. To enlist us in the race to bland stability, it is necessary to destroy the rental market. There are many ways to do this and all are succeeding.

First, keep talking about that "drawerful of rent receipts," as if it were a drawerful of snakes. Second, put "Own," and "Rent" blocks on every form and cast a cold eye on anyone who checks "Rent." Keep this up until everyone thinks like the Virginia suburbanites interviewed by the *Washington Post*: "Many . . . expressed a deep-rooted scorn for renters, and said they thought they should be isolated somewhere far from people who own homes."

Third, destroy landlords. This is the easiest because the very word *landlord* is anathema nowadays, but if the vocabulary of Anglo-Saxon hierarchy won't deter them from offering apartments, open-housing laws will. If we applaud vicious idealists who pose as prospective tenants to catch "bigoted" landlords, fewer and fewer people will take on the legal risks of the rental business. Soon there will be no landlords left, and then a triumphant federal bureaucracy will force me to buy a house through HillaryHome.

October 10, 1994

O N MY GOOD days my definition of a conservative is someone who has ordered a book from Liberty Press and knows who Irving Babbitt was, but as you know, I have very few good days. I have defined some other conservative types of late and they all make me sick.

1. Gump Cons prove that conservatives are like a box of chocolates: you never know when something mushy is going to ooze out.

I met Forrest Gump eight years ago, having read the Winston Groome novel before it was published—i.e., I reviewed it for the *Washington Post*, which fact alone tells us something: if the book had contained the seeds of a great conservative revival, the *Post* never would have assigned it to me.

Screenwriters always change things, but even so I'm having a hard time understanding why the movie made Pat Buchanan deliquesce in print. In the novel, Forrest is a grits 'n' gravy version of Inspector Clouseau—which is why I gave it a rave. Farce as farce, farce for its own sake unhampered by lessons and deeper meanings, is a conservative art form. Liberals are the ones who demand that their entertainment be didactic and "worthwhile," but We the Guiltless shouldn't need a message-bearing Forrest Gump. Yet Gump Cons obviously do; they're so busy finding their favorite symbols that they sound like readers of existentialist literary quarterlies.

I am also tired of hearing them attribute Forrest's nobility of character to his IQ of 75. Anti-intellectualism is a tropism of the Right having much to do with the fact that most intellectuals are liberals. Gustave Flaubert, a conservative to the nines, yielded to the same impulse in *A Simple Heart*, his story of a slow-witted but great-souled maidservant who still reigns as France's Forrest Gump, but hosannas to admirable idiots are not sanctified by being French. Say what you will about Ayn Rand, she always connected virtue to intelligence.

2. Irish Tenor Cons are conservatives with a tear-in-the-voice speaking style. Personified by Oliver North, the Chauncey Olcott of the mawkish Right, this type would rather move hearts than minds. That he succeeds in doing so is the cause of his biggest problem; stuck with a constituency composed largely of people who can be swung like a lariat, he must keep on gulping and swallowing and choking up until cerebrally based conservatives can't stand the sight of him.

3. Connube Cons think you can't be a conservative unless you're married. The Republican Party of Virginia is overrun with Connube Cons. When Democrat Mary Sue Terry ran for Attorney General, a Connube announced that the GOP candidate had more legal knowledge in his little finger than spinster Mary Sue had "in all five [sic] of her ringless fingers." I voted for two-handed Mary Sue just for spite—the only time I've ever voted for a Democrat.

Virginia's Grand Connube is Gov. George Allen, of whom a local reporter wrote during the campaign: "While Allen never missed an opportunity to say he was married, he never mentioned that this is his second marriage." When an Allen aide stated that his candidate was better qualified to be governor because he's a husband and father, Allen repudiated him, but then Oliver North chimed in with a tremolo warning that the governor's mansion must not be "a sterile house."

To spot a Connube candidate, look for the little blond kid—democracy's

Plantagenet—on the dais. Supposedly these are sons, but there are so many of them and they all look so much alike that I think the candidates rent them from Little Blond Kid, Inc. Simply give them a call and they'll say, "Yeah, we've got that," just like Staples Office Supply.

C ONNUBE Cons have some odd blind spots. They adore Ozzie and Harriet and bray about the other wonderful family shows of the Sixties, even though critics of that era complained that the fathers in these sitcoms were portrayed as hapless Dagwoods perpetually outwitted by women and children. But that's okay: *Dagwood is married.*

4. Entreprenoor Cons, so called for the way they pronounce "entrepreneur," define a conservative as someone who owns his own business—period. That's all it takes; you don't even have to be married. It's a good thing Entreprenoors are self-employed; if they had a boss they would get fired for spending three hours a day dialing the Rush Limbaugh show. Many get through, which is how America learned to mispronounce "entrepreneur."

5. Con-Con Macoutes wreck Clifton Fadiman's theory that conservatives are wittier than liberals because our freedom from earnestness gives us a deft touch. Deftness dwells not in columnist Sam Francis, who called FDR "Old Rubberlegs" and descended to flat nothingness when he nicknamed the GOP the "Stupid Party." Con-Con Macoutery is the bane of many male conservatives, who associate whiplash retorts with foppishness, but they should remember that the art of the insult is still touched by Versailles.

The best American example of it, which Con-Con Macoutes would do well to study, is Charles Francis Adams' opinion of William Jennings Bryan: "He is in one sense scripturally formidable, for he is unquestionably armed with the jawbone of an ass."

November 7, 1994

W RITERLY soul-searching has struck the *Washington Post.* Last month they had a huge Style piece called "Thinking Out Loud" in which print journalists debated the morality of going on television and hitting the lecture circuit.

Crossfire's Michael Kinsley, justifying his decision to abandon writing for screaming, reflected that the essay is no longer "the real world" because "people make up their minds watching TV." And besides, "I like the fame and fortune." As for lecturing, "I didn't do it for years, but it became more socially acceptable. Then I thought, no one seems to think there's anything wrong with this . . . It's amazingly lucrative."

Time's Margaret Carlson rues having to "skim the surface" on *Capital Gang*, where the "nuances" of her written work are not welcome. "I want to talk in paragraphs," she sighs, but what's a girl to do when being on the Gang Show has upped her speaking fee to $10,000?

Syndicated columnist Chris Matthews, who is on TV so often that millions of channel surfers think something is wrong with their remotes, made forty speeches last year. "Three speeches match your syndicated column income," he explained.

To Fred Barnes, having less time for "real journalism" is "very frustrating," but playing Freddie the Beadle on *The McLaughlin Group* has its consolations: "You have a certain visibility and get your calls returned." And its compensations: "Magazine articles don't generate speech requests." Barnes, whose speaking fee is about $5,000, gives six to eight speeches a month and thinks anyone who disapproves of this racket is simply jealous. "You only hear 'Aren't you degrading yourself' from other people in journalism, who aren't on shows," said he jauntily.

Oh, really? Before I saw the light I toured three books; I was interviewed on ABC by Barbara Howar and CNN by Marilyn Ringo, did Barry Farber's radio show with Martha Mitchell, and appeared as the mystery guest on *To Tell the Truth*. I still get speech requests, most recently a $5,000 offer from the University of Tennessee that I turned down. Once in a while a TV offer dribbles in because TV people still can't believe that any writer would say no, but I always say no because I refuse to be a Writing Head.

The distinction between Talking Heads and Writing Heads may not exist, but it ought to. The former are primarily television personalities who do no harm because television is their natural milieu. But the latter, by laboring in the wrong vineyard, risk spoiling precious grapes.

A Writing Head is a writer who encourages people to listen rather than read, and thus contributes to the destruction of his own metier. The warning signs of this unforgivable sin are evident in Chris Matthews's description of his new show, inexplicably named *In Depth*: "I don't spend any time thinking about it before I get here," he confesses. "If anything comes into my head, I basically can go with it. It's first draft."

That sounds like a workshop in the Theodore Dreiser Sentence: "The, to Carrie, very important theatrical performance was to take place at the Avery on conditions which were to make it more noteworthy than was at first anticipated."

Knowing what talking constantly on television does to the syntax of politicians, one has no reason to suppose that the same thing can't happen to the syntax of writers who talk constantly on television. It's happening to some Writing Heads already, and it produces a sensation that every Fifties-era woman will recognize: Trying to read their prose is like trying to dance with the man who took $10,000 worth of Arthur Murray lessons and still can't lead.

The writer's ear is sharpened by isolation and solitude, not by a little electronic plug carrying the disembodied voice of a producer counting off the seconds to commercial break. Heard often enough, the countdown will stay with the Writing Head when he sits down to his word processor, until the leisurely habit of polishing his prose deserts him. No longer will he heed Boileau's injunction, "Make haste slowly." No longer will he take the time to weigh the difference between the sturdy traction of "I've got" and the smooth glide of "I have" and decide which one his sentence needs. Alone in his atelier but with his mind still back at the sound stage, he acquires the habit of writing like someone who is trying to finish a thought before Eleanor Clift shrieks or John McLaughlin roars "Mor-TUN!"

F AME and money aside, I suspect that the lure of Writing Head-dom is tied up with America's desperate quest for "well-roundedness" and our concomitant fear of its antithesis, the one-track mind. Intense concentration looks a lot like loneliness, so we deliberately scatter our shot to prove how well-adjusted we are. Our ideal is the straight-A student who is also a class leader and an "all-round athlete." Aware that intellectual triumphs alone would mark him as "weird," he hurls himself into extracurricular activities so no one will suspect him of studying too hard. When writers indulge this national tic, "extracurricular activities" translates into TV and lecture gigs.

I'll keep my one-track mind and indulge no tics but my own. The late novelist Jean Stafford expressed my brand of patriotism perfectly when she declared, "I pledge allegiance to the English language." To that I would add my religious credo: "Hail English, full of grace." I will mount no stages, sound or lecture, and if my book sales suffer for it, then so be it. I have no interest in fortune beyond earning enough to support myself, which I already do. As for celebrity, I trust John Keats:

> *Fame, like a wayward girl, will*
> *still be coy*
> *To those who woo her with too*

slavish knees,
But makes surrender to some
thoughtless boy,
And dotes the more upon a heart
at ease.

December 5, 1994

'**M**IS.MIS" is computerese for "Miscellaneous Misanthrope,"
the disk file where I store the incipient thoughts I jot down
while eating dinner, watching TV, or brooding. The listmaking season is now upon us, and so, in lieu of New Year's Resolutions,
I wrote up the file.

■ Permissiveness and liberalism are ever linked. I spotted Rudolph Giuliani
for a weak-sister Republican the moment I saw the way he let his son disrupt
his inaugural address. That brat should be whipped until his nose bleeds but-
termilk.

■ For whom the Bell Curve tolls: Feminists are worried that Charles Murray
will follow his study in black and white with one on male and female IQ differences. Let the geniuses fall where they may; I'm glad my IQ is only 126.
If it were higher I would like math and science, and I don't want to. An IQ in
the 120s is as convenient as wearing a B-cup bra: anything larger or smaller
spells trouble.

■ Caveat Creep: Rush Limbaugh's TV show now has a dress code requiring
"skirts and dresses for ladies." I haven't owned a dress since 1970. I spent the
Fifties in high heels, girdles, wired bras (32B), and waist pinchers called
"Merry Widows." I earned my stripes—literally—and now I intend to stay
happily unbound and trousered. I would remind traditionalists that the flowing, bell-bottomed pants suits of the Seventies were quite elegant. Moreover,
pants cover a woman far more than the skimpy thigh-highs that pass for
dresses today. If you doubt it, watch Jane Wallace on *Equal Time* or Marcia
Clark on *O. J. Simpson.* The views stop just short of Van Diemen's Land. The
only difference is that Marcia Clark has good legs.

■ An aspect of sexual harrassment that no one, to my knowledge, has considered is "shop talk." Something about laboring in the same vineyard reduces sexual tension between men and women and replaces it with an oddly chaste camaraderie. When I began publishing, I quickly learned the paradoxical lesson that sex isn't sexy. The loftily named "editorial conference" more often than not consists of "Is there a synonym for clitoris?" and "They go to bed in chapter five," uttered with the serene detachtment of medieval copyists working on the Psalter.

I think Clarence Thomas and Anita Hill really did discuss Long Dong Silver and the hair on the Coke—as shop talk that Miss Hill later twisted and used as a weapon. The hair on the Coke is from *The Exorcist*, a novel that pitted enraged church groups against defenders of the First Amendment's protection of blasphemy, but incredibly, both of these lawyers claimed they didn't read it. After Thomas so testified, he quickly and needlessly added, "I saw a clip from the movie, the part where the bed moved." Shakespeare would have loved that compulsive little slip. I believe both of them read *The Exorcist*, and if I know anything about shop talk I'll bet that the hair on the Coke was a running joke for weeks.

Orrin Hatch revealed that a case involving the porn movie *Long Dong Silver* was filed in the Western District, making it more likely that the Oklahoma-based Hill, rather than the Easterner Thomas, would have known about it. Thus, Hatch suggested, she used her knowledge of the case to invent a prurient conversation and then accused Thomas of initiating it. In the ensuing either–or debate no one stopped to think that the two might have had a long conversation about Long Dong Silver that wasn't all that prurient.

■ Instead of nominating Clarence Thomas, George Bush should have renominated Robert Bork and resigned the Presidency in the face of a second rejection. It was the only honorable thing to do, but white plumes don't wear well in democracies.

■ Incidentally, if Thomas is such as conservative, what was he doing working at EEOC? I'd rather dynamite it.

■ I have been in an irritable mood ever since Vatican II. A Protestant expects the Catholic Church to act like the Catholic Church the way a woman expects a man to act like a man.

■ In my student days nobody talked about school prayer per se; it was simply part of the decorous rite called "Opening School" whose benefits were clearly secular. Ritual and ceremony develop the habit of doing the same thing at the same time in the same way, inculcating over time an orderly, systematic approach to everyday life. This is something that children from today's hectic homes need desperately. I see a definite connection between Opening School and my undeviating routine before leaving the house: I stand in front of the stove, checking each burner and intoning, "Off, off, off, off." If religious conservatives promoted school prayer as a way of training kids to pull themselves together, instead of insisting that prayer means praying, the GOP would be a lot better off.

■ The ultimate measure of American ignorance is the one-word headline WHY? that we put on dire news. Next comes TRYING TO UNDERSTAND, followed by A TOWN WITHOUT ANSWERS, followed by a special with Connie Chung, who keeps her brow furrowed for half an hour. Perplexity on this scale bespeaks our preference for education over learning. The legions of ribbon-tying hysterics pole-axed by the Susan Smith infanticide could benefit from exposure to Euripides' *Medea*, but Americans believe any amount of learning is a dangerous thing. The egalitarian Left says it isn't "relevant" and the philistine Right says, "It won't help you make a living." Probably not, but it makes life livable.

■ I'm not prejudiced, I'm "postjudiced." Postjudice is the compliment that common sense pays to experience.

■ Never look on the bright side; the glare is blinding.

December 31, 1994

1995

T HE latest battle cry among conservatives, picked up from Rush Limbaugh, is: "Words mean things." You may have noticed that it started cropping up in soundbites some months ago. Well, now it is the soundbite. I was dutifully watching the news when suddenly some triumphant Republican loomed up and gleefully announced, "Words mean things." Just that, nothing more. I waited to find out what things words mean, but I had heard all I was going to hear. That was it. Over and out. Me gone.

This is destined to be a lost cause. The American approach to words is willfully Druidic: Words mean . . . things. Years ago in one of his language books Edwin Newman noted that airlines were offering passengers "a cup of *au jus*." People ordered it blithely, amid murmurs of "I love *au jus*" and "*au jus* really hits the spot." It had nothing to do with their grasp of French; rather, it was that nobody saw anything wrong with ordering "a cup of with gravy," or saying "I love with gravy" and "with gravy really hits the spot." Not to worry, America said to Newman. Some day, when *au jus* has been on menus as long as *à la mode*, people will get it right. Meanwhile, shut up and drink your with gravy.

Champions of Words Mean Things must also combat America's ingrained democratic responses to malapropisms. There are two. "It doesn't matter how you say it as long as people understand what you mean" is our linguistic divining rod; each time it quivers a raving lunatic is upgraded to a spokesperson for the homeless. The other response, "It's not polite to correct people," is our sole remaining form of etiquette, punctiliously adhered to by all, especially English teachers.

Another stumbling block is our tacit concurrence that imprecise speech is an island of safety in a disintegrating society. Using certain words incorrectly cloaks some parlous truths about American life. The current fad among pundits for calling Lloyd Bentsen *patrician* has paralleled the descent of the Clintons back into the Erskine Caldwell novel whence they came; *patrician* now means "not awful."

The way we sling *erudite* around says everything about our non-existent intellectual and educational standards. Reviewers have been calling me erudite for twenty years. It means someone who likes to read. It means "acting white" when you already are. It means knowing how to work in quotations without using footnotes. All you have to do is write "Socrates said the unexamined life is not worth living" and somebody will call you *erudite*.

Using *cancer* literally instead of metaphorically would wreck American discourse Right and Left. Ayn Rand told her doctor that cancer was caused by "bad premises." She had no bad premises; therefore she did not have cancer. Liberals think the same way; their definition of cancer is any growth on the body politic that challenges their premises. For example, if I keep smoking three packs a day I will die of lung racism.

The now-ubiquitous *choose*, birthed by the abortion movement, has been used so much and so automatically that it is no longer even a word, just a speech habit similar to throat clearing. It is now a fixture of public-service announcements and rebuttal ads. Newspapers contain full-page letters addressed to "People Who *Choose* to Drink and Drive" (people who drink and drive!). Philip Morris U.S.A. defends "Americans who *choose* to smoke" (who smoke!), saying they "have the right to make a personal *choice*" (the right to smoke!). And of course, there is no such thing as a plain old college; the operative phrase is "the college of your *choice*." This fixation on choosing may mean that Americans are groping for the Christian concept of free will, but it sounds more like another dung hill of democracy to me.

Words cannot mean things to people who have learned to filter them as well as we have. Political correctness has breathed new life into the paralepsis, the rhetorical device whereby we make a statement by first announcing that we are not going to make it. When pundits write, "No one is suggesting . . ." the American eye reads "I'm suggesting." When we hear, "This is not to say . . ." we translate it as, "I'm saying." The standard formulas of feminism, such as "our fighting men and women," have trained us to regard words as nothing but aids to fantasy, and the Clintons have reduced us to infantilism: *agenda* means something bad; *plan* means something boring; and *ideology* means something dumb.

W ORDS do mean things. Take *fungible*. The dictionary defines it as something that can be exchanged for something else when paying debts, as when a farmer pays a shoemaker in eggs instead of money. Not true; *fungible* is the sound you make when the periodontist says "bite down"— proof that you have eschewed flossing.

Or take *gravamen*. The dictionary defines it as a legal term, from the Latin *gravare*, "to burden," meaning the most serious charge in an indictment. Wrong. It's actually an eponym.

Count Manfred Gravamen (1835-1906) was a trusted Hapsburg minister ordered by Emperor Franz Josef to spy on Empress Elizabeth. A firm believer in getting the worst over with, Count Gravamen always kicked off his imperial reports with, "First, the bad news."

Every day brought fresh evidence that Elizabeth was one Sacher torte short of a full tray.

"First, the bad news: she gave a tea for the Hungarian revolutionists."

"First, the bad news: she ordered her ladies to speak nothing but Magyar."

"First, the bad news: she communes with the spirit of the poet Heine, whose works Your Majesty has banned."

"First, the bad news: she's collecting Gypsy midgets for her private circus."

"First, the bad news: she's hanging upside down on a trapeze."

"First, the bad news: she's eating sand."

Finally, Franz Josef began greeting his minister with, "Well, what's today's gravamen?" and a word was born.

February 6, 1995

M Y MAILBOX has become an arena of conflict. The people who want to save the National Endowment for the Arts have put me on their mailing lists because I'm a writer, which fact leads them to assume that I'm an alienated, left-wing intellectual just like them.

Meanwhile, the people who want to abolish the NEA have put me on their mailing lists because I'm a conservative, which fact leads them to assume that I'm a normal American who doesn't hold with all that elitist arty stuff—i.e., a fellow Gumplican.

Naturally I'm on neither side, for reasons guaranteed to provoke both. To savor to the full my troubling stance, consider my enduring love affair with two

Masterpiece Theater classics: *Upstairs, Downstairs* transported me into a world where equality was an aberration; and *I, Claudius* never plugged family values.

Nonetheless I have some thoughts on the NEA controversy. First, the general question of whether governments should support the arts:

Don't try it at home unless you live in Versailles. Only an absolute monarch can do it right because he wants his reign to be called the Age of Himself. Culture piped through great vanity emerges as great culture, but democratically elected leaders must pretend to be no better than anyone else. The pretense, which seldom strains credulity, elevates the lowest common denominator and produces cultural poobahs like Maya Angelou, whose writing makes one weep, not for Shakespeare and Austen, but for Zane Grey and Olive Higgins Prouty.

Second, the question of whether deserving individuals should receive grants:

It's extremely unwise to give creative types anything; we'll just break it or drink it. Our self-destructive streak has been endlessly romanticized but it is very real; easy money and freedom from want, far from solving our problems, tend to bring out the worst in us.

In my own experience, supporting myself with hack writing was my salvation. As a secure grantee I would have worked dilatorily on the usual turgid, plotless first novel, but instead I wrote, from necessity, three true-confessions stories a week. They trained me to keep the seat of the pants on the seat of the chair, without which a writer is nothing, and to make myself instantly clear to the simplest audience. Churning out opening sentences like "Brad waved the letter in front of my face, accusing me of unspeakable things" might not be art, but what it taught me is recorded in Horace's *Ars Poetica*: "Capture your reader, let him not depart/From dull beginnings that refuse to start."

The worst aspect of the NEA controversy is its false either–or and obscured battle lines, which brings me to my third and most important point.

Remember the flutist who was pushed in front of a New York subway train by a "youth" about ten years ago? She lost a hand. They sewed it back on but her musical career was ruined. That girl symbolizes the real issue here. The parlous state of the arts in America is directly and almost solely related to urban crime.

Arts are inseparable from cities, and our cities have been destroyed. You have to go home in the dark after the opera and the play, and fewer and fewer people are willing to take the chance. It's becoming increasingly hard to satisfy a craving for pizza, much less string quartets, now that the drivers are afraid to deliver at night. If television has lowered cultural tastes, it has been able to do so because it offers people a chance to stay in the (relative) safety of their homes instead of venturing out into the urban kraal.

We wouldn't need an NEA if cities were the vibrant and glorious cultural enclaves they once were. One of the most insidious effects of urban crime on art is the way it inhibits artists themselves.

I often wonder what my writing would be like if I could live the way I was meant to live, in a raffish bohemian neighborhood in a flourishing city, surrounded by my own kind, instead of the hybrid life I lead now. I would love to be able to live in New York, or my hometown of Washington, D.C. I long to do the crazy, spur-of-the-moment things that writers have always done: run around in the middle of the night with kindred spirits, getting drunk without worrying about creating a spectacle that might attract a mugger, or dull the reflexes needed to fight him off.

A ND THEN there's that wretched car. I would have much more time and energy for my work if I could stroll down the block to buy groceries. I want to shop at Jewish delis, Italian greengrocers, Greek fish stands, preferably at four A.M., but instead I have to drive out to a shopping center. No writer should set foot in these child-seat hells, but I'm dependent on them, and hence on the car that I don't want. I can't take a bus because we don't have them where I live—and won't. Public transit is dying right along with the arts, for the same reason: crime. A bus provides criminals with an ideal captive audience; just get on and go down the aisle, robbing the victims row on row and sending them where the poppies grow.

So I really am an alienated intellectual, but not the kind the arts crowd likes. The feeling is mutual; the pro-NEA people are the same liberal masochists whose permissive politics have resulted in urban anarchy, and I hate them.

Nor do I have any use for the cowardly anti-NEA Gumplicans who think conservatism consists of a philistine bray instead of a stentorian roar. I detest the anti-intellectualism that pervades the Southern and Midwestern GOP and I resent being tarred with their small-town Rotarian brush. I'm not one of their Babbitts; I'm a right-wing intellectual—the correct definition of "elitist" in my opinion. If hostile liberal reviewers wish to call me, as one did, "the thinking man's redneck," then so be it. I want crime stopped and I'm not fussy about how it's done, because I think one bar of Puccini is worth more than our entire population of urban goths.

March 6, 1995

I F YOU WANT to hear the ultimate feminist horror story, I've got it. This past Christmas season I had my annual telephone gabfest with my best girl-friend from college. These calls are always very informative because she keeps up with everybody and goes to alumnae events. It's never long before we turn very girlish, starting sentences with "You'll never guess" and exclaiming "Oh, honestly!" Last year was no different, except that one of her news items kicked off with: "You'll never guess who's thinking of going to law school."

That's an easy one if you're talking about the general population; of 260 million Americans, only 17 are not thinking about going to law school, so you could name just about anybody and be right. But we weren't talking about the general population. We were talking about girls who were in col-lege from 1953 to 1957, now the target audience for bladder-control products advertised by June Allyson. Or to put it another way: tempus fidgets.

My friend named a name that rang a faint bell. I thought back in what I used to call "mounting dread" when I wrote gothics, until I placed her. She was a junior when we were freshmen, so that meant she was sixty. S-i-x-t-y.

Now that I had a new Ultimate Feminist Horror Story, I had to bump an earlier one back to Penultimate Feminist Horror Story. The previous one was about the uproar over the laxative commercial that featured a roll of unused toilet paper.

You remember it. It was one of those new understated ads, like the luxury car sitting in the middle of nowhere, that are supposed to make everyone feel subtle. The camera zoomed in on a full roll of toilet paper in a bathroom dis-penser, and a sign reading "Day 1." The sign changed to "Day 2 . . . Day 3 . . . Day 4 . . . " and so on, but still the roll remained full, obviously untouched because unneeded. Then the laxative was shown and extolled, whereupon we saw the roll unrolling at top speed, proof that the laxative worked.

Feminists were "outraged." The ad was sexist, they said, because the sce-nario was obviously limited to constipated men. A constipated woman would still use a certain amount of toilet paper every day, they said, but by ignoring this fact, the ad implied that constipated women were not only unimportant, but invisible.

"There's no woman living in that house!" wailed one feminist, as if that in itself were sexist. "Don't they even have women guests?" demanded anoth-er, then compared the bathroom in the ad to the male huts of Polynesia. At no time in the brouhaha did they consider that for the ad to work, the toilet paper had to remain untouched. Several talk-show opponents reminded them of this, but the outraged feminists replied, "That doesn't matter. Women use toilet paper every day."

"But it's not a toilet-paper ad, it's a laxative ad."

"That doesn't matter. Look at the pissoirs of Paris. There're no compara-ble conveniences for women because men think it's funny when a woman has to go and can't. Men don't want women to go, that's why they refuse to stop on long car trips. Look at Jean Harlow. She died of uremic poisoning because they wouldn't let her go."

That's when I lost it. Forgetting that I was sitting beside an open window, I yelled at the TV, "Her mother was a Christian Scientist! The toilet paper has to keep still!" The next day, a neighbor gave me an odd look and thereafter left the laundry room as soon as I walked in.

The toilet-paper debate was such that it bumped back everything else that had ever sent me around the bend, making it impossible for me to identify my Antepenultimate Feminist Horror Story. It's just as well. My Latin is rusty; I don't know what, if anything, comes after—or rather before—antepenulti-mate, and I need a lot of categories to continue in this vein. Women are han-dling feminism so badly that I would have to spend all my time bumping things back to secure my Ultimate Feminist Horror Story before something else came along and dislodged it.

I have no quarrel with feminism as long as it's real feminism, but what we have endured this past quarter-century is pseudofeminism.

Pseudofeminists talk aggressiveness but practice timidity. Take sexual harassment. Every time I turn on the news some woman is describing, with murky insouciance, that terrible day ten years ago when her self-esteem was shattered because her male boss kept looking at her "body parts" instead of her face. A real feminist would say, "I'm up here, Mr. Crabtree," and that would be the end of it. If you say it right, you only have to say it once.

A REAL feminist understands that men cannot be expected to admire in the female sex the very qualities they despise in their own. They may sing the praises of "femininity" but in truth they have nothing but contempt for softness, restraint, and suffering in silence. The woman who makes it clear that she also is contemptuous of these traits reminds men so much of themselves that they will admire her even as they thank God they're not married to her.

Pseudofeminists also have infused sexual harassment with their signature tunnel vision. In Muriel Spark's novel *Loitering with Intent*, the heroine, ana-lyzing why she liked a foul-mouthed man that other women found offensive, thinks: "Vulgarity I could take from him or, if he had been alive today, the sixteenth-century Benvenuto Cellini, because these were big sane men."

That some men can get away with anything while others make even

"damn" sound dirty is a fine distinction beyond the analytical powers of pseudofeminists. Instead they think like Susan Faludi, who wrote in *Backlash*: "If
the American man can claim no ancestral coat of arms on which to elevate
himself from the masses, perhaps he can fashion his sex into a sort of pedi-
gree." There you have it. Equality is why women aren't equal; American men
do bad things for heraldic reasons; the bar sinister creates the bastard instead
of the other way around.

April 3, 1995

I AM AT war, fighting to save the dying practice of letter writing from the
iniquities of "communications resources." Mind you, I'm not a Luddite.
I love computers for making letters easier to write, and I love fax
machines for getting my letters to their destination instantly. My quarrel is
with America's attitude toward the epistolary art. I call it Scriptophobia.

Other commentators on this subject have been content to blame the telephone, but there's more to it. The telephone merely made letter writing
unnecessary; our era of special prosecutors and independent counsels has
made it fatal. "Paper trail" has not only entered the language, it has replaced
"albatross." Letters, if they are written at all, are something to be shredded.

None but the brave and the dumb write letters in an era ruled by the politically correct. Those people pass things around, and they're so wired for
insult that their Xerox machines switch on all by themselves. Caught between
lawyers and monomaniacs, Americans have become so paranoid that our collective subliminal ear is starting to hear the word "letter" as "anonymous letter." Soon someone will run it together and the compound spelling will catch
on, giving us a new "damnyankee" in time for the millennium.

The media have a vested interest in Scriptophobia. Unlike a tape, a letter
can't be spliced to produce the desired effect. People who develop the habit
of writing letters also develop the habit of organizing their thoughts, thereby
endangering the gaffe industry. And if illicit couples still wrote love letters,
there would be no "he said-she said" contests to drag out for weeks.

Scriptophobia is part of our larger preference for ephemerality that
extends beyond letters to a disdain for the written word in general. A prime
example is the "oral history" craze spurred by Alex Haley's *Roots*. Haley did
not introduce the form—the Federal Writers' Project preserved slave narratives in the New Deal, and Studs Terkel later made a career of the genre—but
it was Haley's sainted Gambian griot who gave oral history new meaning.

At least Terkel and the Federal Writers wrote their findings down, but the griot had memorized a thousand years of Mandinka history that he had to recite from the beginning or else he could not keep it straight. Haley tried to get him to start at 1767, but no, he took it from the top, and if anyone interrupted him he had to start all over again.

How wonderful! said liberals. No nasty old printing press for the griot. No divisive European categories and specializations. This was living history for real people who refused to destroy their environment by cutting down trees. Oral history was proclaimed holy, and anyone who said the griot's obsessive-compulsive fits were the verbal equivalent of "Step on a Crack, Break Your Mother's Back" was called a racist.

Scriptophobia is winning. Computer jocks predict with relish "the decline and fall of print." Body language now speaks louder than words, so courtroom stenotype is yielding to videotape, or the griot again the Stenomask, worn like a feedbag, into which the recorder repeats every word spoken by all parties. Joggers make calls from portable phones while listening to an audio book with the other ear, and I fight on.

To give you a taste of my war, here is a letter I wrote last year to the Symantec Corporation, makers of Q&A Write, the word processor I use:

> Recently I faxed your office to find out how to order a user's manual for a Q&A upgrade I received free when I replied to your offer. All I wanted was the price plus postage so I could send you a check. What I got was a five-page fax (a sixth page was blank) listing all sorts of things—800 numbers, 900 numbers, regular area-code numbers, and various support membership fees, including one for $5,000. Besides leaving me feeling overwhelmed, it used up my fax paper.
>
> I tried to call one of the 503 numbers that seemed to be the one I needed, but I got an incredibly long message about press this, press that, and then a period on hold with music. Knowing how this sort of thing goes, I hung up and decided to write you this letter.
>
> I realize you're trying to centralize your support services, and obviously your company is growing, which I'm glad to hear, but I submit that you have achieved self-parody. The reply I got from you is straight out of a *Saturday Night Live* skit about the frustrations of high-tech life.
>
> As a Q&A user for seven years, I have conducted a running argument with other writers who swear by WordPerfect, telling them, "If I couldn't use Q&A I'd go back to a typewriter." I am a walking ad for you, so I hope you will be good enough to send me a personal reply telling me how I can order the user's manual.

I FAXED this so I know it got there, but I never heard from them. In Scriptophobic America, people who write letters are regarded as weird, maybe even dangerous, or at the very least, quaint pests. Since all three of these characteristics hint at intelligence, a letter—any letter—strikes many people as an elitist put-down regardless of what it actually says. A letter also is formal, which means cold. A letter is dutiful, which means polite, which means cold. Above all, a letter is adult, which means—guess what?—cold. Stack all this up against American insecurity and you have, by Gump, a nation of Scriptophobes.

I'll lose my war because the whole country is aligned against me, but for one whose motto is, "Whatever the majority is doing has got to be wrong," there are worse things than defeat. At least I have the satisfaction of knowing I'm in good company. Mary McCarthy rated the men in her life on a scale of epistolary prowess: "He writes a good letter." Jean Stafford's hilarious correspondence with Con Edison over a disputed light bill is part of her literary papers, so maybe future generations of graduate students will get a kick out of the letters in mine.

St. Augustine, asked what he would do if he knew the world would end tomorrow, replied, "I would go on working in my garden." I'll go on writing letters because I'm a devout high-church Epistolarian.

May 1, 1995

T HE definition of "elitist" is spinning out of control. Nailing it down is much harder than mastering French verbs. If you say "*baiser*" instead of "*embrasser*" and somebody takes you up on it, you can have a lot of fun being wrong, but elitist means so many things to so many people that you are damned if you do and damned if you do. Soon it will be possible to list on a three-by-five card all the things that are *not* elitist and still have plenty of room left for the phone numbers of liquor stores that deliver.

This never happened with "elite." Like "deluxe," it was an advertising word that generations of Americans took in stride. Sometimes they got it mixed up with its opposite, "hoi polloi," but it never became a hot button; its few conversational uses were lighthearted, as in "where the elite meet." Perhaps it was protected by the French acute accent (élite) it used to carry— after all, back when "fantasy" was spelled "phantasy" people did not describe their own in public. But elitist never had a French accent mark. Starting life with nothing but a good old American politicized suffix, it pulled itself up by its rootstraps to become the epithet of choice for both sides of the political spectrum. Left or Right, elitist means . . . something bad.

To liberals, elitist is a synonym for racist and sexist. Like the eager swain in fairy tales sent forth by the princess to find three of something, liberals go forth to find conservatives who fit all three. Their stumbling block is the populist Right. Liberals have no trouble accusing this group of racism and sexism, but elitism? Thwarted, the liberals must be content to pin the elitist rose on traditional Republicans only. But where to pin it? All the traditional Republicans have removed their suit jackets to placate the populist Right. Country clubs in shirtsleeves have defined elitism down.

To the populist Right, liberalism and elitism are two sides of a Janus face that never loses its symmetry: the further left a liberal moves, the more elitist he becomes. Offended by the British accents and classical music of public broadcasting, the populist Right hurled a blanket charge of elitism at all PBS supporters, unmindful that the lunatic fringe on the tote bag consists of "elitists" who also support the abolition of IQ tests, the replacement of Jane Austen with Alice Walker, and art scholarships for graffiti daubers. Making silk purses out of sour socialists has defined elitism up.

To feminists, an elitist is a fascist is a pro-lifer. When the Supreme Court put restrictions on federally funded abortions, a NOW member said: "It's an elitist position. It denies abortion to the poor and the young." But if elitist meant what she wants it to mean, pro-lifers would favor abortion-as-genocide to reduce the underclass population. What pro-lifers actually favor is their own definition of elitist: a feminist who looks down on full-time motherhood.

No one can fling charges of elitism around like a paleoconservative going after a neo-con. To columnist Samuel Francis, an elitist is anyone he disagrees with—like George Will, who once suggested that gun control might be a good idea in a nation of people unable to program their VCRs. Francis called this "prim elitism" and worked himself up into a lather, saying "elites despise, fear, and hate . . . the law-abiding non-elite," and launched a fusillade at "the gun gestapo's hidden agenda of elitism and statism" that promotes "criminals and their elite allies."

I am tired of the distortion and disparagement of this honorable word. To me elitism means a love of excellence and superiority, but America has declared war on both and developed a sick love of the lowest common denominator to make sure no one becomes too fine for our touted democracy. We are almost at the point of regarding every virtue as elitist. Pride and dignity are now signs of haughty detachment; beggars and hysterics prove their humanity by their faults and become tests of our ability to love. By expecting nothing we get nothing except the chance to go on loving.

Let's face it: elitism lends life a patina it sorely needs. God may have loved

the common people but He made far too many of them. As the protagonist of
Mary McCarthy's *Birds of America* put it: "I've decided that may be why
Parisians are so sullen and why they drink. They thought of equality first."

Elitism also does wonders for vice. The public raucousness we think of
as homosexual behavior is actually low-class behavior. Before gay rights and
"inclusion" opened the closet door, overt homosexuals were the kind of people one enjoyed knowing socially, but now, as my New England friend
observed scornfully, "Vermont is filling up with lesbian goatherds."

T HAT would not sit well with the renowned eighteenth-century lovers
known as the "Ladies of Llangollen." Lady Eleanor Butler, daughter of
the Duke of Ormonde, and the Hon. Sarah Ponsonby, niece of the Earl of
Bessborough, ran away together and rented a run-down Welsh farm.
Financially strapped, begrudged only two small legacies by their families,
they nonetheless did good works among the poor—"the duties of our birth,"
said the imperious Eleanor. Their guests were "people like ourselves." They
did not mean other homosexuals; "I speak of breeding and education,"
Eleanor explained. As the fame of the Llangollen chatelaines spread, the
luminaries of the age—Wordsworth, Walpole, Scott, Burke, Mme de
Genlis—made pilgrimages to their farm, proof that tolerance and acceptance
await not those who lower their standards but those who raise them.

This was echoed by a resident of Ovett, Mississippi, when that supposedly unsophisticated backwater was invaded by lesbian communards. "I have
lived here all my life," she said, "and there are gay couples here, and everyone knows it. The difference is they don't go around hugging and kissing and
holding hands and going on TV to talk about it."

ELITISM: the attitude that dares speak its name in politically correct times.

May 29, 1995

T HE American attention span always has gotten a lot of attention. The
first to note our easy distractibility was Alexis de Tocqueville. His
findings were echoed by Frederick Jackson Turner, but being an
American, Turner used the more tactful and romantic "restlessness." Other
commentators were people with a stake in concentration, such as teachers,
inventors, bridge players, and Jobean old salts who made boats-in-bottles.
These earlier critics, who tended to use words like "stick-to-itiveness," held
that Americans could not concentrate because we could not sit still. This

opinion prevailed until the television age, when a new kind of critic announced that sitting still was destroying our ability to concentrate.

Sociologists of the Fifties warned that TV viewers were falling into the habit of thinking in clumps of ten or fifteen minutes, until a commercial came on and temporarily shut down the cognitive process. Actually this was the Golden Age of the American attention span. Early TV had some meaty shows such as *Hallmark Hall of Fame* and *Playhouse 90* that were presented live within the traditional boundaries of the drama, so the resultant thought-clumping was not very different from what playwrights had been doing for thousands of years.

The logic-friendly format of the theatrical act went out of style around the same time that more artistry went into commercials. Our attention span consequently shrank to about five minutes, according to the sociologists. It went on like this, with a new official attention span announced every few years, until it was down to thirty seconds. It stayed at that for a while, long enough to begin acquiring the cachet that attaches to permanence, but then the soundbite came along and turned thirty seconds into an eon.

No one has announced our new attention span yet, but there are hints. Bill Clinton promised to "focus like a laser beam" on the economy. A current bumper sticker, "Practice Random, Senseless Acts of Kindness," effectively says that if you help more than one old lady across the street, instead of leaving the second one standing there while you rush off to hug the squeegee man, you are in a rut. Computers are getting faster and faster, with each new speed advertised as "blazing," and Internet messages of "snail f---!" greet those who still use a 386.

Movies are becoming increasingly incoherent as scriptwriters strive for new ways to keep the restless interested. Gone is the orderly approach that Old Hollywood called "backstory"—filling us in on the action up to the point where the movie begins. It's a technique as old as storytelling. *Hamlet*: the king has died; *Rebecca*: the first wife has died; *The Odyssey*: the hero is setting off for home after a long absence. This is all we need to know to follow the plot, but we need to know it right away.

Apparently feeling that logical narration is for snail fanciers, today's movie makers eschew both backstory and the traditional flashback in favor of the staccato technique known as "cutting in and out."

The movie opens with a scene of bankers in conference. We barely know who everyone is, when suddenly the dreary discussion of loans is interrupted by a split-second shot of a naked smooth leg draped over a naked hairy leg. This means that an affair was had, but we have as yet no idea who had it. Back to the bankers for a few minutes, then another split-second shot of a knife on a kitchen counter. When the bankers adjourn for lunch we see the entwined legs again. This time the hairy leg fades out and immediately fades in again, covered now in prison orange. The orange-leg shot is mixed with a shot of a boys' baseball team in orange socks; back and forth, faster and faster, man's leg, boy's leg, bad orange, good orange, while the soundtrack emits whirring, clicking noises to suggest someone snapping still photos as fast as humanly possible.

Never mind the popcorn, the best accompaniment for today's movies is a surge protector. Other cinematic devices designed to nail our elusive attention are the split-screen telephone conversation and the zoom shot that pulls a human dot on the horizon into an extreme close-up so fast that our stomachs turn over. But of all the techniques for concentrating the mind, the most ironic is the freeze frame. A character who stops dead in his tracks and assumes a basilisk stare is probably supposed to remind the audience to focus like a laser beam, but in fact it resembles nothing so much as that menopausal dilemma of standing motionless in the middle of a room, trying to remember what it was you came in to get.

M UCH of our flagging attention is a natural reaction against the unnecessary tedium we create for ourselves. As the country that enshrined the clarion call of "quick 'n' easy" and still believes ads promising mastery of a foreign language in only "ten minutes a day," wouldn't it make sense for us to be on the parliamentary system? We could have got rid of Bill Clinton long ago, but no, we wait out the whole grinding, nerdy, petulant four years, and then wonder why we can't keep our minds on anything.

Our distractibility is also the inevitable residue of our undisciplined feelings. The American proclivity for leaving our emotional lights on has drained the battery of our attention span dry. The human spirit can take only so much of 24-hour coverage, memorial services, ribbons, teddy bears, crisis counseling, and moments of silence. We pay such obsessive attention to disasters and tragedies that we end up seeking respite in forgetfulness. (Quick, name one Teheran hostage.)

Welcome to America the Flea Circus. We now have a new disease, Attention Deficit Disorder, and like all democratic diseases, it does not discriminate. The good news is that by the time we run the gauntlet of ADD resources, clinics, programs, workshops, seminars, CBS Specials, and Sally Struthers promos, no one will remember what it is.

June 26, 1995

A MERICA'S latest excess, far worse even than compulsive hugging, can now be identified. We have entered the Whatnot Stand mode. A whatnot stand, for those of you who are younger and/or better born than I, was a triangular shelf hung eye-high in the corner of humble parlors up until about the end of the 1940s. On it stood glass figurines, made-in-Japan miniature saucers, plaster statuettes of prone babies with bare bottoms peeking from open pajama flaps, rosebuds made from glued sawdust, never-used souvenir ashtrays, a Mexican-sombrero pin cushion, and a no-evil monkey trio that glowed in the dark.

Hanging from the whatnot stand were made-in-Japan miniature paper fans, and stuffed behind it were brittle sheaves of Palm Sunday palm, enough to build a hut, brown with age and covered with dust—naturally, for how can you dust cracked palm? Everything on the whatnot stand was undustable, as was the whatnot stand itself with its jigsaw-cut scalloped edges and knobby trim.

The thing defied control, and so much the better, for its owner liked it that way. The whatnot stand was her monument to chaos-as-sentiment, tangible proof of her subconscious belief that to be overwhelmed is to be alive. Order of any kind would have made her feel emotionally truncated, which is why she enjoyed wrecks and fires and her sister's insanity, and why she never threw anything out.

The most egregious manifestations of America's Whatnot Stand mode are the ad hoc memorials that deface the sites of tragedies and disasters. The prize for hysterical excess surely belongs to the maudlin detritus currently piling up at the John D. Long Lake in Union, S.C., where Susan Smith drowned her two sons. It has gotten so bad that the police have had to create a roped-off section with a sign instructing, "Please place all memorials in this area." It contains, writes David Finkel in the *Washington Post Magazine*:

> a large color photograph of the two boys. There are hundreds of flowers, some fresh, most fake, some dead. There are homemade crosses, and deflated balloons, and a Bart Simpson doll, and an old toy police car, and a giant stuffed clown, and two faded Christmas angels, and rotting Easter candy, and a scratched-up *Beauty and the Beast* glass containing $14.36, and a broken toy helicopter, and smeared notes, and, under a dirty American flag, a toothbrush.

Other examples are the AIDS quilt, only slightly smaller than Rhode Island, that gay activists unfold every year on the Mall; whole streets and walls turned over to chalk artists; computers with slews of pre-loaded junky software; and those personal-design bank checks advertised in the Sunday papers. Geared to hobbies and professions, they are so cluttered with pictures of fish, golf paraphernalia, and firemen in full battle dress that there is hardly any room to write (the one for barbers has a black comb across "pay to the order of").

But it's not only the masses who play at whatnots; the classes are doing it, too. PBS's *Three Tenors* are two tenors too many, and Judge Ito's hourglass-strewn desk looks like a made-in-Japan old curiosity shop (what's he doing up there, cooking rice?). These pale, however, beside the antics of Maryland's certifiably gimcracked governor, Parris Glendening, who inserted a love song to his wife in the middle of his inaugural address.

The Whatnot syndrome sounds like the tastelessness that invariably overtakes a democracy. It's that, but also something more. Its deeper significance was inadvertently expressed by Robert Fulghum, the national periwinkle who wrote *All I Really Need to Know I Learned in Kindergarten*. Deploring the emotional paucity of people who don't have notes all over their refrigerators, he advised: "Get your stuff up there. Disorder is love."

We need to counteract this mindset, but the best friend American rationalism ever had now seems to be in extremis from its own folly.

Baseball is predicated on Occam's Razor, the philosophical principle that states, "Hypotheses must not be developed beyond necessity"—i.e., don't gild the lily, quit while you're ahead, enough is enough. If the home team is leading 1–0 and the visiting team does not score in the top of the ninth, the game ends then and there. They don't play the bottom of the inning because the home team, having already won, could only win by more.

The guys in the bleachers don't know Occam's Razor from Gillette's, yet if a baseball novice remarks that the bottom of the ninth was not played, they will shrug and say with a pleased grin, "'Course not." Their pleasure comes from a deep certainty, never articulated but always there, that baseball's spartan restraint and pristine logic help life to make sense—what erudite baseball fans such as George Will and Jonathan Yardley call "symmetry" in their April and October columns.

But baseball has lost face since the players' strike. It's being edged out by a game that recalls George Eliot's phrase, "much of a muchness," an ideal game for Whatnot America because the ball is two different colors and you can go berserk afterwards: soccer.

Conservatives are supposed to be patriotic, but I find myself increasingly repelled by America. A few years ago I reviewed a novel about a man in the throes of a nervous breakdown who makes a motel reservation for the purpose of committing suicide in the room. The moment he walks into the lobby, flashbulbs go off, a camera crew rushes him, a band strikes up "Lucky

Me," and a bevy of cocktail waitresses in Greek chitons pelt him with flowers. Turns out he's the One Millionth guest, fated to be feted all weekend, or as the Official Greeter puts it: "You won't have to be alone for one second!"

Reader-identification works in unprofessional ways, its wonders to perform. Except for this scene, the novel wasn't very good, but I gave it a rave anyhow.

July 31, 1995

P LAGIARISM has become so commonplace that the *Washington Post* reported an instance of it this past March with the lead sentence: "The plagiarism virus has claimed another prominent journalist."

I have never been plagiarized in the full legal sense of having long verbatim passages lifted, but I have been "plagiaromped," to coin a word for a practice widespread enough to need one. The worst offender was a leading news magazine whose reporter used the standard technique: she quoted me by name once, and thereafter closely paraphrased passages from my book.

I also found a well-known catchphrase of mine in a book I happened to review, proving my contention that the plagiarist's identifying trait is stupidity. Everyone knows literary editors match reviewers to books. Having been typed as a Southern humorist, I am routinely offered books of Southern humor. This particular book was an ostensibly humorous work by a Southern woman, so wouldn't you think it would cross her mind that I might be asked to review it? (I praised the phrase she swiped, calling it the funniest line in the book, and left her to her conscience.)

I found real plagiarism in a Lizzie Borden book I reviewed. Here we see plagiarists' stupidity on a grand scale. Anyone who writes about the Borden case knows he is writing for a cult whose obsessed members have read every word ever written about our heroine. The victim book happened to be a particular favorite of mine and one that I know practically by heart. Finding five nearly verbatim passages, I went into avenging-angel mode and did a side-by-side comparison. It caused a small stir in literary circles, resulting in a squib in *Book World* headlined "Lizzy Tizzy" that credited me with "five whacks."

My file on plagiarism has now grown so fat that I have had to divide the gall into three parts, with separate folders for journalism, books, and academia.

Accounts of journalistic plagiarism all sound more or less like the *Post*'s recent one. First the plagiarist issues a melodramatic apology; he is "horrified and heartbroken" by his deed. Next comes the excuse: the deadline made him do it; "I was not mindful that I was breaking the rules of my craft." Finally we hear from the plagiarist's editor, who explains: "He succumbed to the pressures of the moment and did an absolutely aberrational act." Free will yields to spontaneous combustion.

The creative writer who plagiarizes needs something more ivory-towerish than deadlines. When Alex Haley was sued by two novelists who found their work in *Roots*, he first blamed his "research assistants," but the boiler-room imagery clashed with his well-publicized claim that *Roots* was a solitary labor of love. In the end, he settled out of court for $650,000. But it doesn't matter, his defenders insist, because he helped blacks find their history.

Academic plagiarism is the easiest to pull off because bad writers stick together. Martin Luther King was dead by the time his plagiarism of Paul Tillich was discovered, but his defenders rallied. Said one: "He was trained in the black folk pulpit, which is an oral tradition. In this tradition, language was seen as common treasure, not private property."

I also have a fourth folder labeled BEYOND PLAGIARISM whose contents represent one small step for infringement of copyright but one giant leap for demonic possession. The practice of writing "sequels" to dead authors' books was only the beginning; now we can write new ones for them. California computer expert Scott French devised a program that mimics the style of dead authors, producing a novel entitled *Just This Once* as it might have been written by the late Jacqueline Susann, author of *Valley of the Dolls*. Defending his technique, French said: "I didn't copy her words or even sentences, but her way of thinking. And I don't think you can copyright the way a person thinks."

It is significant but not surprising that few people outside the publishing world are shocked by any of this. Americans are prone to excuse plagiarism even at the risk of sounding Aristotelian ("There are only seven plots"). More to the point, we have a flippant maxim that is a bald defense of plagiarism: "Great minds think alike." We may think we hold private property sacred, but we subconsciously make an exception for plagiarism—the subject simply doesn't turn us on.

In the first place, it concerns so few people. Nearly everyone owns a house, but how many own copyrights? How many people even know a copyright owner? (Hint: how many conservatives know someone with AIDS?)

Second, it's so subjective. To Americans, "property" evokes the scene in *Dr. Zhivago* when the Bolsheviks move in and start chopping up the furniture for firewood. But what, exactly, is intellectual property and how, exactly, do you steal it? This is not a subject likely to inflame a people with a fetishistic preference for practical knowledge.

Third, we are a nation of conformists. We take a dim view of the very thing that a copyright preserves, protects, and defends: originality.

THE siren song of situation ethics pervades the subject of plagiarism. At a panel convened to discuss novelist D. M. Thomas's use of whole pages from another book in *The White Hotel*, a participant said:

> What is plagiarism, apart from legal questions of ownership, copyright, or financial gain? How, for example, does it differ from repetition, reportage, quotation, paraphrase, exposition, and other ways of reproducing previously existing material? Plagiarism is closer to pride, a sin of the spirit, than to the criminal activities of the burglar.

In other words, "There are no easy answers." But there are. I can think of one. In a properly run Republic of Merit, Alexandra Ripley, "author" of *Scarlett*, would be sent to the salt mines along with the two nephews of Margaret Mitchell who cooked up the sequel deal.

August 28, 1995

I HAVE never read any books by the Italian novelist Carl Coccioli, but I ran across a quotation from one in 1979 that I have been saving ever since. The clipping is yellowed now but the message is ominously fresh: "The only thing that Americans have not done in their masochistic games is to declare war on themselves."

Masochism is not all whips and chains and twisted sexuality. The most insidious kind has nothing to do with sex, nor even with the new brand of sex that feminists call gender. It is, in fact, one of the few destructive neuroses left that does not require a bedroom.

I refer to parlor masochism.

A parlor masochist is anyone, male or female, who prefaces every opinion with "Correct me if I'm wrong," who betrays an eagerness to accept the views of others, who placates his enemies and strives for their good opinion, who explains too much and is always apologizing.

Parlor masochism is the dominant (as it were) force (as it were) in American life. Deflecting hostility has become our national art form. Nothing more accurately measures our diminishing strength of character than the way we settle our differences. Where once we said "Let's step outside," we now say "Let's have lunch."

Clintons come and Clintons go, but the master mold of parlor masochism is still George Bush. Whenever he caught himself in a moment of strength, horror seemed to set in at once. Whether it was his press conference on the Panama crisis ("I didn't get angry, I didn't get angry . . . I wouldn't mind using force if it could be done in a prudent manner") or his panicky haste in ending the Gulf War, he always recalled the bride in the doggerel: "Oh, mercy, look what I've done! / Married the father instead of the son!"

His staff covered his kinder-and-gentler compulsion with a multitude of spins, usually attributing it to good breeding, but after the 1992 election the truth peeped out. Commenting on the cloying amiability that Bush showed Clinton during the transition, a senior administration official told the *Washington Times*: "It's like they've been dating or something." Another said simply: "It's getting sick."

It is. A checklist for parlor masochism must begin with the United States Navy, which is so eager to help feminists destroy American sea power that it has changed its rallying cry to "I have not yet begun to cooperate with the investigation."

Marine colonel Fred Peck, testifying before Congress against gays in the military, personified unswerving realism when he said that his own gay son should not be allowed to serve. But then came the well-publicized meeting with his son's lover. "By the end of the weekend," young Peck told the media, "my dad was introducing him to his friends as his son-in-law."

Florida Supreme Court judge Rosemary Barkett, vacating a death sentence, observed that the defendant "is a good man, except that he sometimes kills people."

Reginald Denny, pulled from his truck in the Los Angeles riots and beaten nearly to death, said of his attackers, "They don't look like bad guys. They look like guys I could hang with." He didn't want them to go to jail. "I'd give them a chance," he said, and recommended community service. The prospect of seeing them again at their trial did not disturb him; "I'll crack them a smile and wink at them," he promised. Then he hugged their mothers. Could anything make this man mad? Yes: the "white supremacists" who supported him. "They're nuts," he ruled. "They're definitely a brick shy of a load. It's a human issue, not a racist issue."

In Richmond, mothers of children molested by a brutal 13-year-old boy met with the boy's parents for a "dialogue" described in the press as "rage turned to compassion." Rage is always turning to compassion in Parlor Masochist America. Whenever furious citizens form groups with names that begin "Save Our," "Take Back," or "Stop the," stand by for an ad hoc *agape*.

Mary McGrory demonstrated the parlor masochist's favorite logical fallacy. *Post hoc, ergo propter hoc*—"after this, therefore because of this"—permits the transfer of appeasement between unconnected events. In a column on the confirmation battle of Dr. Henry Foster written shortly after the Oklahoma City bombing, Miss McGrory speculated that Foster would, after all, be confirmed as surgeon general because of the "Oklahoma effect, that immeasurable but unmistakable shift in the public, that after the ultimate in violence and hatred, has lost any taste for mean and negative."

L IKE every good American disease, parlor masochism does not discriminate: conservatives catch it, too. Columnist Charles Krauthammer has recommended scrapping affirmative action, which benefits minorities who are not disadvantaged, and replacing it with a monetary reparation for blacks only. Forget Aleuts and Pago Pagoans; "America's sin was against blacks," he wrote in *Time*, and suggested a one-time payment of $100,000 for every black family of four, the money to come from a ten-year 75-cent gas tax.

Can America's "turn to the Right" survive such abject cringing? George Will has identified "four facets of the nation's fraying" as conservatives see it: affirmative action, illegal immigration, welfare, and crime. These are the same four subjects that scare all too many conservative politicians into backpedaling chatter about "big tents." Will they follow through and abolish these scourges? Or will they decide that they have married the father instead of the son and recoil from their initial resolve?

As our gorgeous mosaic comes uncaulked, parlor masochists are trying so hard to keep the multicultural peace that they have fallen into the habit of simply keeping the peace, any peace, without even knowing why they're doing it. The day after my local paper quoted me as saying, "College professors are incapable of earning a living with either their minds or their hands," a college professor phoned me—and invited me to lunch.

September 25, 1995

A S the culture war heats up and the attacks on Hollywood decadence mount in anticipation of the 1996 election, I find myself remembering the Hollywood that started me off on the road to cultural polish. The memories are especially poignant at this time of year. On October 7, 1959, I was devastated by a newspaper headline: "Mario Lanza Dies in Rome." My first crush, the man who had aroused my romantic and musical passions in such exquisite tandem that I could not tell one from the other, was dead at 38.

The young now ask: Who was Mario Lanza? Born Alfredo Cocozza in Philadelphia, his powerful tenor voice and extraordinary good looks won him the title role in *The Great Caruso* in 1951. His success began in the hearts of teenage girls but it went straight to the heart of something much deeper. As a music critic of the time put it: "Mario Lanza is the symbol of America's cultural democracy." Because of him, anyone who was in high school in the early Fifties stands an excellent chance of being an opera lover regardless of background or education.

My own story is typical. I was born into the class that no one admits to: the lower middle. People brag about being poor but nobody brags about punching two holes in a can of Carnation evaporated milk and calling it coffee cream.

My family's musical tastes were what you might expect, only worse. My father, a free-lance musician who had played the banjo in speakeasies during Prohibition, was fixated on the popular tunes of the Twenties. His favorite shaving song was "Don't Bring Lulu," which he sang while conducting a contest with himself to see if he could arrive at his upper lip when he hit the line, "You can bring Rose with the turned-up nose."

My mother, who grew up in World War I, was partial to "We Don't Want the Bacon, We Just Want a Piece of the Rhine," and that anthem to the orally challenged, "K-K-K-Katie." (She also knew the sequel, "Sthop Your Sthutterin', Thimmy.")

But it wasn't all Tin Pan Alley pep. My grandmother favored us with lugubrious Victorian ballads about fallen women who realized, too late, the error of their ways when a letter edged in black was delivered to the brothel: "And sadder she seems / When of Mother she dreams / In the mansion of aching hearts."

I was less than transported, and growing up in the Forties didn't help. When "Mairzy Doats" came out I decided that I hated music.

To people like us, opera was music for rich people, music to laugh at, the subject of cartoons about fat ladies in horned helmets. But then along came Mario Lanza, with his deep dimples, burning black eyes, and crystal-shattering high Cs. His first two movies were musicals containing some opera, but *The Great Caruso* pulled out all the stops. The film was saturated with the major tenor arias in the Italian repertoire, plus the sextet from *Lucia di Lammermoor*, the quartet from *Rigoletto*, and the final duet from *Aida*.

Lanza hit me like whiskey hits . . . well, you know. I saw *The Great*

Caruso over and over. My favorite part was the *Rigoletto* aria whose first line sounded like "the doughnut is moppylay." Wanting to know what it meant but having no one to ask, I got *The Victor Book of Operas* from the library and learned that it was "*La Donna e Mobile*": woman is fickle.

In this way I pieced out the name of every aria and ensemble piece in the movie, and learned the plots of all the operas. I spent my modest allowance on Lanza's records (among the last 78 rpms), but soon the tenor arias were not enough; I wanted to hear whole operas. Thanks to the craze Lanza had started, they were being recorded on the newly invented long-playing records. We didn't have an LP phonograph so I listened to them in the public library, sitting for hours in the stuffy little audio room, following the librettos. By this time I was in fourth-year French so the Italian made sense; I learned to pronounce it and acquired a small vocabulary.

This sounds like weird-kid behavior, a specialty of mine, but for once I was a conformist. All the other girls had crushes on Lanza too, so everybody was into opera. We sang the easy-to-carry "*M'appari*" from *Martha* in the gym locker room, and even tried the famous tour de force from *Pagliacci*, laughing and sobbing so maniacally that the teacher came running in to see what was wrong.

A RTURO Toscanini called Mario Lanza "the greatest voice of the twentieth century," but he was much more. Those presently engaged in a Diogenean search for heroes should stop and reflect that Lanza was the only person in the history of the world to succeed in elevating teenage musical tastes. He did it, moreover, without creating snobs. Although my generation were products of a decade notorious for status seeking, having a crush on an opera singer pointed us toward the higher goal of self-improvement. Inspired by girlish passion, we earned our status the old-fashioned way: we "bettered" ourselves.

Today I am a fair connoisseur of opera, knowing what to listen for in important spots, such as the end of "*Di Quella Pira*," and, after sufficient martinis, able to sing "*Alerte!*" from *Faust*—quite a feat, since it's a trio. I've come a long way from "We'll crown Bill the Kaiser with a bottle of Budweiser," and I owe it all to Mario Lanza.

A candle always flares up before it goes out: after Lanza, the next teenage idol was Elvis. Our entertainment is now so debased that it will take more than election-year growls from Bob Dole to set it right. We have carried egalitarianism to such a maniacal extreme that we now regard beauty as an affront. The national anthem must be sung at ballgames by tone-deaf croakers, and actresses with classical faces have been replaced by cross-eyed

Karen Black and pop-eyed Susan Sarandon. What is needed is a Minister of Culture—but we're not supposed to say that.

T HE O.J. verdict and the Pope's visit should not have anything in common, but they do. As throngs cheered John Paul II, a poll found a majority of American Catholics favored "the dictates of their own consciences" over Catholic doctrine.

The Simpson jurors, encouraged by their own Pope John, ignored the evidence and followed the dictates of their own consciences.

The rogue conscience is a uniquely American development, as we can see by the characteristic oxymoronic twist of the words themselves. Take two words that do not go together (e.g., diversity/strength) and put them together anyway, and you will get something that is tearing us apart.

The rogue conscience was an idea whose time had come before most Americans even got here. The country was settled by people who made a fetish of "individual conscience" and pioneered by people who made a fetish of staring grimly off into the distance and intoning, "A man has to do what he has to do." Conscience as open-ended compulsion took root, becoming the wellspring of inspiration and energy for our most tumultuous social causes. Abolition and Prohibition were about conscience; slaves and drunks were the "what."

The 1960s were the golden age of the rogue conscience. The civil-rights movement turned the white conscience into the eighth wonder of the world, a marble colossus that loomed over cocktail parties and transformed swizzle sticks into tridents of the heart.

Draft dodgers gave us the cafeteria conscience, picking and choosing their ethics carefully as befits those with weak stomachs. The conscience du jour was the fruit of the grape and lettuce boycotts. Then feminists replaced conscience with consciousness and diddled it in "consciousness raising" sessions, a group effort in which the search for truth became simply a matter of listening for "clicks" in one's head.

The machinations of the Sixties softened us up for the next faddish distortion of conscience, one that would make Hester Prynne turn to Hamlet and say, "They've got to be kidding." It was the pseudo-conscience of sensitivity, which has made cowards of us all.

It was a foregone conclusion that Lance Ito had to be the judge on the Simpson case. They could not give it to a white judge because blacks would get mad; they could not give it to a black judge because whites would get mad;

and they could not give it to an Hispanic because Hispanics are either white or black—unless they're brown, in which case everyone would get mad. What was left but an Asian? And not just any Asian. It could not be a Korean because they own too many stores; nor could it be a Chinese or Vietnamese, both synonyms for valedictorian. Ito, whose parents had been sent to a Japanese internment camp, was a twofer for the ages: an Asian victim.

Once Ito was on the case the problem of his wife came up. There was a time when "The judge's wife is a cop" would have been the punch line of a dirty joke. But Ito's wife really is a cop, and the feminist consciousness on which we are impaled made it impossible to fire her after she married a judge. We used to prohibit married couples from working for the same firm out of a prudent distrust of human weakness and a wariness about emotionalism on the job. But now we tell them, "It's between you and your conscience"—hence the outlandish spectacle of Ito examining his conscience from the bench.

Americans talk about our consciences the way Frenchmen talk about their livers, but at least they know what a liver looks like. We must reify our obsession.

"To reify" means to regard as concrete and material that which is not. The vitamin has been reified; a chemical intangible originally defined as a unit of nutritive value, it is now a pill and thus "real": I swallow it, therefore it is. Most reification consists of cartoonish mental pictures of things like the calorie and the kilowatt. Freudian terms are especially easy to reify; we imagine the "id" as a grinning demon and the "ego" as a large fragile bubble.

W HAT does our rogue conscience look like? I see it as a glistening silvery cloud, about the same size as the dark green cloud in foot-odor commercials, rising out of our brows. Two hundred and fifty million American puffs of amorphous adjudication; making a difference, sending a message, separating the message from the messenger, and skywriting "Everybody's gotta right to be Sir Thomas More for 15 minutes."

The rogue conscience has made all too many people lose sight of what real conscience is.

Conscience is the transmission system that enables us to shift into empathy. The reaction to the Simpson verdict reached a nadir at a mostly black cosmetology school in my town. Our local paper, after describing the taunting, flaunting, and high-fiving, recorded something even worse: "Others made fun of the sad look on prosecutor Marcia Clark's face or mocked what victim Ronald Goldman's father was going to say next."

Conscience is what makes us conscientious. We haven't heard that word much lately; it's been replaced by "meticulous," which is not quite the same thing. A compulsive picture-straightener is meticulous; conscientiousness corrects more important irregularities.

In 1977, as I watched the scene in *Roots* in which Kizzy is punished for learning to read, I experienced a rare burst of idealism, visualizing millions of black youngsters taking a solemn oath: "I vow to become the best reader in America, to honor my ancestors who were forbidden to learn." I was sure it would happen—how could it not, when the obligation was so clear?

Now, a word to Catholics who would follow the dictates of their consciences instead of the dictates of the Vatican.

Congratulations, you're Protestant. Practice your singing, and remember to say "gambling" when the pollster asks you which sin you hate the most.

November 27, 1995

T HANKS mainly to this column, most people now believe me when I say I'm a misanthrope. A few even believe me when I say I favor absolute monarchy and the divine right of kings, but nobody believes me when I say I have a visceral aversion to children. I've stated it unequivocally in several books but people still pass it off as a curmudgeonly pose.

Okay, I'll try again: I consider pedophilia an unforgivable crime. How could anyone be sexually attracted to a shapeless, hairless, falsetto runt?

Americans have made such a fetish of children that adults no longer count—not even in body counts. Janet Reno approved the Waco assault because "there were kids in the compound." Afterward she was castigated because "there were kids in the compound." A CNN broadcaster watching the conflagration cried, "My God, there are kids in there!"

Last summer a Philadelphia ice-cream vendor was shot to death by a robber. A cop told ABC News: "It was lucky that no children were killed."

Jeff Smith, TV's "Frugal Gourmet," dropped a skillet and immediately said: "I don't mind accidents in the kitchen as long as there aren't kids around to hurt themselves."

Recently, my little corner of the world was shaken by the discovery of a man with fifty pet cobras in his basement. Quoth a neighbor in our local paper: "My God, there's kids around here!" (My God, there's a great line in Elsa Lanchester's autobiography: "I held a baby once. It felt like a bag of hot snakes.")

The same disregard for adults marked Democrat attacks on the Contract with America: "They're abandoning America's children! . . . They want to take food out of the mouths of children! . . . They're coming for the children!" Even PBS funding was cast in puerile terms. It was *Sesame Street* and *Sesame*

Street alone, they implied, that the GOP was gunning for. *Rumpole of the Bailey*, the most adult show on all of television, was never mentioned.

Network commercials portray children as the only reason why adults should avoid accidents. First we had Goodyear's "So much is riding on your tires," then "My daddy loves me so much he bought a Volvo," but the prize goes to the Aetna insurance company, which simply displays a list of the kinds of coverage it offers, with no sound except a baby gurgling off-camera.

The same theme runs through public-service ads. Think you might have cataracts? Better get them taken care of so you can see your grandchild (gurgling sound off-camera). As for smokers, who have been at the bottom of the triage list all along, we are now warned that the danger we pose to co-workers is nothing compared to the danger we pose to children, to which I say, "Reach for a Lucky instead of a sweet."

America has gone beyond the child-centeredness of the Fifties. Now we are child-defined, a condition that makes many adults sound as if they have actually turned into children.

Bill Clinton on Whitewater: "I didn't do anything wrong."

Hillary Clinton on Whitewater: "I know nothing bad happened."

FBI Director Louis J. Freeh, advising local and federal police to stop competing with each other: "Play with your friends, be fair and honest, and share your toys."

Every major newscaster now employs the infantile euphemism, "the N-word."

Defending Lani Guinier, Dana Cunningham of the Legal Defense Fund said of the queen of racial gerrymandering: "Lani is the kind of person you want at your children's birthday party, because when the kids start fighting over a game, she will figure out a new game. A game nobody loses and everybody loves."

A househusband writing in *Newsweek*'s "My Turn" calls paternity leave "a spicy stew of belches and smiles" and describes the fun of grocery shopping with his little one ("We squeal at the celery"). This joy was made possible by the Family Leave Act, without which he would not be "trading coos with my daughter." He ends with a coo to his readers, explaining that he must stop writing now because "little wet slimy hands await."

No wonder we tolerate pornography. It's the only way left to say "Adults Only."

P OLITICIANS can no longer get away with kissing one baby per campaign stop. Now they must visit nursery schools and sit in tiny chairs with their knees under their chins. The spirit of enforced diminution is evidently hard to shake off. George Bush worried that Anita Hill's lurid testimony might have been heard by "little children," which was topped by Ross Perot speaking in another context about "tiny little children." How much smaller can they get?

A politician, says Wesley Pruden of the *Washington Times*, must "demonstrate that he loves children more than Mother Teresa loves children." The hands-down winner is Rep. Robert Dornan, who, in the middle of a C-SPAN tirade against Long Island Rail Road gunman Colin Ferguson, suddenly interjected, apropos of nothing: "I remember his name because it's my grand-kid's—Colin."

Child worship is the American woman's gross national product. She thinks she's the sexiest creature on earth, but sexy women have better things to do than swarm over children.

They are more like Queen Victoria, who, far from being repressed and frigid, possessed that rare form of female maturity that enables a woman to love a man more than a child. In a letter to her oldest daughter she freely admitted: "I often grudged you children being always there, when I longed to be alone with dearest Papa. Those are always my happiest moments."

American men are desperate for women like this, but what they get is a self-inflated neurotic growling Joan Crawford's signature line: "I'll do anything for those kids, ya hear me? Anything!"

December 11, 1995

L AST year my December column was given over to "Mis.Mis," computerese for "Miscellaneous Misanthrope," the disk file where I store material that did not make it into columns during the year—frequently because a little voice in my head whispered "Uh-uh."

This is America. Everybody's gotta right to start a tradition, so I've decided to do another Mis.Mis. We might as well begin with some uh-uhs.

■ Capt. Scott O'Grady, the pilot downed in Serbia, is our most embarrassing "hero" yet. An American officer does not describe himself as "a scared little bunny rabbit." Patton would have slapped him.

■ Have you noticed how many political cartoonists depict the generic teenaged welfare mother as a white girl? I clipped one showing a ponytailed blonde. Even more far-fetched is the depiction of male criminals as 1930s comic-strip "crooks"—burly, tattooed white men in masks and working-class caps who look like Victor McLaglen in *The Informer* or Sluggo in the "Nancy" comic strip.

■ Courage is in short supply nowadays. American drinkers defied the Eighteenth Amendment to the Constitution but American smokers knuckle under to the health lobby's agenda.

■ "A military chest seems to suit the ladies best," goes the old song. We need to get women out of the military, and then redesign men's uniforms to make them more dashing.

Democracy's tailors have destroyed the charms of male martial plumage. The present Army uniform looks like a forest ranger. Putting officers and men in identical green pants and tunics makes it impossible to distinguish rank at a glance. That, of course, is the whole point. Army officers used to wear "pinks and greens"—light tan pants with a dark tunic—while enlisted men wore khaki top and bottom. But that was too hierarchical, implying that some men are officers and some are not, so out it went.

The Air Force uniform looks like a Greyhound bus driver. They should copy the French flyers of World War I, whose uniforms were dyed to match the skies of Provence. The Marines have clung to their incomparable dress blues, but they should bring back the Sam Browne belt and swagger stick that they abandoned.

Naval officer whites are smart but the winter blues are too "suitish." The Navy especially needs a morale boost after what feminists have done to it. They should revive the officer's cocked hat and frock coat for full-dress occasions. As for the sailor, remove that silk hanky from his neck and give him a tie made from a thin strand of rope, along with collars of contrasting colors and a hard blue cap with his ship's name in gold.

Barbara Cartland: "The man in women's sexual fantasies is not nude, he's wearing a uniform."

■ A few days after the O.J. verdict the old-movie channel ran a 1952 British courtroom drama, *Eight O'Clock Walk*. I imagine they ran it because of the jury-selection scene: the first 12 names out of the box were the jury, and the first name called was automatically the foreman—that was that. My mouth dropped open. I've always known that the English did it this way, but evidently the O.J. trial had erased my memory.

■ Watching Atlanta Braves games, one catches glimpses of the new, chastened Jane Fonda whenever the camera pans to her and Ted Turner in their box. She's always snuggled up to him, gazing at him adoringly and giving him impulsive little kisses. His contempt is unmistakable. He married her to prove that he could do what the government could not; she married him because he looks and sounds like Henry Fonda.

■ One day when I was about seven, I opened a box of raisins and lifted out a nice fat clump. I was about to eat it when I saw that it was a huge dead bug. After restoring order among the female hysterics, my father flushed the bug down the toilet and wrote a letter to the company. They replied with a prompt letter of apology and said they were shipping us a complete line of their products. Several big cartons were duly delivered: canned fruit, vegetables, juices, cookies, and crackers. They sent us so much it took us weeks to eat it all.

It never occurred to us to sue them, and it never occurred to them to doubt my father's word and demand to see the bug. The incident was a study in civilized behavior all around. Can you imagine what would happen today? The aggrieved parties would rent a safety-deposit box for the bug, take the kid to a psychiatrist, and demand $100 million in damages. And to think we were grateful to get all that free food.

■ Call the spin doctor! The following individuals have come back from the dead to run for President of the United States:

W. Somerset Maugham: "Love is, essentially, only for the very stupid or the very poor."

Friedrich Nietzsche: "Wives and children have killed more artists than the cholera."

George Fitzhugh: "If women wore trousers, men would use them to plow with."

Henry Adams: "Journalism is the last resource of the educated poor who could not be artists and would not be teachers."

William Garrett Brown: "Africa still mocks America from her jungles. Still she jeers: 'With the dense darkness of my ignorance I confound your enlightenment; still, with my sloth, I weigh down the arms of your industry. Still with my supineness, I hang upon the wings of your aspiration. And in the very heart of your imperial young republic I have planted, sure and deep, the misery of this ancient curse I bear.'"

John Dryden: "Here lies my wife / Here let her lie / Now she's at peace / And so am I."

December 25, 1995

1996

T HE death of actress Butterfly McQueen three days before Christmas hit me hard. Part of my shock was due to the way I heard about her passing. As I was watching the late news, they announced that she had been badly burned in a fire at her Georgia home and was not expected to live. Then, seconds later, they got a bulletin that she had just died.

The two reports coming one on top of the other gave me a disturbing sensation of telescoped time; *is* and *was* were crowding each other. To separate them and regain a sense of cosmic order, I mentally thumbed through some *Gone with the Wind* chronology. "Olivia De Havilland is the last one left now," I mused. "Melanie died at 29 but she's outlived everybody except the young bit players . . . the little girl who played Bonnie must be about five years older than I . . . the baby Bonnie is three years younger."

My sensation of telescoped time stood revealed for what it was. My own mortality is too neatly measured by *Gone with the Wind* for comfort. The book and I both came out in 1936, so the death of anyone connected with it diminishes me. Especially Butterfly McQueen, who made a unique impression on my four-year-old mind when I saw the movie for the first time in 1940.

I'm told that I sat through all three hours and forty minutes as still as a stone, impressing several audience members who complimented my mother on her well-behaved little girl. Evidently I concentrated very hard, but I retained nothing except four discrete scenes: the silhouette of the wagon against the backdrop of flames; the horse dying in the traces; the shot of the looming fence that foreshadows the riding accident—and Prissy shrieking "I don't know nuthin' 'bout birthin' babies." The only human image that stuck in my memory was Butterfly McQueen.

I was offered a Scarlett doll but I turned it down. I wanted a Prissy doll but they didn't make them, so I was offered a "colored" baby doll as a consolation prize. You'd never know it from Kenneth Clark's statistics but colored dolls were very popular with little white girls back then. Not, however, with this little white girl. I detested all baby dolls regardless of race, creed, or color. I wanted a Prissy doll to go with my Charlie McCarthy doll because even then I was drawn to quirkiness.

Later on, as I read and reread the novel, I paid special attention to the Prissy passages. Liberals have always held her up as a minstrel-show character inserted into the story purely for comic relief. They're usually the same liberals who make a point of boasting that they have never read, or could not finish, the book. That many of them are also English professors adds irony to ignorance, for by refusing to take Prissy seriously they miss an exquisite example of literary apposition.

The movie necessarily omitted several interesting minor characters but the most significant omission was Prissy's mother, Dilcey. Unless we know her, we cannot understand Prissy.

As the novel opens, Dilcey belongs to the Wilkes family and serves as midwife at Twelve Oaks. When she marries Pork, Gerald O'Hara's valet, Gerald buys her so that the couple can live on the same plantation. Being soft-hearted, Gerald also buys her feckless 12-year-old daughter by an earlier marriage.

Dilcey is the salt of the earth and the rock of Gibraltar rolled into one. Described as "an unsmiling bronze giantess," she is half Indian and very proud of the fact, attributing her marble stoicism to this genetic infusion. "Mist' Gerald buy my Prissy so I wouldn' grieve and I doan forgit it," she tells Scarlett. "I is part Indian and Indians doan forgit them as is good to them. I is sorry 'bout my Prissy. She mighty wuthless. Look lak she all nigger lak her pa."

Liberals call this gratuitous racism, but in fact it replicates the good mother–bad daughter dynamic between Scarlett and the saintly Ellen O'Hara. Dilcey and Ellen are a matched pair, differing only in color, selfless paragons of virtue who never bend, never complain, and never shirk their duty. Scarlett worships her mother and longs to emulate her, but she possesses none of Ellen's honor and goodness, nor her resigned acceptance of martyrdom. Lacking self-insight, she suffers periodic guilt seizures as she wonders, "Why can't I be a great lady like Mother?" The obvious answer crops up throughout the book:

"In her face were too sharply blended the delicate features of her mother, a coast aristocrat of French descent, and the heavy ones of her florid Irish father."

"It was Gerald's headstrong and impetuous nature in her that gave them concern, and they sometimes feared they would not be able to conceal her damaging qualities until she had made a good match."

"No, I don't love you. But I do like you tremendously—for the elasticity of your conscience, for the selfishness which you seldom trouble to hide, and for the shrewd practicality in you which, I fear, you get from some not too remote Irish-peasant ancestor."

"Lordy, 'twus right funny how de older Miss Scarlett git de mo' she look lak Mist' Gerald and de less lak Miss Ellen!"

"I often wondered what she was like. You seemed to me so like your father."

L IKE Prissy, Scarlett takes after her pa. Once we understand this, the ostensibly racist "birthin' babies" debacle becomes instead a deft display of parallel characterization. Like all good writers, Margaret Mitchell does not overexplain. She doesn't tell us that Prissy feels inferior to Dilcey and wishes she were more like her, but the artistic balance in the portrait of the two perfect mothers and the two erring daughters leaves us with no other conclusion. Scarlett longs to be a great lady because Ellen was one, and Prissy lies about her knowledge of midwifery because Dilcey was a midwife.

Madge Sinclair, who died shortly before Butterfly McQueen, could have played Dilcey to a turn. Hail and farewell to them both.

January 29, 1996

P AY no attention to what *Burke's Peerage* says about Princess Diana's lineage. Any woman who goes on television and discusses her affairs, betrayals, suicide attempts, and vomiting habits, and then says "I'm a very strong person," is an American.

The Enid Waldholtzing of the Princess of Wales and the debate over the future of royalty remind me of the running battle between my English father and my American mother that dominated my childhood and ultimately shaped most of the political opinions I hold today.

My parents dwelt on opposite sides of a yawning philosophical gulf. He would speak of his "betters" and she would snap "You're just as good as they are!" When he tried to explain the difference between the American usage of *better* and the English usage of *betters*, she automatically upped the ante to "You're better than they are!" without having heard a word he said.

Monarchy was a special sore point. He tried to explain why Edward VIII had to abdicate, going over each constitutional point in his precise way, but he got nowhere.

"Malarkey. He was the King, he could do anything he wanted, and if anybody didn't like it he could throw them in jail and cut off their head," said the great republican.

His favorite illustration of noblesse oblige was the story of Queen Alexandra, who sent a car for King Edward VII's mistress as he lay dying so the lovers could say goodbye. My Yankee-doodle-dandy mother was unimpressed.

"She should have sent a car to run over her."

They had their most memorable clash over the tiny pieces of lead sewn into the Queen's hems to keep her dress from flying up: Oh, for God's sake! Do they think she was born without knees? Of course she has knees, but we don't want to see them. Why not? Because she's the Queen. Oh, for God's sake!

I always sided with my father. The psychobabblers no doubt will say that I'm "threatened" by Princess Diana, that her lèse majesté has unearthed my "unresolved conflicts" and "buried anxieties." Maybe so, but a recent book claims that eccentrics have no unresolved conflicts or buried anxieties, and I have reason to believe the book. In any case, I am an unabashed anglophile; if Paris is worth a Mass, London is worth an Electra complex.

Currently, I side with Prince Charles and think he deserves a feminist award. Most men ditch their dear old Dutch for a trophy wife but he ditched the trophy wife for his dear old Dutch. No one gives him credit for preferring time-ravaged Lady Camilla Parker-Bowles to firm-fleshed Di, or realizes her ladyship's value to the state. Plebeianized England needs Queen Camilla: any woman can ride a horse but it takes a true aristocrat to look like one.

Charles is regarded as an odd duck because his hobbies of architecture and the cello fall outside the Pale du jour. Diana, on the other hand, is considered normal because her hobbies—throwing up, hurling herself into glass cabinets, hating her husband—conform to acceptable feminist standards of assertiveness and self-expression.

Actually she's one diamond short of a full tiara. Not like those royals of yore called the Mad and the Simple; full-bore insanity with its connotations of blue blood would offend our anti-elitist age. Democracy demands neurosis and Diana delivers. So far she has indulged in common-garden masochism, but falling through glass eventually loses its charm. Needing bigger and better crashes, she is courting self-destruction by assaulting what she dimly realizes is her only identity: the monarchy itself.

Diana the Masochist is history's most problematic regicide. Even if it were still possible to torture her in the Tower, it would be pointless because she already tortures herself on her Nordic Track. Safe from the scaffold, she insists upon losing her head on sound stages, mounting her *coup d'état* by overthrowing herself on television. Edward II's adulterous consort was driven into exile by an outraged nation screaming "She-Wolf of France!" but when Diana admits the same sin the telly-paradise bleats, "She's only 'uman." It's a revolution for the Nineties: the clenched fist holds a sodden Kleenex. Diana will never tell viewers to eat cake because it's fattening, but it's only a matter of time before she demonstrates her technique for having her cake and eating it too, and who better to bring it up than Barbara Walters?

Diana is a monster of plebeianism who needs to take a leaf from the story of a woman who started out very much like herself.

Henriette-Lucie Dillon, daughter of an Irishman and a French noblewoman, was a lady-in-waiting to Marie Antoinette. Famed for her magnificent blond hair, she married the dashing Marquis de La Tour du Pin and threw herself into the pleasures of Versailles.

WHEN the Revolution began, the young couple fled at once to the United States. It was on this voyage that the giddy Henriette changed suddenly and completely. Finding her glorious hair so tangled and matted that she could not get a comb through it, she cut it off and tossed it into the sea. "I dropped my hair overboard," she wrote many years later, "and with it all the frivolous ideas which my pretty blond curls had given rise to."

The couple bought a farm near Albany and the marquise went into the dairy business, making butter stamped with her family crest. She took great pride in producing only the best, showing herself to be, as Peter Gay noted, "the great lady she had always been."

When the Revolution ended she and her husband returned to France. On the voyage back, this sociological anomaly volunteered to be the crew's tailor, mending their clothing and generally making herself useful—and hence beloved. Where her new traits came from is one of the mysteries of personality, but what she did with them is called "making the best of things." She was not only a real aristocrat but a natural one as well.

February 12, 1996

R EADERS of this space often write me asking where I get my ideas and how I put a column together. It's a hard question to answer in a letter but I can tell you the genesis of this column here and now.

It was a morning in mid-January and I was enjoying my definition of heaven: coffee, cigarettes, and the *Washington Times*. The intense silence imposed by heavy snow made me feel even more alone than usual, and it was good. Peaceful and magnanimous was yours truly, sipping and inhaling and turning pages—until I came to the story about the female Episcopal bishop who consecrated a slice of Wonder Bread.

A traditional parish in Maryland that opposes the ordination of women had boycotted the bishop's visit and stripped the church of wafers and wine to prevent her from offering Holy Communion. A minority of progressive parishioners rallied round her, one contributing an unpretentious little merlot, and another, who must be a convert, contributing a loaf of Wonder Bread. Her Grace made do with the substitutes and was photographed with arms upraised, "breaking" the squishy slice (you can see her fingerprints on it).

Afterward, she was photographed receiving a violent, miter-threatening hug from a female supporter. Two traditionalists in the back of the church who had videotaped the event also were included in the love feast when another progressive female made a point of shaking hands with them, telling the reporter: "It seemed to me that understanding could happen if we shook hands and touched each other's bodies."

At that, the pin-drop hush of a snowy morning was shattered as I yelled "Kill! Kill!" and a column was born.

I've always had a bleak opinion of my poor, feeble sex but I used to be detached and rational about it. Back in the Seventies I scrutinized arguments on the Equal Rights Amendment for logical fallacies; did the same with abortion arguments in the Eighties; and filled the margins of feminist books with austere little notes that would have done any bluestocking proud.

No more. I have turned into St. Jerome as he might have been portrayed by Jackie Gleason. I went ballistic when Anita Hill, professor of law, said, "I look forward to the day when just one woman's word is enough"; and again when Enid Waldholtz said, "I was tired of being the strong one," and then cried for five hours. My reaction to the lady bishop was but the latest manifestation of the crumbling fortress that once was my nervous system. Any day now you will see me starring as the egg in a public-service ad, "This is your brain . . . this is your brain on women."

Looking back on the feminist movement, I wonder if it might not have been better if the Equal Rights Amendment had been ratified. That way, the feminists would have disappeared, as the suffragettes disappeared after the ratification of the 19th Amendment. Except for the remnant that formed the League of Women Voters, which quickly became an enclave of conventional matrons, it was hard to tell that suffragettes had ever existed.

But ERA was defeated and out of the ensuing frustration the horror show called post-feminism was born. The dependably middle-class Betty Friedan beat a hasty retreat; Susan Brownmiller and Germaine Greer, the most intelligent and talented of the Seventies' feminists, moved to the Right, leaving the field to the hot-gospel genderoids who are giving us ERA on a case-by-case basis.

All of the dire results that Phyllis Schlafly predicted are coming to pass, without the solemnity of a Constitutional amendment to discourage actions that are more ridiculous than dangerous. We already have gay marriages in Hawaii and unisex bathrooms in coed dorms, but would a ratified ERA have inspired a suit to force Hooters restaurants to hire men as cocktail waitresses?

When Mrs. Schlafly was campaigning against ERA she was often confronted by talk-show hosts who solemnly read out the words, "Equality of rights under the law shall not be denied or abridged by the United States or by any state on account of sex," and then asked her, "What's wrong with that?" She always replied, "Read the other part"—meaning the second clause with its nightmarish scenario of eternal litigation: "Congress shall have the power to enforce this article by appropriate legislation."

Her technique caught on. When NRA members recited "The right of the people to keep and bear arms shall not be infringed," gun-control advocates demanded their favorite other part: "A well-regulated militia, being necessary to the security of a free state. . . ."

I HAVE a favorite other part, too. Feminist literary critters love to recite Virginia Woolf's plea for "a room of my own," but there's more. What she said was: "Give me 500 pounds a year and a room of my own and you can keep the vote."

We conservatives have a tendency to box ourselves in with Aristotelian formalism and a Jesuitical approach to argument, but when the subject is feminism the best thing to do is get right down there with Jean-Jacques Rousseau and Bill Clinton and just let it come.

I'm sick of women. I'm sick of their wombs, I'm sick of their breast tissue, I'm sick of their lawsuits, I'm sick of their glass ceilings, and I'm sick of those made-for-TV female-victim movies about stalkers, anonymous callers, and buried memories of childhood incest. I can't bear to watch them but I always read the listings faithfully, in a spirit of self-flagellation, to see what they'll come up with next.

As far as I can tell, there's only one plot left: a white-male fetus rends his father's penis while the parents are making the beast with two backs; the father bleeds to death, and the white-male fetus, conveniently situated within reach of his mother's G-spot, stimulates her until she becomes his sexual slave.

If anyone wants to write this screenplay, I offer, free of charge, a title: *Umbilicus Rex*.

March 11, 1996

BOB Dole's habit of referring to himself in the third person is having such a disconcerting effect on the primaries that they will have to be renamed the tertiaries if he doesn't cut it out. He sounds as if he really doesn't want to be President, he just wants Bob Dole to be President.

My nerves gave way during his post–New Hampshire news conference when he told supporters, "You're going to see the real Bob Dole from now on." I turned him off and surfed around for an old movie to take my mind off politics. Under normal conditions I never tire of *The Third Man*, but this time I skipped it. I finally settled on *Wuthering Heights* but my respite was brief. When Merle Oberon cried, "I *am* Heathcliff, he's more myself than I am!" all I could think of was Bob Dole.

Object to his age and he will say "Bob Dole is rested and ready." Call him a Washington insider and he will say "Bob Dole has been tested." During one particularly bad week in January when he had to counter speculation that his campaign was bringing forth Lazarus, he said: "I don't think people think Bob Dole is that bad."

Hearing him say these things on television can be either comical or irritating, depending upon your mood; seeing them in print accompanied by the reporter's attributives is positively eerie: "'We must reach out to more and more people, and Bob Dole can do that,' Dole said tonight."

I wait for the day when he objects to the verb that reporters routinely use in describing him. Then we'll read: "'Bob Dole doesn't snarl,' Dole snarled."

Welcome to the Doppelgänger school of American oratory. At the rate Dole is going, his rhetorical onanism soon will become so deeply embedded in the soil of American politics that Pat Buchanan will have yet another abomination to rip out "root and branch"—except that Buchanan has begun using the third person, too.

How long has Dole been doing this? A search of my files turned up a clipping from November 1992 in which he assured gloomy Republicans that Bill Clinton would not have a legislative honeymoon because: "Bob Dole is going to be his chaperone."

From what is known about speech habits, it probably started much earlier than a mere four years ago. This is a question for a serious scholar to explore. If Dole wins the nomination, Linda Bloodworth-Thomason can do a film biography to show at the GOP convention. After the sunny optimism she brought to *The Man from Hope*, she can demonstrate her versatility by producing *The Pronouning* in collaboration with Stephen King.

The camera pans over Russell, Kansas, following the candidate through his formative years . . .

To his mother: "Bob Dole's hungry."

To his father: "Can Bob Dole have a quarter?"

To his teachers: "Bob Dole didn't do it."

To nice girls: "Would you like to go to the picture show with Bob Dole?"

To bad girls: "If you did it with all those other guys, how come you won't do it with Bob Dole?"

Neither Dole nor his advisors seem to realize that referring to oneself in the third person has a dark history. Psychopaths are especially prone to it. When Lola Montez wanted to make an impression on King Ludwig of Bavaria, she burst into the royal presence, tore open her bodice, and cried, "Lola has come!"

Worse, it's undemocratic. Given the more-populist-than-thou desperation of Campaign '96, why would a politician risk a usage associated with absolute monarchs, dictators, and supreme egoists like Douglas MacArthur?

Maybe it's Dole's way of avoiding the dreaded "I" word—that is, "I," the selfish pronoun outlawed by the collectivist government in Ayn Rand's *Anthem*. When her hero escapes from the re-education camp he has to practice arduously before he is once again able to pronounce "I" properly, a therapy that may become necessary for Bob Dole.

Another possible explanation is a misreading of Middle America's favorite self-help book, *How to Win Friends and Influence People*, by Dale Carnegie. The author recommends repeating the name of the person to whom one is speaking, working it into the conversation as often as possible to serve the dual purpose of flattery and memory training: the listener gets to hear the sweet sound of his own name, and the speaker gets to remember what it is.

T HIS is invaluable training for a politician, but repeating names year after year carries the same risk as singing "God Bless America" at Kiwanis luncheons year after year: if you hit the wrong note on the final *home* you automatically swing into another refrain, and then you can't stop. Fortunately, Elizabeth Dole works for the Red Cross. She'll know how to handle such emergencies if she becomes Third Lady.

Significantly, Dole not only uses the third person, but the Third-Person Diminutive. Now that Americans have exchanged the backslap of the first name for the verbal goose of the nickname as the ultimate sign of equality, he must take care to remind us that he no longer has a full, formal name. He would never say "Robert J. Dole is not imploding" because he knows that voters are threatened by aloofness. To reap the psychological value of his nickname he must say "Bob Dole is not imploding." This, so help me Tocqueville, is America's definition of a soothing statement.

Considering how rapidly language horrors spread in this country, the Third-Person Diminutive is likely to catch on, but before it gets carved in marble we should test it on a sampling of notables and listen carefully:

"Nat Hale only regrets that he has but one life to give for his country."

"Johnny Paul Jones has not yet begun to fight."

"It's a far, far better thing Sid Carton does than he has ever done."

"Here stands Marty Luther, he can do no other."

"*L'état, c'est Lou.*"

April 8, 1996

I HAVE figured out a painless way to follow Campaign '96. Instead of suffering through CNN and C-SPAN, I watch old movies. The current politicos turn up in them like figures from Greek mythology who assumed different forms.

Anything starring Miriam Hopkins also stars Hillary Rodham Clinton, especially *Becky Sharp*. The symbol-rich love scenes between Garbo and Gilbert in *Queen Christina* feature a cameo appearance by George Stephanopoulos as the grape. Al Gore plays the title in *Raintree County*, as well as the romantic lead in post-war flicks starring the Great Stone Stone of the late Forties, Guy Madison.

The late Forties were also the years of the Rat, the character actor who always made the woman sitting in the row behind you whisper, "I don't like his face." Rats came in three types. The Handsome Rat was Zachary Scott, the two-timing chiseler in *Mildred Pierce*, but sadly, he has no counterpart on today's hustings. He was too slimy for even the most disaster-prone campaign, so unequivocally feral that Bob Dole would take one look at him and say, "He's the only thing about America that America isn't about."

The other two Rat types are well-represented in Campaign '96. The Obnoxious Rat was played by nasal, prematurely balding Dan Duryea, the silver screen's ubiquitous cocksure nephew; his heir is nasal, prematurely balding James Carville, who plays the cocksure nephew in *The Little Foxes*.

Arthur Kennedy was the Weak Rat, a part he owned after playing Branwell Brontë in 1946's *Devotion*. He spent thirty years making Weak Rat movies, all starring White House press secretary Mike McCurry, whose washed-out blondness and unsteady gaze make him an Arthur Kennedy lookalike.

Bill Clinton? Remember Sonny Tufts? He was the big bashful lug who operated on the principle that the way to a woman's bed is through her maternal instinct. However, limiting Clinton to Tufts's light comedies overlooks the great tragic role he was born for.

In *Letter from an Unknown Woman*, Louis Jourdan plays Stefan Brandt, a celebrated Viennese pianist and dedicated roué who seduces the young Joan Fontaine and leaves her pregnant. She eventually marries a rich, kindly older man and resigns herself to a passionless life. Fifteen years pass. Suddenly, Stefan turns up again and she is promptly consumed by passion. So is he, but when she goes to his room she makes a shattering discovery: the dissolute Stefan has had so many women that he doesn't remember her and proceeds to seduce her from scratch.

The mother of all Campaign '96 movies, as I discovered the other night, is *Come Back, Little Sheba*, with Shirley Booth and Burt Lancaster.

Doc Delaney is a well-bred man whose life has been ruined by a shotgun marriage to his social inferior, the slovenly Lola. Forced to quit medical school, he is now a chiropractor and a member of Alcoholics Anonymous. Though outwardly neat, polite, scholarly, and well-spoken, he is one drink away from mayhem.

Trouble starts when Lola rents a room to Marie, an art student and her opposite in every way: young, slim, energetic, fastidious, and an early riser. Doc idealizes Marie as a symbol of his own youthful promise until he sees her in a compromising situation with Turk, a crude jock intent on giving her the old lock-and-load. Mistakenly thinking that Marie has yielded to this male version of Lola, Doc goes on a bender, busts up the house, and tries to stab his wife.

Why did this seem so familiar to me? I had seen the movie many times before, of course, but that wasn't why. This was another kind of familiarity. . . .

Suddenly, it hit me. Grabbing pen and paper, I scribbled furiously, intent on capturing the inchoate associations tumbling through my mind before they slipped back into the misty subconscious regions they had occupied ever since the New Hampshire primary.

Doc Buchanan is a well-bred man with a fatal addiction: campaigning. A columnist by profession, he has put aside writing and thinking to follow his new ambitions, and now he is an unrecovered candidate. Though his friends attest that he is neat, polite, scholarly, and well-spoken, he is one caucus away from mayhem.

The measure of his addiction is what it has done to his wife. She's starting to look like Shirley Booth: the same full, fleshy face, the same expression of tired sweetness, the same lingering traces of the pertness she must have had once, but has no more.

HOW could she be pert? She's been standing in high heels ever since Doc Buchanan went on his bender. Even Pat Nixon was allowed to sit down while she gazed in adoration at her speechifying husband, but poor Shelley has to stand up.

Every woman who has worn high heels can interpret the look on Shelley Buchanan's face. It's subtly different from the other female "look" that signals menstrual cramps. That one contains a glimmer of hope because we know we will have a nice flat stomach the next day. The high-heels look is one of unmitigated despair because we know our feet will be swollen the next day. Hopelessness of this magnitude conjures up Shirley Booth's Lola Delaney, flopping down the stairs in her bathrobe, eyes at half-mast and tired all over.

Adding to Shelley's exhaustion is a woman who is her opposite in every way: Bay Buchanan; lean as a pitchfork, flat as a drawbridge, a quivering longbow of energy, a human alarm clock without a snooze button made sleepless by her lust for the votes of America's Turks, those professional peasants of the Buchanan Brigades more accurately called Little Sheba Republicans.

Doc and Bay Buchanan deserve to spend ten thousand years in Purgatory massaging Shelley's feet, except that would require Shelley to be in Purgatory with them. She deserves to go straight to Heaven, there to receive from St. Peter himself a pair of golden Hush Puppies in which to wiggle her toes through eternity.

May 6, 1996

G AY marriage is a consummation devoutly to be missed, but it's a dead cert. If you doubt it, try to remember the last time America turned down a vocal minority. In the Sixties we were the Girl Who Can't Say No, but she was a font of virtue compared to what we are now. Overcome by the miasmic gases of diversity and inclusion wafting from the Nineties swamp, we have turned into the Punchdrunk Kid, a twitching lummox with cauliflower ears who mumbles "Sure, Jake, sure" to everybody.

The preliminary stage of brainwashing is already underway. "Husband" and "wife" are yielding to "spouse," a vague usage that benefits no one but gays. Gov. Roy Romer recently vetoed Colorado's proposed anti–gay marriage law, calling it "mean-spirited," a word that functions in America like the bell in Pavlov's laboratory. And now Bill Clinton has announced, through his gay-liaison office, that he is "personally opposed" to homosexual marriage. This phraseology, a staple of the abortion debate, is a reminder not to let our premises stand in the way of our conclusions.

The major brainwashing, soon to begin, will proceed as follows.

Magazines will run cover stories that thinking Americans—all 17 of us—recognize as that brand of persuasion called "nibbled to death by a duck." *Time* does "Debating Same-Sex Marriage" and *Newsweek* does "Rethinking Gay Marriage." Lofty opinion journals weigh in with "A Symposium on," "In Defense of," and "Voices from," while *Parade* does "If They Say 'I Do' . . . Will We Say 'You Can't?'" Cover art consists of a pair of wedding rings sporting identical biological signs: two arrow-shooting circles for men, two mirror-handle circles for women. We will start seeing these logos in our sleep.

Next, the pundits. Molly Ivins writes "Bubba, Hold Yore Peace." Ellen Goodman waxes earnest about tradition *versus* change in "Something Old, Something New," Ruth Shalit writes something borrowed, and Richard Cohen, Victim America's identifier-in-chief, does a column called "We're All Single."

Arianna Huffington will figure out a compassionate way to be against gay marriage, but most conservatives stand to fare badly in this debate. Will Durant wrote, "When religion submits to reason it begins to die." In a media-saturated society teeming with talk-show producers casting dragnets over think tanks, proponents of gay marriage win merely by being scheduled. By contrast, the conservative instinctively recoils from analyzing eternal verities. He may know the words to legal arguments such as "the need to show a compelling state interest, etc." but he doesn't know the tune. In the final analysis he believes in the sanctity of marriage "just because."

To liberals, the just-because mindset betokens racism. Therefore, anyone who opposes gay marriage must hate blacks. Anti–gay marriage laws will be equated with the old anti-miscegenation laws, producing tortured sophistry about "the difference between race and sex." The liberal will claim that all differences are the same, forcing the conservative to claim that some differences are more different than others. Caught in an Orwellian trap, terrified of being called a racist, he will seek safety in a soundbite of chortling folksiness.

"When a baby is born, people don't say 'it's white' or 'it's black,' they say 'it's a boy' or 'it's a girl.'"

Because this makes no sense, it becomes instantly popular. Repeated incessantly on talk shows, it starts running through our heads like the beat-beat-beat of the tom-toms in "Begin the Beguine," intensifying when Bob Dole soundbites it into a back-to-basics vision of blood and sex and whatever in a prime-time press conference.

Then Jesse Jackson and the feminists change the word order, ostentatiously placing "black" before "white" and "girl" before "boy." Remembering to say it the PC way becomes such an overriding obsession that we forget what it has to do with gay marriage, especially after Clarence Page points out that in slave days the color of a baby was indeed the first thing people noticed.

Soon, Republicans panicked by mounting accusations of racism suggest that gay couples be allowed to register their unions and establish common-law marriages based on seven years of cohabitation. But gays reject these half measures, comparing them to the irregular marriages of slavery, when couples "jumped over the broom."

All attempts at compromise elicit cries of "Second-class marriage!" and lead to lawsuits under the Americans with Disabilities Act. Calling themselves "connubially challenged," gays will sue the Christian Coalition for forcing them to lead immoral lives. Arguing that marriage will keep them from promiscuity, which will keep them from getting AIDS, they will equate prohibition of same-sex marriage with capital punishment. A Clinton judicial appointee will find the "right" to gay marriage lurking under a constitutional penumbra, and CNN will give a 900 number so viewers can vote yes to prove they aren't racists.

I FIND it ironic that gays are now singing the praises of wedded bliss in terms that were the bane of my existence forty years ago, when "settling down" proved you were "mature and responsible." If they keep it up, they will corroborate the English prostitute who plied her trade in the States and wound up in a book about American sexual attitudes. A great many of her clients, she said, showed her photos of their wives and children. Clearly bemused, her sigh almost audible on the page, she added: "Yanks are born married."

My personal opinion of marriage reflects my status as a pariah in the

Fifties snuggery of joined-at-the-hip Togetherness. "Rather a beggar woman and single be, than Queen and married," said Elizabeth I, and so say I. My objective opinion, however, conforms with Timothy Dwight: "It is incomparably better that individuals should suffer than that an institution, which is the basis of all human good, should be shaken or endangered."

June 3, 1996

I WISH baby boomers would stop telling me what I remember about Franklin D. Roosevelt. Ever since the wheelchair controversy erupted over his planned memorial, a chorus of know-it-all media goslings has been saying, "People of his time didn't know he couldn't walk."

Of course we knew. We saw photos and newsreels of him clinging to the arm of one of his sons, usually James, with his other hand gripping a cane. We saw pictures of him seated with his leg braces visible around his ankles and bulking squarishly under his trousers at the knees. True, we never saw him in a wheelchair, but we didn't have to. It was an era of starch and vests; "foundation garments" and "best dresses." Common sense, born of our own experience, told us that when his public day was done he removed the heavy braces and slipped into something more comfortable: in his case, a wheelchair.

Only the most benighted optimist would have thought FDR able to walk. Those were the days of annual polio epidemics, and we knew all too well what they presaged. Members of the post-Salk generation can't begin to imagine what life was like then: the ever-present worry, the dread of summer, the suspicions surrounding swimming, the panic that arose over a child's slightest sign of lassitude. Polio was a national obsession and a seasonal monomania, fed by newsreels and picture spreads in *Life* of paralyzed victims in wheelchairs and iron lungs. No one ever seemed to recover, so if they couldn't walk, it followed that FDR couldn't either. If the White House had decided to spell it out in a press release, we would have received it with universal bemusement: Why are they telling us what we already know?

The most inarguable proof that we knew has never been mentioned by media boomers. They must have heard about it, but they probably put it out of their minds as the politically correct are wont to do. It was something men used to say whenever the subject turned to Eleanor Roosevelt: "If he could stand up, he'd knock her down!"

The debate over whether FDR's memorial should show him in a wheelchair is drawing comments that say nothing about the Thirties and Forties and everything about the Nineties. A sampling from the pro-wheelchair contingent:

Doris Kearns Goodwin: "Roosevelt's polio made his special relationship with the American people possible."

Christopher Roosevelt, grandson: "His disability gave him his character."

Maureen Dowd: "It is perverse not to celebrate Roosevelt for the remarkable effort it took simply to get out of bed every day."

Hugh Gallagher, polio victim and author of *FDR's Splendid Deception*: "They are trying to steal our hero from us."

Michael Deland, wheelchairman of the National Organization on Disability, says that not showing FDR in a wheelchair is "misusing history."

A Harris poll of those unswayable independent thinkers known as the American people found that 73 per cent favor a memorial with "visible recognition of FDR's disabilities."

Roosevelt's special relationship with the American people sprang from something that pre-dated his affliction, was unaffected by it, and would be viewed as intolerable today: his absolute superiority and blessings on all fronts.

He was better than we were, and we all knew it and felt safe because of it. He may have governed for the Common Man but he never pretended to be one, and we relished his aristocratic flair and the patrician assurance that flowed from him. We loved it that he was rich and had an estate on the Hudson. We loved it that he was so handsome, and we loved his having what we called "that voice" because it so unmistakably proclaimed his advantages. F. Scott Fitzgerald was right: you can hear it in the voice; not just money, but background and breeding, the caste superiority that people crave in a leader whether they know it or not. We were the last generation of Americans to know it, and the last to get it. The Kennedys tried but the reek of the parvenu was on them, and we knew that, too.

The always wise Somerset Maugham wrote: "It is not true that suffering ennobles the character; happiness does that sometimes, but suffering, for the most part, makes men petty and vindictive." Roosevelt's character was shaped not by polio but by his Roman matron of a mother—"Ole Miz Roosevelt," as approving Southerners called her—who devoted her entire life to him. A man sure of his mother's love is girded for the battle of life, said Freud, but our feminist age regards Sara Delano Roosevelt as perverse.

M EANWHILE, real perversity flourishes. We live in a society that worships weakness, though its promoters carefully call it "vulnerability." Any kind of weakness will do—physical, mental, moral, social—as long as it advances the twisted notion that the unhalt, unlame, unstupid, unvulgar, unpoor, and uncriminal are somehow not playing fair.

We talk incessantly of "heros" and seem to have a plentiful supply, but they're a far cry from Horatius at the Bridge. Ours is the age of the passive hero. Get yourself taken hostage, shot out of the sky, buried in an avalanche, trapped on a runaway roller coaster, or wander off and fall in a hole, and you are sure to end up on the morning shows as the latest hero, having done nothing but been in the wrong place at the wrong time or blundered into a situation that an earlier America associated with Dagwood Bumstead.

The memorial flap is an attempt to diminish FDR's legacy of noble stoicism until he fits the mold prescribed by Hillary Clinton's ex-guru, Michael Lerner, in *The Politics of Meaning*: "If the world needs to be healed, it will be done by 'wounded healers,' people who themselves are in need of healing."

Now the Procrustean banditti are after Bob Dole, urging him to talk about his arm, and he, poor fool, is going along with it.

July 1, 1996

THE best story about what can happen when a politician tries to flatter the masses comes from England, but fittingly enough the politician was American-born Lady Nancy Astor. Standing for Parliament during a period of personal unhappiness, she visited a women's prison and told the detainees: "You're luckier than I am; you're wanted and I'm not."

The season of "the real people" is upon us, and if the rest of Campaign '96 is anything like the shirt contest we've already seen, Oliver Stone will be forced to quit the movie business and find other work. Not that Campaign '96 won't inspire movies; merely that it won't inspire the wordy, three-hour character studies that Stone likes to make. Conservative politicians are courting the Common Man with such unshaded artlessness that we will have to regress to the silent era and make two-reelers with titles like "The Pickup Truck," "The Gun Show," and "The Tractor Pull," starring Buster Keaton as a beset Republican candidate desperately trying to cultivate a populist image.

Title card: "I love the smell of grease!"

Close-up: chain breaks.

Music: "Ride of the Valkyries."

Something like this almost happened to George Bush in '88 when he lost control of the 18-wheeler he was trying to drive, and again to the GOP senatorial candidates in last month's Virginia primary. John Warner tried to operate a textile loom, only to have the gears seize up. His opponent, Jim Miller, was admiring a pickup truck and chortling, "My Daddy had one just like this!" when the thing took off under him. The gentleman had started his engine without realizing that Miller was patting his mudguards.

The possibility that someone will get killed on the hustings grows daily, as does my hunch that the candidate who has to be removed from a threshing machine with a spoon will be a Republican, because Democrats don't have to run this man-of-the-people obstacle course to deflect charges of being "for the rich."

GOP strategists don't seem to realize that trying to out-lout the proles contradicts what everyone knows about human nature. I should say "used to know" because this kind of knowledge is rooted in home truths, maxims, and adages, which are reactionary by definition and hence suspect in our hyper-democratic age. These pithy guides to living have been dismissed as "simplistic"—a condition of pre-bigotry something like HIV—while the person rash enough to claim that "everyone knows" anything at all is now accused of trafficking in "easy answers."

People who reject the accumulated wisdom of the ages have no way of knowing when they're going about something all wrong. Take, for example, those shining stars of ass-backwardism, the feminists. Blow hot and cold? Keep a man guessing? Play hard-to-get? Certainly not, they huff; such ploys "reinforce stereotypes" and imperil "equal partnerships." Maybe so, but everyone knows they work.

The worst casualty of the New Ignorance is the psychology of class.

Title card: "John Warner spends his time in fancy restaurants having lunch with Barbara Walters instead of cleaning his hunting rifle."

Close-up: eye squints into end of barrel.

Music: "The Vacant Chair."

Jim Miller actually said this during the Virginia primary, which may be why John Warner tried to operate the textile loom. Eager to play the class card, Miller forgot the joker in the populist deck. Psychologists call it "identification with the aggressor" while Nancy Mitford expressed it with, "The masses love a lord," but they mean the same thing: the great unwashed side with the washed.

Bubba doesn't want to have lunch in a fancy restaurant himself because he would feel out of place, but he thinks it's great that John Warner can: "God bless the squire and his relations and keep us in our proper stations."

Earlier generations of politicians could brag about their non-existent log cabins without damaging themselves, but the faux populists of Campaign '96 are stirring the acrid juices of contempt. The difference is television, which takes us close enough to see their pleading eyes. Miller's, like Lamar Alexander's, were positively plangent, while Dole's roll around like marbles whenever he feels unsure of himself.

They're starting to look horribly familiar to me, and I know why: they remind me of "poor Lloyd."

Every woman has had a poor Lloyd in her life. He's the adoring suitor she despised, the one who adored her so much that she turned into Mildred in *Of Human Bondage*. Everything poor Lloyd did got on her nerves, but the more she screamed at him the more he proposed, the more she slapped him the more he apologized, the more she insulted him the more he loved her.

E VERY human interaction contains an unconscious erotic element. Regardless of the age and sex of the parties, despite the unerotic nature of their business, when one party has something the other party wants, a symbolic battle of the sexes is on. If Republicans want to win the blue-collar vote they should stop wooing it so slavishly. They should stay out of pickup trucks, avoid heavy machinery, ignore country music, stop making placating references to their father's overalls, stop talking about "the real people," stop saying "That's what America's all about" every time they see a lunch box, dare to keep all their clothes on, and campaign with the self-assured dignity and air of command that Bubba secretly admires. It might even help close the gender gap; after all, as everyone knows, "Faint heart never won fair lady."

As for my vote, it goes to Laurence Olivier for his remark about serving in World War II: "When I joined the Air Arm I thought, 'How marvelous, now I shall know real people, instead of this froth that I've been living amongst all my life.' My God, give me the froth every time."

July 29, 1996

A T last Hillary has done something I can identify with. Before you swoon, let me say that an interest in psychic phenomena is not incompatible with conservatism. That old rip of the Old Right, novelist Taylor Caldwell, believed in reincarnation. Shortly before she died she wrote a book describing her former life as a kitchen maid in the home of George Eliot.

My main objection to Hillary's psychic quest is her taste in ghosts. Why would anyone want to talk to Eleanor Roosevelt and Mahatma Gandhi? Unless the spirit world has turned them in the direction of rational thought and logical discourse—not something a spirit world is likely to do—they must make even less sense now than they did when they were alive.

Moreover, they're too new. People I can remember, who were on the earth during my own sojourn, just don't seem metaphysically respectable. That's the difference between liberal necromancers and conservative necromancers; the former will commune with anybody but the latter snub *arriviste* ghosts.

Hillary and I also have different reasons for conjuring. She does it for guidance but all I want is information. For example, I would love to ask Eleanor of Aquitaine if she invented flossing. This is a theory of mine that I've taken up with several dentists, all of whom seemed to think I was a little odd. Nonetheless, I believe I have a point.

Consider: Living to the age of 82 was amazing enough in the 12th century, but Eleanor (1122–1204) kept almost all of her teeth as well. I believe she accidentally discovered flossing while embroidering. Medieval women embroidered miles of tapestries so we can be sure they developed the bad habit common to all women who sew: biting the thread when they couldn't find their scissors.

One day in the bower, Eleanor got the thread caught between her teeth and couldn't get it out. A crisis ensued, with lots of ladies hovering in trepidation as Eleanor worked the thread up and down and around until it came out. When she saw specks of rotting food clinging to it, a good habit was born.

I'd welcome *anyone* who attended the funeral of the Duchesse de Montpensier in 1693. I've read about it in Saint-Simon's memoirs and biographies of Louis XIV, but no mere printed page can do justice to this story. It's the kind of story that people dine out on, the kind of story that makes those privy to it friends for life, the kind of story accompanied by a fond shaking of the head and a nostalgic sigh, "I'll never forget the time. . . ." I think of it whenever I see the beer commercial with the "old times, old friends" motif. It's that kind of story.

The Duchesse de Montpensier was the daughter of Louis XIII's younger brother, and thus first cousin to Louis XIV. As the oldest female of royal blood at court, she was called "Grande Mademoiselle." According to the custom of the time, when she died her heart was entombed in a chapel, while her entrails went into a sealed urn that was placed on a sideboard in the mourning room at Versailles, where pairs of noblewomen chosen by the king took turns watching over it round the clock. It was all done with exquisite taste; from the solemn major domo to the susurrating murmur of the nuns at prayer, the occasion exemplified punctilious court etiquette and stoic neoclassical grief.

Malheureusement, Grande Mademoiselle's badly embalmed entrails had fermented, producing enough gases to turn the sealed urn into a bomb. Suddenly there was a deafening explosion, followed by a hideous stench. Pandemonium erupted; ladies screamed, chevaliers fought each other to reach the doors, fleeing priests trampled doddering old marquises as, gasping for air, the mourners poured onto the lawns in abject panic.

When they found out what had happened they reverted to type. "All was perfumed and restored," writes Saint-Simon, "and the commotion was made light of." It was that kind of story, and I'd love to hear it.

M Y welcome mat is always out for Adelaide Bartlett, she of *Regina* v. *Bartlett* (1886), one of the great English murder cases.

Edward Bartlett was a prosperous wholesale grocer with some very advanced ideas. Hankering presumably for a threesome, he introduced his wife, Adelaide, to a wispy young clergyman named George Dyson and encouraged them to spend time together while he was away at business. As a maid later testified, they spent a great deal of time together, none of it wasted.

That winter, Edward got sick. Adelaide nursed him, relying on Dyson to run errands to the chemist. When Edward died suddenly, his father, who had always hated Adelaide, told the police she had poisoned him. An autopsy was ordered. When the doctors opened the body, they nearly passed out from the fumes it gave off: Edward's stomach was awash in liquid chloroform.

The police soon discovered that Dyson had bought two bottles of chloroform from the chemist. When questioned, Adelaide explained that Edward was afflicted with satyriasis, and that to escape his ravenous lust she sometimes had to knock him out with a chloroform-soaked handkerchief held to his face. As to how it got into his stomach, she said he must have mistaken it for his medicine and drunk it.

Many more lurid sexual tidbits came out at her trial, but the defense focused on the core issue: whether it was possible to cajole or force someone to drink such a large quantity of a liquid as volatile as chloroform, which would vaporize during the struggle. A parade of forensic witnesses testified that she simply couldn't have gotten it down Edward's throat. The jury concluded that he had somehow drunk it on his own, and Adelaide was acquitted.

I'm not alone in wanting to talk to her. Afterwards, a member of the Royal College of Surgeons said, "I think that in the interests of science, she ought to tell us how she did it."

September 2, 1996

R EMEMBER the "Voluntary Simplification Movement"? The trend-spotters fingered it a couple of years ago and Style editors duly responded with features. Practitioners of Voluntary Simplification, we learned, threw out their microwaves and talked a lot about "stopping to smell the roses." Their goal was to break their dependence on machines that go *ping!* and revert to simple household items like scrub boards, clothes lines, carpet sweepers, rug beaters, and, if they could find one, a zinc box to replace the fridge.

They seemed to be a composite of Luddites, nostalgia freaks, and environmentalists, but a closer examination revealed some stark differences. Take the matter of automatic transmissions *versus* stick shifts:

Luddites hate both.

Nostalgia freaks hate automatics for being new and easy to drive, which spoils what they call "real driving." They drive a stick shift for pleasure.

Environmentalists hate automatics for being wasteful and easy to drive, which spoils their sense of duty. They drive a stick shift for pain.

Voluntary Simplificationists drive a stick shift because it's simpler. Not easier—simpler. Not simpler to drive, but simpler to make. All they care about is the amount of technology at the engineering end. The stick shift is hard to drive because its engineering is simple; the automatic is easy to drive because its engineering is complicated. Thus, automatics are harder and more expensive to repair, which complicates the lives of people who own them. So shift gears or die, because the complicated life is not worth living.

When the Voluntary Simplification Movement first cropped up in the news, I created a "Simp" file and kept an eye out for further articles, but they stopped abruptly sometime back around January. The VSM has disappeared from the radar screen.

I can think of two reasons for the sudden blackout. First, of course, is the Unabomber. Another is advertisers. Writing about Simps for daily newspapers is a good way to get fired. You can't have features about people who toss their washer and dryer turning up next to the Sears ad. Worse, some Simps also toss their clothes: men make do with the "one good Sunday suit" of Booth Tarkington heroes, and lady Simps, who refuse to play the sartorial shell game known as "accessorizing," limit themselves to one—God help us, *one*—handbag that goes with everything. This is not what America is all about.

On the other hand, it is. Ambivalence toward possessions and a hankering for the simple life have been staples of our national discontent since Henry David Thoreau took to the woods. By the middle of the present century it was known as "getting away from it all" and "quitting the rat race." Essentially a male urge, it takes a terrible toll on women unless they're like Betty MacDonald, who saw the comical side and wrote *The Egg and I*. But most escapists are too idealistic to have a comical side, which is why they miss the Catch-22 lurking in all simplification rites.

The protagonist of *The Man in the Grey Flannel Suit*, in abandoning the corporate power ladder for an undemanding job, will also abandon rage for pique.

The big-time journalist who buys a little country weekly ends up worse off, the heart attack he was trying to avoid brought on by two aspects of journalism he never had to cope with before: letters-to-the-editor and mothers-of-the-bride ("It didn't get in!").

Bohemian intellectuals of the Fifties got their simplicity fix from Arthur Frommer's *Europe on Five Dollars a Day*. The bible of the freighter elite, it was packed with ecstatic advice on how to live like an earthworm, but the blithe spirits who devoured it soon discovered that an American without a "nice bathroom" is in serious danger of going insane. Frommer's unique style, a kind of Franciscan hard sell, inspired millions of aesthetes to resolve to "need nothing," but frustration dodged their paths. One couple reportedly kept trying to throw their clothes away, only to be pursued by thrifty French concierges who kept trying to return them.

My own simplicity fix is a medieval fantasy: I'm a cloistered nun in a thirteenth-century Kentish convent. My cell contains nothing but a straw pallet, a prie-dieu, and a nail in the wall for my poor tattered cloak. I like this part because I'm no longer tied down by writerly detritus marked *Keep!* stacked in the corner, but a Catch-22 emerges when I flesh out the details of convent life. I have no trouble faking piety at group prayer, but when I sneak food into my cell to keep from going hungry on fast days, there's no place to store it, so I have to stack it in the corner.

I T'S a fact of human nature that people overwhelmed by problems always try to bring symbolic order out of chaos by cleaning out their closets and bookshelves; discarding things makes us feel better, or as current parlance has it, "in control." Such is America's present mood, perfectly captured in a line from Christopher Frye's play *The Lady's Not for Burning*: "What's a halo? Just something else to keep clean."

The Voluntary Simplification Movement did not disappear. It merely became superfluous when other, more comprehensive downsizing movements turned it into small potatoes.

Why throw out your clothes when you can throw out your congressman? Term limits is our national sock drawer. Why give everything to the Salvation Army when the Tenth Amendment says you should give it to the states? Why take the Simp vow to stay home rather than travel with more than one suitcase? Join the flat-tax movement and hang out with people who are less interested in taxes than in the postcard they want everything to fit on.

The ultimate simplifiers are the growing number of Americans who survey the country and grumble, "Tear it down and start all over." At the moment they're at the movies: *Independence Day* is spring cleaning writ large.

September 16, 1996

L   AST month the PBS women's talk show, *To the Contrary*, inter-
      viewed some woman who had written a book about traveling alone in
      foreign countries. I was struck by the déjà vu nature of the questions.
Is there a "taboo" about women traveling alone? How are women traveling alone "perceived"? That's an updated version of "What will people
think?" but the tone of voice was the same. They tried to put a feminist spin
on it with earnest pronouncements that "women travel differently from men,"
but it didn't work. The telltale signs of female insecurity were evident: the
searching look, the eager smile, the too-quick nods of agreement, the little
gusts of laughter-as-punctuation. It was the same old same old, going back
not only to my day but to Victorian times.

I went to Paris alone in November 1969. I dreamed of going when I was
taking French in school, but I couldn't afford it then, nor for years afterward.
All I could afford was a passport so I got one for inspiration, something to
take out and look at once in a while. I also used it for I.D., since, unable to
afford a car, I didn't have a driver's license.

When finally, at the age of 33, I started making real money, I decided one
night on the spur of the moment to fly to Paris. It was characteristically
impetuous, but airline reservations were no problem in late autumn. Three
days later I was there.

The airport bus put me off at the terminal near Les Invalides. I hadn't
made a hotel reservation, so I walked around the side streets until I saw a
small hotel where I got a room for $5 a night.

I went immediately to the Eiffel Tower. It was too cloudy to go to the top,
but I didn't care. I centered myself underneath it and bent my head back and
gazed up through the intricate web until my eyes played tricks on me, the
hypnotic sensation of being encinctured by those steel bands satisfying my
peculiar claustrophilic need to be literally *in* Paris.

The next day I went to Notre Dame. On the gargoyle roof I met a woman
from Rochelle who asked if I would like to see "Le Bourdon," the big bell. It
was a lecture given only on request, with a tip to the guide afterward. She
seemed to know all about it so I followed along. I didn't catch all of the lecture but the guide's dramatic finale needed no translation. He tapped the bell
ever so lightly with his baton, producing a reverberation that made us both
scrunch our shoulders.

At the Conciergerie I saw Marie Antoinette's cell. I knew her in high school—the girls who thought of nothing but clothes and were always combing their hair—but here in this wretched place she behaved at last like a Hapsburg archduchess. From Stefan Zweig's biography I knew the route her tumbril took from the prison to the guillotine. I followed it on foot, the closest thing to a pilgrimage I've ever made.

Later I browsed a bookstore and bought the two-volume paperback of *Autant en Emporte le Vent* (*Gone with the Wind*). That night I saw *Midnight Cowboy* with French subtitles, afterwards discussing it with the young woman serving behind the lobby bar. It was my most successful conversation of the trip; I managed to tell her how the movie differed from the book, and compared it to the author's other filmed novel, *All Fall Down.*

It was foggy and drizzling the day I went to Versailles. Three or four other people were in the Hall of Mirrors, but the gardens were deserted. Wishing my old social-adjustment teachers could see me, I sat down on a bench by the statue of Bacchus, utterly content. At last I had a playground all to myself.

Given my constant need for coffee, I had to buy what I didn't even know the name of in English. I told the hardware clerk, "It's shaped like an eagle's claw (*le talon d'un grand oiseau*)," feeling proud when he promptly produced a "*thermoplongeur*": immersion heater.

Shopping for shoes was harder. Everything I tried on felt like a 5EEE. I kept saying "*plus long, plus mince,*" but nothing fit. Finally the salesman said, "*Vous avez les pieds anglais, Madame.*" I left on my English feet, clutching my new idiom.

In a tiny restaurant near the Place d'Italic I had beef burgundy for 18 francs. The best thing about the meal, aside from the food, was that it was Thanksgiving and nobody knew or cared. Nobody saying, "I hate to think of you being alone on Thanksgiving." Nobody assuming I was just being brave when I said, "I like being alone." Nobody inviting me to share their tumultuous family gatherings and having to accept because there was no way out of it. Culture shock was now a thing of the past.

I GOT picked up in Montmartre, but my motives were purely linguistic. As we sat in a cafe sipping vin rouge, he leaned across the table and confided that he loved playing pinball machines. I couldn't think of anything to say in either language.

As it turned out, the heart interest of my trip was the hotel owner's son. His name was Marc and he was six years old. You heard me: six. A child. As in "CNN Breaking News." Evidently being in a country notorious for aloofness and formality had a relaxing effect on me, because Marc and I clicked.

He showed me the ball he was making from tin foil, to which I contributed some cigarette-box liners. I told him about making a ball from rubber bands when I was his age, and started one for him. He liked keys, so I described the key to the Bastille at Mount Vernon and gave him the key to my typewriter case for his collection. I had to break the lock when I got home, but it was worth it.

I thought about my Paris trip as I watched *To the Contrary*'s show on women who travel alone. A week later I watched a longer, louder version of it called the GOP Convention. Four solid days of listening to Republicans take on the Herculean task of making women feel secure convinced me that the female sex was a foreign country and I had a language problem.

September 30, 1996

O N the final night of the Democrat convention, a glowering Robert Novak assessed today's kinder, gentler version of the old quadrennial bash: "It's been feminized!"

I said the same thing in one of my books, but the poet Wallace Stevens said it better than both of us: "It is the sun that shares our works; the moon shares nothing: it is a sea."

A rising tide of tears and amniotic fluids sank all boats in San Diego and Chicago, leaving everyone convention-tossed. Never before have so many people had the menopause in public. The soggy narratives that floated the podiums in bathos even repelled some touchy-feely liberals, to judge from the tortured spins they put on them. Thomas Moore, who writes spirituality books, called them "cultural bonding experiences" and equated them with ancient myths. He was seconded by George Stephanopoulos, who said stories of travail and tribulation have been the stuff of myths "from time immemorial."

Maybe it helps to be Greek. The only potential myth I saw was Elizabeth Dole, condemned to roam the world throughout eternity telling people how wonderful her husband is, only to discover at the last that her mike was broken the whole time and she has to start all over again.

It makes little difference which convention was worse, though it was only to be expected that the Dems, having the later date, would try to exceed the GOP's excess. They did. Evan Bayh's twins are one baby more than Susan Molinari has; the wounded New York cop is a paraplegic but Christopher Reeve is a quadriplegic, etc.

Anyone who doesn't recognize this as the feminization of one-upmanship should have been with me back when I worked on the *Raleigh News & Observer* and got caught in the crossfire between two rival sponsors of the North Carolina Mother-of-the-Year contest. Each felt her candidate merited my lead story, and shrank not from telling me why.

"That poor brave soul had three bedridden people in the house at once, and they all wore bags!"

"Bags! Bags make it easy! Mine had to change her epileptic son's diapers and use a catheter on her husband after he lost his privates in the hunting accident. I said to her, I said, 'Honey, you're just a Christian martyr,' I said, but she just smiled and shook her head and went on feeding her retarded nephew."

Female morbid eroticism presented Democrats with a problem. The sensuous sickroom has changed since the halcyon days of flat-on-your-back helplessness. The word "victim" has acquired so many positive associations that women must now do their bearing-up and burden-toting at Wheelchair Basketball and be seen cheering at Special Olympics. Today's handicapped are self-sufficient, athletic invalids are "challenged," and the old male saw, "If you get sick, she's got you good," is heard no more.

You can really hurt a girl this way. To atone, the Democrats scheduled two deathbed arias so that women who feel sexually rejected could say, "That's what America's all about," and really mean it.

What happened in San Diego was the fulfillment of a prophecy. When women first demanded the vote, men argued that politics was too rough-and-tumble for their refined sensibilities. The suffragettes turned the argument around, saying the participation of women would make politics more refined.

The media called the GOP convention "carefully orchestrated," which is a carefully orchestrated way of saying "feminized." To see how their refined show was playing, Republicans turned to the exquisitely named ABC News Pulse, a hand device equipped with buttons used by focus-group participants, who record their reactions to politicians' words, facial expressions, and tones of voice as they watch TV.

Letting women press a button whenever something upsets them is bound to be edifying. The Pulse became an electronic spider web that trapped the tiniest gnats of gruffness and sarcasm in the silken strands of female finer feeling and delivered them up to dessication—even the Big Mac joke.

Personal stories are in now, so here's mine.

When I was nine, my grandmother's Cousin Elva came to tea. Granny prepared my mother and me carefully for the visit because Elva had had a tragic life, and Granny, the soul of tact, did not want anything said that might remind her of it. Specifically, Elva's son had drowned.

"Don't you-all mention water, you hear me? If poor Elva even hears the word she just goes to pieces. Don't bring up anything that has to do with water. Boats, piers, oars—"

"What are you going to make the tea with?" asked Mama.

"Don't be smart, Louise, you're as bad as the child."

Suddenly she remembered my goldfish and made me move its bowl into the kitchen. As I came back there was a knock at the door.

"There she is. Remember: no water!"

L IKE rope in the hangman's house, the forbidden topic pressed in on us from the start. Our upstairs neighbor ran a bath, the janitor watered the lawn, and my goldfish did one of his splashy flipflops. I had to go to the bathroom but it would mean flushing the toilet.

To complete my agony, I had just finished reading *Anthony Adverse*, notorious for its "water symbolism" sex scenes. I couldn't understand why Anthony swam so much, and my usually mentorish father had refused to explain. Now, in spite of myself, the confusing passages came back to me: "sinking into a warm lagoon" . . . "the waves were cresting, cresting" . . . "the sea was calm now, lapping gently around him."

Just then I made the fatal error of catching my mother's eye. As the giggle hit, a piece of cookie went down wrong and I started to choke. Galvanized by my violent wheezing rales, Cousin Elva leaped up and gave a desperate cry.

"Water!"

With luck this will happen at the next GOP convention.

October 14, 1996

I 'M writing this column on drugs. Just ask Bill Clinton, he'll tell you. I write everything on drugs—books, articles, reviews, and thank-you notes to literary critics who praise the grace and clarity of the writing that issues from my perpetually drugged brain.

There is only one time, aside from sleeping and eating, when I don't use drugs. My grandmother always said, "A lady never uses drugs on the street," and I never have. Otherwise I use one drug after another, because a delivery system tastes good like a delivery system should, and I have no intention of forgoing the pleasure.

Now I've done it. Every time I say something good about cigarettes I get bombarded with letters. The prize came from a couple who opened with "Miss King"—no "Dear"—and informed me that tobacco is "more addictive than heroin." After lingering sensuously over such words as *foul*, *stench*, and *disgusting*, they promised to pray for me to quit, which they were sure I would try to do, since: "Everyone we know who has ever smoked has tried to quit and almost all are ashamed and embarrassed to let it be known that they smoke." As fanatics always do, they enclosed clippings.

The virulence of the anti-smoking movement has always hinted at something bigger than smoking. When the first Surgeon General's warning came out in 1964 amid the marches and bombings of the early civil-rights movement, many people saw it as a calculated attempt to threaten the economies of tobacco-producing Southern states to force compliance with racial integration.

As things turned out, the South caved anyway, leaving a nascent anti-smoking movement by the wayside, waiting to be picked up, as Napoleon said of the French crown, on the tip of somebody's sword.

Subsequent events suggest that this is exactly what happened. Smoker-bashing has proved immeasurably useful to multiculturalists and diversity hustlers who understand the importance of a safety valve in campaigns of enforced tolerance. Taking their cue from American League baseball, they instituted the designated-pariah rule: If you intend to make everyone love everyone else whether they like it or not, be sure to give your useful idiots someone they can hate openly without fear of being called mean-spirited. Take care, however, that they don't catch on, or else they might start hating the people they really hate, and then all Hell will break loose.

The useful idiots haven't caught on—useful idiots never do. They're so gullible they even believe all drugs are created equal, and support the Clinton Administration's plan to lump tobacco, marijuana, cocaine, and heroin together in pursuit of an outcome-based addiction that recognizes no difference between a glassy-eyed degenerate with arms like sieves and a tired waitress on a cigarette break.

No difference, that is, except one: it's okay to hate the waitress.

Redirected emotion—what psychoanalysis calls "displacement"—is the crowning achievement of anti-tobacco propaganda. A majority of Americans are now in the grip of this disorder, providing a perfect out for a government helpless against hard drugs. We can't invade the inner cities without starting a race war as well as a mutiny in our multiracial army. Opening fire on the

Mexican border would provoke Hispanics, declaring war on supplier nations would provoke Asians, but bankrupting North Carolina will play in every focus group in Peoria.

My letter writers always demand to know why I keep smoking when I know it's bad for me. Aside from the simple fact that I enjoy it, I have three reasons: misanthropic, nostalgic, and subconscious.

On the misanthropic front, smoking gives me a perfect excuse not to go anywhere. People used to invite me to things, but now I've got them trained to leave me alone, and I owe it all to second-hand smoke.

On the nostalgia front, my childhood inured me against dire warnings about fatal illness. My grandmother belonged to the last generation of women who washed and dressed their own dead, and it left them with a morbid streak. They all knew, or claimed to know, someone whose hair "turned white overnight," or someone who "turned to stone" ("It starts in the feet and works up"), or someone who died when "it" hit their heart— "it" being an air bubble from hiccoughing, or a tiny sliver broken off from a toothpick that somehow "got into their bloodstream."

I was supposed to die from reading: ink, which was poison, would get into a finger cut and thence into my bloodstream. But Granny's best warning, recited whenever she saw me scratching, concerned shingles: "When the two ends of the rash meet around your waist, your heart stops." If you grow up hearing things like that, nothing Henry Waxman says could possibly make an impression.

M Y subconscious reason can't very well be subconscious or I wouldn't know about it. I just call it subconscious to confuse the buzzword-addicted crowd who claim smokers are "in denial." Nothing upsets them more than a smoker who knows exactly what he's doing, so I made sure I nailed down my subconscious reason.

It's this: I think suicide *qua* suicide is weak and shameful, but maybe, if I just keep smoking, I can hasten my exit from this Walpurgisnacht called America and escape the mephitic cultural collapse that Nice-Nelly conservatism is powerless to stop.

This is probably wishful thinking in view of my family's medical history, but it points up another benefit of cigarettes we no longer hear about: consolation. Even the word is gone from the language now, but it was what came through in World War II newsreels showing weary soldiers and refugees lighting up. In their most despairing moments a cigarette was all they had, and increasingly I feel the same way.

There goes my chance at Keynote 2000, even if I work on my perkiness and arrange to rent a baby.

October 28, 1996

' YOU can pretend to be serious," wrote Sacha Guitry, "but you can't pretend to be witty." True, you can't pretend to be witty because wit is dry, subtle, lacerating, cynical, elitist, and risqué—all impossible to fake. Humor, on the other hand, is broad, soothing, positive, inclusive, and smutty—to make sure everybody gets it. Pretending to be humorous is easy and a great many people are doing it.

The "happy talk" associated with local news has now permeated the media. Network anchors are stretching and straining for jokey leads, none with more gravid insouciance than Dan Rather, whose ineffable opening statement, "President Clinton was as relaxed as a pound of liver," earned Dan the Cyrano de Bergerac Award. *"Oh, sir, what you could have said, had you some tinge of letters or of wit. But of wit you never had an atom, and of letters you need but three to write you down: a-s-s."*

No yuk is left unturned, even in the unlikeliest places. Crime shows and violent movies, once limited to a few stoic wisecracks, now brim with constant quipping, banter, genial insults, and playful asides. This is not comic relief, which is defined as a separate scene or subplot, but comic accompaniment for murder and mayhem.

Even the print media have joined the bray. Newspaper headlines increasingly run to juvenile puns ("Katie Kicks Dole's Butt"), while ads are silent versions of the basic elements of hysteria. Models in print ads used to smile to show their pleasure in the product, but now as they gather round to exclaim over the computer or the fridge or the optician's wide selection of frames, they simulate bladder-busting laughter; heads thrown back, eyes bulging, mouths stretched into rictuses, both rows of teeth exposed all the way back to the molars. The computer isn't that funny. The user's manual is, but they're not reading it.

Americans now ache to be funny the way previous generations ached to "sit down and play the piano without notes," as matchbook ads used to promise. It was guaranteed to make you the life of the party; all you had to do was forget about being tone-deaf and send away for 12 easy lessons on how to play the piano without notes.

The hopes of today's would-be comics are just as unrealistic, but they are sustained by a powerful influence that did not exist in the matchbook era.

After nearly fifty years of television, our population now contains more people who have listened to laugh tracks all their lives than people who haven't. It has trained them to laugh when somebody says something funny whether it's funny or not, and to expect every bon mot of their own to be greeted by gales of mirth whether it's bon or not.

Being funny is now part of the American Dream. You know what that means: everybody's got a "right" to be funny. Don't laugh; anything is possible in the land of liberty and penumbras for all. It would be easy in today's climate to invent agendas for outcome-based humor and comparable-worth jokes and connect it all up to self-esteem. The Norma McCorveys are ready and waiting, as an observer of life among the Yuks can testify.

A few weeks ago I was in a variety-store checkout line whose cashier was yukking it up with a desperation reminiscent of those poor souls who knock themselves out on a first date to be sure of getting a second. To a customer buying a red shirt, she caterwauled, "Better not wear this around a bull!" and then bellowed with laughter. The customer was momentarily taken aback but quickly rallied, saying gamely, "I don't know no bulls, but my husband's full of it!"

Encouraged, the cashier let loose with a hearty guffaw and stepped up her efforts. "Looks like it's curtains for you!" she told a woman buying a curtain rod. To a woman buying three paring knives she said, "Gonna cut up, huh?" Then it was my turn. I put my pancake turner on the counter and braced myself.

"Ready to flip out?"

"Any minute now."

I said it in the spirit of "Fine, thanks," a conventional rejoinder to round off the exchange and ease my escape, but the cashier heard it as a cue. Suddenly a great wheezing rumble rose up out of her and exploded in a yelp of mirth that was almost feral. Having a perfunctory comment received as devastating wit is embarrassing. I shifted feet and tried to strike a nonchalant pose while other customers peered around the gum stand to get a better look at us; one of them whispered, "What happened?"

This question is best answered in one of those upbeat human-interest segments about ordinary Americans doing extraordinary things. I imagined the cashier being interviewed while walking through a field with Charles Kuralt, explaining why she wants to turn the housewares department into a comedy barn. "Yeah, healing power," she agrees, as he prompts her gently. Then, as both pick weeds and chew on them to look sincere, she flashes her hectic grin and says, "I just want to show that everybody has a sense of humor."

I T'S not a bad idea in a time of mounting social tension and incipient civil insurrection. Like most Americans, the cashier's definition of a sense of humor is based on our national ideal of the chortling toastmaster "putting people at ease." This is how she sees herself.

She was so busy playing toreador with the red shirt that she neglected to fold it, so busy sharpening her one-liners that she dumped the knives blades-first into a plastic bag they could slice through, but good service is not what our jesters are striving for. Their object is a universal feeling of safety and security—beginning with their own—which they try to achieve by neutralizing everyone who crosses their path.

Americans are behaving like people subconsciously obeying the dictum, "Eat, drink, and be merry, for tomorrow we die," but since the first two will kill you, we are pouring all of our inchoate fears into being merry.

November 11, 1996

F OR the past year my local radio station has been running an ad for a mental-health clinic. It begins with a somber voice-over reciting statistics about depression, then launches into a minidrama featuring a teenager sobbing, "I can't take it anymore!" In another version, a man dissolves in tears and blubbers, "It's no use! Nothing helps!"

Whenever they came on I always yelled a string of unprintables at the radio, but sometime in October I lapsed into an oddly placid silence. I knew why. Campaign '96 had turned me into what the South calls a "good soul," meaning crazy, but not enough to commit; the kind of craziness that involves rocking back and forth, smiling absently, and not bothering anybody. I stopped yelling at the radio because I knew how those people in the ads felt: I couldn't take it anymore either.

Meanwhile, I had a column to write—this one—due October 29 but scheduled to reach you after the election. The dates called for a brilliant last-minute analysis that would turn out to be stunningly prescient, but try as I might, I got nowhere. "Nothin' helps," croaked the Clinton in my head. "It's no use, it's no use, it's no use!" barked the Dole trio lodged in my ear. A writing block loomed.

Most columnists confronted with this problem wing it by writing about their children, but as you know, I've never been blessed. I was up against it, so I decided to kill two birds with one stone and answer my *NR* fan mail in print.

First I'd like to thank the two readers, whoever you are, who sent me roses anonymously back in February when I called Princess Di a masochistic peasant. Unfortunately for me, you sent your floral tributes to *NR*'s New York office, but I don't work there. No matter; the staff enjoyed the roses and I enjoyed the deliciously mysterious unsigned cards, which are now in my scrapbook.

Something similar happened ten years ago when I raved Oleg Cassini's autobiography in *Newsday* and he sent me a bottle of Dom Perignon—to *Newsday*. I told the book department to send me the card and donate the champagne to anyone with a big romantic evening in the works. That was lavishly optimistic of me, knowing book departments as I do, but I didn't dare let them mail it.

"G.B." in Dallas wrote me about his daughter, a graduate civil-engineering student who has just moved into her first apartment and doesn't like living alone. To boost her spirits, he asked me to write her and give her a pep talk about the joys of independence.

I appreciate the trust but I question the wisdom of asking me to comfort an extrovert: I wanted my own apartment when I was four. I like winter better than summer, rain better than sunshine, night better than day, silence better than sound, and secession better than union. *NR* parents! It's 10 P.M. Do you know who's cheering up your children?

In any event, G.B., by studying civil engineering your daughter has exhibited an independence far superior to my own. I was raised by a grandmother who said, "A lady never adds fractions if they have different bottoms."

"H.J." in Baltimore is worried that I have "joined the feminist effort for equality by sacrificing the rules governing pronouns." His alarm bells sounded on reading my Paris column when, describing the joys of spending Thanksgiving in a foreign country, I wrote: "Nobody inviting me to share their tumultuous family gatherings." Did I, asks H.J., "use *their* to avoid the crime of using the masculine *his*?"

I never join feminists in anything. I stand by the masculine singular but sometimes it's impossibly awkward. Whenever it is, I do what George Orwell recommended: "Break the rule sooner than say anything outright barbarous." Sometimes you have to go by ear. The Paris column, like this one, was more colloquial and anecdotal than most, and lent itself to a more relaxed, conversational style. The grammar, though technically incorrect, was "right."

H.J. suggests that dropping the pronoun entirely would have been better. Yes, I could have done that, but it would have thrown the tempo off. Writing and keeping time to music are related somehow. I can't explain it, but I can feel it all along my nerve endings and right down to my feet. Unrhythmic prose reminds me of the boy I dated in college who spent $5,000 at Arthur Murray's and still couldn't lead. He followed beautifully, though.

Speaking of my feet, "R.B." in Chicago wants to know what size shoes I wear. This, too, comes from the Paris column, when the French shoe sales-man told me I had "English feet."

I N Paris in 1969 I wore a 7½ AAA, but I was lithe and young then, and still wearing high heels. Lately I've had to wear 8W sneakers without laces because my feet and ankles are swollen. I have no idea why, but I'll ask *NR*'s David Klinghoffer to look it up in his *Hypochondriac's Handbook* and tell me what I'm supposed to be worried about. You may remember David's article in our Health Care issue wherein he confessed to keeping a blood-pressure gauge in his desk. They say that once, after an editorial phone call with me, he took his pressure and the cuff exploded.

"L.E." in Minneapolis wants to know why I never write about foreign policy. That's easy. If it doesn't involve England, it didn't really happen.

What, asks "P.K." in Richmond, do I think Virginia Military Institute should do now that the Supreme Court has ruled it must go coed? I think VMI should do to itself what Rome did to Carthage in the Punic Wars: tear it down, brick by brick, stone by stone, and sow every acre with salt rather than give in to the diversity dictatorship.

"J.J." in Seattle has several bones to pick with me. "Don't you care about the infrastructure? How would you feel if a bridge collapsed?" That would depend upon who was on it at the time. "What should the government do about tobacco?" I would love to see the day when President Bork abolishes all anti-smoking groups by fiat. Don't worry, that's just a car.

November 25, 1996

N IGHT thoughts on the election. . . . First of all, I didn't vote. How could I? I'm a Baseball Spinster, not a Soccer Mom. I might as well be a Transmontane Whig or a Free-Silver Albigensian.

Add "archconservative" to my profile and it's obvious I had no place to go. No one remotely resembling a conservative was on the ballot. During the campaign I withheld my unvarnished opinion of Bob Dole out of whatever shreds of GOP loyalty I had left, but here it is: he's George Bush with a mas-culine voice. I was disgusted by the eager appeasement of his farewell Senate speech trumpeting his support of every liberal hissyfit from the Martin Luther King holiday to the Americans with Disabilities Act, and infuriated by his bouncer number in San Diego when he invited all who resist equality at any price to note that "the exits are clearly marked."

I have so noted and no longer count myself among Republicans. They're pussyfooting, henpecked invertebrates—all mouth and no gonads—and I'm through with them. That, of course, is wishful thinking in view of their sole area of dauntlessness. I refer to mailing lists. I'm on all of them, and the bombardment of pitches I received all summer and fall played no small part in my decision.

One in particular sticks in my mind. Sent under Bob Dole's signature, it said: "Because the RNC-State Victory '96 Battle Plan is a confidential GOP Members-only document, I have assigned it a code number. Please make sure this number, 004-07-073, matches the one on your Battle Plan."

This throbs with boys-in-the-treehouse arrested development, the glee of grown men assuming that everyone gets a kick out of being called Double-O-Four. It made me think, not of James Bond, but of the Tom Mix Clubs of my childhood, when we got a Secret Whistle Ring for three boxtops and the password was "Shredded Ralston for your breakfast."

Almost as hard as getting off GOP mailing lists is resigning from the female sex. I'm working on it. The extent to which women disgraced themselves in Campaign '96 and did serious damage to the political process can be measured by the hints, not entirely tongue-in-cheek, recently dropped by three respected conservative women commentators—Mona Charen, Kate O'Beirne, and Danielle Crittenden—that maybe giving women the vote was a mistake. Add my ongoing potshots on this subject and we are four musketeers.

The old chestnut that women voting for the first time elected Warren Harding in 1920 is false: he would have won his overwhelming victory anyway. But women did re-elect Bill Clinton, by an edematous 54 to 37 per cent, a nicely metaphorical margin of victory inviting images of premenstrual bloat approaching the watery-grave level.

Besides electing Clinton, women have made emotional meltdown a condition of office in a manner not seen since Jean-Jacques Rousseau persuaded the French aristocracy that "I feel, therefore I am" was an improvement on Cartesian logic. The priorities women have foisted on the political process have so filled the public forum with tears, intuitive insights, and hysterical particularism that we are in the throes of another Romantic Movement without the art and literature that made the first one worthwhile.

Women lack an objective point of view, and have not the inclination or ability to weigh and dissect dispassionately. As female political dominance has increased, our august national watchwords of life, liberty, and property have yielded to "You're being mean to me!," "Don't you dare touch that child!," and prissy reprimands of "incivility" directed against anyone with a rigorous, unequivocal manner of speaking. The male politician wishing to keep one step ahead of the ad hoc female nervous system must do what the male protagonist did in the famous short story "The Lady or the Tiger?" Just hold your breath, open the door, and see what comes out.

Women also harbor a resentment of grandeur, of the imposing and imperious in any form. For this reason, and despite feminism, women's political agendas evoke drab visions of unemancipated drudgery, as when my fellow spinster Gloria Steinem predicted during the Pope's visit: "We will live to see the day when St. Patrick's Cathedral is a child-care center." Having already lived to see political conventions turned into child-care centers, I believe her.

H ISTORY seems to suggest that whenever women get something, either it's no longer worth having, or, if it's still valuable, women's acquisition of it signals the beginning of the end. Women in major countries got the vote after two wars that left democracy in serious disrepair; English, American, and some European women after World War I, the rest of Europe's women after World War II. Democracy got back on its feet, but its heyday of pure republican vigor was gone for good, and once women started casting make-nice votes for social programs, small-"r" republicanism was forgotten about entirely.

Teaching lost status after women took it over, but that can't compare to the wrecking crews at work today. Women in the military? Too brutal and hardening, said men, but women persevered and now we have a sensitive, vulnerable Army and a Navy so crazymaking that its readiness state is Ethelred. Law? Women are too emotional and subjective, said men, whereupon all the girls went to law school and now everybody is suing everybody else and going to jail on the testimony of children.

What would an America of disfranchised women be like? As a native of Washington, D.C., I couldn't vote until I was 26, so I'm already used to the idea. I don't expect it to happen, but as I said at the start, these are night thoughts. They shroud the glare from shining bridges to the twenty-first century and the rosy cheeks of Mrs. Clinton's village insurgents. As for the lush green promise of inclusion, I say it's spinach and I say the hell with it.

December 9, 1996

T
HE *Titanic* is one of the two things that make me cry (the other is "*La Marseillaise*"). It's also the only thing that can make me knock off work and ignore a deadline. Whenever the 1952 movie starring Clifton Webb and Barbara Stanwyck comes on TV, I drop everything and prepare to dissolve.

I have a first-hand connection to the *Titanic*. My father was taken by his father to Belfast to watch her being built. He used to tell me about it, then launch into the story of the doomed voyage, wiping away a few tears of his own while my irrepressible mother interjected, "Why didn't they put it in low and pump the brakes?"

As I write this, I have just seen the latest *Titanic* movie, the CBS two-part miniseries starring George C. Scott as Captain E. J. Smith. Scott, of course, was superb, and so were the navigation scenes, but I didn't shed a tear, and frequently yelled at the TV with the choleric abandon I usually reserve for network news.

A comparison of the various *Titanic* movies reveals more about our current cultural confusion, spiritual brittleness, and artistic mediocrity than the endless symposia on values emanating from conservative think tanks.

The 1952 movie with Clifton Webb and Barbara Stanwyck is a personal drama with a nautical backdrop. Webb plays a rich American expatriate and bon vivant who married poor-girl Stanwyck and made a fashionable lady of her—but at a price. His cold sophistication and sharp tongue have hurt her once too often, and she has gotten even by making him rock another man's cradle. Norman, the 13-year-old son he adores, is not his child.

Stanwyck has left Webb and is taking Norman and his older sister back to America on the *Titanic*, but Webb books passage at the last minute and demands custody of Norman. In the bitter argument that ensues, she blurts out, "He is not your son." She immediately regrets it, but it's too late. To her guilty horror, Webb takes it out on the boy, changing overnight from a loving father to a snarling stranger.

On the night of the disaster, Norman is put into a lifeboat with his mother and sister, but longing for his father and conscious of wearing his first pair of long pants, he gives his seat to a woman and returns to the ship.

As the lifeboat rows away, the band on deck begins to play "Danny Boy." Stanwyck, looking around in panic, realizes her son is not in the boat and gives a despairing scream. Up on the foundering ship, Webb finds Norman and tells a crewman to put him in a lifeboat, but the last one has just left. The lesson of "the sins of the fathers" could not be made clearer.

The movie ends on the theme of "Greater love hath no man than to give up his life for a friend." Gazing worshipfully at his father, Norman says, "I thought we could make a swim of it together, sir." Webb embraces him and replies, "I've been proud of you every day of your life, but never so much as I am at this moment. I feel as tall as a mountain." As the band plays "Nearer My God to Thee," Webb and the boy, their arms round each other, sing the hymn with the stranded passengers—John Jacob Astor, Mr. and Mrs. Isidor Straus, men in white tie and coal-blackened stevedores—until the end comes.

The 1958 British documentary *A Night to Remember* is an excellent film, but it contains the first hint of something that was destined to get worse. Once again the band plays "Nearer My God to Thee," but instead of the melodious church version heard in the earlier movie, they inexplicably play the complex choral arrangement. Not surprisingly, the passengers do not sing.

The made-for-TV *R.M.S. Titanic* came out in the late Eighties and starred Donald Sutherland. Told from the viewpoint of liberal academics in second class, it was predictably political, and had the Countess of Rothes, who displayed such courage in the lifeboats, fondling herself in the Turkish bath. It was also factually off: the ballroom dances were surreal slow-motion shots completely unrelated to the lively turkey trots and bunny hugs of 1912.

This movie had no "Nearer My God to Thee" at all. The band played a dreary dirge called "Autumn." Here we have a curious arbitrary bow to historical accuracy. At the inquiry held after the disaster, some survivors testified that the band played "Nearer My God to Thee," while some said it was "Autumn," described in several *Titanic* books as an "Episcopal hymn." I never heard of it, but I do know the difference between spring and fall. Why would the band, playing on an April night for people about to die, choose the mournful "Autumn"? They were playing without sheet music—could they possibly have known this obscure number by heart?

THE new CBS miniseries also gives us "Autumn," along with a band that has been reduced to a string sextet whose thin efforts are barely audible. The emasculation of this scene over the years is a perfect example of the movie industry's conscious refusal to let people have their cultural myths. We needn't look far for the reason. If I can respond emotionally to a full-throated rendition of "Nearer My God to Thee" with every atheistic fiber of my being, imagine the effect it would have on millions less warped. The resulting spiritual rejuvenation would bankrupt the sex-and-violence business overnight.

The CBS miniseries also tries to downplay first-class passengers and give equal time to steerage, but it doesn't work. Tragedy is *supposed* to discriminate. Audiences have always been more interested in the high and mighty because they fall farther and harder: it simply makes for better theater. As Aristotle said in his rules for the classical drama, tragedy is what happens to the best people; melodrama is what happens to the rest.

The CBS *Titanic* is more faithful to the rule laid down by Oscar Wilde: "One would have to have a heart of stone to read Dickens's account of the death of Little Nell without bursting out laughing."

December 23, 1996

T EMPUS fidgets, as Cicero used to say. It's the end of yet another year and time for my "Miscellaneous Misanthropy" column, the fruit of a computer file called "Mis.Mis" where I dump all the opinions and observations I didn't have room for in previous columns. When the time comes, all it takes is a couple of keystrokes and up pops an effortless year-end roundup.

This year we have a problem. Now that my column appears in every issue I don't have all that many notes left over. I do have a lot of unused news items, such as my favorite Richard Cohen-ism of 1996—"person-eating shark"—but so what? Political correctness is now so widespread that you could probably top it with an even more idiotic clipping of your own.

The situation calls for a new kind of Mis.Mis, and I have found one: the annual Christmas letter. You know—they come in red or green envelopes addressed in silver or gold metallic ink and open with "Hi, Everybody!" It's the preferred form of communication of people who have so many friends that there is no other way to keep in touch with them all. The Christmas letter used to be laboriously mimeographed, but now a simple computer mail merge can send the identical letter to thousands, all of whom feel disoriented after reading it because writers of Christmas letters typically try to mix the oil of good cheer with the water of stream-of-consciousness. But that never happens to me, so sit back, relax, and begin. . . .

Dear Gentle Reader:

I'm writing this on Thanksgiving Day, a holiday I celebrate with scrupulous attention to its central place in French history. I had two fried pork chops, a baked potato with sour cream, and turnip greens fried in the pork-chop grease. No Southern cook wastes grease. Besides, in case my plan to commit passive suicide with tobacco doesn't work, I'll need a backup.

I woke up in a bad mood because I knew there wouldn't be anything in the morning papers except columns and editorials about Thanksgiving, and features about local families with something mind-boggling to be thankful for. One of the latter contained this headline: "LUNG TRANSPLANT KEEPS ALIVE A MAN WHOSE BROTHER'S ORGANS WERE DONATED 6 YEARS AGO." I've written headlines, and that's not a headline, it's a fugue.

No faxes today. I love faxes. Yesterday I got one from an editor at another conservative magazine who wanted permission to quote something I said to him in a phone conversation last summer. I asked him not to, explaining that *viva voce* quotes are dangerous; they might be picked up and requoted wrong, either by accident or design, and there would be no published version under my byline to prove what I really said.

Afterwards I felt guilty. How could I be so rigid? So unfair? So cruel? Searching for a way to make it up to him, I hit upon a simple solution. Here it is. In his phone call last summer he asked me what I thought of the Democrats' convention, and I replied: "Poor white trash of all races." There. Now he has a published version under my byline that he can quote whenever he likes. Never let it be said that I'm not thoughtful of others.

No mail on holidays, either, but yesterday I got a beaut. It was a chiding note from the Crippled Chipmunks, my generic name for those charity outfits who make return-address stickers and send them out unsolicited, along with a request for a donation. Yesterday's note said: "We hope you're enjoying your new stickers. There's every chance that your donation is in the mail right now. Naturally, you don't have to send us anything. The stickers are a free gift from us, but . . ."

It reminded me of the time I wrote for *Penthouse* and a reader sent me nude photos of himself, with a note saying "Please return the photos." If the Crippled Chipmunks sent out an order blank and a price list I'd buy their stickers, but I won't be diddled.

These particular stickers were guaranteed to irritate me because they said "Florence F. King." My middle name happens to be Virginia, but that's not the point. A spinster never uses a middle initial; if I signed myself "Florence V. King" I would be signaling that I am either married to or divorced from a man named King, and that my maiden name begins with V. Observing this simple point of etiquette would have made "Ms." unnecessary.

R EMEMBER Taki's *NR* piece about what makes a woman alluring? I was going to write a similar piece on men, but the only alluring man I could think of was Aleksandr Lebed. That is less a measure of my libido than of the debilitating effects of Campaign '96 on my life-force in general. Let's just say, in the passive spirit of "mistakes were made," that permanent damage was done.

The sound of male voices talking, talking, talking, made me want to run away and join the ladies' auxiliary of the French Foreign Legion. Politicians are naturally garrulous but something new has entered the picture. Desperate to close the gender gap and capture the women's vote by proving that they, too, can "open up" and "articulate their feelings," they have turned into female impersonators.

The prize for the season's great leap forward into transsexualism goes to Lamar! Alexander. Back in October he floated his idea of using vouchers to send inner-city kids to suburban schools. Asked how he would handle the certain protests of suburban parents, he said, "I'd ask them: would you rather have them walk into the front door of your school, or climb into your window at night?"

He's turned into Gracie Allen. The rhetorical roots of his argument can be found in the routine in which George Burns makes her return the $10 lamp she put on their charge account. When the store gives her a credit slip, she thinks she has $10 more than before and tells George he can now afford to take her out to dinner.

Shine, perishing republic. Talk to you next year.

December 31, 1996

1997

G IVEN my absorbing interest in interplanetary wonders, I pay close attention to the activities of compassionate conservatives. By far the most active star in this alarming constellation is Arianna Huffington, chairwoman of the Center for Effective Compassion, who puts Halley's Comet to shame. You don't need a telescope to see her, just a TV remote. Hold down the surf button and she goes by every 75 milliseconds.

When not chairing and guesting, La Belle Dame Sans Respite writes a syndicated newspaper column that has a way of ending up in my files much more often than a conservative column should. The latest one to catch my eye appeared shortly before Christmas under the headline, BLESSINGS BORN OF A CHARITABLE TAX CREDIT.

"Passion replaced number-crunching last week at the Cannon Building on Capitol Hill," she begins rivetingly. The Republicans were there to talk about balancing the budget, but to her delight, Rep. John Kasich and Sen. Dan Coats stripped off their green eyeshades and just let it come.

The ensuing orgiastic revel consisted of a heartfelt discussion of a tax-credit proposal that would allow "families" (as usual, no mention of other types of citizens) to give up to $1,000 of what they owe in taxes to a poverty-fighting charity of their choice. Say your federal tax bill is $8,000; you could give $1,000 of it to somebody besides the government. Do you then get to take a $1,000 deduction on the $7,000 you still owe the feds? As best I could tell after three re-readings, the answer is no. You are still out

$8,000; your reward is knowing that you helped privatize welfare.

"I cannot think of another piece of legislation that would achieve in one fell swoop three crucial objectives," Mrs. Huffington effuses. First, "it would establish a hierarchy of charitable priorities," i.e., promote the charities that make conservatives look compassionate instead of just conservative. Here she quotes Kasich at his plaintive-beagle best: "We love the symphony, but we have to have priorities. You have to examine your heart and ask: 'What is the greater crisis—the symphony or crime?'"

Mrs. Huffington's idea of worthy charities are those underfunded little rabbit hutches of Trad Vals idealism where people chomp on grass roots and quiver at the mention of "community." One such is the National Center for Neighborhood Enterprise, whose founder, Bob Woodson, told her: "If the 105th Congress does nothing else, it's got to pass this bill. Can you imagine what a boon it would be for poverty fighters to be able to recruit millions of Americans to give directly to those in need?"

Turning over our taxes to our local Bob Woodsons would effect her second crucial objective: "strengthening the frail bonds of community" by giving us a chance to become "personally involved" with the welfare mothers and homeboyz we never got to meet when we paid our taxes directly to the government. The woman's insight is astonishing; how did she know this is just what I've always wanted?

"Will everyone follow giving a check with giving time—like mentoring a neglected child or a fatherless teenager?" she asks. "Of course not. But many more will, until a critical mass is reached that will begin to transform society."

Critical mass is a euphemism for the pressure of conformity, which brings her to her third crucial objective: the charitable tax credit will make us better people. "We become generous by the practice of generosity and compassionate by the practice of compassion—not by the practice of lobbying the government to be compassionate. There are certain things that just cannot be delegated. In fact, giving our taxes to government to practice compassion for us has the same character-building effect as paying someone to pray for us."

What kind of conservative confuses taxes with charity and taking with giving? Anyone who spends much time with Mrs. Huffington, apparently; Dan Coats stated that her latest monomania would mean "taxpayers will have a choice in terms of how they direct some of their charitable giving." What charitable giving? They're taxes, damnit! Choosing who gets to twist our arm for the same amount of money is not a choice, nor is being allowed to pick out the rathole down which it gets poured.

M RS. Huffington and her half-cocked confrères on the bleeding-heart Right are turning compassionate conservatism into privatized liberalism. If they continue their panicky mobilization schemes, they will loose the few remaining dogs of the poverty war that have not yet been sicked on us. The slavery-reparations crowd will demand that we give at the office. Jesse Jackson will want to "invest" our IRA interest, and each of us will be assigned our own personal illiterate to tutor in the brave new world of compulsory volunteerism—and if you doubt that phrase could catch on, you don't know America.

Mrs. Huffington does, judging by her impassioned credo: "Let me make it quite clear that I am not neutral on the subject. In fact, to paraphrase Kenneth Tynan's review of John Osborne's landmark play *Look Back in Anger*: 'I doubt if I could love anyone who does not love the charitable tax credit.'" This, as any writer will tell you, is an unconscionable stretch; you don't make your point with a 1956 British play that most of your readers have never heard of. So why did she haul it in?

Maybe because it's about middle-class masochism. Act One opens with the well-bred Alison ironing while her prole husband Jimmy loafs in bed carping at her, her family, and her background. Enter Helena, Alison's old school chum, who urges her to divorce the loutish Jimmy, whereupon Alison leaves him. Act Two opens with Helena ironing while Jimmy carps at her, her family, and her background. In Act Three, Alison, having discovered that she can't live without her compulsory volunteerism, returns and takes up her old post at the ironing board as the curtain falls.

January 27, 1997

M Y solution to the Ebonics question is simplicity itself. As far as I'm concerned its proponents can take a flying phucllddyrhc (a Greco-Welsh patois learned at my mother's knee and other low joints), but I am fascinated by the psychodynamics surrounding the controversy.

The moment the media reported that the president of the Oakland school board had called black English "genetically based," honchos of color heretofore famed for their support of any and all things African launched such a swift and unequivocal attack on Ebonics that they sounded like H. L. Mencken. Jesse Jackson called it "an unacceptable surrender bordering on disgrace" and predicted Oakland would become "the laughingstock of the nation." "The very idea," Maya Angelou huffed, was "threatening," and NAACP president Kweisi Mfume contemptuously dismissed it as "a cruel joke."

This unexpected switch from the excellence of self-esteem to the esteem of the excellent self took white America, and particularly white punditry, by surprise. Among the latter the chief reaction was intense relief, the kind of relief that makes people giddy. While blacks were sounding like Mencken hurling thunderbolts, pundits were sounding like someone who just found his lost wallet and discovered that all his money was still there.

Whimsy and gaiety ruled. Before congratulating Jesse Jackson ("Bravo, Jesse"), Mona Charen confided that she loves the black-English song, "Is You Is or Is You Ain't My Baby?" Mary McGrory went on a *My Fair Lady* kick, rattling merrily on about 'Enry 'Iggins, Eliza the "squashed cabbage," and Alfred P. Doolittle doing the old soft shoe to "A Little Bit of Luck." Clearly ready to burst into song herself, she called on Education Secretary Richard Riley to get "an emergency company" to perform the musical in Oakland. "Who knows," said she gulpily, "everybody might do a little laughing and singing and open up to the idea that learning can be fun. . . . Give them *My Fair Lady*, send AmeriCorps to the rescue, and they'll be all right."

Be still, my heart. I find no cause for relief in the furious black opposition to Ebonics. Quite the contrary. When a people who have demanded separate congressional districts, separate government contracts, separate admissions policies, separate IQ tests, separate history, and separate justice suddenly recoil from a separate language, my first instinct is to look for an exposed nerve.

Afrocentrism flatters blacks and affirmative action mollifies them, but telling them that English is their second language makes them feel like the one thing they have never had to worry about being: foreigners. Throughout our history, whenever nativists and immigrants have squared off, blacks could savor the satisfactions of being on the entrenched side for a change. The tacit pleasure they took in being on a genealogical par with the most jurassically credentialed members of Colonial Dames and First Families was finally spelled out in *Roots*.

Ebonics threatens this cachet by putting blacks on a par with Hispanics, whom they resent and whose numerical encroachment is much on their minds. When I combine what every white Southerner knows about black snobbery with the Menckenesque quality of the broadsides hurled by the leadership, I am persuaded that the exposed nerve is, if you will, "black nativism."

But who cares about my theory now that Jesse Jackson has changed his mind? He just attended a public forum in Oakland to lead his new chant— "Limited-English proficient funds!"—even as Mary McGrory was clicking her computer mouse to simulate a castanet accompaniment for her solo about the rain in Spain. Now all of the formerly relieved white pundits are up the creek and everybody's wallet is missing again.

As with every racial controversy, the repositioning, backpedaling, and caving have begun. The clippings promise to be a bonanza for anyone who writes "GOD!" in margins, so to save time I'm using the new rubber stamp I just had made. Herewith a couple of already sanctified items:

"If I was Hispanic and spoke no English, you would communicate with me in Spanish and help me make the transition to English," said Robert Williams, who invented the word "Ebonics." This was quoted by the *Washington Post*, which tactfully ignored the missed subjunctive: If I *were*.

Stanford linguist Merritt Ruhlen: "If history had gone differently and Africans had come over and founded America and raided Europe and brought white slaves over, and this country ended up with a 10-per-cent white minority that was kept in ghettos and spoke white English, you'd find the same problems in reverse. People would be saying, 'Why can't whites learn good black English?' We spend all our time in school learning 'good' and 'bad' grammar and can't see that it's an historical accident that white English is called the best." (So help me, I copied that right.)

I T'S not generally known, but an Ebonics glossary was compiled in the 1920s by an amateur linguist who later became famous as "J.R.M." Ring a bell? Hint: His initials have appeared in print more times than any other set of initials in the history of mankind, second only to "I.N.R.I.," always with the word "To" in front of them. Now can you guess his identity?

Okay, I'll tell you. J.R.M. was John Robert Marsh, and his initials appear on the dedication page of his wife's book, *Gone with the Wind*. He got into Ebonics when Margaret Mitchell needed to differentiate between the speech of house servants and the speech of field hands. Marsh drove all over Georgia talking to blacks and taking notes until he had a glossary that enabled his wife to write her precision dialect scenes. You can read about it in a 1993 book I reviewed, *Margaret Mitchell and John Marsh: The Love Story behind Gone with the Wind*, by Marianne Walker, who located the glossary. I offer this as a belated Kwanzaa present to the Oakland school board.

February 10, 1997

E VERYONE of a certain age is familiar with the phrase "nice people." Not just the words, but the tune; the myriad layers of meaning and innuendo, the trenchant pauses, vocal inflections, and quirked eyebrows that flesh it out. It's our original code word and our only natural one, predating today's awkward euphemisms by many decades, which is why you must be of a certain age to appreciate it.

The Cult of Nice People was the means by which Americans of an earlier time assessed the "civility" so avidly sought and interminably discussed by Americans of the present day. The niceness it involved bore no resemblance to the niceness of Nice Guys; still less to the spastic niceness of "compassion," "sensitivity," and "reaching out." Based on what psychology calls "consciousness of kind," it was a finicky, rejecting niceness activated by an early-warning system of mental bells and whistles that went off whenever the need to be judgmental arose.

I should stress that it was never tied to the "American standard of living." Nice People did not necessarily have a three-car garage—or even a garage. I know this for a fact because I was born into the most dedicated fifth column of Nice People ever to undermine America's egalitarian ideal: the pre–World War II shabby-genteel class, urban division, who lived in rented apartments.

Nice Peopling may have made the rich exclusive and the middle class snobbish, but it gave the shabby genteel a means of self-respect that is now illegal: the right to identify and discriminate against the shabby uncouth.

Today, if I close my eyes and concentrate, I can hear the words as they must have sounded to me as I lay in my crib: *nispeepul*. I think of it as my primal sound. Most children raised in crowded apartments hear their parents making love, but I probably heard late-night discussions about nispeepul.

I certainly heard plenty in the daytime. "The new tenants in 2B are nice people. . . . I just saw that couple down the hall and they aren't nice people." I remember our door opened on the crack as my grandmother, a human radar gun, peered out at our neighbors' visitors to assess the cut of their jib. "Their friends aren't nice people," she ruled. A month later they proved her right by having a free-for-all, so we moved. Before we vacated, she and my mother, normally the most indifferent of housekeepers, spent the final days scrubbing the old place "so the landlord will know that nice people lived here." Nothing in our apartments became us like the leaving of them.

The niceness of Nice People was not strained. It consisted of a few simple standards such as being quiet and clean, and an idiosyncratic standard called "having things nice." This varied according to individual taste and temperament, but basically it meant going to a little extra trouble for little extra niceties: cloth napkins instead of paper, for example. Another idiosyncrasy, not to be confused with "having things nice," was "having one nice thing." This referred to the Cinderella piece that survives the most straitened circumstances. Our dishes were chipped and mismatched but we had sterling; the Nice People upstairs had a piano but no rugs.

Nice People in really dire straits often cultivated a comforting eccentricity, like the poor but proud Nolans in *A Tree Grows in Brooklyn*. Francie Nolan hates coffee but her mother, Katie, gives her a cup at every meal so that the child can enjoy pouring it down the sink afterwards. When Katie's shocked sister protests, Katie replies: "I think it's good that people like us can waste something once in a while." Thanks to her mother's shrewd psychology, Francie feels a notch above her real station and thus never succumbs to the hopelessness that goes with grinding poverty.

The eccentricities I cultivated during my years of writer's poverty illustrate Nice Peopling carried to the *n*th degree. Loath to buy booze in half-pint bottles, I always splurged on several fifths at a time, and labeled my scabrous mail box with a raised-engraving calling card to stand out from my neighbors, who penciled their names on Band-Aids, telling myself that if the police came they would know at once who was *not* drunk and disorderly.

Today Nice Peopling is practiced chiefly by the government, which has expanded the "regardless of" list to include citizenship status, language preference, political affiliation, gender, sexual orientation, marital status, parenting status, animal-companion preference, and previous or ongoing condition of communicable disease. Being choosy now means renting to the stateless lesbian with TB instead of the Marxist pedophile with the boa constrictor.

W HAT private-sector Nice Peopling still exists is practiced by those scourges of Republican country clubs, the liberal media. Yuppie pundits toss off casual references to the "born loser," their only unabashed acknowledgment of congenital traits. *Time* has a weekly elite–prole test: maps of the U.S. with differently colored areas showing the degree of popularity of various trends or practices. My favorite is "People Who Eat Hostess Twinkies," featuring a chocolatey South and a white, Twinkie-free Northeastern urban corridor.

Their worst offense has been the Nice-Peopling of Paula Jones as "trailer-park trash." They've since apologized, but they could have saved themselves a lot of trouble if they had consulted me in the first place. I could have told them what every liberal should know.

I knew a Paula Jones in high school. We called her the "Too Girl": too much makeup, too much perfume, etc. One day our homeroom teacher asked someone to take the flag home and wash it, and the Too Girl volunteered. The next day she struggled in sideways with what looked like a sheet of plywood. She had starched the flag. It stuck straight out from the pole.

As we laughed, a hurt look crossed her face. Then she lifted her chin proudly and said, "I did it because I wanted to make it nice."

February 24, 1997

U NDERSTANDING female misogyny requires a taste for paradox. A female misogynist is an exceptionally independent, self-confident woman who starts out assuming that other women are just like her and gets dismayed and impatient when they aren't. Eventually, after years of watching the majority of her sex snatch defeat from the jaws of defeat and call it femininity, she realizes that women capable of leading women are also capable of despising them.

Nineteenth-century suffrage literature is replete with examples of female misogyny. In a letter to Susan B. Anthony, Elizabeth Cady Stanton called housewives "the mummies of civilization" and boasted that "such pine knots as you and I are no standard for judging ordinary women."

Elizabeth Blackwell, America's first woman doctor, diagnosed the illness and blamed the patient: "I believe that the chief source of the false position of women is the inefficiency of women themselves—the deplorable fact that they are so often careless mothers, weak wives, poor housekeepers, ignorant nurses, and frivolous human beings."

Florence Nightingale was made apoplectic by neurasthenic Victorian women who cultivated the morbidly romantic image then in fashion of woman as fragile flower. "It is a scene worthy of Molière," she wrote scathingly, "where people in tolerable health do absolutely nothing and persuade themselves and others that they are victims."

Caroline Norton, who pushed the Married Women's Property Act through Parliament after being legally robbed of chattels and children by her estranged husband, blasted other women for their "feeble, supine, docile natures." Josephine Butler, who campaigned against Victorian England's brutal prostitution laws, looked down on women who shrank from using such words as "rape" and "hymen" as casually as she. Emily Davies, founder of the first women's college at Cambridge, coined the acronym "LOA"—lack of ambition—to describe women less erudite than she.

The most unexpected blast came from anarchist Emma Goldman, the most freewheeling woman in America, who kicked off the fastest backlash in political history when she published her famous essay, "Women Need to Be

Emancipated from Emancipation," almost as soon as the ink was dry on the newly ratified Nineteenth Amendment.

The women's-studies crowd treats female misogynists gingerly, either censoring them outright or else attributing their outbursts to temporary losses of equilibrium brought on by overwork. The one who defeats them is Ida Tarbell, the Queen Bee.

Ida Tarbell's exposé of John D. Rockefeller's Standard Oil monopoly forced President Theodore Roosevelt to take up trust-busting. A member of the New York State Association Opposed to the Extension of Suffrage to Women, the star reporter of *McClure's* magazine forged a second career advising women not to have careers. Posing as an unfulfilled spinster who missed out on the joys of dirty diapers and varicose veins, she wrote a series of articles called "The Business of Being a Woman" in which she proclaimed, "Women lack the vision necessary to achieve greatness." Deploring "the essential barrenness of the achieving woman's triumph," she preached marriage, motherhood, and homemaking for all.

That Ida Tarbell was one of the boys is clear from the lavish approbation she collected. Said her *McClure's* colleague Lincoln Steffens: "She was another fellow, a nice fellow—we didn't have a feeling of man or woman in that office."

British writer Arnold Bennett awarded her the ultimate backroom laurel, "just like a man," which recalls Zbigniew Brzezinski's assessment of Margaret Thatcher: "In her presence you pretty quickly forget that she's a woman."

THESE accolades describe a "virago" according to the original definition of this now-debased word: a woman of stature, strength, and courage who is not feminine in the conventional ways. Feminists know a virago when they see one, and they don't like what they see.

Mention Lady Thatcher and they sneer, "You call that a woman?" Mention Joan of Arc and they sigh, "Yes, but she wasn't really a woman." Boadicea fares a little better because she was raped, but the fearless assassin Charlotte Corday, who rid France of Marat, "wasn't really a woman."

The current feminist claim that Hillary Clinton is unpopular because "Men don't like strong women" is a classic example of projection. *Feminists* don't like strong women because too many viragos would put them out of business. To prosper they need a steady supply of women who exemplify the other V-word, "victim." Their all-time favorites are Sylvia Plath, the Brat of Endor, and Virginia Woolf, the Andromeda of the small press. As far as First Ladies go they probably would prefer Mary Lincoln, who went crazy—

always a winner with feminists. But at least they have Mrs. Clinton, who got where she is by being a clinging vine in the most literal sense.

The philosophical divide between the woman-as-virago and woman-as-victim camps was exposed by Election '96. The lemming-like spectacle of women voters washing up on Slick Willie made female misogynists cringe, but feminists regarded the gender gap as a triumph of distaff political savvy. Thus the paradox of female misogyny is that things are the opposite of what they seem. "Feminists" who prefer victims are the real female misogynists, and "female misogynists" who prefer viragos are the real feminists.

Given the attraction of opposites, it is also a paradox that men never admire in women any trait they despise in themselves, e.g., timidity. Men and viragos admire women like Elizabeth I, who forbade English diplomats to accept foreign decorations because: "My dogs wear my collars."

There was a broad! Shall we ever see another?

March 10, 1997

M Y ideal candidate for President fits the mental picture I get when I hear the words "confirmed bachelor": Lionel Barrymore playing Cardinal Richelieu with gout, his swollen foot propped up on an ottoman as he signs *lettres de cachet*.

My compromise candidate is Sen. Fred Thompson of Tennessee, frequently mentioned as a possible contender for the GOP nomination in 2000. Divorced but not remarried, Thompson is the closest thing to a bachelor we have. If he stays single and runs for President four years hence, it would be a glorious setback for the Noah's Arking of American politics.

The difference between married and unmarried Presidents is aptly illustrated by one who was both. Grover Cleveland entered the White House as a bachelor. His Presidency began on a rarefied plane thanks to his sister, who served as his hostess. Miss Rose Cleveland was pure disembodied intellect. An erudite spinster, she mentally recited Latin declensions to relieve her boredom in receiving lines. Her impenetrable self-containment left our national penchant for mawkish excess with nowhere to go.

Her astringent tenure did not last. When Grover Cleveland married 22-year-old Frances Folsom and the couple produced the first baby born in the White House, a daughter named Ruth, a bottled-up America popped its top. The sugary sentiment and treacly hysteria inspired by "Baby Ruth" are still with us in the candy bar named for her, but the ablative absolute hasn't been the same since.

The last unmarried man to run for President was Adlai Stevenson, who, like Thompson, was divorced. His marital status became a burning issue in the 1952 campaign, and the Republican camp made the most of it. In a newsreel that is seared on my memory, Ike and Mamie Eisenhower came out on the back of a campaign train in the middle of the night in their bathrobes, the calculated imagery of a still-warm connubial bed augmented by his calling her "Darling." At that moment, political marriage turned into *marriedness*.

Marriedness is a form of overkill similar to delivering the State of the Union speech in person instead of sending it up to the Hill to be read by a clerk in accordance with the modest intent of the Constitution. Let one President do something like this and subsequent Presidents are afraid to stop doing it—the American definition of "tradition" in a nutshell. Woodrow Wilson started the personalized State of the Union and the Eisenhowers started marriedness, and now we're stuck with both.

The latest forms of marriedness are familiar to all. Marriedness is the husband being sworn in on a Bible held by his wife instead of the unobtrusive Supreme Court clerk of old. Marriedness is the political couple holding hands in public. Marriedness is a convention podium turned into an overwrought snuggery. Marriedness is the Biblical command to become one flesh carried out under the auspices of the truncated conjunction, resulting in wives named "Tipper 'n' I" and "Bar 'n' I," after Mrs. Nixon, whose name was "Pat 'n' I."

The only ticket out of this molasses pit is a bachelor President. It would do America good to be governed by someone who is not in love or pretending to be. How? Let me count the ways.

It would be an object lesson to the millions who believe they are "not really alive" and "only half a person" if they don't "have somebody."

It would thwart foamy activists who assault the political process with emotional appeals. Married men are easy to get around because they already have been gotten around so many times that caving in is second nature. By contrast, when was the last time you heard a bachelor say, "All I want is a little peace and quiet"?

It would give pause to the gay-marriage advocates who use the Noah's Arking of politics as a wedge. Having a bachelor in the White House would make it much harder for them to go on asking their check-mate question: "If marriage is as wonderful as you say, why don't you want us to have it, too?"

Finally, a bachelor President would represent the ideal of male celibacy. I speak of the form, not the fact. I would expect him to enjoy the consolations of a discreet mistress, but that would not affect his symbolic value as an unmarried leader.

C ORNELIA Otis Skinner said, "Woman's virtue is man's greatest invention." True. No one is more icily pragmatic than a girl who has made up
her mind to be good. Plunk her down in a society where men insist on marrying virgins and she will say, "Okay, I'll be a virgin." That's that.

Male celibacy has a much more inspiring history as a mature sexual
morality practiced for reasons other than mere "reputation." Proof of worthi-
ness for the priest and philosopher, conserver of strength for the warrior and
athlete, source of creativity for the sublimating artist, male celibacy has played
a central role in civilization's greatest institutions. People know this, if only on
an unconscious level, and respond positively. A man without a woman makes
them feel secure because they know they have his undivided attention.

The question is, can Fred Thompson be elected?

Students of the Fifties claim that Adlai Stevenson's divorce hurt him with
voters, but they're only half right. Being divorced hurt him, but being unmarried did him no harm at all among hard-core haters of Eleanor Roosevelt.
Made up of most Republicans and just about all Southern Democrats, this
was the Shellshocked Majority that Stevenson could have cracked had he
been more politically acceptable. They may not have liked other things about
him, but their tirades invariably took an upswing toward the end when they
uttered a wistful sentence that began, "At least . . ."

When the question of his marital status comes up, all Fred Thompson
need do is look rueful and reply, "I deeply regret that America will have no
First Lady if I'm elected," and just let it sink in.

March 24, 1997

I N the past, whenever Europeans made fun of our provincialism and lack
of culture, we could always salvage our egos with tributes to the
"American standard of living."

It referred not to individual incomes but to what made us all rich, even
the least among us. Merely by being Americans, we enjoyed an unpreced-
ed degree of personal cleanliness and hygienic protection made possible by
what advertisers proudly called "modern conveniences." Thanks to the
ASOL, we could get even with our foreign critics, as H. L. Mencken did
when he said, "I'd trade the whole Acropolis for one American bathroom."

To anyone raised in the ASOL heyday, seeing lice treatment kits on the
shelf of a suburban drugstore is traumatizing. I spent 12 years in the D.C.
public schools and never heard of anyone being infested, but now more and
more schools are lousy in the literal as well as the figurative sense. Even more

shocking, no one seems horrified. Newspapers report the problem with cute headlines about "nit-picking" and parents take it in stride, like the mother who told my local paper: "When I grew up, it was the poor, dirty kids who were thought to have it. That's not true at all. Anybody who comes in contact with someone who has it can get it."

But of course. No American louse would dare discriminate, but that still doesn't explain how it knew where the nice, clean kids were, or why the interviewed mother reacted with such nonchalant fatalism. My own mother would have gone to pieces.

The fact is, we're not nearly so clean as we used to be. The ASOL has taken some big hits in the past few decades. The Sixties gave us dirt and called it "authenticity." Manic individualism proclaimed a "right" to be dirty, incense replaced ammonia, and thoroughness was renamed "uptightness." The Age of Aquarius was in fact the Age of the Missed Corner, and we're still in it.

The ASOL took its next hit from feminists. Housework, said the Marxists, was a propaganda tool of male capitalists, who invented labor-saving, push-button machines so women would think of themselves as "domestic engineers" instead of the unpaid scullery maids they really were.

Housework, said the doctoral candidates in etymology, was an arena of sex hatred because dust balls under the furniture were called "slut's wool" in seventeenth-century Yorkshire.

Housework, said Betty Friedan, was driving women crazy. Housework, said Gloria Steinem, consisted of saying, "Pick it up yourself."

It worked. Women exchanged brooms for brief cases and we got a revised ASOL tailored to the needs of the working wife: Complaining about dirt is sexist.

The last hurrah for the old ASOL was sounded by Jimmy Carter, of all people, when he paid an inadvertent tribute to gringo plumbing in his "Montezuma's Revenge" speech at the Mexican state banquet. Shocked commentators professed not to know what came over him, but it's not hard to guess. Sick and tired of being made fun of by foreigners, he had a sudden unconscious urge to get even.

He was in fine philistine fettle that day; if his wife hadn't flinched he might have gone on to the Elyseé Palace and told the one about the midget and the bidet. That was how Americans talked in the golden age of the ASOL; in epitomizing what was assumed dead, Carter became his own Dracula, driving in the stake until it was really dead this time, once and for all, forever.

The ASOL was replaced by the American Standard of Coping, a friendly defense mechanism free of imperialistic overtones and guaranteed not to offend anyone. Fierce displays of disgust are not permitted. If we are faced with a bare homeless bottom positioned over a curb, or beset by someone who gets more sensual pleasure out of saving water than using it, we must do as the Lice Moms do: take precautions, follow the directions on our treatment kits, and never get mad—just "concerned." Above all, we must never blame others.

THE American Standard of Coping would fascinate Henrik Ibsen. In his play *An Enemy of the People*, Dr. Stockmann discovers that his town's water supply is poisoned, but when he tries to warn the townspeople, they turn on him. The mayor, who happens to be Dr. Stockmann's brother, sides with the people; assuring them that their water is safe, he blames "progressive" science for spreading the poison of doubt. Having heard what they wanted to hear, the townspeople ostracize Dr. Stockmann.

The play as rewritten by the ASOC opens with a chorus of Education 'n' Awareness, i.e., ten tips on water safety proffered by the perky chemist on *Good Morning, America*. This starts a ratings war and a search for perky chemists ensues. Once every network has one, the burning question is not water but who will become the Greta Van Susteren of the test tube.

The second act is about Coping Chic. Kitchens fill up with countertop distillers and filters—already available from catalogues for people who cope with crime by shopping from home. Soon there are three filters on every faucet to go with the three locks on every door. Meanwhile, when bottled water is found in a construction worker's lunchbox, offended yuppies buy $500 divining rods and ABC manages to find and hire the country's only perky dowser.

Sensing that his point has been lost, Ibsen's ghost comes out on stage and recites the moral of the play as he wrote it: "You should never wear your best trousers when you go out to fight for freedom and truth."

Obviously, he didn't know Americans. Bombarded for years with warnings about everything we put in our mouths, we have developed a masochistic need to hug the messenger. In the third act, the ASOC's Dr. Stockmann is lauded as a "whistle blower" and gets to spend weeks on TV saying, "I was just doing my job" and "Larry, I thought about all the kids."

I would drink from the Ganges just to see Ibsen's face.

April 7, 1997

I T all started when I went to the mall to buy a new toaster. It should have been a day off, which in my case means not writing about America, not taking notes on America, not thinking about America. But such days don't exist. I got a column out of my day off, and here it is.

Shopping at the big discount chains is a painful experience for me because I'm scared of the Official Greeters, especially the one in the wheelchair. As soon as she sees you come in, she revs up and zooms in on you, shrieking, "How can I help you have a fun-filled shopping experience?" They had her in a TV ad once, racing through the aisles and burbling, "I love people! I love people! I just love people!" Having been stalked by irony all my life, I know an omen when I see one. If there's the slightest chance of someone being run over by a people-loving disabled American, it's a dead cert to be me.

My first task was getting into the store without being seen by the cadre of Official Greeters. There's a way to do this. Lighting a cigarette, I stood outside the door smoking until I saw a covey of Fam Vals approach: distracted parents, three or four kids, everybody dropping things and talking at once. If there's one thing OGs love even more than human beings it's kids, so I got behind the Fam Vals and surged in with them. It worked. As soon as the OG on duty saw the munchkins she shrieked, "Hiya, fellas!" and immediately engulfed them, allowing me to sneak past on my little cat feet.

I hadn't bought a toaster for twenty years so I was unprepared for the new four-slot models (one even had six) that had come on the market since then. Fam Vals again: the bigger the toasters, the better we feel about ourselves. Finally I found a two-slotter and bought it.

Back home, I plugged it in and was about to throw the packing away when I noticed the "Use and Care Guide." I started reading it, and in minutes I was underlining my favorite passages and making marginal notes in typical workaday fashion.

It opens with "WARNING: A risk of fire and electrical shock exists in all electrical appliances and may cause personal injury or death." Next comes "IMPORTANT SAFEGUARDS: When using electrical appliances, basic safety precautions should always be followed to reduce the risk of fire, electric shock, and injury to persons, including the following."

What follows is a list of 17 Dos, Don'ts, precautions, safeguards, warnings, and dire caveats that leave nothing to the imagination, common sense, or sanity itself. Not even those unrivaled connoisseurs of peril, Jewish mothers and grandmothers of all stripes, could come up with a list like this. Things happen here that could happen only in a "Pink Panther" movie.

"Do not use appliance except as intended."

"Do not use outdoors or while standing in a damp area."

"Do not place on or near hot gas or electric burner, or in a heated oven."

"Do not place any part of this toaster under water or other liquid."

"Do not insert over-sized foods, metal foil packages, or metal utensils into the toaster."

"Do not clean with metal scouring pads. Pieces can break off the pad and touch electrical parts creating a risk of electrical shock."

"Use toaster in an open area with 4–6 inches air space above and on all sides for air circulation. A fire may occur if toaster is covered or touching flammable materials including curtains, draperies, towels, walls, and toaster covers."

"Failure to clean crumb tray may result in a risk of fire."

Is Paris burning? You bet; Inspector Clouseau has done with one toaster what von Choltitz failed to do with a whole German army.

Meanwhile, non-klutzy toast lovers are stymied by two SAFEGUARDS that never before crossed their minds: "Do not use appliance unattended" and "Unplug from outlet when not in use." You don't really have to go to the bathroom, it's all in your mind; just stand there and watch the toaster toast and everything will be all right as long as you remember to unplug it before going downstairs to get the mail.

At this point the guide dissolves in repetitive babble. SAFEGUARDS is followed by a CAUTION about extension cords, which "may be used if care is exercised in their use. If an extension cord is required, special care and caution is [sic] necessary." CAUTION is followed by another WARNING ("Unplug before cleaning. . . . Do not immerse in water"), followed by a four-point CAUTION, only two of which are new. One says: "Avoid using items with 'runny' frosting, fillings, icings, or cheese. This includes pre-buttered foods. When these substances melt, they cause a sticky build-up and may result in a risk of fire." The other new CAUTION says, "Do not physically hold down the toast lever," which, when combined with "Do not operate unattended," raises the distinct possibility that there are people in this world who get their kicks from hanging around toasters.

The purpose of this frenzied flyer is to protect the manufacturer against lawsuits, but there's more to it. The surface of American craziness is only the beginning; the really good stuff is found underneath. Looking at my day off as a whole, I would venture to say that there would be no litigiousness or Official Greeters if we had real Family Values, instead of the fake kind that hangs over everything from shopping malls to focus groups like a damp shroud.

I mean, for example, grandmothers who did not dye their hair and date, but lived with their married daughters and enlivened breakfast with: "If you stick a fork in that toaster you'll be burned to a crisp. There'll be nothing left of you except a little pile of ashes and everybody will say, 'Do you remember that poor little girl who electrocuted herself?'"

That's called a "loving warning," and if you grow up hearing them you won't have to sue people or hug strangers to get attention or prove that somebody cares.

April 21, 1997

G ET out your vocabulary cards, it's timid–wimp–cave time again. Michael Reagan has quit the Republican Party and says that he won't return until it "acts like a winner and not a loser."

He was fairly temperate as conservative GOP-bashers go—and we go pretty far. He used "cave in" only once, eschewed the real Roget stuff like "pusillanimous," and came nowhere near Wesley Pruden's regular references to the "Gelded Age." Still, his remarks pulsated with the unmistakable glee of the conservative scorned. Nothing gives us more pleasure than going after "moderate" Republicans as immoderately as possible. To air is human, to lambaste is divine.

GOP-bashing looks a lot like the "Revolution of Contempt," Lamartine's name for the overthrow in 1848 of Louis Philippe, who called himself the "Bourgeois King" and removed the fleur-de-lis from the Palais Royal to show people how nice he was. "Louis Philippe afforded France some of the happiest years in her history," wrote André Maurois, "but the French do not live on happiness." Once their contempt for Louis Philippe was aroused, they ignored the widespread prosperity of his reign and had a revolution anyway.

Conservatives don't live on happiness either. Our Louis Philippe was Bob Dole, who so aroused our contempt that we developed an irresistible impulse to strike out at him. It was easy to do thanks to the Dole persona. Every man who ever felt awkward and square could get back at himself by kicking Dole. Every woman who ever feigned raptness while a boring date droned on in a monotone could give Dole the gate. Every old person who ever forgot a name or fell to rambling could call Dole senile. It was his bad luck to be the universal frame that fits the memory picture known as the Worst Night of My Life.

Expressing contempt for "Poorbobdole" soon became more important than winning the election. Each time yet another leading conservative columnist called on him to withdraw from the race, our secret pleasure—admit it—was palpable. So was the columnist's. Cal Thomas almost succeeded in swaddling his in sanctimony, but Arianna Huffington was obviously having fun when she wrote that Dole's insistence on doing the same wrong things over and over was "getting perilously close to the definition of insanity," and that if he did not withdraw, convention delegates "will be forced to consider patricide." She meant to deny him the nomination, but metaphors like this cropped up in too many columns by too many writers to be entirely syntactical in scope.

Unspent contempt for Dole is behind the current wave of GOP-bashing, but getting over him won't help. We'll always have a Poorbobdole because contempt will continue to breed as long as television supplies the familiarity.

The up-close and personal view of our leaders puts us in such proximity to every facial tic, nervous gesture, and unconscious habit that we react in ways once limited to the custom-staled marriage bed and the jaundiced view across the breakfast table. Does Pat Buchanan whicker after a triumphal statement? "Stop making that noise!" Does Pete Domenici purse his lips when temporizing? "If you do that one more time I'll scream!" Liberals are immune to this because they don't crave loftiness, but conservatives feel forlorn at the merest hint of clay feet. You know the sinking sensation I'm talking about. If it weren't for C-SPAN I never would have known that Newt Gingrich talks like a term paper in heat, but I know it now.

The Revolution of Contempt is as old as television, but interestingly, it never touched Nixon, whose gift for inspiring towering emotions never flagged. The hatred was pure and the pity was Aristotelian, pulsing with talk of "hubris" and "tragic flaws." The temptation to shine the lamp of antiquity on Nixon proved irresistible to his critics and ultimately armored him: a man called "Agonistes" simply does not invite contempt.

Ford got a little but it was good-natured; Jimmy Carter got a lot but it was couched in the word "impotence," if you can call that couching. Reagan was contemptuous of contempt, in contrast to Bush, who seemed almost comfortable with it, as if he had been registered for it at birth.

B ILL Clinton is so much more contemptible than Louis Philippe that we must turn to another upheaval of 1848 to find an apt comparison. It happened in placid Bavaria when adventuress Lola Montez seduced King Ludwig I into spending the state treasury on her. Casting discretion to the winds, Ludwig followed his mistress around Munich like a puppy, forbidding the police to arrest her when she horsewhipped the postmaster and tried to run over the butcher. Finally, when the army was near mutiny and the prime minister had threatened suicide, a howling mob of once-stolid burghers ran

Lola out of town and forced the sexually enslaved Ludwig to abdicate.

Something like this should have happened to Clinton by now, but he has deflected contempt in Nixonian fashion by displaying traits that tempt his critics to explain him in terms drawn from another sacrosanct field of classical studies: Freudian psychoanalysis.

People have begun to sense that there is something wrong with the man; apart from his "distinguishing characteristic" and well north of it, he is not as others are. The telltale adjectives are showing up; his lying is "affectless," his appetites are "compulsive," and *Human Events* has been running a huge ad for a book that calls him a psychopath. Stand by for "mirthless" smile (he's got one).

This is not contempt but fascination, which may explain the strange helplessness that has come over Republicans, and the recent upsurge of anti-anti-Clintonism that has even made some conservatives call off their dogs. We don't want to impeach him because if we got rid of him we would miss the end of the movie: a remake of *Spellbound* with Bubba as the Gregory Peck nut case and Janet Reno as Ingrid Bergman.

May 5, 1997

P ARENTS of the pre-television era kept children quiet indoors by handing out pencils and paper and paying a penny for every word we could get out of jawbreakers such as "sesquicentennial" and "antidisestablishmentarianism."

As the twig is bent, so grows the tree. To see how many things America has democratized, I completed the sentence, "Everybody's got a right to . . ." for hours of rainy-day fun.

My first answers came quickly and held no surprises. Everybody's got a right to fame, wealth, self-esteem, genius, creativity, true love, multiple orgasms, home ownership, and law school—the self-evident truths, if you will. The pleasure-and-profit aspects of American leveling were fairly constant, and, notwithstanding some new cupidities, as banal as ever.

My second-tier answers revealed a bizarre side to our leveling urge that was more interesting. Between daytime TV and the welter of magazine covers containing a diagram of the human brain, Americans have begun to envy people with multiple personalities, buried memories, one-of-a-kind genes, and yet-to-be-understood medical "disorders" with an easily remembered name that goes with "My Fight Against . . ."

Peel away the modern scientific trappings and we see the fine hand of democratization at work. Ancestral memory tells us that peasants are strong as oxen; rare ailments are the mark of an aristocrat and outright decrepitude is found only in royal houses. Pulsing through the American subconscious is the passionate conviction that everybody's got a right to the Wittlesbach Taint and whatever it was that hit every third Hapsburg. Moreover, the newly formed anti-circumcision society is a clue that somebody out there is striving for Capet Foreskin.

As my mind ranged over the upscale magazine ads that promote the ghostly pallor of decadence and new lipstick shades named "fungus" and "internal bleeding," I wrote: "Everybody's got a right to be a nihilist." Oh, surely not, I amended silently, it wasn't possible. Nonetheless, it's happened. We have democratized nihilism.

Naturally we have refashioned it to conceal its traditional connection with openly unhappy intellectuals—because even nihilism must be "unthreatening." Once restricted to characters in Russian novels who took twenty pages to say "Nothing matters"; later associated with solitary anarchists who cooked over canned heat and expatriates in black turtleneck sweaters who started little magazines called *Flux*, nihilism is now as American as the baseball strike zone, which has disappeared.

You remember the strike zone. It's one of those things that generations of us learned so early in life that we sometimes got it mixed it up with other sacred texts and wound up saying, "Now I lay me down to sleep, over the plate between the shoulders and the knees."

Today's strike zone is wherever a particular umpire feels like putting it. Having already shortened it to somewhere above the belt, some umpires are now widening it, calling strikes on pitches well off the plate, as the above-the-plate camera angles clearly show. It all depends upon which umpire is calling the game. An arbitrary strike zone is no strike zone, but few find it disturbing and sportscasters even include it in their patter. "He's got a tight one . . . he's got a wide one," they quip in matter-of-fact monotones, as if meaninglessness were merely our beloved independence writ a little larger.

All American movements have subdivisions. If baseball is ruled by Populist Nihilism, Nihilism Chic has women in its grip as dress sizes abandon even a nodding acquaintance with basic arithmetic and turn literally into the "little nothing" of fashion legend. Women have always wanted to wear a smaller size than they actually took, so designers accommodated them by cutting small sizes big. This was a manageable deception back when the ideal figure was "a perfect 12," but then women decided that double-digit sizes sounded fat, so down they went to 8, 6, 4, and 2, any of which might be the same size as the old size 12 depending upon who designed it.

S O WHAT happens to women who already wear a size 2 when legions of plumper women decide they like the sound of it? Washington boutique owner Betsy Fisher found out when a designer said his company might introduce a size 0, "which is insanity," she told the *Washington Post*.

Do not put it past women to boast of being "a perfect zero." Nothing can restrain them except the U.S. Bureau of Standards, but it stopped regulating clothing sizes in 1942. When the government cancels one of the few useful services it ever performed, we have as good a definition of nihilism as any in the dictionary.

America is engaged in the pursuit of nothingness as if it were a new right that just turned up under a penumbra. Dumbing-down, audio books, the contents of anything labeled "-free," especially when consumed by women trying to be a perfect zero, are all nihilistic in spirit, but we reserve black-hole status for our legal system. The only jury that can be impaneled is one that knows nothing, never heard of anybody, and has no opinions whatsoever on any subject under the sun. Media commentators help it along by putting "alleged" in front of everything, conveying the notion that there is no criminal, no victim, no police, no witnesses, no crime, no case.

Nihilism's first cousin is passivity, as in the recent case of the Massachusetts teens who got their kicks from the muscle relaxant, Robaxin, evidently the latest thing in recreational drugs. I happen to know something about Robaxin, having taken it years ago when I hurt my back—never mind how—and I can testify that only a nihilist would consider it a turn-on. I felt like an empty wet suit, like one of Salvadore Dali's limp watches; a *rasa* without a *tabula*, a *schmerz* without a *Welt*, a *raison* without a *d'être*. In retrospect, however, it seems I was *avant* with a *garde*.

May 19, 1997

T HE attempted restoration of the Republic of Texas is looking better and better since the President's Summit gathered in Philadelphia to finish off the Liberty Bell. Another country would come in handy now that Bill Clinton has redefined citizenship to include compulsory volunteerism.

Billed as "bi-partisan," the summit attracted as sorry a band of Grand Old Compassioneers as ever was seen. There was George Bush, the reason why of the GOP Light Brigade, doing his impersonation of a grasshopper trying to be a regular guy. There was Barbara Bush, all wifed-out and breathing on cue; there was Gerald Ford, looking happy as only the seriously dumb can; and there was simpering Nancy Reagan, securing her husband's Place in

History with the vacuity of a teenager wrapping thread around her boyfriend's oversized class ring.

A Lott was missing, but the enervated little tableau serves well enough as a symbol of what happens when the Right abandons its native sternness and tries to operate on the oxymoronic principle of "conservatism with a heart."

Both the summit itself and the press coverage gave off that quality of upbeat malice that marks all socialist dictatorships, a "Be my brother or else" tone that no one but Jimmy Carter could miss. Gone were the customary euphemisms as Colin Powell rejoiced, "It's good to have an army again," and *Newsweek* pondered how to "prod" and "embarrass" us into mentoring the Great At-Risk and Felix Ungering their littered streets.

The most riveting semantic switch came at the end of *Newsweek*'s story when it was asked "whether the American people can be inspired to hold themselves accountable for the future of their children." The longstanding avuncular reference to "our children" has now been replaced by "their children," a rhetorical first conveying the message that this time they really are ours.

How can I help? According to Powell, "You gotta reach out to people who don't look like you, don't talk like you." How about don't write like you? Mary McGrory, who thinks government workers should be *ordered* to tutor in the D.C. public schools, visited an elementary school and watched "our little strugglers" being mentored by volunteers from an elite law firm, who were "laughing and talking and throwing them up in the air." Unfortunately they caught them.

The summit had much to say about Corporate America (Powell: "I'd like to give them a guilt trip") and their duty to practice *noblesse oblige*, now known as "giving something back to the community." The philanthropy of the old robber barons is out now. They filled America with libraries, museums, and concert halls, but they let us alone and we let them alone, and that won't do at all.

Socialist levelers use charity to force big business to give at the orifice. If the robber barons had really cared they would have granted their geologists paid "release time" and bused them to the slums to fiddle while the oil fields burned, and kept a few blast furnaces idle to use as "safe havens" for the Great At-Risk, as Kmart has offered to do with 2,150 stores. Never mind that most of their customers moved to the suburbs to get away from these same swarms of budding superpredators and may now decide to avoid Kmart. Stockholders be damned; turning stores into indoor street corners is a "challenge" that must be met.

The real value of volunteerism to liberals was expressed in *Newsweek*'s gloating observation: "It's put-up-or-shut-up time for those who have urged the private sector to take a greater role." Except for a few moist sentimentalists like Mary McGrory, liberals want volunteerism to fail and take conservatism down with it so they can proceed unimpeded with their agenda for Big Socialism.

T HEY could not have picked a better petard to hoist us on. The failure lurking in mass volunteerism is not the ordinary failure of Women Strike for Peace or Take Your Daughter to Work Day. It's more along the lines of the Lost Colony or the Flight to Varennes.

Consider the possibilities:

A volunteer will be murdered, giving "release time" new meaning.

Pedophiles will flock to serve, giving "at-risk" new meaning.

The retail safe-havens scheme will produce a phantom of the opera. What was that tinkling sound coming from Electrical Fixtures? Why are the curtains swaying in Housewares? Someone is in here . . .

Mentors who are thinking of taking their charges home should rent *The Man Who Came to Dinner* and *Crawlspace* at their local video stores, and drop by the library to look up Truman Capote's first published short story, "Miriam," about a kindly benefactress and a little house guest who gives "roots" new meaning.

Companies forced to hire welfare mothers will be forced to give them paid release time so they can be forced to volunteer to read to the children of mothers still on welfare, who in turn will be forced to volunteer to read to the children that the ex-welfare mothers left untended when they were forced into the labor market.

Fiery adoption controversies will erupt as volunteers get attached to children. If thwarted, some unstable mentors will turn to kidnapping, giving "little strugglers" new meaning.

Philadelphia's "48-hour graffiti-free zone" pledge that commits volunteers to remove new defacements in two days will turn out to be the greatest artistic inspiration since sunsets. As volunteers with turpentine labor to stay one step ahead of kids with spray cans, whole neighborhoods explode the moment someone lights a crack pipe and a $1.2 trillion class-action suit is brought against Glidden and Dutch Boy.

By Election 2000, "Bring back Big Government!" bumper stickers are everywhere. The Democrats win 435–0 and conservatives console ourselves with the thought that at least we can't paint ourselves into another corner because there is no paint.

June 2, 1997

W HAT do you do when you've got a stalemate on your hands? When you've tried everything and nothing has worked? When patience is depleted and you hear the sizzle of a lit fuse at the base of your skull?

The answer depends upon your brand of conservatism. Most conservatives would pray. I know some of you even pray for me because you've said so in your letters, proving that your faith is above rubies or something. Another kind of conservative would get drunk. This is easy because we don't drink liberals' sissy concoctions; it takes forever to get drunk on wine coolers but we can get there on a few belts. Some of us would hire a lawyer, but not many. Litigation is a liberal's game; a conservative's first instinct—after prayer, of course—is to slug somebody, but I couldn't do that because it's a man's world and I'm but a Southern lady in it. Booze was also out because it works against my fighting instincts. Paradoxically, I'm a happy drunk, prone to love everybody and lead a singalong in "Wait Till the Sun Shines, Nellie." What, then, could I do? There was only one route, so I took it.

"Pedantry in distress" describes my actions at such times. Whenever I'm at the end of my rope, my thought processes zoom in on the problem and ignite a relentless intellectual craving for a succinct articulation of it. Somewhere in this apartment is the perfect quotation; all I have to do is find it. Memory stirs and I see it in my mind's eye. Is it in my quotations notebook where I copy favorite passages from books? Or is it in my ever more apocalyptic files? The search begins.

The quotation I was looking for this time turned up in the file labeled LICK & PROMISE. It's from Rudyard Kipling's observations on America:

"A certain defect runs through everything—workmanship, roads, bridges, contracts, barter and sale and so forth—all inaccurate, all slovenly, all out of plumb and untrue. So far, the immense natural wealth of this land holds this ineptitude up; and the slovenly plenty hides their sins unless you look for them."

My problem concerned a receipt I needed for a tax-deductible purchase made for me in New York by someone else. My efforts to get it started in February and went on for two months. At first I stayed out of it and let my stand-in pursue the matter with the salesman. At one point the words "The receipt is in the mail" were actually spoken, but of course it never came, and shortly the salesman vanished into the black hole of "sales conference." When he surfaced, the promises began again: the receipt would be mailed in two weeks . . . in ten days . . . next Tuesday . . .

Finally I got fed up and called him myself. "That receipt wasn't mailed to you?" he asked wonderingly. Just then the phone faded out. Not a cut-off sound, just a sudden gentle nothingness that would have appealed to Emily Dickinson. Next, I got a Bell recording saying "Please hang up and dial again." I did, but the salesman didn't answer his page then or the next three times I called. The operator asked me if I wanted his voice mail; I said yes, but then she remembered that he had no voice mail. I asked her for his fax number and faxed him, but he never called or faxed back.

I called three more times, but he wasn't answering his phone, his page, his pager, his cell phone, his car phone, his fax, or his computer. He had no answering machine but he did sell them—why, I wondered, didn't he put one aside for himself?

At last I got him on the phone. I asked him why he had not responded to my fax and he said he never got it; when I told him where I had sent it he said the operator had given me the wrong number. To make a long story short (*NR* couldn't print the best part of the conversation anyhow), I got the receipt three days later. There was only one thing wrong with it: the dot-matrix print-out was so faint that the purchase price was unreadable.

Multiply my experience by the number of Americans who endure something similar every day and it adds up to millions of rides on the Vortex at Kafkaland. The cumulative effect on the national nervous system has given rise to the Stress Industry, but it would be a mistake to think that the how-to-cope books, aerobics classes, breathing workshops, shower massages, and competing brands of indigestion pills will solve anything. When the bookstore clerk can't find *Stop Complaining and Start Living*, when the receptionist at the aerobics center gets the appointments mixed up, when the windows won't open at the breathing school, when the new shower head won't spray, when the sealed bottle of Gutlox is found to contain rat droppings, then we know that Kipling was right.

A MERICAN shiftlessness has worsened since his time. I can think of four reasons why.

World War II instilled a fear of efficiency-as-fascism that joined forces with our blotterlike capacity for taking everything in and getting it all backwards to give us words to live by: "He made the trains run on time" meant that late is good.

Fifties conformity produced a lust for "creativity" (the forerunner of self-esteem) that excused wool-gathering and sloppiness as signs of artistic destiny in children who grew up to be salesmen.

When pop psychology ruled that meticulous people are sexually frustrated, screwing up a simple task proved that you got boompsed regularly.

In the maelstrom of noble causes and idealistic movements driving our Age of Guilt, martinets have been overwhelmed by fanatics and lofty conscience has driven out simple conscientiousness.

According to current idiom, the opposite of a procrastinating slacker is a "control freak." You are looking, so to speak, at one right now. I do everything yesterday, triple-check it, worry about it, and keep files on people who give their jobs a lick and a promise.

I can find anything.

June 16, 1997

WILL Durant said all great nations begin stoic and end epicurean. America has been on this well-traveled road to Rome for some time, but we can also measure our decline by another yardstick that is uniquely ours. We began as sympathizers and will end as empathizers.

The Nineties have blurred the original distinction between sympathy and empathy and the dictionaries have followed suit, but just for old times' sake, here it is: We sympathize with people whose troubles are different from ours; we empathize with people in the same boat. "I feel your pain" is empathy, but "I can imagine your pain" is sympathy.

That sympathy is obviously the nobler emotion explains why it has fallen out of favor with Americans. In the first place, it's too hard, demanding not only thoughtful reflection but a certain amount of serious reading. Second, it smacks of elitism. Lastly, sympathy compels us to touch the third rail of egalitarian democracy: the generalization. Once we utter the words "I can imagine" we enter the realm of broad, sweeping thought, which tends to produce broad, sweeping statements, which, as we all know, tend to hit the multicultural fan with a horrendous splat.

How much safer, then, to trade the wide-ranging heroics of sympathy for empathy's nonjudgmental inclusiveness and reassuring common touch. We made the switch the way we always do, by constant repetition of the word, until everybody was empathizing with everybody else and reciting "I identify with" and "I can relate to" over every conceivable foible and calamity that flesh and spirit are heir to, all in the name of a level suffering field.

The people most likely to go on an empathy jag are those who personalize every problem, reduce every experience to its most pedestrian component parts, and get so caught up in the particulars of a situation that they cannot see the universal principle.

Reading Margaret Carlson's column on Lt. Kelly Flinn is like reading half of Charles Lamb's essay on roast pig: we are left wondering whether the Chinese peasants will ever figure out fire, or will they just go on burning down their barns whenever they want cooked meat.

Painting Lt. Flinn as the victim of "a louse so low he makes George Costanza look like Sir Galahad," Miss Carlson asks: "Why wasn't she given counseling, a reprimand, or reassignment?" Reassignment? Doesn't she know that no matter where they stationed her, every wife on the base would empathize with Catherine of Aragon?

The level suffering field erupted last year when baseball star Roberto Alomar spat in the face of umpire John Hirschbeck, who flew into a violent rage and threw Alomar out of the game. In an attempt to get off the hook by feeling Hirschbeck's pain, Alomar told a press conference he understood why the umpire was so upset: Hirschbeck's son was dying of the disease that inspired the movie *Lorenzo's Oil*.

This is how the word "empathy" made its unprecedented appearance in the sports pages, where it remained for several weeks as Hirschbeck's defenders accused Alomar of a "lack of empathy" for raising the painful subject, while Alomar's defenders insisted that his heart was in the right place but that his being a bachelor made it hard for him to "empathize" with a father.

Empathy is a female game designed for boffo displays of intuition and finer feeling. Its greatest impact has been felt in our legal system. The difference between the empathetic female mind and the sympathetic male mind is the difference between the jurisprudence of an earlier age and the juris without prudence that prevails today.

When Albert DeSalvo, the Boston Strangler, was tried for his other "Green Man" sex crimes in 1964, women could still be excused from jury duty on the grounds that they would hear things "unfit for female ears." That's sympathy.

DeSalvo consequently had an all-male jury, which returned in just three hours with a guilty verdict. By contrast, the Menendez brothers got off when the female jurors at their first trial concluded that yes, they did it, but no, they didn't, not really, not if you understand them and relate to what was going through their minds. That's empathy.

Somerset Maugham got it right when he said, "There's not much kick in the milk of human kindness." Empathizing with everybody is like sleeping with everybody: eventually it makes you frigid, at which point you decide it's a lot less trouble and just as much fun to empathize with yourself.

M ANY Americans are indulging in this vice. Soccer Moms contended that because the Doles had no children, he could not govern "for families." Military men regularly call talk-radio shows to declare that anyone who has not "worn the uniform" has no right to send troops into battle. The most enthusiastic self-empathizers, however, are Congress Moms whose idea of legislating is to pass laws against their own problems.

Rep. Marge Roukema is pushing for family leave because she had to quit graduate school to nurse a sick child. Rep. Connie Morella is pushing for breast-cancer research because her sister died of breast cancer. Sen. Mary Landrieu, who has a five-year-old, wants to overhaul the school-lunch program, and Rep. Cynthia McKinney hints, "I can relate to the single mom at the bus stop at 5 A.M. with her baby because I've been there." As for Congress Dads, Sen. Pete Domenici demanded that the Kennedy-Kassebaum health-care bill be amended to cover mental illness because his daughter is mentally ill.

In a column on personalized agendas, Margaret Carlson chided, "One-on-one conversions are no substitute for empathy." They ARE empathy! What is missing is the broad, sweeping thought of a wide-ranging sympathetic mind. Without it, all we will get are more versions of the Americans with Disabilities Act, which has robbed us of sympathy's most precious jewel, "There but for the grace of God go I," and replaced it with "The goddam gimps towed my car."

June 30, 1997

I T'S a start, but it's not enough. The apologies tendered by Bill Clinton for the Tuskegee experiments and Tony Blair for the Irish famine only point up the need for volunteer apologists to aid in this great work.

Words cannot express how deeply I regret the Annexation of Schleswig–Holstein. Many say there's no point in discussing it because only three people have ever understood it—a Heidelberg professor who went mad; Prince Albert, who died at 42; and Lord Palmerston, who forgot what it was that he understood—but it's actually quite simple.

As every schoolboy knows, the dispute over the duchies began in 974 when the forces of Cnut of Schleswig and Baldur of Holstein captured so many women from each other that the Danish province of Schleswig filled up with Germans and the German province of Holstein filled up with Danes. Ethnic tensions increased in 1106 when Lothair of Supplingenburg became Duke of Saxony and created German counts to rule Holstein, a policy that was challenged in 1404 when Eric of Pomerania claimed the titles for

Denmark, thereby incurring the wrath of Frederick III, who added Dithmarschen and Stormarn to Holstein over the objections of the House of Gottorp–Delmenhorst. He was reversed by the German Diet, which awarded Lauenburg to Holstein and put Schleswig under the suzerainty of the Margrave of Sonderburg–Augustenburg, who, being but eight years old, was subject to the regency of his mother, Landgravin Johanna of Oster Jutland, until her overthrow by Oskar Tremendus, who, as every schoolboy knows, abandoned the German Diet.

The Tremendi prevailed until the Congress of Vienna declared the duchies independent and named the Danish king Duke of Schleswig–Holstein, an edict later revised by the London Protocol which stipulated that the King of Denmark be recognized as Duke *in* Schleswig–Holstein but not Duke *of* Schleswig–Holstein. Faced with this most grievous of insults, King Christian annexed the duchies, whereupon Prussia and Austria declared war on Denmark.

It is abundantly clear to a gender-sensitive age that the key figure here is the Landgravin Johanna of Oster Jutland, the rightful Queen of Denmark who was denied the crown by the sexist Salic Law that prohibited women or matrilineal claimants from reigning in any land once part of the Holy Roman Empire. So to Salic Moms everywhere who have found their inner Dane, I offer my sincerest apologies and my solemn promise that Schleswig–Holstein will never, ever be annexed again.

A nation that obsesses daily about the use and abuse of "body parts" must come to terms with the War of Jenkins' Ear. It began in 1731 when a Spanish captain, angry that England had reneged on her promise to give back Gibraltar, boarded an English merchant vessel and cut off the ear of its captain, Robert Jenkins. At least that's what Jenkins claimed when he turned up in the House of Commons with an ear in a jar. A few cynics said he really lost it in the pillory, but cynicism was in short supply once Pitt waved the ear around and declaimed "the honor of England."

Spain denied the ear story and countered it with a charge that an English captain had cut off a Spanish captain's nose and forced him to eat it, but no one believed it. Whipped into a white heat of patriotism, the English people demanded a war with Spain. When it came, church bells rang out and everyone was so pumped up that James Thomson wrote "Rule Britannia" and novelist Tobias Smollett joined the navy.

It was shaping up into a great little war when something strange happened: it went away. As historian Carl Becker explains: "How the War of Jenkins' Ear might have ended we shall unfortunately never know, for it was soon submerged and lost in the War of the Austrian Succession." In other words, as wags delight in pointing out, since no peace treaty, armistice, or surrender was ever signed, it must still be going on somewhere.

I regret to say that "somewhere" is the United States. Remember Lorena Bobbitt, the Hispanic who sliced off her WASP husband's member? In the name of the Prudential Insurance Company, I hereby apologize for their inflammatory logo of the Rock of Gibraltar which has done so much to prolong this 258-year-old war.

I'll never forgive myself for the Sepoy Mutiny, whose cause ranks as the most insensitive act of cultural imperialism ever committed by the usual suspects, i.e., Anglo-Saxons. In 1857, the new Enfield rifles that England distributed to her native Indian troops (sepoys) required greased cartridges. The manufacturer was supposed to use mutton fat, but to save money had used instead the cheaper fat of cows and pigs. Since every sepoy soldier was either a Hindu or a Moslem, certain defilement awaited any man who so much as touched an ammo box. Do you wonder that I can't sleep?

T HE Apologizer Bunny keeps going and going and going. I wish to express my heartfelt regret to Lt. Kelly Flinn for what Emperor Augustus did when he discovered his daughter, Julia, committing mass fornication in the Forum on Amateur Night. Instead of simply reprimanding her, he exiled her to the island of Pandateria in the Adriatic—the Minot, North Dakota, of antiquity—and supplied her with a staff of servants and guards consisting entirely of eunuchs.

To Madeline Morris, who advised the military to abandon its "masculinist aggressivity," I apologize for Lord Cardigan, who calmly observed the first casualty in the Charge of the Light Brigade and said, "Imagine the fellow screaming like a woman when he was hit."

Lastly, I apologize to Brian Lamb of C-SPAN and the personality-deprived everywhere for what Charles II said about Prince George of Denmark, the husband of his niece, the future Queen Anne: "'Tis fortunate that he snuffles, else the footmen would think him dead and carry him out."

July 14, 1997

T OWARD the end of his life when his health had begun to break down, my fellow misanthrope Evelyn Waugh wrote his friend, Nancy Mitford: "I'm quite deaf now. Such a comfort." I wish I could say the same as we prepare for our national conversation on race, but unfortunately I have ears like a lynx.

I didn't always hate the sound of the human voice. As a college student in the Fifties I ran with arty bohemians, a dependably garrulous breed, staying up all night in shabby apartments amid Toulouse-Lautrec posters and orange-crate bookcases, drinking muscatel and talking intensely about "life."

By "life" we really meant our own lives, which is what made our marathon soul-searching so enjoyable. We were the last generation of wannabe intellectuals to celebrate selfishness. We thought Gauguin was right to abandon his wife and children and run away to Tahiti, we cheered Sherwood Anderson's walk down the railroad tracks into a new life, and we did not care how much adulterous havoc George Sand wreaked. Nothing mattered to us except cultivating the garden of our salad days; we would have sacrificed anybody for a chance to live in Europe "for a year," justifying it with the self-evident principle that creative people must put themselves first.

Then came the Sixties. Suddenly, intellectuals were no longer selfish and soul-searching was no longer arty. As altruistic hippies and utopian radicals replaced bohemian blithe spirits, discourse among the avant garde degenerated into self-flagellating confessions, consciousness-raising, and wrangles about bus schedules for Freedom Rides and which Safeways to target for boycotts of lettuce and grapes.

When the black-turtleneck-sweater crowd donned tie-dyes and took up selfless martyrdom, I found myself cut off from the writer's natural milieu. I enjoyed blithe spirits and outrageous nonconformists, but now their opinions set my teeth on edge. I liked the freemasonry of artists with their easy assumptions of superiority, but now they all believed in equality. I wasn't cut out to be a hippie, but neither was I cut out to be a Republican committeewoman. Where could I turn for stimulating conversation?

I solved the problem by keeping a foot in both camps, becoming an anti-intellectual intellectual, a right-wing feminist, and an elitist conservative—three guaranteed ways to end up with no one to talk to at all, which is probably why I did it.

Giving up talking is the smartest thing I ever did. Take, for example, the widespread assumption that writers need to talk often with all kinds of people to master the "give and take" of human exchange. I believed this myself for years, but now I know it's not true. Writing and talking don't mix, and in fact war against each other. Every fledgling writer soon learns that trying to reproduce "the way people really talk" results in unreadable dialogue. It also works the other way around, as the Rambling Wreck from Arkansas has demonstrated. Bill Clinton's 1969 letter thanking the ROTC colonel for saving him from the draft was full of repellent sentiments, but they were well-expressed. It was a good letter because it did not sound like the way people really talk. But now, after years of incessant talking, everything Clinton says sounds like bad writing.

"It's really about listening," said John Kasich of the proposed national conversation on race. Exactly. A writer who listens to America talking does so at his peril. The first principle of art is selectivity; "Achilles' rage alone, when wrought with skill, abundantly does a whole Iliad fill," advised Boileau. American conversation being all about healing power, its first principle issues from therapists, facilitators, and every woman's best girlfriend: "Start at the beginning and don't leave anything out."

For all our eagerness to heal with words, the average American utterance can be jarring. This is probably caused by continuous exposure to bereaved families trying to cram into a sound bite their pleas for a) mercy, b) justice, or c) privacy.

"Remember always never to bring a tame in union with a savage thing," advised Horace. When a prisoner on Maryland's death row chose gas over lethal injection to force the authorities to witness painful capital punishment, Kathie O'Donnell of the Public Defender's Office explained, "This is a brutal act, he doesn't want them to sort of redefine the act by making it seem like he's going to sleep."

YOU don't say "sort of" when talking about savage things, but Americans always insert these stool softeners to avoid sounding too blunt and direct. Even some columnists are doing it now. I have seen the softening "sort of" in columns, along with "Correct me if I'm wrong" (Okay, you're wrong), and "I hate to say it" (Then don't).

"Neither a talker nor a listener be," advised King. My decision to go Trappist was reinforced last year when I got a message from Mary Matalin's show inviting me to "talk about your review of Hillary Clinton's book." This should not have hit me as strongly as it did. I get enough requests for personal appearances to have kept my cool, but I reacted instead like the heroine of a gothic novel who has to get thrown down a well, locked in the attic, and smothered by a fallen canopy before she finally says "Suddenly, I realized . . ."

How can you talk about what you have already written? How can extemporaneous speech possibly improve and clarify something that took you three days of revising, polishing, and fine-tuning to get exactly right? Writing is the ultimate self-expression, but letting an idea stand in pristine—i.e., written—

form offends an oral culture. Nothing is final until we render it fleeting; nothing makes sense until we confuse it; nothing is lively until we kill it.

Nonetheless, there's hope. Have you noticed how often the new buzzword, "closure," has been cropping up lately? It may be a subconscious way of saying everybody shut up.

July 28, 1997

I N AN effort to prove that Americans have an innate reverence for the arts, Hillary Clinton recently told the story of Dolley Madison's priorities on the night the British burned the White House in 1814. Did the fashionable Dolley think to save her wardrobe, including all those *Empire* turbans? No, indeed. She saved Gilbert Stuart's portrait of George Washington.

Therefore, implied Mrs. Clinton, the National Endowment for the Arts is, and of right ought to be, first in the hearts of her countrypersons.

Never mind the logic. I'm tired of uncoiling the serpentine corkscrews of the Clintonian mind. Besides, the interesting subject here is art per se. If we look at the Gilbert Stuart portrait of Washington in the light of recent art controversies, we can see just how awful democracy is.

Framed prints of the Gilbert Stuart portrait hung in every public-school classroom once, leading generations of children to suppose it was a picture of Washington in Heaven because of the white clouds at the bottom. The clouds are the unfinished part; according to one story, Stuart was so awed by his subject that he remained unsatisfied with the work and left it incomplete.

Think of it. A portrait of a white male, by a white male, who left a white hole. Empty canvas going to waste when so many people have never been done in oils. Since there's still some room left in it, why not fill it up? Stick something in there—an Aztec priest performing open-heart surgery, a lesbian hooked up to a dialysis machine, Marion Barry hooked—something, anything. It doesn't matter what, as long as it celebrates our Great Diversity and atones for the Great Unpainted.

Sound insane? It shouldn't—it's precisely the approach to art that We the Connoisseurs tolerate without a peep. Take the "Three Suffragettes" statue that languished in the Capitol cellar for so many years. It shows Lucretia Mott, Susan B. Anthony, and Elizabeth Cady Stanton in what appears to be a box seat at a baseball game. It was kept under wraps because it did not "fit," artistically speaking, in the Rotunda, but since when has asymmetry ever bothered feminists? The NOW cows wanted that statue out front where everybody could see it, by God, and never mind sissy stuff like balance and proportion.

They were on the verge of victory when suddenly Rep. Cynthia McKinney and other hob-nailed aesthetes of the #3 sepia persuasion objected to the work because Sojourner Truth (#6 burnt umber) was missing from it. The solution? It got to be inclusive! Whittle a statue of Sojourner Truth and put her in. Where? Don't make no nevermind, just so she in it. But what about the artistic prerogative of the original sculptress? Don't make no nevermind—she white. Well, then, since we're wrecking creative intent, would you prefer Ms. Truth to be whittled in black marble in contrast to the white marble of the rest of the work? Ooooeeee! That be cool! You tellin' it now, sista!

Artistic prerogative and creative intent are no longer sacrosanct, even when inspired by political correctness. Sculptor Lawrence Halprin scrupulously included Braille panels in the FDR Memorial, only to come under fire from blind tourists who complained that the panels were too big to read with fingertips and that some were eight feet off the ground. A Halprin assistant explained the aesthetic reason—the panels must be big enough to be appreciated at a distance and draw the viewer (whoops!) in—but it did no good because what was once called "perspective" is now called discrimination. There is only one way to satisfy the blind-fury crowd. Chop those panels off the top and put 'em on the bottom where people can reach 'em, and make the big dots little dots, you dumb bastard, or we'll tie you to your cement and throw you in the Potomac.

I T IS significant that the general public expressed no surprise on learning that giant Braille panels had been included in the memorial. That's because We the Connoisseurs of the United States, being in huddled masses assembled, were no longer capable of being surprised by anything to do with the FDR Memorial. The artistic despotism and aesthetic usurpations committed by both sides in the controversy had already rendered us numb. A decent Respect to the Opinions of Mankind requires that I declare the causes which impel me to say this, and so let Facts be submitted to a candid World:

They threatened to tie up traffic with piles of wheelchairs.

They compromised on the wheelchair by putting casters on FDR's regular chair, then gave him a cape as rigid as a piece of sheet metal to hide the casters from all but the most vigilant paranoids, who are now flocking to the memorial to see the casters as tourists once flocked to the Erechtheion to see the fragile marble drapery falling in soft folds from the bosoms of the Karyatids.

They modeled statues on portraits painted from life, then removed the cigarette holder, leaving FDR with two stiff fingers holding nothing.

They took away Eleanor Roosevelt's fox fur piece to prevent animal-rights protestors from dynamiting the site, an everpresent danger that evidently unsteadied the hand of her Praxiteles because she looks exactly like Bess Truman.

They have sized and placed statuary to encourage "interaction," creating what amounts to a petting farm that sooner or later will attract bronze fetishists who will try to hump something.

They have included so many "rooms" and so many pools, including a waterfall, that the site is a humid maze, making it an ideal bathhouse for the homeless, who can escape detection merely by freezing in place and pretending to be one of the statues of the Depression homeless. Who but the bronze fetishists would know the difference?

We can predict where this is headed. *Tableaux vivants*, once the pastime of Victorian maidens, will be revived. The homeless will be assigned to the memorial as salaried "living statuary," and the Clintons will call it art.

August 11, 1997

T HIS seems to be the season for chipping away at the diminishing rock of my childhood. First Jimmy Stewart died, and then Woolworth's five-and-ten announced that it was going out of business.

To be honest, Stewart was the antithesis of my taste in men. The lovable boy-next-door type has always irritated me, and physically he turned me off because he was too tall and skinny. Solitary, poor, nasty, brutish, and five-foot-ten is more my style, but I liked Stewart anyway because he was *there*. Where childhood memories are concerned, thereness is what counts. I probably wouldn't shop at a Woolworth's today, but I want it to be there, and now it won't be, not ever again.

Woolworth's needed no Official Greeters. The moment you walked in you were enveloped in an overpowering aroma of hot sweetness issuing from the sugary batter in the doughnut fryer, the boiling caramel in the candied-apple machine, the flavored syrups that were drizzled over crushed ice to make snowballs, and the mountains of candy corn, butterfingers, and chunked-up chocolate in the cavernous food bins.

The sweet smell was a year-round fixture. In summer when the doors sat open, it wafted out to the street. In winter the hissing steam heat trapped it inside and mixed it with the cloying scents of the cosmetics counter, where they sold big blue bottles of Evening in Paris perfume, cans of dusting powder named Quelques Fleurs and Djer Kiss (which no one could pronounce), and tiny satin bags of gardenia sachet to scatter in bureau drawers—or, for serious wafters, to tuck into bras.

The hardwood floors were black with age and squeaked, just like the floors of our apartment. The store served our regular needs—a ten-cent envelope of phonograph needles, Granny's advanced knitting books with instructions to rival the quantum theory—as well as some highly irregular ones, e.g., the glittery earrings my father bought to decorate the head of the banjo he made, the oil my mother used to soften her baseball glove, and my penknife fixation.

It was at Woolworth's that I got my first pet: a miniature turtle that I persuaded Granny to buy me before we went to the movies. They put him in a white pasteboard carton, like Chinese take-out, and I named him Mergatroyd after a cartoon character.

During the movie I kept whispering "Hello, Mergatroyd" and sticking my finger in the box to pet him. I couldn't wait to get home and make him a rock garden, but Granny was absorbed in *Back Street*, which met her definition of a good movie ("She dies in the end"). At long last, when the movie ended and the lights came on, I opened the box to check on Mergatroyd, but he was as dead as Margaret Sullavan.

I burst into tears and ran up the aisle. "She's not old enough to understand about kept women," somebody whispered in disapproval, which made me cry harder. Granny offered to buy me another turtle but I wanted only Mergatroyd. Nor would I let her ask for a refund because that put him on a level with light bulbs or a can opener. I wanted to give him a funeral, so back we went to Woolworth's to buy a soap dish for a coffin and two tongue depressers to make a cross.

The orgasmic transports that today's retailers call a "shopping experience" swept through Woolworth's on December 8, 1941, when a man began smashing everything stamped "Made in Japan." No security guards converged on him and no one worried about lawsuits. As the crowd cheered, the manager winked and said, "I needed to get rid of this stuff today anyhow."

It would have been futile to expect my mother to stay out of the fray. Grabbing an illustrated teapot, she was about to sidearm it, shortstop-style, against the wall, but just then Granny showed up, waving a length of hat veiling she had been inspecting when she heard the ruckus.

"Oh, Louise! I turn my back for a minute and you act like whitetrash!"

"I'm going to break every piece of junk those sneaky grinning runts ever made!"

"Then go home and break your ashtrays where nobody can see you!"

She did—and bought new ones stamped "Made in U.S.A." from Woolworth's.

B ESIDES the infinite variety of its stock, Woolworth's offered the masses
an ongoing morality tale in Barbara Hutton, the Woolworth heiress who
went through six husbands and $50 million. Her Babylonian highjinks were
chronicled regularly in newsreels, and since the dimestore was a block from the
movie theater, the audience usually was eating something from her redolent
candy bins as we watched her exchange vows with yet another playboy.

"Money cwan't buy happineth," said Granny through her salt-water taffy.

"Oh, s—!" Mama snorted. "It can if you do it right. She should have been
made to work in a Woolworth's for a few years, find out where her money
comes from and learn the business from the ground up so she could run it herself. Then she wouldn't have time to get mixed up with all those lounge
lizards." Leave it to Mama to define real feminism and responsible capitalism in one breath: an unassisted double play.

Such easy lessons are impossible in a non-Woolworth's economy; how
can you have a Barbara Hutton if you have to do research in *Forbes* to find
out who really owns a store? It also takes plutocrats of variegated swath to
personify the titanic ruin that makes for a really effective I-told-you-so
morality play. Bill Gates could become another Jack the Ripper but it's doubtful that anyone could think of anything memorable to say about it.

Today I shop from catalogues whenever possible to avoid characterless
suburban malls. "I found a million-dollar baby in FootLocker" lacks something. "Diamond bracelets Wal-Mart's doesn't sell" scans, but despite their
eternally falling prices Wal-Mart's comes up short in that raffish gypsy-push-
cart atmosphere I loved.

September 1, 1997

O F all the self-defeating things Americans do, our practice of renaming eternal verities to make them sound more user-friendly wins the
booby prize.

Like all societies, we acknowledge the need for certain people to "set an
example" so that others will have someone to "look up to," but we don't dare
put it that way. Instead we call them "role models," a compound now so
deeply embedded in our cliché lobes that no one stops to think that both
words connote superficiality, ephemerality, and pretense.

Earlier generations of Americans looked up to Better Thans, as in "better than we are," people who were a cut above them, such as teachers or business owners, and those who were several cuts above them, such as doctors,
lawyers, and clergymen, once known as the "learned professions."

It's all over now. Better Thans preserved the stability of black neighborhoods in the Jim Crow era, but now the only blacks who call them role models are those who attend conferences on "Role-Model Flight and the Creation of the Underclass."

Among whites, the loss of esteem for the learned professions has been less dramatic in that it has not resulted in actual mayhem, but the psychological shocks mount daily. The doctor who cut off the wrong foot plays golf with the lawyer who advertises his services in commercials that open with the deafening crunch of a head-on collision and a close-up of a teddy bear on a rain-drenched road. Both say "Between you and I" and neither has any Latin—nor does the clergyman who confessed to molesting boys: the difference between "*Noli me tangere*" and "*nolo contendere*" now escapes him.

It could be argued that these male Better Thans have self-destructed under pressure from the flood of women into the learned professions. It certainly can be argued that women have damaged the Better Than Mystique by fritzing the "not-rightness" wire in our brains. This is the wire that makes children insist that their favorite bedtime story be told exactly the same way each time; leave out the pig's hat and the child will wail, "You didn't tell it right!"

The not-rightness wire remains connected throughout our lives, governing our expectations and pre-conceived opinions and giving off a hot sizzle when they are thwarted. Like most unfair reactions, this one is universal and immutable, and hence important.

My not-rightness wire sizzles when I see an Episcopal priestess in a reversed collar. When I see the politically correct commercial with the middle-aged construction worker who says: "My doctor told me to take Dynamitol for my constipation. I trust her [wink], she's my daughter." And when I see a picture of the full Supreme Court containing two huge white spots—the jabots worn by the lady members to lend a feminine touch. Justice O'Connor's lacy number reminds me of the fanned-out handkerchief pinned to the shoulder of a friendly Midwestern waitress, but Justice Ginsberg's stark, foot-long Geneva bands are even worse: she looks like John Calvin gone wrong.

Most Better Thans are no longer better, and many are not even equal. Two messages left on my answering machine are a case in point. Both were from local public-school teachers unknown to me. The first one sounded like a 911 call, a rush of words from a woman with a shrill, cawing voice just this side of hysteria.

"I'm calling Florence King! I have a high-school English class that needs your help fast! A workshop, a speech! Something, anything!"

The other message was a wrong number. Thinking she had reached the mother of a student, this teacher launched into a long, rambling explanation about a schedule change. Again I was struck by the voice: flat, whiny, unconfident, muddy diction. Different in temper from the first frantic caller, yet they were alike in one way: they both sounded common.

I felt oddly betrayed. The teacher as grande dame was a fixture of my school days, and lest you think I'm warming myself in the glow of nostalgia, cold mathematics bears me out. All of my elementary-school teachers were born, roughly speaking, between 1885 and 1910, meaning that they came of age when college was still a preserve of the comfortable class. Teaching was the only career open to women then, and so generations of ladies became teachers. They had a way of speaking and a general demeanor that their public-school charges, who usually did not belong to the comfortable class, instinctively recognized—and so did our parents. The effortless discipline these women maintained and the automatic respect they commanded had less to do with school prayer and other touted traditional values than with frank class-consciousness.

T HE truth about role models that we go to such lengths to hide can be summed up as "Sweet are the uses of elitism." A role model is someone who is superior in a worthwhile way, whose power of example transcends the fickle transports of hero-worship. He cannot be too far above us. He must be someone we don't actually know but do come into contact with, or at least see from time to time as the old-world villager saw the squire.

Thus, a valid role model is an accessible Better Than from the comfortable class. That used to mean the middle class when we had only three classes, but democracy works in mysterious ways its chaos to perform.

Today's middle class is yesterday's "blue-collar class," which was the New Deal's "working class," who were Huey Long's "little people," who were Bryan's "simple people," who were Lincoln's "common people," who were Hamilton's "masses," who were Marie Antoinette's "them." Thanks to government scholarships, college loans, educational tax credits, and affirmative action, millions of would-be Better Thans are pouring into the fake middle class convinced that everybody's got a right to be a role model—which is Hillary Clinton's "It takes a village."

September 15, 1997

 PERCEPTION is a terrible thing to waste" is the motto of the Robert Torricelli College of Liberal Artifice, where students major in time-warping so they can give eyewitness accounts of humanity's long history of bigotry without being constrained by chronological realities.

The Torricelli method does not involve stretching the truth, merely stretching one's mortal coil over eternity and walking across it without a net. The Great Torricelli, who is 46, recently demonstrated his technique when he recalled the pain and humiliation he felt in 1951 when, having just progressed from being a gleam in his father's eye to being a mass of unviable tissue, he watched the Senate hearings on organized crime and heard ethnic slurs against Italians. "It is among the first memories I have of government of the United States, and probably the first hearing of the United States Senate I ever witnessed," he said. "It was only on a flickering television screen, but I will never forget it, and even if I tried, my family would never allow me."

I know the feeling well. I'll never forget that hot August morning in Paris when I went with my Huguenot family to the palace reception. My mother dressed me in my best bib, the one with a ruff, and a diaper with a four-foot train. Young as I was in 1572, I knew that an invitation from Catherine de Medici, who was not only an Italian Queen of France but the mother-in-law of Mary Queen of Scots, meant that the Catholics had accepted us at last.

As we set out for the Louvre we heard church bells throughout the city. "Why are the bells ringing?" my father asked a passer-by. "Today is the feast of St. Bartholomew," he replied. I did not see the sign he made behind our backs, but as later events would prove, I perceived it.

The Louvre courtyard was packed with Huguenots. Catherine de Medici must have invited every Huguenot in Paris, and now they were waiting for her to descend—what a landmark day in ecumenism this would be!

The next thing I perceived was only a flicker, but it flickered in our direction—an arrow fired by King Charles IX from a palace window, a signal to the guards to launch the only interfaith prayer breakfast in history that was not boring.

Cries of "Kill the Protestant dogs!" are the first memory I have of Medici government, but I escaped the flashing swords and daggers by squeezing into a stone niche with Indiana Jones, whose words I'll never forget: "They always do this on saints' days. Remember Chicago in 1929?"

Of course I do, I was there. If you don't believe it, check out the right-to-memory clause in the Constitution. It's under Penumbra XIV and it says "Everybody's got a right to whenever." Thanks to this guarantee enjoyed by a free people, the Great Torricelli is not alone in his chronological hell. Bill Clinton remembers black church-burnings in his Arkansas boyhood even though no black churches were burned in Arkansas then. Hillary Clinton claimed that her parents named her after Mt. Everest conqueror Sir Edmund Hillary even though she was born in 1947 and Sir Edmund did not make his climb until 1953, prior to which he was unknown outside his native New Zealand.

Explaining his support for the Employment Nondiscrimination Act of 1996, Ted Kennedy said, "I remember help-wanted signs in stores when I was growing up saying 'No Irish Need Apply.'" Think about that. He was born in 1932. Some cloaked anti-Irish sentiment no doubt still existed, but the signs, relics of the nineteenth century, were long gone from a state that by his day had become an Irish fief.

A related time warp cropped up in the 1975 TV movie *The Legend of Lizzie Borden*. In a shot of Lizzie entering an 1892 Massachusetts store, the camera lingers on a sign reading "Irish Keep Out." The screenwriter obviously wanted viewers to see it and reflect on how terrible life was for the Irish in those days, but anyone with a sense of history is just as likely to reflect on how terrible life would have been for the Yankee plutocracy if the Irish had been barred from stores. There would have been no food on their tables. Irish servants like the Bordens' Bridget Sullivan did the shopping and ran the errands, and like blacks in the segregated South, were welcomed by merchants as long as they had money to spend.

Americans' lack of a sense of history is what makes the time warp such a useful tool for pandering politicians and guilt-ridden liberals. A black congressman announces that slave ships threw so many African captives overboard that "sharks still swim the route," and millions believe it. Demi Moore interprets *The Scarlet Letter* as "Horny Hester Lap Dances in Vegas," and millions accept it.

C HRONOLOGICALLY shattered by our successful pursuit of what television calls "immediacy," we have even developed a mental block against the pluperfect tense; dozens of public figures say "if I would have" instead of "if I had had," and millions don't turn a hair. Mired in our creepy now-ness, our idea of history is Mike Tyson waiting until they found the ear before going on CNN and saying, "I want to put this behind me."

The time warp that incenses me the most concerns the 1916 "affair" between Franklin Roosevelt and Lucy Mercer. That they slept together is now a given, thanks in large part to Elliott Roosevelt, who claimed in his 1974 book that he had seen a motel receipt for one of his father's trysts. This was taken as gospel and recycled by subsequent writers, whose sense of history should have told them that: a) there were no motels in 1916; b) in the era of the gold standard and a larval IRS, men in Roosevelt's world lent each other hotel suites, yachts, and hunting lodges for trysts; and c) Roosevelt was a Victorian gentleman who never would have compromised an unmarried girl of his own class.

I say it was a romance, not an affair. Of course, I don't actually *know* because I didn't live back then, but oh, how I wish I had.

September 29, 1997

W
HEN Princess Diana made her televised confession in 1995, the press quoted an unidentified Palace official who said, "In the old days we could have beheaded her." In the last few months, however, the real possibility arose that she could step on a land mine.

The once and former Merry England would have found it irresistible, reminiscent of those bizarre historical incidents, like Clarence drowning in a butt of malmsey, that provided material for "Beyond the Fringe." It would have recalled Evelyn Waugh's novel about African missionaries that contains the line, "Come quickly, the Bulanga have eaten Lady Tippett!" Martyrdom to a noble cause on the one hand, while on the other a denouement in the Peter Sellers–Terry Thomas tradition of high farce.

But Diana died a People's death on Labor Day weekend and Merry England is now an oxymoron. I heard the news late Saturday night, just moments after I had finished writing the column that ran in the last issue. My first thought was to scrap it and write a new one on Diana, but to do that I needed to watch TV, so I made coffee and dug in. I stayed there the whole week, including two replays of the funeral, until they were down to interviewing the jeweler who made the ring. I'm now waiting for Barbara Walters to interview the flagpole and ask it, "If you were an English flower, what kind would you be?"

The coverage mesmerized me because it illustrated everything I've been writing about in this space for the last six years: feminization, democratization, emotions run amok, rhetorical chaos, litter as love, familiarity as contempt, vulnerable role models, passive heroes, mass empathy, gimp chic—I felt as if I were leafing through back issues of *NR*. If Diana's life passed before her eyes last week, so did mine.

My saturation viewing helped me make a vital decision. For some time I had been thinking of emigrating to England to bring my nationality in line with my blood, but I have now abandoned the idea. There is no England, just this demi-realm, this scepter'd loony bin set in a sea of rotting flora, this U.K. of Utter Kitsch where the crud de la crud build teddybear temples to a gilded hysteric who was nothing more than Judy Garland with a title. If I must live in a country where people who once tipped their hats now tip the scales, I might as well stay home and save myself the trouble of learning to look right instead of left to avoid an oncoming hug. My hyphen, right or wrong.

So much for sharing my innermost self-doubts. Now to my predictions.

I knew Diana's burial site was a mistake when I read what one Mrs. Irene Randall, interviewed as she pushed her disabled daughter in a wheelchair, told a reporter: "I don't like the idea of her being alone on that island." In 1950, four Scottish students stole the 450-pound Stone of Scone from under the Coronation chair in Westminster Abbey, took it back to Scotland, and kept it for four months. Count the graverobbers in Dickens.

Diana often pulled people up in mid-curtsy, so we can expect an official announcement soon that obeisance is "optional." In democracies that means you don't dare do it.

Titles will be downplayed, something already underway to judge from the crowds of women who imperiously summoned "William, William! to their sides and offered advice to "Charles, Charles!" First to go probably will be "the Honourable" for children of hereditary peers of the lower degree (e.g., the Hon. Nancy Mitford, daughter of a baron). Next to be shorn will be younger sons of dukes and marquesses (Lord Randolph Churchill, Lord Alfred Douglas). And so on and so forth—Tony Blair's version of Bill Clinton's creeping health care: start with the kids.

I also think Blair will try to put in place changes for the next reign modeled on the Bourbon restoration. As a sop to republicans, Louis XVIII, Charles X, and Louis-Philippe were all called "King of the French" instead of "King of France. Blair no doubt prefers "King of the British People."

We can be sure that Diana would champion all of these innovations, both from her stated wish to modernize the monarchy and her demonstrated subconscious wish to destroy it. They will be her legacy in death, but what would have been her legacy in life? Suppose she had lived to old age?

ONE commentator cast her as Elizabeth of Austria, estranged from Franz Josef, wandering the world but returning from time to time to brighten her stodgy husband's life. True, Elizabeth was obsessed with staying slim, ate sand for colonic cleansing, and was attacked by an anarchist while exercising. But she was also an intellectual who traveled with a Greek tutor, a sexual iceberg, and a Wittlesbach, a family too far gone into making brain waves to produce a mere neurotic.

Time's Roger Rosenblatt foresaw a future Diana basking in serenity, "the King's mother . . . the hair whiter, the skin a bit more lined," but it is impossible to visualize her aging gracefully. If you think the funeral coverage was excessive, imagine forty years of tummy tucks, skin peelings, the first face lift ("The New Di!"), the first nervous breakdown, the menopausal spiritual trek to Tibet ("At last I've found peace"), the second face lift, the "Hairdresser Plot," two more nervous breakdowns, the lawsuit over the third face lift, the disappearance from the Swiss sanitarium, and the amnesia attack ("I adore Spokane").

I foresaw her marrying Dodi Fayed ("At last I've found true love") and producing a son. Women and their he-hen accomplices would get so caught up in tremulous analyses of What This Baby Means that they would miss the one thing it actually did mean: a pretender to the throne. Trouble for the monarchy, yes, but a dream come true for the London bag lady who told CNN that she came to Diana's funeral because "I just want a bit of 'istory."

'Ere it is, ducks: Bonnie Prince Mohammed.

October 13, 1997

T HE other day a woman I ran into at the post office asked me to stop by her apartment and autograph a book. She was neither friend nor acquaintance, just someone I knew to speak to, but by the time her "few minutes" had stretched into the hour of chaos that it became, she had worked her way up to Nemesis.

We walked over to her convenient downtown building that I had often thought of moving to and now can't. On the day in question, however, I was eager to see whether the rooms were as big as people said.

I never saw the rooms. It was impossible to get a feel for the place because her apartment was in a state of cyclonic chaos. She was a yuppie careerist who lived alone, not a beset mom, but the living room looked as if someone had forgotten to child-proof it. The end tables were cluttered with coffee cups and empty Coke cans. The coffee table was strewn with unopened junk mail, old newspapers, and a skein of tangled knitting wool that looked like a hair ball from a giant mutant cat. There was no place to sit; the sofa was taken up by a picture frame, an open tool box spilling out loose nails, and dry cleaning still in plastic bags. There were two armchairs but one contained a boom box with a broken antenna and the other a cardboard box full of withered potted plants, their leaves covered with dust.

She gave a merry laugh. "I won't apologize for the mess because I know writers understand." Here she threw her arms up in the air in the Unshackled Slave pose and sang out, "Creativity!"

She started looking for my book but couldn't find it. While she searched I stood there looking at the floor. It was littered with crumpled cellophane wrappers, empty envelopes, cards with empty plastic domes that had contained bobby pins or cosmetics, and a couple of yellow GE light-bulb sleeves with nothing in them. Evidently whenever she opened something she just tossed the wrapping on the floor.

"Oh, where is that book?" she wailed. "Would you mind helping me look for it? It'll jump right out at you."

Fool that I am, I looked in the bookcase but of course it wasn't there. "Try the bedroom," she called from inside the hall closet. I did. The bed looked like the mounds of Nineveh before the archaeologists arrived, heaped with bulging laundry bags, a cordless telephone, a TV remote, loose CDs, a CD player, a hair dryer, and six weeks' worth of TV schedules. Clothes were flung everywhere: over the top of the closet door, across the lampshades, and, of course, on the floor. The crowning irony was her vanity table, a cluster of gummy bottles in whose encrusted midst sat that quaint tribute to Victorian fastidiousness known as a "hair receiver."

My book finally turned up under a sack of plant food in the foyer, bringing forth an "Oh, no wonder!" from my hostess. I found it wondrous myself. Desperate to leave, I reached into my purse for a pen before she could start looking for one and signed the autograph, but I was not free yet.

"Listen, I'm going to drive you home. I insist."

That's when I saw the ultimate detritus. The back seat of her car and most of the floor was full of labels from canned food. No cans, just labels, dozens and dozens of them in a spreading heap. "I save them for my group," she explained. "We're making food maps of the world—we cut out Mexico from a chili label, Germany from a sauerkraut label, and so on. We're distributing them to the schools." I didn't ask what kind of group; I could imagine.

As we turned a corner she slowed down and pointed with pride. "Look, there's my spot." Seeing my bemused look, she pulled over to the curb beside a sign that said ADOPT-A-SPOT. "It's my group's," she said. "We take turns making sure it's not littered. Last week I caught a man throwing away a cigarette pack and made him pick it up. Cigarettes! Yuk! Dirty, filthy, disgusting! Fwooey!"

She was making me crave. I hadn't had a cigarette since the one I smoked outside the post office before I went inside and met Typhoid Mary.

She let me out in front of my building. As I dragged myself up the stairs there was a crinkly sensation on the seat of my pants. I reached around and peeled off a can label that said, inaccurately, NO FAT. Opening the door, I looked around with relief and satisfaction. My little home, neat as a pin.

T HE point of this story is not that I'm a fussy old maid. You already
know that. The interesting thing here is what my contretemps says
about America.

Robert Fulghum, author of *All I Really Need to Know I Learned in
Kindergarten* and other infantile credos, writes that people without magne-
tized messages all over their fridge doors are unfeeling. "Lighten up," he
advises. "Get your stuff up there. Disorder is love."

The lovable slob is a fixture in American popular culture. Neil Simon
gave us Oscar Madison in *The Odd Couple* and Betty MacDonald gave us Ma
Kettle in *The Egg and I*. But the slob alone is obnoxious. To be lovable he
needs to play against his opposite number, the neat neurotic. Oscar's foil is
peevish, honking Felix Unger who alienates his poker club when he washes
the cards with ammonia; Ma Kettle's is the tight-lipped, disapproving Birdie
Hicks, who scrubs out her henhouse with so much lye that she kills her hens
while the Kettle hens roost in the parlor and flourish.

Americans have a neurotic need not to be neurotic. The lovable slob scenario is a winner because it shows bad things happening to uptight people.
The thing to be is a slob, and if you don't have a neatnik foil to make you look
lovable you can Adopt a Spot and be your own Felix often enough to deflect
criticism.

Then you can live amid disordered piles of love, great gobs of feeling,
and tumbling heaps of emotion in an apartment from Hell that is a microcosm
of America—or now, a corner of a foreign field that is forever England.

October 27, 1997

I TRIED to watch the Promise Keepers Washington writhe-in with an
open mind, but I didn't last long. Barely an hour into it, my various reactions settled into the narrow end of my mental funnel and took on a unified familiar shape, until I saw not 700,000 men but one man. The man every
Southerner knows, the man no Southerner can avoid, especially in August
when the Revival comes to town.

In short I saw Earl, who just got Saved.

Earl gets Saved every August and falls from grace sometime in
November in the male-bonding excesses of football or the autumnal batch of
hard cider that starts him drinking again, but in the meantime he is everyone's
cross to bear, starting with his wife.

You can spot Earl on sight because the first thing he does after he gets
Saved is get cleaned up. Between his new haircut and his lethally close

straight-razor shave he's a red, scraped, pulpy mass from the neck up. Watching him shave, hands still shaking, is his wife's first endurance test. Normally he uses a throwaway Bic but for his August tonsorial nothing but his granddaddy's razor will do, and since it's a Southern razor, there's a long story behind it. This Earl recites in masochistic detail while he shaves: how Alvin Lee used it to cut Billy Lee "to ribbons" in a fight and then accidentally fell on it and bled to death; how Uncle Clay Lee used it to slit his own throat when the burden of his sins grew too heavy; and how Granddaddy got it back from the sheriff and used it to mark his place in the Good Book as a reminder to go and chase nooky no more.

The second endurance test awaiting Earl's wife is his fervent pledges of deathless fidelity: "I'll love you till the ocean wears rubber pants to keep its bottom dry" is about par. Nor are strangers exempt. Stand next to him in the Piggly-Wiggly line—inevitable, since he has volunteered to do the grocery shopping—and he will point to the six-pack of Bud in your basket and say, "I usta drink that stuff before the Lord stopped me. I tell you, I was so worthless they shoulda stood me up against the wall and shot me. No good! I tell you, I was the no-goodest sinner you ever did see till I went to the altar and turned myself in to Jesus, and He said to me, He said . . ."

Analyzing the psychological effects of Revivalism in the small Southern town where she spent her life, Lillian Smith wrote: "I cannot remember one time when the banker or millowner or principal of the school, or cotton broker or politician went to the altar. They were always among the Saved. Perhaps it is as well—for one little penitent journey might have caused a run on the bank or a cultural panic."

Earl's penitent journey has a similar erosive effect on his wife. Listening to his non-stop self-abasement, she begins to wonder: what has he done that she hasn't already caught him doing? What might he do that she hasn't yet suspected him of? Can it be that she has underestimated his capacity for ruinous mayhem? A terrible tension is born: when will Earl crack?

She can't, of course, acknowledge these dark thoughts because she must keep up a happy front as the wife of a Saved man, but she would be happier if he were not quite so Saved. She misses grocery-shopping, and she would just as soon put the dishes away herself instead of finding the turkey platter sitting on top of a tea cup. Truth be told, she agrees with the women in *A Tree Grows in Brooklyn* who said the ideal husband was a fireman because: "He made good money and wasn't home much."

The tension snaps when she goes to the bathroom in the middle of the night. Used to Earl leaving the seat up, she automatically reached back and lowered it without looking, but this time the newly solicitous Earl had put it back down, and she, half-asleep, realized too late that what she had lowered and sat down on was the lid.

When he woke up and found her mopping the bathroom floor he offered to do it for her, but she screamed at him. Overcome by a powerful thirst, he tore up the kitchen looking for his booze until he remembered that he had poured it all down the sink the day he got Saved. There was nothing in the house to drink except the vanilla extract he had bought at the Piggly-Wiggly. He was on the last bottle and yelling something about nooky when the sheriff arrived.

A LL right, so I'm a cynic. That's better than being a desperate idealist like most of my fellow conservative columnists, who let themselves be persuaded that PK's gospel according to the T-shirt signaled the ultimate victory for family values. When will we learn that religion does not a conservative make, nor atheism a liberal? Like all people driven by emotion, PK could be swung like a lariat; the Right is in trouble if we think that 700,000 weeping men is good news in an era that is already close to rule by hysteria. Whatever happened to our traditional distrust of the mob?

I also reject the view put forth by several gleeful conservative pundits that PK dealt a fatal blow to radical feminism. After three decades of male bashing, what is there to gloat about in the spectacle of 700,000 men curdling with guilt and begging for forgiveness? It sounds like successful brainwashing to me.

Then there is PK's apples-and-oranges comparison of marital problems and racism. They vow to help their wives, spend time with the kids—and end racism? We're headed for an all-purpose, automatic agenda. *The Home Accessories Catalogue*: "Everything you need for kitchen, bath, and ending racism." "Subscribe to *The Model Airplane* and learn to build miniature replicas, exchange ideas with other hobbyists, and end racism." Another triumph for Bill Gates: "Windows '95 made your life easier with the Start key. Now Microsoft introduces the Stop Racism key." On and on it will go, until the humble vacation postcard reads: "The scenery is beautiful, wish you were here to help me end racism."

November 10, 1997

E XCEPT when insanity or America intervenes, there is no such thing as an illogical mind. The mind is by definition logical, as Socrates demonstrated when he took an illiterate slave boy and led him through the solution of a complex mathematical problem by asking him the proper questions in the proper sequence.

What a glorious moment it must have been for those present, one of those clean, sharp times when cold comfort is the best comfort of all. If I could travel back into the past and pick one historical event to witness first-hand, I would skip the legendary battles and boudoir intrigues for a front-row seat at this triumph of the reasoning process.

Socrates would have an even more edifying time-capsule experience if he and his slave boy could be fast-forwarded to our era to re-enact the demonstration for us.

He would discover that to Americans the point of it all is to make the slave boy "feel good about himself." Everyone keeps saying this even though it conflicts with another incessant chant, "It doesn't take a rocket scientist," a favorite of television blondes who utter it in tones of self-satisfied relief as they interview Socrates on the morning shows.

The home schoolers ask him for tips on how to do-it-yourself. The Bell Curvers insist on giving the slave boy an IQ test. The geneticists insist that he isn't really a slave boy. A well-shod Walter Coppage proclaims "Socrates never walked here" as he drags a barefoot kid through a Haitian open sewer in a new sponsorship ad. Child-abuse watchdogs try to put the slave boy in foster care, the American Psychological Association discovers Sudden Attention Concentration Disorder, and *The Weekly Standard* does "The Slave-Boy Crack-Up."

My interest in Socrates' demonstration of logic was triggered by a letter I received from a young man who described himself as a libertarian-conservative, Christian homosexual (he dislikes "gay" because it refers to a left-wing political agenda). That he is intelligent and well-educated is indisputable; his letter is a model of syntax, spelling, punctuation, and vocabulary, but his reasoning is something else.

Taking issue with my column against same-sex marriage, he offered the following thoughts:

1. The argument that children are the primary purpose of marriage is negated by the fact that not all heterosexual couples intend to have children, yet are permitted to marry anyway, and to remain married despite their childlessness.

2. The argument that nothing prevents homosexuals from living together also applies to heterosexuals, so why do the latter need to marry?

3. How could homosexuals devalue marriage more than, say, Elizabeth Taylor?

4. Since marriage is an honorable estate instituted by God, and since God created us heterosexual and homosexual, He cannot have intended His blessing to be bestowed on some of His creatures and withheld from others.

5. The argument that homosexuals will marry solely to collect spousal benefits is negated by the age-old heterosexual custom of marrying for money. "Keep in mind that, if we are going to prohibit homosexual marriages of convenience, logic obliges us to impose the same restriction on heterosexual marriages."

6. "Since homosexual marriage neither harms the rights of others nor does anything to diminish the public good, there is no compelling interest to forbid it."

Fuzzy thinking yields easily to classic reasoning. Points one, two, and five are each a *reductio ad absurdum*; or, to paraphrase the Vietnam general, "We had to destroy marriage to save it for homosexuals." Point three is an *argumentum ad verecundiam*, "to the shameful," an argument based on an unworthy authority or example—poor old Liz, who at least had three children along the way. Point four brings God into the reasoning process, thereby clouding the distinction between faith and knowledge made so abundantly clear in the old adage, "A woman knows it's her child; a man can only have faith that it's his." And point six is a *petitio principii*, "begging the question," an argument that asks us to accept the premise so that we can agree with the conclusion.

A LL well and good, but today's single-issue logicians are hostile to classic reasoning. The clean, sharp feeling of cold comfort cuts no ice with them if it threatens to blow away their perceived "rights," and so, in the interest of greater security, they have invented American reasoning.

American reasoning arises from a molten pit of gluey psychodramas and steaming monomanias surging like blisters on the surface of cooked cereal. It invariably leads to the kind of disjointed, who-struck-John arguments heard on talk shows. Take, for example, the debate at my last public appearance. The question was why every society, even Nazi Germany, has been more tolerant of lesbianism than of male homosexuality.

"The lesbian sex drive has no effect on society," I said. "A woman may be exclusively attracted to women and repelled by men, but she can still reproduce the species. All she has to do to conceive is be present, but if a man feels no desire for the female, conception won't occur and the race will die out."

That's an *argumentum ad equinam* but horse sense has no place in American reasoning. I was attacked.

"You're saying women are passive!"

"You're emphasizing our differences instead of the ways we're alike."

"Do you want to force lesbians to bear children?"

The best was the woman who kept asking ominously, "Suppose you substituted the word 'black' . . . ?" I wish I could have heard the rest of her pinch-hitting strategy but she was drowned out in the uproar. How my remarks about the lesbian sex drive could be transferred to blacks is one of the mysteries of the universe, but the *argumentum ad africanum* is such a cornerstone of American reasoning that as soon as she heard the word "race," out it came.

November 24, 1997

B RACE yourselves, this is an upbeat column. The Virginia gubernatorial election and the reaction to the verdict in the "Au Pair Murder Trial" put a song in my heart.

As you know, our new Republican governor-elect, James S. Gilmore III, won a thunderous victory with a single issue: his promise to abolish the "car tax," an annual levy based on the assessed value of cars and trucks.

I doubt Gilmore can do it, but that's not the point. What has my toes curling is the dud Bill Clinton fired when, campaigning for the Democrat candidate, he warned that school budgets would suffer without the car-tax money: "This really is a question about whether Virginians will be selfish in the moment or selfless for their children and the future."

Weepy, the eighth dwarf, made a boo-boo. Instead of generating guilt he infuriated people. Letters columns filled up with vituperative rejoinders ("How dare he?") and talk radio turned into one big sputter of rage. For once, no one melted at the sacred word "children."

The same week, the second-degree murder conviction of au pair Louise Woodward triggered a spontaneous outpouring of support for her, along with demands that the verdict be dismissed and her sentence reduced to time served. As I write, the judge has not yet ruled on the requests, but again, that's not the point. What energizes me here is the spectacle of child-worshiping Americans rallying behind an English girl accused of infanticide. YESSS!

I see a light at the end of our tunnel vision. Americans are beginning to understand that adults count, too.

How they lost sight of this fact in the first place is not hard to fathom. A glance through my files makes it abundantly clear.

Headlines: STARVATION IN N. KOREA; REPORTS OF CHILDREN DYING.

Mary McGrory on Waco: "Nobody except their families would much care about the fiery deaths of the cultists if it weren't for the children."

Firefighter Randy Woods of the Oklahoma bombing: "Grown-ups, you know, they deserve a lot of the stuff they get. But why the children? What did the children ever do to anybody?"

It so happens that children are the source of the blanket of fear that now hangs over the head of every American adult.

Ann Landers on child sexual abuse: "I urge all who have a strong suspicion to act on it. You will have performed a humanitarian service."

The ubiquitous public-service announcement: "Concerned persons can report abuse anonymously. If they give their names, confidentiality is guaranteed by law."

The abuse witchhunt has given children power over adults to a degree never before seen in any society. False accusations are always blamed on overzealous social workers or prosecutors who supposedly planted the idea in the children's minds and coached them through their stories, but to believe that this is always the case is to spurn what W. C. Fields and I have worked so hard to establish.

The Sinless Child ranks with the Noble Savage as a repository of cracked idealism. Unable to think in the intellectual sense, children twitch and flicker in response to the stimuli of the moment like nocturnal creatures on the Discovery Channel, sensing with unerring instinct the perfect moment to strike.

They have a knack for locating adults' soft spots and a sense of timing that can set up an embarrassing moment to the millisecond. The evident nervousness parents exhibit when they bring adult strangers home suggests that the words "Oh, you mustn't say that!" have been spoken before, probably not for the last time. It is a known fact, always denied, that handicapped people, people with scars, homely people, and bald men don't like to be around children because the little fartlings have a mean streak wide enough to drive a truck through.

Since child abuse became the bee in every bonnet, children have caught on to its usefulness as the fork in every tongue. Taught in "awareness" lectures how to report anyone who so much as looks at them crooked, they know they have adults in the palms of their grubby little hands.

Adults also know it, which is why they are nervous wrecks. Teachers, camp counselors, day-care workers, sports coaches to whom the pat on the backside is second nature are all scared to death. So even are kindly souls who actually love children and enjoy making friends with them, like the editor of my local paper whose column about a misinterpreted action concluded: "It is sad that I, as well as other men I know, have stopped smiling at children in supermarkets."

Others have stopped frowning and yelling. The curmudgeonly retirees who used to chase children away from their flower beds and demand that the paper boy hit the porch now don't dare open their mouths, knowing that where revenge once was limited to overturned ashcans, it might now be a charge of child abuse.

W HAT we fear, we hate. I don't claim that Americans have risen to my level of child-hatred—many are called, few are chosen—but signs indicate that they are fed up enough to admit that all it takes is one child to raze a village.

That Bill Clinton's trick of using the little battering rams for political purposes blew up in his face in Virginia suggests that the Diaper Gap finally may be closing. To take advantage of this, Republicans should stop protesting, as Orrin Hatch did, that the GOP "does not hate children." They should ignore the "talking points" their consultants give them, such as using "children" in every other sentence, and they should take Robert Novak's advice to "find a national application of the no-car-tax principle."

I suggest abolishing taxes on savings interest. If they stand fast in the face of dire predictions about its impact on "children's programs," they may find that when Americans have a choice between hostages to fortune and fortune, they'll choose fortune.

December 8, 1997

Y OU see before you, as it were, a woman who has yielded to the forces of change. It rarely happens but there are some things we just can't fight, so I gave up and moved the red flag in my quotations notebook.

This is the little plastic gizmo I use to mark my all-time favorite idiotic statement by a brain-dead American leader, to help me find it fast amid the cluster of slightly less idiotic statements by American leaders still capable of registering an occasional blip on the EEG machine. One must discriminate in this life.

The red flag had been on the same page for 28 years. I remember the day in 1969 that I put it there. Richard Nixon had just had his first Supreme Court nominee, Clement F. Haynsworth, shot down. He named another, G. Harrold Carswell, but the flak started again. Citing the many times Judge Carswell's decisions had been reversed on appeal, the Democrats called him a "legal mediocrity."

Into the breach rode Nebraska's Sen. Roman L. Hruska, who proved that he had been shortchanged of more than a vowel when he said in defense of Carswell: "Even if he were mediocre, there are a lot of mediocre judges and people and lawyers. Aren't they entitled to a little representation and a little chance? We can't have all Brandeises and Cardozos and Frankfurters and stuff like that. I doubt we can. I doubt we want to."

Compared to today, this could be said to represent a Golden Age of American public discourse. At least he got the subjunctive right, though that may have been an accident, but except for the descent into "stuff" it wasn't all that bad; his sentences parsed, he did not ramble or equivocate, and his thumping anti-intellectualism did not really offend most Americans. His only mistake was voicing what oft was thought but ne'er so baldly expressed.

But enough of nostalgic longing for Hruska of the silver tongue. It's 1997 now and my little red flag has passed to Sara Lister, the latest fallen woman in Army Secretary Togo West's Department of Ill Repute, who said: "The Marine Corps is—you know, they have all these checkerboard fancy uniforms and stuff. But the Army is sort of muddy boots on the ground."

I'm waiting for the translation. I looked at my checkerboard and I looked at a picture of a Marine in dress blues but I still don't get it. Did she mean that both feature two colors? Did she mean that the Marines are squares? Hardly, since she also said: "I think the Army is much more connected to society than the Marines are. The Marines are extremists. Wherever you have extremists, you've got the risk of total disconnection from society, and that's a little dangerous."

Why did she pull back to "a little" dangerous after saying "extremists" and "total"? Probably for the same reason she tossed "sort of" in front of the muddy boots. Public statements are such minefields nowadays that speakers sprinkle their sentences with these adverbial sweetmeats to keep from sounding mean, but in fact they sound like coy zealots in the manner of Newt Gingrich, who called the Rush Limbaugh show and said of Bill Kristol: "I've concluded that he thinks he has to make news by pandering to the liberals every week and has become sort of the most destructive element on the right."

As a long-time collector of idiotic statements I've noticed that where race once inspired the most sublime idiocies, today's Best Of are inspired by women in the military. They are also much easier to find. Key phrases fairly leap off the page: "pregnant sailors . . . Army called too aggressive . . . lighter and less dangerous hand grenades . . . stepladders added to obstacle courses . . . a training program to stamp out profanity at Fort Hood . . . the possibility of single mothers taking babies to war . . ."

These are statements to read through spread fingers, the way jurors look at autopsy photos. Morning papers are especially dangerous because sudden movements can make you spill hot coffee in your lap.

Maj. Cindy Sito, Army spokesman in Haiti, where our male and female soldiers sleep in the same tent: "In my opinion, it's easier to run a unit if you're able to reach out and touch everybody."

Capt. Rosemary Mariner, naval aviator: "No amount of nostalgia over manly warriors protecting fair maidens erases the fact that this country cannot go to war without women on the front lines."

The Rand Corporation report on how female sailors improve life at sea: "We used to hear stories of men who used to be quite malodorous due to infrequent bathing; now their male peers appreciate that such men seem to take better care of their hygiene when working in the presence of women."

Annapolis man to James Webb: "I like women at the Academy. They've brought a measure of refinement to the place."

Somebody else said the best way to stop sexual harassment is to create an incest taboo between male and female troops. I can't find the clipping so I can't give you chapter and verse, but I remember it only too well because of the coffee blister.

W HAT kind of statements are issuing from fearless Republicans on the pro-military side? Most of them sound like Dan Coats, President Pro Temporizer of the Senate: "Whether or not it's better to have a female drill instructor, as the Marine Corps does, work in the initial training phase with women, and males with males, and then integrate those into the services, I think it's something worth exploring."

And explore he will, on a Magellanesque scale. "I am ready to talk to the Secretary of Defense, to talk to military leaders, to continue to visit training units and others around the world," he vowed, bloviating a sailwind for himself rather than face down Pentagon feminists who are submitting our military men to the kind of surgery performed by the Magellan of the famous exam paper, who, said its schoolboy author, "circumcised the globe with his clipper."

December 22, 1997

D EAR Gentle Readers: It's time for my Christmas letter. I just read all about how to write one in a family-holidays supplement that came in the newspaper. The key to success, it said, is to imagine an embroidery sampler and strive for the same upbeat tone. Okey-dokey, here we go: YOU CAN ALWAYS FIND SOMETHING TO COMPLAIN ABOUT IF YOU BUT TRY.

As always I spent the year yelling "Kill! Kill!" at TV and radio newscasts. What irritates me the most is the stun-gun metaphor. First introduced by Dan Rather in 1989 when he opened his story on the collapse of East Germany with "The Berlin Wall is still standing, but it doesn't stand for much," the stun-gun metaphor is designed to capture the fickle American attention span by making the audience wonder if they heard it right, and if so, what the hell does it mean?

So many newscasters have copied Rather's disjointed insouciance that we now hear dozens of jarring leads every day. An organ-transplant story kicks off with: "A girl who died is still living." Is a jury going to see a vital piece of evidence? If you put it that way it will make sense and no one will listen. To get everyone's undivided attention, start with "The Unabomber's cabin is on the move." If your next story is about a cat lady who got evicted, begin by saying "Moving is something Mrs. Mabel Pfunknagel is not about to do" before mentioning the 75 cats, the health-department citation, and the city in which the stand-off is taking place. Then you can segue into the latest story about John Berendt's book on Savannah, which contains people even odder than Mrs. Pfunknagel. This is how the networks promote "connectedness"—meaning that we are all links in a common chain of humanity going nowhere except mad from listening to news about houses with feet.

I did a print-division "Kill! Kill!" on reading Kelly Flinn's book excerpt in *Newsweek*. After smashing all her framed awards, her framed Air Force Academy diploma, and framed pictures of all the planes she flew, she says, "I curled up in a fetal position, holding a stuffed elephant . . ." The next day, "The house was still full of glass, and I was still holding my elephant."

What is it with the New Woman and stuffed animals? Check out feature-story photos of teenage girls in their rooms, college girls in dorms, and Gen-X careerists in their apartments and there is always at least one teddy bear in sight, more often whole slews of them lined up on the bed. To my generation of women, who collected transparent black negligees, this regressive mountain of button-eyed fur is incomprehensible. The Kelly Flinns of the Nineties might have hyperactive sex lives but there isn't a femme fatale among them. What do they do with their teddy bears during assignations? Hide them before he comes over? Wait and let him help move them? Since the New Woman usually sleeps with the New Man, maybe they all pile in together in one big vulnerable heap. The subject cries out for a *Cosmopolitan* article: "Should You Tell Him About Pooky?"

Now to my Gentle Reader Awards. The prize for Most Interesting Letter of 1997 goes to a retired merchant seaman who explained how all the men on the *Titanic* might have been saved. Permitting each man to wear a life jacket was, he wrote, a waste of life jackets. If Captain Smith had been as calm and British as legend claims, he would have ordered the crew to construct rafts from life jackets and oars, something taught in basic seamanship that all of the crew would have known how to do, and that would have taken them only minutes. I had never heard of this before but the common sense of it overwhelmed me.

The prize for Nastiest Letter of 1997 goes to the goodwife who took umbrage at my anti-Promise Keepers column. Her letter opened with "Dear Citified Person" and consisted of two pages of questions such as "Have you ever milked a cow? Slopped hogs? Helped with the butchering? Cleaned out a barnyard?"

Of course not. I don't know any Episcopalian who has. Her letter had less to do with Promise Keepers than with cramming conservatism into the narrow end of a populist funnel, a homey task helped along by Republican politicians who run around in workshirts and fall into public ecstasies over pickup trucks. But not all politicians cater to the Common Man. When Randolph Churchill, son of Sir Winston, ran for Parliament, he was heckled by a farmer who took the same tack as my correspondent. "How many toes has a pig?" challenged the farmer. Whereupon Randolph shot back: "Take off your bloody boots and count!"

The Craziest Letter of 1997 was not a letter but a brochure from E.T.H.I.C., "End the Horror of Infant Circumcision." I read it in a typical nightowl interlude at 3 A.M. after washing my hair. All was calm until I came to the statement that circumcision robs men "of what would, if left alone, eventually become approximately 15 square inches of erogenous and protective tissue."

Math and I don't mix. I learned square footage in school, but only long enough to pass the exam, after which it went completely out of my head. Fifteen inches? No, no, it couldn't be, but what was a square inch? I was so transfixed by mental pictures of a Scotsman's sporran that I couldn't think.

Suddenly I remembered that Home Depot had run a tile-sale ad with a measuring chart in the paper that week. My papers were in the recycling box out at the curb, but no matter. Unmindful of the hour, unmindful that I was wearing half of an old pair of pantyhose as a stocking cap to batten down my cowlicks, I crept downstairs and into the night.

After much rummaging I finally found the ad and crept back inside, noiselessly so as not to disturb my neighbors. Unknown to me, however, the morning-paper courier had slipped in behind me and was coming down the stairs as I tiptoed in.

"Jesus!" he gasped, flattening against the wall.

Black negligees or stocking caps, I still get a rise out of men.

December 31, 1997

1998

A CARDINAL rule of writing is never interrupt yourself to explain something. If you must bring up an obscure topic, drop informative hints about it as you go along so that you don't end up with the entire explanation all in one place. This keeps you from skidding to a stop and sounding teacherish. Otherwise it's better to omit the obscure topic altogether, or as mothers might put it: If you can't say it interestingly, don't say it at all.

The American way of history turns this rule into a crapshoot, as I discovered recently when I reviewed a biography of John Quincy Adams. A full explanation of what happened would make me sound teacherish, so I'll just quote the note I faxed to the editor:

"Re: JQA and *Amistad*.

"I wrote this review before the publicity about the movie hit TV. I didn't want to go off on a tangent about what was then a little-known slave mutiny, so I decided to leave it out, but now it's all over the tube. If there's still time, stick in a sentence about it so they won't think I live in the Gobi Desert."

I would love nothing better than to live in the Gobi Desert provided the Mongolians stayed snubbed. I can see my yurt now, and myself curled up in a yak skin, reading my new seven-volume, unabridged *Decline and Fall of the Roman Empire*. I haven't even started it yet, but reading every word of Gibbon is my life's ambition because I love history, but as usual I'm in the wrong country.

Americans hate history. "You're history!" screamed the girl as she threw her engagement ring in her fiancé's face. "That's ancient history!" snarled the ad director to the un-hip copywriter. An exception to our aversion might be "social history," the offshoot discipline concerned with everyday life. It's useful during nostalgia trips when we yearn for the decade du jour, usually the Fifties, or during periodic offbeat fetishes like the recent Jane Austen revival, when we develop an intense curiosity about dead customs, usually female virtue. Otherwise we would rather keep on thinking about tomorrow and consign history to the dust bin of history.

But we can't. It is a fact universally unacknowledged that there won't be any tomorrow unless we think constantly about history in terms of its new definition: material for commemorative minutes for Black History Month.

Our age of bigger and better apologies is unsuited to the traditional methodology of history. The meticulous sifting and weighing practiced by Gibbon is much too slow for people in the throes of multicultural panic, so we take our history like those freshmen who are so desperate for acceptance by a frat that they drink a whole quart of whisky all at once and then drop dead.

Our discovery of the voyage of the *Amistad* is typical. In the sea lanes of the American publicity machine you can sail from total ignorance to total saturation in about two weeks. Every slavery movie is launched full speed ahead and proceeds so steady on course that the promotion for one movie is interchangeable with any other.

First we get the interviews with the forthcoming movie's producer or director, who explains how he stumbled upon an obscure historical incident that he had never heard of but which immediately began to obsess him. "I felt wrung out and, yes, haunted." Soon we will all know the feeling well.

Next come the interviews with the cast, who look studiously grim—or if white, studiously wracked—as they describe how they felt during the filming. "It left me depressed and, yes, angry" . . . "I felt numb and, yes, sick." After the last of the clips has been shown, we hear from the white psychologist from Berkeley who was invited on the show to analyze how depictions of whippings and massacres affect race relations. "Total honesty leads to mutual trust and, yes, oneness."

Thanks to all the film clips and spot ads, the *Amistad* was soon ubiquitous and, yes, a household name. Once the movie finally opened we had to endure the "dialogue," America's two-ish name for a cast of thousands all sounding off at once on op-ed pages, Sunday shows, and hastily called forums. Meanwhile, in Akron, Bill Clinton was dialoguing with Abigail Thernstrom about Colin Powell, our own Scipio Africanus, adding a little touch of Gibbon in the night.

T HE crisis in slave-movie dialogues comes when whites think they have made amends, only to learn that blacks are offended and, yes, angry. Take the dialogue between *Time*'s Richard Schickel and the *Washington Post*'s Courtland Milloy. In Schickel's rave review of *Amistad*, he wrote that showing the slave leader Cinqué with "the wild rolling eye of what might be a desperate and panicked animal" captured the dehumanization of slavery.

An infuriated Milloy countered that Spielberg used the same crazed-eye shot for the T-Rex in *Jurassic Park*, and suggested that he equates black men with bloodthirsty dinosaurs. Furthermore, "There are really no bad white people in the movie," which "is essentially about how two white guys . . . come to the rescue of some Africans bound for slavery," making *Amistad* merely "a tribute to the American justice system."

Then, suddenly, America changed boats. *Amistad* was sunk, as it were, by *Titanic*, the whitest event in history, and there's going to be hell to pay. The *Washington Post* has already shored up against the gathering tempest with a Style feature of remarkable desperation, "The Toast of the Titanic: Oral Tradition Carries On Legend of Lone African American," about a mythical black stoker named Shine (the *Post* writer interrupts herself to apologize for the name) whose fictitious shipboard heroics were recounted in raplike toasts drunk in Harlem in 1912.

Crowding out a black slave ship with a white luxury liner is bad enough, but naught will atone for the scene in which Kate Winslet climbs on the *Titanic*'s prow and poses as the timeless symbol of the Great White Goddess: a ship's figurehead. Après moi le dialogue.

January 26, 1998

I WISH it were 1959 again. Not for the creamy complexion and svelte figure I had then, but because it was the last year of my pre-Kennedy life, before I had ever heard of them.

Nobody I knew had ever heard of them. Old Joe's stormy prewar ambassadorship rang a faint bell with my parents but they didn't make the connection until the 1960 campaign. Ethnic Northerners remembered JFK with pride from the Veepstakes of 1956, but we were not, to put it mildly, ethnic Northerners. We didn't even know he was Irish; my English father thought of the name as Scottish thanks to an old British military march called "Sir Alexander Kennedy." As for my mother, she didn't even know about Boston. The first time she heard JFK's voice she said, "He's got guts to go into politics with a speech defect like that."

O Time, cease in your headlong flight, make me pre-Kennedy just for tonight! Those were the days. Golden days, before America got moving again. Palmy days, when the tough went back to bed when the going got tough. Halcyon days, when getting mad trumped getting even. Salad days, when no adult had more than 32 teeth. Bliss it was to be alive when Camelot meant Tennyson, compound meant syntax, tragedy meant Oedipus, and curse meant time-of-the-month.

Some will say the Roosevelts were just as bad, but I was around then, too, and I disagree. Unlike Joe Kennedy, FDR did not shove his children down our throats. On the contrary, he downplayed them, did little to grease their paths, and seemed unperturbed by the mounting evidence that they would not amount to much.

Americans subconsciously picked up on his detachment and reflected it in our own attitudes toward his children. We learned their upper-class nicknames and kept up with their traffic tickets, divorces, and madcap entrepreneurial schemes, but we did not idealize them. We never thought of them as a "dynasty," not even when Franklin Jr. won what turned out to be a single term in Congress, and the idea of one Roosevelt scion picking up the torch dropped by another would have inspired a sheaf of jokes with Elliott as the punch line (he used it as collateral to start the Dropped Torch Dude Ranch, etc.). As objects of obsession the Roosevelts were, as usual, not up to snuff, and we knew it.

It might be argued that some Kennedy-style push would have made winners of them, but this skirts the larger question of the assault the Kennedys mounted on America's accepted definition of greatness and achievement.

In his introduction to *The Education of Henry Adams*, James Truslow Adams wrote:

> By the time the line reached Henry, the accumulated weight of great abilities and great offices had become crushing in a democracy. In no other American family, and in few anywhere, have ability and service been so conspicuous generation after generation without a break. In an aristocracy such a family would have been given a title, and have become a continuing entity as a family in the political and social life of the country. In a democracy there could be no such scaffolding built. The members of each generation would have to stand or fall by their own abilities . . .

In other words, merit and merit alone is the American way of greatness. FDR accepted it when he let his children sink or swim, and we the public accepted it when we declined to make a fetish of them.

By contrast, Joe Kennedy rejected it and built a privileged scaffolding for his sons, instilling in them an appreciation for the ancient perquisites of primogeniture, *carte blanche, noblesse oblige, le roi le veult, l'état c'est moi,* and—the Kennedy favorite—*droit du seigneur.*

The privileged scaffolding is now occupied by the third generation, wearers of the Order of Celebrity, a media knighthood whose motto, "Famous for Being Famous," was painted over with "Public Service" as needed. Whenever a Kennedy 3 was hit by scandal, the claque industry trotted out the whole thundering herd of human-rights activists and makers of documentary "films" to prove that the torch was still being passed, but the strain was evident. Kennedy 3 was top-heavy with gilded losers; running a charity oil company and founding a university in Angola sounded like something Elliott Roosevelt would do. The claque needed a punchier explanation for our endless Kennedy worship, and Michael Kennedy gave them one on New Year's Eve.

THE explanation would intrigue James Truslow Adams, whose family had the opposite problem in later generations. Analyzing why America *stopped* worshiping Adamses, he wrote: "They had little respect for the mind or opinions of the common man. They always got their own light from their own guiding stars and not from the will-o'-the-wisps of the marsh of 'public opinion.'"

The Adamses thrived in an early America of limited suffrage when the remnants of Old World hierarchy were still in place, but as egalitarianism took root their aloof personalities, their introverted habits, and their general "differentness" sank them like a stone. "A certain failure had become noticeable by the time of Henry's father, [who] had not become President . . . the failure in adjustment to environment had begun."

Michael Kennedy's death made pundits think hard about environmental adjustment. *Newsweek's* Jonathan Alter was rendered breathless by the Kennedy genius for it. The clan is "a mirror of America," "a metaphor for the American Century"; they have an "uncanny connection to the times," each generation has "absorbed the Zeitgeist," and Michael's death is "entirely in context."

In context of what? "If judged by its tabloid throw-weight, the dynasty is alive and well and yielding the racy and heart-wrenching stories so in tune with the times."

It's come to this. We not only identify with a man who died doing what Daffy Duck did in a thousand cartoons, but we call it a tragedy and blame it on a curse.

Kennedys 'R' Us, Adamses 'R'nt.

February 9, 1998

I T'S deadline time and I'm winging it. Usually it takes me four days to do a column: two days to write it, one day to revise it, and one day to polish it. But there's no time for that now because I waited too long.

I should have started this column a week ago but I have been glued to the TV watching the Come Again Kid deny non-adultery in the wrong verb tense. My deadline is the same day as the State of the Union speech; there's no telling what will have happened (future perfect) by the time you read this, but I have to write *something* so I'll ask you to forego my usual carefully prepared food for thought and take (ink)potluck: a free-associative mélange of some of the things that went through my mind as I watched fate close in on Deep Croak.

. . . It is 1952. Now 16, I have lost my baby fat and gone from duckling to swan, and my mother, who normally pays no attention to anything except baseball and her hero, Sen. Joe McCarthy, is being uncharacteristically maternal. We are washing dishes when suddenly, out of the blue, she says:

"If a man ever asks you to do something funny to him, you tell him to go to hell, you hear?"

"What do you mean, 'something funny'?"

"Never mind, just promise me."

Mystified, I promised. The mystery deepened as she swung off on one of her patriotic tangents.

"That's why the French can't win a war without our help! It saps their strength! They're so busy doing something funny to each other that the Germans just walk right in!"

I got A's in history but I couldn't sort that one out. I tried my grandmother.

"What does it mean when a man asks a woman to do something funny to him?"

"Your grandfather was a perfect gentleman."

I might have known. It was her standard reply to all sex questions. Next I consulted my best girlfriend, who drew a blank.

"Maybe we could look it up in the dictionary?" she suggested hopefully."

"Oh, sure. If it isn't under 'something funny' we can try 'funny comma something.' "

She had an older married sister who had come through with several tidbits we couldn't pry out of our mothers, so we dropped by her place for an intelligence briefing, but this time she balked.

"You two don't need to know about such things. Just remember that men have a terrible name they call women who do something funny."

"What?" we chorused.

"I wouldn't repeat it."

. . . It is 1956. Now twenty, I finally figure out what Something Funny means from, of all things, a supplementary text my history professor put on reserve in the library.

Félix Faure, president of France 1895–1899, died during a visit from his mistress. Hearing her terrified screams, his aides broke down the door and found him seated on a sofa with the mistress kneeling in front of him, her long black hair clutched in his death-locked fingers. After freeing the hysterical woman, the aides put the fallen leader in bed with his hands folded over a crucifix, a scene immortalized by a newspaper drawing of the time that was reproduced in the reserve book under the title, "Death of Faure (Official Version)." My mother was right.

What strikes me about today's oral-sex psychodrama is where the kooky thinking is coming from. My generation of women had our rationalizations, but they were *ours*, not men's. The erotic contortionism we called "Everything But" made us the Keystone Kops of heavy petting, stripping gears and kicking holes in dashboards with high heels, but our dates not only put up with it, they respected us for being virgins because we had them convinced that nice girls never got in the back seat.

That kind of female power vanishes when men do the kooky thinking. The emerging theory that fellatio does not "count" as adultery or even constitute a sexual relationship proves that letting men get hold of rationalizations is like letting Wrong Way Corrigan get hold of aviation.

Whether or not Monica Lewinsky brings down the Clinton Presidency, she has certainly succeeded in weakening the "womyn" wall of political correctness. One commentator after another referred to her as a "young lady," a "girl," a "kid," and even, once or twice, a "child." Each time these diminutives emerged, Clinton seemed to get older and older.

Another point of linguistic interest was Lewinsky's taped statement, "I've lied all my life." Male commentators took it literally, but most media women made less of it. I daresay they were thinking, as I was, of the hyperbole of girl talk. You have to add mental italics—"I've *lied* all my *life*!"—to hear the giggle and the long disjointed story about nothing in particular that usually accompany statements of this sort.

Whether Clinton goes in disgrace or stays under a cloud will make little difference to serious lovers of language because either way we are in for it. Face it: no matter how many women have done something funny to Clinton, not one of them will ever be called a fellatrix, and it's a dead cert that "sexual addiction" counselors will do their tone-deaf best to give satyriasis a bad name.

I must admit that the tumult is expertly plotted. The best-loved novels always contain two very different women who play off each other: Scarlett and Melanie, Becky and Amelia, Anna and Kitty, the angel and the hussy, the blonde and the brunette, good sister/bad sister. Now we have Paula Jones with her signature line, "Ah jes' wanna git mah good name back," and Monica Lewinsky with "Schmucko"—Daisy May meets Marjorie Morningstar.

Now to spin one for my mother: I don't believe the "sophisticates" who keep telling pollsters that a President's sex life is his own business. It's merely a roundabout way of excepting themselves from the charge of puritanism regularly hurled at Americans by—the French.

February 23, 1998

THE Karla Faye Tucker case was a defeat for conservatives, the latest example of the many-splintered thing our movement has become and more proof that our ranks are heavy with people who either cannot or will not think.

On the clemency side was the Christian Right, who wanted to save her because she had found God. On the execution side were the Law 'n' Orders who wanted to kill her because they "believe in capital punishment" period-paragraph, and the populist yahoos who chanted "Use a pickax!" outside the death house. But this was only the official scorecard. To fully understand conservative thinking we must consult the Tacits, those fearless mainstream Republicans who never say what they think. Presented with a white woman on death row, the clemency Tacits wanted to save her because she was a woman but were afraid of being called sexists, while the execution Tacits wanted to kill her to prove they weren't racists.

We could have extracted a political benefit from the case if we had approached it not as a controversy with sides, but as a chess problem with moves: the clemency move or the execution move? My own views on capital punishment are nothing less than bloodthirsty, but as soon as I started thinking like a chess player everything changed.

The clemency move would have checkmated feminists with a double standard of death and handed conservatives a valuable fait accompli in the debate over women in combat. But the execution move checkmated conservatives with an equal right to die and handed feminists a government-sanctioned "body bag."

Unfortunately for Karla Faye Tucker, thinking like a chess player takes time and concentration, always at a premium in America and even scarcer than usual during the last week of her life. Had we not been so obsessed with Monicagate we could have concentrated on Karla Faye, but timing, as they say, is everything.

Ideally, an ax murderess should be a pillar of the church *before* the fact, like Lizzie Borden, but we can't have everything to our taste. On the matter of Karla Faye's religious conversion, I was of two minds. I was leery of her Born Againism purely on aesthetic grounds because I oppose the separation of church and stateliness. Unbelieving writers nearly always harbor this high-church tic. As my fellow agnostic, H. L. Mencken, put it: "One might easily imagine an intelligent man yielding himself to the voluptuous Roman lure but there is surely nothing to seduce him in Protestantism. . . . The news that a poet had been converted to Presbyterianism would be first-page stuff anywhere."

Faith, hope, and snobbery aside, I believe Karla Faye's conversion was sincere, in part because the Born Again stance is so exhausting that no one could fake it for very long. Remember, she was Saved in 1985 and spent 12 years witnessing, praising, and thumping, not to mention perfecting the Pat Robertson art of smiling, laughing, and talking all at the same time. "Protestantism," said Mencken, "converts the gentle and despairing Jesus into a YMCA secretary, brisk, gladsome, and obscene." Without the lube job of sincerity working in mysterious ways she would have dislocated her jawbone.

Her conversion could have won her much more general sympathy if only Robertson & Company had been willing and able to take it beyond its strictly Christian meaning. Savvy conservative supporters could have connected it to the magic word that has always underpinned the American Dream and now drives Bill Clinton's politics and the self-help industry: change. Pull Yourself Up by Your Bootstraps; Go West, Young Man; Don't Stop Thinking about Tomorrow; Ten Ways to a New You! are all secular versions of being Born Again that are calculated to make Americans' identification juices flow.

Her irreparable mistake was boasting that she had orgasms while killing. A woman can get away with murder or she can get away with sex, but if she tries to get away with both she collides with the male idée fixe that Tacitus articulated when he wrote: "A woman who has lost her chastity will shrink from no crime." Monica Lewinsky is now bearing the brunt of this on the lesser levels of perjury and obstruction of justice, but did it describe Karla Faye? True, she was a prostitute, but the orgasm claim was surely a lie.

THE murder occurred in 1983 when the multiple-orgasm craze was going full-tilt, when it was impossible to turn on the TV without hearing feminists talking about the female's "superior capacity," or read *Cosmopolitan* without finding an article on the mighty G-spot. I would bet anything that enough of this pop carnality filtered through to Karla Faye to inspire the trendy lie that sealed her doom.

The fresh-faced sexual desirability of her last days thrust feminist columnists into one of those guarded situations when everyone knows everyone is thinking the same thing. Judging from the tension that crept into their prose, they knew men were thinking what men know women know they think whenever they see a pretty nun, a pretty lesbian, or a pretty condemned prisoner: "What a waste!"

I was taken by her looks, perhaps because she fit one of my favorite lost words: "winsome." Believers attributed her physical metamorphosis to the glow of salvation but it's more likely that it came from the regularity of prison life and the first normal routine she had ever known. Alarm clocks and mealtimes are next to godliness.

She reminded me of a girl in high school who was always volunteering to wash the blackboards, beat the erasers, empty the pencil sharpener, fill the inkwells, and water the plants, earning the teachers' affection and straight A's in "citizenship" to balance her dismal academic record. At first I despised her because she was so "sweet," but then I discovered she really was sweet.

So, finally, was Karla Faye. May she rest in peace.

March 9, 1998

AMERICA has no peer when it comes to contradictions but we surpassed ourselves with our recent creation of what has to be the last of the red-hot oxymorons: the helpless, insecure femme fatale who never grew up. Delilah is now a poor kid who needs counseling.

Our sensuality is sealed under an adult-proof cap and any attempt to pry it off leads to failure and frustration. Monica Lewinsky's porn version of spin-the-bottle moved one columnist to quote wistfully from Ben Franklin's letter in praise of sex with older women, but nowadays that means Mary Kay LeTourneau, the 36-year-old Seattle grade-school teacher who gave herself to her 13-year-old pupil and had his baby. Authentic female voluptuousness is so scarce that we don't even have anybody who can do the Carmen number right. If you want a fiery temptress with a knife in her stocking, you have to make do with Diane Zamora, identified in news stories as "the diminutive former midshipman."

It all goes back to Bill Clinton's arrested development. If you want an 'R'

Us, he's it. In an earlier column on the White House sex scandal I predicted that Monica Lewinsky will never be called a "fellatrix" because Americans do not love language, but I see now that I was wrong. Why should we take up a hard-edged Latinate word when "oral" connotes children fixated on perfect safety and security? I take it all back: "oral sex" is the perfect description for this act, in this place, at this time. Say it to yourself and you can hear the gurgle of a contented thumbsucker and the promise of "comfort food": sodomy as macaroni-and-cheese.

Reading matter? Any adult deeply moved by *Leaves of Grass* has an assygassy mind ruled by an achy-breaky heart. Walt Whitman belongs to the interlude Clinton admirers call "youthful idealism" and do their best to stretch into an eon. This is when Ravel's "Bolero" sounds wanton instead of monotonous, when *Lady Chatterly's Lover* comes across as spontaneously free instead of unconsciously funny, when Mary Queen of Scots is a romantic heroine instead of a self-destructive idiot. *Leaves of Grass* is a State of the Union message in verse: unstanched puerile prattle with every scheme but a rhyme scheme.

The return of the gifts was pure rite-of-passage, the teen steadys breaking up: "I don't think we should see each other anymore," the thumb through a stack of 45 rpms, unwrapping the adhesive tape from the too-large class ring. Mike McCurry's observation that this could, after all, be a "very complicated story" only added to the Ricky Nelsonness of it all. Parting steadys can never remember whose records are whose or agree on what to do about birthday presents. I half-expected the next trumpet fanfare of "CNN Breaking News" to open on Clinton toeing the dirt and mumbling, "I want you to have it."

White House infantilism is so relentless that whenever someone accidentally strikes a note of maturity it produces sudden weird images and a kind of out-of-sync joy. Clinton's grim reference to "that woman" rescued the femme fatale from therapy and put her back before a Middle European firing squad. That word "compromising" transferred her to the Old Bailey, and "hatpins" became weapons of female self-defense for a few puzzling seconds, until I realized that what I call a hatpin is unknown to Monica, who has taken the Fellatrix Oath: First, do no harm.

What turns the scandal into a primal bog of arrested development is Clinton's selfish sexual preference. It's on a par with the innocent selfishness of an infant whose world is its wants, the blind selfishness of a fetus battening on its host. I can't understand why a woman would tolerate such one-sidedness. Back in my wild youth, men were so solicitous of female pleasure. "Do you like this? . . . Does that feel good? . . . Here? . . . There?" They went on and on, sometimes irritatingly so, but their hearts were in the right place even if some other things weren't. No man ever asked me to service him as an isolated act, but evidently today's men expect it—or they will now.

This is what feminists call liberation, but not all of them are playing the indulgent mother to our ageless P. One of them—the one that too many conservatives love to hate—laid into him like Carrie Nation. Interviewed in England by the *Guardian*, the underappreciated Andrea Dworkin said:

"Bill Clinton's fixation on oral sex [is] the most fetishistic, heartless, cold sexual exchange that one could imagine. . . . The second issue that concerns me is what Hillary Clinton is doing, which I think is appalling. She is covering up for a man who has a history of exploiting women. It's pathetic. She should pack her bags and leave."

Here comes the best part: "I have a modest proposal. It will probably bring the FBI to my door. But I think that Hillary should shoot Bill and then President Gore should pardon her."

W HEN Clinton's post-scandal approval ratings soared the Left saw blasé sophistication and the Right saw moral corruption, but Americans are neither sophisticated nor corrupt, just childish and democratic. What they really approve of in Clinton's behavior is the way he takes the adult out of adultery and the in out of sin. If he had kept a soignée thirtyish mistress and visited her discreetly the whole country would have felt threatened. Mistresses are for kings and discretion is elitist by definition, but love on the rope line suggests a limitless participation that reduces adultery to the minor crime of tumescence in office.

To prevent his kindergarten from swelling beyond the acceptable class size that concerns him in tranquil moments, he ought to reconsider a woman he met a few years ago: the five-hundred-year-old Peruvian mummy he said he'd like to date.

She might not be bad if he put his mind to it. As Agatha Christie said: "An archeologist is the best husband any woman can have. The older she gets, the more he is interested in her."

March 23, 1998

' I WANT to spend more time with my family" has long been the failed politician's favorite cover story, but Trad Vals hypocrisy reached a batty zenith on Ash Wednesday when Congressman Bill Paxon gave up his identity for Lent.

Two years ago Paxon and his wife, Congressman Susan Molinari, were the GOP's "golden couple." Beaming partners in a two-career marriage brimming with give-and-take, they gained national fame with their cloying performance at the 1996 Republican National Convention when Paxon sat in the gallery taking care of the baby as wife Susan, invariably described as "perky," delivered the Keynote Address.

The first fissure came last year when Mrs. Molinari abruptly quit Congress before her term was up to anchor *CBS News Saturday Morning*, giving as one of her reasons a wish to spend more time with her family.

Two months later, Paxon joined the plot to topple Newt Gingrich in hopes of succeeding him as Speaker, only to emerge as the scapegoat when the plot failed. But soon another plot beckoned: toppling Dick Armey and succeeding him as Majority Leader, which would give Paxon another crack at the Speakership when Newt resigned to run for President in 2000.

Paxon was toppling away, working the phones and lining up votes, when suddenly it hit him: he didn't want to be Speaker, he didn't want to be Majority Leader, he didn't even want to be a congressman. It meant nothing, nothing, you hear me, nothing! He had been in politics all his adult life starting with the Erie County legislature when he was just out of college, but now all that was over, over, I tell you, over! The upshot of his epiphany was his stunning Ash Wednesday announcement that he was quitting Congress and turning his back on politics forever to spend more time with his family.

Except that he didn't put it quite that way. As his plangent explanations over the next several days proved, it wasn't so much his family that he longed to spend time with, but his baby, Susan Ruby, now 21 months old. The baby's mother, however perky, entered into the picture only insofar as she lent force to his explanations, as when he told a clearly nauseated Chris Matthews on *Hardball*: "I saw Susan getting lots of hugs and kisses and I wanted my share."

After his wife quit Congress, he told the *Washington Post*, "she never looked back, and she is happy with being home with her daughter and that inspired me too." Furthermore, it was his wife's trips to New York to prepare for her Saturday show that had made him realize what he was missing: "Thursday and Friday I'm home alone with the baby and I realize that's what I wanna do. . . . It's out of pure joy I'm doing this. . . . I'd rather be home."

Much of his *Post* interview consisted of what he said to himself. "I asked myself, 'How do you possibly do justice to this child and still do the job?'" He thought he might be like an old firehorse, able to respond automatically to his congressional duties once he heard the bell, but no. "This horse wanted to be in the stables, with the colt."

His wife had been great about his career, he hastened to point out, willing to "make allowances in her schedule" if he had run for Leader, but "it is still very hard to have a young family, with Susan going off to New York for her work." Besides, they wanted to have more children, and so he asked himself, "Who is going to raise the babies?"

He made the rounds talking obsessively about his daughter, doing such a bang-up Stella Dallas schtik that the ghost of Barbara Stanwyck must have turned green with envy. Facing Washington reporters, he announced gulpily, "This is not a fall. This is a rise." He told his fellow members of Congress, "This little girl has helped me turn what has always been unthinkable, leaving office, into an easy choice." When he addressed his staff in his office amid Susan Ruby's toys and playpen, "His voice cracked and trailed off. He began to cry. He took a handkerchief from his pocket and dabbed his eyes."

At press conferences in his constituencies of Buffalo and Rochester, he was absorbed in the baby. "At both stops, Paxon basked in her antics. At both stops, he choked with emotion." Over and over he reminded audiences how time-consuming is the job of Majority Leader, reiterating, "It's not fair to my 21-month-old daughter."

Asked what she thought of it all, Mrs. Molinari made a suitably perky reply: "As an American I am sorry. As a wife and mother I couldn't be happier." In one sense she probably meant it since she now has a full-time, native-born nanny, but even the perky can recognize a hostile takeover when they see one.

I F Paxon had anything left in him of the Irishmen in his own ancestry or the Italian men in his wife's, he would order her to get her perky tush back in that house and raise her child. But being a New Man shaped by the creeping feminization promoted by the GOP at Convention '96, he is punishing his careerist mate by out-housewifing her. She quit Congress? He not only quit Congress but the Leadership as well. She wants to spend more time with the baby? He's going to spend so much time with the baby that he'll look like a politician with a constituency of one: Poot Paxon, the Baby's Friend. And don't bet on him getting a job. At the rate he's going his next statement may be "My place is in the home."

The marriage will probably break up, but what of little Susan Ruby? Paxon predicts, "Twenty years from now, my daughter won't give a hoot if I was Speaker or Majority Leader or on a highway crew. She wants to know if her daddy's there."

Don't be so sure. Status helps. The style and flair that made Tallulah Bankhead were not the dowry of a road mender: her father was Speaker of the House. In any case, faint heart never won fair lady; Susan Ruby may well grow up to despise him.

I know I do. If he's the New Man, I'll take Vlad the Impaler.

April 6, 1998

ACCORDING to the rules of what is lately called "full disclosure" I should ask everyone who loved *Braveheart* to leave the room now, but since that includes nearly all conservatives there would be no one left to read what I'm going to say. Let me stipulate, then, that my quarrel is not with macho heroes or patriotism but with the lack of discipline, self-indulgence, and carelessness of today's moviemakers.

Going to the movies is no longer an option due to my distaste for being in dark auditoriums with my so-called peers, but I finally saw *Braveheart* a few weeks ago on NBC. It was "edited for television" but that just means they cut some sex and violence. Otherwise the version I saw reinforces the first of my several objections: even with cuts it still was so long that it took two nights to run.

I expected it to kick off with Robert Burns's electrifying "Scots Wha' Hae Wi' Wallace Bled" sung by a male chorus like the one that sang "Men of Harlech" in *How Green Was My Valley*. Instead, the interminable title sequence was accompanied by a soloist playing a tuneless air on the Celtic uilliann. It was the kind of music I associate with free concerts at art galleries.

Establishment shots are stock footage of an instantly recognizable location to let the audience know where the story takes place. One establishment shot will do, but *Braveheart* never stopped establishing the fact that we were in Scotland. Mist-covered braes (See? That's Scotland). Mountain tarns (Look! Didn't I tell you it was Scotland?), Moors, moors, moors (Now that's really Scotland!). Heather, heather, heather (Hey, the Scottish national flower, right?). Cairns, peat fires, wee cots (You better believe it, this is Scotland, man!).

These atmospherics involved no action or anything to hold the viewer's interest. *The Quiet Man* contained a long shot of a steep Irish hill but Maureen O'Hara was walking up it, which made all the difference. In *Braveheart* we get a lot of ethereal stalling designed to camouflage what is, despite all the praise it won, a badly flawed script.

The backstory that opens the movie is a case in point. All we need to know is that William Wallace's father was killed by the English, and that he was adopted by an uncle who was something of an intellectual. John Ford could have wrapped it up in five minutes max, but Mel Gibson drags it out with rambling dialogue and static shots of the boy Wallace blinking and thinking of Scotland as he stares off into space at the moors and the cairns and the mountain tarns.

So much attention is paid to the where that the who, what, why, and when are given short shrift. With a third of American college students unable to place their own Civil War in the right century, a movie about the Middle Ages must explain historical facts and figures in quick and vivid ways, but *Braveheart* presents an unnamed English monarch as a generic king out of a fairy tale with nothing to identify him except the sobriquet "Longshanks."

Those of us raised in the bad old days of rote learning know that he was Edward I (1272–1307) of the House of Plantagenet, a family that ran to tall, lanky physiques. He was known as the "Hammer of the Scots" and the "English Justinian" for his contribution to the development of law, but his popular fame rests on two things that even the most untutored audiences have heard of. Both would be very easy to bring out in a movie and would serve to "place" him, evoking that shock of recognition that makes historical characters come to life.

The first concerns the "Eleanor Crosses." When Edward's adored wife, Eleanor of Castile, died on the Scottish border while accompanying him on his wars, he escorted her body back to London and ordered a stone cross to be erected wherever the cortège stopped for the night. The last and most elaborate of these monuments to the woman he called his "*chère reine*" was erected in a village outside London afterwards called Charing Cross.

The second story concerns the world's most famous title. Early in their marriage Queen Eleanor accompanied Edward on his Welsh campaigns and gave birth to a son in Caernarvon Castle. When the Welsh barons demanded that their country be ruled by "a Welsh-born prince who speaks no English," the wily Edward supposedly held up his new son and said, "Here is your Prince of Wales."

A UDIENCES reminded of these stories would say, "Oh, *that* king!" instead of "Which king?" Connecting the historical dots also would have solidified the identity of the movie's burlesqued homosexual prince: he was that baby.

On the second night, near the end of Part II, I finally yelled, "They can take our homes, they can take our women, but they can't take our common sense!" What set me off was the scene in which Princess Isabella visits Wallace in his cell and, saying she has something to make his execution painless, transfers a mysterious liquid from her mouth to his during their final kiss.

What, pray, was the liquid? If a soporific to deaden the pain of his scheduled evisceration had been available in 1305 it would have advanced surgery by centuries and taken the medieval out of medieval dentistry. If it was poison, how did she transport it orally without poisoning herself? If it was in a vial or a goose bladder why didn't she just hand it to him? How was she able to talk with something like that in her mouth?

Confusing, overlong movies are a major cause of the crude audience behavior that keeps me out of theaters. The only way to make a large group of strangers behave in the dark is to keep the leash of artistry taut around their necks, but don't expect today's moviemakers to do it. Selectivity is the first principle of art but the last principle of democracy. The artist's duty to pick and choose, to include and eliminate, to put things in their proper place is inimical to our times. It was a war waiting to happen, and art lost.

April 20, 1998

' **C** LASSIST," you may recall, is a neologism meaning someone who makes judgments based on social class. It's a perfectly good -ist, no better and no worse than any of our other -ists, -ites, and -phobes, but it never quite caught on. The only people who use it are the Marxist-feminist lunatic fringe and far-out black ranters who get on a roll and can't stop. To the latter, "classist" is a code word for whites who use "underclass" as a code word for blacks.

Everyone else has problems with it. In the first place, it's hard to pronounce and turns into a squirty hiss, tempting ableists to assume a speech defect and go through a drying-off pantomime. In the second place, the people who would normally use it—liberal intellectuals—have a mental block against it. As members of the class laboriously known as "four or more years of higher education," they have already learned that a "classicist" is a specialist in Greek and Roman literature. Try as they might, they can't shake that extra syllable: "classist" simply sounds wrong to them, the product of a typing error like the inevitable "feminity" for femininity.

The third and most important reason why "classist" has failed to catch on is that it turns the unthinkable into a conscious thought. As Midge Decter wrote: "Unconsciously is the only way Americans think about class." The subject skims across our minds like a hair blown across the face: a constant ticklish irritation, invisible but very much felt. If we tossed around a loaded word like "classist," so many strands would come loose from the snarled knot of our classless society that we could never tuck them all back in neatly; to make ourselves presentable we would have to unpin the whole business and start all over again. But since counterrevolution is another unthinkable good idea, we play it safe and impugn class-conscious people with a name that connotes self- rather than natural selection: "elitists."

Conservatives have shown a special fondness for calling the media elitists but recent events suggest that we need something stronger. We should take up "classist" and pin it on the talking heads and ink-stained wretches who described Kathleen Willey as if she were the Infanta of Castile.

The *60 Minutes* interview was barely over when the cheekbone obsession started. Willey's were "sculptured," "delicate," "pronounced," "winglike," "aristocratic." I haven't heard so much about cheekbones since 1945. Whenever I read another Willey story I felt as if I were back in our old neighborhood movie theater watching *Laura* with Granny, who kept jabbing me in the ribs and whispering, "Look at those cheekbones—you can tell she's got good blood."

Patrician adjectives flew as commentators ennobled Willey as though their lives depended on it. Her manner was "refined," her grammar was "cultivated," her diction was "genteel," her makeup was "understated," she had a "Junior League" wardrobe, "finishing-school" posture, a "ladylike" modesty, an "upper class" lifestyle," a "Richmond society" background, and "Virginia aristocrat" written all over her.

Between these lavish accolades and what we already knew about Willey lay a glaring contradiction that altogether eluded the social arbiters: airline stewardess is not a post-deb job. For well-born Southern women of Willey's age the Big Three sinecures were the historical society, the state archives—both stamping grounds for legions of Daughters and Colonial Dames all talking about high cheekbones and good blood—and the society page of the local paper. We had a post-deb when I was on the Raleigh *News & Observer*. Typical of the breed, she couldn't write but she was invaluable because she knew where all the bodies were buried—whose wedding date had to be put back three months, why we must never photograph Mrs. A with Mrs. B, etc.

I wasn't surprised, therefore, when the shabby-wacky truth about Willey came out. When she fell from grace a subtle mood of let-down, even betrayal, seemed to pass over the media, invisible but very much felt. They had taken pains to point out that Willey did not have "big hair" but she had enough so that a single strand from her First-Families-of-Virginia coif had lain for a brief time across their collective face and made them quiver with joy. In spite of themselves, maybe without even realizing it, they had savored their interlude of unrestrained class-consciousness and were crushed when their Infanta turned out to be Pretender Spice.

T HE most fascinating aspect of the media's fling with social hierarchy was the way they turned into Southerners. No one else uses words like "aristocrat," "genteel," and "lady" with such plummy abandon—or uses them at all. The Yankee upper crust, according to Joseph Alsop, simply say "nice people" and let it go at that. Nor do they elevate females to the peerage; the preferred Northern word was "gentlewoman" until the last generation that used it died out. But the Southern lady lives, along with her entourage of cheekbone fanciers, diction coaches, and shintoists so hung up on maiden names that conversing with them is like opening a bank account.

The only Southern quality kick missing from the media's investiture of Willey was the "fine-pored skin" number.

"She has such fine-pored skin that you can see evra vein in huh body," Granny announced.

"Every vein?" said my father. "She must look like a doctor's chart."

"Evra vein!"

Mere elitists don't carry on like this. Southerners have always been clas-sists and now it seems that Americans of the better sort are, consciously or not, following suit. Even liberals can take only so much; a yearning for social hierarchy is natural to civilized people and ours has been frustrated for too long. Nowadays, all you have to do to pass for an aristocrat is wash your face and sit still. If the citizenry gets any commoner it won't be long before the cheekbone of an ass starts looking good to us, and given Bill Clinton's catholic taste in females, we may get to see one.

May 4, 1998

I F you think the sublime classical world of antiquity could not produce an American neurotic, guess again. In 356 B.C. the Temple of Artemis at Ephesus, one of the Seven Wonders of the World, was set ablaze by a man named Erostratus who confessed that he did it because he wanted to be famous.

Boy, what he missed. America has long been the natural home of celebri-ty wannabes, but Erostratus would be in clover if he could see the liberating benefits they enjoy in the Nineties. Earlier on, when we merely democratized fame, we defended the right of any mouth-breather to rise from deserved obscurity on the strength of his God-given hebetude, but that's now consid-ered limiting, even elitist. Fame, once democratic, is now socialistic.

From each according to his hebetude, to each according to his bad taste in friends. Why should Erostratus be the only one to go on CNN? If Erostratus is famous then so is his roommate, who lent him the arson car. So is his squeeze, who tells Larry King what the real Erostratus is really like. So is his 11th foster mother, who gives us the skinny on early-warning signs. And so is the manager of the convenience store where Erostratus bought out the entire stock of kerosene and Bics, whose name became a household word after he strolled through the aisles with Diane Sawyer, straightening cans of Spam while analyzing nervous gestures and problems with eye contact.

Our most disconnected fame socialist is Ellen DeGeneres's mother, who seems unaware that her raison d'être is no more. She first hit the tube during the publicity barrage for the coming-out episode of *Ellen*, making herself available for a spate of interviews about parenting an overt lesbian, handing out how-to tips, and presenting a picture of matter-of-fact acceptance and nonjudgmental serenity.

It may have been an act but it soon became sincere when Mrs. DeGeneres saw her chance to get in with the gay-rights crowd and began doing guest appearances at their functions. She's still at it—I surfed across her on a C-SPAN panel the other night—but there's a small problem: *Ellen* has been canceled and its star has made such a fool of herself that her career is on the skids. Yet Mrs. DeGeneres marches on, ignoring her aging daughter's bad ratings and worse press in her eagerness to make a name for herself.

This could get ironic. As a Louisianan she is subject to the Southern practice of identifying an obsessed woman by adding the word "lady" to her obsession. The equestrienne who's never out of the saddle is "the horse lady," the spit-and-polish housekeeper is "the ammonia lady," and Mrs. DeGeneres will be "the Ellen Who? lady."

Besides fame socialists we also have fame anarchists. William Ginsburg quickly achieved more or less conventional fame as Monica Lewinsky's lawyer, but then he wore out his welcome and had to start all over again. To regain the limelight he had come to crave, he made the most revolting public statement the country had ever heard: "I kissed that baby's inner thighs when she was six days old." Never mind the creepy pedophilic allusion, never mind the suggestive connection to the act that made his client famous; never mind the sneaking suspicion that lawyer and client just might be a textbook case of *folie à deux*. Never mind anything except the only thing that mattered: Ginsburg had made a comeback.

The world has always had show-offs but America has fame-seeking missiles. Michael Portnoy disrupted the Grammy Awards when he charged the stage, tore off his shirt, and broke into a wild dance, the words "Soy Bomb" painted in black letters on his bare chest. Nobody knows what it meant originally but it doesn't matter because Portnoy has turned pro and the words are now a verb: "to soybomb" means to disrupt for pay. "I soybombed the National Association of Record Manufacturers," said Portnoy, who is weighing other offers. "My work on the Grammys introduced me to the public. My injection of pandemonium on an organized agenda has made me a lasting entity."

Anonymous fame-seeker sounds oxymoronic but we have those too. They're the people who want to sink into a famous crowd. Taking part in a mass protest movement used to be a gesture toward the future; the media coverage may have been satisfying but idealistic selflessness was the primary reason for getting involved. Now the opposite is true: the past is what matters and the media are essential to its preservation.

Ask any participant in any mass happening on the Mall why he is there and he will say: "I want to be a part of history." The answer has a center-stage quality suggesting a lust for anonymity of a special kind: the anonymous fame-seeker actually wants to be the anonymous English soldier who whittled a cross for Joan of Arc at the stake; the anonymous spectator who picked up the shoe Richard II lost as he was carried aloft from his coronation; or the anonymous Spartan boy who let a fox gnaw out his entrails rather than show pain. This way, if Ted Koppel doesn't call, at least you can be a legend.

O UR lust for fame springs from a suffocating commitment to equality, a need for secular immortality to replace a lost belief in Heaven, and feminization, which gives equal importance to anything as long as it's personal: "What's the real Erostratus really like?" would be of no interest whatsoever in a civilized patriarchy.

Whatever the cause, I have a question. As more and more celebrity wannabes wander from green room to green room like mendicants with begging bowls, offering up their privacy and dignity for enough fame to keep body and soul together, what will happen to the concept of the Unknown Soldier? Think about that. We already have a Vietnam Memorial that looks like a telephone book. Now that we have discovered the unanonymous joys of DNA, when will we insist on knowing who is in that Tomb so we can track down their families and put them on television?

And worse, how many of them would jump at the chance?

May 18, 1998

A T LAST I'm running with the herd and swimming with the tide and being a good little conformist. Americans, once gregarious and other-directed, are crawling into their shells and turning into shut-ins. In fact, they're turning into me.

The gated community is edging out open-hearth suburbia, and gates are only the beginning: there is talk of moats and drawbridges. Children once thought to need the give-and-take of classroom and playground to keep them from growing up warped are being home-schooled, never mind their social adjustment. And people who used to feel sorry for writers because we have to sit alone in a room all day are now moving heaven and earth to become self-employed so they can sit alone in a room all day.

This is glorious-new-dawn stuff, but what really makes me feel like a pioneer is the soaring popularity of catalogue shopping. According to a spokeswoman for the Direct Marketing Association, a majority of Americans now do some or most of their shopping from home, and the numbers are rising. The trend is attributed to gridlock traffic and time constraints on two-career couples and single parents, but the spokeswoman alluded gingerly to another reason: "people's growing disdain of crowded places."

Welcome to MisanMall. No spaced-out teenagers, no music, no Official Greeters, no NO SMOKING signs, no endless war-refugee hiking, no parking-lot kidnappings, no bomb scares, no "disgruntled employee" of the food court brandishing an AK-47 and ordering everybody into the icebox just as you're sitting down to lunch. It's just you and your thumb and your own private dreamland, the way it was when you were a child poring over the most famous catalogue of all.

Marketing analysts ignore it but I think one reason for the rise in home shopping is the Sears, Roebuck catalogue phase that children used to go through. It was like the dinosaur phase: every kid got hooked. I discovered the Scars catalogue at age six when we visited rural relatives. I spent the whole visit thumbing through it, fascinated not only by the bicycles and BB-guns but by merchandise I had no use for, such as baling wire and manure spreaders. I was in the throes of that universal childish delight in treasure hunts that Sears satisfied with one huge book.

Afterward I asked Granny if we could shop from it but she said, "We don't have to, we can go downtown." That was the trouble. Whenever she made me try something on in a store the saleswomen gathered round and gushed, "Isn't she just the sweetest little thing you ever did see?" It's terrible to be that misunderstood so I associated catalogues with succor at an early age.

I've been catalogue-shopping for a decade now and I love it. My first purchase was a $600 dual-floppy Sharp laptop from the Damark catalogue. Nothing has ever gone wrong with it and it has the best keyboard of any computer, laptop or desktop, I've ever owned. From the same source I also bought both of my fax machines, and nothing has ever gone wrong with them either. Thanks to the Damark and Lyben catalogues I never have to talk to smart-aleck techies.

Catalogue-shopping has even made me a better cook. Stores don't deliver anymore so if you buy an imported cast-iron Le Creuset pot you have to lug it out to the car and then up the stairs. The temptation to make do with your old cheap pot is great, but if you buy an expensive Le Creuset from a catalogue, UPS does the lugging and you end up with better coq au vin.

Good kitchen knives also make all the difference. Not even Vulcan could snap the blade of my $75 German carver, but I never would have learned as much about knives standing on my feet in a store as I did reading a detailed and attractively presented catalogue over breakfast. When the knife arrived I also had the time and energy to enjoy the brochure, learning how to say "Please don't use the knife to cut bones" in five languages. My favorite is: *"Bitte verwenden Sie das Messer nicht zum Hacken von Knochen!"* That's really telling 'em. I'm going to bellow it at the top of my lungs if I ever see another airhead salesperson in the flesh.

D ID I just hear you grumble that once you start buying from catalogues you get bombarded with more catalogues? You're right. It's called "niche marketing" and I got my first taste of it when I sent for the gel-filled insoles. One foot product was all it took; now I get catalogues for crutches and wheelchairs. After I bought the moist heating pad I started getting neck-brace and traction catalogues, but my most memorable experience was landing in the niche from whose bourne no traveler returns.

It happened when I discovered a mail-order garment I've never seen in any store: they're 100 per cent white cotton, with legs extending three inches down the thigh. After misspending my youth in seductive lingerie the comfort is indescribable. You've had paper cuts on your finger? Well, I used to get lace cuts not on my finger, and now I'm being punished for my sins with thunderbolts of memento mori: I had no sooner ordered three dozen pairs of comfies than I was inundated with catalogues for liver-spot cream, bladder-control pills, write-your-own-will kits, and 911 neck alarms.

I welcome niche marketing because in my business you can't have too many catalogues. A foremost rule of writing, now largely ignored, is never call any object a "thing": you must name it. While reading one of the landscaping catalogues that started arriving after I bought the outdoor thermometer, I learned the name for a solution to a problem I don't have. You know how rain gushes out of the drainpipe and keeps hitting the same place beside the house until it makes a hole in the ground and water seeps into the cellar? To prevent this you buy a vinyl sleeve or polyethylene tube called a "downspout diverter." Why do I need to know this? I'll never buy a house but I do write about Bill Clinton, and something tells me it has the makings of an apt metaphor.

June 1, 1998

' H ER voice was ever soft, gentle, and low—an excellent thing in woman." Shakespeare never saw an Alice Faye movie but Lear's tribute to his daughter Cordelia perfectly describes the actress who died May 9 at the age of 86.

Living in the Madonna era would be unbearable if I didn't remember Alice Faye. Her 1940s musicals set in the Gay Nineties and World War I were my favorite movies, not only for their foot-tapping tunes but for their effect on my seatmate. For once Granny did not get a chance to jab me in the ribs and whisper "She's got consumption" or "She's losing her mind." The only tragic event in an Alice Faye movie was the requisite interlude of boy-loses-girl, but since the characters were always in vaudeville the show had to go on. Hearing the songs she remembered and seeing the fashions she had worn kept Granny's mind out of the grave for the whole show.

There were two Alice Fayes but the first was before my time. When she arrived in Hollywood in 1934 they made her a Jean Harlow clone with platinum blonde hair but the effect was all wrong. Harlow was the bad girl with a heart of gold but Faye suggested an intriguing contradiction at once less and more: a good girl with a heart of gold. As balancing acts go, this one is almost impossible to manage without becoming cloying or ridiculous, as Doris Day would later prove, yet it was the elusive essence of Alice Faye: she was the girl men could imagine themselves respecting in the morning.

By the time I remember her the studio was letting her wear her natural honey-blonde hair and showcasing her rare quality of choosy sensuality in period musicals. Her pretty but not beautiful face framed in big flowered hats made her believable as the girl from a bygone age that men called a "peach" and a "corker." She starred as Lillian Russell in the biopic of the Gay Nineties legend with Edward Arnold as Diamond Jim Brady, but her best movies were vaudeville sagas in which she played the good-sport singer to a pair of songwriting partners played by John Payne and Jack Oakie or Tyrone Power and Don Ameche.

Her singing voice, like her speaking voice, was described as "husky" and "throaty." After seeing her in *Alexander's Ragtime Band* the famously difficult Irving Berlin said he would rather have her introduce his songs than anyone he knew. She had a tangible effect on movie audiences. I remember the shuffling vibration as patrons tapped their feet in a carpeted version of the old soft-shoe when she sang "On Moonlight Bay" in *Tin Pan Alley*. She got another impromptu response later in the same movie. It was about World War I songwriters but it came out in 1941 when we knew we would soon be in World War II. The moment Faye started belting out "America, I Love You (and There're a Hundred Million Others Like Me)" a palpable electricity filled the theater and exploded in applause when the last note ended.

Most women can't put across a patriotic song. Kate Smith had a better voice but Alice Faye brought something to four–four tempo reminiscent of Nora Bayes. Her signature song, however, was "You'll Never Know" from *Hello, Frisco, Hello*. It also had a tangible effect I've never forgotten. The usher had sat down across the aisle from us to watch the scene; as she sang the line, "You went away and my heart went with you / I speak your name in my every prayer," I glanced at him and saw that he was crying.

Alice Faye's last public appearance was an interview six years ago on American Movie Classics channel which was re-run last week. In contrast to other aged actresses with their orange hair and skin stretched so tightly they can barely open their mouths to speak, her hair was frankly white and her face frankly unlifted. She had kept her figure but it was an old lady's rawboned slenderness with a stick-figure quality about it, and she had no waistline left. The famous contralto voice was still ingratiating but it had lost its seductiveness, and her hands were like brown claws.

She had come to what Marilyn Monroe and other sex symbols dread so much that they die young rather than face it, yet as the interview progressed it was clear that Alice Faye had chosen the better part. This was a woman who knew exactly who she was and where she stood, too secure for publicized nervous breakdowns, battles with booze and pills, and maudlin announcements of "At last I've found true love." After a brief marriage to Tony Martin she married bandleader Phil Harris in 1941 and stayed married to him until his death in 1995.

A S FOR "career conflicts," Faye settled hers in one decisive swoop. By 1945 she had tired of doing musicals and asked Darryl Zanuck for meatier dramatic roles. He cast her in *Fallen Angel* as a betrayed wife with Linda Darnell as the other woman, but he was so intent on building up

Darnell that he cut Faye's best scenes. After previewing the completed film
she complained to Zanuck, who said or did something she could neither forget nor forgive. That same day she walked off the lot and out of her contract,
never to return. Blackballed by Hollywood, she stayed home and raised her
two daughters, her career over except for a radio show with her husband and
later a few TV appearances.

What happened with Darryl Zanuck? This is where Barbara Walters
would lean forward and ask plangently, "What dwid he dwo to you?" in
hopes of a lurid confession, but Alice Faye shook her white head firmly and
refused to elaborate, telling her AMC interviewer, "That goes with me."

It was a Cordelia moment. Lear's daughter was also invited to spill her
guts; her sisters did so eagerly, wallowing in verbal excess to prove how
much they loved their father, but dignified Cordelia would say only, "You
have begot me, bred me, loved me: I return those duties back as are right fit;
obey you, love you, and most honour you"—and not one word more.

Hail and farewell, dear Miss Faye. There'll never be another like
you—"Never, never, never, never, never."

June 22, 1998

G OOD timing has never been my long suit but the invention of Viagra
suggests that my luck has changed. Now that I have, shall we say,
retired from the ring, I can appraise the issue with a degree of objectivity that would have been impossible to summon when I was in fighting trim.

When the news of the miracle drug broke my first thought was that a
classic scenario had come to an end. Never again would a woman have to
struggle to keep a sympathetic—or straight—face while a hollow voice said:

"This never happened to me before."

"It's not you."

"I shouldn't come here on the days that I see my analyst."

Also facing extinction was the inevitable quotation from the porter's
scene in *Macbeth*, long a staple of macho intellectuals given to two-fisted
drinking: "Gotta cut down on the sauce. 'It makes you stand to, and not stand
to.' Ha-ha."

The woman could never think of a suitable reply. "It doesn't matter"
meant that it didn't matter; "Don't worry about it" sounded flippant; and "It
happens to lots of men" implied that you knew lots of men. Changing the subject was even more perilous. Diversionary topics are usually drawn from the
day's news but in this case current events had a fiendish way of being awful-

ly current. Eisenhower's heart attack? Fallen warrior. Sputnik? Defiance of gravity. Francis Gary Powers? Shot down. The Paris Summit? Collapsed. Dag Hammarskjöld? Sudden death. U Thant? An unfortunate accident befell his first name, leaving him with a mere bud. The past was even chancier than the present, populated as it was by people named Ethelred the Unready and Pippin the Short. About the only safe topics were the Edict of Bad Ulm or the Venerable Bede, and he was a celibate.

Viagra may eliminate the old scenario but anyone familiar with male psychology can predict with certainty that far worse scenarios are in the offing. As competitive as men are, how long do you think it will take before 100-milligram men launch a concerted campaign to make 50-milligram men feel like 90-pound weaklings? Once they start bragging "I'm a 100-milligram man myself" a kind of arms race will ensue until everybody is a 100-milligram man, at which point it will start all over again with demands for 200-milligram or even 500-milligram dosages.

Next, combine men's irresistible impulse to challenge authority with the know-it-all streak that makes them disdain roadmaps, and figure out how long it will take them to second-guess their doctors and pop a few extra pills "just to be sure."

Now go through *The Guinness Book of World Records* and note the preponderance of male over female names, then contemplate the sheer idiocy of most of the deeds therein and tell me how soon we can expect "Longest Sustained Erection" to be right up there with "Longest Held Breath."

We are headed for an epidemic of priapism, a cherished male fantasy as fatally flawed as that other cherished male fantasy: dating a nymphomaniac who owns a liquor store. The new scenario will feature the same old despair, but because the bladder cannot be voided while the penis is erect, "This never happened to me before!" will be spoken in considerably louder tones, and the lady in question will not have to worry about making tactful conversation because what's left of her will be busy calling 911 for both of them.

Of course not all men will brag about being on Viagra. Quite the contrary. Some men—the *über*competitors, if you will—are eager to take the opposite tack. Larry King, 64, has already kicked it off, asking in his newspaper column: "Is it boasting to say that I don't need Viagra?" No, it's just lying.

A certain number of men are going to take Viagra on the sly and then proudly display the result with the boast, "This is no pill," as in Pearl Harbor's "This is no drill." The lady in question is supposed to be flattered, and she might be if only he would shut up. But he keeps saying it—each time, over and over, until she realizes that he's protesting too much. And so it's back to the old scenario and the old cliché, with only a slight difference: "It's not you, it's Viagra."

A corollary problem is what will become of the woman whose *amour-propre* rests on being the only woman who can make an impotent man perform. The classic example of the breed was the Duchess of Windsor, said to possess some mysterious lubricious "technique" that women's magazines spent the sexual revolution trying to define and pass on in endless how-to-turn-him-into-a-stud articles. We need only imagine the Duchess forced to co-exist with Viagra—no uproar, no King, no legend—to predict the effect it's going to have on her *Cosmo*-reading wannabes: millions of unraveling female egos.

N OTHING can happen nowadays without running into the natural-versus-synthetic argument. Dare to call Velveeta cheese and the same people who make fun of polyester will snarl that Velveeta is not "real" cheese, just as polyester is not a "natural" fabric. Lest you think these people would not mar erotic interludes with comparisons between natural erections and those induced by Viagra, guess again. In the movie *John and Mary*, about the morning after a pick-up, Dustin Hoffman cooks breakfast for Mia Farrow and solemnly intones, "This is a natural egg." To his way of thinking, their future hinges on her response.

Velveeta-hating wool gatherers can lay the K-Mart curse on anything. Comes the day when the majority of American men are taking Viagra and praising its wonders, the high priests of environmental awareness will *stop* taking it and start talking incessantly about how much better they feel now. Sex? Why, it's better now, too. It's like sweaters—one good one is better than lots of synthetic ones.

And for those times when sex is not so good—indeed, nonexistent—they have an explanation at the ready: "I shouldn't come here on the days that I buy hard cheese."

July 6, 1998

T HE woman of mystery has never been an American type. Maintaining a vague "past" runs up against high-school yearbooks, friendly seatmates asking "Whereya from?," and TV shows such as *This Is Your Life* where everyone we would prefer to forget comes crashing through a rose-covered trellis.

We have always associated the woman of mystery with unstable Middle European governments that fell a lot and citizens with forged "papers" who went underground a lot, but that's all changed now. Monica Lewinsky has taken the woman of mystery and painted her red, white, and blue all over, especially red. Thanks to her *Vanity Fair* photo-op and the reception accorded it, American women have learned how to be mysterious in a democracy: do something so idiotic that people from all walks of life lie awake nights racking their brains trying to figure out why you did it.

The racking and figuring got off to a rousing start when *Time* published the fan-dancer picture. Normally blasé talking heads cawed "How could she?" and "What possessed her?" like querulous chaperones, while tolerant-or-bust Richard Cohen fumed, "What was she thinking? What was Ginsburg thinking? Where were Lewinsky's parents?"

William Ginsburg, self-described "avuncular family friend," took credit for the whole idea, saying Monica needed the photo spread to boost her morale and renew her sense of herself as a desirable female after her months as a shut-in. This was believable in that nothing Ginsburg says is beyond belief, but then, true to form, he gilded the lily. Setting himself up as a Moses with one Israelite, he blamed Monica's psychological captivity on Pharaoh Ken Starr and thundered, "Let her libido go!"

I suspect the libido he wanted to liberate was not Monica's but his own. The first lurid hint of disquiet on the avuncular front was his claim to have kissed her infant thighs. Combine this with her only outings, when the two of them hit every steak house in Washington, and what do you have? The eating scene from the movie *Tom Jones* in which the Deadly Sin of gluttony symbolized the Deadly Sin of lust.

Each outing brought him one steak house closer to immolation in the charcoal fire in his loins, but knowing his chances were nil, he dreamed up the photo session as another vicarious way to possess her. That he masterminded the whole thing, from the clothes to the poses, seems obvious. The flouncy, flirty, Fifties-era motif could not have been Monica's idea; only the most provincial Southern girls still think it's cute to fling sidelong glances and peek from behind feathers. These are the fantasies of a man for whom a stripper in baboon-hindquarters red was an overworked law student's idea of hot.

The debate over why Monica went along with it left me wondering why anyone should even ask. Why do 35-year-old divorcées remarry in formal church weddings wearing long white dresses and veils? Why do people walk over graves at cemeteries? Why do women breastfeed and change babies' diapers in public—and even at restaurant tables? Because nobody knows how to behave anymore. The collapse of savoir-faire pervades Monica's photo shoot. You don't wear a diamond if you're not engaged because you just don't. You don't wear dark polish on short nails because you just don't. You don't play with the American flag because you just don't. And you don't expect Monica's America to understand because the only just-don't they recognize is political incorrectness.

She reminds me of two other girls about her age who made more history than was good for them when they got involved with famous men. The first, born almost exactly a century earlier than Monica, was Marie Vetsera, whose new-money family wanted into Viennese society. Since the pinnacle of that society was Hapsburg royalty, Marie's mother turned a blind eye when an influential friend placed her daughter's zaftig teenage charms in the path of Crown Prince Rudolf.

Historian Betty Kelen's words could be the accompanying text for Monica's photo spread:

> Not even the soggiest retelling of her story has ever insisted that Marie was intelligent. She is instantly recognizable as one of those plump girls whose moods alternate between bubbling affection and moping depression. Had she been put in a box with a lid on it until she was older, she might have brought to some bureaucrat the enchantment of a submissively amorous and soulful wife with excellent judgment in cooks.

Marie was put in a box all right. Rudolf decided to shoot himself, so he asked if he could shoot her too and she said okay. Much racking and figuring has gone into learning her reason, but as far as historians can tell she went along with it because she went along with it, leaving posterity no choice but to turn her into a romantic heroine.

AN unnamed media consultant quoted in the *Washington Times* said the photos show "the new, contemplative, take-charge Monica . . . much more serious, much more down-to-earth, much more intelligent, much more in charge of her own affairs. . . . It gets her away from this image of a helpless damsel. You are definitely seeing the birth of the new Monica."

This could be the accompanying text for the original drawings of the Gibson Girl, the "new woman" of the early twentieth century who threw off Victorian shackles to become man's equal. One of the models used by Charles Dana Gibson was a creamy brunette named Evelyn Nesbit who posed on the beach in a black bathing dress. The mistress of famed architect Stanford White, who built her an indoor playground in their love nest, Evelyn later married Harry Thaw, an insanely jealous millionaire who found out about White and shot him dead during a musical revue on the roof of Madison Square Garden in 1906.

Harry got off scot-free but Evelyn was ruined. For years she was the object of smirks and jokes until, at long last, a movie of her life treated her sympathetically. It was called *The Girl in the Red Velvet Swing.*

July 20, 1998

I WAS planning to write about the Y2K crisis this time, but then I stopped by my new post-office box and found a batch of letters wanting to know my opinion of the American Film Institute's "100 Best Movies." Ask and ye shall receive. I'll start with the ones I hate.

Citizen Kane: Too long, too dark, too talky, too arty. Orson Welles was a ponderous overrated bore, the cinematic equivalent of William Faulkner.

The Maltese Falcon: Does anybody really know what was going on? I don't. It's so overplotted that following it is like following Ariadne through the labyrinth after she runs out of string.

The Grapes of Wrath: Wherever there's a democrat singin' the praises of the People, I'll be there. It's not Ma Joad we revere, but the actress who portrayed her, Jane Darwell, Hollywood's premier commanding dowager. In the book, Ma was as primitive as the rest of the family, barring only Grandpa, who masturbated at the table.

The movie is a love letter to the New Deal. When the mistreated Joads arrive at the migrant labor camp run by the Department of Agriculture, the administrator is so kind and polite that they can only stare at him in poleaxed disbelief. As they stand there with their jaws sagging, he explains how self-government in the camp works. To me his speech is worse than any abuse the Joads have endured. The smiley officiousness that comes over him as he rattles off a list of mandatory committees recalls that classic moment in mimicry when the parodied bureaucrat says, "I'm from the government and I'm here to help you."

Forrest Gump: It came out after I had stopped going to the movies because of the cretins in the audience, but by the time it ran on television Pat Buchanan had ruined it for me with his columns linking truth, honor, patriotism, pure love, home, and mother to room-temperature IQs.

This is a conservative movie, my friend. The smart people do stupid things and the stupid people do smart things, proving that the elitists don't know half as much as the working-class guys named McGowan, Schultz, Hernandez, Lucetti, and Leroy Johnson in that foxhole out in Nam who don't think it's funny that Forrest got confused and mooned the President at the Medal of Honor ceremony because it's love of God and country that counts, not making

Phi Beta Kappa at Berkeley with a bunch of peacenik intellectuals.

Buchanan followed his Gump either–or with another in praise of Sgt. Alvin York, who "never got out of the third grade" and was not a member of the "cognitive elite." Alger Hiss was, therefore he committed treason. It stands to reason, folks, because "In America, character, not IQ, is destiny."

Wherever there's a populist beatin' up on brains, I'll be there. Both of these columns came out in 1994, giving me two years to resolve never to vote for Buchanan, whom I once adored, and a full three years to nurse my loathing of a movie I finally got to see.

Identifying conservative movies is a tricky business. They are loosely defined as those in which John Wayne says "We're goin' in" and "We're movin' out" at least once each, but these scripts usually center around a spoiled rich boy who is forced to shape up. He always does, and even becomes a hero, but he's invariably rich.

Another misleading genre is the traditional-values extravaganza featuring the banker with a heart of gold who approves loans with no collateral so that the little people can own their own homes. Two such films made the 100 Best list.

It's a Wonderful Life: As you no doubt guessed, this is a movie I love to hate, but not for the reasons you thought. I can take the unceasing self-sacrifice, I can take the shambling good cheer, I can even take the angel, but that raffish Building & Loan reminds me of the Women's Bank of early feminism.

The Best Years of Our Lives: Democratized by the army, banker Frederic March abandons the Hooverish fiscal prudence of his pre-war career and makes an unsecured loan to a penniless fellow veteran who wants to buy a farm. Defending his new practices in a speech at a financial banquet, he delivers a drunken harangue on the heartlessness of "stuffed shirts" who don't believe in humanitarian lending.

Ayn Rand wanted to cite this as anti-capitalist propaganda when she was called as a friendly witness by the House Un-American Activities Committee in 1947. Richard Nixon supported her, but Parnell Thomas, afraid to criticize such a popular movie, limited her testimony to *Song of Russia*, a heavy-handed and comically obvious piece of Communist propaganda that flopped at the box office.

Y OU already have a pretty good idea of the kind of movies I like, but two of my more obscure favorites did not make the 100 Best.

Sylvia: A 1965 black-and-white starring Carroll Baker as an intellectual prostitute with a character of gold. A daughter of the slums, she pulls herself up by her library card, doing whatever she has to do but reading the whole while—even in the brothel parlor as she waits for her next john. When her friend is run over and needs a lifesaving operation, Sylvia risks the ultimate degradation to pay the medical bills. Emerging triumphant and as self-contained as ever, she and the friend escape the life and Sylvia becomes a respected poet. This movie is unsurpassed as a statement of female autonomy and sisterhood but there's not a word in feminist film critiques about it.

Theater of Blood: A 1973 British black comedy starring Vincent Price as a Shakespearean actor who murders, one by one, the critics who panned him, copying the murders from the plays. One is beheaded in his sleep, one is drowned in a barrel at a wine-tasting, and the frustrated spinster who flirts with gay men is electrocuted under the dryer as Price, disguised as a hairdresser, recites Joan of Arc's death sentence from *Henry VI, Part I*: "Because she is a maid, spare for no fagots, let there be enow."

August 3, 1998

I T TAKES an optimist like yours truly to see the bright side of the Year 2000 computer glitch. For example, the language alone is heartening. The doomsayers are predicting it will be a calamity, a disaster, and a catastrophe, but so far nobody has called it a "tragedy." The mere fact that Y2K seems to be immune to the most misused buzzword of our time makes it a consummation devoutly to be wished.

According to the worst predictions, planes and elevators will stop, dams and bridges will jam, banks will fail, the stock market will fall, the global economy will collapse, nuclear missiles will launch themselves, and the world will be destroyed, all because computers think it's 1900.

That's how pessimists see it, but I have a song in my heart, a rainbow in my pocket, and sixpence in my shoe. Show me a cloud and I'll show you a silver lining. Show me a darkness and I'll show you a dawn. Show me a King with a January birthday and I'll show you a dreamer.

I have a dream. Suppose we wake up on New Year's Day 2000 and find that the computers are right—it really is 1900. . . .

At a rock concert celebrating the brave new century a heavy-metal artiste tries to sing "Punchin' Out My Ho" but a strange thing happens: each time he tries to pronounce "ho" it comes out "lady of the evening." He gives up and launches into "My Black-Leather Bitch," only to find himself singing "Sunbonnet Sue." Next he tries his award-winning Nineties pimp song, "Sent My Ho to Sell Her Bootie," but it turns into "Seeing Nellie Home." He can't understand it; all the songs he used to know have been wiped out of his memory and replaced with a whole new repertoire. Stranger still, the crowd loves it and demands an encore, so he sings the most sexually explicit song his reprogrammed brain can come up with: "You Are My Honeysuckle, I Am the Bee."

The new-old pop sound of 1900 solves problems we thought would never go away.

Monica Lewinsky's father finds his manhood: "Every man standing by had a tear in his eye, for some had a daughter at home."

Viagra suddenly becomes unpopular and soon vanishes from the pharmacopoeia: "Her beauty was sold for an old man's gold, she's a bird in a gilded cage."

Nina Burleigh learns to tone down her slutty expressions of gratitude to Presidents who brush her bicycle-scarred legs under card tables: "I gambled in the game of love, I played my heart and lost, I'm now a wreck upon life's sea, I fell and paid the cost."

Sexual-harassment lawsuits stop as women relearn the lost art of righteous indignation: "My mother was a lady, like yours, you will allow, and you may have a sister who needs protection now."

The number of dead babies found in toilets and dumpsters drops dramatically: "Over my slumbers your loving watch keep, rock me to sleep, mother, rock me to sleep."

Public schools change overnight: "Reading and writing and 'rithmetic, taught to the tune of a hickory stick."

Our eardrums are no longer blasted with regular reminders to dial 10-10-321, but long-distance service is not interrupted and in fact improves: "Hello, Central, Give Me Heaven."

Our long national nightmare of hypochondria ends as Americans stop obsessing about the perfect health-care plan: "The doctor has said that she will be dead when the leaves from the trees start to fly." Now that health is no longer regarded as a "right," we develop a realistic acceptance of the bleak truth that sometimes things can go very wrong even when there is no Amtrak: "Baby's face brings pictures of a cherished wife that's dead, but baby's cries can't waken her in the baggage coach ahead."

No more cases of anorexia or bulimia are reported. In the new 1900 the toast of Broadway is Lillian Russell, who at five-foot-five and 165 pounds is said to have the best shape in America—the word "figure" is now obsolete. When the Russell dimensions are reported, England is rocked by an earthquake registering a perfect size 16 on the Richter scale, said to have originated as a rolling movement under a small island at Althorp.

Best of all are the public notices of the new 1900. LADIES ENTRANCE . . . UNESCORTED WOMEN WILL NOT BE SERVED AT THE BAR . . . THIS SUBWAY CAR RESERVED FOR WOMEN ONLY . . . LADIES DAY! WOMEN ADMITTED FREE! Even better are the signs at City Halls. POLL TAX DUE ONE MONTH BEFORE ELECTION DAY . . . LITERACY TESTS GIVEN IN REGISTRAR'S OFFICE . . . JURY ROOM—MEN ONLY.

S UCH is my dream. The feminist website that recently cited me as a "force for reaction" got it right. I freely admit that I'd like to dismantle the whole shebang and start all over again, but many others share my anarchic urges. I don't mean the survivalists, who are bound to be in clover. Nor do I necessarily mean vengeful computer nerds, though any unusually intelligent person in Regular Guy America is bound to be a little dangerous.

I mean the earnest Op-Ed Cassandras with their apocalyptic quotes from "experts" advising us to buy gold, dried food, and shotgun shells in case of Y2K "social disorders." The note of glee under their "concern" takes me back to the Cuban missile crisis of 1962, when people raced through the supermarket in their brand-new farmers' overalls, buying enough dried beans to lift the *Hindenburg* and trying to look solemn when they said "Isn't this terrible?"

Our winter of discontent had barely begun in 1962 but the America of today is an unsolvable problem enclosed in an inescapable conundrum wrapped in a curtain of charity. Anarchy may be tempting, but there's a catch. Suppose, come January of 2000, the President has to declare martial law and assume emergency powers, and uses Y2K as an excuse to stay in office indefinitely?

Many a heart will be aching, even the girls once in thrall, we thought he'd be gone but now breaks the dawn and he's still there after the ball.

August 17, 1998

Y OU can tell a lot about a people by what they absolutely will not forgive. It's a matter of ideals, but more often than not it's a matter of sore spots.

Take the French. Sanche de Gramont tells the story of a rich gentleman who shot his maid dead when he found her decanting wine with a metal funnel. If the official ideals of liberty, equality, and fraternity had prevailed he would have paid the ultimate penalty, but his nation's most renowned sore spot carried the day and he was found not guilty on grounds of justifiable homicide.

Linda Tripp is the American counterpart of the luckless maid, the perpetrator of a deed so unforgivable that our official ideals of empathy on tap and runneth-over compassion have dried up, leaving her stranded in an arid desert of relentless vilification and pitiless mockery.

Mike Downey of the *Los Angeles Times* wondered if Monica Lewinsky "is someone who will sell a confidant down the river, which would make her every bit as much an injudicious Judas as that gum-flapping back-stabber Linda Tripp."

Time's Calvin Trillin wrote: "Just because your behavior calls to mind Victor McLaglen in *The Informer*, there is no law that says you have to look like him as well. . . . Gypo Nolan, the character Victor McLaglen played, may have been, all in all, more admirable than Tripp; at least he had pangs of remorse for betraying his friend."

Something is fishy here. At first glance it seems entirely plausible that friendship should be an American sore spot, but when we think about it we come up against the self-evident truth that it is friendliness, not friendship, that matters to us. We are not the *De Amicitia* type; such thoughts as we have on the subject are found in ads for friendly loan companies, articles on how to tone the smile muscles, and headlines about friendly victims who loved people slaughtered by unfriendly psychopaths who kept to themselves.

Anyone familiar with the nine-to-five world would hesitate to call Linda Tripp and Monica Lewinsky friends. It sounds to me as if they were office mates, workaday pals, something less than colleagues and something more than ships that pass in the night. True, they got very close, but closeness is not necessarily friendship. To say that Tripp was close to Lewinsky is to say that Jean Valjean was close to Inspector Javert when in fact it was a case of being unable to shake him off.

Another argument against friendship as the sore spot that Linda tripped is that both she and Lewinsky are women. Watch closely as male pundits hand down the now clichéd verdict, "Friends don't tape friends," and you will see the trace of a smirk. Even more telling are the male columnists who cram references to backstabbing, throat-slitting, Judas, Iago, the Borgias, Munich, and Pearl Harbor all in the same paragraph. Men have never believed in female friendship and now they are secretly overjoyed that all the old adages are proving true. If they use male symbols of treachery to describe Tripp, it's only because they know they can't get away with comparisons to cats and claws. The only reason men object to Tripp's betrayal of Monica is that "tape" won't fit into "Telephone, telegraph, tell a woman."

If friendship is not the operative sore spot in the war against Linda Tripp, what is?

As the naked displays of fury against her mount, there comes a point when we must ask ourselves who among us is most prone to make a sore spot of friendship. The answer, of course, is adolescents. When Tripp-haters get worked up they give off ominous gusts that collect into an atmosphere of gathering tumult familiar to parents, who recognize it as a sign that an hysterical teenager is getting ready to scream "You hate my friends!"

In the stripling world of never-ever-as-long-as-I-live, loyalty between peers is as absolute as it is mystifying and infuriating to those outside the peerage. If ever there were a credo that perfectly expresses the values of this closed circle, it is E. M. Forster's corrupt emollient: "If I had to choose between betraying my country and betraying my friend, I hope I should have the guts to betray my country."

This sentence first appeared in a book Forster published in 1951. Lillian Hellman used it as a sacred text when she refused to "name names" in her appearance before the House Un-American Activities Committee. It frequently was quoted by enemies of "McCarthyism," but it did not become generally known until the Sixties, when "alienated" hippies and draft-dodgers turned it into the catchphrase of the day to rationalize their behavior.

Society, they explained, demands loyalty to family and country whether deserved or not, but coerced loyalty is immoral and therefore not binding on the truly moral person, who is loyal only to the people and institutions he deems worthy.

T HE Sixties inundated us with this kind of thinking. It's called "situation ethics" and we are so used to it that we don't know how we ever lived without it. It's ever so handy for distinguishing one trimester from another, one perjury from another, one adultery from another. Indeed, we use it all the time now.

Linda Tripp did not use it. Instead of making "moral choices" she made a moral choice and in so doing reminded the entire country of the difference. Confronted with a woman who opted for the non-binding loyalties of law and truth and the unworthy institution of Ken Starr, the liberal media, a fortress of situation ethics, unleashed its rage. It was the relentless rage of protestors, blood-throwers, draft-card burners—a Days of Rage rage staged by greying ex-flower children who now manage the news. Their updated version of Forster's credo, "Friends don't tape friends," is copied from a public-service announcement, but his twisted notions of loyalty and betrayal come through loud and clear.

Linda Tripp uncovered a sore spot that turned out to be a grease spot: the dissolving American character, spreading slowly across the floor.

September 1, 1998

Z ZZZT! Foiled again. Today is Testimony Eve and my deadline is the day after Testimony. I can't very well write about what hasn't happened yet, so I'll tell you about the two weeks I've spent glued to the TV.

Be forewarned: the phrase "Testimony Eve" is all wrong. An "eve" is calm and still, with that quieter-than-quiet hush that tells us it's snowing even before we look out the window. I can't look out my windows because the air-conditioners are in the way, and one of them has started making a raspy squawk that sounds just like Bay Buchanan.

Watching the talking heads on CNBC took ten years off my life, a dangerously close shave for someone old enough to remember *Information Please* on the radio. My favorite panelists were Clifton Fadiman, whose name tickled me, and Cornelia Otis Skinner, whose name fascinated me. I was too young to follow the questions and answers but what impressed me then and still sticks in my mind were the easy chuckles and relaxed freemasonry of the polished, the cultivated, and the learned among us. It was a purely instinctual reaction on my part: they seemed to be having a good time, so I did, too.

Bay Buchanan's *Equal Time* also triggers an instinctual reaction in me: I want to watch it through spread fingers like a queasy juror looking at autopsy photos. The morbid streak in human nature explains why the show has lasted as long as it has: we tune in to see how much worse it can get.

No other show on television has been rerigged so often. Conceived as *Crossfire* for girls, its original hosts were Mary Matalin on the right and Jane Wallace on the left, but Wallace laughed constantly and Matalin did not open her mouth wide enough to be understood, much less yell at anybody; Edgar Bergen moved his lips more.

Bay Buchanan took over on the right but her tortuous efforts to imitate her brother without being unfeminine doomed the format to the psychological ambidexterity of the female condition, making it seem more like one of early feminism's assertiveness-training films about coping with recalcitrant home repairmen.

The left-wing chair has seen such a rapid turnover that it now has been held by just about everybody. The reason is not hard to guess. Many a husband has vanished without a trace when a female voice became intolerable, a career move described in the old punchline, "He went out to buy a newspaper and never came back." The producers of *Equal Time* inadvertently discovered how to get rid of liberal women: sit them next to Braying Bay until they run away and join the ladies auxiliary of the French Foreign Legion.

Then there are the guests. Tony Blankley, who keeps his mouth open in readiness while waiting to get a word in edgewise, swishing his tongue around in limbering-up exercises clearly visible to the viewer. Susan Estrich, who cackles to herself off-camera and nearly demolishes the set with her flailing arms. Joe Conason with all the aplomb of an ax murderer. Michael Isikoff, whose open collar and askew tie project that air of danger treasured by English majors who carry a razor to cut the pages of foreign paperbacks. Jonah "My Mom Says" Goldberg, and Mandy Grunwald, hunched and tragic, the gypsy in every opera, trying to make her whispery deathbed hexes heard over Bay's hoarse screams of "Hold on! Let her finish!"

After *Equal Time* I watched *Hardball*, where the leisurely atmosphere of pensive reflection is reminiscent of the *Titanic* at 2:20 A.M. The machine-gun nest that Chris Matthews calls a mouth is the reason why so many people who loathe Geraldo Rivera watch his show anyway: it comes on after *Hardball* and we're too wrung out to move.

Testimony Eve and Testimony Day have now passed but Post-Testimony will usher in another eight months of special reports, extended editions, and "Lemme finish!" I'll watch them because I have to, but what I really would enjoy is hearing Bill Clinton discussed on a revived *Information Please*. The networks aren't interested so I'll have to produce it myself. Here goes:

We should not limit our comparisons of Bill Clinton to history's male rogues, for in behavior and turn of mind he most resembles Caroline of Brunswick, who married the Prince of Wales, later George IV, in 1796.

That Caroline was oversexed from earliest girlhood is evident from her family's efforts to control stud eruptions. According to one source: "They say her passions are so strong that when she dances, a governess must follow behind to prevent her from indecent conversations."

THREE weeks after their marriage the royal couple separated, permitting Caroline free rein for her compulsive bawdiness. She aroused a naval attaché under the table with her foot, displayed a pair of wind-up dolls that simulated coitus, and had unconsummated intimate contact with future prime minister George Canning. Being still married, and aware that adultery against the Crown was treason, Caroline protected her loophole.

When later she moved to Italy and had full-fledged affairs, British consuls took charge of the stud eruptions and kept London informed of her lovers, but soon there were so many that one envoy gave up and reported: "I don't know who is rogering the Princess now."

When George became King in 1820 he warned her that if she returned to England and insisted on being crowned Queen she would be tried for adultery in the House of Lords, but Caroline the hair-splitter had a ready answer.

English law defined an adulteress as the accomplice of an adulterer, but foreigners could not commit treason against England; thus, since all her lovers were Italian, she was innocent.

Never one to go quietly, she returned to England and pounded on the doors of Westminster Abbey during George's coronation, but they would not let her in. Shamed at last, she died three weeks later.

Max Beerbohm summed her up in words that will do for Bill Clinton's legacy: "Fate wrote her a most tremendous tragedy, but she played it in tights."

September 14, 1998

O KAY, you win. I aim to please. I had another subject planned but I got a bundle of letters asking about the Gay Nineties songs in my Y2K column so it's back to the gilded cage.

First, the requests. I can't accept collect calls to sing over the phone so you can learn the tunes: my singing would not necessarily convey them. Appearing in concert on the next *NR* cruise is out, and I modestly decline to record a cassette with WFB accompanying me on the harpsichord. Not that I never sing; the third martini will do it but it has to be spontaneous.

How did I learn such old songs? From my grandmother; we used to sing while I held her knitting wool. There was also a radio show around 1940 called *The Gay Nineties Hour* with an Irish tenor named Frank Munn who sang all three verses to songs that are known today, if at all, only by their choruses.

"In the Shade of the Old Apple Tree" has a happy chorus but a sad verse: "Father, if you'll tell me where she's lying, if the grave be far just point it out to me. Dear boy, she said to us when she was dying, to bury her beneath the apple tree." By the same token, "I Wonder Who's Kissing Her Now?" has a sentimental chorus and a cynical verse: "You have kissed 'neath the moon while the world was in tune, then you left her to hunt a new game. Did it ever occur to you later, my boy, that she's probably doing the same?"

Granny's favorites were about fallen women, and some of them were harrowing. "I stopped then to see what the object could be, and there in the gutter did lay, a woman in tears from the crowd's angry jeers, and then I heard somebody say . . ." The reminder that "She may have seen better days" changes the jeers to tears in the second verse and leads to streetcorner group therapy in the third.

The understanding male is a fixture in fallen-women songs, a fact overlooked by feminists obsessed with the Victorian patriarchy's madonna–whore distinction. The most touching was composed by Paul Dresser, né Dreiser, who, like his brother Theodore, was haunted by memories of their erring sister.

In the first verse a carefree young man in the big city is leaving work at the end of the day when suddenly—and with perfect grammar—"I saw a girl who shrank from me in whom I recognized my schoolmate in a village far away." She tries to avoid him but he persists. "Don't turn away, Madge, I am still your friend! Next week I'm going back to see the old folks and I thought, perhaps a message you would like to send."

Her answer is a chorus of regret. "Just tell them that you saw me, she said, they'll know the rest. Just tell them I was looking well, you know. Just whisper, if you get a chance, to Mother Dear and say I love her as I did long, long ago."

Refusing to let her go, he takes her home with him in the second verse, and in the third reunites her with her dying mother. Theodore handled the material differently in *Sister Carrie* but it was the same story.

Most of these tunesmiths were uneducated men who had knocked around vaudeville but their lyrics were models of English. Take the little boy whose sister is dying of consumption. Overhearing the doctor's verdict that she will be dead when the leaves fall, he finds a ball of string and climbs a tree, telling the curious: "I'm tying them on 'ere summer be gone so my dear little Nelly won't die." When did you last hear a subjunctive verb in a popular song?

The loving and protective brother was another fixture. Girls always seemed to have them, and were they ever handy. "I've come to this great city to find a brother dear, and you wouldn't dare insult me, sir, if Jack were only here!" In the second verse of "My Mother Was a Lady," the harasser discovers that he knows Jack and offers to take her to him. "He'll be so glad to see you, and if you'll only wed, I'll take you to him as my wife, for I've loved you since you said . . ."

Or try this one. In the first verse a little girl asks her bachelor uncle why he never married. He replies in the second verse with the story of the long-ago night when he took his beloved to a ball. During the evening she becomes thirsty and so he leaves her in an anteroom and goes to get her a glass of water, but when he returns he finds her in another man's arms. "Down fell the water, broken was all, just as my heart broke after the ball."

The third verse tells of her attempts to explain and his refusal to listen. They break up, she dies, and he nurses a grudge until: "One day a letter came from that man, he was her brother, so the letter ran. That's why I'm lonely, no home at all, I believed her faithless after the ball."

HOW did the songs influence me? In various ways, good and bad. They helped me break into the true-confessions magazines. The confessions formula of sin, suffer, repent and the Gay Nineties formula of first verse, second verse, third verse are essentially the same. I was fine as long as I stuck to pulp fiction, but my attempts at serious novels foundered on the long arm of coincidence, the nick of time, and the deathbed clarification.

They gave me a sentimental streak to balance my otherwise bleak temperament, but it can produce some bizarre reactions, as when I ghosted a book for a famous lady of the evening.

Professionally, it went well—she was nothing if not forthcoming—but meeting her triggered an uncharacteristic depression I could not shake off. I was in full mope when my agent called.

"So how'd it go?"

"She doesn't have a heart of gold."

"So what else is new?"

He thought I was kidding but I felt so sad that I got drunk and sang what I now think of as the Ballad of Monica Lewinsky: "She's more to be pitied than censured, she's more to be helped than despised. She's only a lassie who ventured on life's stormy path ill-advised. Do not scorn her with words fierce and bitter, do not laugh at her shame and downfall, for a moment just stop and consider that a man was the cause of it all."

September 28, 1998

THE Home Run Chase promised to be the perfect antidote to the first anniversary of Princess Diana's death. As late August approached, all signs pointed to a shutout of female compassion by male competition and the victory of cold dry statistics over hot moist emotions. Vulnerability was out, virility was in. Pecs were in, pathos was out. The inner child was out, the outer hunk was in. This year, I told myself, things would be different; these guys would eat teddy bears for breakfast.

My prediction had the same stuff on it as the pitching of Wild Man Williams, the Phillies closer who fell off the mound in the '93 World Series and almost got lynched after blowing the game. No sooner did I make it than the sports pages filled up with plangent accounts of the long rocky road of self-discovery traveled by Mark McGwire in his painful quest for the overflowing warmth, spontaneous affection, and unselfish caring that are now his trademarks.

Thomas Boswell: "McGwire has to work hard to let those qualities out.

He was in therapy for four years, trying to pry his feelings open. Now, they are. The public senses it and loves it."

Not only is McGwire the equal of Babe Ruth in batting, Boswell reiterated three days later, "But he has also become, perhaps, the most open, demonstrative and sharing slugger since Ruth as well. That emotional largesse came naturally to Ruth. For McGwire, it has been hard won—through divorce . . . and several years of therapy."

Lest we think the point has been made, Boswell stated it a third time the following day: "What other famous player is proud to say he spent four years in therapy so he could understand himself better? . . . For the past week, McGwire's been the first to acknowledge that the blame for his failed marriage was largely his. He's given many versions of his deep self-doubts. . . . "

Indeed he has. This is what he told *Sports Illustrated*: "I was all closed in. I didn't like myself. I wasn't a very secure person. I could never face the truth. I always ran from it. It's like, sometimes I look back at myself in those days and think, 'Who was I?' "

And what did the Home Run Chase tell him about himself? "That I'm a pretty strong person. I knew I was strong, but I don't think anyone understands what I've been through the last two weeks. . . . Right now, it's unbelievable how strong I've stayed through this, mentally and physically. . . . My life has not been easy even though people look at me and see where I am right now. It has not been easy professionally or personally to get to where I'm at right now. I'm a perfect example of a person that is normal and that can conquer things if they believe in themselves."

Psychobabble like this gives introspection a bad name. What the newbaptized never understand is that no amount of therapy can teach someone to be introspective. Introspective people are born that way, and since nature insists on package deals, they are also destined to be another kind of intro: -vert. But introverts and birth memberships are un-American so we have democratized introspection. Now everybody's gotta right to look deeply into theirself, but like all our other adventures in leveling, this one gets everything bass-ackwards. The pensive skepticism and self-containment of the bona-fide introspective mark them as neurotics, while the faux introspective are deemed well-adjusted because they display the isn't-it-wonderful glow of shallow therapeutic good cheer.

Mark McGwire's mask slipped once, most refreshingly, when he blew up at an umpire and got tossed, but it only made matters worse as his subsequent efforts to atone became Clintonian in scope. Smiling, laughing, winking, twinkling he went, chatting up the opposing catcher at the plate and greeting everyone who arrived at first base like the host at a garden party. Nothing could stale his infinite isn't-it-wonderfulness, not even going without a homer in Cincinnati. On the contrary, the dry spell upped the ante to isn't-it-ecstatic. When the Reds' Dimitri Young got a single after homering in his previous at-bat, Big Mac welcomed him to first with a hug.

Tom Knott: "Baseball has come a long way from cleat-wielding Ty Cobb to sensitive sluggers who hug."

By this time I was ready to root for Big Mac's rival Sammy Sosa, but it was too late. He was going around the country telling sportswriters, "McGwire is the man. Every day is a happy day for me. I love it. I'm enjoying every minute." Good sportsmanship, that jewel in the masculine crown so lacking in my own sex ("I'm not going to throw the ball to *her*!") had degenerated into an Alphonse–Gaston nightmare.

I N the first week of September the battle of the asterisk took on new meaning. When Roger Maris broke Babe Ruth's home-run total, baseball's record books carried an asterisk beside his name noting that his season was eight games longer than Ruth's. Since Big Mac was set to render that asterisk moot, we decided he was the man to eliminate the plethora of asterisks that Bill Clinton had scattered throughout your average English-language dictionary.

Jack McKeon, manager of the Reds, on the wisdom of not walking McGwire: "I've been getting all these calls on my voice mail wanting me to heal the country. So we pitched to him."

Tom Knott on September 9: "America has averted its eyes from Bill and Ken, if only momentarily, to follow the ball's flight. The nightly news is G-rated again."

Two days later Starr pitched his report and Clinton took a mighty therapeutic swing, vowing to go on a journey of contrition to the rock-bottom of truth where breaches are repaired, pride is renounced, help is sought, and the magic of change, lovely change, will fix everything up just fine.

Isn't it wonderful? Mark McGwire is our good angel and Bill Clinton is our bad angel, and they have met in the middle of the New Age playing field. One of them is Princess Di with a bat and the other is Princess Di with a potus.

October 12, 1998

F INDING my inner First Lady is easy: Mrs. Warren Harding's maiden name was Florence Kling. When Carl S. Anthony's biography of her came out this year I vowed to read it purely for pleasure so as not to be distracted by the underlining and note-taking of reviewing, but I found so many parallels between the Hardings and the Clintons that my four-color pencil ran out of lead.

Flossie Kling's strident Midwestern accent was never more pronounced than when she barked "Wurrn!," though later on when he was President she carefully purred "my husband." Five years his senior, she was a frumpy girl with the strongest jaw in Marion, Ohio, and, said the daughter of her beautician, "she was self-conscious about her piano legs." Thirty when she wed the philandering 25-year-old Harding, she hid what at first were imaginary throat wrinkles and later real ones with a black-velvet neck band. It would become her trademark.

Politically she was a solid Ohio Republican but her instincts were feminist. "I never wore a wedding ring," she told the press. "I don't like badges. And perhaps it's just a crotchet of a woman who knows women's province but insists on having a personality. . . . I do not like to cook. I hate fussing with food. . . . I'd rather go hungry than broil a steak or boil potatoes. I love business."

Her physical and domestic shortcomings did not bother her husband. "Some men choose women to marry because of sexual passion, others for social prestige, still others for money, but Warren recognized that with Florence he could create a superb partnership. He could count on her." And Florence, despite her occasional insecurities, knew it: "If she could never entirely control him, she continued to boss him with the confidence exhibited only by the sort of wife who knows her husband will never leave her."

Warren came from a close-knit doctor's family whose happiness was marred when his mother was accused of medical manslaughter. Trained in homeopathy, Phoebe Harding acted as her husband's assistant, mixing potions and dosing his patients, one of whom died when her pepsin concoction was found to contain arsenic. She was acquitted on the testimony of Dr. Charles Sawyer, whom her grateful son would one day name White House physician.

The other Harding family scandal was Warren's insatiable appetite for female flesh. His transitory hits included farmers' daughters, sporting-house girlies, and maids, but he also seduced Florence's childhood friend, carried on with the widow next door, and had a 14-year affair with Carrie Phillips, wife of a Marion businessman.

Stimulated by risk, he made love to Carrie on the Phillips's kitchen table, in the yard, and, when the two couples sailed to Europe together, on the deck a few feet from Florence's cabin. He also left a paper trail. "Warren's recklessness in writing love letters seems at times almost pathological, as if he were secretly hoping to be destroyed by them." One particularly steamy letter to Carrie was written on Easter Sunday while Florence dressed for church.

When he was elected U.S. Senator in 1916 he wrote to Carrie on Senate letterhead and made love to his secretary, Grace Cross, who later tried to blackmail him, telling his go-between, "I can describe a birthmark on his back." Meanwhile, he was being stalked by twenty-year-old Nan Britton, a Marion doctor's daughter. Known as "a very nervy person," Nan told everyone in town that she had a crush on him and asked him to get her a job in New York.

Their daughter was born in 1919 but Nan refused to give the baby up for adoption and hinted instead at marriage, eliciting from Warren the same vague promise he had given Carrie: he might be alone in the future, given "the probability of Mrs. Harding's death in advance of his own." Nervy Nan later visited him in the White House. In her 1931 book, *The President's Daughter*, she revealed that they had "a tryst in a large closet, the sitting room actually, adjacent to the Oval Office."

At the 1920 GOP convention a pol said of Florence: "No step was taken without consulting her, and her advice was rarely, if ever, ignored." A reporter wrote: "If Warren G. Harding is elected there will be two p— well, *personalities* in the White House."

F LORENCE adored show-business people and had her own Barbra Streisand in Fanny Brice, who called her plastic surgery "getting my nose back to normalcy." Evalyn Walsh McLean, owner of the Hope Diamond, became such fast friends with Florence that rumors of lesbianism flew. Also on tap were Madame Marcia, Washington's leading clairvoyant, and Dr. Charles Sawyer, the Harding Administration's answer to William Ginsburg, who so craved attention that he told a reporter the President had three testicles.

And then there are the unreleased medical records. Harding had two nervous breakdowns, one in 1889 and another shortly after his marriage in 1893, but no details are known. He died on a trip to Alaska, where his lassitude lifted only once, when he asked, "How do the bull seals control their extensive harems?" His heart attack was misdiagnosed by Dr. Sawyer but a young Navy physician had seen it coming and later wrote: "He played too many holes [of golf] on a single outing when under great mental strain and pressure of official responsibility," and "He loved to play cards and there were times when doing so, he lost too much needed sleep."

The haunting similarities between Florence and Hillary are overridden by one huge difference. Florence was given to bluff raillery and had a "Hiya, boys, have a drink" manner that put men at ease, a quality Harding captured in his touching tribute, "She's the best pal a fellow ever had."

The difference between the two Presidents is found in the poem Warren wrote to Carrie Phillips: "I love your knees, their dimples kiss / I love your ways of giving bliss / I love your poise of perfect thighs / When they hold me in paradise."

It's not Keats but it's normal.

October 26, 1998

A N anonymous Englishman once said with charming accuracy that French sounds like a woman flirting with a man, Italian like a man flirting with a woman, Spanish like a saint praying to God, and German like a stableboy swearing at horses. How, then, do foreigners hear English? This question has intrigued me all my life.

Conducting experiments is a good way to go mad, and several times I almost have. I've tried self-hypnosis with Olivier's recordings, falling asleep to Churchill's recordings, and reciting the Gettysburg Address as fast as possible while drunk. Nothing worked; it still sounded like the same old native tongue to me.

Now at long last the revelation has come. Thanks to the Clinton scandals I not only have experienced English as a second language but as one somewhere in the neighborhood of fourteenth. I don't mean his "parsing" or his redefining of sex. Sophistries are old hat; what I'm talking about is the dawn of a whole new linguistic era.

Remember the flurry about whether UN Ambassador Bill Richardson was pressured by the White House to find a job for Monica Lewinsky in New York? At the Senate confirmation hearings for his new post as energy secretary Richardson was asked if the job he offered Monica had existed before he interviewed her, or if he had created it especially for her. Richardson swore it was an old job but UN sources said he created it, and that when the scandal broke in January he panicked and juggled his staff around to make it look as if the job had existed all along.

He was backed up by his chief of staff Rebecca Cooper, who satisfied my lifelong curiosity when she told the *Washington Times*:

> It's a fungible slot. You can trace a slot, but you can't say this person
> held that particular position because the position has evolved. It's such a

nuance. What the senators were focused on—I mean, I gotta tell you, you're kind of getting into things that are really splitting hairs. People who held this job previously shouldn't regard themselves as the people who held the Monica slot. The job has evolved. All the allegations that people try to suggest, for example, that we created the job just for Monica, that doesn't hold up. Because regardless of Monica and prior to me ever knowing that Monica Lewinsky was ever going to be anyone in the newspaper, I continued to have that need and I filled it.

Welcome to the Age of the Fungible Nuance. Now that I've named it I'll have to define it, which is impossible. The Fungible Nuance will never be included in a dictionary of literary terms because it eludes the straightforward definitions required in reference books. Malapropisms are incorrect words that come in the middle of otherwise correct speech, such as "the clink in his armor." Spoonerisms, or the transposition of the letters or sounds of two words, come from the sermons of English clergyman William Spooner, who traded "a mess of pottage" for "a pot of message."

A Fungible Nuance does not come in the middle of anything except itself because its operative form is the circle. Like beachcombers playing with pebbles, Fungible Nuancers drop words into the speech pool and let them widen into sentences until they have a mess of pottage in a pot of message.

The easiest way to define it is to substitute sound for meaning. "Fungible" means interchangeable but it sounds like a gum disease. "Nuance" means a subtle degree of difference but it sounds like a gas leak. Both ooze.

The best Fungible Nuances are found in print because their baggy unwieldiness can defeat attempts to mine them for soundbites. Rather than cut through whale blubber with embroidery scissors, television producers murmur "Let go, let God" and pass the whole slab on to newspapers, whose readership is declining.

To spot a Fungible Nuance, look for high grammatical crimes, lots of perceive-for-see and purchase-for-buy misdemeanors, and a whiff of the occult. "The ambassador is not a personnel officer," said Bill Richardson's spokesman Calvin Mitchell. "He is not to sit in front of the Senate and answer questions off people's personnel files. And he described, in his mind, what the job was to him and how it was perceived and how it was going to function."

The more self-conscious Fungible Nuancers will suddenly drop an awkward, uncommon verb in the midst of softly lapping cliched sludge, like Barney Frank:

If you're not going to tell the truth about the sex, if there are things you feel you can't tell the truth about, it's unrealistic to expect that you'd tell the truth to seven people. It's hard to segment that. And I also think, in this context, he did not set out to deliberately trap these people in deception. He himself was caught in a bad situation.

A FUNGIBLE Nuance need not be wordy. One tin-earred simile will suffice, as in Jesse Jackson's analysis of Chelsea Clinton's role: "In some sense, her knowledge of what has happened and yet her will to embrace them in the midst of it has been like a big piece of glue in this situation."

The worst Fungible Nuances resemble the "word salad" of schizophrenia or the cascades of Tourette's syndrome. Obsession-compulsion may also be a factor. Orrin Hatch must have been in the throes of "Step on a pronoun, break your mother's back" when he advised Clinton to seek help:

> There's no doubt in my mind that he has a problem, or problems, and that he needs some help with those problems and that he ought to get some help with those problems, because you can't keep doing things like this and have that kind of reckless conduct without it being a very serious problem.

The future of the Fungible Nuance was glimpsed when practitioners began to imitate their own incoherent rambling with onomatopoeic interjections. In her new book, *Bitch*, Elizabeth Wurtzel substitutes "blah-blah-blah" for arguments. Talk-show guests sum up their views with "yadda-yadda-yadda." And Lanny Davis, First Spinner, analyzed his psyche thusly: "I distinguish those feelings from other feelings of betrayal, anger, fill-in-the-blank."

November 9, 1998

I T happened again. The same thing that happened with *Braveheart*, the same thing that always happens when I try to escape into a movie. As usual, I drew a red circle around the TV listing and looked forward to it all week. When the big moment came I turned off the phone, got my coffee and cigarettes, and arranged my new Chinese neck pillow (*1,000 Pillows Catalogue*). I was ready for lift-off but Masterpiece Theatre's adaptation of *Wuthering Heights* was Mission Impossible.

It was introduced by Russell Baker, who announced with solemn pride that while other film versions covered only the first 17 chapters of the book and ended with Cathy's death, this one was filmed "the way Emily Brontë wrote it." That could mean only one thing: they had tackled the part in which Brontë got so carried away with soul-mingling that she created a second generation of characters and gave them names almost indistinguishable from the first.

The heroine of the Gen-Xers is Cathy Linton, daughter of Cathy Earnshaw and Edgar Linton. It would help to call her "Little Cathy" but we are not in Alabama. She marries her first cousin Linton Heathcliff, son of Heathcliff and her Aunt Isabella Linton, but he soon dies and she comes under the gaze of her other first cousin, Hareton Earnshaw, son of her Aunt Cathy's brother Hindley Earnshaw.

No seasoned writer would do this but Brontë was a one-book genius. Structurally, *Wuthering Heights* is a crick without a pillow that needs the services of an Old Hollywood story conference where some supposedly insensitive philistine growls "Enough already! Get rid of the kids."

I didn't recognize any names or faces in the all-English cast and have no idea who played whom, nor do I care. The only memorable thing about them was their ordinariness. Everyone seemed to have wandered in from Tony Blair's England, always emoting but never convincing, their fine Yorkshire madness flattened into the eurodollar of neurosis.

The well-bred Edgar Linton, tragically uncomprehending of Cathy's need for savagery, is presented merely as a polite coward. The wretched Hareton, who has been reduced to an animal state in revenge for his father's like treatment of Heathcliff, comes across as a soccer yob whose big grievance is the foul that Manchester committed against York. No matter what he said I heard it as "Oi, booger you, mate." So, apparently, did Little Cathy. Acted by a Judy Geeson type—the English version of a Tuesday Weld type—she seemed less like the designated restorer of his humanity than a North Country bleached-blonde bird nervously trying to kid him out of tearing up the seats so he won't get sacked from the factory and become "redoondant."

What of the romantic leads, the unforgettable lovers, the eternal sweethearts—Big Cathy and Big Heathcliff? She has sharp, irregular features to go with her nervy shrillness and he has a face like a sadistic potato. The channel is all-passion, all-the-time, but chemistry never once rears its head. In fidelity to the book there are no sex scenes, but neither are there any love scenes. He expresses his devotion by decapitating six baby birds but he never says "My sweet, wild Cathy" and she never says "Fill my arms with heather." The famous despairing lines are also left out. We never hear him howl "I can't live without my life, I can't live without my soul!" And the best-known line in the book, "I *am* Heathcliff, he's more myself than I am," is changed to "I *am* Heathcliff, I can't bear to live without him," or some such empty-calorie cliché.

So it's not "the way Emily Brontë wrote it" after all, but we should not be surprised. Watch any re-make of an old movie and you will find the same sort of tamping down and blanding out because modern man is embarrassed by consuming passion unless it be about class or race.

The love story is downplayed in favor of a Kitchen-Sink drama with Heathcliff as the Angry Young Man of the working class who breaks furniture and gentlewomen to get even for his origins, which just might involve Africa. His original classification as a gypsy is quickly dropped in favor of unspecific slurs about his dark complexion and a gratuitous taunt about Isabella's "blonde hair and fair skin," but the viewer can't help noticing that the actor who plays him is not dark at all. He has brown hair and green eyes and is fairer than the brunette Cathy.

Since the script made such an issue of it, why didn't they dye his hair, make up his skin, and give him sable contacts? Why am I asking foolish questions? There was no need to change his appearance because we have entered the age of saying-is-believing. The credits went by too fast to tell if Toni Morrison served as consultant but I guarantee her heart was with them.

THE storyteller's job is to grab us by the scruff of our concentration and glue us to the plot, but like so many modern movies, this one keeps us distracted and jumpy with scenes that turn our stomachs. We see Heathcliff digging up Cathy's grave and embracing her 15-year-old corpse; the drunken Hindley falling in his own vomit; and a kiss that leaves a band of saliva stretched between the lovers' mouths, glistening like a steel bridge at dawn.

They also overdo the eighteenth-century rustic squalor. Anyone who wants to know about wallowing in the wuthering can read the Late Georgian volume in the *Everyday Life in . . .* series (highly recommended), but laboring this point in a love story leaves the audience unable to concentrate on anything except "God, they must smell."

Take it from a confessed escapist: the Old Hollywood practice of prettying up a story beats realism any day. I also plead guilty to "lookism." Democratic inclusiveness has made Laurence Olivier's godlike handsomeness suspect but it is precisely what makes *Wuthering Heights* work. Heathcliff must be a paragon of manly beauty and romantic dash in order for Cathy to find the rich, kind, well-bred Edgar Linton unbearable. If Heathcliff is a potato-face lout, Edgar comes across as what grandmothers used to call "good husband material," which would demolish Brontë's whole point.

November 23, 1998

I AM one of the .07 per cent of pundits who predicted the November elections correctly. Other practitioners of the beige arts confidently opined that the GOP would pick up anywhere from seven to 15 seats, but I said they would lose seats and that the Democrats might even take back the House.

Trouble is, I didn't say it publicly, but in a letter to Andrew Ferguson, my former roommate, so to speak, who shared this page with me when his "Gimlet Eye" column ran in alternate issues. Only Andy can prove my powers of prognostication so I'm having him served with a subpoena *duces tecum*: come and bring the letter. What a great day it will be for CNN. First a shot of the now-familiar D.C. courthouse emblazoned with the name E. Barrett Prettyman, then the great bronze doors open and out comes Andy. Flanked by his legal team, he steps up to the bank of microphones and starts reading, so awed by my accuracy that he neglects to stop and reads straight through my gossip and dirty jokes.

I arrived at my prediction via my usual unscientific method of letting my mind wander. This is especially easy to do while watching political talk shows. I ranged hither and yon, reflected on this and that, toyed with a fragmented thought here, a filigree of memory there—what champions of the scientific method call "staring into space" and being "a thousand miles away." But it only looks that way. Something will come to me, and then all the fragments and filigrees suddenly spring out and wrap around it like those jungle vines that squeeze people to death. Or to put it more fastidiously: an idea is born.

The GOP pundits' favorite claim was "The country is conservative," varied with "The Democrats have turned to the Right," "Clinton is governing from the Right," and Rush Limbaugh's hubristic signature line, "We've already won."

As I listened to this drumbeat I stared into space and thought about what happened in October when a private school in Georgia tried to expel a 14-year-old boy who looked so pretty in girls' clothes and makeup that everyone thought he was a she. When the school board found him out and tried to expel him the student body rose up in protest. "What's so weird about that?" asked one boy. Other boys wore hair bows to show their support and confronted the principal with their student handbook, quoting back to him a section about respecting "diversity in opinion, culture, ideas, behavioral characteristics, attributes, or challenges."

I don't care who governs from the Right, when eighth-grade boys defend effeminacy anywhere in the country, the country is not conservative. The spectacle of beribboned Penrods invoking the student handbook to save their transvestite from the officials who issued the handbook bespeaks the rife confusion of a country that has lost the innately conservative principle contained in the expression "the nature of things."

The Left, aware of the value of a confused electorate, has succeeded so well in destroying this principle that Americans can no longer distinguish "hate crimes" from the propensity of schoolboys since time immemorial to shun sissies. The old idea that we are endowed with the capacity to outgrow childish cruelty is gone, replaced by today's credo, "There but for the diversity handbook go I."

No country can exchange the nature of things for the diversity handbook and still call itself conservative. I knew the GOP was doomed the moment I read about the peachy he–she.

Listening to Republicans say "The American people want small government" and Democrats say "The American people care about education," I knew the cares had it. A care count is much more accurate than a vote count and will soon replace it. The word "care" has taken on so much emotional water that it is now impossible to pronounce without an involuntary catch in the voice, hence the Irish-tenor quality of our political debate. The GOP is on the losing end of the want–care axis because we can't say "The American people care about small government" without triggering visions of overwrought volunteers enrolling the poor little government in an outreach program.

I T was while some Republican was intoning "The American people want small government" that I was attacked by a hemp-strength filigree. Suddenly I remembered the first Wednesday in November 1952, the day after Eisenhower's landslide ended twenty years of the New Deal. It was the day I walked into a shellshocked high school.

The smell of fear was in the air. None of us had been alive the last time a Republican was in the White House but we had heard plenty about him and he was still booed in newsreels. We were all born in the mid-1930s so we had no memory of the Depression but we were raised on stories about it and knew that a Republican caused it and Roosevelt cured it. In short, we were New Deal babies and we were scared to death.

Our first chance to panic came at lunchtime. "We won't have enough to eat . . . We'll have to put cardboard in our shoes . . . We'll freeze in the winter . . . Daddy said he's going back to resharpening his old razor blades." Finally somebody sobbed, "We'll have to eat margarine!" That was much worse than it sounds today. Margarine was still sold uncolored and looked like lard, which we associated with poor people. Nice people might cook with margarine but they always put butter on the table.

Such attitudes do not fade away. One way or another they are passed on, reemerging in new guises with new names, such as "middle-class entitlements," to seduce a new generation. I have a hunch that the New Deal is now a string on the American DNA.

Professional pollsters would never use one school in Georgia, Irish tenors, and margarine hang-ups to draw conclusions about the entire country, but then I would never talk to three thousand people, much less believe what they said, so we're even.

December 7, 1998

A S soon as the Jefferson DNA story broke I got numerous calls from editors asking me to write about it. I declined for my usual reason—my first duty is to this column—but in truth I didn't really want to write about it.

My reluctance was twofold. In the first place, I don't like Jefferson. As readers of my misanthropy book know, my favorite Founding Father is Fisher Ames, who loathed Jefferson for supporting the leveling ideals of the French Revolution and considered him a crackpot liberal. Whenever anyone quoted "All men are created equal," Ames shot back: "And differ greatly in the sequel." That's my kind of guy.

Second, I had nothing to say. I've heard the Sally Hemings story all my life and I believe it. I daresay most Southern women do, even the ladies in the Monticello ancestral societies who go around twittering about the man they unfailingly call "Mr. Jefferson." I've known several such types who served as costumed hostesses in historical shrines and they are not the serene, white-crowned grandes dames that tourists see. One, who worked at our local Mary Washington House, told me she was so tired of ignoring the enmity between Washington and his mother that she longed to announce: "And this is the room where George Washington shot his mother dead!"

I can state my opinion of the Sally Hemings story in three words: these things happened. Trying to come up with tortured rationalizations and extenuating circumstances is not my style, so I decided not to write about it. But then, instead of putting it out of my mind entirely, I yielded to my fatal habit of thinking around the edges of a subject and ended up with notes for a Jefferson DNA column with a difference. Instead of writing it, it might be simpler if I just showed you the notes.

Note #1: Jeff news made to order for hysterical, insecure, ignorant, sheeplike masses, a/k/a "the American people." Stand by for ultimate media-driven guilt trip: we're all black.

Note #2: How it will work. Constant repetition as per already established parallels. "We're all immigrants" (orig. FDR? Check Wilson, W. J. Bryan). "Everybody is bisexual" (avant garde in 20s & 50s, hippies in 60s, cocktail-party staple by 70s). "We're all guilty" (suitable for most historical events as well as a wide selection of murders).

Media already repeating most-favored statistic: white–black marriage rate increasing, now at 10%, up from 2. Only thing heard more often is crash-test dummies singing "Ode to Joy" in Audi commercial.

Note #3: Much propaganda already in place. Frances Cress Welsing's theory: whites have "pigment envy" (e.g., tanning). Got big play on Phil Donahue show 1988. Said blacks are "sun people," whites are "ice people." Donahue v. impressed.

Shirlee Taylor Haizlip's 1994 book, *The Sweeter the Juice* (explain title is from old black saying, "The blacker the berry, the sweeter the juice"). Claims "some 95 per cent of 'white' Americans have widely varying degrees of black heritage." Quotes Adrian Piper: "The longer a person's family has lived in this country, the higher the probable percentage of African ancestry—bad news for the DAR, I'm afraid."

Note #4: Pioneers. Whites in California & Southwest already making false claims of Hispanic heritage to get jobs under affirmative action. Monticello tourist comment on Jeff–Sally in *Washington Post*: "There should have been more mixing like that. It would have made the country a more interesting place."

Note #5: Ripe conditions. Lionization of Tiger Woods, self-described "Cablinasian," coincides with effort to change racial-classification questionnaire on Census form. Add "Multiracial" box to prevent discrimination (Otherism).

Note #6: Lust for fame. White descendant of Jeff–Sally son on TV enjoying her 15 minutes of blackness. If that's what it takes to get on TV, then so be it.

Note #7: Trend power. Gentiles wearing yellow stars after *Holocaust* miniseries in 1978. Now trendy whites decide to "pass." Trend-spotter Faith Popcorn names it "One-Drop Chic." One-drop T-shirts, one-drop baseball caps, one-drop coffee mugs (Maxwell House sues), and a one-drop screen saver from Microsoft that freezes if touched by an ice person. One-drop personal ads appear in newspapers, blonde cheerleaders form Iowa One-Drop Drill Team. Use old African-American compliment for cadence count: "Light, bright, damn near white!"

Note #8: Trend sweeps country. Two reasons for success: a) The Choose Factor. Constant use of word by feminists makes choosing race seem normal. b) Ingrained habit. Under P.C., anti-gay remark brings rejoinder, "Suppose you replaced *gay* with *black* in that sentence?" Misogynistic remark? "Suppose you replaced *woman* with *black*?" Anti-immigrant remark? "Suppose you replaced *immigrant* with *black*?" Suppose you replaced yourself with black? Might as well, I've replaced everybody else.

Note #9: Political effect. White hold-outs demand old Census form, organize "Other and Proud" march. Inevitable GOP split develops between the Other Right and the Drop Right. Bob Dole: "You want me to be a berry? I'll be a berry." Drops try to unify party with whispering campaign: "It's a short-cut to Compassionate Conservatism."

Drops win platform fight, vow to strike Big Tent and reach out to each other. Bob Dole: "Bound to work. We're all berries." Dole's Keynote speech preceded by Iowa One-Drop Drill Team marching to "Light, bright, damn near white!" Dole gets his old African-American sayings confused and comes out with: "Nothing sweeter than a bright white berry with dropsy." GOP accused of Dropism. Reappearance of ubiquitous headline: WHAT REPUBLICANS MUST DO TO REGAIN INITIATIVE.

Note #10: Numbers. Once everybody is black, Colin Powell's 750% approval rating drops and Granny's ceremental turnover registers 942.7 on the Richter scale.

December 21, 1998

D EAR Gentle Readers: Here we are again, the last issue of the year and time for my Christmas letter. I always look forward to it because it's the only time I don't have to argue a point or prove anything. I can just relax and write an ordinary letter, the kind I write to Andy Ferguson—minus the unprintable jokes, of course—and be as meandering as I wanna be.

I'll start with the cheerful news. I've stuck to my Passive Suicide Diet and am thinking of writing a cookbook called *This Will Kill You*. Here's a sample menu. B: two fried eggs with scrapple; L: chili over rice; D: three martinis, ham steak, creamed corn, and cheese rolls. My object is an obit containing words like "suddenly" and "massive." Before you start chiding me, ask yourselves this: Can you see me in a nursing home, playing bingo, watching soap operas, and being called "honey" by the arts 'n' crafts lady?

This year I had a golden opportunity to dabble in my favorite anthropological hobby of idiom-dating. Did it strike you as strange that Monica's famous soiled dress was invariably called a "cocktail dress" by media people in their twenties and thirties? They don't even drink cocktails; where did they get that anachronism? It conjured up a picture of Monica rustling around in a taffeta number with a circular skirt down to mid-calf and a halter neck that bared the back—i.e., the dress I had in 1953, which I called a cocktail dress. Now tell me this: Who, of all those involved in the scandal, is exactly my age? Answer: Lucianne Goldberg.

Judge not, lest ye be judged judgmental. That's okay, I don't mind. The year brought three new hatreds, or at least clarifications of old ones. I finally put my finger on what it is about Geraldo Rivera that makes me recoil. He reminds me of the street stud in *The Roman Spring of Mrs. Stone*, Vivien Leigh's next-to-last movie, based on a Tennessee Williams novella about a rich American widow who buys love from European gigolos. Although able to afford the best, she cannot shake her fascination for the scruffy young tramp who follows her on her fashionable rounds and stares at her through the windows of five-star restaurants. The lower she sinks the more often he turns up, a symbol of her fate. Finally one night she sees him under the windows of her house. Zombie-like, her will gone, she tosses her key down to him.

I tried to like Ken Starr but his interview with Diane Sawyer finished him for me. What I feel now is not hatred but contempt, which is worse. The open-collar plaid shirt, calling his wife his "spouse," the whole dimple-flashing, soft-voicing, imploring routine made me want to throw up. We're going see a lot more of this when Compassionate Conservatism starts cranking up for Campaign 2000. What is this terrible need to be liked by liberals? If you have the good fortune to be a real S.O.B., don't spoil it.

Anybody who hates Windows as much as I do is bound to hate Bill Gates, but I have another bone to pick with him. He's neither eccentric in the Ford–Edison–Carnegie mold, nor a striding, steely-eyed psychopath of industry in the Ayn Rand mold. He is simply the living, breathing, whining personification of the word "brat."

I bought a ball of string the other day, and would you believe? It has a warning label: "Do not use in situations where personal safety could be endangered. Never use this product to secure large flat surfaces or objects which could 'airplane.' Misuse could result in serious injury or death."

Thank God for my diet. At least it will save me from one of those ignominious finales insurance companies call "household accidents." Imagine some graduate student of the future looking me up in *American Women*

Writers of the Twentieth Century and reading: "She died suddenly from a massive misuse of string."

The mailman can't get all my catalogues into my box so I had to put an old card table in the lobby for the overflow. I've gotten expert at separating the wheat from the chaff, though I enjoy browsing through the latter for sociological insights.

A whole group of catalogues plays into the feeling of being overwhelmed. There's an organizer box for every conceivable kind of clutter, including the clutter that comes from having too many organizer boxes.

Another group plays into our desire to have *all* our problems solved by magic bullets. In the world of gizmo catalogues, utopia is a universal pot lid. No matter what is plaguing you, there's a non-stick, scratch-begone, wipe-away, wrinkle-free, iron-on, add-a-shelf cure for it. My favorite is the Bra Bridle: "At last! No more bra or slip straps sliding off your shoulders!" I suppose this would have been useful once, but nothing slides off me now; even water gets stuck.

N OW for my Catalogue-of-the-Year award. I bought a tam in the Lindsay tartan (no relation, I just like the colors) from a Celtic woolens catalogue. A month or so later I got the bagpipe catalogue, but the best was yet to come.

It came. Now I can order everything I'll need to take part in a reenactment of the battle of Bannockburn from *Medieval Warfare Replicas*: claymores, maces, poleaxes, chain mail, bevor sallets (helmets), and a complete suit of Duke of Burgundy armor ("fully articulated and wearable") at the unbeatable price of $2,495.

I'd rather tilt at language abusers. If it's "just sex," is it also *Just Psychopathia Sexualis* by Richard von Krafft-Ebing? If there are no absolutes, why does everybody keep saying "Absolutely!" instead of yes? Now that "seeking closure" is the latest thing, why hasn't it occurred to anyone to look in the thesaurus for "write finis to"? And if Clinton would not let Monica soldier on to "completion," does that mean he's in control, out of control, a control freak, or just a freak?

Now for my New Year's Resolution. I will not try any more obscure POTUS jokes. From now on I'll confine myself to the one about the traveling salesman and the farmer's daughter.

December 31, 1998

1999

I AM writing this column at the end of the year so it is axiomatic that I am in a foul mood. Not that I have anything against the end of the year—on the contrary, I'm in favor of the end of just about everything—it's the reading matter that comes with it that gets me down.

I refer to "Year in Review" magazine round-ups and the TV equivalent known as "Best Of."

Once upon a time, Americans were not crammed full of news. Today's journalists wax nostalgic about the heyday of newspaper readership, when every big city had at least two dailies and circulation wars were fought to capture a well-informed public, but it wasn't quite that way. People *bought* a lot of newspapers but they didn't necessarily read them. It was more a case of needing them.

Before $200 toys and Saturday morning cartoons, children needed what were then called the "funny papers." Before the average woman owned two dozen cookbooks she needed recipes from the "woman's page." Lacking scientifically calibrated baggies for every conceivable sort of waste, households needed a lot of newsprint. And men who felt the need to carry *something* but were not yet bold enough to buy briefcases bought newspapers, rolling them up like walking sticks and slapping them against their legs—a twice-daily male ritual, to and from work, that circulation statistics rendered as a morning and afternoon paper in every home.

We got our news from radio and newsreels, but we still came up short.

Even if you went to the movies every time the picture changed, you saw only three newsreels a week, plus an occasional *March of Time*, always hideously boring. A chain of theaters called the Trans-Lux showed nothing but news-reels, but only big cities had them and the audiences were overwhelmingly male, meaning that women wouldn't go if they were alone and couldn't go if they had children with them, which they usually did.

Into the breach rode *Life* magazine with "The Year in Pictures." Nearly everything in it seemed new, including the spreads on the ubiquitous Dionne quintuplets. Some photos were standard but they were never stale; even the obligatory shot of professional debutante Brenda Frazier closing the Stork Club showed her slumped in a different direction from last time.

Now, thanks to instant replays, pool reporting, looping, and other marvels of communication, year-end round-ups show us not what we have missed but what we have already been saturated with. Open a Year in Review or tune in to a Best Of and you are in Kafka's castle, a beset "K." wandering back and forth between a picture of Ken Starr's coffee cup and a picture of Ken Starr's garbage bag, pursued by Barney Frank lisping his eternal riddle, "What did the Moving Finger touch and when did he touch it?"

Like a looming execution date, seeing and hearing the same thing over and over concentrates the mind, but instead of eliminating mental detritus, it enhances it and gives it center stage. Somewhere in the middle of my third Year in Review issue I concluded that nothing much had happened in 1998 that could compare in importance to Newt Gingrich's lapel pin.

That huge, silvery rune held, I was sure, the key to the universe. I stared at it every time I saw his picture, wondering what it was, what it said, why he always wore it, and why it was so big. A lapel-pin round-up would have helped—"Who's Stuck with What?"—but nowhere in the endless pages of lists, up-and-down arrows, and broken picture frames could I find one. *But I had to know*! That's when I went a little crazy. Like the dog in the Beggin' Strips commercial who's sure he smells bacon, I got out my magnifying glass and ransacked all my round-ups, looking for pictures of Newt to try to read what was on the pin, to no avail. The one thing I wanted to know was the one thing nobody had rounded up.

If you've read one Quotables round-up you've read them all, or rather heard them all, since most are printed soundbites recycled by the 'zines and then re-recycled on Best Of television specials. Quotables come in two mod-els: the All-Purpose and the Rosebud. The first lends itself to a build-your-own-quotation kit consisting of key words that can be put together to form whatever sentiment the speaker wishes to express.

T AKE, for example, those popular building blocks of the scintillating sentence: Feel, Sort of, Move on, Heal, Children. Liberal wordsmiths can say, "I sort of feel we should heal and move on for the sake of the children." Moderate Republican wordsmiths can say, "I feel we should sort of move on to heal America's children." The articulate pedophile can say, "I sort of feel I heal when I move on children," and yours truly can say, "Keelhaul children."

The Rosebud is a quote associated with a single individual and contains the essence of his personality. Unfortunately, Rosebuds are fragile flowers. The original Rosebud was uttered once and never came our way again, but the Quotable Rosebud is repeated so often that it becomes the last Rosebud of summer. Lucianne Goldberg's "I love dish!" is dead on the vine, an essence of nothing except the women Marie Antoinette made the mistake of cultivating: the Duchesse de Polignac comes to mind.

Now for my own Year in Review. I think I've found the bribery charge needed for removal. Why did the White House transfer Monica Lewinsky to a Pentagon office containing a Republican woman known to harbor intense anti-Clinton feelings? Was she perhaps instructed to befriend Linda Tripp and bribe her with that condo in Australia?

I have always believed that Hillary was an emotionally insecure man's insurance against abandonment. When Clinton married her she was a plain Jane that no man, particularly no Southern man, would try to take away from him. Now she is no longer plain, and Al Gore may need to appoint a vice president soon.

Why not? The country is finished anyhow so we might as well have some fun.

January 25, 1999

M Y peace has been disturbed. An institution of higher learning and fine madness has asked me to teach a course in book reviewing. Naturally I said no, but not in my usual fashion, i.e., with intent to wound. I didn't tell them to have their heads examined, and even stifled my favorite rejoinder, "I'd love to but I just don't want to." (Note: works like a stun gun; highly recommended for all invitations.) I simply gave them a polite excuse because I felt a column coming on and did not want to enervate my thoughts in a pointless fight with strangers. I saved them, Gentle Reader, for you.

Why in hell do undergraduates need a course in book reviewing? We're so busy "making education a priority" that most of them can't even read. A few lit. crits. earn a full-time living from reviewing, but basically it's a cottage industry, a sideline that you fall into because you're a compulsive reader.

I started while working for the Raleigh *News & Observer* and wasn't even paid (newspaper staffers aren't). There were no "educational requirements"; the books were stacked in towering piles on the editor's office floor and I was told to pick out whatever I wanted. I still remember my first review—*Dearest Vicky*, the letters of Queen Victoria to her eldest daughter. I had no idea what I was doing but I kept on doing it, eventually receiving my first thank-you note from an author: John Quirk, whose novel about the Detroit auto industry, *The Hard Winners*, I can still recommend.

Now, 35 years later, I know what I'm doing, but there's no way to teach it. That, of course, would not faze the Educationists, who promote the theory of "learning by doing" only when it serves their anti-intellectualism; in practice, they demand academic credits, paper credentials, and incessant course-taking before anybody can do anything. If they ever got hold of reviewing it would suffer the same fate as the public schools. We would have licensed graduates of Advanced Book Reviewing, Book Reviewing Dynamics, Book Reviewing Resources, Book Reviewing: An Overview, and no book reviewers.

For what it's worth, here are some tips on reviewing, offered free of tuition charges to anyone who is interested.

1. A book review is NOT a book report. It's a news story about a book and needs a brisk journalistic lead. DO NOT think you can just "tell what it's about." That's how you describe a book to a friend; a review must analyze.

2. DO NOT use the word "compelling" or the phrase "quite simply," as in: "This is quite simply her best novel to date." DO NOT say "I loved . . . " as in "I loved the description of the sunset." It's cloying—what the British so aptly call "twee." If any author describes a sunset, hit him with the anonymous editor's advice: "There are two things that cannot be described. One of them is a sunset." DO NOT call any author a "national treasure," even if he is.

3. DO NOT review murder mysteries. If you can't get out of it, stop reading just before the end when the murderer is revealed and write the review from a position of ignorance: Once you know whodunit the strain of trying not to tip the author's hand will make you tense and affect your writing.

4. DO NOT review every book you are offered. The editor will lose respect for you and think you're broke, so be fussy. A really awful book can be stimulating; it's the mediocre ones that will kill you, so learn to spot them quickly. Flip through them for certain signs, such as authors who use "folks" and "my friends" in every other sentence: That's not writing, that's talking. Checking out novels is harder; it depends on what just happens to snag your eye, such as "rosy pink nipples." Usually I read about 50 pages before reject-

ing a novel, e.g., the one based on a 1787 Scottish infanticide case that introduced so many characters so fast that it should have been called *The Thyroid of Midlothian*. Occasionally you can spot a bummer at once, as when I faxed my editor: "I need a substitute for *The Last Virginia Gentleman*. A woman has sex with a horse on page two and I refuse to read it."

5. DO NOT try to be kind. Remember Ambrose Bierce, who "wondered about the possibility of someone doing an English translation of the works of Henry James." If you are hard to please, your praise will be worth something.

6. Reviewing for the *New York Times* will drive you nuts. Whenever you quote directly from a book, you have to give them the page number so they can check it in their copy. It hung over my head like a cloud, ruining my reading pleasure. Finally, when they began requiring page numbers for quotes summarized by reviewers in our own words, I quit. Just as well, since they never assigned me the meaty stuff I enjoy. I'm strong in history, but being neither a historian nor a history professor, I was considered unqualified to review it because my bona fides don't show up in my biog blurb. Reviewer and author must be in the same "field" to convey that sense of lofty expertise the *NYTBR* treasures. My only regret in leaving them is that I did not get the last word. Had they offered me Germaine Greer's *The Change* I was planning to blurb it: "Miss King, a columnist for NATIONAL REVIEW, has had the menopause."

7. DO NOT judge a book by the press releases that come with the review copy. In fact, don't even read them if you think you might have a drinking problem. The surest way to fall off the wagon is being reminded that publishing houses employ people who write " . . . the author's stunning eptitude for martialing words to sew the seeds of revolution."

8. DO NOT review any book about Ayn Rand. Even if you rave it, her gremlins will find something to go bananas about and write you a letter: "Dear Social Metaphysician! Examine your anti-Objectivist premises and you will see that your epistemology stinks!!!"

9. If you ever review me, DO NOT call me "erudite." They all do, but it's no compliment. By American intellectual standards, you are considered erudite if you have read *The French Lieutenant's Woman* and *Ivanhoe for Young People*.

February 8, 1999

THE cry of terror seldom varies regardless of time and place. Take Scarlett's "The Yankees are coming!" and substitute the Huns, the Roundheads, or the "Melech-Ric!" of Saracens fleeing Richard the

Lionheart and you have the voice of raw fear through the ages.

Lest you think that voice will be heard no more as the touchy-feely Nineties turn into the compassionate Aughts, think again. We are already living in a reign of terror and it's going to get worse, but the identifying cry will change. Unlike earlier ones, it will lack vigor and martial clangor and offer no dramatic possibilities whatsoever because you can't make a movie about people screaming "Help! The volunteers are helping me!"

My own history of volunteerism grinds exceeding small, having been compulsory. Growing up during World War II meant taking part in endless school-sponsored collection drives for old newspapers, "tin foil" from chewing-gum wrappers, and empty toothpaste tubes. The latter, being lead-based, were supposedly used to make new bullets, so we had to take them to school where they were piled on a table beside a sign reading "Brush Away the Japs!" supplied by the visiting dental hygienist.

The newspapers we made into hospital bags which, we were told, would be used for the disposal of bloody bandages as well as "bed pockets" to hold the personal belongings of recuperating wounded soldiers. To prove it, they showed us a newspaper picture of a man in a bed with a newspaper bag fastened to his pillow with a clothespin.

Nobody ever questioned it, or asked why, if tin and lead were so scarce, they were used to package gum and toothpaste in the first place. We kept quiet because volunteerism, whether voluntary or compulsory, cats rapidly into the human psyche and sends it on warped paths. One path is the Little Napoleon complex manifested by air-raid wardens during the war and Neighborhood Crime Watchers now. Another is the Little Engine That Could complex that motivates eager beavers. Still another is the Patient Griselda complex found in people eager to prove how much punishment they can take. These are the three faces of volunteerism. Most schoolchildren tended naturally toward group two, while I simply laid low. After the war, when it came out that the stuff we collected was useless and the drives had been devised to make civilians feel that we were "doing our bit" and "pulling together," my natural inclination to pull apart received a terrific morale boost.

The Fifties were a golden age of selfishness, which is the real reason they have been enveloped in nostalgia. Volunteering as we have come to know it today began in the Sixties with Kennedy's "Ask Not" trumpet fanfare. The Peace Corps was a triumph of purified ulterior motives, combining salaried wanderlust with a government-approved odor of sanctity that no one dared sniff too hard for evidence of escapism or desperation. Why else would a widow of 62 like Mrs. Lillian Carter of Plains, Georgia, risk cholera in India if not to do good? It was only much later when we met her family that we caught on.

Ronald Reagan upped the ante with his fondness for folksy stories, constantly telling the one about Alexis de Tocqueville and the volunteer firemen, and stashing selfless neighborly heroes in the VIP gallery at every State of the Union until volunteerism became a bee in the national bonnet, buzzing frantically in the manner of half-understood American ideas, ready to swarm.

The first wave hit in 1992 when Ross Perot turned "volunteer" into a code word for pseudo-democracy, insisting that he could do nothing without his followers' permission because they, not he, really ran things. Whenever he was asked an awkward question he had only to squeak, "Gotta ask the volunteers," and all dared call it populism.

Perot primed us for Hillary Clinton, whose book, *It Takes a Village*, describes a nightmare of volunteerism in which everybody sponsors everybody else until we have tutored, sustained, and affirmed each other to death.

To this end she sings the praises of her ideal volunteer, Brianne Schwantes, a 13-year-old invalid who helped battle the 1993 midwestern floods. Brianne suffers from brittle-bone disease; her bones have broken so easily and often that her growth has been stunted, yet when she heard about the floods she persuaded her parents to take her to Iowa to help fill sandbags. There she was, barely four feet tall, volunteering her all for her fellow citizens. Hillary doesn't say, but was there a loud *crack!* that went unnoticed amid all those collapsing levees? Where is this kid now, and how many pieces is she in?

A MERICANS now believe that it takes a village to do everything. We are in the midst of a volunteering frenzy, especially in the suburbs, whose residents have dislodged artsy-craftsy and enshrined grassy-rootsy in an effort to revive a lost sense of "community."

Senior citizens get the worst of it. When not dodging con artists who claim "I just like to help people," they are expected to "mentor" the young like the retired couple in the PaineWebber commercial who invested in no-load mutual funds so they could "work with kids." Open the paper to the Metro Area section and you will find the Mentor Feature. It alternates with the Exhausted Mom Feature about the woman who runs a consulting business from home, gets only four hours' sleep, cooks nothing but fish sticks, irons skirts while wearing them, and volunteers to do the bulletin boards at her children's school so the teacher will have time to mentor the mentors.

The ultimate volunteerism is the medical-research participation ads that begin: "If you are at least 18 years of age and have . . ." All ailments are represented and volunteers are paid, so they can work their way through college. My favorite casting calls are Diarrhea and Chronic Constipation because I can just see Bill Clinton signing up for both and compartmentalizing his way clear with "It depends upon what you mean by *go*" and "Define *fan*."

February 22, 1999

Y OU really shouldn't encourage my sociopathic tendencies. I've been in a normal frame of mind, relatively speaking, for some time now, but it ended last week when I got a letter from a Gentle Reader thanking me for helping him realize that he's a misanthrope.

This in itself is not unusual. I've gotten numerous letters thanking me for making misanthropy acceptable, and I've saved them all as proof that, like some other people I could name, I work in mysterious ways. What made this latest letter different was the writer's confession of something that had been buried in his subconscious until I came along and dug it out.

In earliest boyhood, he wrote, he had had a fantasy of waking up one morning to find that some unspecified disaster had caused the rest of the human race to vanish into thin air, leaving him the only person in the world. As time went on, the fantasy receded and he forgot about it, but now, thanks to me, it was back.

And now, thanks to him, so is mine. I've had the identical fantasy off and on for years. The full-feature presentation took a while to produce but the story idea was there as far back as I can remember: specifically, the kindergarten "free-discussion" period when the teacher asked us to name our fondest wish and I said I wanted my own apartment.

As time went on, I noticed a widening gulf between the conventional definition of hardship and my own. In seventh grade when we read *The Man without a Country*, I didn't see why my classmates groaned and shuddered at the sentence meted out to the traitorous lieutenant. Spending the rest of his life aboard ship, sailing around and around the world, fed and clothed and allowed to amuse himself, but left completely alone by all those aboard, who were forbidden to speak to him—was punishment?

Later, as a history major, I came up against the same question time and again. Studying ancient Greece and Rome, I couldn't help noticing that people who were ostracized and banished invariably got their own islands. Admittedly, it was hard on Julia, daughter of the Emperor Augustus, who found herself in the middle of the Adriatic with a staff of eunuch guards and servants whose tongues had been cut off as well. To Julia, a nymphomaniac, this presented a desperate problem, but a misanthrope would take the view that they couldn't *talk* either.

It was immediately obvious to me that being thrown in the Bastille was a godsend. The cells were not cells at all, but some of the best apartment deals in Paris, furnished with curtained beds, rugs, tables, chairs, stoves—plus, you could bring in your own stuff, including all the books you wanted. Inmates could send out for their meals, but even the prison food was good; the writer Marmontel lovingly described the marinated artichokes. Best of all, there were no restrictions against alcohol and tobacco. It lasted until liberty, equality, and fraternity came to the . . . rescue?

Nothing is so frustrating as studying the heyday of the British Empire on an American college campus. Among the soldiers of the Queen, all you had to do to be left alone was cheat at cards. Produce that fifth ace and you were avoided, shunned, and drummed out of the Family of Man. Never again would anyone say, "You looked so lonely I thought I'd join you." Nobody would care. They'd all be too busy giving you the silent treatment to make sure you spent the rest of your life playing solitaire. That would be your . . . punishment?

All this eventually led to my last-man-left-alive fantasy, which goes like so:

Once I realize what has happened, I take stock of the situation and start planning. In this version, my picky writer's mind interferes with my escapism. After years of proofreading and looking for loose ends and contradictions, I'm compelled to stop and point out that there's enough bottled water on store shelves to last the rest of my life, and that expiration dates on canned food are good for about two years, giving me time to learn how to garden and fish. Heat and lights are easy; I simply move into a house with a fireplace and pick up plenty of candles when I raid the supermarkets (they were already open when the disaster struck) of canned food and bottled water. Transportation is a snap; cars and trucks with full tanks and keys in the ignitions are everywhere (but not clogging up the roads; the disaster struck just before the start of morning rush hour).

A T other times I just lie back and enjoy it. In this version, *still* finding America too friendly, I decide to return to my roots. How to get to England? No problemo! I drive up to Alaska, row across to Russia, and head west in whatever abandoned vehicles I can find, including one of those railroad handcars that you pump, even though I can no longer bend over and pick up a piece of paper from the floor without groaning, "Oh, God!"

After resting up in Paris, I drive to Calais to cross the Channel. I could walk the 21 miles through the Chunnel but the English are a seafaring race, and the Calais harbor has plenty of boats with full tanks, so I wait for a warm, calm day and set out. Naturally I make it and spend the rest of my life summering at Balmoral and wintering at Osborne.

Call me abnormal, but the last-man-left-alive fantasy is more universal than misanthropic or else it would not have been used so often in fiction and movies. Therein lies the rub, however, because it's a static theme that must be compromised before it can succeed as entertainment. The first part of *Robinson Crusoe* is interesting, but it does not become exciting until he sees the human footprints in the sand and realizes he is not alone after all. Only then does the journal stop and the novel begin.

So who emerges from the mists of Balmoral? Is it John Kasich, who always looks as if he's about to bleat? No, it's somebody even worse. The warmest, friendliest, talkingest, smilingest, huggiest extrovert who ever lived, that's who.

My man Friday, Bill Clinton.

March 8, 1999

HI, EVERYBODY, this is Bill Clinton. Bet you never thought I'd be a guest columnist for "The Misanthrope's Corner" but Florence has a hang—I mean, she's been on a spiritual journey renewing her commitment to those amber waves of grain she loves so much, so I told her I'd be happy to spell her this time around.

The way it came about was, Florence called Vernon Jordan and asked him to find somebody to fill the job. Man, that was really a switch. Usually ol' Vern hears about the warm body first and then comes up with a job, but this time he heard about the job first and then had to come up with a warm body. And is mine ever warm. . . . Justice isn't the only thing that's obstructed around here. It's been such a long time between affidavits that I'd suborn a rock pile if I thought there was a snake under it.

Anyhow, ol' Vern was so taken aback to hear from a woman who already had a job that he had to stall while he got his thoughts together, so he goes (sorry about that verb but I got it from Monica), "Do you play golf?" and Florence goes, "Golf is an exercise in Scottish pointlessness for people who are no longer able to throw telephone poles at each other."

Well, ol' Vern is like, "Hello?" (he spent so much time talking to Monica that he turned into a Valley Girl too). There was a silence on the other end, then Florence is like, "You already said that when you answered the phone." Well, that got ol' Vern steamed, so he goes, "Do you dislike Scottish people?" and Florence goes, "Don't think small."

He told me later, "Mission aborted. That woman is a stranger to networking. She's also a racist and a golfist. Golfism is tearing this country apart."

That's when I felt challenged. Hillary always says I've never met a stranger, and the other week at the prayer breakfast that GOP jock Steve Largent told me, "I care for you and I love you," so just for the heck of it I decided to give Florence a call and turn her into an FOB.

"Hi, Flo! I hear you need a caddy."

"Golf is tiddlywinks played while standing up and wearing a hat."

"Aw, shoot! I bet I could have you on the golf course in ten minutes."

"I'm Vernon's age."

" . . . Oh. Well, I mean . . . well, at least I can write your column for you "

So that's how I ended up as guest columnist. Sid's already figured out how to spin it: Appearing in NATIONAL REVIEW proves how bipartisan I am. Besides, it'll be good therapy for me, like doing the *New York Times* Sunday crossword, which I always do with one hand while . . .

Why did the White House architect have to go and make this office *oval*? It always keeps me from concentrating. Whenever I'm in here I feel like I'm sitting smack-dab in the middle of a great big little ol' . . . That's why I hit on Monica and Kathleen and the rest. It wasn't my fault—the office made me do it.

Well, that's all DNA under the bridge now. I'd better read a few of these sample columns to see what I'm supposed to do here. Hoo-boy! That Buckley sure is nig—chintzy. They only give her one page. It's the last page, too. Wonder how she boils it down to make it fit? You can't say "continued on" because there's nowhere left to go. That's what I call too much closure for comfort. Short means clear, which is not good. When I work on my State of the Union I like to put in lots of padding so I can bull my way through . . . I mean, so I can lead the American people to a thorough understanding of new programs to improve their lives and help them invest in their children's future.

Hmmm, I wonder if her asking me to be guest columnist is part of a plan to worm her way into the White House as a speechwriter? I'll have to remember to tell Bruce to give her the gate. Trouble is, my memory's so bad I might forget. I'd better tie a string around my finger. No, I'd forget to remember that too. Hey, I know where I'll tie it! That way, somebody's sure to see it.

The difference between Florence and me as writers is that she's a verticalist who goes from beginning to middle to end, whereas I'm a horizontalist who expands outward from my innermost core. The first thing I do is write down the key words I'm going to use: renewal, change, reconciliation, families, personal, comfort, healing, focus, understand, communicate, share, save, touch (say exactly *what*).

Second, I write down the key phrases: "the most vulnerable among us," "our fighting men and women," "not a single child," "come together" (change that to *interface*), "good for our country," "build a new world," "I need to get back to work" (delete *back*).

Third, I write down the ping-pong balls: old answers to new questions; yesterday's solutions to tomorrow's problems; present dreams and future goals; going forward and turning backward; giving much and taking little; building up and pulling out (Note: fix).

Then I go back and put in the ideas. That's how you expand outward from your innermost core.

Well, I'd better get back to work—I mean, to work—on this column. Wonder if they'd change the title just this once, as a special favor to me? Not that anybody would ever take *me* for a misanthrope, but presidents are people too. "Peepul, peepul who need peeeee-pulllll". . . That Barbra's got a great bod. The face . . . well, who sees women's faces? True beauty is found in the back of the neck.

More bad news on the legacy front. Ever since Paula Jones described my seduction technique I've tried to avoid Frenchmen, but Jacques Chirac showed up and said he was glad to be back "in the country which constantly surprises the world." What you reckon he meant by that? Then we got into fruit imports and it turned into the Banana Summit.

The good news is, I'm secretly pushing for a bill of attainder to tighten up congressional residency requirements in case Hillary runs for Senator from New York. Then she'll be in Elmira and I'll be in Fine Fettle! SOOOO-EEEEEE!

March 22, 1999

F LASH: Juanita Broaddrick's story is "credible." That's the official buzz-word and it has caught on like wildfire, allowing the media to believe Broaddrick, doubt Clinton, and stay neutral, all at the same time.

After years of claiming to be "balanced" they finally are, but it's the kind of balance that has less to do with journalism than with the Flying Wallendas. Like the acrobat who knows his life depends upon emptying his mind of all distracting thoughts, the media will not risk their balance with an in-depth investigation of Broaddrick. They would rather risk the wrath of the gods and be condemned to spend eternity perched motionless in the middle of the high wire knowing that to think is to die. (See Bulfinch: "The Myth of Punditeion.")

I'm used to working without a net so I've been thinking. Part of me believes Broaddrick simply because I wouldn't put anything past Bill Clinton, but another part is skeptical.

First, her weeping. She sobbed and wiped but there were no tears to speak of, just two little wet spots at the corners of her eyes, the kind of moisture that comes from yawning. I believe she faked it, but for an entirely understandable reason: You're supposed to cry on television. Like the rest of us, she has seen countless shots of people crying, not only over their own troubles but over remote events that "touched their lives"—the kid needing a transplant waiting for the liver that never came, the asthmatic running the marathon with an oxygen tank strapped to his back, Princess Di. We live in the age of the teddy bear on the sidewalk; Broaddrick knows it and tried to present herself accordingly, but it was a mistake. Tears don't last 20 years. Pride does, but icy dignity gets you nowhere in America, and besides, she isn't the type.

As for what happened in the room, I believe the part about Clinton pointing to the ramshackle jail as an excuse to sling his arm around her shoulders. He embraced Monica the same way in the now-famous ropeline shot, reaching around her to shake hands with the crowd until she just happened to be in his arms.

What I don't believe is her depiction of a tough, macho Bill Clinton in total control of the situation. It is abundantly clear that his nature is skewed sharply toward the feminine-passive. His gabbiness and teariness are flagrant but there are other, more subtle signs, such as the platonic company he keeps. Male bonding holds no charms for him. Friends of Bill are legion but as a group they are androgynous—lots of little husband-and-wife sets to play with for a man who has no wish to be one of the boys.

He has never once used a sports analogy to explain a political position. Chalk talks are second nature to most politicians but Hail Mary passes, punts, bunts, and first downs have no place in Clinton's repertoire. His supporters see this as evidence of New Age values, while his detractors see it as political correctness, but seen in context it more closely resembles a woman's instinctive disinterest tinged with resentment. His gross appetites notwithstanding, he has an overly fastidious side that comes out in his persnickety lip pursings, slow-motion lid lowerings, and dismissive little sniffs, which, when added to all the rest, makes him the most unmacho president since Benjamin Harrison.

Even if such a man were to commit rape, chances are it would not proceed with the Hun-like dispatch Broaddrick describes because Clinton is President Clouseau, a Charlie Chaplin forever pratfallen upon sexual hard times. This may be why America can't hate him. The person who misses his calling in life is always sympathetic, and Monicagate leaves no doubt that he could have been a legendary comic actor.

He could have played all the Big Lug parts of Jack Carson and Sonny Tufts. A W. C. Fields look-alike, he's got a red nose and an unflagging sunniness that would have made him perfect as Mr. Micawber, thriving on chaos and upheaval, at his best when everything is at its worst.

He could have transmuted his farcical private life into art as Chaplin did with an incident at a party: Flirting with a girl, he took her rolling hip movements and little squeals to mean he had aroused her, only to discover that he had backed her up against a hot radiator. This scene triggers instant visions of Monica because the kind of women Clinton goes for are classic comic foils. Add screwed-up pizza orders and wrong-number phone sex and the Big Creep, like the Little Tramp, could have had the world laughing with him instead of at him.

Rape is concentrated, coldly efficient, and grim, but a Clinton rape would resemble his foreign policy: threaten to send troops, start to send troops, recall troops, talk about troops, try another country.

The logistics of the alleged rape bother me: How do you "tear" pantyhose? Those things stretch. You can run them but you would have a hard time tearing them. Could Clinton, who has never done hard manual work, manage it with his small, pasty-white, graduate-student paws? Or did he use just one?

I believe he bit her lip, maybe as a means of sadistic control, maybe in the heat of passion, but what really riveted me were the sunglasses and the "Better put some ice on that." It was too Vegas, too citified, too against type, as if an urbane Unclinton had suddenly risen from the dead.

That's when déjà vu hit. He had turned into the rat in a Joan Crawford movie. Usually played by Zachary Scott or Steve Cochran, rats were always beating up Joan Crawford—or Ida Lupino or Ruth Roman—because she broke some sacrosanct rule of gun-moll etiquette such as falling in love with a rival gangster. When the rat found out about it he snarled, "You two-timing, double-crossing little tramp!" and let her have it. The manhandling scene ended in various ways; sometimes she was rescued, sometimes she shot him, but in one movie, as she lay bloodied on the floor, the rat walked calmly to the door and said, "Better put something on that eye," and left.

What was the movie? I can't remember and it's driving me crazy, but I bet that either Clinton or Broaddrick saw it.

April 5, 1999

AMERICA has a time problem. I don't mean our obsessive need to "save" time that foreigners have long joked about. We aren't like that anymore; the American in a hurry has slowed to a crawl and now uses what little Yankee ingenuity he has left to figure out how to get more "leisure" time to spend with his family.

Now that we are no longer speed demons or efficiency freaks, we might reasonably be expected to develop the richer, fuller attitudes toward time that we profess to admire, but the opposite has happened. We are still in a time warp, only this one is even worse than the one we shed. Now it's not merely clock time but our whole concept of time—past, present, and future and their links to each other—that has been shot to hell.

Chronological eeriness lurks everywhere. Mark McGwire's pursuit of Babe Ruth's record was almost overshadowed at one point by talk of what pitcher would become "immortal" by giving up the big one. Masochistic debates about enduring a lifetime of pity to get to the good part tend to spring up when a nation's population is in the habit of spending much of its day hitting Rewind and Fast Forward buttons. For the time-warped it's a matter of personal preference, and Reds pitcher Brett Tomko is a Fast Forward man. "If it's hit off me," he said, "I'd be on every highlight film for the rest of my life. I'd be part of history."

Another Fast Forward favorite is the expression "lame duck." It used to refer to a defeated incumbent during the period between his loss of an election and the inauguration of the victor. Now it means a President entering his second term. The moment he wins re-election, a feat once once regarded as an ultimate triumph, he's called a lame duck.

To see the Rewind set in action, turn to any Op-Ed page and you will find that of the five syndicated columnists featured, four will attempt to make their points by quoting Yogi Berra's "It's deja vu all over again," while the fifth, more literate than the rest, quotes Faulkner: "The past isn't dead, it isn't even past."

The past may not be dead but we do our best to kill it while simultaneously wallowing in nostalgia. During the late unpleasantness a parade of White House flacks went from talk show to talk show comparing Ken Starr's investigation to the puritanical, sexually repressed, hypocritical, hysterical, paranoid, Commie-hunting days of McCarthyism, only to be interrupted by pictures of drive-ins and T-Birds and Dean Martin singing "Memories Are Made of This" in the ubiquitous commercial for tapes from the Nifty Fifties.

Among the chief killers of the past are, of all people, writers. The increasing number of novels written in the present tense ("She takes off her bra and moves her hands down her hips, knowing that he is watching") are defended on grounds of "immediacy," but in fact their authors choose to hit the Record button because it saves them from getting tangled up in auxillary verbs.

We have developed a mental block against using past tenses correctly. Even educated people say "If he would have sent the letter. . . . if she would have gotten the job . . . if I would have had time. . . . " Damnit! A past action that precedes another past action takes the pluperfect: "If he *had* sent . . . if she *had* gotten . . . if I *had* had . . . " This is more than bad grammar: No longer willing or able to cope with anything unequivocal, we skirt the pluperfect and substitute the past-conditional to give ourselves what we imagine to be chronological wiggle room.

The word "past" has become a virtual synonym for bigotry and hence must be avoided by any means necessary. Everybody in publishing knows that Alexandra Ripley was chosen to write the sequel to *GWTW* because she came up with the craziest plot. An authentically rendered past makes a novel hold together, so to be on the safe side she opted for shattered, dragging the story to Ireland to avoid dealing with the ex-slave characters and substituting a caesarian performed on Scarlett by a Celtic witch.

Our time conflicts have produced an intense interest in the past alongside an utter contempt for it. Editors used to write "off-chron" in the margins of manuscripts to call attention to errors of this type but now nobody cares how many howlers end up in print, and reviewers who do care are called "picky."

Among my shoot-the-messenger experiences was a biography of Clark Gable which claimed that while shooting the 1953 movie *Mogambo*, Grace Kelly called Gable a "male chauvinist pig," an expression born in the 1970s. The heroine of a novel set in 1938 spoke of looking "sexy," a word not in use 60 years ago. She also put on a brand-new pair of nylons straight from the box even though women of the stocking era always washed new nylons first to keep them from running. I've found a blouse in 1910 that should have been a "waist" and a record player in place of a "Victrola," but the worst was finding a 1955 scene in my own memoir updated by a proofreader who was blindsided by her own terminal now-ness: She changed "t—d" to "nerd" to conform to my 1985 publication date.

W E HAVE lost our grip on the rhythms of life. In the Middle Ages there were no clocks, just church bells ringing the canonical hours: Matins, Lauds, Prime, Terce, Sext, None, Vespers, and Compline. It was unhelpful for making precise appointments but as psychological accuracy it was unsurpassed. The sonorous bells literally reverberated within medieval man, cleansing his soul. By contrast, we get to watch a miracle take place when the detergent removes a stain from a T-shirt in ten seconds while the Elapsed Time ticks away at the bottom of the TV screen.

We have met the Y2K problem and it's us. If chaos ensues on January 1 it will simply be the climax of the time warp we are already in. In fact, it may happen even earlier. We always go around mumbling "Spring forward, Fall back" to prepare for the time change, but this year we could get it mixed up with "Put it behind us and move on" and go crazy before the computers do.

April 19, 1999

T HE spirit of recycling in all its vainglory was expressed by John P. Marquand, author of *The Late George Apley*. He did not live to see recycling as we know it, but as a scion of Old Yankee Massachusetts he was an expert on the battier aspects of New England thrift.

Engraved on his mind was a boyhood chiding he received from an aunt. One day as he was cleaning out his desk he found half of an old pair of scissors, a single rusty blade with a single rusty thumbhole. He was about to toss it in the wastebasket when his shocked aunt told him that it would make a "perfectly good" letter opener.

This woman walks among us today. We have all heard her condescending voice, seen the high-cut nostrils of her long, thin nose flare with indignation, watched her go so stiff with righteousness that you could pick her up by her feet. Though she is long dead, she has been reincarnated—another form of recycling—as the star of a comedy of errors that has taken America by storm. The play is now in its sixth year and expected to run for ten more, so we might as well open the envelope. Ladies and gentlemen, the winner is . . . Al Gore in *Marquand's Aunt!*

The recycling movement has now passed through the cute good-citizen phase and progressed to the point where it is virtually impossible to throw anything out. I grew up in an apartment building where old appliances, venetian blinds, and the like were disposed of in one sentence: "Leave it out for the janitor." We put it beside our door and the next day it was gone. What the janitor did with it we neither knew nor cared; some janitors sold stuff for parts, some sold it by the pound to junk dealers, and Mr. Fix-It types had a nice little sideline in secondhand goods. Castoffs were an unwritten fringe benefit of being a janitor and everybody was happy.

The alternative was "Throw it down the incinerator." I would give anything for an incinerator now. They were a wonderful invention; there was one on each floor and all you had to do was walk down the hall. You could throw anything down them provided it fit, and if it didn't you could chop it up. We threw a whole armchair down the incinerator when my mother set fire to it with a cigarette. First the pillows, then the stuffing, then the wood a few pieces at a time, then the springs a few coils at a time, until it was all gone.

Our chair's cremated remains took up a lot less room than today's environmentally correct burials. To get rid of useless furniture today you must hire a trash hauler to take it to the landfill, or else take it yourself, provided you own a truck and, if a woman, can lift a bureau and don't mind driving to desolate places like landfills. Otherwise, you have to rent a truck and find two strong young men you aren't afraid to let into your home. The only guaranteed way to get rid of old stuff is to buy new stuff from a store that takes your old stuff to the landfill for free.

Then again, the landfill may not take it. Environmental guilt is so widespread that your landfill could be run by someone in the last stages of Marquand's Aunt syndrome. I bought a new air conditioner from a store that promised to take the old one off my hands. I thought it was a free service but they said they had to charge me $25 labor to take the condenser out before they would be allowed to throw the AC away; otherwise the landfill "wouldn't accept" it. Waste not, want not condensers.

My attic storage room is full of 15 years' worth of fritzed appliances and electric fans, but with neither janitor nor incinerator I am now faced with taking them unspayed to the landfill and finding out what it feels like to be rejected by a dump.

To encourage people to recycle cardboard, the garbagemen will not pick up cardboard boxes—but neither will the recycling truck. You have to cut them into flat pieces, which is why every hardware store now sells box cutters, a particularly vicious instrument once used only in warehouses but now de rigueur for every good little recycler—and the weapon of choice of preteen inner-city thugs who do not yet own guns, who would not now own box cutters if hardware stores did not stock them for good little recyclers.

The one item I was glad to recycle was newspapers, not for patriotic Gore but for personal convenience, but this too shall pass under a bureaucracy. You can't tie the papers with string and put them directly on the ground by the curb. You must use the recycling boxes provided by the city, which have themselves been recycled from what feels like old bus tires; they're heavy even when empty and their handles, instead of being rolled or flat, are so sharp that lifting a week's worth of three daily papers is like getting a good grip on oyster shells.

I have to take the box down first, then make two more trips with the papers, which intrigues the local liberals who teach at the college up the street from me, who gaze at my struggles from their car windows with quizzical, pensive expressions, obviously thinking, "How come *she's* recycling?" followed by, "Maybe she's not so bad after all."

R ECYCLING as a political litmus test goes back to the late Fifties when Vance Packard published *The Waste Makers* and made "planned obsolescence" the buzzword of the decade. Packard, the darling of liberals since his earlier attack on advertising, *The Hidden Persuaders*, now became the darling of beatniks and other hippies-in-waiting eager to flaunt their capacity for needing nothing, wanting nothing, and living like the "real people," i.e., Europeans.

They hated anybody who bought anything and quoted Packard's findings on how much whipped cream went to waste in the bottom of the aerosol can because *They* want to *make* you buy more! Their heroes were people who took the trouble to puncture the can, like Packard's son, and get *all* of the whipped cream.

This is the spirit of recycling: little people elevating little virtues to make themselves look bigger. Welcome to the Age of Marquand's Aunt.

May 3, 1999

H AVE you noticed? America has a new all-purpose word: "surreal." Derived from *Surréalisme*, the French literary and artistic movement known for fantastic imagery, improbable events, and incongruous juxtapositions, it means "having an odd, dreamlike quality."

It got its start in the Gulf War when it was used to describe the greenish glow that filled our TV screens when we bombed places at night. At that time our all-purpose word was "awesome" but the rockets' green glare subjected it to overkill so some commentator varied it with "surreal."

It turned out to be an ideal Nineties word; foreign enough to qualify as multicultural, sensitive enough for a neutered poet, and, from the onomatopoeic point of view, its unmistakable sound of something writhing quietly made it a natural addition to the vocabulary of political correctness.

"Surreal" proved so popular that it quickly worked its way up the food chain—literally—serving as a description of everything from the nocturnal shine of crocodile eyes to Dolly Parton's bust. Its popularity was perfectly timed to enable us to describe things that really were surreal, such as the photos of Mars, but as the decade progressed the word degenerated into a synonym for "unusual."

Clinton's definition of sex, Monica's definition of love, Hillary's definition of marriage, Linda Tripp's definition of friendship, Lucianne Goldberg's definition of literary agent—all were called surreal. We built up such a head of surrealism that Clinton, to distract us from his surrealistic troubles, began bombing places at night, filling our TV screens with another round of greenish glows that everybody promptly dubbed surreal.

We always do this. Give us a catchphrase or a concept and we pounce on it, grind it down, wear it out, and leave it in pieces like a toy on Christmas morning without ever finding out what it was. This is how the Numbing of America works. It just so happens that we are surrounded by things surreal but we have lost the ability to react to them.

Making Americans react used to be a simple task. William Randolph Hearst ruled that readers of his papers must say "Gee whiz!" when they saw the front page, "Holy Moses!" when they read the second, and "God Almighty!" when they turned to the third. He could never get a rise out of us today because when everything is surreal, nothing is surreal—not even the following:

"The Navy has maintained that pregnancy at sea does not hurt readiness."

"Some female Marines are complaining they can't stand in formation at the six-month mark of their pregnancies because the Corps doesn't provide an ample maternity uniform."

"Arkansas agreed yesterday to hire 400 more female guards in men's prisons and let them do everything from stopping rapes to monitoring the showers."

"In some respects, companies view affirmative action as a helpful management tool to keep them from getting sued."

Don Imus on Mike Barnicle's plagiarism: "He's obviously sloppy and lazy. But you shouldn't be fired for that."

Laurence Leamer, author of *The Kennedy Women*: When Eunice Kennedy Shriver's husband was ambassador to France, a French secretary on her staff said, "If you're not mentally retarded, you can't even get invited to this embassy."

Surreal begets surrealer. The numbers-game charge that blacks have been irretrievably harmed by "400 years of slavery" means that slavery began in the 1590s and remains on the books today.

The "fighting men and women" construction of pundits bending the knee to the feminist thought police has infected the general public, producing letters to the editor with such statements as "the men and women who fought at Iwo Jima and Belleau Wood." Stand by for Veracruz and Little Big Horn.

When Michigan became the sixth state to allow the blind to hunt assisted by guides and laser-sighted weapons, Thomas Schermer, a blind hunter, said: "I might not be able to see the deer, but I'll guarantee you that in those last seconds before I shoot, my pulse will be just as high as in the days when I could."

We progress. Fifteen years ago William F. Buckley Jr. was universally castigated for saying that blind yachtsman Jim Dixon should not be allowed to sail the Atlantic alone. Now that institutionalized surrealism has given us the armed and dangerous blind, I predict that drivers' licenses will be next. If you doubt it, consider this: Icarus never said he had a "right" to fly, only that he could. This is the difference between American surrealists and the modest kind.

F ROM surreal to surrealer to surrealissimus invariably leads straight to Mary McGrory, who eulogized one of the toads under the penumbra known as the Supreme Court: "Justice Brennan never was hung up on the Framers' intent."

The most publicized eulogy to Brennan came from Thurgood Marshall Jr.: "He had the biggest heart of anybody in the building." This is the sort of thing that should upset us but doesn't, yet on a deeply unconscious level it does, because even the most brainwashed American instinctively knows that nothing is more dangerous than a judge with a heart—or an emotional surgeon, or a vulnerable engineer, or those "flexible, sensitive" warriors Betty Friedan called for when she lectured at West Point.

So much surrealism is couched in these misbegotten tributes that we can no longer recognize chaos. The anxiety that afflicts Americans comes from the gnawing, inchoate sensation that we are all at the mercy of a society driven by emotional decisions, personalized actions, and subjective thought processes.

A regular reminder that the cold comfort of objectivity is a thing of the past are the terrifying TV appearances of Jo Ellen Demetrius, the "Jury Lady," who earns her living advising lawyers how to pick jurors whose prejudices, disappointments, resentments, fears, crotchets, tics, and twitches will result in a "favorable" verdict.

Gee whiz! Holy Moses! God Almighty! Will no one rid us of this surreal Vestal?

May 17, 1999

I AM constitutionally incapable of shedding a tear, either real or crocodile, over the Littleton massacre. When you've seen one pile of teddy bears you've seen them all; when you've read one cover story blurbed "WHY?" you've read them all; and when you've heard one best-and-brightest "articulate" teenager being interviewed you have heard everything.

This time, however, I am not alone in my cynicism. Everybody is searching earnestly for "root causes" and the "Lesson of Littleton," but under the requisite sensitivity lurks a rogue voice whispering a cold truth: One of the best-kept secrets of American life is the number of people who have fantasized blowing up their high schools.

That this forbidden thought has begun to peep out from some unexpected quarters is proof of how widespread it is. On talk shows devoted to Littleton, numerous guests of the thoughtful 'n' concerned persuasion seemed driven to confess that they, too, were teased in high school, including a plump, yellow-haired psychologist named Butterworth who made a jocular but revealing remark to Geraldo about having been the butt of adolescent jokes because of the combination of his appearance and his name.

Judy Mann, the *Washington Post*'s resident backpage feminist, came across as uncharacteristically brusque in a column called "High Schools Are the Real Problem." Predictably, most of her animus was aimed at the cult of macho jocks and the cheerleader-as-handmaiden that defeats the dream of perfect sexual equality, but she zapped high-school culture as "sick, demeaning, and depressing" and aligned herself with "generations of young people forced to coexist in large public schools that many of them hate."

That's pretty good for a tolerant liberal, but when Bill Maher turns into a crusty curmudgeon we know something is up. The host of *Politically Incorrect* is actually nothing of the kind and neither is his show, but his Littleton outburst was pure H. L. Mencken:

> We now live in a culture that not only glorifies violence, but even worse, glorifies high school. . . . We have this upside-down culture that panders to youth in a way that is harmful to kids and terribly boring to adults. . . . It's okay to adore youth, but to pretend it has something to tell us is ridiculous. . . . [H]igh school isn't real life. It's just four years of

embarrassment and boredom and pettiness, where nothing much happens; sort of like the Carter administration.

If most of Europe's intractable geopolitical problems can be blamed on the idealism of Woodrow Wilson, most of America's social problems can be blamed on our glorification of high school. Interestingly, both started around the same time. Before World War I high school as we have come to know and hate it did not exist. The vast majority of Americans stopped school after the eighth grade, leaving high school to the middle class—the *real* middle class, not today's deluded alpine bell curve. High schools, as their name implied, were essentially public prep schools, and excellent ones at that. The tears I can't shed for Littleton I can easily shed for myself when I read descriptions of third-year Classical Greek in old high-school curricula.

Under this sensible hierarchical arrangement the two groups guaranteed to hate each other parted company before they reached the inferiority-complex stage of adolescent development. The minority of nerds, drips, and brains were in high school, while the majority of studs, sexpots, and dunces were spread out in the working force, making mutually assured psychological destruction logistically impossible.

Then along came the usual suspects, democracy and equality. More and more people went to high school, until a generational peasantry formed. As with all revolutions, everything got a new name. Youngsters became "teenagers"; school, grounds, and diploma became "plant," "campus," and "degree." The resulting Omnium Gatherum was called "the best years of your life," and cliques erupted like zits.

Nearly everyone has been warped by the democratized high school. The rudeness encountered in Tech Support is widely viewed as a revenge of the nerds, but I would go further and attribute computer viruses and even the millennium scare to smart kids getting even; some genius out there has known all along how to fix Y2K but he's not talking.

And then there's me. If I had had private tutors this column might be called "Melanie's Corner," but instead I went to high school where I forged my credo: "Whatever the majority is doing has got to be wrong." High school, where I became an anarcho-elitist from overexposure to friendly "student leaders." High school, where the girls who recited Mickey Rooney's wives in the cafeteria made fun of me for reciting Henry VIII's wives in history class, prompting my development as a misogynistic feminist.

I RONICALLY, the people who are warped most by high school are those golden lads and girls who are *not* warped by high school. Being popular at this stage of life means subscribing to adolescent tastes and priorities that can never be shaken off. When the star athlete's brief gaudy hour is finished he turns into the roly-poly Maytag repairman sunk in puzzled loneliness, wondering why no one needs him. The luscious cheerleader who told brainy girls "I'd love to get my hands on your hair" ends up looking like Medusa top and bottom, her varicose veins springing in all directions just like her frizzy home-dye job. Voted "Most Likely to Succeed" in high school, they end up as lost winners who can't figure out what hit them even though they were once forced to memorize it for the lit test: "Golden lads and girls all must, / As chimney-sweepers, come to dust."

A generational peasantry, their country's pride, when once unleashed, can never be denied. If we really want to save "the culture" we should decentralize adolescence by abolishing the democratized high school and return to the eighth-grade diploma. It's all my parents had, and they were more literate than today's "college" grads.

It won't happen, of course. Our schools are finished along with everything else, but never let it be said that I don't have an occasional constructive fantasy.

May 31, 1999

U NLIKE book reviewing, book blurbing is based on that deathless feminine principle: "If you can't say something nice, don't say anything at all." This would seem to disqualify me but I've been blurbing books for a quarter of a century now. I was born to blurb thanks to a sourtempered honor that manifested itself when I was six.

One day as I was thumbing through *Collier's* I came to a celebrity endorsement of a then-revered product.

"Look, Mama! Ben Hogan smokes Luckies same as you."

"Oh, that means nothing. They pay him to say that."

As she explained how the endorsement business worked I went into full glower. The truth about Santa Claus hadn't bothered me a bit but this was different.

"I don't like Ben Hogan," I muttered darkly.

"Well, plenty of people do, that's why they put him in the ad."

"If he doesn't mean it, he shouldn't say it."

The first rule of the blurb business resembles the first rule of Pentagon business: "Don't call it a war." The publishing equivalent is "Don't call it a blurb." Privately everyone does but officially it's called a "comment," or more descriptively, "A word from you . . . " as in: "A word from you will call attention to this important book."

Requests for blurbs come from the editor or the publicist of a book in production and are usually based on the author's list of good blurb prospects—i.e., friends. Think of a bride registering her silver pattern.

Fax machines and e-mail did not exist when I started blurbing so I always replied in a gracious letter beginning, "Thank you for giving me the opportunity to read . . . " I was so polite, but, to extend the marriage metaphor, kissin' don't last. Discovering that blurbing could adversely affect my income I devised a form letter:

> The books that make people think of me when they need a blurb tend to be the same books that make literary editors think of me when they assign reviews. Since blurbing a book obligates me to eliminate myself as a reviewer, I am put in the position of working against myself.

At this stage of the game I was reviewing regularly for the *New York Times*, where they give you a lie-detector test if they even suspect you are friends with an author. Otherwise, invoking the blurb–review clash was merely a tactful ruse to get out of blurbing static Southern novels in which three generations of women sit on the porch and talk for 400 pages. (To get out of reviewing them I told *NYTBR* that I had been asked to provide a blurb.)

Between the Southern-blurb mafia and the rampant confusion that typically prevails in publishing houses, my tact soon collapsed. I reverted to type when I was asked to blurb an oral history about Elvis Presley by a woman who had once interviewed me. The editor said they needed a "quick response" because they were behind schedule, the reason for the delay being that the manuscript was 1,400 pages, but he promised I would be "caught up in the whirlwind of nonstop excitement" the moment I started reading the "enclosed" advance copy. But the letter was in an ordinary business envelope and the post office had no packages for me.

I fired off a typical snappish reply: "I have written so much about my own very different musical tastes that my blurb on anything to do with Elvis would be laughable."

My most embarrassing experience? Finding my 1980 blurb recycled in 1995 by an author who has gotten progressively worse with each book.

My most heartbreaking experience? "Andrew Ferguson's wry worldview, understated wit, and economy of style make him the Buster Keaton of the cultural essay" was how I blurbed *Fools' Names, Fools' Faces*, but "understated" was misprinted as "understanding" on the dust jacket.

My craziest experience? The woman who sent me her huge manuscript with a letter saying, "Here is your chance to share in this historic publishing moment by promoting my groundbreaking book." There was no SASE so I threw it in the post-office trash can. A few weeks later I got another copy and another bumptious letter: "Out of all the prominent authors eager to comment on my book, I have chosen you." This time the trash can was overflowing with discarded junk mail so I left the tome on the table, but on my next trip a postal clerk gave it back to me, explaining that he had seen me walk off without it. He was so proud of having salvaged it that I hated to throw it away in front of him, so I took it with me to put in a public trash bin. But there wasn't any. I could have sworn there was one on the corner but now it was gone. I ended up shleping a seven-pound manuscript through downtown on a broiling hot day, looking for a can. Finding one at last, and by now in a towering fury, I stood there slamming chunk after chunk of manuscript into its maw. A week later the story was all over Fredericksburg that my latest book had been rejected and I had tried to set fire to it on Caroline Street.

My favorite blurbs? Probably this schizoid pair. *A Nation of Victims*: "Charles Sykes's acridly funny exposé of those solitary, poor, nasty, brutish, huddled [m]asses known as the American People warmed my compassion-deprived, differently sensitized heart. This book is the best news I've had since Ayn Rand came out in favor of factory smoke."

Fried Green Tomatoes at the Whistle Stop Cafe: "Watch out for Fannie Flagg. When I walked into the Whistle Stop Cafe, she fractured my funny bone, drained my tear ducts, and stole my heart."

A writer I would love to blurb is Christopher Hitchens. I know, I know, he attacked Mother Teresa, but I have relished his writing ever since we were regular reviewers in *Newsday*'s daily book section. I was Tuesday, he was Wednesday: ships that pass in the night, or more likely, trash-compactor buddies like Steve McQueen and Ali McGraw in *The Getaway*.

I've already written the blurb: "If Christopher Hitchens is a Marxist, I want to be one too."

June 14, 1999

I COMPILED an interesting list the other day: All the men in my life were subject to the military draft. That figures for a woman my age, but what is interesting are the memories and reflections my listmaking triggered.

Now that Americans are incapable of putting up with anything and think nothing of launching multimillion-dollar lawsuits over spilled coffee, it is almost eerie to recall my generation's matter-of-fact acceptance of the draft. Lives were built around it, cheerfully and optimistically for the most part. Boys jotted figures to see how much of their military pay they could save and how much they could earn afterward if the service taught them a good trade; girls automatically factored two years—three if he enlisted to avoid induction—into wedding plans; and everyone spoke knowledgeably and hopefully of the most desirable postings: Montauk Point Lighthouse meant weekends in New York for lucky Coast Guardsmen.

For college girls there was the tempting prospect of marrying an officer and going with him to a foreign country at government expense. I was so desperate to see Europe I might have done it if I had had the chance, but both of the boys I was dating chose to enlist after graduation. They wanted, in the parlance of the day, "to get it over with," but their resignation was mixed with relief All three of us were sunk in that familiar senior-year depression brought on by the realization that we had been in school for 17 of our 21 years. The psychological situation called for a purely physical interim in which we did not have to think. Thanks to the draft the boys had one, and I envied them.

My beaux were part of the palely loitering bohemian crowd, all arty intensity and nascent alienation, the kind of boys drill sergeants love to get hold of, the kind of whom fathers say, "It'll do him good." When I saw them again a few years later it was obvious that they had been gotten hold of and that it had done them good. Not that they had learned to love the Army; on the contrary, they hated it. But they had lost the palely loitering look and their bohemian petulance had been replaced by jaunty cynicism.

I thought of them when I read the ruminations of editor Max Perkins on the self-image of the untested male:

> A man who wends his life with his knees crooked under a desk is not more than half a man, and we all know it. And Dr. Johnson said, when they were running down the military, "If a general walked into this room now we'd all be ashamed." And if a good workman, a mechanic, walked into a boardroom at a directors meeting, the directors would all feel ashamed. And if old Zimmerman, foreman at our press, a man like Adam Bede, in a striped apron, walked into our directors meeting we'd all feel ashamed. And that is true and must mean something, but what, I don't know.

Nothing in female psychology can compare to this. The career woman and the Mommy Tracker, the bluestocking and the sexpot, are well aware of their differences but the reaction they rouse in each other is mutual contempt, not shame. You will never find a woman executive watching busy diner wait-resses with envious admiration the way male executives watch construction workers at a building site. It's the Adam Bede syndrome, the overcivilized man's need to prove himself the equal of earthy men that was satisfied to a large extent by universal military service.

The draft produced the kind of men that today's girls have never known, and relations between the sexes were better for it. What sticks in my mind about them is their self-sufficiency and competence in fixing things that broke and figuring out solutions to emergencies. Thanks to the draft I belong to the last generation of American women who could scream "Do some-thing!" and get results. Most of my men were intellectuals but they had been taught in basic training to change a tire in 90 seconds, rig up electrical wiring, tie knots that stayed tied, and take a rifle apart and resassemble it while blind-folded. This last was never necessary in civilian life but it made for a self-assured deftness that was awesome.

Nowadays the Adam Bede syndrome has been turned on its head; awe is reserved for women and their "great strides" and middle-class young men have turned into tentative, palely loitering computer jocks whose idea of "Do something!" is reloading the software.

Proof that American men want their Adam Bede syndrome back is abun-dant. Al Gore's hysteria-tinged boast of working on a farm, shoveling manure, castrating hogs, and delivering calves "with my bare hands" is straight out of George Eliot, recalling those passages that Victorian reviewers of *Adam Bede* condemned as "startling horrors of rustic reality." After six years in an administration incapable of feeling ashamed of anything, least of all the entrance of a general, Gore might need psychological comfort more than votes.

The best description of the Adam Bede syndrome as it applies to the draft comes from poet Michael Blumenthal. Writing in 1981, he compared his fel-low Vietnam draft-dodgers to those who served.

To put it bluntly, they have something that we haven't got. It is, to be sure, somewhat vague, but nonetheless real, and can be embraced under sever-al headings: realism, discipline, masculinity (kind of a dirty word these days), resilience, tenacity, resourcefulness. . . . There is something miss-ing in my generation of hypersensitive, "untainted" men. It is something that cannot simply be dismissed with so emotionally loaded a word as "macho." . . . It has to do, I think, with camaraderie, with shared purpose, with self-transcendence. It has to do with going into the dark tunnel of danger and mortality and emerging on the other side. . . . Ultimately, it may have to do with everything that follows: with having a family, with making commitments, with knowing what it means to sacrifice, with being an adult.

If this was true in 1981, think how much truer it is now. Maybe it's time to scream "Do something!"

June 28, 1999

W HEN Geraldine Ferraro ran for vice president in 1984 I was bombarded with requests for articles on how women would react to her. Now Campaign 2000 is threatening to turn into a political bake-off, but so far nobody has asked me to write about Elizabeth Dole. It's just as well because I couldn't possibly do it.

In the first place, I don't have any notes on her. After her ding-a-ling performance at the 1996 GOP convention I dutifully started a file called E. Doli so as not to mix her up in her husband's (poorbobdole.com), but the only thing in it is the envelope from an old gas bill on which I scrawled: "Betty Crocker before they made her look ethnic."

I need a subject that lends itself to detached analysis, but E. Doli gets me into knee-jerk reactions, déjà vu, and late-night speculation on whether there might be something to this karma business after all. The only way I can write about her is to practice Freudian free association.

E. Doli is the woman who keeps cropping up in my life as a vacuous nemesis. Note the only-in-America aspect here. A nemesis by definition has enormous psychic heft and menace; a silly, shallow nemesis is oxymoronic but that's the kind we produce, and they find me every time.

A classic vacuous nemesis of the Fifties was the young, progressive dean of women who was brought in to replace the septuagenarian, traditional dean of women. Hailed as "a breath of fresh air," Mrs. Progressive—she was usually married—vowed to "replace suspicion with trust" and emanated waves of empathy, in contrast to Miss Traditional, who had all the give-and-take of Torquemada and emanated nothing except memos banning patent-leather shoes lest boys see up our dresses in the reflection.

Instead of summoning girls to her office like Miss Traditional, Mrs. Progressive came to us, strolling through pajama-clad throngs at slumber parties and encouraging intimate discussions on "Should you French kiss?" and "Is petting wrong?" Let a hand go up and she was beside the questioner like a shot, pouring on empathy like pancake syrup. Miss Traditional's only open reference to sexual desire was her memo about never letting a boy sit in a chair we had just vacated lest he feel our body heat, but Mrs. Progressive took pride in no-holds-barred girltalk and assured us that we could say anything we liked.

Well, yes and no. Despite her seeming spontaneity she somehow always managed to end discussions on her terms with one of her signature lines, her favorite being "If you love him, you *won't*." She could always work them in, and we got so we could tell when one was coming: Her wide crinkly smile grew crinklier, her head tossed gaily, and she winked. But if any girl tried to continue the discussion beyond the signature line, Mrs. Progressive's crinkly gaiety vanished, replaced by the blank-eyed stiffness of an actress who has lost her place.

That's what happened when she counseled me about running around with bohemians. This time her signature line was "Mr. Right is looking for you, too!" but I didn't take the hint.

"I don't want to get married. I'd rather live in Paris and have affairs like George Sand."

That did it. The back went up, the wall came down, and she set an Olympic uncrinkling record that stood until the media started asking E. Doli unscripted questions.

E. Doli's refusal while transportation secretary to believe anything bad about air bags or anything good about raising the 55 mph speed limit reminds me of the dream world inhabited by the North Carolina clubwomen I covered when I worked on the Raleigh paper. Sunk in an inferiority complex over the South's image as a cultural wasteland, they convinced themselves that it was a potential cultural mecca that could flower at any moment if only everyone else realized what they themselves already knew.

Their saving wisdom was supplied by the professors of history and classics who spoke at their luncheons, and went like this: Culture does not require big cities. Ancient Athens had a population of only 90,000, about the same as Raleigh's at this time. Therefore, Raleigh could become another Athens. The professors didn't believe it but they knew it was what the clubwomen wanted to hear. I didn't believe it because I could admit that Socrates and Plato were not wont to say "Les' git some beer an' go rustle up some nooky." But the club-women believed it and repeated it like a chant because it was such a nice belief.

A MERICA can't afford to elect E. Doli but the craven GOP will nomi-nate her for veep unless her mask drops with a resounding crash, so I'm hoping she follows in the footsteps of Granny's friend, the "Side Lady."

She was a little old spinster with a vision problem who had to turn her head to the left to see properly. Timid and unworldly, she had been dominated by her father, who broke up the closest thing to a romance she ever had: a flirtation with a Richmond streetcar driver. She met him when she took his trolley to her music lesson and soon invented excuses to ride around all day with him, sitting directly behind him so they could talk. But Big Daddy found out about it and locked her in her room, and she never saw him again.

At 70 she had a stroke and lay unconscious in her hospital bed, head still turned to the left, attended by her minister and a brace of Confederate Daughters.

Suddenly, she stirred and tried to speak. Everyone gathered round the bed, each expecting to hear what he wanted to hear. The minister wanted transfiguration, the Daughters wanted a match for the famous deathbed apocrypha, "I'm going to see General Lee and Jesus," and Granny, who wholeheartedly believed that the Side Lady turned her head to the left in memory of the driver's side of the streetcar, wanted treacly sentiment.

"Say something, honey," she urged tenderly.

Whereupon the Side Lady opened her eyes, straightened her head for the first time in anyone's memory and said: "We gonna sit raht heeah till all you colored git back of that line!"

July 12, 1999

ARE you sitting down? I ask because I'm getting ready to say something nice and I don't want you to sustain any injuries from crashing suddenly to the floor.

To get right to it, I love the post office. You heard me. The post office, officially known as the U.S. Postal Service, a name that has never caught on because "post office" triggers more positive associations than we know we have until we sit down and think about it. That's what I did recently when I got up at 4 A.M. and sat at the table drinking coffee, smoking, and staring into space. Writers are constantly asked "Where do you get your ideas?" and this is the answer: letting your mind roam free in the middle of the night until it brushes up against an unlikely subject.

As with any exercise in nostalgia, good post-office associations are usually found in those of a certain age, though this one holds out a possible exception: Children still seem to go through a stamp-collecting phase. Whether it will be enough to form a rich marrow of memory remains to be seen. Today's plethora of stamps, first-day covers, and gift shops in main branches may reduce the post office to just another mini-mall. That would be a tragedy because your true post-office aficionado is in the grip of a mystique.

The post office of my childhood was a Greek temple with institutional floors of a speckled black-and-brown pattern and high ceilings that drew heat and captured rising sounds, sending them back as a steady hum of humanity reminiscent of the bustling excitement of a train station.

The first thing you saw, whether you wanted to or not, was the New Deal mural painted by an unemployed artist under the Works Progress Administration. A huge panorama of workers and farmers with bulging muscles and noble brows, the mural was said to contain cryptic socialist messages passed to the artist by Eleanor Roosevelt, a rumor that gave Southern dowagers something to do while standing in line and led to cryptic stamp orders when they got up to the window and barked, "Twelve hammers and seven sickles!"

Another famous sight was the Rogues' Gallery of the FBI's most-wanted criminals. Post offices still display them but they stir no excitement in the era of *Unsolved Mysteries* and live interviews with the latest beneficiary of jury nullification. We pored over them because they were our only close-up look at big-time criminals, and they gave sweet little old ladies who wouldn't hurt a fly a golden opportunity to practice their favorite science: eugenics.

"You can see they don't have good blood," said Granny. "Look at those weak chins. Short necks, too—that's always a bad sign. And shifty eyes! Remember, always look people straight in the eye so they'll know you're honest. Except men, when you get older. Then it means something else. That's how they can tell."

"Tell what?"

"Never mind."

The post office of yore imparted a feeling of security that made no sense, but then feelings of security rarely do. Few today remember Postal Savings Accounts but to the Depression generation they were the one bank that could never fail. Many people, including my father, clung to them well into the Fifties because "The post office will always be there." Others, more bold, put most of their money in the bank but kept about $300 in Postal Savings "just in case."

The certificates added to the aura of substantiality by being bigger and fancier than paper money, which appealed to that squirrely instinct of children to have something they can take out and look at. I had my own little account, and would have one now if they still existed because, you see, Banks Are Bad But The Post Office Is Good. This is the sort of New Deal-planted idée fixe that small-government conservatives keep running up against, but even the gruffest of them make an exception for the post office in their favorite maxim: "The federal government has only three duties: print the money, deliver the mail, and declare war."

It is no accident that the title character in Kevin Costner's *The Postman* is the allegorical savior of a ravaged, post-revolutionary America. The movie flopped because it was confused and poorly written but the concept was on target. We harbor a subconscious postal patriotism that is tied up with Ben Franklin, the Pony Express, and the idealistic good-guyness contained in the motto: "Neither snow, nor rain, nor heat, nor gloom of night stays these couriers from the swift completion of their appointed rounds." That these words were written by Herodotus in the fifth century B.C. makes the post office more of a "traditional value" than much else that we have.

THE postman and the FBI agent are the only two government employees to figure regularly in movies, but while the G-man is the admirable star, the postman is the lovable bit player—the comic relief, the separated lovers' Cupid, the sympathetic messenger of the gods bearing the letter edged in black, a bit of human contact for lonely Shirley Booth in *Come Back, Little Sheba*. And if the movie is very old he sports a badge of office certain to set off a childhood obsession. Kids still crave the fireman's hat and the cop's billy but in my day we also would have killed for the postman's leather shoulder bag.

The place of the post office in American psychology is what lies behind the Luddite hatred of faxes and e-mail, which, we are told, "will never replace the letter." That's nonsense; I save my faxes and print out my e-mail because they *are* letters. The loss mourned by the Luddites, who are often right-wing anarchists, is the still-powerful concept of "the U.S. mail." The phrase was too long a symbol of stability to be completely powerless now; sending obscenity through "the mail" or using "the mail" to defraud was worse than doing it in person, and on a subconscious level we still think so.

We may succeed in privatizing Social Security, but I predict that any attempt to privatize the post office will rouse American ire as neither Whitewater, nor Chinagate, nor Kosovo, nor Monica by night had the power to do.

July 26, 1999

IT must be nice to be one of those big-gun columnists with a research staff to gather notes for you. How painless, said she longingly, to have the day's news clips put in front of you, already marked and summarized by hired minions who are easily replaced when their minds snap from direct contact with the morning papers. This way the columnist has the news broken gently to him, enabling him to ease gradually into a temperate reaction to the day's big story.

Contrast it with my way: staggering up when I hear the Washington papers hit the door and juggling a cup of coffee, a cigarette, and a red Scripto over a front-page story about the Navy's plan to put women on submarines. This is why you will never find George Will trying to light a pen, or Anna Quindlen writing "I can't think of a worse place to have cramps."

The proposed destruction of the Navy's last all-male haven promises to hew to the familiar three-pronged pattern established by feminist assaults on the military:

1) A crazy idea is put forth.

2) Elaine Donnelly objects to it.

3) It happens anyway.

The coed-submarine idea was put forth by Navy secretary Richard Danzig, an incomparable prose stylist like all of the Clinton cabinet, who said: "The most Narcissus-like thing about creating something in your own image, about being in love with your own image, is the continued and continuous existence of this segment of the Navy as a white-male preserve." Read that at 5 A.M. and it becomes a multicultural minute celebrating Moby Dick as a Greek myth.

Not that Danzig was advocating affirmative action—perish the thought. He was merely pointing out, he said, that when a democracy changes, so must its military. Otherwise, "if the submarine force remains a white-male bastion it will wind up getting less and less support when it requires resources, when it has troubles, be they accidents or personnel issues or other kinds of things."

As the not-so-subtle threat of uncooperative white men being left to drown lingered in the air, Danzig's spokesman popped up with what the Pentagon calls a clarifying statement. There were no plans for coed subs in the "near future," he said; the secretary merely wanted to prompt submariners to start thinking about "future changes."

The table was now set for Elaine Donnelly, the longsuffering head of the Center for Military Readiness, who objected on cue: "The submarine force is being targeted for really harmful social change for no particular reason. It is clear what is happening here is happening in stages."

As usual, she was right; this summer 144 women officers on orientation tours will remain aboard subs instead of being returned to shore at the end of the day. The phrasemakers at the Pentagon claimed this was "not inconsistent with the policy of not assigning women to submarines," a statement not unlike the examples given by George Orwell in his essay on the politics of obfuscation, but one not without value since it gave the *Washington Times* a golden opportunity to untie the nots in their headline: WOMEN TO SPEND NIGHTS ON SUBS.

This is how it starts. The next step will be congressional hearings featuring so-called "enraged conservatives" who will, as usual, swallow their rage and make their classic mistake of adopting the enemy's language, delivering fervent opening statements on why "women have a place in our military" and heartfelt testimonials to "our fighting men and women." Not to be outdone in the art of standing up and caving in, populist conservatives will protest that only "elite" career-path women officers stand to benefit from coed subs while enlisted swabettes will bear the brunt of the hardships. To prove it, John Kasich will announce yet again that his father was a mailman.

Meanwhile, crusty old salts will try desperately not to sound crusty, old, or salty as they counter feminist claims that mashing your boobs against a man in a narrow passageway is no big deal. The mention of space is fatal, bringing on an army, so to speak, of measurers to explain how to convert a 30-foot-wide tube into an oasis of privacy.

A Navy briefing document on this problem already exists. Outfitting coed subs "will require removal of operational equipment reducing war-fighting effectiveness." So be it. Why worry about war-fighting when you have already converted the entire military to peacekeeping? Take out the torpedoes to make room for individual shower stalls. Operational equipment? On coed subs? Don't be silly. Get rid of the periscope. Who needs one when you've got female intuition aboard? "I have a feeling something is up there . . . "

T HIS, discounting my punch-drunk exaggerations, is how it will end. At the moment we are at the same stage we were in back when everyone was saying, "They'll never put women in fighter planes." I give yellow-bellied, polka-dot submarine warfare about three years to become fully operational, which is to say, capable of being sunk by the *Lusitania* traveling at ramming speed.

If we put women on submarines, history will record it as the time we defied human nature once too often. If feminists think Tailhook and Aberdeen were bad, wait till they see what happens underwater. For a preview they can watch a German movie called *Das Boot* and substitute a coed crew for the all-male one. This has to be the most tension-racked movie ever made, unbearable to watch yet so masterfully plotted it's impossible not to. Without a single recourse to tedious exposition, we are made aware of the loathing that builds up between people as mutual disgust exposes neuroses they never even knew they had.

It's not a matter of claustrophobia. Claustrophobics weed themselves out of the submarine service by not volunteering for it. The danger lies in the feral instinct to lunge at people we can't get away from, and for men in today's military that means women. So far they have submitted, but if we seal up the sexes and submerge them, we may wish we had heeded Dryden's warning: "How ill my fear they by my mercy scan / Beware the fury of a patient man."

August 9, 1999

J FK JR. WEEK produced evidence of the existence of Hell powerful enough to make believers of us all. It came to pass on CNN when Bernard Shaw, breaking for a commercial, said, "Our continuous coverage will be right back."

At last we've done it. Continuous Coverage has become a real person—"anthropomorphized," as English majors are fond of putting it, 50 million words made flesh and brought to us live, a world without end, amen.

Who is Continuous Coverage and what does he or she look like? We need not agonize over the pronoun. As the driving force behind the yentafication of America, Continuous Coverage is most definitely a she such as Somerset Maugham had in mind when he said, "It requires the feminine temperament to repeat the same thing three times with unabated zest."

Show Ms. Coverage a picture of a locked and deserted gate or a motionless grey ship parked in the middle of the ocean and she will say: "We don't know exactly where she is at this time or whether the family has received word of her plans, nor are there any indications at the moment that she will shortly issue a statement soon, but as of now what we can tell you is that so far Caroline Kennedy Schlossberg hasn't arrived yet."

Ms. Coverage issues some version of this bulletin so often that it begins to sound as if Caroline Kennedy Schlossberg is the second member of the family to vanish from the radar screen, but before another continuous coverage can get started, Ms. Coverage returns with something new: "Here are Caroline Kennedy Schlossberg and her husband bicycling at their summer home on Long Island. Apparently they decided to go out for a bicycle ride. Behind her you see her husband, Edwin, on a bicycle."

The difference between mere coverage and Continuous Coverage is immense. Take, for example, the word "family." It has been grating on our nerves for a long time but its normal irritation quotient is as nothing compared to what Ms. Coverage can do with it. Somewhere around her 356,748th usage the viewer concludes that the human race should spring from widely spaced test tubes stored in hermetically sealed underground laboratories in secret locations scattered throughout Greenland.

Continuous Coverage is a jealous mistress and a blindly loyal one, though not a particularly democratic one. Even though JFK Jr. was never called a "prince" by anyone in or out of the media, he suddenly became one, and by exquisite coincidence was immediately bumped up to "People's Prince" lest the Brits think that Ms. Coverage had a better orgasm during the Dianalia than she was having now. The problem was, real royalty has what this particular member of "America's royalty" lacked: frontage.

Like so many New York apartments from the outside, JFK Jr.'s looked like a dump. The approach to Kensington Palace offered plenty of room to build an endless vista of flowers, candles, balloons, and teddy bears, but when this same crud was piled in front of a converted warehouse it suggested nothing so much as a New York garbage strike in its eighth week. What to do? A pull-back shot would have shown nothing but the dump next door, so Ms. Coverage came in for extreme close-ups so extreme that you could read the size labels on the teeshirts.

All slavishly adoring lovers kill the thing they love. When Ms. Continuous Coverage called JFK Jr. a prince, she effectively called his father a king, which did more damage to the Camelot myth than all of his tawdry sex scandals combined. JFK was always Lancelot, never Arthur, but once Ms. Coverage inadvertently crowned him, his picture in our memories underwent a Dorian Gray transformation. Gone was the handsome, debonair president blessed with the privilege of remaining young throughout eternity, replaced by an old man who seemed to grow more gnarled and spotted each time Ms. Coverage said "prince," until nothing was left of him but a desiccated shell on the attic floor.

The Irish in general came in for regression thanks to Ms. Coverage's compulsive political correctness. Having come to America before anyone bothered about such things, they were simply called "the Irish." They also were called "Irish Catholic," but this was almost always a compound noun rather than a compound adjective, so they never really had a hyphen.

They do now. They acquired it, along with today's de rigueur minority-huddle word, when Ms. Coverage reported on the Gaelic Mass at Old St. Patrick's Cathedral and referred over and over again to "the Irish-American community."

DESPITE Ms. Coverage's sleepless, round-the-clock, repeating-rifle approach to the news she manages to miss a lot of things both large and small. Most of the latter probably can be traced to the sheer ignorance of a younger generation of researchers and caption writers who assume that St. Thomas More Church was named for Thomas Moore. This same generation draws many of its college graduates from social strata unfamiliar with niceties, which probably explains why Bobby's oldest son, Joseph P. Kennedy II, was invariably identified as Joseph P. Kennedy III, making him the son of his uncle, Joseph P. Kennedy Jr., who died a childless bachelor.

The larger oversights are things that Ms. Coverage refuses to mention, such as the number of women snuffed or otherwise destroyed by Kennedy men, a list that has just been upped by two. A sensitive topic I wish someone would discuss is JFK Jr.'s appearance. Not his hunkiness, but the fact that he didn't look at all like either of his parents, nor even like his own childhood pictures. It got even eerier when he became a teenager. We saw very little of him then, and the few photos flashed quickly on the TV screen this week reveal coarser, almost loutish features that cannot be entirely explained by the awkward age.

Did he have plastic surgery? Now that I've said it I had better bid you adieu. America's royalty plays rough, and Lord High Sycophant Mike Barnicle may throw me in the Tower.

August 30, 1999

THE time has come to write about something I have never written about before. I've kept silent for three reasons: The story did not fit my usual themes, it had no point when standing alone, and I could not include it in my memoir without arbitrarily switching locales and introducing too many characters with no continuous function.

Now, thanks to Hillary Clinton, my themes have expanded, my story has a point, and switching locales is the latest thing, so I will announce my candidacy for senator from New York and tell you what happened in Watertown.

It all started in 1944 when my mother's foster sister married a man from a little town 18 miles north of Watertown called Philadelphia. My mother and grandmother, who had never been north of Maryland, were dismayed, but I, who had never been north of Maryland either, was fascinated.

As the family letter-writer I scrupulously marked the envelopes "Philadelphia, New York STATE," underlining "state" three times so it wouldn't go to Pennsylvania. From my aunt's letters I learned the phrase "upstate New York" and latched on to it obsessively in my weird-kid way. Being a map freak as well, I sent away to Esso for a free road map, telling them that I wanted a map of "UPSTATE New York." When the map of the entire state came I carried it everywhere and read it until the folds split, becoming an expert on UPSTATE New York by the time we spent our first vacation there in the summer of 1946.

We took the train. Granny didn't go, which was just as well. We had to change trains in Manhattan so we stopped for lunch at the Automat. We were on our way in when my mother and I skidded to a stop and peered through the window in disbelief at something neither of us had ever seen before: an integrated restaurant.

"Look at them," Mama marveled. "Just sitting there, big as life."

My father, who had lived up North, hustled us in, but we almost missed our connection at Grand Central from stopping and peering in every other restaurant along the way.

("Miss King, what is your first memory of New York?")

The train to Utica passed Yankee Stadium, which thrilled my tomboy mother, and FDR's Hyde Park mansion, which thrilled us all. It sat on a bluff high above the tracks so that we had to look up, adding to the religious awe we felt. Secular reality returned when we saw Utica.

"What a dump," said Mama. "It looks like it's full of those run-down hotels where bums eat sardines out of the can and keep milk on the windowsill."

("Welcome to Utica, Miss King. Instead of a press conference, our local media have prepared a word-association test.")

The train from Utica to Watertown was a local that got us in after midnight, two hours late. My aunt and her husband met us and drove us to "Philly," as they called it, but I remember nothing except being carried upstairs to bed clutching my cracked New York map.

The next morning we awoke to a perfect movie set of a small town, with a Main Street, a grammar school, a white frame church, big square saltbox houses with barns instead of garages, and a town bad girl whom my aunt's mother-in-law pointed out first thing.

The second thing she pointed out was her hatred of FDR. We couldn't believe it, I least of all since I had known no other president until the previous year. It wasn't just that she was a Republican; what really bothered her, she said, was that "He brought back liquor." That made two more shocks: I had never met a Republican, and I had grown up hearing Southerners say, "At least he brought back liquor." My life was opening up, but unlike Hillary's, it was opening up in New York.

My aunt's husband had to hide his stash of Genessee Cream Ale from his mother. At first she approved of me because I was "such a quiet little thing," but then my life opened up some more. I had tasted my father's beer at home and hated it, but Genessee Cream Ale was so ambrosial that I drank two bottles and sang "I'm Looking Over a Four-Leaf Clover." Hillary, baby, give up: I got plastered at age 10 in upstate New York on upstate brew.

We borrowed a car and went exploring: Alexandria Bay, where we toured Boldt's Castle, other little towns in the area—Theresa, Antwerp, Gouverneur, Evans Mills—and Watertown, where we marveled over the beauty and stability of the residential streets with their huge McKinley-Queen Anne houses and towering shade trees. All three of us loved it and wanted to move there.

Mama caused episodes coming and going when we went to Canada. As native-born Americans she and I had no trouble entering, but when my father could not produce his naturalization papers the border guard grew officious.

"Listen," Mama piped up. "He ought to get in quicker than anybody. He's English and England owns youall."

My father's old passport was finally accepted but we had to listen to a rote recital of Canadian history before we were passed through.

On our return trip Mama was determined not to pay duty on my "real Canadian sweater" so as we neared the border, she made me put it on even though it was July.

"A little warm for a sweater, isn't it, young lady?" asked the guard.

"She's got malaria," said Mama.

When we were safely across she glared in the rearview mirror. "I'm not setting foot in that country again. They can take their maple leaf and shove it!"

("Miss King, what is your opinion of NAFTA?")

Her finest hour came when she got out of a speeding ticket by telling the New York state trooper about her childhood sweetheart, George McQuinn. They were born a week apart in Ballston, Virginia, and went to school together. George played first base for the old St. Louis Browns, when he made the final catch in the 1944 World Series, and was afterwards signed by the Yankees.

September 13, 1999

I T'S been open season on *The Oxford Psychiatric Dictionary* since Bob Woodward invented the "Clara Bow Syndrome" to describe Monica Lewinsky, so I will now contribute my own original entry: LEXOPHO-BIA, "fear of law."

Lexophobia is not merely a fear of being sued and running up Clintonian legal bills, not simply the normal revulsion brought on by the sight of a lawyer, but a burgeoning psychosis that has America in its grip. Its symptoms are three, the first being a paranoid certainty that every law is a potential dragnet.

Propose a law, any law, no matter how sensible and needed, and the air will instantly be filled with howls of despair about a "foot in the door," the "camel's nose in the tent," a "slippery slope," and a place called "down the road." Ban partial-birth abortion and it's back to coat hangers and button hooks; fund abortions for inner-city teens and genocide is just around the corner. Censor *Hustler* and they'll come after *Harper's*. Institute dress codes and the next thing we know women will be forced into purdah. Outlaw assault weapons? Today my elephant gun, tomorrow my son's .22 rifle. Pass an amendment against flag-burning? Do you know what they could do to me if I accidentally dropped a cigarette on my Fourth of July tee shirt? And what about the red-white-and-blue paper cups at the picnic?

The newest kids on the lexophobia block are video-store owners who like to point out that "Big Brother" could, *could* use the V-chip to limit or keep records on what movies people watch; and the anti–metric-system shut-ins who equate steres and litres with the coming of world government and compulsory "harmonization," a fresh scare word that is made to order for the website era.

The second symptom of lexophobia is the belief that laws are so unfairly applied that the innocent get off scot-free.

One of our latest buzzwords is "specificity," yet we condemn every instance of it as evidence of "singling people out." Watchdog groups are doing their best to hamstring the police in the matter of "profiling," which, says *Washington Times* metro columnist Fred Reed, simply means cops noticing things. Attempts to outlaw profiling are attempts to spread suspicion equally among all classes of citizens and build a more just world in which cops stop the CEO of a Fortune 500 company to ask him why he's driving such an expensive car, and arrest the Salvation Army lady for prostitution because she's standing on a corner.

To lexophobes of this stripe, social harmony takes precedence over the science of criminal investigation, but by demonizing its chief tool, deductive reasoning, they have planted the idea that if the country is to hold together, nothing must be allowed to make sense.

By charming coincidence, nothing does. We used to tell jokes about being "a little bit pregnant" but *Roe* v. *Wade* verified the condition and gave it a name: first trimester. Now we don't even notice when someone claims to be "sort of enraged" or "kind of devastated." We have become human punch lines seeking safety in equivocation and teasing ourselves with visions of more and better confusion. Consider Sarah Wunsch, an ACLU lawyer in Massachusetts, who said after Littleton: "I almost wish somebody in a football jersey had done it. What would they do then?"

"They" and "Them" are key players in lexophobia, which is predicated on the midnight knock at the door and the sudden disappearance associated with totalitarian governments. The irony, which lexophobes can be counted on to miss, is that their efforts to stamp out judgmentalism by stamping out cause and effect have turned us into what totalitarian governments love best: a nation of insecure nervous wrecks unable to think straight who will either accept the solace of passivity or else explode, justifying a crackdown.

Lexophobia takes its hardest toll on conservatives. Liberals love gradualism and incrementalism; their idea of fun is petitioning all 50 state governments one by one to effect some tiny change that they proudly call "a step in the right direction." Conservatives, contrary to our name, tend to be go-for-broke people whose natural inclination not so long ago was to *abolish* the National Endowment for the Arts and the Department of Education, *end* abortion, *outlaw* flag-burning, and *rescue* school prayer.

But action verbs are out now that one conservative's litmus test reminds another conservative of those ancient maps marked "Here be monsters." Conservatism is so splintered that it has been forced to abandon its coherent political philosophy and take up the gnomish passions of lexophobia. The latest practitioner is George W. Bush. Yes, he's pro-life and believes in a pro-life amendment, but it would be impossible to get it passed, and besides, *Roe* v. *Wade* won't be reversed anytime soon, so forget about it and concentrate on his campaign slogan: A camel's nose in every tent, and two left feet in every door.

The final and most pervasive symptom of lexophobia is unquestioning support for laws that make people feel good about themselves, i.e., that body of hysterical ukases known as political correctness.

Contrary to current received wisdom, nothing is more compassionate than detached, impersonal fair play, and there is one place where it has always been practiced. In her biography of Henri de Toulouse-Lautrec, Julia Frey writes:

> In the brothel, "kindness" was eliminated. Nothing was given away there; there was no pretense that the women loved their clients. The interactions were straightforward; everything was for sale. No one was being nice to him because they felt sorry for him. He, like any client, paid for drinks, amusement, sex. He owed no emotional debts and could choose to accept or decline what was offered.

Then there's the Houston City Council, where the affirmative-action director was suspended, ordered to undergo sensitivity training, and forced to apologize for referring to a councilman, who is a dwarf, as a "midget."

September 27, 1999

I T is not in the nature of ghouls to get a grip on themselves, but the grief junkies and sidewalk mourners of the English-speaking world seem to have lost interest in both Princess Diana and JFK Jr.

In view of the close death dates involved I expected them to mark the end of summer with a final commemorative immolation on the twin pyres of hysteria—a double header, so to speak. Mohamed Al-Fayed would fill Harrod's with portraits of Diana, Dodi, John-John, and Carolyn, all together in Paradise; and some enterprising American toy maker would come out with four teddy bears joined at the hip. But it didn't happen. The August 31 anniversary of Diana's death passed almost unnoticed, and JFK Jr.'s demise on July 16 was forgotten so fast it was as if it had never been.

Two factors explain the short-lived death of JFK Jr., the first being the media's delayed reaction when they remembered that dwelling on dead Kennedys invariably leads to discussions of torch-passing. Nobody wanted to get into this because the remaining Kennedy men are so nefarious or inadequate that the only torchbearer the family has left is Kathleen Kennedy Townsend, who is almost as exciting as Al Gore and Bill Bradley.

Now lieutenant governor of Maryland, KKT has a personality that recalls yearbook profiles that say "Honor student, loves animals. Hobbies: thimble collection." Fearing for their ratings if she won the veep spot on an already stuporous Democratic ticket and they had to cover her for months on end, TV honchos decided to censor all further mention of JFK Jr. so that nobody would breathe a word about torches.

The other reason JFK Jr. vanished twice has to do with his sister-in-law, Lauren Bessette. No one quite knew how to react to this third death. The extreme care the media took to include her name in every bulletin screamed afterthought, but to grief junkies, who are connoisseurs of the finer points of morbidity, three in a grave simply isn't done. It was as if Romeo and Juliet had died with Juliet's nurse. They saw Lauren not as a tragic figure but as someone who had made bad travel plans. Their collective subconscious transformed her into the woebegone anti-hero described by the phrase "along for the ride": the naïve teen in a car full of thuggish friends who flee before the cops come, leaving him as the sole suspect. In short, the tragicomic figure known as the goat.

The sidewalk ghouls felt cheated, but they didn't know what to do about it until the news that the Bessette family might file a wrongful-death suit gave them the permission they needed to put JFK Jr. out of their minds.

As the date of Diana's death approached, the world braced for the Brits to writhe again, but they showed instead a restraint bordering on indifference. Various theories arose. Some observers put it down to the chastening nature of second anniversaries; once we can no longer say, "This time last year she was alive," the mourning is complete. Anglophiles insisted that "English blood will tell"; the grief junkies, they said, were so ashamed of their unbuttoned behavior that they had resolved to heed a blast from the past: Captain Smith saying "Be British" to the *Titanic* stokers just before the boilers blew up.

My own theory took shape as I watched *Diana: The People's Princess*, the British television movie that ran on Labor Day weekend.

This may be the worst movie ever made, with wooden actors obviously chosen solely for their clonelike resemblance to the real-life characters. Diana, played by Amy-somebody, keeps running through Mediterranean villages with paparazzi in hot pursuit, wailing, "Why cawn't they give me my privacy?" The little-girl dresses she wears in these chase scenes are intended to underscore the pathos of her situation, but with her long skinny legs pumping away under thigh-high skirts she looks like an aging colt.

In the scenes with William and Harry the hugs never stop and are hard to distinguish from first downs. William flings himself into her arms while Harry takes flying leaps over the back of the sofa into her lap.

Democracy never rests either. Requesting the press to leave the future King of England alone, Diana whimpers, "William will freak out." Announcing dinner to the princes of the blood and their mother, no longer an HRH but still the daughter of an earl, her butler pops his head in the door and says, "Grub's up." Once they're all at the table, sensitivity is served.

Diana: "One in four Angolans has lost a limb to land mines."

Harry: "Really? I didn't know that."

No attempt is made to dramatize the story; the time line consists solely of dates flashed on the bottom of the screen so that we can do the arithmetic and think, "She had only one week to live." Nor are there any flashbacks. It would be sadistic to introduce them because they would disorient the millions who followed the original breaking news from start to finish. Like children hearing a favorite bedtime story for the thousandth time, grief junkies know the precise order of events and won't have it any other way.

Creative imagination is dead. We know Diana wore white capri pants and a black blazer on the night she died; we know Dodi wore blue jeans and a brown suede jacket; we know which arm he had around her; we know the order in which the entourage entered the revolving door at The Ritz; and the movie gets it all exactly, compulsively, obsessively, clonishly *right*, even to the point of casting the actors in a black-and-white security-camera shot to replicate the real black-and-white security-camera shot as seen on TV.

No wonder the Brits didn't go to pieces this year. If they can't do it exactly the way they did it the first time, including another funeral and a Royal Horse hussar whose chin strap comes loose three-point-four meters in front of the Abbey, they won't do it at all.

October 11, 1999

THERE seems to be a journalistic convention that columnists who take Pat Buchanan to task must include a testimonial about how delightful it is to know him personally. Mona Charen was "very fond" of him when they worked together in the Reagan White House, Bob Novak praises his sense of humor, and Jack Germond and assorted other McLaughlinites never screamed with a nicer guy. If you come to bury Pat, you must praise him first.

I don't know him. I was on his radio show some years ago, but it was via telephone, so we never met. We do, however, have two things in common: We're contemporaries (I'm three years older), and we're both native Washingtonians. That being the case, the requisite testimonial may be at hand.

In college, my sorority sisters and I used to go to the Connecticut Avenue Hot Shoppe. In his memoir, *Right from the Beginning*, Buchanan talks about how he and his gang also used to go there to pick fights. One night, some truculent teenagers came in. They were obviously looking for trouble so we decided to leave before a rumble got started. As we were scurrying out, though, one of the boys, sporting dark Fonzie sideburns and a puckish grin, gallantly opened the door for us. Was it Pat? I don't know, but I've often wondered.

There was a time when Pat Buchanan was my favorite columnist, TV personality, and public figure, which is why I broke my ironclad rule about not going on shows to go on his: I simply wanted to talk to him. It's hard to pinpoint exactly when disillusionment set in, but I do know that what began to bother me was not his politics but his writing. I really don't care what views people hold as long as they describe them well, but something was happening to Pat's literary style.

A column that made me do a double-take was the one on the controversy surrounding the FDR memorial. It was, you will recall, an artistic controversy having to do with sculpture and placement, but Pat ignored all that and launched a foaming jeremiad at FDR for destroying the "Old Republic" that went all the way back to 1918, and featured a sentence that even Faith Baldwin would delete: "FDR spent World War I sneaking off into the Virginia countryside with Lucy Mercer, cheating on the mother of his five children, breaking Eleanor's heart."

Matters worsened when he got fixated on movies. His column on the "cognitive elite" controversy growing out of Charles Murray's IQ findings had nothing to do with the cognitive elite or Charles Murray. It was about Sgt. Alvin York, whose few years of schooling in the Cumberland Mountains inspired Pat to extol the moral superiority of ignorance and recycle the threadbare cliché that many a drop-out "hired and fired" college graduates.

A clue to what brought on all this was his gulpy mention of York's modest dream of owning "a piece of bottom land." Since native Washingtonians are not up on plowing problems, I knew he had gotten this from the Gary Cooper movie, which made much of it. It was obvious that instead of taking the time and trouble to write 800 carefully reasoned words, he had spent deadline eve in front of his VCR and then dashed off a disjointed column from his reveries.

His writing already in jeopardy, his thinking went to pot as well after he saw *Forrest Gump*. He became the movie's self-appointed publicist, heaping such clamorous praise on Gump's multitude of virtues that he inadvertently equated loyalty, duty, honor, country, morality, hard work, and true love with an IQ of 75. "How on earth," he asked incredulously, "did this film get through the PC screeners?" It didn't; it just got through Pat. It was a satire on the American success story: Gump as the dumb sports star, the dumb patriot, the dumb businessman, and the dumb politician, landing on his feet every time.

Pat next turned his blind eye to *Braveheart*. Predisposed to flack it as a right-wing patriotic saga, he missed its uncanny similarity to the left-wing *Spartacus* written by Hollywood Ten member Dalton Trumbo: Prole with inborn gift for military strategy raises army, yells "Freedom!" a lot, suffers horrible death, lives on in hearts of oppressed. Memo to Mel Gibson: Change Cassius to Edward I.

His cinematic obsessions are the key to his strange behavior of late. Why did he publish a soft-on-Hitler book in the midst of a political bid? Why did he cozy up to Marxist stormy petrel Lenora Fulani? There is a simple explanation, and fittingly, it comes from a movie: Pat Buchanan has a Walter Mitty complex. What lures him is not running for president, but the fantasy of running for president, preferably against all odds. Under his bombast about

pitchforks and riding to the sound of the guns is a thwarted Danny Kaye figure yearning to exchange the passive pursuits of writing and talking for an
imaginary world of mortal danger, fearless battle, and heroic legend.

At the moment, his favorite movie is *President Pat*, but who knows what
other tapes lurk beside his VCR? *Captain Pat Hornblower*, destroyer of the
politically correct Navy. *Going Pat's Way*, wherein a lovable jaunty priest singlehandedly takes America back to God. *The Great Patsby*, a cautionary tale
about operating without set values. *A Pat for All Seasons*, wherein the hero is
martyred for his unpopular beliefs. When he's up, he watches *Young Pat*,
when he's down, he watches *Pat in Winter*, and for peasant-rallying medieval
moods he turns to *Patanhoe*.

For a change of pace he plugs patriotism as a song-and-dance man in
Yankee Doodle Pat, and even more surprisingly, in *Gunga Pat*. He doesn't
usually see himself as a little brown brother, but he can't resist the scene in
which he uses his last breath to blow the warning bugle. There's also *Pat and
Delilah;* he's not comfortable mushing with Hedy Lamarr, but he has a real
feel for the jawbone of an ass.

He always saves the best for last so we will too. A remake of the George
C. Scott epic: *Pat*.

October 25, 1999

N ORA EPHRON likes to tell a story about the advice she got from
her screenwriter mother: Never regret any experience, no matter
how grisly or boring, because "Everything is copy." Translated
from writer's shoptalk, you can get a column out of anything, and that's just
what I am about to do because I am writing this in the middle of moving to a
new apartment.

I could have told NR about the move and asked them to send in a pinch
hitter until I got settled, but I shrank from doing that. It's simply a matter of
honor: I've never missed a deadline in my life, and I refuse to start now. Even
more important, I don't want any Gentle Readers on my conscience. So many
of you write me heartfelt testimonials such as, "Reading your column keeps
me sane," and, "If I turned to the last page and you weren't there, I'd consider suicide," that I've been experiencing a twinge each time I write *Fragile* on
a carton. Besides, I have no choice: The rug cleaners just left and I can't move
from this spot until everything dries, so I might as well write something.

My new place is only four blocks away, but I feel as if I'm going to the
moon. I've lived in this old apartment for 16 years. You know what that

T HE trend spotters and opinion leaders have fallen down on the job. Here it is February already, and we haven't been sold on "post-Y2K syndrome."

No roundtables, no panels, no two-part specials, no cover stories, no man-in-the-street interviews, no 900-number polls, no lapel ribbons for empathizers—nothing. Just peace and quiet, give or take Alan Keyes, and people going about their business with nobody asking them if they're having an anti-climax.

Something is wrong. When in the course of current events have we been left alone like this? What is behind the strangely mature silence about the calamity that wasn't?

One explanation could be embarrassment, except that the media are incapable of embarrassment. Accuse them of indulging in much ado about nothing and they will simply preempt themselves and do a day's worth of breaking news called "More Ado About Nothing."

A post-Y2K syndrome would have dovetailed nicely with the traditional late-winter-blues syndrome, but this winter is different. Elián Gonzalez has washed up from foreign shores to become the *E pluribus unum* of "Our Children," making it possible for all Americans to obsess over the same kid at the same time. The thrill of having our favorite national neurosis coordinated with such precision makes the successful extermination of the Y2K bug seem as nothing.

It's a shame, really, that we don't feel let down and cheated, because the media-government complex worked so hard on Operation Friendly Panic. As the glitching hour approached, the news was full of sunny John Koskinen, chairman of the President's Council on Year 2000 Conversion, he of the smiling eyes, bald pate, and soothing manner that made the *Washington Times* dub him "the nation's grandfather."

Koskinen is a whole comfort zone unto himself, the balm in Gilead made flesh, the personification of kiss-it-and-make-it-well.

Indeed, Koskinen gave such a virtuoso performance that even the most trusting souls could not help wondering darkly, "How come they picked him?" The answer was easy: He looks exactly like our original designated grandfather, Dwight D. Eisenhower. Picking an Ike clone for a front man was tantamount to saying they were expecting the worst.

It was brilliant, but then they made a mistake.

Ever since the Y2K bug was first publicized a few years ago, the gurus had talked as if all we had to worry about was the actual rollover of the date at midnight on New Year's Eve, but in December they started issuing state-

means: Every word I've written for NR has been written here, plus the last half of *Confessions of a Failed Southern Lady* (I moved in the middle of that too), as well as four subsequent books and God knows how many reviews. A local acquaintance said they should put a bronze plaque on the building. I told her that knowing the landlord, he'd probably say, "How much is a tin one?"

It was also the site of my last fling, at age 48, so the new place will be my first completely chaste home since the going rate for attractive efficiencies in Washington was $75 a month. I have marked the transformation by giving away my old double bed and buying a twin bed to take up less room, but I must admit that the symbolism is perfect.

Still, another kind of excitement may be in the offing judging from a clause in the lease I just signed. It says: "No four-legged pets allowed." When I know the new landlord better, I may suggest a more concise way of phrasing that. Exotic pets are all the rage now; monkeys have two arms and two legs, and snakes don't have any legs at all.

For someone whose powers of mental concentration approach self-hypnosis, the worst thing about moving is the way it interferes with following the news. Gone are my leisurely coffee-filled hours of marking and clipping the morning papers. For the past couple of weeks I have had the attention span of a soccer mom, glancing at a headline here, scanning a story there, and wondering what it all has to do with life's really important concerns, like where the hell is the telephone man.

Being a member of the movers' focus group is like taking that famous history class at Harvard alongside Robert Benchley, who said he learned that Charlemagne did something with the Holy Roman Empire in A.D. 800, but that he had no idea what. Now that I've temporarily joined the ranks of distracted Americans, I've been making do with the gist of the news and shrinking the issues until they fit neatly into my leftover mental niches. That way I can take them out and look at them when I have some down time, like now.

This week, for example, I learned that House Speaker Denny Hastert did something with health-care legislation that made him look more pathetic than ever, like the lug whose perennially embarrassed wife is always jabbing him in the ribs at parties and hissing, "Stop doing that!" Then, right afterwards, or maybe it was right before, Tom DeLay did something with the income of the working poor. What it all means, in the considered opinion of the movers' focus group, is that Republicans can no longer object to anything for fear of being accused of hating whatever it is.

Scientists interested in measuring the effects of moving on the human brain, take note: When the Senate rejected a black judge named White and

David Horowitz came out with a new book called *Hating Whitey* in the same week, I felt positively coordinated. Coming on top of the *J'accuse* Alan Dershowitz hurled at Pat Buchanan, it established the point at which the names of conservatives who have not yet been called racists would fit on a three-by-five card and still leave room for my window-shade measurements.

Before someone accuses me of movism, I wish to point out a surprising discovery I've made: Havoc isn't all bad. Deep thinking is fine in its place, but nothing concentrates the mind like deep cleaning. Being unaccustomed to physical exhaustion, I was unprepared for the almost out-of-body experience of blinding clarity it triggered when I finally finished packing my books and sank down with the morning papers to read George W. Bush's back-pedaling explanations of what he really meant when he lambasted conservatives twice in one week.

"But oftentimes, people only hear the sterile numbers of economic news . . ."

"Oftentimes, people only hear our gloom-and-doom scenario . . ."

"I was making the case that when we'll oftentimes be talking about numbers and economics . . ."

"I said oftentimes our party has been mischaracterized . . ."

His strained venture into the anachronistic poesy of "oftentimes" hit me like one of those sunbursts that bad novelists enjoy describing. I knew approximately how the quotation went but I had to check the exact wording, so I ripped open G.E. Three-Speed Exhaust Fan, the box containing my complete Shakespeare that I had just sealed up, and turned to the beginning of *Macbeth*, where Banquo comments on the meaning of the prediction the witches have just made:

> *And oftentimes, to win us to our harm,*
> *The instruments of darkness tell us truths,*
> *Win us with honest trifles, to betray 's*
> *In deepest consequence.*

If compassionate conservatism corrupts, does absolute compassionate conservatism corrupt absolutely?

November 8, 1999

MANY societies have made life miserable for their citizens, but none has ever driven them crazy. A few, such as Louis-Philippe's self-satisfied bourgeois France, may have bored them to distraction, but sturdy sanity has always held sway among the commonality even when their rulers fell into hereditary fits and had sobriquets like "the Simple" and "the Mad."

Enter America, where presidential candidates dare not admit to seeing a psychiatrist and the masses go on daytime TV to boast volubly about "seeking professional help." Of all democracy's unintended consequences, this one takes majority rule where no one ever imagined it could go.

Driving people crazy is easy to do. You don't have to give them electric shocks or put them in solitary, all you have to do is make them doubt the evidence of their senses until they whimper, "What the hell is going on?" This is where America is now. There's a war on, and it's not in any of the places likely to become Bill Clinton's next Ruritania du jour. It's in our heads, and the enemy is the unrelenting flux of American life. Every day is *Gaslight*, and we're Ingrid Bergman.

Advertisers used to pound home their messages in the simplest possible way, but watching some of today's TV commercials is an experience akin to reading *Beowulf*. There's the one showing a car sitting in the middle of the desert while an Irish tenor voice sings "Home on the Range" in Italian. In another, a geeky guy sits down alone at a set-up chess board and nervously wipes sweat from his face while a clock ticks away menacingly in the background. After a moment, a driverless car pulls up beside him, and he rises and walks off.

At least we can tell these are car commercials. More puzzling are the ones that seem to have no sponsor. These are in black-and-white and feature a man in a white dinner jacket with a satanic goatee who fires off sneering, mocking questions along the lines of, "So you think you did the clever thing, do you? Who would want *you* for an employer?"

Are they trying to convince us to keep up with the sadomasochistic Joneses? Do they believe the economy is so good that we might be willing to buy the product to figure out the ad? It's probably another online trader, but either they don't say or else the name goes by so quickly that it doesn't register. Then, after the program returns, we keep on trying to solve the mystery of the commercial until we forget what's going on in the mystery we're watching.

In a column written shortly after the death of Vincent Price, Alston Chase said that because good guys mumble, Price's perfect diction had gotten him typecast as a villain. Now all movie dialogue consists of bad diction drowned out by background noise. Characters mumble while revving engines, chopping wood, sharpening swords, hammering anvils, and operating machinery. Movies used to muffle background noises when characters spoke, but today nothing is muffled except their lines. Much of this is meant to convey the stress and strain and general unpleasantness under which working-class characters live, but Joan Crawford waitressed, barmaided, and factory-girled her way through dozens of movies in which we could understand every word she said. Today's cinematic noise has the same purpose as the rock music that SWAT teams play for holed-up criminals.

The desire to leave one's mark by cluttering up the works has been the motivation behind petty vandalism since time immemorial. More recently, it has manifested itself in the plangent wish, "I want to be a part of history," uttered by grief junkies on pilgrimages to sidewalk memorials for dead celebrities. Now the ante has been upped to a constitutional guarantee of the right to time-travel. Edmund Morris shows us how to do it in *Dutch: A Memoir of Ronald Reagan*, but Morris is not the first author to hit on the idea of driving his readers crazy by inserting himself in a book.

In *The French Lieutenant's Woman*, a novel of Victorian England published in 1970, author John Fowles imitates the omniscient Victorian novelist's technique of stopping the action cold to deliver homilies. This is no more than what most Victorian writers did, but Fowles goes them one better by climbing into the story as an unnamed character who trails the hero around.

When the two share a train compartment, the author-character confesses to a writing block and studies the dozing hero, thinking: "Now what am I going to do with you?" At the end, he waits outside the Rosetti house while Charles goes in to persuade Sarah to marry him. Does she or doesn't she? We never find out, because the chortling author-character admits that he has no idea what happens. He supplies the book with two endings, either of which we may choose provided we can find someone to turn the pages for us after they put us into our strait jackets.

Now that Morris has gone Fowles one better by climbing into a biography, it's only a matter of time before the teachers' lobby puts pressure on textbook publishers to leave blank spaces in history books so that pupils can insert their own names:

"That first terrible winter, _____ told William Bradford that he or she was starving."

Alternatively, the publishers could just toss in an extra personage that every pupil can identify with.

"Lewis, Clark, Sacajawea, and I stood overlooking the mighty river."

"After I checked with Travis and Bowie I turned to Davy and said, Davy, I said . . ."

The possibilities for political correctness would be endless:

"'For Goddess' sake, stop it! You violent Southern white man!'" I shouted as I grabbed Preston Brooks's cane and wadded my pelisse under Senator Sumner's bleeding head."

Not to mention the possibilities for building self-esteem:

"I was in the play that night, so when John Wilkes Booth leapt to the stage I tackled him and broke his leg."

Ingrid, you don't know what gaslight is. All you had to worry about was a switched picture.

November 22, 1999

THE announcement of Judge Thomas Penfield Jackson's findings against Microsoft was marked by an unprecedented coincidence: Janet Reno and I were both wreathed in smiles. How could it be? I'm a right-winger who favors capitalism and laissez-faire government, and she's a left-winger who favors socialism and meddling government. Somebody was being illogical, and it wasn't Janet Reno.

Conservatives are big on logic, ever conscious of our duty to be rational and objective, quick to pounce on those who lead with their hearts instead of their heads, and unforgiving of anyone who "personalizes" an argument. Nobody has defended logic more rigorously than yours truly. I've held the fort with lofty terms like *post hoc, ergo propter hoc* and Aristotelian discourses on the "feminization" of reason, but when the Microsoft news broke I went slumming in the ghetto of subjectivity, there to learn how the other half lives and appreciate their satisfactions.

It was a lesson I'll never forget, to wit: Aristotle, schmaristotle. When Bill Gates gets his comeuppance, the logical thing to do is let fly with visceral syllogistic mayhem.

The dorky, bloodless, adenoidal Napoleon with bangs, I hope the Justice Department double-clicks on him until he turns into the Sisyphus of the task bar, forever opening, never closing. Better yet, I hope Mount Rainier erupts and turns his headquarters into a high-tech Pompeii, immobilizing his endless stream of "innovations" in obdurate eternity, to be upgraded nevermore.

I want revenge, or to put it formally in the kind of airtight, irrefutable argument you have come to expect from me: I hate Windows; therefore, Microsoft should be liquidated. I want to get even for hideously written user's manuals, for the icons that replaced incoherent words with incoherent pictures, for the way "icon" has tunneled its way into the language like a virtual mole.

I want to get even with every techie I've ever known. Every date who bored me to death with droning explanations. For the engineering majors with slide rules in leather cases slapping against their thighs like cavalry sabers. For the utter contempt in which they held "liberal-arts types." Forget alpha males and beta males, I'm talking about "pi males." They're the real leaders of today's pack, these chest-thumping, trouble-shooting bullies of Customer Support, and Bill Gates is the quintessence of the breed.

I sense that I am not alone in my gleeful reaction to the Microsoft news. For a country with a tradition of worshipping captains of industry, America has always been made strangely uneasy by Bill Gates. The only people who look up to him with unabashed admiration are "entrepenoor conservatives"—talk-radio callers who became Republicans when they discovered the word "entre-preneur" and found a way to apply it to themselves. They use it like a mantra to buck up their faith in small business and their Horatio Alger dream of being their own boss. As one of them told Rush Limbaugh, the government should leave Gates alone because "he started his company in a garage."

For the rest of us, Gates is the source of a conflict so severe that it verges on disorientation. The only thing Americans love more than progress is the old saw, "If it ain't broke, don't fix it," but Gates has emerged as the com-pulsive national fixer for millions who are unlucky enough to own something that works just fine. No wonder we recoil from seeing him as the new Henry Ford. He's caused a nationwide nervous breakdown with his unnecessary and endlessly upgraded bells and whistles. Think what would happen if he designed cars.

People shifted gears for decades before the automatic transmission was introduced. Since then, there has never been a time when you couldn't buy both; the stick shift did not become a "dinosaur," as it would have if Gates had dominated Detroit. The same holds true for telephones. First came "Number, please," then the dial, then the push-button, but you can still get by with a rotary phone today; you have to do a few things differently but it doesn't "crash."

A fear and loathing of Gates and his products has begun to emerge. Back in the early Eighties, columnists wrote funny pieces about their first attempts to use a PC, but now the humor has changed to outright rage. Commenting on the Windows error message, "Your computer has malfunctioned. Click O.K.," the *Washington Post*'s Rob Pegoraro snarled, "No, it's not O.K.!"

There are hints that Judge Thomas Penfield Jackson himself may be in a similar mood. In his ruling, described by the AP as having an "indignant tone," Jackson charged Microsoft with creating "confusion and frustration" that "increased technical support costs," and with selling a complex product that made computers more susceptible to crashing.

But that's not all. "In one final jab at Microsoft," reports the *Washington*

Post, "the electronic version of his ruling was formatted not for Microsoft's industry-standard Word software program for word processing, but rival Corel Corp.'s struggling WordPerfect software."

Judges have PCs too. I bet Jackson got the Windows error message, "Fatal Exception OD, 01FF:000001C4," and woke up his wife when he yelled, "What the hell does that mean!"

I charge Gates and his gang with marketing bundled sadism. Using "Crash," "Freeze," and "Fatal" in error messages is the work of people who get off on being the bearers of bad tidings. The latest, nicknamed by Windows users, is the "Blue Screen of Death" that pops up at the fate worse than fatal. It's royal blue with white letters like an old word-processor screen in DOS. Seeing it made me so nostalgic that I had Windows taken off and my old DOS reloaded. Now I use the mouse pads for drink coasters and the CD drive for an ashtray holder, so let's hear it for Descartes: I am; therefore, I hate Windows.

December 6, 1999

U NINTENDED consequences strikes again. All politicians promise to "do something about education," but now, at long last, one of them has delivered. Thanks to Al Gore's masculine-image problems, Americans are learning the Greek alphabet.

These are dumbed-down times, so we haven't gotten beyond the first two letters, but that's enough to explain Al Gore. A leader must be a dominant, aggressive alpha male, but Gore is a submissive, fear-grinning beta male who never tries to mate because the females would just reject him and the alpha male would kill him.

Women have always instinctively understood this difference. Back when I was a sorority pledge memorizing the entire Greek alphabet, alpha males were called "real men" and beta males were called "drips," but these simple categories vanished in the Seventies when Jane Goodall and Dian Fossey took to the jungle and made faces for the documentary cameras. The contemporaneous emergence of the "gorilla ladies" and early feminism scienced up what women already knew and cast a pseudo-anthropological veneer over girl talk. Men became "males" and watching National Geographic specials replaced perusing old yearbooks.

Alphabetized men are once again in the news thanks to Naomi Wolf, the garrulous sibyl with the *Charlie's Angels* hair who is employed as Al Gore's valet. Whether or not she advised him to be Alpha Gore—she claims she did not—she has given Campaign 2000 a unique twist. Now the whole country is looking at the candidates and wondering, "Which one is the ape?"

When the American woman expresses a desire for alpha males, she means something all her own, an ersatz ideal extending beyond established systems of biology and ethics into a dense jungle of predatory fallacies and feral oxymorons that can change color to blend in with whatever they land on. As in any National Geographic special, first you see it, then you don't.

To survive in this gynecratic terra incognita, the American alpha male must understand that being too aggressive is "unacceptable." He can sow his seed as much as he likes as long as he pays child support. He should be a good father, but under no condition should he be a strict father, because patriarchal dominance must be stamped out. The Alphas have already caved on this point, judging from the raft of TV ads featuring men gazing in limpid adoration at children. The AFLAC Dad buys insurance "Because he has his mother's eyes," while the MasterCard Dad spends his vacation staring intently at his son and intoning, "Remembering who you work for is priceless."

This sounds like bad news for hot-tempered John McCain, but guess again. As McCain's former press secretary explained it, "He gets very angry when people attack his family, his wife." How angry? When the *Arizona Republic* ran a cartoon insulting to McCain's wife, he stopped speaking to them for a year. He got even madder over an article in the *Phoenix New Times*: "He didn't speak to me for five years," said the reporter. Andrew Jackson fought duels over insinuations about his wife, but he was "out of control." McCain drops pins so his enemies will know there's a lot more silence where that came from.

According to Elizabeth Drew, some Republicans are using "temper" as a code word to suggest that McCain is unstable. That "temper" has become synonymous with crazy proves that masculinity has been soccer-mommed to death, so McCain's place in the Greek alphabet is a moot point.

Then there's the scion of the Grecian alphabet. It's instructive to compare him to another George—Georges-Jacques Danton, the French Revolution leader and one of history's premier alpha males.

A son of the soil, the boy Danton was kicked in the face by a cow when he bent under her and squirted milk into his mouth from her udder. His nose was broken and his cheekbones crushed. A few years later, he was kicked in the face again, this time by a bull (today's image-makers would make much of the gender balance), and suffered a broken jaw. By now his broad peasant visage looked like a clenched fist, but it wasn't over yet. A bout with smallpox left him pitted.

He acted on women like catnip; they couldn't keep their hands off him. He bedded them all, but he also adored his wife and boasted that he made love to her every night. When she died suddenly while he was away from Paris, he rushed back as soon as he got word. Going directly to the cemetery, he dug up her grave, pried open her coffin, and, sobbing wildly, covered her corpse with kisses.

George W. missed a New Hampshire debate to watch his wife receive an award from Southern Methodist University. Our only conceivable answer to Danton is Steve Forbes, who has a pitted face.

The surest sign of an alpha male is that he is alpha even in extremis. The spectacle of a powerful man brought low has the somber magnificence of the death throes of a bull elephant, as we see in Nancy Hale's poem on the death of Darius the Great.

> *Then all the frightened generals ran away.*
> *But first they slashed and jabbed at him with knives.*
> *To the invader, and to save their lives*
> *They left him, bleeding, in the early day.*
> *When the impatient Macedonian*
> *Rode up, victorious and strong of heart,*
> *He found this pitiful subject for his slaughter:*
> *Omnipotent Asia, dying in a cart;*
> *The King of Kings, a lone abandoned man,*
> *Who choked, and rolled his eyes, and called for water.*

If the jogging George W. had been fatally buried under a pile of debris from that errant dump truck, the word "tragedy" would have echoed through the land as it always does at such times, but omnipotent Asia dying in a cart would have morphed into Dagwood Bumstead going splat.

December 20, 1999

D ear Gentle Readers: 'Tis that season again, and I'm all ready for it. Most people get out their box of tree lights at this time of year, but I got out my box of quotations to find something suitable to kick off my Christmas letter to you.

It didn't take long. With a new millennium upon us, the winner is Oscar Wilde's accurate prediction that he would die before the end of 1900 because: "If another century began and I was still alive, it would really be more than the English could stand."

The first order of business is to thank you for your housewarming cards and gifts. I love the fridge magnets, potholders, dishcloths, and that fantastic rum-soaked fruitcake: I just drank a piece for breakfast.

The move could not have gone more smoothly. The company charged just $100 an hour for four men, and they all introduced themselves and shook hands when they arrived. They worked so fast that the bill came to only $300, and they were surprised when I tipped them each $10. Civility is not dead everywhere. The next time a Southern newspaper calls me for a comment on that standard Sunday feature, "Is the South Still the South?," I intend to give a resounding "Yes!"

My new apartment is a duplex, 2BR as before, but smaller and newer, hence easier to keep clean. The old one was a huge barn with woodwork and molding that collected dust, and more doors than a Vincent Price movie. The doors also had little decorative ledges that collected still more dust. It would have been an ideal place to test the housekeeping advice of the late memoirist Quentin Crisp ("After the first four years the dirt doesn't get any worse"), but cleanliness, despite the ever-present risk of godliness, is a priority with me.

Not so aesthetics, which explains what I used for a living-room "window treatment," as decorators say. A shower curtain. Not the plastic kind, but the fabric kind that requires a liner when used as intended. I like it. It goes with the rug and it's easy to open and close—just give it a slap.

My old building was tucked into a side street, but now I'm downtown amid the city noises I love. Conservatives are supposed to underwrite William Cowper's "God made the country, and man made the town," but total silence distracts me so much that I need an exhaust fan on at all times for "white noise." One of my earliest memories is the streetcar rattling over the end-of-the-line switch outside our windows, and the driver reversing the wicker seats with screeching slams. Fredericksburg has nothing that good, but I'm on the main drag to the hospital and get a lot of sirens.

Before deciding on this apartment, I looked at another that was really, really downtown—in the balcony of the newly renovated old movie theater. It was practically a penthouse; a circular steel staircase winding up to 2BR, each with a bath; wall-to-wall carpet, washer/dryer, dishwasher, and wet bar, all for $850. But such elegance would be wasted on somebody who decorates with shower curtains, and my object was to have less space, not more. Besides, it involved a long trek through the "galleria"—a veritable mall—to get to the elevator.

I'm on the ground floor now, but since I write and watch TV in the kitchen, I have to walk upstairs to the bathroom. A well-known and respected conservative, who shall remain nameless, suggested a way to make things easier on myself, but I told him I couldn't do it. Lest we forget, civilization emerged not from the grand documents and noble philosophies of men, but from an arbitrary little voice in the female head saying, "That's not nice!"

Other than that, my socio-cultural observations are on hold because the post office does not forward catalogues. I had phone numbers for the ones I've ordered from so I called them with my new address, but the ones I merely studied are lost.

You can learn a lot from catalogues you never order from. How somebody like Bill Clinton ever got elected becomes instantly clear when we view universal suffrage through the prism of three offerings: "Will make your friends scream with laughter!" (toilet seats that play Sousa marches in response to pressure); "A real attention-getter!" (lifelike severed limbs); and, "Guaranteed to liven up your parties!" (*Le Mannequin Pis* drink dispensers).

I moved my NR-idea files myself, clutching them to my heart all the way to the new place. Now that I'm settled, I've gone through them and made column notes. A sampling:

1. The switch from mere age to "age groups" and the relentless use of the word "generation" have convinced me that undifferentiated blobs aren't so bad after all.

2. I detect movement on the virtue front: Apologies are out and forgiveness is in. You might think one could not exist without the other, but it's no longer necessary to have a petitioner in order to have an absolver. Forgiveness, once a sign of a generous soul, is now a sign of individual responsibility and superior awareness. The most committed forgivers need no prompting, which is why their forgiving is indistinguishable from their recycling and flossing.

3. Come the moment in Campaign 2000 when our fancy lightly turns to thoughts of arsenic, I'll be ready with my second-favorite (next to Lizzie Borden) murderess, Madeleine Smith, the well-bred Victorian nymphomaniac who made grand slam with Scotland's unique "Not Proven" verdict in 1857.

4. Recently I got a letter from a Gentle Reader who asked: "If you could repeal one Constitutional amendment, which would it be?" I don't know what I've done to have such cruel limitations placed on me, but I'll give it a try.

5. My most serious column will be about my new book, *A Brou, Not a Ha- Ha*, in which I explain why every country that fought in the War of the Spanish Succession shouldn't have.

December 31, 1999

2000

I SPEAK to you from my bed of pain, felled by one too many millenni-al lists. Somewhere between the 1,000 Most Significant Somethings and the 100 Greatest Whatevers, I lost it. I am now sick of everybody who was anybody, including Churchill.

The trouble with lists is that they are the work of conformists. Take, for example, that old standby, the Ten Most Admired, an annual exercise in lock-step opinion ever since I can remember. Year after year, it was always the same; an overnight newsmaker might occasionally break through the phalanx of acceptable thinking, but otherwise it boiled down to the President, the First Lady, and Billy Graham.

The millennial lists exceeded mere conformity to achieve the most rigid political correctness yet seen. Nelson Mandela was on everything except Entomologists Who Changed Our Lives, Gloria Steinem was right up there with Edison on the one about light-shedders, and Crazy Horse joined Oscar Wilde on Most Misunderstood.

If the cure for democracy is more democracy, then the cure for lists is more lists, so I have compiled People I Instinctively Like for My Own Quirky Reasons Whether I Ought To or Not.

SOCRATES—With a single sentence, "The unexamined life is not worth living," he gave introspection a good name, making it possible for people to figure out, among other things, why they feel it necessary to put the President, the First Lady, and Billy Graham on Most Admired lists.

CARDINAL RICHELIEU—The feline aesthete who pulled France from under the ineffectual Louis XIII is the perfect antidote to presidential candidates who heap praise on "the American people" in every other sentence. "Though he loved France," writes Will Durant, "Frenchmen left him cold."

What I admire most about Richelieu is the guiding principle he called *raison d'état*, the "reason of state" that decided his every move. As he defined it: "A Christian cannot too soon forgive an offense, but a ruler cannot too soon punish it if it be a crime against the state." I've always thought that was a neat way around Nice Guyism.

TALLEYRAND—Usually described, for brevity's sake, as Napoleon Bonaparte's foreign minister, he was actually all things to all men, slipping between the meshing gears of French political upheavals to position himself in the right place at the right time in the manner of Dick Morris.

An aristocrat who was consecrated a bishop, he aligned himself with the National Assembly, the Revolution, the Constitutional Monarchy, the Republic, the Directory, the Consulate, the Empire, the Bourbon Restoration, and finally, the July Monarchy. When Louis-Philippe was crowned, he asked Talleyrand, "How many governments have you sworn allegiance to?" Unruffled, Talleyrand replied, "Sire, yours is the thirteenth."

In an era of despicable amoralists like Bill Clinton, Talleyrand comes across as a likable one. To understand the difference we need look no further than the furious words of the parvenu Napoleon, who called him "a silk stocking filled with s***" At least it was silk.

SGT. ALVIN YORK—The hero of World War I wasn't taken prisoner, he took prisoners—132 of them, to be exact. In this last great military feat before women got the vote, the word "hero" meant exactly that: a man who takes the initiative and does something aggressive singlehandedly.

Today, "hero" must have a passive connotation and involve a group or else we dare not use it. From the capture of the crew of the *Pueblo* in 1968, to the Teheran embassy hostages in 1979, to the current absorption in John McCain's ordeal in the Hanoi Hilton, we have steadily burdened heroism with so many disclaimers that it has come to describe being in the wrong place at the wrong time with lots of great people.

RADCLYFFE HALL—The British author of the 1928 lesbian novel, *The Well of Loneliness*, was not lonely. She had no trouble seducing the breathtakingly beautiful Una Troubridge away from her knighted husband, and lived openly with her for years in a classic butch-femme arrangement. Hall especially enjoyed playing the husband in public, but there the resemblance to today's most famous lesbian couple ends.

Ellen DeGeneres and Anne Heche smooched and felt each other up at the White House Correspondents' Dinner, but Radclyffe and Una celebrated their difference differently. Now that familiarity is breeding contempt like rabbits, I wish I could go back in time to Claridge's and listen in when Hall, after making sure she had the other diners' attention, told the waiter in a loud voice: "Lady Troubridge will have the lamb."

ELEANOR GEHRIG—The Gary Cooper movie about the life of doomed ballplayer Lou Gehrig portrayed Eleanor the way all such movies portrayed the wife: as the keeper of the flame who kept the scrapbook.

The scrapbook scene used to be the backbone of movies about celebrated men. Whenever the screenwriter needed a quick way to show the hero's increasing fame, the passage of time, or his wife's selfless devotion, the camera zoomed in on a huge jar of white paste and a pair of feminine hands pressing down on a newspaper clipping that always fit exactly on the scrapbook page the way real clippings never do. The message was: A good woman always miters her corners.

The Eleanor Gehrig portrayed by Teresa Wright in *The Pride of the Yankees* comes across as someone content to spend her life cutting, pasting, and adoring, but the real Eleanor was not that sticky. A witty, sophisticated woman who knew the score far better than her mama's-boy husband, she was canonized along with him, but one story about her illustrates just how different they were, and raises the possibility that if ALS hadn't killed him, Eleanor eventually might have been driven to do him in herself.

When he was striving to set a record of 2,000 consecutive games, she remarked that stopping at 1,999 would make a much more interesting statistic—and the poor earnest lug didn't get it.

January 24, 2000

BACK when *Roots* kicked off an interest in genealogy, author Alex Haley advised youngsters to keep a tape recorder at the ready when talking to their grandparents so they could gather stories and reminiscences to help them trace their family trees.

This might have been a fruitful exercise once, but today's seniors have achieved the American nirvana known as being "informed." Their overriding interest now is retirement savvy, and their conversation, such as it is, revolves around IRAs, CDs, munis, T-notes, rollovers, no-loads, caps, penalties, and discounts. This is no way to keep your ancestors straight; children taking Haley's advice today would come away thinking they were direct descendants of Louis Rukeyser and Jane Bryant Quinn.

Seniors are equally "informed" about health care, able to hold forth at length on CAT scans, quadruple bypasses, every -itis, -otis, -ilia, -plasty, and -therapy known to science; the fine print about deductibles and out-of-pocket expenses in Medicare and HMO legislation; and the price of prescription drugs at Giant on Thursdays between noon and 3 P.M.—all delivered with heavy doses of "access" used as a verb.

When not talking about how to be shrewd medical "consumers," they regale their audience with "informed" descriptions of the enriching "activities"—jogging, bench-pressing, aerobics, yoga, karate, Ping-Pong, square dancing—available at their golden-age apartment complexes, where nobody has time to reminisce and no self-respecting senior would be caught dead napping unless he's caught dead.

In 1934, when Social Security was being debated, a Republican congressman predicted that it would destroy "the romance of life." New Dealers called him "flinty," the Depression-era equivalent of "mean-spirited," but in one sense he was right: Today's old people are less colorful and entertaining than they used to be, and the big losers are their grandchildren. These poor kids will never savor the galloping eccentricities, unfurled prejudices, and baroque sickbeds of geriatric top bananas who could elevate old age to an art form.

The world of my childhood contained few independent retirees. Grandparents, usually grandmothers, lived with their married children, usually their daughters, because "A son is a son till he takes a wife, but a daughter is a daughter all of her life." This is still true, and old ladies still know it, but now that they belong to an officially designated special-interest group they don't dare say it because it sounds "divisive."

Divisive statements were Granny's stock in trade, as when I told her I had seen Mrs. So-and-So on my way home from school and she said, "She dyes her hair but she's very nice." Keeping up with her Q.E.D. opinions made me feel like the scullery maid in the fairy tale who no sooner scrubs out the three drops of tallow wax than they reappear somewhere else. As a child I could not get a line on her, but when I entered adolescence, everything suddenly fell into place.

My legs had sprouted a veritable lawn and I wanted to shave them. I knew Granny would object, but instead of her usual tragedienne set piece (gaze heavenward, place hand on heart), she merely sighed irritably and said, "Oh, don't be silly, it won't show."

Won't show? I wondered if she was going blind and had assumed, in her imperious fashion, that nobody else could see either. Then I understood: In her day, leg hair *didn't* show. She spent her youth in black cotton stockings and long skirts, and in some corner of her mind nothing had changed.

I displayed the same psychic mechanism recently when, discussing abortion with a woman less than half my age, I said: "What's the matter with you girls nowadays? Why do you keep getting pregnant? Don't you know about diaphragms?"

The young woman's jaw dropped. A querulous note had crept into my voice that had never been there before. It was an old woman's voice, but instead of feeling self-conscious I was hard put not to laugh as I thought of Granny: I sounded just like her.

A child who lives with an old person learns that identity is a calendar. America would be a calmer place if we could all admit this. Ruminating on the time-line of prejudice, besides being interesting, would keep us from dissolving in panicky revisionism when a revered historical figure is discovered to have held a bigoted opinion, and would teach the young that their own standards of tolerance are likewise the product of chronological determinism and no more immune to change than anyone else's.

Despite all the talk about "catastrophic" illnesses, children today have no understanding of what aging really means, as we can see from a chemotherapy public-service announcement that, to me, is incredible. An old man is visited by all of his grandchildren, who range in age "from 3 to 18." He longs to take a picture of them sitting together on the porch eating ice cream, but he doesn't do it because "I didn't have the energy to walk upstairs and get the camera."

Why didn't he send one of the kids up to get it? More to the point, why didn't one of them volunteer? I spent the best years of my life threading needles, looking up phone numbers, and reading out obits. Now it's I who squint, but thanks to my training as an old lady's handmaiden, my own burgeoning infirmities are easier to bear.

My uninformed grandmother taught me all about catastrophic illnesses, though she never called them by their medical names. She just held forth on turning to stone, coughing up chunks of lung, wasting away, goiters as big as grapefruit, and what is now called "osteoporosis." As Granny explained it: "She bent over to button her shoes and just broke right in half. The undertaker tried to put her back together but he didn't do it right and you could *tell*."

Children love this sort of thing, but nowadays they have to go to a horror movie to get it.

February 7, 2000

ments about what could happen on "Monday, January 3, the first workday," and speculating about kinks that could persist for "a few weeks," which soon turned into "a few months," not to mention (except they mentioned them) quarterly crises involving fiscal-year dates.

Then there was Leap Year. Nobody had ever before uttered a word about it as a computer problem, but the Boys of December identified February 29 as a glitch within a glitch, a mini-Y2K on the heels of the big one, when the computers might go crazy all over again. Finally, one consultant cautioned that some problems "may linger until 2001 and beyond."

Around Christmas, the news filled up with airports that looked like dog shows, warnings about packages from Frankfurt, and grim talk about our "porous" Canadian border, accompanied by shots of desolate Montana crossings with nothing but little concrete posts to indicate the line of demarcation between Dull and Duller. The apocalypse menu had expanded to include terrorism.

No wonder we didn't experience post-Y2K syndrome. The media-government complex made the mistake of forgetting Occam's Razor, the philosophical principle that states, "Hypotheses must not be developed beyond necessity." In other words, don't pile on; focus on one main point or else you will lose your audience.

Was Y2K a hoax? A Spanish business official thinks so. Salvador Bellido was quoted in the *Washington Times*: "We're beginning to think that all this has been set up for someone's benefit, I don't know if it was Bill Gates or who."

Much as I would like to blame Gates, he doesn't strike me as the type for a subconscious hoax, which is what I think Y2K was. Yes, computers needed fixing, but so did something else, so why not kill two birds with one stone?

As far back as I can remember, i.e., Pearl Harbor, every American disaster has inspired the sentiment, "It brought us together." Now that we could teach the Balkans a thing or two about Balkanization, maybe a band of goo-goo idealists in the media-government complex saw in Y2K what the flakier Transcendentalists saw in utopian communes and cooperative farms.

Guilty over Our Great Diversity's failure to realize its potential, maybe they began spinning visions of the "inclusion" that could be achieved if a cross-section of Americans found themselves up the same creek. Not that they consciously wanted a Y2K panic, or actively decided to help it along. It was just that they couldn't stop thinking about how it would bring us together—all those chips off the old mosaic taking turns digging cesspits and weeding the communal garden, their imagined differences dropping away as they shared their feelings, their dreams, and their Spam.

The false alarm did produce a post-Y2K syndrome, but it's not the one the media-government complex anticipated, and they are in no hurry to tussle with it. Known as "the boy who cried wolf," it poses a direct threat to another of their creations: the warning industry.

From now on, the nightly scares about insidious apples, death-dealing Alfredo sauce, and cancer of the navel will, with luck, fall on the deaf ears of sneering cynics and seize-the-day blithe spirits, until the health nazis sicken and die and Joe Camel is the Comeback Kid.

February 21, 2000

J OHN McCAIN got stuck in a verbal tar pit in his recent attempt to paint himself as a blasé man of the world. Ironically, it began on his campaign bus, the "Straight Talk Express," and continued in a store selling extra-sharp cheese.

Asked about gays in the military, he stated in his modestly boastful way that he had served with many in the Navy, though he had never discussed the subject with them. He probably thought this proved that "don't ask, don't tell" works, but there was a slight problem: McCain was in the Navy back when gays were barred from the military and faced instant dismissal if exposed. Naturally they never discussed it with him.

That being the case, the reporter shot back, how did McCain know they were gay?

It was a Biblical moment, recalling the world's first Gotcha! question: "Who told you that you were naked?" It's not hard to imagine the sensation that must have slammed through him. Since we're recalling notable moments in gardens, we can go with Emily Dickinson's "zero at the bone" on seeing a snake in hers.

McCain had three choices: He could say his gay shipmates told him they were gay, which would have contradicted his original statement; he could say he found them in flagrante and failed to report them; or he could say he "just knew."

With no choice but the last, he lumbered into a wordy answer about recognizing "by behavior and by attitudes," whereupon gay spokesmen issued their usual condemnation of stereotyping. Their reaction was fairly tepid as these things go, but McCain panicked and made another statement, explaining that he had merely had "suspicions" about certain shipmates, and that someone else had told him they were gay.

Two days later, he went before Katie Couric in the obligatory clarification rite, explaining that a fellow officer had indeed confessed his homosexuality to him, but only after leaving the Navy.

For some reason I have trouble visualizing this heart-to-heart. I think he made the whole thing up and never served with any gays, real or suspected, and furthermore I don't care.

What bothers me about this incident is what our fear of stereotyping is doing to the qualities of insight, perception, and subtlety of mind. The whole country is turning into Scarlett O'Hara. You heard me, Scarlett O'Hara:

> But Scarlett intended to marry—and marry Ashley—and she was willing to appear demure, pliable, and scatterbrained if those were the qualities that attracted men. Just why men should be this way, she did not know. She only knew that such methods worked. It never interested her enough to try to think out the reason for it, for she knew nothing of the inner workings of any human being's mind, not even her own. She knew only that if she did or said thus-and-so, men would unerringly respond with the complementary thus-and-so. It was like a mathematical formula and no more difficult, for mathematics was the one subject that had come easy to Scarlett in her schooldays.

Every American is expected to be a "people person," yet we dare not go from A to B in assessing them, on pain of death from our internal censor. Instead we must judge each person we meet "as an individual," a parlor version of reinventing the wheel that precludes drawing conclusions, playing hunches, or learning anything at all that might come in handy the next time we meet an individual.

Like John McCain, we pass insight around like a hot potato, and palm perception off on "someone else" so we will not be suspected of putting two and two together. Our goal is nothing less than willful obtuseness, a condition that was displayed in all its glory by a woman on *Hardball* who illustrated the pitfalls of gay stereotyping by drawing what passes these days for an analogy.

Suppose, she said, you entered a room and saw there a man in a kilt. You would assume he was a Scotsman, wouldn't you? But he could be "an extra from *Braveheart*, [or] it might be Halloween."

Our rejection of wide-ranging ruminative thinking is a key factor in many of our woes, such as the "crisis in relationships." Men who don't generalize about women will be even more dumbfounded than those who do, while women who generalize about men will be somewhat less furious than those who don't. Every little bit helps.

Public confessions of personal behavior are deemed offensive by many, but they may serve as R&R leave in our war against stereotyping. Someone who knows himself to be an incestuous foot-fetishist might well find it a strain to be judged "as an individual" and pursued by the blockheaded furies of equality. Going on Jerry Springer with the other incestuous foot-fetishists is a way of saying, "*Now* do you get it?"

Gays especially are made uncomfortable by unanalytical people and often confess to them for reasons unrelated to braggadocio. They may simply be tired of waiting for the truth to sink in, or they may find it necessary to clear things up when a determined tabula rasa mistakes them for extras from *Deliverance*. Gays prefer heterosexuals who are worldly, raffish, nonconformist, and eccentric, not out of snobbery or decadence but because these types never meet a thought they cannot entertain—royally.

The worst damage inflicted by our fear of stereotyping is in the arts. A creative artist "just knows" things. When this river flows unimpeded the result is a Shakespeare, but when it's dammed up we get the eighth wonder of the American global village, the nonjudgmental novelist.

They're a lot like politicians. Afraid to exclude, they throw in so many characters that they end up with the big tent of Republican dreams. Afraid to differentiate, they make everybody talk alike. Afraid to dominate, they refuse to plot. Afraid to instruct, they dumb down their language.

And afraid to think, they display the insight of Scarlett O'Hara.

March 20, 2000

T HIS past February's miniseries, *Sally Hemings: An American Scandal*, marked a turning point in race-based entertainment. It arrived on television with almost no fanfare, did well enough but broke no ratings records, inspired no agonized debates, and raised no fears of ensuing riots.

What a difference 23 years makes. When *Roots* premiered in 1977, the streets were deserted every night it aired, and you could walk down an apartment hallway and hear it coming from every TV. News shows ran footage of grim-faced patrons in Harlem bars watching the whipping scene, pundits tied themselves in masochistic knots of white guilt, and a resolutely upbeat Joan Rivers, guest-hosting the Johnny Carson show, kept count of the babies named Kunta Kinte and Kizzy born in L.A. hospitals.

I did not expect a rash of newborn Sallys; the name is as "out" as out can be in today's world of Meaghans and LaToyas. But otherwise the silence is deafening.

Less than two years ago we were roiling in controversy over the DNA report that a "Jefferson male" fathered Sally's last child, Eston Hemings.

When the story broke, the Monticello Association closed ranks, traditionalist Jefferson scholars turned cartwheels attributing paternity to his brother or nephews, and the morning shows bristled with Hemings descendants, including a white one seeking her 15 minutes of blackness.

Now comes the definitive movie treating the affair as established fact, and there's not a peep out of anybody. How come the ho-hum?

It might be our notorious attention span: Having taken in the original DNA news, we are now in "been there, done that" mode.

It might be the power of foregone conclusions, which work in not-so-mysterious ways. About three weeks before the new miniseries aired, the Thomas Jefferson Memorial Foundation quietly admitted that Jefferson probably did father all of Sally's children. It was an uncharacteristic move; ancestral societies are famously inflexible, but with the movie in the can they no doubt decided that it was pointless to go on denying the story in the face of American neo-Cartesianism: It's on TV, therefore it is.

My own theory is that the movie was too good for its own good. It drew the curtain of charity over the sex scenes to keep traditionalists happy, yet contained enough surprises and Catch-22's to thwart the guilt-ridden white liberals and race-card-playing black activists who participate in the overwrought debates that get controversies going. There is something here to neutralize everybody.

It opens with a subtle but effective touch. *Sally Hemings: An American Scandal* cleverly employs a subtitle that de-emphasizes the racial aspect and establishes a certain national affection for the heroine reminiscent of the English attitude toward Nell Gwynn. It's as if a collective historical voice were saying, "A good sort was our Sally." Not exactly the kind of white attitude that Al Sharpton & Co. groove on.

The script contains three literary elements, all well done: satire, irony, and parody. The satire rears its head in a bent *Roots* moment. Once again we see a newborn baby held up in the air, but instead of the slave father lifting it up to a starry sky and sonorously intoning, "Behold the only thing greater than yourself," a midwife does the honors in broad daylight as the baby's slave grandmother shrieks, "What color is it?" and Sally's slave brother replies, "White as snow!"

The irony finds that elusive balance between incongruity and believability. Sally, who was taught to read by Jefferson, reads his own words back to him from the essay in which he expresses his distaste for blacks' physicality and his belief that they are intellectually inferior. Ignoring his pleas to stop, she presses on, until he shouts, "You're taking it out of context!" Jostled by the familiar modern phrase, we glimpse the spectacle of a Founding Father trying to spin his way out of a gaffe.

The parody disarms attempts to identify the politics of the moviemakers. The parodied figure is James Callender, the gossip-mongering newspaperman who first broke the scandal in 1802. The film Callender is obnoxious enough to please the most conservative media-hater, yet he is played with a touch of prissiness and a soft, smiley way of speaking certain to please the most liberal Ken Starr-hater. This is not the stuff of lively debates; mouthy commentators would shut off in mid-sentence once they realized what they had gotten themselves into.

The Washington assignation goes far to explain why the movie caused no stir. No proof exists that Sally was ever in Washington, but no proof exists that she wasn't, so to give the story movement the screenwriter takes artistic license and has Martha Jefferson eject Sally from Monticello, whereupon she turns up at the White House and spends the night with her presidential lover. The next morning, his secretary knocks at the bedroom door to remind him of his appointment with a waiting ambassador, but Jefferson says, "Tell him I will be at least another hour" and climbs back into bed with a drowsily smiling Sally.

This is déjà vu at its stun-gun best, triggering the time-traveling viewer's memory of that future day when another president and his inamorata let a foreign dignitary cool his heels while they had at it. Naturally nobody wanted to talk about this movie. It's the "been there, done that" of Clinton Fatigue.

But you can't keep a good neurosis down. Trained in displacement and projection by years of code words, we have found a way to talk about Tom and Sally after all. It's called "deploring the ban on interracial dating at Bob Jones University," and everybody has put in his two cents' worth.

The results are in, and it's unanimous. All Americans approve of interracial dating, so now our attention span can flit on to Protestants vs. Catholics, which is so old it's new. It's been ages since we've been there and done that.

April 3, 2000

S OUTH CAROLINA'S Confederate-flag controversy has pushed me over the edge into a full-blown case of Rebel Fatigue.

"Fatigues" are the road rage of a political journey, those critical times when you can't stand it any longer and need to pull over and have an epiphany. Rebel Fatigue is the third Fatigue of my political life. The other two struck in the '60s.

My Ayn Rand Fatigue did not emerge as long as I did nothing but read her books. The trouble started when I attended a discussion group and found myself in a roomful of Randites. The meeting was held in the apartment over mine, hosted by a neighbor I had never met but had seen in the lobby when she strode purposefully by me in a black cloak and snatched up her mail with one of those swift, sure gestures I had read so much about.

Her floor plan was identical to mine but she had no furniture; for a split second I thought I had been robbed. We all sat on the floor and listened to tapes from the Objectivist Institute. There were no refreshments, as the hostess was above all that. A couple of people went into the kitchen to get a glass of water, striding purposefully across her rugless floor and my ceiling, which explained a lot.

The discussion period consisted of people saying "A is A" and drawing dollar signs in the air to signify approval. The few tepid arguments that arose were settled by the hostess, who read aloud from her heavily underlined copy of *Atlas Shrugged*. Next, we listened to Rachmaninoff, Ayn Rand's favorite composer. Then all the individualists got up and went home.

My John Birch Fatigue was strikingly similar, except there was something to sit on. The room was full of funeral-parlor folding chairs and the fragrant smell of freshly sawed wood from the unpainted planks they used as bookcases for their stacks of "literature." Dominating all was the biggest coffee urn I had ever seen outside of a diner. The woman next to me, a tired bleached blonde, saw me looking at it and leaned over and whispered, "The first time I came here, I thought it was an AA meeting."

That was the night LBJ announced that he wouldn't run. When the news came, the tired blonde heaved a deep sigh and said, "They've gotten to Johnson." "They had to get to him so they could get to Bobby Kennedy," said someone else. "They've already gotten to Nixon, so it's all set."

"None dare call it treason!" snarled the moderator.

I had had it with folding chairs, bare floors, purposeful strides, and barrel-of-fun cell meetings. I wasn't cut out for the conservative fringe, yet the conservative mainstream was just as incompatible: God-'n'-country platitudes, suburban families, and Julie Nixon's wedding dress. That was the clincher, the symbol to end all symbols, an apocalyptical fifth horseman named Sweetness 'n' Light: I hadn't worn little puffed sleeves like that since I was 6.

I went into alienation panic. It was 1968, not a good year to look for the all-of-a-piece, elitist conservatism I craved, defined so exquisitely by T. S. Eliot: "classicist in literature, royalist in politics, and Anglo-Catholic in religion." It fit me like a glove—even, in my fashion, the last. But it was not to be found in American conservatism, and so I gave up my citizenship, as it were, and settled for being a Southerner.

The Southern woman's Rebel Fatigue starts the first time a man takes her on a tour of a Civil War battlefield. Yankee women don't have dates like this. He always picks the hottest or coldest day of the year, and his chivalry is superseded by his need for a pack horse. You have to help carry stuff: maps, binoculars, the works of Bruce Catton.

It takes about eight hours because he must stop and reflect in orotund tones. "Here" is never simply "here," but "right here" (raht'cheer) or "on this spot." His language comes completely out of character, as oddly formal poetic locutions and archaic word reversals start popping out of him. "Here stood Lee." "Here it was that Lee stood." His vocabulary suddenly expands. When he describes a fight in a bar he chortles, "There was blood all over the place," but when he tours a battlefield he speaks grimly of "carnage." Afterwards he turns quiet and melancholy. It's like sex.

Speaking of which, you also spend a lot of boozy time listening to his Civil War music. This tends to stimulate Southerners, who respond to martial music the way normal people respond to love songs. Chances are excellent that you will end up in bed, boompsing your little hearts out to the strains of "The Bonnie Blue Flag." (A more suitable beat, by the way, than "Dixie," almost as good as "The Light Cavalry Overture.")

Granted, this stage of my life was an improvement on the folding chairs, but it was no substitute for T. S. Eliot's credo. My political alienation eventually returned and I developed Rebel Fatigue, but it remained dormant until the South Carolina flag flap forced me to admit three things.

First, whitetrash have captured the Confederate flag. For every Walter Scott-reading history buff who sees it as heritage and tradition, there are thousands more who have it painted on their black leather jackets and tattooed on their arms.

Second, pro-flag arguments are getting insane, e.g., the letter to the *Washington Times* insisting that the flag does not symbolize slavery because Julia Dent Grant, wife of the Union general, was a slaveowner.

Finally, an aspect no one has yet mentioned: aesthetics. Flying three flags—national, state, and Confederate—on one pole is clutter, an unfurled whatnot stand. It puts me in mind of a clothes-crazy woman who, constantly running out of hangers, hangs one garment over another until she can't find the first one, and then sues the dry cleaner before she discovers what happened.

For God's sake, take it down before things get any sillier.

April 17, 2000

I NEVER knew how strained the quality of mercy could be until I read the "Advice for George W." roundup in NR's April 3 issue. It had the distinct sound of people whistling past the cemetery.

Even the most optimistic advice was shot through with tense reminders to do this or avoid doing that, to remember such-and-such but avoid thus-and-so, to go here but don't go there; while the various well-meant admonitions to be "active" and stay "on the attack" merged into a household hint about scooping up dropped ice cream in one piece before it loses its firmness and melts into the carpet.

Some of the pessimistic contributors tried to be lighthearted, but their recurring allusions to frat boys, recommendations of "English-language-immersion lessons," and paternalistic reminders to "Stand up straight" and stop acting the class clown made him sound like someone who has to be wiped off before being sent out to mingle with guests.

Other pessimistic contributors were simply pessimistic. "Be real" is the end of the line for advice; once you have said that, it doesn't matter what else you say. The gloomiest pessimists made lists of all the things Dubya should do, then effectively took them all back. Using the poker player's metaphor for an impossible task, one said that even if Dubya did everything he was told, "he will still be drawing for an inside straight," while another ended his list of Do's with: "[I]f he doesn't, he's finished."

Were I advising Dubya, my first caution would be, "Be careful how you describe things, because you just might hit the nail on the head." This was the unfortunate result when he said he would not debate until fall, giving as his reason: "America is now going into a hibernation period when it comes to politics."

In other words, the Bores of Summer are upon us and there's no relief in sight. As long as Bradley was in, there was a chance that a candidate would go crazy and pull a Sherwood Anderson, walking off the podium in mid-speech the way frustrated businessman Anderson walked out of his office in the middle of dictating a letter and became—what else?—a writer. It would be the best thing that could happen to us, forcing us to do something about our tortuous political process, but we'll have to wait for another time.

Meanwhile, somebody could liven up the campaign trail by training attack dogs to react to "reformer" and "results." America's whistle-stops would resemble the comedy skit about the economist whose dogs tore out throats, or not, depending upon whether they heard "stock" or "bullion." Then his wife hosted her cooking club and all the girls started talking about "stock" and "bouillon."

In one sense, Dubya's language problems are less severe than Gore's. Everything that comes out of Gore's mouth sounds like the e-voice that says "You have mail!" but Dubya's utterances are entirely his own.

His English prepositions are straight out of a foreign-language lab: "America wants somebody not of Washington" sounds like a flailing student of French taking turns between *à* and *de* in hopes of getting at least some of them right.

His worst preposition problems have to do with body parts, e.g., "I don't have all the facts at my hand." Then there are the heart metaphors: Look at his heart . . . look in his heart . . . don't judge his heart . . . only he knows what's on [in, with, next to] his heart. An Aztec priest could settle this very quickly, and deliver, posthumously, the Hispanic vote.

His stabs at parallelisms land him in *mot juste* trouble: "Our party is enthused and excited. John deserves credit for bringing people into the party, and I deserve a lot of credit for exciting the party." Unnerving the party, yes; agitating the party, yes; but not exciting the party.

His most interesting verbal tic has gone unnoticed, though it surely is unique in the annals of blue-blooded scions: He sounds as if he is trying to "better" himself. His overexacting pronunciation of the "t" in "Clint-ton" exemplifies the habit of the socially unsure of going overboard in polishing their diction. In Dubya's case, it's more likely a subconscious way of achieving the verbal precision that he knows eludes him. By the same token, clinging to poetic archaisms such as "amongst" and "oftentimes" may make him feel more literary than he knows himself to be.

The heat he has taken over his anti-intellectualism may have given him a shadow slogan, "A Goof-off with Guilts," but his efforts to atone only make him sound even more like a middle-class striver, as in his latest utterance, when he changed pronouns in midstream: "You cannot lead America to a positive tomorrow with revenge on one's mind." There's pathos here, but the average Reagan Democrat will hear nothing but a Yalie putting on airs.

Dubya's most worrisome speech habit concerns something more important than making the dean's list. People plagued by crippling self-doubt invariably give themselves away with cockiness and flippancy. Dubya's displays of these have been widely noted, but another compensatory technique of the self-doubter that has gone unremarked is his use of "double emphasis."

Asked if McCain's candidacy had damaged the GOP, he replied: "I don't think the fracture is much of a fracture. I really don't."

Answering Forbes's criticism, he said: "I've got a good strong record. I've done well in office. I've performed."

To tell when he's trying to convince himself, look for the print media's insertion of "he added," as in his defense of his Bob Jones appearance: "'I gave the right speech,' he added." It always comes after he has rattled off five or six other things he did right.

I have some advice for him. He should stop talking about being "energized." Nobody is energized, we're all prostrate and ready for the Second Coming because what this country needs is a Redeemer with Results.

May 1, 2000

I SWORE up and down to everybody, including WFB, that I absolutely, positively would not write about Elián Gonzalez. It was a matter of perverse pride, the way I used to feel back when we native Washingtonians were not allowed to vote. Like being disfranchised in a democracy, being a columnist who ignores Elián is the sort of thing that suits my temperament.

I knew that finding something else to write about would make me what the politically correct tactfully call "subject-matter challenged," but just how challenged I had no idea. This, then, is the story of what happened to me on my way to deadline.

Elián's centrality has reached the plateau once associated with the expression, "the bride at every wedding and the corpse at every funeral." Updated for the cable era, it is now rendered as "all Elián, all the time."

We have been through these monomanias before, but this one puts our earlier obsessions to shame. O.J. and Monica might have overwhelmed other news, but they did not appropriate it and make it their own. Events that had nothing to do with decapitation or oral sex simply remained non-decapitation and non-oral-sex news stories.

This time is different. Non-Elián events have an eerie tendency to turn into Elián events, especially when they promise to be good column material, such as Rep. James P. Moran's brush with an 8-year-old alleged carjacker.

According to the congressman, he had just pulled into the rec-center parking lot to pick up his sons, when suddenly he was confronted by a little black boy with an "icy stare" who said he had a gun and told Moran to give up his car keys or else he would shoot him. Moran overpowered him, picked him up, and carried him into the rec center, where the gun was found to be a baby bottle.

The story was actually about racial profiling of children, but it was caught in the undertow du jour and fitted out for a sea change. Right on cue, the kid said, "I thought he was going to kidnap me or kill me." His parents threatened to sue Moran for false imprisonment, and Moran threatened to press charges if, after consulting the authorities, he decided it was—are you ready?—"in the best interest of the child."

This phrase has turned into an entrance cue on a par with "Hark! Here Gloucester comes!" As soon as I came to it, my mind filled with visions of backyard slides, and I had trouble concentrating. Nor, it seemed, was I alone. The story normally would have been red meat for the *Washington Times*'s vigilant black metro columnist, but her mind appeared to be in Little Havana too. "Heaven save us," she wrote, "from the messes adults create when they get so caught up in their own agendas that they lose sight of the fact that they are using children as political pawns." Moran, a former heavyweight boxer, had morphed into macho Lázaro González or macho Fidel Castro, take your pick.

Nothing gets my writer juices flowing like an idiotic apology. We were treated to a real corker recently, but a column no sooner came to me than I had to scuttle it. Why did Peter Benchley pick this, of all times, to apologize to the great white shark? Life was imitating art—the art in this case being Little Havana's garish poster crammed full of gulls, crosses, Jesus, flowers, the Virgin, boats, rosaries, flags, rainbows, saints, and dolphins, and in the middle of it all, Elián on his inner tube.

One look at Benchley's guilt-ravaged face told me that he had seen it too, and was doing penance for *Jaws* because the sharks had miraculously left Elian alone, proving that they had been misunderstood all along.

The trouble with trying to figure out how to avoid writing about Elián is that you have to keep thinking about him. He becomes the prism through which everything must be viewed, until the cable of your mind is all Elián, all the time.

It does no good to switch from the news to escapist fare because you will only come up against the iron laws of mathematics just in time to watch them melt: Parallel lines might never meet, but parallel Eliáns do. *Masterpiece Theater*'s new *David Copperfield* stars Janet Reno as Betsey Trotwood, Greg Craig as her simpleminded factotum, Mr. Dick, and Maxine Waters as Miss Murdstone.

When you've had enough of that, try the old-movie channels. If you're as lucky as I am, you can catch *Boy on a Dolphin*. Cousin Marisleysis is played by Sophia Loren, who was miscast; when she emerges from the sea in a wet blouse, you know she doesn't need to be hospitalized for anything.

My eeriest experience came while watching one of International Paper's black-and-white commercials featuring children talking about their fathers' jobs. This one shows a grimly determined little girl with a bloodless, Nurse

Ratched air about her, making her father an enormous ice-cream sundae and taking it to him in the yard. We've all seen it dozens of times, but this time I really saw it.

The father isn't in a yard. He's seated all alone at a bare picnic table in the middle of a treeless nowhere that looks like the steppes of Asia or a moonscape. Then it hit me: This ad is about Cuba, a banished father, and a kid who is just beginning to understand power.

Child-struck America is not ready for a Helen of Troy. Our idea of a sexy geopolitical crisis is a custody battle, but since Elián's stay might last as long as Helen's, what shall we do with him?

PeoplePC can hire him to do the Spanish-language version of little Marc John Jeffries's spiel. He already has a cellular phone and enough gold chains to sink him and his inner tube as well; the logical next step is having an agent.

Better yet, the Clintons have talked of adopting a child. Why not Elián? If we're lucky, it would reprise "The Ransom of Red Chief," the O. Henry story about a pair of klutzy kidnappers who snatch a kid so bratty that they end up having to pay his parents to take him back.

May 22, 2000

WELCOME to *The Eliad: Book II.* The dolphin-gathering hero from the wine-dark sea cavorts now at Wye of the bigger backyard, guarded by picture-taking Greg Craig of the rhyming name. I didn't intend to write about Elián again, and certainly not twice in a row. Since my last column was about my refusal to write about him at all, I was relieved when the INS packed him up and took him away. I thought his removal from Miami would spell *finis*, or at least anti-climax, to the whole affair, but the aftermath of what is now being called "The Raid" has stirred my juices.

The conventions of the Homeric epic demand a plot that pits a protagonist who is trying to get back home against antagonists who are trying to stop him. The antagonists must be outlandish enough to stick in the mind to ensure their place in crossword puzzles thousands of years hence when the epic is still being read by civilized people everywhere. *The Eliad* is certain to endure because its antagonists are the Cyclopses of the Sledgehammer Right.

I have had it with hysterical conservatives. To hear some of them tell it, "The Raid" was the equivalent of the sack of Rome. They went ballistic over "The Picture" showing one of "Janet Reno's jack-booted thugs" pointing what was variously described as a rifle, an Uzi, or a machine gun at the "head [heart, chest, face, throat] of a six-year-old." If you don't believe it, look at

"The Picture." I did, and it distinctly shows the agent holding the gun at an angle away from the closet.

This scenario was rehashed in scores of rabid letters to the editor, but the most unsettling was a frenzied screed in the *Washington Times* about "the wicked, smiling face of the INS agent clutching a terrified and screaming Elián. . . ." I looked at this picture too, and it's obvious that the woman is *grimacing*—as well she might.

I regret to say that the editor-in-chief of the *Washington Times* went his correspondents one better. In his column about a probable secret deal between Clinton and Castro, Wesley Pruden wrote: "Mr. Clinton, who would sacrifice his own child's freedom if political expediency demanded it . . ." He follows this incredible statement with a parenthetical comparison: "(just as he sacrificed his own child's peace of mind for his cheap sexual gratification over the years). . . ."

These unfortunate words mark a sharp departure from the Right's treatment of Chelsea. Ever since she flowered into an appealing young woman, conservatives have gone out of their way to praise her as the Clintons' only achievement. Even the most virulent Clinton-hater readily admitted that Bonnie and Clod, as Pruden calls them, did one thing right. Now, fair play is out and Chelsea has been subjected to a stupid comment that is more shattering than any account of her father's sex life could be.

The seizure of Elián was just what the NRA deserved. Talk-radio conservatives brayed that "The Picture" would be an ideal ad for the group, but in fact it belies the blizzard of patriotic alerts America's most tireless junk mailer sends out. They urge their members to think of themselves as latter-day Minutemen exercising their Second Amendment right to open fire on a would-be dictator's secret police, but one look at "The Picture" restores reality. The NRA's vision of armed citizens prevailing against a modern tyrannical government is a romantic fantasy, and I'd rather know it than dream on.

In view of this, "The Raid" should disturb me, but it doesn't. In the first place, I am getting impatient with the hatred of government of some on the right. In the second place, I have been fed up with dithering ever since Jimmy Carter spent 444 days on the Iranian hostages. This time we got it right, and I could not help being impressed at seeing an adroit, no-nonsense show of strength for a change.

I also saw that without the Cold War, some conservatives have nothing to be conservative about. Abortion doesn't really do it for them, perhaps because it takes place in the female pelvis, nor do the family values they were so quick to put aside in favor of separating father and son. But fighting Communism takes them back to a time when there were no women's issues to speak of and no soccer moms to speak to. The Cold War was their raison d'être and *The Eliad* exposed their subconscious wish that the USSR will rise again.

Nobody can be a scapegoat as long as Janet Reno without garnering some sympathy. I feel a twinge, mainly because I can't help thinking how much worse off we might be had Clinton's first or second AG pick been approved. Zoe Baird and Kimba Wood were both babes. If he had had a dishy AG, considering what the added element of sex does to power-madness, who knows what else they would have done together? Maybe he was planning to get a Svengalian hold on Baird or Wood and use her to help him take over the country. It's happened before: Look what the uncorrupted Queen Isabelle did after she got boompsed by the Earl of March. On second thought, don't look. Suffice to say she was thereafter called "the She-Wolf of France." Poor homely Janet Reno might be the only thing standing between us and a Castro of our own.

Every Homeric epic needs a Siren, and *Human Events* supplies one. Flat-singing Ann Coulter of the tone-deaf ears put Elián's custody up for grabs by revealing that he was conceived after his parents were divorced, meaning that Juan Miguel González has no legal claim on him, but is simply "the man who impregnated Elián's unwed mother." To keep us in belly-laughing Zeus mode, the hard-trying Coulter of the arch-fallen wit called Juan Miguel a "posterboy for Cuban family values," a "Cuban Lothario on a mission for Castro," and the "poor man's Hugh Hefner." In sum, Elián is, in Coulter's word, a "bastard."

Run that past voters, and compassionate conservatism will see its electoral hopes snatched from the rosy fingers of dawn and handed over to November's bat-wing night.

June 5, 2000

T HE breaking news of recent weeks has prevented me from commenting on an event that affected me more than either *The Eliad* or that dazzling new opera, *La Donna è Giuliani.*

Claire Trevor died on April 8 at the age of 91. The name probably means nothing to you if your baby pictures are in color, but mine were in black and white, like her movies. A quick 'n' easy way to bring you up to speed is to give you my old seat between my mother and grandmother and let them talk across you:

"She's the bad woman."

"Yes, but she has a heart of gold."

Actually she didn't always, but bad women had a good image in those days, and moviegoers cut them a lot of slack. People believed in the power of redemption then, and the bad woman was in charge of proving that it worked; if having a heart of gold helped things along, we issued her one.

We were not complete romantics, however, nor were we entirely naïve. We knew that a bad woman struggling against society's opinion had to have a few other metallurgical qualities going for her: a steely disregard of pain, a character threaded with an unsuspected vein of iron, and a brassy combativeness that became her protective shield against the world.

Claire Trevor displayed them all, playing a diseased streetwalker in *Dead End*, a fallen woman in *Stagecoach*, a drunk in *Key Largo*, and enough gangsters' girlfriends to be a moll for all seasons. She won an Oscar for best supporting actress for her *Key Largo* drunk, a performance so harrowing and heartwrenching that watching it is almost unbearable. She stole the show from lethargic Lauren Bacall, who went on to stardom while Trevor spent her entire career in secondary roles.

In another time and place (which usually means France), she could have been one of the great tragediennes, but she defied Hollywood's idea of a leading lady. She was not beautiful, or even pretty, but starkly attractive and soignée, one of those women who skip untrammeled girlhood and look 35 for twenty years. It made her an adult, which made her a bad woman, which made her a supporting actress.

She never had a spread in the movie magazines, but to say she wasn't a star is to disregard the ultimate compliment couched in the debates that moviegoers of the '40s used to have as we stood uncertainly outside the theater, reading the posters and wondering whether we'd like the feature. "Oh, Claire Trevor's in it" always settled the matter: It had to be good.

Watching her movies today always sets me to imagining her in roles she should have played. She would have been perfect as Belle Watling in *GWTW*. Ona Munson was too blowsy and torpid to be believable as Rhett Butler's courtesan, and comes across as too put-upon. Trevor could have brought an energetic toughness to the part as well as a more convincing physical presence.

I wish she had played Alma, the prostitute in *From Here to Eternity* whom Montgomery Clift falls for and decides to marry. Donna Reed, of all people, got the part and won an Oscar for it, but I have never understood why. The instant she appears on screen, limpidly beautiful and seated posture-perfect in the brothel parlor like a debutante waiting for someone to fill up her dance card, we doubt that this is your average enlisted man's cat house. Trevor would have given Alma a stylish tawdriness and infused her yearning for respectability with scorching vehemence and smart-mouthed despair.

I can also think of a starring role that cried out for her: Sadie Thompson in *Rain*. Both Joan Crawford and Rita Hayworth sashayed too much, and neither got the reversion to vice right. Hayworth reacts to the minister's suicide like an automaton going back to square one, while Crawford oozes complacent snideness, as if the suicide had merely allowed her to have the last word. Trevor would have infused the moment with sultry flint, taking grim pride in this final proof that she had been the better human being all along.

After the '40s, the bad woman fell upon hard times. First, she was demoted to bad girl (Jennifer Jones in *Duel in the Sun*), but all that smoldering and chest-thrusting gave the bad girl a bad name, so she was recycled more sympathetically as the bad girl with problems, a category that broke down into various subgroups: the vulnerable bad girl (Marilyn in *Bus Stop*), the misunderstood bad girl (Liz in *Butterfield 8*), and the sick bad girl (Marilyn in *Niagara*).

In the '60s, the sexual revolution took a leaf from Father Flanagan and proclaimed, "There's no such thing as a bad girl," and so the bad girl with problems was replaced by the good girl with problems. There was the oversexed good girl (Julie Andrews in *The Americanization of Emily*), the dumb good girl (Shirley MacLaine in *The Apartment*), and the neurotic good girl (just about everybody in just about everything).

The advent of the neurotic good girl was the final nail in the bad woman's coffin, because neurotics are always selfish, which automatically rules out a heart of gold.

Gone too are the other precious metals that Claire Trevor mined so well. Iron character and steely endurance prevent us from sharing our pain, and brassy combativenesss trips our psychological security alarms, so classy badness has been outlawed and the bad woman is now known simply as a woman who has made "bad choices."

She is found in redemption's new venue, the confessional talk show, analyzing her recovered memories, pinpointing her cry for help, and explaining why promiscuity is such a fantastic learning experience. Do not hold out hope that she will come to appreciate the allure of mystery, because democracy won't permit it. Being "a woman with a past" has too many connotations of closed doors and brusque distance, and you know what that means. If today's Americans met a Claire Trevor character in the flesh, they would call her an elitist tramp, an elitist blackmailer, an elitist smuggler, an elitist card shark, and an elitist drunk.

June 19, 2000

A GREAT debate is currently sweeping the land: "What've you got? Clinton fatigue or Clinton nostalgia?"

We like to think that we line up squarely on one side or the other according to our politics, but, as with everything involving Clinton, it's not that simple, especially since he fashioned triangulation into the new Gordian Knot. We have all turned into hard little bumps of tangled threads, unable to tell our strands apart.

Liberals, who should be nostalgic, are secretly fatigued. Civil-rights mavens saw our first black president cut off welfare; the working classes saw our first Marco Polo Democrat put their jobs on the take-out menu; and feminists saw themselves blame victims right and left to keep our first feminist president in office.

Conservatives, who should be fatigued, are secretly nostalgic. Economic conservatives have got it into their heads that the departure of Mr. Wall Street will somehow hex the market; libertarians are leery about "restoring decency"; and social conservatives are showing signs of Slouching Withdrawal Syndrome, like the champion of family values who recently mesmerized a call-in show with a classic Freudian slip: "Bill Clinton has turned America into Sodom and Good Morning."

A measure of our unresolved conflicts is the attention being paid to his leaving office. Not speculations about future jobs or books, but the actual moment when he will no longer be president. Pundits frequently spell it out, as in "at 12:01 P.M. on January 20, 2001"—what will happen to Bill Clinton?

It's not a bird, it's not a plane, it's Cinderella Man hovering like an animated sword of Damocles, making sure we realize how much he loves being president. Since his final-year countdown began this past January 20, he's been spelling it out every chance he gets, marshalling batteries of wistful smiles and plangent tones to express how much he dreads the day when this best of all possible jobs comes to an end and he is forced to leave his beloved White House.

These performances have given rise to an inordinate amount of what-iffing about a third term. Even though the Constitution forbids it, pollsters have been asking—just for fun—if people would vote for him again, and pundits have been analyzing—just for fun—the responses. But underneath all the fun there courses a murky underground stream. So far, no one has identified it for what it is, but Cinderella Man threw out a hint when reporters asked him—just for fun—if he would like a third term. His reply: "I'd do it forever if I could."

Did anybody but me hear the off-key zither music that horror movies use to cue the maniac? I can't be the only one, because back when Y2K loomed, several commentators speculated—just for fun—that he might use the crisis as an excuse to declare a national emergency and cancel the election. There have also been some jokes and cartoons lately about carrying him, kicking and screaming, from the White House, so I am not alone in thinking what I'm thinking, only in giving it a name:

Presiphrenia.

Given his known emotional fragility, the nostalgia-vs.-fatigue chatter comes across as a parlor game we have devised to distract ourselves from a subconscious but widespread uncertainty about what he might do if he's not president. The situation is rife with possibilities. Even if he vacates the White House peaceably at the appointed time, he still could form a government in exile and become a rallying point for partisan malcontents for years to come. If you think it can't happen, repeat after me: Bonnie Prince Charlie. At least Charlie was called a "pretender to the throne." Our practice of calling ex-presidents "Mr. President" is a can of worms ready for parsing, the ultimate hair begging to be split.

Since he may well be more dangerous out of the White House than in it, I have devised a plan to neutralize him: Make him President Without Portfolio for life. He would not have any duties, but he could do all the things he enjoys: live in the White House, fly on Air Force One, go to Camp David, and be serenaded with "Hail to the Chief." To keep busy, he could make himself useful in small ways, such as raising and lowering the flag. The sight of him up on the roof, tugging ropes at precise hours each day, would solidify his legacy for all time: the American Quasimodo.

My plan is based on the "hair of the dog" principle of hangover cures; we've had too much Clinton, so what we need now is more Clinton, not a new president. Let's face it: We're afraid to elect another president because neither candidate is even bearable, much less admirable. We used to be philosophical about our mediocrities, telling ourselves that someday a great leader would emerge and we would have another Adams or Roosevelt, but now we know it's never going to get any better. We don't even have a choice between the lesser of two evils anymore; it's boiled down to which one is less nerve-racking.

To give ourselves a much-needed vacation from presidential politics, we should cancel Election 2000 and every presidential election thereafter until Clinton leaves the White House feetfirst in, say, a quarter of a century or so. As for who will do what is laughably called "running the country," we could try a rotating office of National Manager to be filled by the nation's governors. If we restricted the terms to six months, we wouldn't have time to get sick of anybody.

Who knows? We might even find that we don't need a president. I know for a fact that D.C. doesn't need a mayor. When I was growing up, we were governed by three appointed commissioners whose names nobody could remember, plus the members of the District Committee, who might be anybody, but were usually Southern congressmen whose names we also forgot. We didn't know who appointed whom or who did what, and we didn't care. The city worked fine, and nobody pestered us about getting out the vote because there wasn't any.

Self-government is rewarding, if we just keep our heads.

July 3, 2000

FOR as long as I can remember, "sensible" has been the word most often used to describe the English. Despite their dotty vicars, unleashed doggy ladies, and the residual feyness evident in their pub hours, when all was said and done, the world called them "sensible."

It had to do with their unique cheerful stuffiness, which enabled them to spot the false and the foolish instantly and discard everything but the humor. To hear a supremely confident Englishman dismiss something out of hand with a single withering retort was to know that "sensible" was a virtual synonym for Englishness. There was no doubt about it; they owned the word.

No more. The hysteria surrounding the death of Diana was the first erosion to strike this green and sensible land, but now comes an obtuse bureaucracy to finish plowing it under. Tony Blair's munchkins in the Department for Culture, Media, and Sport recently issued a directive ordering state-supported museums and art galleries to see to it that at least 12 percent of their visitors are minorities, or else lose their funding.

Once upon a time, this would have made the entire country rise up as one and huff "Nonsense!" in the best gouty-squire tradition, but Cool Britannia discourages the temperament associated with gouty squires. So far the only classic English rejoinder has come from the conservative Lord Tebbit. "My first reaction is one of joy," he said, "because those whom the gods wish to destroy, they first make mad, and these ideas have been fermented in minds which are gravely imbalanced."

For the rest, stunned curators and directors are huddling, trying to figure out how to rustle up enough homeboy aesthetes to fill their quotas, hoping desperately that they will be allowed to count Jews, and wondering if putting up signs reading "To the Egress" would be the best way to get rid of surplus whites.

The sheer impossibility of coping with the logistics has so dominated their minds that no one has stopped to consider a much more sensitive aspect of the controversy, one so sensitive that we can only marvel that Tony Blair's quivering antennae missed it.

The ruling, reports the London *Daily Telegraph*, is "intended to stimulate interest in the nation's heritage among young blacks and Asians." All right. Suppose they do start going to museums. What will they see but the entire canon of Western culture spread out before them? Canon to the right of them, canon to the left of them, masses of dead white males raining down on them, all shot out of the same canon:

Fragonard—Satin-clad white people without a care in the world, frolicking the hours away in verdant copses pruned by somebody else.

Romney and Gainsborough—White ladies of leisure in big hats and lace fichus, all of whom look entirely capable of saying, "Beulah, peel me a grape."

The Venetian School—Noble white ladies being fanned by their personal "blackamoors," who are dressed as caliphs and carrying the pet monkey.

Dutch Genre Painters—White people who demand spotless kitchen floors.

The Elgin Marbles—White people robbing white people of people even whiter.

Nativities, Annunciations, and Crucifixions—White Christians far in excess of the white-Christian quota. These are the same haloed people whom the museum directors are trying to steer toward the Egress exhibit.

Brueghel—Mobs of beer-swilling poor white trash, all of them falling-down drunk.

It all adds up to neo-imperialism in the service of inclusion, but left-wingers have never been in the habit of thinking their brainstorms through. I will bet that whoever dreamed up the 12 percent ukase was captive to the Shining Faces syndrome. This is the theme of cultural-messiah stories such as *To Sir, with Love* or Pat Conroy's *Conrack*. An idealistic teacher takes a job in the slums and resolves to introduce the dregs of society to the finer things in life; after a semester of crisis-laden field trips, he is rewarded when his Verdi-humming, van Gogh-digging charges decorously take their seats on the last day of school and gaze up with shining faces—at him.

How can England's shell-shocked museum directors fill their minority quotas? My sympathies are with them, because as a college student I had a summer job selling prints and postcards at the National Gallery of Art and I know something about what museum people have to put up with. I also feel a certain sympathy for the minorities, thanks to my baseball-loving mother, who formed her opinion of museums while dating my cultivated father: "They're full of dumb pictures."

I have therefore devised a plan to help both the directors and the minorities over the quota hump. Italy has professional mourners for hire to the friendless or kinless who want someone to pull out all the stops at their funerals. Why couldn't enterprising British minorities shake down the government and hire themselves out as professional culture vultures and get paid for hanging out in museums?

To turn street kids into convincing museum visitors, the directors could start a school, like Fagin, to teach the reluctant aesthetes everything they need to know about looking at art. How to step back and shutter the eyes, squeeze the bridge of the nose, measure with an erect thumb, pace up and down, and master an ethereal vocabulary ("infinity," "spatial," "vastness," etc.) so they can do a quick shining-face number in case Tony Blair's cultural messiahs show up unannounced at the latest exhibit.

England is finished. I thought we would go first, but I was wrong. It's a relief in a way, because I am now rid of the longing that used to come over me back when *Upstairs, Downstairs* was showing. I watched it twice every week, once on each PBS channel. I wanted to walk into that house and never come out; it was a microcosm of a sane society that I craved so much I would have even changed places with Ruby. Afterward, I would get depressed and think about emigrating, but now that the green and sensible land is no more—I don't have to look for the Egress.

July 17, 2000

I F pundits want a really penetrating subject to toss around on Sunday-morning shows, they should contemplate those members of the electorate who are least likely to come through Campaign 2000 all in one piece.

We, the Doomed Remnant, are the people who remember when vice presidents were rarely seen or heard, when they got our attention only if they became president the old-fashioned way, and when, in the words of John Nance Garner, the vice presidency wasn't "worth a pitcher of warm spit."

This genial disdain for the second office of the land was a measure of our civic health. It meant we could be casual, even careless, about the way we governed ourselves and still come out all right. Having someone high up who was unimportant, someone big who was routinely ignored, translated into an eccentric balance of power such as existed between absolutist kings and court jesters. Vice presidents, like jesters, were designated safety valves who kept the body politic supple.

The body politic is now straight as a ramrod, and the new measure of our civic health is the silent scream rising in our throats as we behold the tortuous writhings of Al Gore.

Conservatives who give Bush credit for his widening lead in the polls should guess again. It's not that Bush has gotten better, but that Gore has begun to inflict real psychic damage. Personally, I sense that he shares the affliction that novelist James Gould Cozzens, who liked unusual words, diagnosed in himself: "anhedonia," the inability to experience pleasure. While this can profit an introverted writer like Cozzens, in a politician it boils down to waiting for a crackup.

This is what we are presently doing, and it's taking its toll. Wondering what would happen if the real Al Gore stood up triggers visions of a campaign ad. It's "Sleepless in America" time. Twilight is spreading over the fractals . . . tinkling sound as lantern jaw crumbles under full moon . . . cut to Lon Chaney speaking v-e-r-y s-l-o-w-l-y.

Members of the Doomed Remnant know that it doesn't have to be like this. The inevitability of vice presidents came about when the Twenty-second Amendment made reelected presidents lame ducks from the moment of their reelection, which removed the guesswork from a sitting president's plans and turned the vice president into an heir apparent.

Proposed in 1947, the amendment contained a courtesy clause excepting the then-sitting president from its conditions. "Otherwise," explained my junior-high civics teacher, "it would be an insult to Mr. Truman."

This is why the last of what I call our "normal" vice presidents was Truman's 1948 running mate, 71-year-old Sen. Alben W. Barkley of Kentucky. We didn't notice him until he performed the only notable act of his tenure: He got married, which produced an unforgettable newsreel of a White House party welcoming him back from his honeymoon, in which Truman was heard to mutter, "You old fool."

The good times ended when the first administration covered by the Twenty-second Amendment took office. It seemed to us that Nixon went at the vice presidency like the houseguest who insists upon making himself useful. He was everywhere, in newsreels, on magazine covers, invariably headlined "A New Kind of Vice President." It was this, not only his reputation and personality problems, that generated the famous inarticulate revulsion contained in "There's something about Nixon. . . ." No doubt he was thorough, but there was something about Vice President Felix Unger that we couldn't stand.

When, after two terms as vice president, he ran for president in 1960, the pattern was set. Nixon's loss that year did nothing to dislodge the fait accompli: The vice presidency now was not only a heartbeat away from the presidency, but a mere eight years away from it as well.

Several reasons suggest that the metastasized second office leads to more vice-presiding than the freight will bear.

1. A favorite rationale for putting vice presidents to work is "the need to utilize all available talent." But as Nixon demonstrated, the vice presidency, like Betty Friedan's housework, expands to fill the time available. To get round this vicious circle we invent veepish jobs—commissions, blue-ribbon panels, Project-this, Target-that—which waste money and may gel into permanent bureaucracies.

2. From hyphenated Americans to hyphenated administrations: Reagan-Bush, Bush-Quayle, Clinton-Gore. It's one thing to see it on a campaign button, but to hear it spoken in a formal speech or newscast is to sense that we are moving, heartbeat by heartbeat, toward a co-presidency. Considering what the Constitution has already failed to protect us from, we can no longer use the old rubric, "It can't happen here," to rule out a power struggle.

3. Now that vice presidents are high-profile heirs, presidents have no way to get rid of them. Unsensational reasons for switching nominees no longer exist. Picking a new running mate for a second term is tantamount to saying that really big mistakes were made. The party in power has no choice but to keep the booby on the ticket, thereby helping him wear out his welcome and emerge as a compulsory presidential candidate that nobody can stand.

Conservatives inclined to delight in the Democrats' predicament should put a lid on their schadenfreude. The Veep Who Came to Dinner is an equal-opportunity disaster waiting to happen to either party. This time around the nerve-racking compulsory candidate is Al Gore, but the last one was Bush the Elder, who drove Reaganauts up the wall and tapped Dan Quayle, who drove everybody up the wall.

We need a Warm-Spit Amendment: Limit vice presidents to one term and impose a four-year moratorium to prevent them from running for president until they have made themselves useful somewhere else.

July 31, 2000

B Y the time you read this, the GOP convention will be under way, but right now I'm getting ready for it. I've already made a run on the liquor store and hidden my guns; now all I have to do is buy a can of something called "DeeStickee," guaranteed to remove all gummy, sugary, syrupy residues, in case I have to wash down the TV.

I'm not looking forward to this. What I'd really like to do is go where no Republican has ever gone before, but they go practically everywhere now. The only way to avoid Republicans these days is to go to the one place where they wouldn't dare set foot, but I don't have a country-club membership.

I can tell what I'm in for by the key words in the convention program schedule. It defies reading; but you don't really have to read it: Just squeeze it and it squirts out enough Renewal, Progress, and Purpose to drown a double stack. It's shaping up like my Christmas visit years ago to the home of a beau made desperate by the strain of living with a repressed, suicidally conventional family who were determined to believe that people wanted to do the right thing, that everybody got along with everybody else, and that nothing was wrong when, in fact, everything was wrong.

Whenever anybody asked his mother what she wanted for Christmas, she smiled brightly and said, "All I want is a big box of love." When she said it for the twentieth time, I got an idea. I told my beau about it, and we drove out to Sears and went around back to the loading dock, where he persuaded them to sell him a crate that had contained a refrigerator. When we got back home, he hid it in the garage, and we went to work on it. When he unveiled it on Christmas morning, his mother took one look at what we intended as gibes—LOVE! THIS END UP! LOVE! POST NO BILLS!—and invited the whole neighborhood over to see the proof of her wonderful boy's dedication to family. "You can't win," he muttered. No, you can't. The world is full of people like this, and most of them are Republicans.

In most election years there's so much competition for the GOP Tunnel Vision Award that it's hard to decide on the winner, but this time it's a snap: Christie Todd Whitman, who allowed herself to be photographed frisking a black criminal suspect. It happened when she went out with the cops, which, said her damage-control people, was one of her gubernatorial duties: getting hands-on experience of the policeman's lot.

That's all cops need, some woman in the back seat chirping, "Ooh, can I do it?" Men welcome this sort of thing only when a woman is under 25 and wants to see what it feels like to hold a boat or a plane on course just for a minute, giving them an excuse to press against her and put their hand on hers to steady it. Substitute a gaunt post-post-deb cruising around Camden in the middle of the night, and instead of a delicious frisson all they get is a shudder.

At least the photo of the smiling white socialite patting down the spread-eagled homeboy will keep Whitman off the ticket and, with luck, send her permanently out to pasture, but it's the top of the ticket that worries me. He's turned into Lyndon Baines Bush. Instead of throwing money at problems, LBB throws tax credits. His $42 billion "New Prosperity Initiative" would give the "working poor" a tax credit to buy health insurance, but lest anyone call it welfare, the Bush camp insists that "the governor hasn't proposed any wealth transfers," as if the revenue lost in tax credits did not have to be made up for by higher taxes on somebody else.

His New Prosperity Initiative even creates $750 million in tax credits for teachers who use their own money to buy classroom supplies, but none dare call it Great Society II. "The reason you haven't heard any criticizing," said Sen. Rick Santorum, "is because these are tax reductions, not new government programs."

Oh. . . .

Keeping track of LBB's blizzard of billion-dollar initiatives is slow business because so many news stories have to be read twice, like the one about the "American Dream Down Payment Fund," in which LBB proposed a program to give poor people money to put into savings accounts so they can buy a house.

After rereading this to make sure it said what I thought it said, I came across a column by Cal Thomas praising it. "But his objective is not to maintain people in their dependency," Thomas explained. "He wants to emancipate them. It is a subtle but important distinction." It certainly is, and if you reread Thomas you will grasp it: Democrats give people money to spend, but Republicans give them money to save.

The definition of "compassionate conservatism," once so elusive, can now be pinned down: It's new government programs masquerading as tax credits. That won't pour, however, so Republicans at the squeeze-me convention, like my beau's mother and Cal Thomas, will define it as they wish it to be, using great big gobs of emotion and happy talk to sing of the miracles of self-sufficiency that rugged individualism can achieve if you just spread around enough handouts.

Grover Norquist, president of the conservative Americans for Tax Reform, is impatient with complaints such as these. "Look," he said, "the governor is going to spend money. I find nothing troubling about it, and it certainly sounds more cheerful than the Republicans saying they want to abolish the Department of Education."

Norquist the cheerful is obviously looking forward to the convention, and so, in my fashion, am I. I'm hoping LBB will announce a Classroom Compassionate Discipline Initiative so he can screw it up and say, "No child's behind was left."

Meanwhile, I believe in DeeStickee so strongly that I want everybody to have some, especially CNN's Jonathan Karl, who reported that LBB pinched his cheek. I had no sooner read that twice than I came across an item about a brawny ABC cameraman whom LBB greeted with: "Big boy, are you a golfer? You must shank it a mile." I read that three times but it still sounded like Mae West.

August 14, 2000

I T won't last, of course, but for the moment I'm in a wonderful mood. In fact, I'm happy, and if you want to credit (or blame) somebody for this unusual state of affairs you need look no further than Dick Cheney.

It has nothing to do with politics per se. Although I like his controversial congressional voting record, my reaction to him is a matter of what psychologists call "free association." He has become my personal, walking Rorschach test and I would have the same positive images of him whatever his politics were. They're the kind of deep-down personal reactions that campaign operatives try to dig out in focus groups, but since I'll never be chosen for a focus group (people who pick juries never want me either), I will bare my soul here for the purpose of showing why Cheney is the only good reason to vote in November.

The moment W. unveiled him, my life turned into one big inkblot. Each time I saw him on TV another sliver of memory emerged from the mist, fragmentary sights and sounds grew sharper, and lost tactile and olfactory sensations returned with a visceral twist of recognition.

I saw white shirts, a whole drawer full of them, each crisscrossed with the blue strip of paper the Chinese laundry put around them like a bandolier. I saw a vest with the gold chain of a pocket watch curving down across the stomach. I saw myself standing on tiptoe to plant a good-night kiss on the cheek of a man who gave off the pleasing scents of witch hazel and starch, and the sterner metallic smell of barber's clippers. Then, somewhere, a fast-forward button was pressed and I heard that same man's voice yelling "Put some clothes on!" and "Who is that boy?"

The TV was on throughout my Proustian time travels, which made them even more satisfying. Every time a querulous talking head said, "It's Daddy pick" and "This is your father's Oldsmobile," I pumped my fist and said, "Yesssss!"

Cheney is nothing like my father, who was as skinny as Fred Astaire and had the personality of the characters played by Clifton Webb and George

Sanders. But Cheney is Everyfather, the consummate figure who has been missing from our national life long enough to make his absence felt in the chaotic statistics about single moms, gay marriage, and deranged teens that are recited daily.

But now, miraculously, he's not missing anymore. W.'s announcement of a running mate thrust the entire country into an old black-and-white family sitcom. Suddenly, America's collective front door opened and in walked Mr. Central Casting himself, a little pudgy, a little rumpled, a little tired, to send shock waves of recognition through the millions who could have sworn they heard him call out "It's me!"

Not all of the shock waves were positive. Most of the media, unable or unwilling to acknowledge the overnight emergence of a universal father symbol, talked around the point, dredging up a word that would mean what they said without saying what they meant: "gravitas."

The Gravitas Hour swung into high gear. Not since *Amos and Andy* dominated radio have so many Americans listened to the same thing at the same time. From every discussion show on every channel of every TV in the land there poured forth testimonials to Dick Cheney's gravitas. Gravitas was what he had; gravitas was what he was. On and on it went, until gravitas meant Cheney and Cheney meant gravitas. Now he was not only a symbol but a synonym.

Identifying someone as the incarnation of solidity and seriousness is risky business. When it dawned on the media that all their talk of gravitas might be having an unintended effect, they followed it up with the dismissive assertion that "People don't vote for vice presidents." Don't they? If we keep seeing dais shots of a fidgety W. darting his pleading eyes over the crowd while a patiently resigned Cheney waits with his hand in his pocket, it's only a matter of time before someone asks, "Who's that standing next to Gravitas?"

I am savoring Cheney while I can, because it won't be long before the hand comes out of the pocket to grasp that of his wife. I liked the way she took his arm instead, but the GOP image patrol will soon put a stop to that. Hand-holding by political couples is one of those new traditions that we hew to so religiously; Jimmy and Rosalynn Carter started it and now none dare call it low class.

Indications are that the overhaul of Cheney's reassuringly inhibited self has already begun. He dropped his g's on *Nightline* and backpedaled on his conservative congressional votes with a suspiciously worded defense. Left to his own devices, he probably would have responded as his former boss did when confronted with his old congressional votes. "Forget the record," Gerald Ford said cavalierly during his first week as president, "the record reflects Grand Rapids." But instead, Cheney said that if he had it to do over, he probably would "tweak" his.

The word didn't sound like him. Whoever heard of "tweaking" a voting record? It sounds like something a plastic surgeon does. I bet it was dreamed up by some fax-happy Bush operative assigned to squish recognizable personalities into shape.

Democrats are using gravitas to mean boring, white male, and arch-conservative, while Republicans are using it to mean a hard-working nice guy, but its original meaning was something quite different, as F. R. Cowell describes in *Cicero and the Roman Republic*:

> No Roman in any circumstances could regard himself as vanquished. This was the key to the real strength of the Republic. The other well-known virtues of the Romans followed from it; their manliness and courage in battle (virtus), their sobriety, their consciousness of their responsibilities, their disciplining of the emotions (gravitas), and their readiness to give single-minded attention to the practical needs of the hour (simplicitas). With it all went a precise formality by which almost all their other actions were guided.

This is what we need after eight years of President Peter Pan. Too bad we can't vote for Cheney-Bush, or better yet, Cheney-Thompson.

August 28, 2000

AMERICAN punditry has a new literary genre: the "Campaign Diary." Everybody is writing them and it's easy to see why. The format is ideally structured for unstructured thoughts. The lead-ins—Day One, Day Two, etc.—hide the fact that you no longer know or care what day it is, and imply that you are actually on the campaign trail when in fact you are slumped half-drunk in front of the TV wishing you were dead. They also eliminate the need to make everything dovetail into a logical conclusion. When the brackish waters of Fallacy 2000 threaten to swallow you up, just insert a new lead-in and change the subject. Readers will simply think something new happened. Who knows? Maybe it did.

DAY ONE: In the interests of pretending to be a new kind of misanthrope for the next three months, I'll start with the good news. Laura Bush comes along just in time to prevent a complete break in my family's susceptibility to gorgeous brunette First Ladies. My grandmother was wild about Frances Cleveland, my mother was wild about Grace Coolidge, but Jackie Kennedy left me cold. I was just about resigned to letting down the side, but now there's hope.

Laura won my heart with the way she handled the outdoorsy, unintellectu-al Bushes on one of her first visits to Kennebunkport. As the clan prepared for a vigorous game, someone asked her, "And what do you do?"—i.e., what sport she played. Laura serenely replied, "I read, I smoke, and I admire." Unfortun-ately, she has since quit smoking, but there's hope on that front too. Living in the White House is stressful, and stress must be relieved. If she starts smoking again and W. starts drinking again, it could spell the end of the Health Nazis.

Fallacy 2000 could be our first First Lady election. With many in both parties wishing their tickets were the other way around, the continuing con-trast between the worrisome front-runners and their reassuring running mates might cause millions to end the war of nerves by voting for the wives instead.

It's not impossible. Hillary has traumatized Americans so much that they now ache for a bona fide First Lady more than they realize. Tipper Gore's bubbliness harkens back to irrepressible Dolly Madison, but this is not a good year for blithe spirits. Tipper also has a whiff of Zelda Fitzgerald about her, and America wants normal. Laura Bush would win in a landslide, for all the obvious reasons, plus a subtle one that would deliver a record male vote: She comes across as a woman who can make a man settle down without making his life miserable.

DAY TWO: Nothing beats a week of tributes to compassion interrupted by the AFLAC talking-duck commercial. Two yuppie businessmen are eating lunch on a park bench when behind them a bicyclist falls with a loud crash, followed by a scream. Without so much as a backward glance, one business-man says to the other, "When I had my accident, my supplemental insurance kicked in." Why don't they go see what happened and try to help?

DAY THREE: I could swear that mentor/tutor/volunteer newspaper fea-tures increased after Colin Powell's speech. The photo always shows a white soccer mom suffused in a moist glow of self-sacrifice, seated beside a minor-ity kid staring at a Little Golden Book. How long will it be before it's like jury duty? Being a writer always saves me from that, but from tutoring reading?

DAY FOUR: During the New Deal, GOP stabs at compassion were called "Me Too-ism." Now, bolstered by white guilt and obsessed by black votes, Republicans may well become the "Me First" party. Considering their demon-strated eagerness to challenge Democrats to feats of racial one-upmanship, it's only a matter of time before a GOP honcho, probably Bush strategist Karl Rove, wakes up some morning, thinks "Nixon went to China," and calls for slavery reparations.

This has a certain terrible beauty. America's oldest racial entitlement is the post–Civil War reparations scheme dreamed up by the GOP called "Forty

Acres and a Mule." Confronted with this first, Democrats will say "Me Too" and call for a national surtax.

Rove has already announced the end of the GOP's "Southern Strategy," dismissing it as an "old paradigm" inimical to the spirit of Fallacy 2000's incessantly lauded "positive agendas." Pat Robertson took umbrage at this, saying, "You have to give people a reason why this party is different from the other party." That goes double for southern Democrats turned Republican, who are like the catechism pupil in *The Cardinal*. Assured by Father Fermoyle that Protestants can go to Heaven too, the boy asks, "Then why do we have to go to all this trouble to be Catholic?"

DAY FIVE: I always sing after three martinis. This time I made a special effort to choose something inclusive.

> *From Britain's shore the English rose,*
> *The shamrock and the heather!*
> *God save the Queen and Heaven bless*
> *The maple leaf forever!*

They left out Welsh-Canadians, but outside of a stew pot there's not much you can do with leeks.

DAY SIX: My eye is swollen and itching. Boric acid didn't help so I used Preparation H and it cleared it right up. Why not? Swelling and itching are swelling and itching. Preparation H didn't discriminate, it didn't say, "Hey, this is an eye, I'm outta here." It's a new kind of Preparation H that reaches out beyond its base to touch every willing agenda.

DAY SEVEN: Earnest pols take the fun out of diversity. I prefer the Jewish southern belle I knew at Ole Miss. Each weekend her mother burst into the dorm with new clothes, crying, "Leah Lee, honey, where you at? Try on this darlin' shmatta!" Then her boyfriend would come down from Memphis and they'd fight. "Murray Lee, Ah'm sick 'n' tard of listenin' to your magilla! You're a nebbish, 'deed you are, just a l'il ole nebbish!"

September 11, 2000

DAY ONE: Another load of cow flop, another Campaign Diary. My coverage of the Dems' convention got off to a bad start when I inadvertently missed Hillary's speech. I say inadvertently because it was Shark Week on the Discovery Channel and I didn't realize I wasn't watching her.

I switched back in time to see Bubba's interminable trek through the bowels of the convention center. Choreographed by Harry Thomason, it was widely interpreted as a "lone gladiator" entering the Colosseum for the last time, or Gary Cooper as Lou Gehrig heading stoically for the Yankees locker room, but what it actually suggested should bring Harry Thomason's career as a choreographer to a rapid and merciful end. Whether subconsciously or deliberately, this touted Friend of Bill was getting even for the ostracism he and his wife suffered after the travel office and haircut episodes of 1993. It requires the brain of a convention delegate to find anything heroic or flattering about this cinder-block hegira. To me it symbolized the instinctive dread of labyrinths that pervades mythology, or the universal nightmare in which we try to reach an unnamed something that keeps getting farther away. A Clintonized interpretation might be the condemned prisoner's last mile; specifically, the French lady-killer Landru marching to the guillotine. At the very least it suggested JFK's rake's progress through the subterranean passageways and boiler rooms of hotels he used for assignations.

DAY TWO: Now we know what happened to the Play-Doh the INS gave Elián González: It turned into supple, flexible, malleable, pokeable, pullable, stretchable Joe Lieberman, the conscience of the Senate. The potter was Maxine Waters, who could make even strong white men weak; give her five minutes alone with Louis XIV and she'd have him saying *L'état, c'est vous*. It was only to be expected that poor, eager, grateful Joe Lieberman developed spinal deliquescence at the first sign of her displeasure and reshaped himself into the Little Affirmative-Action Engine That Could. It was the greatest proof yet of the power Waters wields. She's a one-woman shadow government who can issue a call for racial "disturbances" anytime she doesn't get what she wants. If the convention had run a week longer into August she could have ordered her forces to mount a floor demonstration on St. Bartholomew's Day.

DAY THREE: If either of the Liebermans says "Only in America" one more time. . . . George Will beat me to the punch when he pointed out that England had a Jewish prime minister 132 years ago, so I am left with pointing out that England's first Jewish knighthood was bestowed on Sir Solomon Medina by William III in 1699, in gratitude for his financing of the wars won by the Duke of Marlborough. So far as is known, neither Sir Solomon, nor, later on, Baron Nathan Rothschild, screamed "Oh, my God! I don't believe it!" like a Lotto winner.

DAY FOUR: The Kiss. Polls and pundits are divided on whether it was planned or spontaneous, but the either-or restricts our understanding of what actually happened. Clearly it was both.

It started out scripted. The idea was for Gore to encircle Tipper's waist and for her to place her hands on his shoulders while they exchanged a quick, sweet peck. This they did, but then something happened, and I know what it was because I wrote the same scene countless times back when I was hacking out paperback Gothics.

The hero of a Gothic is always an emotionally warped squire whose rigidly arranged life is disrupted when he hires a plucky governess intent on uncovering the secret tragedy that has made him so cold. Nothing daunts this girl; she's game for anything—locked rooms, hidden passageways, bat-infested attics, whatever it takes to solve the riddle of his shrouded past and bring him out of his shell. As she draws closer and closer to the truth, he panics, feeling his defenses crumbling, and decides that sex is the only way to control her. His chance comes when he pulls her out of the abandoned well she has just fallen into. Since his arms are already around her, he suddenly yanks her against him and snarls, "Come here, you little fool!"

The Gore clinch was a classic Gothic kiss, a last-ditch attempt at self-preservation by an aloof man content in his aloofness, asserting that aloofness to the whole world by momentarily cutting off the air of the woman who never stops doing whatever it takes to bring him out of his shell.

Writing Gothics is as bad as watching conventions. I took a course in court transcribing, so I used to write them on the Stenotype machine when drunk and transcribe them when sober. "Come here, you little fool" in Stenotype is: KOPL HER RBGS U HREUTL TPAOL. (That's faster to take down than it looks.) If you want to bombard Gore campaign headquarters with this coded message, I am powerless to stop you.

Never let it be forgot that every silver lining has a cloud. A noticeably lowering presence at Bathos 2000 was 17-year-old Albert Gore III. It has since come out that he had been arrested for reckless driving and speeding (97 mph), but the look on his face betokened something more than just being grounded.

Nobody can sulk like a teenage boy. That kid was furious and nobody who remembers the '92 convention can blame him. That was the year Gore used him to flaunt his paternal sensitivity in a blubbering account of the boy's brush with death. Next came the '96 convention, where Gore used his sister's cancer to flaunt his fraternal sensitivity, and now at Bathos 2000 he was using the whole family to prove how loosey-goosey he is.

The whole family, that is, except his namesake. He was ostensibly left out of the show to punish him, but it could be that the Gores know he sees through the old man and is hellbent on sabotaging him—hence the merry chase he gave North Carolina's controlling legal authorities.

September 25, 2000

I AM writing this in bed, where I am recovering by proxy from Al Gore's 28-hour nonstop Labor Day campaign marathon, "Sleepless in Wherever." Somebody has to rest and since he isn't about to, I'm doing it for him in my capacity as a veteran of the next worst thing to political campaigns: book tours.

The Constitution sets the minimum age for presidents at 35, but the candidates we end up with are nearly always in their 50s—the heart-attack age. Never mind all the Diet Cokes, it's still the heart-attack age, which makes Gore a candidate in more ways than one.

Pols used to enter a hall by walking up the aisle and waving decorously. Now the aisle has turned into a ragged serpentine with crowds on opposite rope lines. Gore runs in smiling maniacally and zigzags from one rope line to the other like an infantryman dodging bullets. At one stop he and Lieberman staged what appeared to be a modern-dance recital, entering from opposite ends of the hall and loping toward one another in a wide arc, meeting in the middle like an ecstatic Daphnis and Chloë. All that was missing were the diaphanous chitons.

In his round-the-clock trial by ordeal, Gore marched in a Pittsburgh parade, visited a truck factory in Michigan, watched football in a Philadelphia pub, ate breakfast with firefighters, ate lunch with construction workers (buying 100 cheesesteak sandwiches), and drove Louisville's Motor Speedway in his limo. Afterward, he made a point of rubbing it in to groggy reporters during a night flight on Air Force Two. "I can't believe that you guys are sleeping back here," he gloated, all bright-eyed and bushy-tailed. "I'm loving it."

Some sensible advance man scheduled his final campaign stop at a 911 emergency center where he signed autographs, but he probably wished he could wind it up by going a few rounds with Tipper. They couldn't do it publicly, of course, but he could have picked her up and thrown her on a gurney in the back of an ambulance and climbed in after her. It would have looked like Emma and Léon making out in the swaying coach in *Madame Bovary*. This way, if he had had a heart attack, the rescue squad wouldn't have needed to go and get him because he was already there.

Never mind campaign-finance reform, we need to reform campaigning itself before some candidate drops dead or causes a calamity. The possibilities are endless. Suppose a punch-drunk Gore tries to slap high fives, misses, and hits a little old lady in the head and kills her? Or, working a diner at 4 A.M., he reaches across a table to shake hands and knocks a woman's coffee in her lap. He grabs a napkin and tries to pat her dry, but just then her husband returns from the men's room, misconstrues the scene, and socks Gore in the nose. The

Secret Service agents panic and shoot the husband, rumors spread that citizens are being executed, riots erupt nationwide, and Clinton declares martial law, cancels the election, and stays in office for the duration of Civil War II.

Gore's insane Labor Day marathon was supposed to show how hard he will work for the American people, but to me it hinted darkly of a taste for self-punishment that could make a Gore presidency perilous in a way that a Clinton presidency is not and never could be.

Despite his libido, Clinton is cerebral rather than physical; lazy, self-protective, and soft. He never went out for sports in school, and now that his jogging regimen seems to be on hold, only golf interrupts the flow of his inactivity. JFK's obsession with "vigor" is one aspect of his hero that he hasn't copied, as when he told Monica that intercourse would be too risky. True, he had an ulterior motive, but the result was the same: He avoided exertion and took his pleasure the easy way.

Nor does he follow JFK's lead in going coatless to prove that he can "take it." Clinton has a heavy, unusually long black overcoat that makes him look like an undertaker, but he wears it anyway for the sensible purpose of keeping warm. Like all true voluptuaries, he is a finicky indoorsman who loves his precious, pasty-white self too much to place any demands on it. He hurls himself into campaigning because it gives him pleasure, but Gore does it because it gives him pain. Given the choice of a Sybarite or a Spartan in the White House, I'll take the Sybarite every time.

Next to Gore on the scale of neurotic campaigning is Lieberman, not because he's a Spartan but because he is so eager to please that he would sing "I'm a Little Teapot" in 50 kindergartens a day if that's what it takes. As for W., he's a casual campaigner, but for the wrong reasons: He's lazy and diffident without having the excuse of being a reader.

Ironically, the only confident, psychologically healthy candidate is the man described by the *Washington Post*'s David Von Drehle as "grouchy," "snippy," "taciturn," "shy," and "visibly irritated." The man who enters a room with downcast eyes, trails off in a mumble, and "smiles as if his lips were sewn shut."

Dick Cheney on a campaign is like me on a book tour. When we say what a pleasure it is to be wherever the hell we are, it comes out sounding like Dorothy Parker's monologue: "Would I like to waltz with you? Would I like to be caught in a storm at sea?" W. would advise that you gotta let 'em look in your heart, but that, in my case at least, would only compound the problem.

The kind of personality Americans now demand from public figures is alluded to in the political reporter's familiar phrase, "wade into the crowd."

Anyone who has ever been in the spotlight, whether Cheney's big one or my modest one, learns firsthand the shattering effect that aloofness has on Americans. You must radiate naked emotional neediness or they will hate you; the slightest pulling back will set them off and trigger an onrush of panicky hostility that must be experienced to be believed. So ask not why we can't restore maturity and sanity to campaigns. This is why.

October 9, 2000

I F you're sick of politics too, here's an "October surprise." For sheer escapism nothing beats a classic British murder case, so let's time-travel to Glasgow in 1857 for a front-row seat at *Regina* v. *Madeleine Smith*.

She was 21 when she was tried for the arsenic murder of her lover, Emile L'Angelier. He was 34, a tousle-haired, liquid-eyed French adventurer who had taken part in the Revolution of 1848, making him in modern terms an ex–Vietnam War protester and hippie has-been.

That and his job as a clerk in a Glasgow factory office made him an unacceptable suitor for a rich socialite like Madeleine. She came from a family of architects; her father was renowned in the field and her maternal grandfather was David Hamilton, designer of the Royal Exchange.

She had been prepared for the life of an upper-crust society hostess at a select English finishing school, where she acquired all the fashionably useless accomplishments. Her academic learning was sparse, but she did pick up one valuable fact: Arsenic, all the girls said, did wonders for the complexion when used as an astringent, producing that deathly pallor so prized by Victorian ladies.

After graduation, she returned home and marked time, waiting to marry. Her father already had a husband picked out for her, a friend of his named William Minnoch. Little is known about him, but the name alone inspired one commentator on the case to conjure him up as "ginger whiskers and tedium." I conjure up Mr. Minnoch as that sterling impediment of indigestible rectitude known as "good husband material." It's possible that the thought of spending the rest of her life with him drove Madeleine around the bend and into L'Angelier's arms. Considering the deconstructive effect of unflagging male virtue on female nerves, Mr. Minnoch emerges as an accessory before the fact.

Under normal Victorian conditions it would have been impossible for Emile even to meet Madeleine, but he was a social climber and a tireless practitioner of what we call "networking." By making himself agreeable, doing little favors, and stroking everyone who crossed his path, he finally met somebody who knew somebody who knew a friend of Madeleine's sister. A carefully calibrated meeting took place on the street when the Smith girls were out walking, and he was formally introduced to her.

Emile came late at night and stood at the window of Madeleine's street-level room, talking with her while she served hot cocoa on the sill. She was able to bring him into the house a couple of times thanks to her mutual-aid pact with one of the maids—Madeleine looked the other way when the maid's boyfriend slipped in—but nothing happened, so to speak, because her sister shared her room.

The act that the High Court of Justiciary would call "connexion" took place when Emile followed her to the Smiths' summer home in Rowallen and they had at it in the garden, the orchard, the riverbank, everywhere but in the house. This daughter of architecture liked her sex alfresco.

She also liked to write letters. All Victorians did, but there is nothing Victorian about Madeleine's. They were more like today's phone sex. "I am much excited tonight," she wrote. "It is a pleasure, and no one can deny that. It is but human nature." She even described finding blood on herself.

Her splendor in the grass was short-lived. Like many a woman before and since, she soon discovered an unpleasant truth about men: As soon as they've had you, they try to boss you around.

Emile started criticizing everything about her: clothes, friends, habits, her letters, even her sexual submission. He turned into a prude, condemning her for yielding to him and making her promise not to do it again. His object was a rich wife, or, in lieu of that, money and improved status; his method was to break her down until she was putty in his hands. But he went too far when he threatened to show her letters to her father. Deciding to fight back, Madeleine went to the chemist's.

After a cocoa-on-the-windowsill date, Emile became ill. Two more sessions at Madeleine's bar did the trick: He was found dead with 82 grains of arsenic in his stomach (4 to 6 is enough). The police searched his room and found stacks of Madeleine's letters, all "crossed" in the fashion of the time: After finishing a page, she turned it sideways and wrote across her own words. One crime writer has suggested that reading them drove Emile to suicide.

Madeleine's icy poise in the dock, even while her letters were read aloud, was grudgingly admired. Her raven-haired beauty and pale complexion didn't hurt either. The Crown had to show that Emile saw her the night before his death, but she was saved by a smudged postmark and an all-male jury, who brought the dour Scottish verdict of "Not Proven," the Presbyterian way of saying "We know you did it, but . . ."

She was free, and only 21. What happened to her? A recent book, *Murder in Victorian Scotland* by Douglas MacGowan, tells us she moved to London, married the designer George Wardle, and lived in raffish Bloomsbury, where she charmed George Bernard Shaw and, according to Sacheverell Sitwell, posed for Rosetti. She also invented the place mat, inspired perhaps by her windowsill snacks. She got on with the Socialist set but we can bet she was contemptuous of them: They were theory, she was action.

In 1910 she emigrated to America where her son, Thomas Wardle, had settled. Then 75, she married 49-year-old William A. Sheehy, who died in 1926. Madeleine died two years later and is buried in Mount Hope Cemetery in Hastings-on-Hudson, N.Y., under the name Lena Wardle Sheehy. She was 92. The good die young, except Mr. Minnoch, who became president of the Glasgow Chamber of Commerce.

Madeleine Smith, R.I.P. A cad took the fuzz off her peach and she took the lining off his stomach. Some women just don't need the vote.

October 23, 2000

I HAVE frequently made tongue-in-cheek statements about repealing the Nineteenth Amendment. Now I say it again, but with a straightened-out tongue. The women's vote is making idiots of everybody and we'd be better off without it.

It's hard to pick a defining moment when all roads lead to Waterloo, but mine is probably the minivan commercial. It's been running over and over all summer; interestingly, on a lot of political shows. It opens with a chiding kid asking, "How far would you go to protect your children?" and then features more kids asking more chiding questions. The one that gets to me is "Would you face a charging grizzly bear?" I'd pour honey on the little bastard just to make sure, but then I'm not focus-groupable. The correct answer is an affirmative upward surge of the wriggling yellow line on pollster Frank Luntz's Female Emotion Machine.

This yellow line has replaced the fate line in our national palm, threatening to decide Election 2000 and those in the foreseeable future. It has been serpentining and corkscrewing its jaundiced path across our TV screens ever since the primaries, measuring the instinctive reactions and knee-jerk opinions of the soccer moms and their feminized mates that Luntz assembles for the edification of the candidates.

What the yellow line has writ, let no man put asunder. Not that any man would dare, least of all Frank Luntz, whose cherubic features fairly tremble with uncontainable joy as he explains its progress. See? It's dipping down to Gore's red line! But now look—it climbed suddenly up to Bush's blue line! [Clap hands and turn to camera in triumph.] Do you know what that means?

The slightest movement of the yellow line is enough to make weak men weaker. Did it go up at "community"? Shove that word into every speech as often as possible until the broads think you're going to put the superintendent of schools in charge of the army and navy. Did it take a sudden sharp plunge at "statesmanlike"? Get Dick Cheney a pet caterpillar and make him carry it around in a jar and sing to it at day-care centers. Did it stay steady on course in burrow-like contentment? W.'s incessant repetitions of "education" must be working, so make him pronounce it "ed-ju-kay-shun" to drag it out.

Special attention must be paid to the wavering yellow line that goes up, then down, and then up again. This is the silent visual version of a female voice saying, "I'm not mad, just hurt." It means that she liked what you said, but not the way you said it. The usual culprit here is an edgy distrust of declarative sentences, so train your candidate to insert an adverbial stool softener such as "sort of." Joe Lieberman used this to great soothing effect when he said, "This is a time to sort of knit the country together," about why he looked forward to meeting with Louis Farrakhan. The dropped stitch of "sort of" was so humanizing that the gals didn't even notice that he was talking about knitting with a monster. This statement was a twofer for Soft-Stool Joe because he also remembered that "look forward" is catnip: The yellow line goes straight to it.

It also goes straight to humor, provided it's the gentle, unthreatening kind of humor favored by the "healing power" crowd, who like to think you can laugh your cancer away. Say something with bite, however, and you will lose all 50 states and the District of Columbia. The Yugoslavian election upheaval was a perfect cue for W. to announce that his favorite sandwich is Kostunica on rye, but the yellow line would have deep-sixed. I know because it happened to me on a daytime TV show during a book tour. The hostess was talking about the teeny-tiny stone in her engagement ring, and I said, "It must be a recondite." You just can't say things like this around conventional women. Even though they don't get it, they still know that something was said, and that's all it takes for them to conclude, "You're making fun of me." W. was wise to stick with peanut butter and jelly on white: It's been tested.

The yellow line is woman at war with herself and it was squiggling through our cultural life long before Luntz put it on a screen. One daffodil-bright manifestation of it affected my book-reviewing career. In the early '80s I got my first review assignment from the *Philadelphia Inquirer*, and before the year was out I had eight papers calling me regularly. What began as a sideline turned into a full-time job that kept me too busy to write another book of my own for four years. I found out why when one of the literary editors explained why he called me. "We'd like to have more women reviewers but a lot of them don't work out because they can't bring themselves to attack a bad book. They pull their punches and bend over backwards to say something nice. But you don't."

The pundits who gather nightly to analyze the wildly fluctuating polls can't afford to be that blunt, but they must be thinking the truth even if they don't dare speak it. If you want to know why Bush is three points ahead of Gore on Tuesday and Gore is three points ahead of Bush on Wednesday, listen:

"I'm not going. They'll be angry with me, but I don't care. I've made up my mind. On the other hand, if I don't go they might think I'm angry with them. Not that I care, but . . . Oh, I might as well go. The only thing is, they'll think I'm worried about what they'd think if I didn't. Why should I care? That settles it—I'm not going. My mind's made up."

The typical woman voter is convinced that she makes up her mind based on "the issues," but in truth her overriding concern is who is most "personable." She should reflect on Mme de Staël's assessment of kindhearted Louis XVI, the last king of France: "When the people feel the need for political reform, the private qualities of the monarch are scarcely sufficient to halt the force of that impulse."

And while she's at it, she should also reflect that history's foremost family man was Czar Nicholas II.

November 6, 2000

I AM up that famous creek without a paddle. The deadline for this column falls two weeks before the election, but by the time you read it you will know who won. Now I know how the author of "The Lady or the Tiger?" felt. He solved his problem by ending the story just before the door opened, but I can't create suspense because you know something that I don't. The only way I can write around the last days of the autumn of our discontent is to let my mind range over political loose ends and see what I can tie up—i.e., free association.

I use "mind" advisedly. Yesterday they found me downtown, wandering around muttering, "If Al Gore wins, the only prescription drug I want is a cyanide capsule." A nice policeman brought me home. I calmed down for a while but I lost it again when I turned on American Movie Classics.

You know Al Gore has gotten to you when you're watching *Psycho* and all you can think about is what you wouldn't give for that high-flow shower head. No wonder Janet Leigh didn't hear the old lady come in. The water was rushing and cascading down on her in a deafening roar. So much water was jetting out so fast and furious that her blood washed right down the drain while she was still alive. Those were the good old days when showers worked faster than arteries, but now Leigh would empty before the tub did and Al Gore would take credit for it.

I never realized how monstrous Gore was until the debates. One reason for my delayed reaction is the obsession with Bill Clinton that has consumed conservatives for seven years, making the care and feeding of additional obsessions not only unnecessary but impossible. I was also sidetracked by the new female politics. Women are now expected to assess candidates according to which husband they remind us of, ex or current, but being a spinster automatically disqualified me for membership in the Wronged Caucus, encouraging my natural tendency to swim against the tide until I developed a mental block against considering the possibility that there had been any Al Gores in my life.

But suddenly, during the first debate, the mists of time parted and I found one. I hadn't thought about him for years. Not that I had forgotten him—no mental block could produce that degree of amnesia—but until that moment I had never made the connection between him and Al Gore.

It was 1955. Some of my sorority sisters cooked up a trip to an amusement park. They were all going steady but I wasn't, so they set about getting me a blind date. There was a consultation, then somebody said, "I hear he's really brainy. He'll be perfect for Flo."

He was so handsome it was hard to believe he was a blind date, but even harder to believe was the way he had dressed for a night on the midway. The other boys wore slacks and sports shirts but he wore a cream linen suit, white shirt and tie, fluted monogrammed handkerchief in his breast pocket, black-and-white laced wingtips, and a hat—a *hat* hat with a snap brim, colored band, and creased crown, made of soft summer straw.

He did all the things you do at amusement parks, but he did them differently. At the shooting gallery he pulled a plain handkerchief out of his pants pocket and draped it over his shoulder under the gun butt. At the test of strength he did limbering-up exercises, squatting and stretching his fingers like a concert pianist, until the crowd tittered. Tall and very well-built, he rang the bell, but he had made such an ass of himself that he came off as the 90-pound weakling instead of Charles Atlas. He reversed everything; it was as if he preferred the negative to the photograph.

When he bought cotton candy for us I held my breath, afraid he would ask for a knife and fork. At the merry-go-round, which he called a "carousel," he bypassed the prancing, proud-maned steeds and steered me over to a pair of ostriches, lifting me up onto the inside one. It was reversal time again: Nobody ever rode the ostriches. They were for "drips" and "squares," but now I was on one—sidesaddle.

He mounted the other and launched into an explanation of how a carousel works. It consisted of the usual stuff women have to listen to—gears, axles, valves, rotation—but soon a glottal tension crept into his voice, and with it a different vocabulary. What intrigued him about carousels, he said, was that on the surface all was sweetness and innocence, but "underneath" and "down below" and "in the darkness" under the revolving platform were "the bowels of the machine."

He pointed to the hole in the ostrich's neck that was sliding up and down on the brass pole, and said, "In and out, in and out, in and out."

Suddenly, he handed me his hat, pulled out another handkerchief, and jackknifed sideways until his head projected out over the platform's edge. He vomited quickly, wiped his mouth, and then sat up straight on his ostrich. Seconds later he did it again, stretching himself out like a trick rider until his body was parallel to the platform. It was bend, heave, wipe, resume seat; the cleanest, best-timed, most thoroughly calibrated barf I ever saw.

It happened so fast that few people even noticed him except some children behind us who said, "Oh, look at that man." I had been hearing these words all evening, but this time the tone was laudatory. Obviously unaware that he was throwing up, the kids thought he was a trick rider.

He gestured for his hat and I gave it to him. I was afraid he would make a pass later on but he did not. At 19 I couldn't psych him out, but I can now: It wasn't me he wanted to sodomize, it was that wooden ostrich.

And so now we have a new president. I hope it's the one with an instinctive appreciation of the great tradition of normal, fun-loving frat boys: Wait until you're at the top of the Ferris wheel, then everybody throw up at once.

November 20, 2000

I STILL don't know who's president. The deadline for this column is none other than Tuesday, November 7. I could wait and turn it in a couple of days late, but I have a Miss Goody Two-Shoes streak. Not as big as Al Gore's, but still big enough to make me loath to break my ten-year NR record of never missing a deadline. This way I can go on giving my supercilious sniff of "*I'm* never late" whenever the editors are slow sending me a galley proof.

Besides, I don't want the column hanging over my head while I watch the returns. I plan to spend all day Tuesday cooking so I can spend all night eating. Everything is from my *Passive Suicide Cook Book*: vichyssoise, Stroganoff, macaroni and cheese, and raspberry dumplings. I'd love to invite Ralph Nader to find out if he eats food. Whenever I start to admire him I remind myself that integrity without sensuality is just as bad as sensuality without integrity.

Speaking of sensuality, I'm wondering if the Gore Kiss will enter our tradition of instant traditions. According to the iron laws of American insecurity, what once is started cannot stop. Take the State of the Union message. Presidents used to send them up to the Hill to be read aloud by a clerk, but once Woodrow Wilson decided to deliver his in person, all subsequent presidents followed suit.

The tradition of instant traditions also governs bad taste. LBJ was the first to refer to his wife by her first name; Jimmy Carter was the first to hold hands with his, as well as the first to walk part of the way up Pennsylvania Avenue on Inauguration Day, and now they all do it. It's democracy's version of "the law of the Medes and Persians, which altereth not."

Will the Gore Kiss become de rigueur, at least for Democrats? Will non-kissers be accused of not loving their wives as much as Gore loves Tipper? And if so, how long before the Republicans cave? Probably no longer than it usually takes them to cave.

Tipper's situation is cause for alarm. He's been kissing her again at various campaign stops, sometimes to shouts of "Let's see the kiss!" One newspaper ran a front-page panel of photos showing him kissing her in three different places (i.e., geographic locations). If foreplay on the hustings becomes an instant tradition, Tipper will be remembered as the first political wife to be forced into the role of a Zola heroine, a woman aroused but left unsatisfied, the Thérèse Raquin of the whistlestop, consumed by pelvic furor as she gazes out over a sea of cheese-wedge hats in the middle of the night, somewhere in Wisconsin.

An aroused but unsatisfied woman is pitiable, but a man in the same condition is the last word in virility. Gore initially tried to use double entendres to pioneer male arousal as an instant tradition, but it takes a talent for indirection and understatement to put double entendres across. Tearing off his jacket and bellowing "I'm HOT!" at the top of his lungs didn't work, so he opted for frank tumescence, appearing on the cover of *Rolling Stone* with his

Dingell-Norwood so prominently outlined that they had to airbrush the front of his pants.

Meanwhile, Clinton posed for *Esquire* sprawled out like a male odalisque, his tie forming an arrow pointing to his Potus. Welcome to the future: Henceforth, in the cherished tradition of instant traditions, whenever Americans look at a presidential candidate we will see not only Tippecanoe, but Tyler too.

Another arena of instant tradition is the political gaffe. Since gaffes are inevitable, the candidate can only hope that his will be the lovable kind, like Truman's threat to beat up the music critic who panned his daughter's singing, or else the kind that enter the language and become titles for history books, like Harding's "normalcy."

This is exactly what W. pulled off. His malapropisms are, after all, a direct link to Mrs. Malaprop, Sheridan's most beloved character. He also crafted "More and more of our imports come from overseas" to go with Calvin Coolidge's "When a great many people are unable to find work, unemployment results." Best of all, he poached on the liberals' sacrosanct hunting ground: public television. His appearance in Florida, where a pumped-up, cheering audience inspired him to shout "This place is on fire!" in a crowded gym, was straight out of *Fawlty Towers*.

Gore's gaffes, on the other hand, are one of a kind, arising from an eldritch landscape of quicksand lakes that no one else would ever wade into. Typical is his reference to the "extra-chromosome Right" that has haunted him for six years. Everyone assumes he meant Down syndrome, but being a keeper of odd knowledge, it is much more likely that he meant the "criminal type" as defined by the 19th-century Italian physician Cesare Lombroso: brutish men with sloping foreheads and overlong arms whose XYY chromosome was thought to predispose them to violence. This is just the sort of thing Gore would know.

I believe his union-lullaby story. As a '60s college student he must have heard Pete Seeger's recording of old union songs. The only one that stood out was "Solidarity Forever," set to the tune of "The Battle Hymn of the Republic." The rest all sounded alike, as do Baptist hymns, barracks ballads, sea chanteys, and all the songs people sing when they're fired up, homesick, or drunk.

We can guess what happened. His parents, being Gores, were probably capable of singing union songs to a baby, and Al's speaking voice hints of tone deafness, which might also run in the family.

Whoever wins will need a defense against the media's gaffe patrol, so here it is:

Legions of intellectuals have poked fun at Louis XVI for writing the single word, *"Rien,"* or "nothing," in his diary on the page for July 14, 1789, the day the Bastille was stormed. It's supposed to prove how hopelessly stupid he was, but what his critics overlook is that it was not his personal diary but his hunt diary. Louis, who hunted every morning, merely meant that he hadn't bagged anything.

December 4, 2000

A MERICA is not a banana republic. We are a banana democracy, a system with all the problems of absolute monarchy and divine right but none of the benefits. Now we have our very own Lady Jane Grey, but we have no quick way to get rid of her, and we don't even know who she is yet.

At least I don't. The deadline for this column is the day after the Florida supreme court meets, but I am not going to wait and see what happens because I now have a reputation to consider. This is, you will recall, the third column on the election that I have written from a position of ignorance because of deadlines. In the first, I compared myself to the author of "The Lady or the Tiger?" while the second opened with the eerily prescient words, "I still don't know who's president." Now everybody at NR thinks I'm clairvoyant, so I decided to go ahead and write this mother because Madame Florenza waits for no one.

The most intriguing aspect of the Florida mess is Bill Clinton's unabashed joy in it. In a speech last week he yukked it up, saying, "The American people have spoken, we just don't know what they said yet." The words themselves were conventional enough, a solemn cliché paired with the kind of gentle irony we think of as Lincolnesque, but they were belied by his delivery and demeanor: A chuckle bubbled through his voice and his eyes sparkled with merry contempt. One-dimensional commentators will credit him with staying calm and upbeat, but Madame Florenza knows something they don't: He has found his legacy at last. That flash of glee revealed the far side of his self-centeredness in all its glory as, savoring the percolating constitutional crisis, he said to himself, "After me the deluge."

The movement for an easy-to-use national ballot will go nowhere because we already have an easy-to-use national ballot. The butterfly is now the most famous piece of paper in American history, displayed on TV so often in such intimate closeups that no voter could possibly make a mistake on one now. Also helpful is the sexual symbolism of chads. The hymen is back, and being discussed as obsessively as it was in girltalk circa 1953. There are intact chads, missing chads, and chads that are a little worn, proving that somebody has been fooling around. In girltalk this was called "Men can tell." In Florida it's called "Democrats can tell."

I see a Chadgate in the future. Somebody among the ballot counters—or more likely, some lawyer—is going to realize their souvenir value and start selling them to the millions of acephalics who go around saying "I want to be a part of history." First, though, we will be treated to McChad. Some counters are eating the little buggers, so it stands to reason as we now define it that chadophagiacs will be rounded up, charged with destroying evidence, and dosed with Metamucil—Mussolini's castor oil has no place in a democracy—so that Jimmy Carter can inspect the contents of their bed pans for undigested votes. These, known as "gentle chads," will become collector's items, as valuable as Ty Cobb baseball cards. Coincidentally, laxative stocks will take off and go through the roof, proving that a rising tide of crap lifts all boats.

If we must vote, we should go back to pottery shards. To extend the metaphor, the shattering has begun. My spirits tell me the Electoral College's days are numbered. The pundits currently pooh-poohing the possibility with glib assurances that "The small states will never stand for it" have obviously forgotten how the liberal meltdown works. Constitutional arguments will be drowned out by endless charges that the Electoral College is elitist, patriarchal, anti-majoritarian, and, of course, racist, since the same rich white males who fashioned it also counted blacks as three-fifths of a person. We will be bombarded by quotations from Hamilton about the danger of "popular passions" and Elbridge Gerry's warning about "the ignorance of the people." Jesse Jackson will word-search the *Federalist Papers* for every instance of "mob," while Maxine Waters will quote Fisher Ames's "All men are created equal but differ greatly in the sequel" to prove that supporters of the Electoral College oppose affirmative action.

By the time it's all over the floors of America will be covered with little grease spots, human chads that used to be us, rendered down now in the blast furnace of political correctness to the manageable deliquescence that liberals demand in a citizenry. It won't matter whether the floors are in populous New York or sparse Utah; once we have been browbeaten into pretending that the Electoral College contains 538 John Rockers, an amendment abolishing it will sail through, propelled by the winds of self-preservation.

This is all set forth in the Network Solutions commercial about the sociopathic roommate and the toothbrush that I kept seeing as I watched the Florida news.

A nice, polite, middle-class girl has answered the wrong ad and gotten a low-class slattern for a roommate. As she's watching TV, the slattern shuffles out of the bathroom, brushing her teeth. She stands directly in front of the nice girl, blocking her view. The nice girl peers around her and hintfully says "Hello?" but the slattern ignores her and continues brushing.

Suddenly an expression of horror crosses the nice girl's face. "Is that my toothbrush?" she exclaims. The slattern takes it out of her mouth, looks at it without interest, and says, "Yeah. Yeah, it is," and proceeds to scrub her tongue.

It ends happily with the nice girl starting her own online roommate-finder company, but otherwise it is a microcosm of life in America.

What can you do about the encroachment of thugs? What can you do when rights keep trumping restraints? What can you do about people who don't know how awful they are?

Nothing, because a bold peasantry, with gall a mile wide, when once unleashed, can never be denied.

December 18, 2000

DEAR Gentle Readers: Here it is, Christmas-letter time again. Usually I e-mail my columns to NR, but I'm having this one delivered in a Ryder truck. If they have a flat tire and I miss my deadline, I'll appeal to the International Court in The Hague.

The first order of business is choosing a famous quotation that best expresses my view of the past year. I found two. Naturally they're tied, so I'll give you both:

Catherine the Great on the wisdom of democracy: "How can shoemakers meddle in affairs of state?"

Bonaparte on the best way to settle a recount: "I found the crown of France in the gutter and picked it up on the tip of my sword."

Actually I have no business writing anything at this point because my mind is a jumbled mess from following the news. I tried to watch something else, but it's not that simple. One night when I checked the TV schedule for escapist fare, I found three movies about going crazy: *The Snake Pit*, starring Olivia de Havilland; *Frances*, starring Jessica Lange as the lobotomized actress Frances Farmer; and *Mister Buddwing*, in which James Garner loses his memory.

After all the straitjackets I was ready for a life jacket, so the next night I watched the second half of *Titanic*, timing it to miss the teenage romance and come in at the collision so I could tell myself that I was still following the news. A shipwreck is a shipwreck.

The special effects were breathtaking, but the aura of high school clung to the film like a barnacle. I'm still debating whether one incredible line was included for adolescent comic relief. The intrepid Al Gore, handcuffed to a post with water rising around him, tells the hysterical Tipper to go find something to free him. She doesn't want to be parted from him, but he assures her sweetly, "I'll be here when you get back." Does anyone doubt it? Lines like this are the heart and soul of har-har juvenile mirth. When Tipper returns with an ax and swings frantically at his chains, I half-expected her to chop off his hands by mistake and say "Oops."

It's been a memorable year for mail. Judging from the sheer volume of letters I received, your favorite column was the one in which I said the women's vote is killing us. Everybody agreed with me! Interestingly, the most fervent supporters were other women, but female masochism was nowhere in evidence. Usually, when a writer slams women, the kick-me-again crowd invariably chimes in, but there was none of that. One reader said she would gladly give up her right to vote if it would get Nita Lowey out of Congress and Margaret Carlson off the tube.

At the other end of the scale, my Elián column drew exactly three favorable replies, plus lots of travel advice ("Go back to Cuba!"), and what has to be a first: a charge of encouraging incest. I'm still trying to figure it out.

I got lots of interesting general letters as well. One came from a student who wanted to know why I never write about foreign policy. Write about it? I don't even read about it unless it concerns England, in which case it's not foreign.

I was also cast as Ann Landers by a lovelorn reader who asked for advice on how to survive a grand passion, and a computer expert who said he admired my quips and wordplays and wanted some tips on how to do it so he could banish his inner techie and be popular at parties. I hated having to tell him it was too late. The way to "do what *you* do," as he called it, is to graduate from college qualified to do nothing except crossword puzzles in ink. The way to do that is to take courses whose catalog descriptions kick off with "The flowering of . . ." Especially if they're French lit., which they usually are. Also sign up for "Symbolism in . . ." and "Little-known aspects from . . ." Chart your future like this and you'll be able to quip your little heart out.

I fear I was too discouraging, though, so I'm going to do a column especially for him: an outline for a book called *The War of the Spanish Succession for Dummies.* I was going to use this war last year to send up Pat Buchanan's book, *A Republic, Not an Empire*, calling mine *A Brou, Not a Ha-Ha*, but Pat has faded from the scene now. I only hope that Bay Buchanan has faded along with him. Not many guys have a sister like that, as Cesare Borgia used to say.

Now for my news. I'm puffed in the much-discussed liberal-conversion book *How I Accidentally Joined the Vast Right-Wing Conspiracy (and Found Inner Peace)* by former *Esquire* writer Harry Stein, who said nice things about me and NR on page 60.

I was the subject of the *New York Times* Sunday acrostic on September 24. I was thrilled, though it was downright eerie when I realized it was spelling out my name. I was stuck on it and almost ready to give up when it hit me. The quote they chose, from one of my old books, is not one of my better sentences, but I won't complain.

I was chosen for inclusion in *Who's Who of American Women*, the Millennium Edition. I didn't buy a copy because I can think of better uses for $200. Besides, owning your own reference books strikes me as unseemly; too much like the baronet in *Persuasion*, who kept his copy of *Debrett*'s open to his page on the hall table where everybody was sure to see it. By the way, remember to say "of" American women. The usual Who's Who preposition is "in," but they can't very well use that here, though if they did the entries probably would be a lot longer.

I'm pleased to announce that the new year will feature a new show, *Madame Florenza Predicts*, on The NATIONAL REVIEW Psychic Network. The schedule isn't firmed up yet, but I'm in line for a 3:30 A.M. slot after the infomercial for inflatable scooters. I taped the first segment today so I'll give you a sneak preview:

At W.'s Inauguration on January 20, Al Gore will pull out a gun and try to shoot himself, but won't be able to get the trigger lock off.

December 31, 2000

2001

S HOOT if you must this old gray head, but don't disenfranchise me. The correct word is *disfranchise*. As a woman who favors the repeal of the Nineteenth Amendment, I want that "en" out of there before they do it to me. It's like saying "inextrovert" for introvert.

Well, the election has been decided—"expeditiously," to use another Florida-generated word. It means allowing plenty of time for everybody to become a part of history.

"It's history and we're all here," said the party of vacationers at the Tallahassee courthouse. "We're waiting for history," said the man dug in for a vigil with wife, kids, and mother-in-law. The atmosphere was positively St. Crispin's Day-ish: whole families camped out in front of marble porticos, pointing to the youngest member and declaiming, "Some day his grandchildren will tell their grandchildren what he told them about being here and remembering this."

The locution that struck me was "Years from now . . ." It had a familiar rhythm, like a perfect wave carrying me back to some history of my own. It eluded me until somewhere around the 517th man-in-the-portico interview, when I remembered. It was Deborah Kerr's curtain line in *Tea and Sympathy*, when she gives herself to the sensitive schoolboy to prove to him that he is not the homosexual her macho husband has made him out to be. Unfastening just the top button of her sweater, she sits down on his bed and says: "Years from now, when you talk about this—and you will . . . be kind." Critics of Katherine Harris's mascara, take note.

Even professionals like GOP recount observer Bobby Burchfield saw himself as a fly on the wall. "This is history," he said earnestly. "This is an important juncture not just in this election cycle, but in history. I felt strongly enough about it [that I dropped] my plans for the weekend and came here."

The spectacle of Americans trying to hot-wire themselves into connectedness with their own country somehow does not bode well, but then what does? Anybody with stock in American Bode-Well would be wise to sell it. Nor will things be any different a hundred years from now, because dragging kids into the shadow of Corinthian columns and barking, "Remember this or I'll knock your block off," is simply at odds with the realities of the juvenile memory process.

There are two things to consider. First, the ability to notice and store vivid details during historic moments is adversely affected by having to pee, a priority that can wipe out whole chunks of speeches, vigils, assassinations, and coronations ("What king?") without a trace.

Second, children never remember what they're supposed to remember, but instead latch maniacally onto some minor detail that drives adults wild. As proof I offer the Pearl Harbor Finger. Everybody in my kindergarten remembered Pearl Harbor, but the impact of turning points, ends of eras, and days of infamy never got through to us. What was seared on our minds was the photo that ran over and over in newsreels and newspapers, and still shows up in WWII documentaries to this day: the *Arizona* blowing up, and in the upper right-hand corner a man's index finger pointing toward the mouth of the harbor.

We wanted to know whose finger it was. That's *all* we wanted to know. Like Baby Snooks whining, "Why, Daddy?" we plagued our parents without mercy. They told us it was probably someone directing the photographer's attention to another shot, but that wasn't enough. We wanted his name, and did he know his finger was in the picture, and did he mind, and what was he pointing at? Multiply my kindergarten by all the other kindergartens in America in 1941 and you will have a clear idea of what being a part of history is all about. If AARP polled their 65-year-old members on what we remember best about Pearl Harbor, the overwhelming answer would be our fathers yelling, "To hell with the finger!"

It's a cert that what today's children will remember about Indecision 2000 is the cross-eyed recounter. Did he see two votes instead of one? Was he born cross-eyed, or did he get that way from looking through little holes? If his eyes crossed all of a sudden, did he get sick to his stomach and throw up on the chads? Will he still be a part of history if the doctor uncrosses his eyes? *Why, Daddy?*

Indecision 2000 was a boon to teachers, who were thrilled when their students expressed enthusiasm for studying the Electoral College. Lesson plans were revised to meet popular demand and the the long count was praised as "a great civics lesson."

That doesn't bode well either. The way to understand the Electoral College is not to study it but to feel it, to close your eyes and let it wash over you in a great rushing torrent of Americanness, and then sit back and celebrate it as a national eccentricity.

National eccentricities are the cornerstone of national identity. The Electoral College is to us what cricket is to the English, something that we know in our pores but can't explain to outsiders without making it more complicated than it already is. Out of this failure to communicate grows the sweet fruit of cultural pride. The English are never more happily English than when they can announce, "It's quite simple actually," as a prelude to explaining cricket. The same is true of Germans explaining why their unreadable script is easy to read, or the French explaining why their unnecessary verb tenses are necessary. It's a subtle way of boasting to outsiders that *we* are crazy but *you* are not.

National eccentricities bind a people together and forge the connectedness Americans crave without requiring them to spend the night in a sleeping bag before a marble portico, waiting for something to tell their grandchildren. As a country given to conformity, we don't have enough national eccentricities, but at least we have the Electoral College—so we should guard it well. Don't end it, don't even mend it, because it gives history something to remember us by.

January 22, 2001

T HE other day I made a phone call to reschedule an appointment with a new optician. I sensed something memorable was going to happen as soon as I heard the receptionist's voice. It was trite and flat, incapable of expressing joy or sorrow, excitement or serenity, aversion or ardor: the voice that people imitate when they say, "Duh."

Lo and behold, that's exactly what she effectively said in our ensuing exchange.

"What did you say your name was?"

"King."

"How do you spell that?"

It was a first. I've been through some rough patches in my time, but they were eased by certain small advantages life has dealt me. One is my name. Among the auxiliary reasons why I never married (never mind the main one) is that I hated to give up a path-smoother like King. Many people spend their lives correcting the spelling and pronunciation of their names, and it's hard work, but in this, at least, I've always belonged to the leisure class.

If his receptionist couldn't spell King, what was the optician who hired her like? I wouldn't trust these baby bloodshots to just anybody, to paraphrase Lynda Carter, so instead of rescheduling the appointment I canceled it.

The receptionist was the most extreme example of a human posthole I've yet encountered, but by no means the only one. The Invasion of the Duh People is upon us. Duhs are at the gates, and usually on the telephone. They seem to cluster in that mangled universe known as Customer Service—assigning order numbers, straightening out exchanges and returns, and computing state sales taxes. Our calls are very important to them, which is why I dread buying, subscribing, complaining, or inquiring about anything whatsoever.

Take my catalog order. In the "Color" block I wrote "1st choice, blue; 2nd, green," but all I got was a postcard saying, "We are unable to fill your order. Please call our toll-free number." I did. When the rep came on, I gave her my order number and she pulled it up on her computer and read my name and address back to me. "Right," I said.

Then, silence. A long silence. I thought she had put me on hold but there was no rock music, and it didn't sound like hold somehow. The silence had a nice antiquated sound, making me think of the days when a clerk simply laid the phone down and "stepped away from her desk" to retrieve an actual file from an actual file cabinet.

As my reverie faded, I had an eerie feeling that she was still there. "Hello?" I said.

"Yes." Just that, no more, not even an inflection.

"I got a card saying you're unable to fill my order but it doesn't say why."

"We didn't know what color you wanted."

Nearly two minutes had passed in total silence, yet she had sat there in ox-like placidity, waiting for me to speak first, unable even to bring herself to prompt me. I had to supply all the initiative.

Then there's newspaper delivery. To a Duh, my Sunday-only subscription and my neighbor's weekday-only subscription must be the same subscription, so they placed mine at his door. When, six phone calls later, I finally convinced them that I was the Sunday subscriber, they started putting his at my door. This way, the whole block gets to watch two people stealing each other's newspapers.

Smart people work in Customer Service too, but there's no way to be sure of getting one, and less chance of keeping one. Follow-through is a thing of the past at the "communication centers" where Customer Service reps are stabled. When you call you must talk to whoever answers. If you get a smart one and ask for her name so you can call her back, she'll just say, "Anyone here can help you." But you never get the same person twice, so each time you have to start at the beginning and tell the same story all over again. Take, for instance, my charge-card snafu involving two secret code numbers based on my birthday and one based on my mother's. It makes less and less sense with each telling, so if you happen to draw a Duh late in the game, the result is two Duhs.

I T'S one thing to have a Duh IQ; quite another to have a Duh attitude, like the interviewees in Jay Leno's sidewalk surveys who grin proudly when they have trouble placing James Madison. Leno's use of the Duh attitude as popular entertainment recalls a wildly popular '40s radio offering, *It Pays To Be Ignorant*, a bent quiz show whose theme song went: "It pays to be ignorant, to be dumb, to be dense, to be ignorant, it pays to be ignorant just like me!"

This was such a playground favorite that teachers tried to ban it. At my school you got sent to the principal for singing it, but it spoke too clearly to American ideals ever to be entirely squelched. It's still being sung by such devotees of the Duh attitude as New York governor George Pataki, who derided Hillary for quoting E. B. White during her senatorial campaign.

"Mrs. Clinton," he huffed, "quoted some guy, Wyatt or somebody—I don't think he was from Brooklyn—with some definition of a New Yorker that she must have read somewhere. I don't know who that guy was. I don't know what he wrote. . . . I don't think people from Brooklyn or Peekskill would have quoted that person."

If America were ancient China this would be the Duh Dynasty, but instead of Duh vases and Duh figurines we produce Duh Republicans—they prefer "populists"—who are forever reaching out to "the real people" with the boastful assurance that it pays to be ignorant. If Pataki ever wants to read something somewhere, let it be James T. Farrell's *A World I Never Made*. He will meet Al O'Flaherty, a shanty-Irish traveling salesman from the South Side of Chicago who longs to be a gentleman. To that end he carries his well-thumbed copy of *Letters of Lord Chesterfield* everywhere he goes, quoting from it to prostitutes to reassure them that he'll treat them right.

Al O'Flaherty would break your heart. I don't know about Pataki's.

February 5, 2001

T HE beauty of coming out for the repeal of the Nineteenth Amendment is that I am now at liberty to say "I have a feeling something is going to happen" without worrying about compromising my feminist credentials.

There's a lot to be said for casting off the shackles of logic and reveling in the freedom of female intuition. When men do it they call it "listening to your gut," which allows them to feel tough and realistic as they work in mysterious ways, but women have no compunctions about letting the psychic vibes rock on without restraint, so I'll follow suit.

I waited until after the Inauguration to write this to see if it would shake me out of my mood, to no avail. My sense that the Bush presidency is starcrossed did not budge.

I've had it since election night, when the first hints that something was wrong emerged as though from a script crafted by a master dramatist who has foreshadowing down to a science. Why wouldn't Gore get out of his car? What was making Bush late for his victory rally? And then there was that bleak autumnal rain that began falling in Austin after we learned what had happened. The deserted plaza littered with soggy abandoned signs was nothing less than film noir.

Florida provided just enough comic relief to heighten the tension. As Gore, already established as an odd duck, moved closer to obsession, we had nightly debates about what he would "do" if he lost—"do" being a euphemism for going insane or committing suicide. And if it happened, what of his enraged "base," who gave him 93 percent of their vote? What would they "do"? Nobody spelled that out either, but it was taken to mean what it usually means.

After the Supreme Court stopped the Florida recounts and W. won the Electoral College, I started a count of my own to see how many times the words "Gore won the popular vote" would be spoken and written. I lasted all of two days before it became clear that I couldn't keep up without a full-time staff of elves.

Letters to the editor, talk radio, the-man-in-the-street, and political shout-show regulars all pounded it home. "Gore won the popular vote by 500,000" was given in thousands at first, until the bigger-sounding "half a million" took hold. Then it was reversed to "Bush lost the popular vote by half a million." Liberals questioned his "legitimacy," nicknamed him "President-select," coined "Hail to the Thief," and vowed never to accept him as "their" president.

Then Bill Clinton publicly proclaimed Gore the real winner and thanked Bill Daley for running a victorious campaign. After that, Tom Brokaw could pull out all the stops in his snide interview with W., needling him about losing the popular vote, asking if he wanted to hide under the bedcovers on Inauguration Day, and warning darkly, "No president can govern without the consent of the people."

Commentator Tony Blankley characterized this pummeling as "brutal disdain" and predicted that unless Bush strikes back, "we will face the most vehement political disorder since the years leading up to the Civil War."

I don't know whether Blankley was listening to his gut, but he was certainly listening to mine because I have a feeling that all hell is going to break loose.

Blankley's Civil War comparison is an apt one. A measure of just how close to the edge we are is the sudden rebirth of the Abolitionist movement. You know it can't be long now when the attorney general-designate states under oath that he wouldn't dream of joining the Confederate army, while over in the other hearing room the Interior designee is denying that slavery is the jewel in the crown of states' rights. If you did a freeze frame of the entire Bush team at any given moment, every third member would be caught in the midst of saying "Slavery is abhorrent"—the 21st century's first administration posing in a living tableau of William Lloyd Garrisons and Harriet Beecher Stowes.

Calling slavery abhorrent is the last way left to refute liberal charges of racism, but it is leading them into a trap. If they keep on saying it they will be forced to back reparations; otherwise they will be accused of believing that slavery isn't so abhorrent after all.

Only Houdini could get out of this one, but he's not about to help because it was Houdini who got them into it in the first place. Bill Clinton intends to hang over W.'s presidency like the sword of Damocles, waiting for a chance to be the Comeback Kid. Maybe he can't be Mr. President again—maybe—but the big cheese by any other name would smell as sweet.

A former president, like a deposed monarch, is a rallying point for discontent. In the past, newly crowned kings understood that deposed monarchs had to be gotten rid of, but democracy is a poor substitute for *lettres de cachet* and iron masks. Clinton is now in the same position as the Duke of Windsor in the 1930s: ungone and not forgotten. The unemployed duke was much on the mind of Hitler, who had the idea of restoring him to the throne as England's first Nazi king. But Americans are citizens, not subjects. We don't do royal titles, so if all hell does break loose on W.'s watch and Clinton mounts the Short March from Georgetown to take power, we will have the first warm, friendly Director of Public Safety in history.

If you think a coup can't happen here, consider how the last few elections have accustomed Americans to political happenstance. Carter won because Ford was an appointed president—a nephew adopted by a Roman emperor. Bush the Elder won because he really ran for Reagan's third term. Clinton got his toe in the door because of Perot, and W. won because Gore was a weirdo. As a result, we have the Undecided Voter, in reality the catatonic voter who would rather freeze than decide. Add our 40-year celebration of "civil disobedience" that has jettisoned the civil and kept only the disobedience, and you have what are called "ripe conditions."

Just a feeling . . .

February 19, 2001

THE ultimate test of a civilization's collective character is the value it places on idiosyncratic forms of honor. Ours were on heartening display in the public's reaction to the eleventh-hour kleptomania committed by departing Clintonians aboard Air Force One. More Americans were more shocked by the theft of silverware, dishes, and blankets than ever cared about Monica, Whitewater, and Chinagate combined.

The citizens of Fall River, Massachusetts, reacted the same way when Lizzie Borden was accused of shoplifting twelve years after being acquitted of double homicide. You know God's in His heaven and all's right with the world when rock-ribbed Yankees shake their heads and grumble, "Murder is one thing, but . . ."

Thomas De Quincey understood this phenomenon. In his essay "Murder Considered as One of the Fine Arts," he wrote: "If once a man indulges himself in murder, very soon he comes to think little of robbing; and from robbing he comes next to drinking and Sabbath-breaking, and from that to incivility and procrastination."

In other words, little things mean a lot because they are the things that most people can readily understand. As with all motivations to good behavior, this one is a matter of pride. Knowing ourselves to be incapable of crime on a really titanic scale, we harbor a corresponding dread of being exposed as petty criminals. We might not have the brains or the guts to pull off murder or extortion, but we're by-God not going to get caught swiping pillowcases and suffer the embarrassment of everybody knowing that we think small.

However, if somebody else gets caught swiping pillowcases, our dormant self-disgust suddenly awakens and "reaches out," as Republicans say.

Psychiatrists use the term "projection" to describe the human urge to punish people who remind us of the least flattering aspects of ourselves.

The sure knowledge, evident to all by now, that we will never see the end of Bill Clinton is building up a massive sense of frustration in the country. It would help if an example were made of his light-fingered minions, but the Bushies don't seem to know it, or else are ignoring it.

The absence of righteous wrath on the part of the new administration is a big letdown. Between Air Force One thievery and the sophomoric destruction and defacement of White House property, I was sure that our long national nightmare of compassionate conservatism was finally over, but instead of ending with a bang it is proceeding with the old familiar whimper.

Asked about Bush's reaction to the trashing of the White House, Ari Fleischer said, "He does not consider it a personal affront." The copiers are spitting out cartoons of him as Alfred E. Neuman talking dirty and he doesn't consider it a personal affront?

Fleischer, who is fast shaping up as the man I'm going to love to hate, is a virtuoso on the humility horn, his boss's favorite instrument, which he tooted in a passage of triple-tonguing that approached incoherence: "The president understands that transitions can be times of difficulty and strong emotion. And he's going to approach it in that vein. The question is, Do you have [to] blame somebody in this town? . . . President Bush is not going to come to Washington for the point of blaming somebody in this town. And it's a different way of governing; it's a different way of leading."

Bush's refusal to lower the boom on the Klepto Klintonians is winning him love in all the wrong places, such as the *Washington Post*. Columnist William Raspberry, who never writes about class differences except to condemn them, promptly donned a powdered wig to write: "Bush's no-prosecution decision is both more elegant and more gracious. If this is a class war, then it's the Bush people who are displaying all the class."

This is the kind of self-image that kept Bush the Elder in a state of paralysis. There are only so many battles we can remain above before the enemy decides that we won't fight. Moreover, the compliment has no basis in fact. Aristocrats, being imperious, have a short fuse—witness Coriolanus continually exploding at the plebeians whose votes he must court in his run for consul, at one point even berating them for having halitosis ("You common cry of curs! whose breath I hate"). But we live in democratic times, and "aristocrat" is defined accordingly: It now means someone so polite that he takes crap without protest.

Speaking of class, I have a thought about the stripping of Air Force One.

It might not have happened, at least on such a grand scale, if the presidential seal were not plastered all over everything. It's one thing to have it on the china used for formal White House banquets, but whose idea was it to put it on tote bags, baseball caps, coffee mugs, playing cards, pens, coasters, and bedding?

Could it be someone whose instincts were formed in the class dedicated to the proposition that more is more? The class that can't leave a plain surface alone? The class that sticks skid daisies in the bathtub and wood-burnt signs on the mailbox? If you've got it, don't flaunt it, as the late George Apley would say, but that same someone might even have the presidential seal tattooed on a part of his person that he has been known to flaunt.

Meanwhile, Bush continues to fit himself into democracy's definition of an aristocrat. His latest effort, a presidential first, is tagging along on the opposition's policy retreat. "Some may think I'm naïve to want to rid the system of rancor," he is reported to told have the Dems, "but that's my intent." To angry Republicans he advised, as Tom Delay paraphrased it, "Get over it, guys. Let's not hold any hard feelings. Ashcroft was confirmed. I didn't like the way he was treated. Ashcroft didn't like the way he was treated. But so what? Let's move on."

We're in put-it-behind-us-and-move-forward mode again, a daunting feat when you think about it, recalling that passage in the Bible where somebody "tied his ass to a tree and walked thirty leagues."

March 5, 2001

T HE words "new neurosis" are oxymoronic because the tics and twitches of humankind are eternal. They are also universal, so imagine my joy on finding a twofer: a virgin forest of deadly nightshade with a signpost reading "Only in America."

It's so new they don't even have a name for it yet. Calling it "collecting" or "hoarding," as two recent newspaper features did, is a pathetic understatement. The world has always had collectors—John Fowles wrote a bestselling novel about one—and there are so many people who never throw anything out that they long ago acquired a name: pack rats.

Psychologists who have begun studying call it "OCD," for "obsessive-compulsive disorder," but that pales beside the behavior involved, which is to "disorder" as Bill Clinton is to "fib." Yes, this really is a new neurosis, and so American that the best way to describe it is to lapse into the literary style of Helen Gurley Brown. It's about people who *never* throw *anything* out, who save *everything*, no matter how icky-sticky-poo-poo it is, until somebody calls the *Health Department*!!!

To call such people slobs is to miss the point. Slobs might be messy but they also have a social life, so that when a big date is looming they pull themselves together and neaten up. OCDs, on the other hand, don't have to worry about what people will think because nobody can get in the house, including firemen.

Open the front door and you risk being buried under a landslide of old newspapers. The house is literally packed to the rafters with a mountain range of stuff that normal people throw out. The OCD navigates around it by a series of narrow cleared paths, like the trenches of World War I, past old Christmas trees, stacks of unopened junk mail, empty blister packs that once held baloney and batteries, used printer ribbons (and predating them, used typewriter ribbons), hundreds of expired grocery coupons, plastic forks that come with take-out food, TV-dinner trays, margarine tubs, pieces of broken dishes, burned-out light bulbs, and in some extreme cases, old cigarette butts, used paper napkins, and even used toilet paper.

It's shaping up into a great little mental-health crisis, complete with the usual exculpatory language. It is estimated that OCD afflicts some 2 million Americans, undoubtedly of all races and creeds, but this figure is probably low because OCD is, of course, underreported. Its victims almost never seek treatment, naturally, so only about 5 percent come to light, usually through health violations or eviction.

The problem, needless to say, goes back to their childhoods; most lived in a home with a hoarder and learned bad choices. OCD can be treated, but not with force, like the man who rented an industrial Dumpster and backed it up to his mother's door. Nor does it do any good to offer to help them clear out the mess because they have to reread all the expired coupons. They might also start "churning"—the psychologists' term for moving their detritus from one pile to another to fake tossing it out.

Treatment consists of a long, slow program in which the threatening subject of throwing things away is never mentioned. Instead the facilitator emphasizes the importance of understanding their motivations, taking them on visits to dumps and yard sales, guiding them through a series of mental exercises until they lose their fear of making decisions and develop what will no doubt be called "discarding skills." At the end they mark their successes with little signs reading "This is a flat, clear surface."

But they still won't understand themselves and consequently will slide back into chaos because neither they nor their earnest facilitators will admit that America is the root cause of their behavior:

1. Nowadays, being ready and willing to make a decision about *anything* is all it takes to be called "judgmental."

2. There's a name for thinking that a torn dishrag is worth keeping. It's called "equality."

3. When the word "inclusion" is rammed home in every public statement, some people will develop a warped need to see how much they can include. OCDs are merely insuring that no blister pack is left behind.

4. They harbor a repressed, politically incorrect lust for revenge on the criminal class and OCD is an acceptable form of emotional displacement: They know that if a rapist managed somehow to get inside their houses, he would be suffocated in a barrel of plastic bags or impaled on a splintered mop handle.

Articles about OCD fill me with hungry glee because I have the opposite neurosis: obsessive-compulsive spartanism (OCS). So does one of my favorite novelists, Kathleen Winsor, who described our common persuasion to perfection:

> What a relief it was to have anything done, finished, over with for good. So you could throw it out of your life and forget it and go on to something new. Some of her happiest moments had been spent cleaning out closets or drawers, throwing things away, knowing that whatever the symbolism they had had for her, she was destroying it. Each time she finished with something or someone and knew that she had finished forever, it gave her in some sense the illusion of having been granted a new beginning to life."

Whether it be possessions or people, my motto is "The more there is, the more there is." I ache to hang a "This is a flat, clear surface" sign on the whole world. Give me a box of big green garbage bags and a baling hook and I'm one happy misanthrope. Now that I've donated nearly all of my literary papers, my surroundings are acquiring that impersonal emptiness I've always craved. But it's still not enough, so I've decided to start my own disorderly-house consultation service for OCDs. It won't interfere with my writing; in fact, it will help it by keeping my name in front of the public via my website: www.letmeatyourFKinghouse.com.

March 19, 2001

I HAD never even heard of Dale Earnhardt until he crashed into eternity, but now here I am writing a column about him. What a country!

The outpouring of grief began at once, but this time there were some telling differences. The emotional pitch rose into the Diana–JFK Jr. range, but it was regional, confined mostly to the South, making it impossible for cultural optimists to say, "It brought us together." Another difference lay in the spontaneous memorial: There were no piles of teddy bears on sidewalks. This inadvertently tasteful oversight owes itself to Earnhardt's ruthless reputation as "The Intimidator" and his custom of calling anyone who was not a psychopath a "candyass." Teddy bears, like sidewalks, moved him not.

Instead of the usual static mountain of maudlin bibelots, Earnhardt's spontaneous memorial took the form of motion as some 300 of his mourners turned the Capital Beltway into a stock-car lap and circled once around D.C., a distance of 62 miles. Said one participant: "It's giving back a little of what he gave," which was precisely what the three police jurisdictions involved were worried about. In view of the number of souped-up cars in the solemn cortege, Maryland and Virginia state troopers provided a motorcycle escort to keep the speed down to 25 mph.

Held in the misty rain of a Sunday pre-dawn, it gave off a creepiness not usually found in celebrity wakes. Black, his racing color, predominated, from a row of empty black hats lined up on a dashboard like a headsman's display, to the black balloons held by sleepy children. One man drove an exact replica of Earnhardt's black death car. Another had a doll dressed as Earnhardt in his passenger seat. Another held up his $999 platinum replica of Earnhardt's car as if it were a chalice and made the somber pronouncement, "Auto racing has lost its Elvis. The king is dead." Earnhardt's Number 3, like an updated symbol of the Trinity, was on everything, and when the cortege had run its course, the trucker who organized it told the *Washington Post*: "We're going to try to make this an annual event to keep the memory of him alive."

It was a Black Mass choreographed by Stephen King, lacking only background music from *Carmina Burana*. Stock-car fans, being country-music fans, don't know about *Carmina Burana*, however, so the more polished among us took up the slack.

The most unexpected tribute came from the most polished man in America, MSNBC anchor Brian Williams, himself a stock-car enthusiast and a friend of Earnhardt. Williams's remarks in *Time* had the touching simplicity that comes from controlled writing, but he stood alone. Other eulogists went overboard.

Washington Times columnist Suzanne Fields declared that Earnhardt "did what he did because he had to" and "never forgot his roots"; extolled him for "testing the limits," and compared him to the abstract artist Jackson Pollock, the "anti-hero" who was beset by "demons," yet remained "authentic."

Writing in the *Wall Street Journal*, Brock Yates announced that he does not mourn Earnhardt: "After all, who among us is blessed to die in front of millions of fans, without pain, engaged in an activity that produces wealth, fame, and immortality? . . . Who could go out on a more soaring emotional high?" If the essence of sport is courage, Yates maintained, "he died a noble death."

He did nothing of the sort. He died plastered with ads. He was Goodyear and Winston and Budweiser and Jiffy-Lube and Pennzoil and Coca-Cola and all the other products whose decals were sewn on his suit and stuck on his car, a man turned into a walking billboard named Dale Earnhardt.

This latest catharsis, like all the other wakes and pilgrimages we have come to call Outpourings of Grief, is yet more proof of America's incurable irony deficiency. To understand what we are doing to ourselves, take a look at what neoclassical scholar John J. Enck had to say: "Reason itself, as the 17th century regarded it, tends to unearth in even the most personal and intense suffering, ironies whose very recognition furnishes a sardonic strength."

In other words, solace awaits those who can tell the difference between what they think they are doing and what they actually are doing.

Take the lap around the Capital Beltway: Several hundred racing freaks, all secretly yearning to be what their class of Southerners calls "badass," imitating the chief activity of the trapped family man who spends his life commuting to the female-dominated suburbs, all to honor the thrice-married Earnhardt, who kept his stock cars in an isolated rural compound uxoriously named the "Garage Mahal."

The intensity of the Earnhardt requiem alarmed polished Americans, because it reminded them of the spirit of the '60s, when it was fashionable to condemn "our Anglo-Saxon repression." When Earnhardt's mourners, who are overwhelmingly Anglo-Saxon, proved to be as unrepressed as everybody else, the polished class knew a tendril of fear at the realization that there are now no repressed people left. To vanquish their fear, they lent their voices to Earnhardt's elegiac chorus to placate all those new-minted Anglo-Saxon hysterics.

There is real cause to be afraid of the unrepressed. "The deepest of all human anxieties," said Anna Freud, "is to be at the mercy of one's own impulses." Nobody would dare call for stoicism now, but people know that emotion can snap and reverse course in a heartbeat. By "opening up" we have opened ourselves up to unrelenting insecurity, and it's due to get worse.

The rage that forms the flip side of grief is destined to provide us with an alternative to "suicide by cops." The next time a celebrity dies and the side-walk memorials spring up, go stand in front of a teddy-bear cairn and run down the dead celebrity. You'll be torn to pieces. Guaranteed.

April 2, 2001

FROM time to time over the past few years, I have heard from people who wrote to congratulate me for providing a mailing address instead of an e-mail address at the bottom of this page.

Their letters invariably gave off a tone composed of equal parts of "we happy few," "us against the world," and "hold the fort," and slipped easily into a cantankerous grumble that instantly identified them as the work of a type familiar to anyone who writes for a conservative audience: Luddites, who hate anything and everything new simply because it's new.

Judging by my latest trip to the post office the other day, a new mood has taken hold. This time I got three letters in a single batch of mail, each thanking me for the mailing address in almost plangent terms, without a trace of Luddite grumbling. In fact, all three letters fairly throbbed with weary gratitude.

One correspondent got carried away, taking my P.O. Box as evidence of an exalted level of virtue on my part, saying, "I'll bet you don't even have e-mail." It reminded me of an incident in my teens when a man silenced the audible cussing of his buddies for my benefit, explaining, "I can tell you're not that kind of girl."

Actually I was, I just didn't look it. By the same token, I do have e-mail, but I save it for marriage—i.e., NATIONAL REVIEW. It's how I get this column into their computer, bicker with my editor over commas, and nag him for a galley.

The three mailing-address letters stuck in my mind and got me to won-dering why my P.O. Box came to be transformed into an Edenic niche. As any writer will confirm, getting three letters on the same subject on the same day means you have struck a nerve worth writing about. I told myself there had to be a column in it somewhere and, lo and behold, here it is.

High-tech living has thrust us all into an inescapable state of terror and revulsion that is wearing us out. The ease of computers and the instantaneous reach of fax machines are all well and good, but they are so sensitive and complex that each time we turn them on we brace ourselves, heads cocked like paranoid maniacs, listening for the various hums and buzzes and ding-a-lings to judge whether they sound the way they usually do. If they don't, we go into instant nervous prostration and give vent to the *cri de coeur* of the helpless, cringing souls we have become: "It's doing something different!"

At such times we get an Error Message, which is much worse than hearing a good honest clunk or snap, or even an explosion. At least back when things simply "broke," as it was called, you could understand what happened and why. During the typewriter era when I wrote for *Cosmopolitan*, I used so many italics that one day the underline key broke. It just fell right off. I heard the metallic clatter and saw it lying in the bottom of the machine and fished it out. If I had had the right tools I could have put it back on myself, but nowadays eyesight and common sense will get you nowhere, and the occasional successful poke with nail files and bobby pins is a thing of the past. The very concept of brokenness is gone. The computers our lives depend on "freeze" or "crash" but they never break.

We do. The psychological wounds inflicted by high-tech are the stuff of daily life now.

1. Whenever we have a technical problem, we always assume that our own equipment is at fault. It never occurs to us that the other infernal machine we are trying to connect with might be doing something different, or that the billions of tiny wires and chips in the telecom center might be doing something different as well. Thus, self-blame, followed by self-pity, are the personality traits most likely to develop in low-tech people in high-tech times. Poe had his raven, Coleridge had his albatross, and Thompson had his Hound of Heaven. At least they got some immortal lines out of their agony, but all we can show for ours is "It's doing something different!"

2. Conservatives like to think that the old republican virtues will return if only we make government small and unobtrusive, but in truth, self-reliance and Yankee ingenuity don't have a chance when people no longer have the confidence to snarl, "What the hell is wrong with this goddamn thing!" The respect accorded computers is so total you can almost hear the hush. They are the first invention Americans have been afraid to tinker with; the adventurous experiment on-screen and become proficient hackers, but taking a computer apart "to see how it works" is an idea whose time has gone. As a result, we are becoming a people who are losing sight of what tinkerers used to call the "big picture," voluntarily arranging ourselves into a majority class of computerized helots in thrall to a small priestly class of techno-snot Druids.

3. High-tech is hell on women, forcing us into the worst kind of regression. We used to play dumb when the subject turned to cars and football, but computers have saved us from the need to pretend. Now we really are dumb, and more dependent on men than ever because high-tech has put us at the

mercy of all those Customer Support misogynists lurking behind their 800 numbers, who make the sadistic plumbers and TV repairmen castigated by early feminism look positively supportive.

Worst of all, the male-dominated world of high-tech, where upgrading never stops, has succeeded in upgrading the battle of the sexes with a megagigabyte of irony. Computers are delicate mechanisms whose power resides in mysterious interior places; there is no way of knowing whether or not they will respond; they react with hysteria to some little problem that wouldn't bother anybody but a computer; and they have achieved the status of "can't live with 'em, can't live without 'em." It's only a matter of time before they join ships under the mantle of "she," but the techno-snots will never caress the word as sailors do.

April 16, 2001

H AVE you heard about the fabulous new true-life horror movie? It's called *Revulsion* and it's about a columnist who suddenly and inexplicably finds that she can't bring herself to read another newspaper or watch another talking-head show. The promos are really neat; they show a picture of me curled up in the fetal position, and the voice-over says: "What happens to a cultural commentator when the only comment she can make about the culture is a raised middle finger? This is her story!"

I can't pinpoint exactly when it started, only that it was somewhere between the controversy over the Army's berets and the trial of Puffy Combs. I was able to form an opinion on the berets but I had no idea who Puffy Combs was, except that he was an athlete or something. I did not consider it necessary to follow his fortunes because O. J. Simpson's trial has made child's play of certain kinds of cultural commentary. It's as simple as shifting the cards around on a perpetual calendar—different year, same dozen Black History Months. Whoever Puffy Combs was, the cultural comment was ready and waiting, carved in stone: "Whatever he did, he didn't do it."

At some point in the unavoidable trial coverage I was force-fed the name of Puffy's girlfriend, Jennifer Lopez. I knew nothing about her either, except that she sang or something. Probably "or something" is closer to the mark. Whatever show I tuned in to, whatever newspaper I opened, there the two of them were, until my nerves gave way and I went into an or-something funk.

Innocuous words can sound very seductive if you say them over and over at top speed. As the words "or something" pounded through my brain, they put me in mind of a romantic idyll or an alluring adventure that quickly took on an exotic, east-of-Suez flavor: "The schooner sailed past the sampans into Or Something harbor at dawn." . . . "The delicate carvings on the Temple of Or Something glistened in the tropical rain." . . . "The grenadiers won the Victoria Cross for their gallantry at the siege of Or Something."

In short, I was not myself, but then neither were the Army Rangers and the Pentagon, who had turned into the Duchess of Windsor and Lily Daché arguing about which hat to wear. Telling myself that if they could be frivolous then so could I, I played hooky from current events and treated myself to a vacation of watching and reading nothing except what I damn well pleased.

I did scan the papers and surf the news shows, but only for as long as I could stand it, which was never long. The moment the jungle drums sounded from the Or Something pagoda I was off again on the road to Mandalay, so my take on the latest news cycle is necessarily sketchy. Since I can't attack any subject in depth this time around, I'll do a potpourri of opinions. If any of them strikes you as odd, blame it on the Somerset Maugham remittance man having his twelfth gin and tonic on the veranda of the Or Something Hotel in Pago-Pago.

1. I am anti-beret whatever their color because I don't think American soldiers should look like foreigners. What the Army needs is a distinctively American hat, and one already exists: the "forage cap" of the Civil War era. It's the soft kepi worn by enlisted men (and a few generals; Stonewall Jackson preferred it to the officer's slouch hat). The forage cap being soft, the crown slopes forward at a rakish angle and faces out so that insignia can be pinned on it. The forage cap was also worn by the post–Civil War cavalry, giving it an indelible association with John Wayne, who surely does more for the morale of U.S. troops than Jean-Paul Sartre.

2. Bush's "faith-based initiative" is so unthought-out that it practically screams Arianna Huffington. It's gotten so complicated so fast that they're already tangled up in arguments about how to break down a good deed into its spiritual and temporal components so they can award tax credits for some of the free soup, but not all of it. Let one drunk fail to finish eating before the hymns start, and churches will have to cook the books to save the Constitution. Guaranteeing still more turmoil is the plan to "fund the individual," meaningless buzztalk dreamed up by putative conservatives who have yet to grasp the fact that *all* vouchers are simply the welfare state in single file.

First Amendment conflicts aside, the worst portent of the scheme is its truculent point man, John J. DiIulio Jr., who blasted "predominantly white, ex-urban evangelical" divines for their lack of interest in urban programs. This didn't sit too well down at the church in the wildwood. Retorted

Southern Baptist leader Richard Land, "It would rankle less if he wasn't so ignorant about us and didn't try to stereotype us." If the faith-based initiative is Dubya's idea of reaching out, it won't be long before he has to do a real stretch and reach out to the Cavaliers and Roundheads he has created.

3. Where is Laura Bush? I admit that her silence is blessed after Hillary's din, but she had barely moved into the White House before she left for an extended stay in Texas, supposedly to oversee the decoration of their ranch home. Something isn't quite right. Still waters run deep, so they say. The stillest and deepest belonged to Greta Garbo, who abruptly ended a dispute with Hollywood moguls by saying, "I tink I go home now." She meant Sweden.

4. First there was mad-cow disease, now foot-and-mouth disease. I figure it has to be one of two things, neither of them accidental: Either the Vegans are getting serious about putting a tax on fast food, or else Iraq or some other rogue nation has launched its biological-warfare weapons on the West. If foot-and-mouth can be carried on sole-of-shoe, with all the immigrants pouring into First World countries it would be a simple matter to walk it in.

5. I read that the Taliban were blowing up statues of Buddha or something. When are they going to get around to the Brooklyn Museum of Art?

April 30, 2001

THE new *GWTW* ripoff is the ebonically titled *The Wind Done Gone*, by Alice Randall, a black woman who tells the story via the diary of the mulatto Cynara, daughter of Gerald O'Hara and Mammy. Cynara is thus the half sister of Scarlett, whom Randall names "Other" and describes in a plagiaristic passage boldly lifted from the first sentence in the original book. It's a sentence I know well, having used it for years to test new typewriters:

"Scarlett O'Hara was not beautiful but men seldom realized it when caught by her charm as the Tarleton twins were."

Randall's version: "She was not beautiful, but men seldom recognized this, caught up in the cloud of commotion and scent in which she moved."

That's enough to give us a good idea of other dissonant horrors to come. The book is presently tied up in litigation by the Margaret Mitchell Estate's efforts to stop Houghton Mifflin from publishing it, but anyone who thinks it will never see the light of print should contemplate the bumper sticker that defines our times: "S**t happens."

Helping to shovel the book along is a clutch of concerned literary lights—Harper Lee, Arthur M. Schlesinger Jr., Shelby Foote, and John

Berendt—who have issued an open letter averring, "Now is the time for the American public to hear another perspective of this legend." Note that last word: A novel copyrighted in 1936 has been turned into a myth of antiquity, like Andromeda or Beowulf, too shrouded by the veils of time for anyone to state with certainty who the original author was, and ripe for plucking by any bard who feels like fiddling with it.

Following the arguments of the pro-publication side is like following Ariadne through the Labyrinth after she has run out of string. Race, not intellectual property, is the overriding issue. "Author" Randall takes a flying leap into post hoc, forging a direct connection between the Old South's prohibition on teaching slaves to read and write, and "those who would try to set up obstacles for a black woman to tell her story, and the story of her people, with words in writing."

Someone should explain to "Author" Randall that copyright laws did not grow out of the Black Codes, but Houghton Mifflin's intellectual-property lawyer, Joseph Beck, is too busy practicing literary criticism. The Mitchell Estate wants to censor Randall's book, he believes, because "I think they fear the ridicule that is brought to life. They know the misdepiction of African Americans is a weakness in *Gone with the Wind*."

Margaret Mitchell is regularly accused of ignoring miscegenation, but in fact she addresses it bluntly in Chapter 25 when Old Miss Fontaine, the gruff matriarch of a neighboring plantation, tells Scarlett what happened when Sherman came through.

> "They promised all the black wenches silk dresses and gold earbobs. . . . some of the troopers went off with the black fools behind them on their saddles. Well, all they'll get will be yellow babies and I can't say that Yankee blood will improve the stock."
>
> "Oh, Mama Fontaine!"
>
> "Don't pull such a shocked face, Jane. We're all married, aren't we? And, God knows, we've seen mulatto babies before this."

That "God knows" speaks volumes, and speaking volumes in few words is something that good writers know how to do. In this brief passage, Mitchell is saying that mulattos were a fact of life on plantations. Obviously it was so on the Fontaine place, home to Old Miss's three swashbuckling grandsons, Tony, Joe, and Alex; and probably on the Tarleton place, home to the hard-drinking twins, plus two more brothers who weren't in the movie.

We can only wonder about Tara based on what she chooses to tell us. Gerald O'Hara was a bachelor of 43 when he married 15-year-old Ellen

Robillard. What did he do before that? As the book opens, Gerald is a vigorous 60, Ellen is only 32, and they still share a bed, yet "he knew there would be no more sons to follow the three who lay in the family burying ground." Why not? Would another pregnancy have killed Ellen? Was she barren? Was she frigid? If so, what did Gerald do now? Did he visit the slave cabins? Or was he sleeping with one or both of Tara's young upstairs maids, Rosa and Teena, who—interestingly—were frequently mentioned but never appeared?

There might be a story here but Mitchell wisely refrained from telling it because inclusion is best left to race junkies and compassionate conservatives. When practiced by writers it violates the artistic principle of selectivity; namely, anything that does not advance the plot or the characterization must come out. Accusing Margaret Mitchell of ignoring this aspect of slavery is another way of saying that she avoided distracting subplots and irrelevant digressions, crafted a coherent story by sticking to Scarlett's viewpoint, and kept control over her material for more than a thousand pages.

"Misdepiction of African Americans" is, of course, an unforgivable sin, but if she erred, she erred on the side of inclusion. Race junkies routinely condemn slaveholders for preferring light-skinned blacks as house servants, yet Mammy is described as "shining black, pure African." Pork, Gerald's valet and Tara's butler, is also "shining black," and Prissy, trained originally as India Wilkes's lady's maid, is "a brown little creature."

Mitchell is also accused of making her black characters happily docile, but this is disproved by a trenchant exchange in Chapter 35 that goes by so fast that only real *GWTW* aficionados remember it.

After the war, Scarlett, in Atlanta to entrap Frank Kennedy, tries to send Mammy out to buy rouge, but the shocked Mammy refuses. Furious, Scarlett orders her back to Tara, but Mammy's retort paints a portrait of social change in one brushstroke:

"You kain sen' me ter Tara ness Ah wants ter go. Ah is free."

May 14, 2001

ANOTHER Sunday with the newspapers, another pile of stress articles. This is becoming such a regular experience that if *This Is Your Life* is ever revived and they decide to do me, they'll have to figure out some way to show it. I don't know how they could do it except to heave a file cabinet full of clippings through the rose-covered trellis while the band plays "Auld Lang Syne." The show's format demands a real live person, but it won't be long before every American newspaper has a separate Stress

Section, so they'll be able to bring on a real live Stress Editor to hug me.

Stress as it is now defined got its start when feminists adopted the Nazi motto, *Arbeit Macht Frei,* and ordered wives and mothers to go out to work. I admit to a touch of schadenfreude here because this kind of stress plays no role in my life. I have never had a husband or a child and I no longer drive a car so I am immune to the Big Three, but my advantages are a double-edged sword. Living alone and working at home may sound unstressful, but they have spoiled me so much that the least little thing ticks me off.

My kind of stress dates from the Tylenol scare of 1982, when it was discovered that Americans, the friendliest people on earth, like to poison each other.

Drug companies prided themselves on how fast they "responded" to the problem, i.e., how fast they figured out how to seal everything up so nobody could get it open. The issues of crime and punishment got lost in the shuffle of the Great God Packaging, whose acolytes hit on the solution of frustrating poisoners and headache sufferers alike until they gave up, threw the bottle against the wall, and went out and shot somebody instead.

Now everything is wrapped and sealed to the hilt whether we put it in our mouths or not. Price tags on a loop of rubbery plastic strong enough to leash an Irish wolfhound, appliance boxes wound with steel-belted tape that yields only to wire cutters, and stubborn decal labels that leave a sticky residue that you can't get off no matter what.

I have to be careful about coping with packaging in public. Stress has become such a big-ticket item that one "g**d*** sonofabitch!" is all it takes for somebody to say, "She has a lot of anger." Profanity (though not obscenity) is now considered a "warning sign," the kind we are given lists of in stress articles, like "Ten Things to Look for in an Out-of-Control Loved One."

It would be undemocratic if some people had less stress than others, so America sees to it that no stoic is left behind. One way to achieve this goal is with the ubiquitous phrase "quality-care professionals." As soon as I hear it my stomach knots up because I know that some ungodly snafu is imminent and I will end up on the phone with someone named Pam or Debbi.

Another way is forcing us to listen to a nervous wreck conversing with a megalomaniac. The talk-radio format, which has spread to TV, is virtually unavoidable now. The tension begins when a caller, who has been on hold for two hours, gulps and gushes, "I can't believe it! I'm really talking to you! I've been trying to get through for years!" Having provided listeners with a mental picture of a prisoner dragged up from a dungeon and thrown at Pharaoh's feet, the caller tries to repeat what he has already said to the call screener in pre-talk, but, conscious of the looming commercial break, he stumbles through an incoherent stew of fits and starts until the host booms, "Hold your thought!"

The best way to make sure we are all equally stressed out is to run, suspiciously often, the traveler's-checks commercial about the hysterical woman who left her handbag in a foreign cab. "You don't understand! I'm on vacation!" she shrieks into the phone. "This has never happened to me before! My wallet, my husband's wallet, a thousand dollars!" Then the scatty voice sinks to a tremulous whimper. "Everything is in that cab. . . ." This is supposed to persuade people never to leave home without traveler's checks. It persuades me never to leave home.

The American way of stress is comparable to Freud's "beloved symptom," his name for the cherished neurosis that a patient cultivates like the rarest of orchids and does not want to be cured of. Stress makes Americans feel busy, important, and in demand, and simultaneously deprived, ignored, and victimized. Stress makes them feel interesting and complex instead of boring and simple, and carries an assumption of sensitivity not unlike the Old World assumption that aristocrats were high-strung. In short, stress has become a status symbol.

Blessed are the stressed, for they have inherited the earth. The "air rage" defendant who broke a ticket agent's neck when he picked him up and used him as a pile driver owes his acquittal to our stress worship. Air rage, road rage, and any other collapse of self-control is simply trendy.

This is why so many people liked Clinton. The constant turmoil, the 24/7 crisis mode, the sleeplessness, his hyper approach to everything fit the Stressing of America like a glove. Bush, on the other hand, has let down the side with his orderliness, punctuality, smooth delegating, and early bedtimes. He's just not playing fair with the zeitgeist. This will not stand

The solution? Drawn, tense Bob Kerrey, eyes blinking uncontrollably, voice quavering like the traveler's-checks lady's, in a breaking-news press conference billed "One Awful Night in Thanh Phong" and featuring words like "haunted," "nightmare," "subconscious," "secret," and "heal."

This is more like it. It even has the right name: "post-Vietnam stress syndrome." Kerrey claims he has no interest in running for president, but he's establishing his bona fides whether he means to or not. Now that we have become a nation that judges presidents according to whether they "understand the problems of people like me," a man with Kerrey's stress-test scores would be in like Flynn.

May 28, 2001

T HE movie *Quills* has come and gone, but this sympathetic portrait of the Marquis de Sade will turn up on TV in a year or so. It will be "edited for content," of course, but cutting the worst of the sex and violence will not diminish its disastrous overall message, to wit: Sade was a misunderstood genius who was persecuted by a hypocritical establishment.

This is a good time to review a murder case in which the writings of Sade played a precipitate role.

It happened in a place that most Americans know only as the setting of a famous love story, Emily Brontë's *Wuthering Heights*, but Brontë also penned some lines of poetry that are chillingly prescient in view of the macabre events that would one day unfold there: "I dream of moor and misty hill . . . what have these lonely mountains worth revealing?"

England's "Moors Murders" were committed between 1963 and 1965 by a young couple, Ian Brady and Myra Hindley, who worked together in a chemical-supply firm in Manchester, he as a stock clerk, she as a typist. They lived together as well, first in her grandmother's grimy row house in the city slums; later, when the slum was cleared, in a "council house" on a faceless suburban "overspill estate," i.e., public housing. The only atmospheric touch in this dreary corner of the Welfare State was a sweeping view of the moors.

Brady, a Scot, was the illegitimate son of a Glasgow waitress named Peggy Stewart. She farmed him out to a slum family named Sloan, whose name he was given, and visited him from time to time in the guise of a family friend, not telling him that she was his mother.

Three incidents from his childhood are noteworthy. He was drawn to pictures of vast empty spaces, he buried a cat alive, and he became obsessed with the movie *The Third Man*, memorizing Orson Welles's line as he looks down from atop a Ferris wheel at the people below: "Would you feel any pity, old man, if any of those dots stopped moving forever?"

In his teens he was arrested for petty crime and sent to a reformatory. He was released on the condition that he live with his mother, now married to a man named Brady and living in Manchester. He had already guessed that Peggy was his mother, and so he moved to Manchester, took his stepfather's name, and got a job at the chemical-supply firm, where he stayed six years.

To people of this class, reading books is proof of seriousness, if not stodginess. Everyone thought he had settled down, but his books were pseudo-scholarly paperbacks like *The History of Torture*, and sensational treatments of the Holocaust. His displays of lunch-hour studiousness impressed the new typist, Myra Hindley, who found him "deep."

Myra's dissatisfaction with her life was expressed by regular changes in her hair color. She went through every shade of blonde and even, once, pink, teasing it into a huge, elaborate bubble. The only other remarkable thing about her was her morbid reaction at 15 to the drowning death of a childhood friend; inconsolable, she wore black until it had to be taken from her.

Myra Hindley did more than sleep with Ian Brady. She turned into him, exchanging her flat Lancashire vowels for his Scottish burr, parroting his Nazi views, and sharing his fascination with the vast, empty moors. They drove there in rented cars, always with a shovel in the back, ostensibly so that Brady could dig peat for her grandmother's garden.

Of the five children who went missing between 1963 and 1965, two were found buried on the moors by police diggers who matched the loci to the snapshots Brady and Hindley took of themselves standing on the graves. Other incriminating evidence included nude photos of their ten-year-old female victim, a tape recording of her screams with Christmas carols playing in the background, and a dog-eared paperback of Sade's *Justine*. Among its underlined passages were "Murder is a hobby and a supreme pleasure," and "The crime of destroying one's fellow man is non-existent."

The only study of the Moors Murders published in the U.S. is *Beyond Belief* by Emlyn Williams. Noting that the paperback edition of *Justine* came out in England shortly before the first murder, he makes a convincing case for charging Sade as an accessory before the fact.

The very first sentence of the Foreword is an example of the indoctrination of an immature mind: 'This is one of the great forbidden books of all time . . . stimulating, mind-prodding . . . its publication at this time is an important cultural event.' . . . *Justine* is a dirty book without dirty words. If anything, the language is pretty lofty, one of the reasons why the work is defended as literature. The flights are as high in translation as in the original, often reading like bad Walter Scott. The idiocies in the text will pass right over the head of this particular reader, because Brady and his author have in common two negative traits: a want of literary taste and a lack of humor.

Questioned on the witness stand about his pornography, Brady sneered, "Ye'll find worrse in lairds' manors." This is probably true, but there are far fewer lords than stock clerks. The danger of making pornography universally available in cheap editions challenged the socialist views of novelist Pamela Hansford Johnson, who, while covering the Moors trial, saw a paperback of Krafft-Ebing's *Psychopathia Sexualis* in a railway-station rack. What need, she asked in her commentary on the case, has the general public for such books?

Thirty-five years ago, progressive literary figures like Emlyn Williams and Pamela Hansford Johnson saw through malignancies like Sade, but today's Hollywood liberals are as gullible as Ian Brady. "Half-baked pickers-up of unconsidered truisms," in Williams's words, "just sharp enough to acquire surface knowledge and a run-of-the-mill vocabulary embellished with threadbare turns of speech."

A better description of the guardians of our popular culture was never penned. Barbra Streisand, Alec Baldwin, and Rosie O'Donnell, take a bow.

June 11, 2001

NOW that *The Wind Done Gone* has been cleared for publication by the court of appeals, I present my own version, *Gone with the Hurricane Activity.*

Scarlett O'Hara was not a physically ideal human being, but men seldom perceived it when informed by her life-enhancing qualities as the Tarleton twins were.

"What does it matter if we were expelled from the college of our choice, Scarlett? The hostilities are going to start any day now. You don't think we'd seek career enrichment with hostilities in progress, do you?"

"Hostilities, hostilities, hostilities! This hostilities dialogue has caveated every party this spring. Besides, there aren't going to be any hostilities."

"Why, honey, after the first-strike shelling situation we instituted at Fort Sumter, the Northern Americans will have to engage in hostilities. Violence always begets violence."

"If you boys don't address another issue I'll go in the house and vent!"

"How about if we tell you a privileged communication? You know Miss Melanie Hamilton who's based in Atlanta? Ashley Wilkes's cousin? Ashley's going to marry her. You know the Wilkeses always have meaningful relationships with their extended family members."

"I'll ask Pa if he has any input."

"Do you mean to tell me, Katie Scarlett O'Hara, that you neither advocate nor condone home ownership? Why, it's the only viable alternative worth living for, worth fighting for, worth dying for, because it's the only comprehensive program for social mobility."

"Oh, Pa, you talk like a Hibernian-American."

"'Tis proud I am to be Hibernian-American, and don't forget, Missy, that you're half Hibernian-American, too, and to anyone with a drop of Hibernian-American blood, the land he or she lives on is like his or her mother."

"Ashley, I—I love you."

"You mustn't say that, Scarlett. It serves no useful purpose."

"But Ashley, I know you have a felt need for me!"

"Yes, I have a felt need for you, but it has no growth potential. Oh, Scarlett, can't we put a voluntary ban on these things?"

"Don't you want a one-on-one commitment with me?"

"I have a one-on-one commitment with Melanie."

"But you just said you had a felt need for me!"

"I misspoke. My dear, why must you make me verbalize things that will only give you a negative self-image? Love isn't enough to construct a positive orientation for two people as polarized as we are. You, who are so autonomous and assertive—"

"Why don't you articulate it, you wimp! You're threatened by me! You'd rather live with that submissive little nurturer and parent a network of passive role players just like her!"

"You mustn't say counterproductive things about Melanie. She's part of my gene pool and we interact."

"She's a pale-faced, mealy-mouthed ninny and I'm unsupportive of her!"

"Scarlett, promise me that if I'm killed and Melanie becomes a single parent, you'll reach out to her."

"Miss Scarlett, I don't have no baby-birthin' skills!"

"The Northern Americans are coming! The Northern Americans are coming!"

"As the Supreme Being is my witness, I'm going to take charge of my life and develop survival techniques so that I will never be without my basic nutrients at any subsequent point in time. If I have to fabricate, prevaricate, discriminate, or stereotype, as the Supreme Being is my witness, I'll never be inadequately nourished again!"

"Ashley, the Northern Americans want three hundred dollars in taxes on Tara."

"Why tell me? You know I can't cope."

"But Ashley, this is a worst-case scenario!"

"What do people do when they're faced with a worst-case scenario? Some initiate direct action to achieve full humanity, while inadequate personalities succumb to the winnowed-out syndrome."

"Ashley, let's relocate! They need non-combat advisers in the Mexican army. We could have a restructuring experience!"

"I can't leave Melanie, she has no job-training opportunities."

"She has no reproductive capabilities either, but I—"

"Scarlett, this is unacceptable!"

"Then . . . we have no options?"

"Nothing except . . . self-esteem."

"Rhett, Ashley and I didn't have a sexual encounter at the lumberyard. We were just building bridges of understanding within a platonic framework."

"Oh, I don't begrudge him recreational sex with you. I can identify with that. After you denied me access to your body I reaffirmed myself with surrogates like Belle. But I do begrudge him your consciousness because our value judgments are so alike. We could have communicated so well, Scarlett, but I couldn't deal with your insecurities so I bonded with Bonnie. I'm into fathering now."

"Promise me?"

"Anything, Melly."

"Look after Ashley for me. See that he gets counseling."

"But Rhett, if you leave me, what will I do about re-entry?"

"Frankly, my dear, it doesn't impact me."

I'll go home to Tara and monitor the situation, she decided. I'll think of some way to reestablish connectedness. After all, tomorrow is another time frame!

June 25, 2001

HEARING that Nepal's Crown Prince Dipendra had murdered his father the king, his mother the queen, his brother the prince, his aunts the princesses, and assorted other royalty at the dinner table, the spirit of Lizzie Borden was heard to say one word.

"Damn."

Lizzie wasn't the only departed member of the sanguine elite to express envious dismay. Catherine de Medici, who thought she had thrown the dinner party to end all dinner parties on that famous St. Bartholomew's Day, showed the first blush ever known to stain her cheeks and muttered, "Now I'm no better than Martha Stewart." Crown Prince Rudolf could have kicked himself over his measly little murder-suicide—one of each—out in the sticks at Mayerling. "If only I had stayed in Vienna," he sighed, "I coulda had a V-8!" Even Roman Empress Livia felt outclassed. "It took me years to do mine piecemeal," she reflected, "but Dipendra rubbed out a whole royal family all at once."

If the ill wind of Katmandu blew anybody any good it was yours truly, because it jogged me out of my recent funk and reawakened my interest in current events. I even went so far as to buy a new TV with a nine-inch screen that fits on my desk so I could watch the news and take notes at the same time like a big-shot columnist. Not many people can say they were saved by Prince Dipendra, but I've always done things differently.

Katmandu was my idea of a story and I was ready to roll, but nobody else was. It was reported, yes, but it wasn't covered as we have come to understand coverage—no "CNN Breaking News," no "Fox Alert," no tortuous analysis, no dizzying zoom lens making a whooshing sound as it comes in on the words "The Lessons of Katmandu." Granted, there was a lot of other news to cover that week, but I still got the distinct impression that the media were doing all they could to avoid saying any more about Dipendra's bloodbath than was absolutely necessary. Why?

A news director would claim the story had no American angle, and in one sense this is true. Most Americans probably could not locate Nepal on a map, and if they ever heard of it they probably thought it was the generic name for a prescription tranquilizer. Nonetheless, the Lesson of Katmandu is so apropos that it belongs in "News You Can Use." Every aspect of the story topples some comfortable American assumption, rubs some American nerve, or complicates the usually blissful American subconscious.

The classic American touch was supplied by Prince Dipendra himself: camouflage combat fatigues, which he changed into before he began shooting. After three decades of feminism, Alpha males with Omega grievances have made the G.I. Joe look the outfit of choice at gun shows, stock-car races, and wherever testosterone simmers. We are told incessantly that we are the "only remaining superpower" and that "the world looks to America," but being the arbiters of dress-to-kill is hegemony gone wrong. Who else could make a Buddhist shop at Army Surplus?

In its first official explanation of the royal slaughter, the Nepalese government described it as an "accident." Their bland insistence that a gun had suddenly gone off by itself and killed nine people threw the liberal media into a panic. They had to downplay it because it sounded as if Bill Clinton had gone to Nepal to help them spin.

The media also were afraid of the story because it harbored unintended consequences for the triumph of multiculturalism. As the ever more farcical details emerged, Americans might be tempted to slap their thighs as of old and chortle, "Those excitable foreigners!" Nobody has said this for years, but given today's tension levels, one chortle, taken at the flood, could lead God knows where.

A Monty Python-style regicide in the mountain fastness of a storybook land is bound to be problematic unless it is better timed than this one was. These things should happen in a world that regards dissension as a natural condition, such as the 14th century when there were two popes, or the heady days of pre-nationalism when countries consisted of clots of warring duchies, each given to coining its own money. But Dipendra struck while the iron was cold, his fury muffled between the spongy bookends of a soon-to-be-unified Europe fading into undifferentiated single-currency "harmonization," and an America full of people so terrified of not getting along with each other that an unspoken but concerted effort is afoot to turn everybody into a moderate.

Of *course* the media downplayed Dipendra. Calling attention to his crisis-management style would jeopardize our carefully constructed fantasies of cooperation, mangle the anti-competitiveness agenda of the "everybody wins" crowd, and spike the already-scheduled 814,675 articles, books, and prime-time specials on ending bullying.

Conservatives were just as eager to join the Dipendra blackout. In the first place, it was no time to remind Americans that we have a Nepal of our own, a storybook land in a mountain fastness called Vermont where madness reigns with unchallenged absolutism. Moreover, the White House wanted no talk of Dipendra's camouflage fatigues while Dubya was doing his green-on-green environment number. Whenever he planted himself in leafy national parks in his green jacket you couldn't make out anything except his face and hands, and that was too apt a metaphor for an incredible shrinking president for his handlers to deal with.

If the media had gone all out with Dipendra's royal bloodbath and run "The Lesson of Katmandu" into the ground in typical exhaustive fashion, the need to fill air time would have led to an ethical crisis requiring yet another special, "Covering Katmandu," so they could talk about whether they should have talked about what they talked about, e.g., "Will this help or hurt Tony Blair?"

July 9, 2001

B ACK in February I wrote a column about the "Duhs," those human postholes in the barren landscape of Customer Service who mangle mail orders and can't spell King. Now I bring you even worse tidings. This column is about the Ignos.

An Igno is a Duh with a college education. There's nothing wrong with their gray matter, it's just that it remains virgin soil. They sow it not, and neither do they reap it. It just lies there undisturbed, as fallow as the day it was born, until at last, like other overdue virginities, it loses all capacity for response and you can't do a thing with it.

Ignos are the chief crop of Diversity Ed, what sprouts when Western Civ's Dead White Males are eliminated from college curricula and replaced with African oral historians, Aztec vivisectionists, and the diaries of Anaïs Nin.

Columnists have made hay with dumbed-down curricula. I've written my share of polemics, but I made the mistake of confining myself to arguments against multiculturalism per se. The narrower but more intriguing subject of Igno psychology is one that I left unexplored until two recent incidents convinced me that we are witnessing the spread of a new kind of stupidity that developed nations have never before had to deal with.

The first incident came about when I had to correct a public record involving my Social Security number. I dealt with an administrative assistant, a cordial, seemingly competent woman in her early thirties. She assured me that my problem was all straightened out, but given my natural pessimism, I automatically said, "I can see the handwriting on the wall." That's when she looked at the wall. Turned around and gave it the old up-and-down once-over. Looked back at me with eyes as big as saucers. "It's just a figure of speech," I mumbled.

The second incident involved a group of Gen-Xers who moved into, and then out of, my apartment complex. I never talked to them and I'm not even sure how many there were, but I do know one thing about them—the whole place knew it: They had a red light over their door. Each apartment has a faux Gay Nineties gas lantern for use as an entry light and they put a red bulb in theirs. It was not why they moved out; that had to do with unforeseen financial problems when one of the group lost her job. They weren't really operating a brothel, so all was innocent.

Was it ever. After they left, a neighbor told me that they didn't know what a red light over a door meant. "I told them and they were dumbfounded," she said. "I don't think they believed me."

At first I found it incredible that these heirs of the sexual revolution did not know what a red light symbolized, but then it hit me: I had run into the first principle of the New Stupidity—the inter-generational idiom was dead.

When you grow up, as I did, hearing about "houses of ill repute" and "ladies of the evening" from older members of an extended family, you not only find out what a red light means, but you sign up for an ongoing course in the brand of informal history known as "lore," or, what "everybody knows."

Like the extended family that watered it, America's lore pool has dried up. What "everybody knows" has gone the way of every other certainty because we can't even agree on who "everybody" is. Our obsessive commitments to diversity and radical individualism have encouraged Ignos to practice a self-segregation of the intellect governed by the credo "Everybody's gotta right to his own everybody." The mind of the Igno resembles the tables in their college cafeterias where races and ethnicities voluntarily huddle with their own kind. The typical Igno can seem intelligent and informed as long as he doesn't budge from his educational salt lick, but let him stray and there's no telling what will go over his head.

What happened with the red light promises to engulf the phrase "bully pulpit," which comes from the same era. Ignos have only a foggy idea, if that, of who Teddy Roosevelt was, so they can hardly be expected to know that in TR's day "bully" was an expression of enthusiasm comparable to "cool." It won't be long now before the Ignos get it all mixed up with day-care aggression and conclude that bullying is a presidential perk.

The woman who searched the wall for the handwriting I saw thereon personifies the Igno condition from the religious conservative's point of view: People who don't read the Bible will believe anything.

I'll concede that Diversity Ed imperils the Igno's soul, but I'm more interested in what else it does to him, and by extension, to all of us.

When people stop reading the Bible and Shakespeare they cut themselves off from an enormous number of figures of speech used in the English language. Growing up without these models, they never develop the habit of using simile and metaphor themselves. Eventually they develop a fear and loathing of all such literary conventions and a conviction that anyone who uses them is being somehow "insincere." No wonder ringing political orato-ry is dead. No candidate would dare.

The uneducated have always been prone to paranoia because so much that they don't understand is always swirling around them. One "whom" and they think they are being snubbed; a speaker who alternates "if it was" and "if it were" is tricky; and people who use "big words" are making fun of them. Uneducated people with college degrees are even more touchy, and their numbers are steadily increasing.

The American way of solving problems like these is to turn everybody into an Igno so that nobody will know the difference. Moviemakers are doing their part by promoting Igno literal-mindedness, replacing subtlety, indirec-tion, and symbolism with writhing nude bodies and oceans of blood.

It was bound to happen. When there are no imaginations left, nothing is left to the imagination.

July 23, 2001

I'VE been sitting here trying to calculate how many times I've seen Gary Condit run down the Capitol's back stairs.

I tried multiplying the number of days since the story broke by three (CNN, MSNBC, Fox News), and then multiplying by three again for the number of times a day I watch the news. But wait. What about all the talk shows? Some have been using the stairway clip as a lead-in, repeating it after every commercial break, while others have been putting it in a miniature box in a corner of the screen where it plays over and over during updates, often in slow motion. How could I get an accurate count of that?

It was no use. The only thing I could be sure of was the wisdom of America's leading cliché: It was time to put it behind me and move on, so I turned off the calculator, turned on the TV, and promptly saw Condit running down the stairs again.

Writing about breaking news for a fortnightly publication is risky, but several aspects of the Chandra Levy case have taken on enough permanence to allow for commentary, and one in particular is already etched in marble. I refer to the unidentified "law-enforcement source" who told reporters from the *Washington Times* that Condit had as many as six other women on the string, adding, "They are all types and ages."

Has inclusion come to this? Chandra is Jewish and Anne Marie Smith appears to be a WASP. Who else will surface? Maybe Condit studied the new Census form and went down the list so he would have one of each . . . Pacific

Islander, Inuit, Nordic-Cambodian, Hispano-Amerind, Other. Men used to have a "type" and talked volubly about the distinctive charms of "my kind of woman," but if diversity gathers any more steam they'll soon be walking on eggs about what will no doubt be called the "bedmate community."

One thing you can say for discrimination: It reduces the scoring to manageable proportions. A baseball love life is one thing, but it sounds as if Condit has been playing midnight basketball.

A little discrimination might have kept Chandra out of his orbit. One of the few personal facts to emerge about him is his attachment to his Harley. Here we come to an example of the power of reasonless, rockheaded prejudice in all its vainglory. Chandra's mother, being Jewish, Californian, and younger than I, probably rejects this kind of thinking, but I was raised on it.

It goes like this: "Men who ride motorcycles are white-trash." Period. Paragraph. Q.E.D. Fiats like this are usually delivered by a formidable Southern dowager who holds facts instead of opinions and thus has never felt the need to explain herself. In my case, my grandmother, who had only to see or hear a motorcycle to launch her one-woman class war. She never missed a chance to fire a volley; once, at the movies during previews of *The Wild One*, she jabbed me in the ribs and whispered, "See?" She made an exception for motorcycle policemen (she loved cops), but any other man who rode one was DOA.

Unfair? Of course. Did I free myself from my prejudiced upbringing and adopt enlightened thinking? Nope. If I were Chandra's mother I would have put her under citizen's arrest, house arrest, and any other kind of arrest I could dream up the moment I found out about that motorcycle. For that matter, if I had been Chandra, I would have snubbed him myself, congressman or no.

The point is not motorcycles per se, but our steadily shrinking willingness to act on preconceived opinions. Today's constant drumbeat of universal acceptance is a big reason why young women become crime victims. Hunches, sixth sense, all the inexplicable wisdom of "just because" and "not quite right" that once served the cause of female safety are now condemned as judgmentalism. I can think of several things about Gary Condit that lend themselves to speculative analysis under "Men who . . . ," but I doubt that girls like Chandra Levy are even capable of starting a sentence that way.

This case may be solved by the time you read this—or two minutes after I e-mail it to NR—so I won't go out on a limb with predictions, but I will tell you (1) what I hope happened, and (2) the déjà-vu scenario that could have been set in motion by accident.

My hope is springing eternal right now because I haven't been so solidly on a woman's side since Mrs. Harris shot the Scarsdale diet doctor. Gary Condit was made to order for my gut-reaction approach to human relations. Motorcycles aside, one look at him was enough because I've been against teeth since the Kennedys, but what really infuriated me was his warning to Chandra that if she breathed one word about their relationship, it would be "done, over, kaput."

I hope she staged her own disappearance to get even with him. Female guile carried off in the grand manner of Delilah and Lola Montez would give us a much-needed antidote to feminist victim studies, harassment lawsuits, and the whole dreary equality scene, and re-educate young women on the lost art of how to cause trouble like the big girls do.

The déjà-vu scenario popped into my head when Fox News reported the allegation that Condit hobnobbed with the Hell's Angels crowd.

Simplistic trogs know they are simplistic trogs, so when a man of superior social rank deigns to hang out with them, they sometimes develop a dumb loyalty to him in gratitude for his attention.

Do you remember the story of how Henry II accidentally ordered the execution of Thomas à Becket? Or maybe it was accidentally on purpose. Nobody knows for sure, but Henry supposedly wailed, "Will no one rid me of this troublesome priest?" and a band of eager-to-please trogs showed up at Canterbury Cathedral and did exactly that.

It's just possible that Condit innocently let drop some casual remark about the troublesome Chandra at a bikerfest, and somebody took him too literally.

August 6, 2001

GLOBAL warming, anyone? Anyone? Just as I thought, so let's get to Condit-Levy.

This is the first time in the ten years I have been lurking back here that I have written on the same subject twice in a row, but there are reasons for my fixation.

The simplest reason is a nostalgic one going back nearly 60 years. I've been in Gary Condit's love nest. It's a condo now, but in my childhood it was an apartment house populated by sherry-sipping Southern widows who made up my grandmother's circle. She took me along with her to train me in the ladylike art of paying calls, and I remember that top-floor corner window they keep showing on TV. I used to gaze out of it with longing while Granny and Old Miz So-and-So gossiped euphemistically about some ailing woman they knew who had "never been well, never," and her invariably "considerate" husband, who "never bothered her."

The case is provoking visceral reactions everywhere, ripping away that thin veneer of verbal prudence known as the civilized response, and shedding light on the national psyche. The most significant outburst so far has come from my favorite blonde-former-federal-prosecutor, the gorgeous Cynthia Alksne, who lashed out at Condit's "little shirt and little tie and little hair, and his little jacket over his fingers!" It had nothing to do with the evidence but it was dead-on, a compendium of the reasonless reasons Condit repels people in a way that Bill Clinton never did or could.

Alksne's heated words recall the scene in *Doctor Zhivago* when the happily amoral, self-indulgent, luxury-loving Komarovsky compares himself to Pasha Antipov, the puritanical, ascetic, dedicated revolutionist whom Lara wants to love but can't. The world pretends to disapprove of men like himself, says Komarovsky, and to admire men like Pasha, "but in fact it despises them!"

America needs the Levy case because it lets us tell ourselves that Clinton wasn't so bad after all, and lets us forgive ourselves for electing him twice. Thanks to Condit, Clinton has once again landed on his feet, rejuvenated in our collective subconscious as the unabashedly sensual rogue the world secretly likes under its pretense of disapproval. Our instinct warns that it is better to have about us men who are fat, and yon Condit has a lean and hungry look that makes Clinton seem safe.

The purists who say they are offended by the media's wall-to-wall coverage are like men who say they buy *Playboy* solely for the articles. This is as close as we have come to a murder rap in Congress since Preston Brooks caned Charles Sumner nearly to death in 1856. The only people who honestly believe it isn't newsworthy are the bigwigs at CBS, but not for the reasons they gave. I will bet anything that the real reason they wanted to keep it off the air was to prevent it from falling victim to Dan Rather's medical problems.

Afflicted with enlarged simile and inflammation of the metaphor, the only way he can relieve his pain is to do verbal stretching exercises with news lead-ins. CBS knew only too well what would happen if they let him report on Condit-Levy:

"The most popular movie in Washington is *The Quiet Man*, but John Wayne isn't in it."

"Gary Condit was seen disposing of a watch box, but he didn't put it in Al Gore's lock box."

"When the Levys hired a preacher to cut their grass, they never imagined he would hand them a clump of deadly nightshade."

My own visceral responses to the case are distinctly Southern, which is about as far removed from the civilized response as you can get. You can take the girl out of the South but you can't take the South out of the girl, e.g., "Why doesn't her father kill him?" Fathers are supposed to do that sort of thing for you, and so are brothers, which is the only reason I regret being an only child. It helps my fantasies along to know that Chandra at least has one brother, though six is the classic number (the oldest is always the one holding the rope).

The way Chandra conducted the affair makes me want to shake her. According to her aunt, she was ever agreeable and accommodating, did everything he told her without question, waited by the phone for him to call, and refused to go out with other men to show him how "monogamous" she was.

This is not how we do it. When a Southern woman is involved with a man, she instinctively behaves like those recalled cars whose transmissions suddenly slip from park into gear and start rolling. The point of it all is to turn him into a mental and emotional wreck.

"Scarlett, realizing that a girl has only two sides and only one man can sit on each of these sides, had elected to sit apart so she could gather about her as many men as possible."

"Usually she made them beg and plead, while she put them off, refusing to give a Yes or No answer, laughing if they sulked, growing cool if they became angry."

"You could laugh softly at them and when they came flying to see why you laughed, you could refuse to tell them and laugh harder and keep them around indefinitely trying to find out."

All women used to acknowledge the strategic value of Southern-belle tactics, but women's magazines haven't published articles on teasing and playing hard-to-get for decades. What they have seen fit to publish was made abundantly clear by Chandra's aunt, who advised her to make herself irresistible to Condit by color-coordinating his closet. Something tells me she didn't get this from the memoirs of Ninon de Lenclos, so where did she get it? She's of an age to have been a *Cosmopolitan* reader back when I was writing for them, so she may have gotten it from me.

My ultimate Southern reaction was triggered by Anne Marie Smith, who affects me the way Belle Watling affected Mammy: "Ah ain' never seed ha'r dat color in mah life. Not even in the de Tarleton fambly."

August 20, 2001

BE forewarned: I'm in a foul mood. America has gotten to me again. I'm sick of "choices." If one more corporate entity offers me a "choice" between this plan and that plan, I'm going to take to the woods like Thoreau. I don't want to be a "savvy consumer," I don't want to "shop around," I don't want to "do my homework." I don't want to be bothered counting up "smart minutes," "bonus hours," and "saver miles." I don't want rebates, whether in-store or mail-in, and I don't want extended warranties, because that means enduring the clerk's painful memorized recitation. I just want to buy what I need as quickly and simply as possible and then leave. The only discount I'm interested in is the one that was traditionally offered for paying cash, but just try and find it today. It's the only savvy consumer option nobody has ever heard of. If you want to pay cash now, they think you're a drug dealer.

Overcomplicated merchandising originated with airline deregulation. To compete for customers, they offered reduced fares if you embarked at 4 A.M. on odd-numbered Thursdays, stayed 11 days, and returned on even-numbered Tuesdays, but that was child's play compared to the higher mathematics now required to figure out ostensible savings. Take the ad I saw the other day for cell phones. They're offering "Whenever Minutes." You get 2000 Neighborhood Weekend minutes and 600 Nationwide Whenever Minutes, provided—it says in the tiny print at the bottom—you have the right number of plan minutes, promotional minutes, and—my favorite—"roaming charges."

Invariably, as with all tiny print, it also says "coverage not available in all areas" and "additional restrictions may apply." So who among us can figure out what it all means? I'll tell you who: our old friends, the Ignos. It stands to reason that the dumbest people in the country are the ones who have what it takes to plow through all the general-services agreements and consumer pricing plans tucked into our utility bills and bank statements. Only Ignos could read, really read, this stuff and understand what it says, which is one big reason why they never read anything else: A day contains only 24 hours, and savvy consumerism consumes all of it, precluding any other form of knowledge. By now it's second nature. Say "Stonehenge" to an Igno and he will assume it's a new security system with a super introductory offer: Change the locks three times a year on even-numbered Saturdays because you give keys to lovers who turn out to be psychopaths, and you get a discount on replacement sets and ten points toward a free "Rape of the Lock" stalker alarm.

Nothing reinforces my confidence like a stuffy bank, but try and find one nowadays. Mine recently introduced a supposedly select, benefit-laden account for depositors who maintain a certain balance. The only perks that

appealed to me were free checks and an extra quarter-point of interest on savings. Since I don't use plastic I was neutral about the credit-card and ATM
benefits, but the other come-ons made my stomach knot up: discounts at 3,000
hotels, discount cruises, discount tours, a 24-hour discount travel agency, discount theater tickets, free home-shopping services, extended purchase warranties, and cut-rate eyeglasses.

As I read the brochure I tried to imagine who would be tempted by all
those hotels and the we-never-close travel agency. Only a retired dromoma-
niac with accumulated bonus roaming charges could possibly do justice to
them. Or maybe the protagonist of Edward Everett Hale's "The Man Without
a Country." Or maybe the half-mad Empress Elisabeth of Austria, the time
she took a notion to search the Mediterranean for Andromeda's rock.

I wrote the bank a letter complaining about their breathless sales pitch,
saying in part: "I submit that I am not alone in my reaction. Most people
won't admit it because they're afraid of being called stuffy, but they feel disturbed when banks go in for such things. This is why cartoons showing bank
customers laden with free toasters and dishes are effective: People laugh at
what secretly bothers them."

I also proposed a bona fide gilt-edged account, one requiring a really
hefty balance, that would offer free checks and bonus interest, but which
would let customers negotiate other perks so that those wanting few or none
could trade them for more bonus interest.

They replied that they would pass along my proposal to "Product
research and development," and include me in the focus group if they decided to do it. I doubt they will. My proposal smacks of elitism and may even be
illegal. Under the rules of American logic, a gilt-edged account must be
"accessible" to all, otherwise a bank might get slapped with a poor people's
class-action suit for not offering free safe-deposit boxes to those who have
nothing to put in them.

Taking care of one's affairs used to be simple and reassuringly familiar.
There was the The Phone Company, The Light Company (which people used
to call the electric company in pre-appliance days), and The Gas Company,
but now all the mergers and buyouts have given them specific names that
keep changing. It's like getting utilities from Liz Taylor. Gone is the old sense
of "thereness." The ingrained errand known as "going downtown and paying
the bills" has been rerouted to a galactic stratosphere where easy-to-remem-
ber 800 numbers all sound alike and behavior is governed by the 11th and
12th Commandments: "Thou shalt visit our website" and "Thou shalt press
the pound sign."

America, once the land of the one-price store, now has the feel of a Turkish bazaar spilling over with bolts of garish cloth and glass beads, echoing with little brass bells and tinny pipes, teeming with hucksters alternately screeching and cajoling as they urge us to dicker constantly over the price of everything amid an atmosphere previously associated with words like Araby and Cathay. "In Xanadu did Kubla Khan a Shoney's discount plan decree . . ."

Note to Ignos: Don't try that last sentence at home.

September 3, 2001

BOY, did I strike a nerve with my "Igno" column. The letters poured in, and every one was positive. Not only did you outdo yourselves in your impassioned support, but some of the hair-raising examples you cited from your own contact with the breed were better than mine.

The letters were also notable for a corollary subject that kept popping up. Many of you asked what caused me to become such a voracious reader. I'm often asked this, so I might as well answer it here and now, but if it isn't the inspirational story you expected, don't say I didn't warn you.

There was nothing unusual about my childhood reading: *Nancy Drew, Lassie Come Home, My Friend Flicka*. Nor was there anything unusual about my pubertal reading: *GWTW, Forever Amber*, Anya Seton, Frank Yerby.

It wasn't until high school that I turned into a case study for a psychiatric conference on bibliomania. The impetus was not high school itself—I was no more miserable than anyone else and a lot happier than some—but an oppressive situation at home. Namely, my grandmother's collection of long-suffering Southern female martyrs who sat in our kitchen talking about how they worked their fingers to the bone "doing for" others without a thought for themselves.

Women in general are susceptible to the selflessness trap, but Southern women get carried away by it, seeing themselves as the plantation mistress going forth to do good on a grand scale. Whilst others sleep, she is abroad in the night, tirelessly nursing the sick and being acclaimed an angel of mercy by adoring throngs of invalids. The reality of her actual social class has nothing to do with it: In her mind's eye she's the lady of the manor and that's that.

I thought of them as the "moist women" because the glow of self-sacrifice seemed to condense on them, though in view of their broad experience with urinals it might have been something else. Most of them had bedridden relatives, usually husbands, whose problems required some form of regular, hands-on help. When I got home from school they would be knee-deep in discussions of "seepage" and "drainage," blissfully unaware of the one-upmanship that pulsated through their accounts. It was obvious that the woman who merely had to empty her husband's urinal felt inferior to the woman who had to change her husband's pads, who in turn felt inferior to the champ who catheterized her father-in-law four times a day.

I recoiled from them with every fiber of my budding womanhood but I didn't know why until the day one of them turned to me with a mournful smile and said, "A bright girl like you should go to nursing school."

That's when I started reading as if my life depended on it—because it did. My instincts told me that if I read enough books, I wouldn't be "like them," so I hurled myself at the classics, starting with *Jane Eyre*, *Wuthering Heights*, and *Madame Bovary*.

My reading had no plan or pattern to it. When the martyrs discussed reaching down somebody's throat to pull out a swallowed denture, I swallowed *A Tale of Two Cities*, *Dombey and Son*, and *Les Misérables*. When they held forth on the various stones and clots somebody had "passed," I took in *The Return of the Native*, *Vanity Fair*, and *McTeague*.

We were shackled together in neurotic symbiosis; when they stepped it up, I had to step it up. Things got critical when they abandoned seepage 'n' drainage for the greater glories of stoppage 'n' blockage. An argument over whose husband's bowels were in worse shape led to a volley of one-upmanship between Ole Miz A, who merely had to empty her husband's bedpan, and Ole Miz B, whose husband wore a bag. But just as she was preening herself, Ole Miz C chimed in with the news that her husband was so impacted that she recently had had to start excavating him "by hand" every third day.

"The doctor said there was a long-handled instrument he could get me, but an iced-tea spoon works just fine."

War and Peace, *Crime and Punishment*, *The Brothers Karamazov*, *Anna Karenina*, *Death in Venice*, *The Charterhouse of Parma*, *The Red and the Black*, *Thérèse Raquin*, *Nana*, *Germinal*, *Jude the Obscure*, *The Mayor of Casterbridge*, *Main Street*, *Babbitt*, *Elmer Gantry*, *Jean-Christophe*, *Fathers and Sons*, *On the Eve*.

I told them about that last one out of sheer devilment, just to see what they'd say. "It's about an aristocratic Russian girl named Elena who marries a Bulgarian revolutionary named Insarov, but he dies of TB and she becomes a nurse in the Crimean War."

I figured it would launch a rousing seminar about gangrene, but to my surprise they responded with expectant little smiles. I realized why when Granny voiced their collective thought.

"An army hospital is the best place in the world to catch another husband. Wounded soldiers get a pension."

Yes, indeed. A smart girl who played her iced-tea spoons right could catch a husband who had only three inches of intestine left, spend the best years of her life scooping him out every hour on the hour, and wind up being called an angel of mercy instead of a dominatrix.

My 16-year-old instincts were on the mark: My reading binge saved me from woman's lot by increasing my natural tendency to selfishness. Reading requires silence, solitude, and inwardness, priorities a woman must guard and cultivate if she is to live in that feminist abode called "a room of one's own." I did, and that's where I live.

It takes a teenager with more energy than taste to get through certain books, e.g., Charles Reade's gigantic medieval epic, *The Cloister and the Hearth*. I couldn't read it today if you held an iced-tea spoon to my throat, but at 16 I didn't skip a word. It has faded from my memory now, except for one perfect sentence in the proper Victorian love scene that it helps to think of whenever I see writhing bodies on TV:

"She came to him glowing with two beauties never before united, an angel's radiance and a woman's blushes."

September 17, 2001

N O day goes by that I am not reminded of the achy-breaky emptiness of my life as a childless spinster. My sources are the endless stream of how-America-lives coverage on TV and the Family Section that no newspaper would dare go to print without. Both outlets regularly run features about mothers who get less sleep at night than I get in my afternoon nap, and who worry constantly about child car seats that eject little passengers, swimming-pool drains that suck out little guts, Cracker Jack prizes that get stuck in little windpipes, pierced teenage tongues that develop infections, exposed teenage navels flashing stop-and-go lights—you name it, I've missed it.

This year, however, I came in for a surprise. For the whole month of August we were bombarded with features about what I always considered a routine errand, but which has now been bumped up to a crisis: shopping for school supplies.

Yes, you heard me right, but your mental picture is all wrong. It's no longer a matter of stopping by Woolworth's for a pack of notebook paper and a few pencils. There is no Woolworth's now, and since "stopping by" Office

Depot or Staples is physically impossible, the typical feature showed a shell-shocked woman pushing a supersized shopping cart down an endless glittering aisle arrayed with a city block's worth of paper clips.

It was a Bataan Death March movie, with the grinning Japs played by children poking and prodding their captive parents through the blister-pack jungle to fill the cart with items they cannot be educated without: daily planners, organizers, calculators, spell checkers, electronic dictionaries, electronic translators, electronic pencil sharpeners, sequin-dappled gel pens, backpacks in every color, theme binders to match the backpacks, index cards to match the theme binders, rulers to match the index cards, and *scented* highlighters.

When you alert Americans to their latest problem you must bring in experts to back you up. The usual bevy of earnest child psychologists and family-relations gurus held forth on how backpacks engender a sense of belonging, what to do when color-coordinating turns compulsive, and how peer pressure "impacts" loose-leaf notebooks (three holes for nerds, two for the in crowd). On the practical side, consumer-affairs mavens offered ten tips on how to make a no-nonsense shopping list and, for mothers who weaken, how to cope with what one maven actually called "sticker shock."

What in the name of Good King Herod is going on? There is more to this than the familiar marketing strategy of creating demand for products that people don't really need. What struck me as I followed these stories was the sense of almost giddy pleasure tinged with relief that came through the comments of experts and parents alike, as if the spectacle of children lusting after notebooks and pens proved something they desperately needed to believe.

It does. Like the doctor's bag and the carpenter's tool belt, school supplies are the outward, visible sign of a purposeful life. The shield hanging over the medieval guildsman's workshop that identified his area of expertise survives today as the backpack hanging over a slouched adolescent shoulder. American parents are only too happy to risk exhaustion and bankruptcy to stuff it with designer composition books and talking thesauruses because they can then tell themselves that if kitting their children out is this much trouble, they must really be scholars.

Self-delusion pervades every aspect of American education. The humble "diploma" is no more; now it's called a "high-school degree," and what used to be the schoolground has been promoted to "campus." The time-honored symbolism of the cap and gown, initially travestied when high-school graduations appropriated it, has been rendered meaningless now that elementary schools increasingly are making it the attire of choice for graduates of the sixth grade. The watchword here is the fancier the better: fire-engine red or kelly green satin gowns and gilt-tasseled mortarboards for little phartlings who can barely read. Stand by for the beneficiaries of social promotion to start wearing master's hoods.

We kid ourselves in these ways to avoid facing an unpalatable truth: Americans love education but hate learning. If you doubt it, parse our revealing catch phrase about the need to "make learning fun." The obvious retort—"Dammit, it already is fun!"—is fatal because it requires you to draw a distinction between education and learning, and once you do that, you threaten everybody, because hatred of learning is our only remaining source of national unity. We can't very well pearlharbor it with the old bromide, "It brought us together," but in fact it has: The egalitarian Left scorns learning as "irrelevant," while the philistine Right chortles, "It won't help you make a living." Actually, it makes life worth living, but if you dare say so, both sides will call you an elitist.

I have tilted at each of these windmills. In 1970, having made some real money for the first time in my life, I decided to go back to college and perfect my French as I wanted to do in my girlhood. I didn't want a degree—I already had one—I didn't want credits; I just wanted the intellectual pleasure. I contacted a department head at a New England college, but I couldn't make her understand. She kept talking about degree requirements and teaching jobs, and I kept talking about my intellectual pleasure, but the phrase meant nothing to her. We were talking past each other. It depressed me so much that I shelved my project.

The anti-intellectual Left may depress me, but family quarrels being the fiercest, it takes the anti-intellectual Right to infuriate me. My particular bêtes noires are the moronic oxen known as "populist conservatives," who turn hostile if you even let it be known that you enjoy public television. Opera and Britcoms set them off the most, prompting their favorite putdown, "The world's richest man is a Harvard dropout."

Farmer in the Dell, anyone? I get to be the Cheese Stands Alone.

October 1, 2001

I N my February 19 column, I wrote, "I can't shake my sense that the Bush presidency is star-crossed," but I never thought female intuition would be this accurate.

As soon as it happened, so many commentators called it "our second Pearl Harbor" that my mind drifted back to our first one. I was not quite six in 1941, so my memory of specific events is sketchy, but the general emotional flavor is engraved on my mind as a classic example of my family's bent dynamic.

My passive father didn't want to go to war and my aggressive mother ached to. As usual, she relieved her frustration with dazzling cascades of profanity, rattling off politically incorrect fivefers such as "little yellow slant-eyed pissant bastards!" She spent four years yelling, "We oughta blow 'em off the map!" and when we did, she cut the photo of the mushroom cloud out of the paper, pasted it over the serenely pastoral "Cottage at Sunset" illustration on our kitchen calendar, and yelled, "Little yellow slant-eyed pissant bastards, BOOM!"

Always sports-minded, toward the end of her life she became, of all things, a sumo-wrestling fan. Thinking she had mellowed with age, I reminded her of her Pearl Harbor sentiments and asked her what she now found different about sumo wrestlers. She thought a minute and then said, "They're not little."

She would be in her element if she were here today. Saber-rattling jingoism is in the air. Stores are selling out of flags, the national anthem is being sung in artsy venues like Washington Square, and there is even talk of issuing war bonds. Enlistments are up, the old knee-jerk caution, "another Vietnam," has faded away, and college boys sound more and more like hard hats as they describe in sanguinary detail what they would like to do to Osama bin Laden.

We are intent on infusing our Second Pearl Harbor with the same unequivocal bloodlust that marked the first—but it won't work. We have been in a psychological lockbox too long and the conflicts that put us there have not gone away for good. They'll resurface, as unresolved conflicts always do, and thrust us back into the same old moral paralysis we were in before.

Most of these conflicts come into view when we couple the new, soon-to-be clichés that have poured from the media since last Tuesday with the familiar, shopworn clichés that were already etched on the national brain before last Tuesday. A few examples will illustrate the emotional taffy-pull we are in for:

1. "Do whatever it takes" vs. "Put it behind us and move forward."
2. "Hunt them down" vs. "police profiling."
3. "terrible swift judgment" vs. "judgmentalism."
4. "righteous wrath" vs. "anger management."
5. "steely resolve" vs. "seek professional help."

Helpists are the keepers of the keys to our psychological lockbox, so it was only to be expected that they would move quickly to defend their turf against any stirrings of steeliness. I saw my first grief counselor on TV bright and early Wednesday morning. A bottle blonde with plangent eyes and a voice made glottal by earnestness, she made me feel as if something hot and wet were crawling all over me. She held forth on how to explain terrorism to "the chillldrunnn." After her came a deluge of grief counselors, including one who lured a sturdy fireman into talking about "survivor guilt," opening the way for the grief counselor to proclaim that victims of terrorism include not only victims and their families, but their rescuers as well.

The Helpist goal of total victimhood produces a mind-set that works against the waging of total war. Since Helpists can't function until something awful has happened, they are more concerned with "aftermaths" than with actual events. For years they have been all over TV assuring us that life is just one big time-lag, that reaction is more important than action, that post-traumatic is worse than traumatic, and that anger is just another "stage" in the "grieving process," waiting its turn in line with denial, guilt, and resignation.

We bought into victimology, and now we are caught between two diametrically opposed rallying cries. Helpists trained us to say "Give me closure," but now we must revert overnight to "Give me liberty or give me death," or else go the schizoid route and adopt both.

That's not as hard as it sounds; we are entirely capable of adopting two of anything. Even as we assured each other that the attacks "brought us together," concerns about anti-Arab bigotry sprang up so fast and absorbed so much of the media's attention that sometimes it almost seemed as if the Twin Towers had been relegated to the status of collateral damage. The subject spilled over into obsession on CNN's extended Saturday edition of *Talk Back Live*. Most of the audience were idealistic twentysomethings who could not discuss Arab terrorists without getting into police profiling, until it was hard to tell what, exactly, the show was about. Their considered opinion, however, was perfectly clear: It's okay to hunt people down provided you have no idea what they look like.

I have saved our most serious conflict for last. Benjamin Netanyahu has written that militant Islam does not "hate the West because of Israel; they hate Israel because of the West." The Muslim world, he explained, has never forgotten the Moorish cultural penetration of Europe and the glory days of Saladin. Once, "Muslim" was synonymous with "civilization," but Europeans destroyed it all and made "civilization" synonymous with themselves. As a result, the words "Western civilization" are anathema to Muslim fanatics like bin Laden.

They are also anathema to many here. Jesse Jackson led chants of "Hey, hey, ho, ho, Western Civ has got to go," and multiculturalists have done their best to eliminate it from college curricula, but we let them all get away with it. Before we declare war on bin Laden we should stop declaring war on ourselves.

October 15, 2001

SHOULD we, can we, ever laugh again? This is the question of the hour, but at the risk of sounding unpatriotic I must admit that I already have—out loud, in fact.

What led up to it was the 653rd discussion of anti-Arab profiling I was watching. Unable to stand any more earnest tributes to color-blind diversity, I turned off the TV and went to the library in search of escapist fare. Needing something to take the pluribus out of the unum, I chose a biography of George V, the present queen's grandfather, who was beset by inept physicians. The worst was Lord Dawson, who is said to have treated a patient for jaundice for six weeks before discovering he was Chinese.

After I wiped up the coffee and changed my clothes it was time to turn on the TV again to see if something new had happened while I was escaping. One of the ubiquitous stress mavens was saying, "I worry most about the ones who haven't started processing the event," and recited the symptoms we should all look for: "irritability, distrust, pessimism, and withdrawal." Since her checklist describes my natural state, I have no way of telling if I'm stressed, but she needn't worry about my willingness to "process events." I call it thinking, and I get paid for it.

The most satisfying thought I've had is that Rudolph Giuliani has rescued us from our adolescent definition of popularity and given us a new appreciation of the individual who "wears well." Abrasive, truculent, aloof, impatient, and blunt, Giuliani was for years a walking compendium of all the traits Americans try to conceal or stamp out to ensure that nobody, anywhere, ever feels "threatened" by us. To this end, we have adopted the fixed smiles and galumphing friendliness of the simpleminded, and taken pains to deny the existence of dark moods with the state-of-the-art boast, "What you see is what you get," which is nothing more than shallowness redefined, another way of saying that if you tap a popular American, all you will get is an echo.

We have painted ourselves into a corner in an everlasting high school of the spirit, but now Giuliani has shown us that what you get is not always what you see. As an amazed America watched, this tense, unappealing man took on the grace of a courtier, the subtlety of a cardinal, the finesse of a diplomat, and the gentle wisdom of Mr. Chips.

It's too soon to tell whether we will retain the lesson—we usually don't—but at the moment, thanks to Giuliani, complexity is in and it's cool to be deep.

The news that fighter pilots will be given authority to shoot down hijacked commercial jets was received with grim acceptance, but the public's stoicism won't last. Americans have heard too much about "human error," as it's politely called. From the doctor who cuts off the wrong leg, to the pharmacist who fills the wrong prescription, to the Marine pilot who accidentally severed the cable on the Italian ski lift, we inhabit the Age of Oops and everybody knows it. Moreover, we have seen so many insane military men in movies that we will soon start imagining some Great Santini is up there just waiting to open fire on us. Finally, there's the little matter of our new, improved, kinder 'n' gentler military. If the order is ever given, I doubt that today's fighter pilots could bring themselves to do it—all that sensitivity training would come home to roost.

I never travel but I do breathe, so I have considered the threat of biochem warfare and come to the following conclusions.

If I were young I'd be scared, but as it is, I find the idea liberating. I'd rather go out now in a dramatic epidemic, à la my beloved medieval England, than live on to die by degrees in a nursing home. It would free me from my dread of encroaching frailty, loss of independence, cheerful nurses urging me to play bingo, and lumpenpsychologists without a shred of insight who have the temerity to assume they can "counsel" a writer. Equally intolerable is the thought of standing in line for inoculations amid hysterical throngs of Great American Moms all screaming "Jason!" I was vaccinated for smallpox and diphtheria before starting school, but, lucky me, it's worn off by now.

Speaking of phartlings, I was surprised to read that a security checker at L.A. International actually searched a baby and its stroller. She must have remembered the scene in *GWTW* (the book, not the movie) when a Yankee cavalry unit appears at Tara, and Scarlett hides her money in Melanie's baby's diaper. It's ingenious; babies are a good hiding place and we are emotionally incapable of persevering in the practice of searching them. They also offer even deadlier possibilities to terrorists who have psyched us out. I would not be surprised if they stole a baby, infected it with a contagious disease, and abandoned it in a crowded public place, knowing full well that Americans who come upon a lost baby will cluster around it, get close to its face, and take deep breaths to give them the wind they need to raise repeated choruses of "Awwwww."

President Bush's plea to get back to normal has been crowned with success. The idiocies have begun:

Blockbuster Video is putting warning labels on its terrorism movies, but shows no signs of changing its own name.

We have a new redundancy to go with our new crisis; Watergate gave us "this point in time" and now 9/11 has given us "credible threat." If Giuliani reverts to his old personality we can call him "credibly threatening."

We have also produced a supreme irony. While the news throbs with stories about the stereotyping of Arab-Americans, a FedEx commercial shows a lantern-jawed CEO asking his executives for suggestions on saving money. A chinless minion replies, "We can open an account with FedEx Dotcom and save ten percent on online shipping," then trails off with an apologetic shrug. Lantern Jaw thinks a moment, and then repeats exactly what Chinless Wonder said, but in a firm voice accompanied by a confident gesture that garners plaudits all round.

Message: Bad guys have weak chins.

November 5, 2001

W E have an emergency. I compiled a sheaf of notes and file-named them Terror3.NR, but faced with the prospect of turning them into a column, I suddenly found that I couldn't go on. Writing three columns in a row about Sept. 11 is like listening to the Three Tenors. It's two tenors too many, or as George Eliot put it: "much of a muchness."

So, you're going to have to take potluck because I invented a new approach to the essay: I decided to open the newspaper at random and write about the first thing I saw that wasn't about terrorism.

I admit I cheated a little, immediately discarding the Business and Sports sections, but when I picked up Style I squeezed my eyes shut, stuck my finger indiscriminately into the pages, and yanked them apart. When I opened my eyes, the first thing I saw were two movie reviews.

Riding in Cars with Boys stars Drew Barrymore, the acting profession's collateral damage, and is based on Beverly Donofrio's coming-of-age memoir of the same name. It just so happens that I reviewed the book, but if you think that's going to get this show on the road, guess again. I've reviewed countless other books just like it, and I never could tell one from the other. Comprising the Funky Feminism school of growth-through-humping, their standard theme is How the '60s Liberated My Personhood, and their titles all sound alike (e.g., Rosemary Daniell's *Sleeping with Soldiers*). I pretty much panned the whole genre, which is why editors kept assigning them to me. I would get a phone call and the editor would say, "Here's one you can have some fun with," which is lit-crit code for "I know you're going to hate it."

The movie reviewer said that *Riding in Cars with Boys* lacks "the honesty and grit" of the book, but I don't remember any honesty and grit. In fact, I don't remember anything about it at all except that I panned it. I read the movie review with great care but nothing in it rang a bell; my mind is a total blank, so chalk up one shaggy-dog story for my new approach to the essay.

The other movie review was *From Hell*, about Jack the Ripper. Now we're cooking. . . . I could fill a whole issue with commentary on this subject.

It's doubtful if the crimes would have become so legendary without the catchy moniker. Nicknaming is an Anglo-Saxon art form born of our need to erect jaunty barriers against emotion, a case in point being the number of WASP men who call their wives "Dutch." The Ripper's nickname invariably gets lost in translation. When the French dramatized the story they called him "Jacques L' Eventreur," which simply doesn't do it. It sounds very fey and very French, a murderer out of a puppet show. I don't know what the Germans call him, but I can imagine. They probably throw together one of their verb-trailing compounds that translates as "Jack who the throats of women who their bodies to men sell cuts." If, as is generally thought, the murderer invented the name himself in his taunting letters to the police, we can clear the two Polish suspects because whoever coined "Jack the Ripper" had an English ear.

The best Ripper book, in my opinion, is Tom Cullen's *When London Walked in Terror*. The worst is Frank Spering's *Prince Jack*, which kicked off the fad of attributing the crimes to Prince Albert Victor, grandson of Queen Victoria and the heir presumptive to the throne until his death from typhoid in 1892.

Prince "Eddy," as he was called (his father was Edward, Prince of Wales, later Edward VII), has to be the sorriest candidate for alpha-male mayhem in criminal history. A study in limpid-eyed lethargy, he was, said Victoria's cousin, the Duke of Cambridge, "never ready, never there." Whatever else we may say of Jack the Ripper, he was smart, but Eddy's mind, said his tutor, was "at all times in an abnormally dormant condition."

To claim a retarded drunkard and drug addict who had inherited his mother's congenital deafness could have pulled off the Ripper's split-second timing and daring escapes is silly enough, but the Prince Jack contingent also insists that the Ripper's surgical skills, good enough to be attributed to a doctor or a Jewish ritual slaughterer, could easily have been acquired by Eddy at royal shooting parties.

It's true that he was always shooting something. In fact, the royal calendar for the August murder dates puts him in Scotland for the sacred annual pursuit of the grouse. He and the other bluebloods shot thousands of birds and animals on any given day, but they did not dress their own kill. That task was beneath even the "ghillies," or gamekeepers; it was done by lowly rustics at a far remove from the royal picnic tables. Eddy would never even have seen it, much less taken a hand in it.

The words "a good English murder" are synonymous with escapism, but we haven't escaped the Ripper. His trademark is the coin of our cultural realm. In the words of Tom Cullen:

> The head had been so nearly severed from the body that the killer had knotted a handkerchief around the neck as though to hold the head to the torso. The left arm had been placed across the left breast, and the legs were drawn up, with the feet resting on the ground and the knees turned outward. The face was bruised and the tongue was swollen and protruded between the front teeth. The body had been disemboweled and, with some show of surgical deftness, the uterus and its appendages had been removed. As a further bizarre note, two brass rings, evidently wrenched from the middle finger of her left hand, and a few pennies and farthings, were laid out neatly at the victim's feet.

Playboy and *Penthouse* arrange a woman the same way: nude except for a scarf or gold chain, gynecologically exposed, fondling her own breast, tongue protruding enticingly, the body air-brushed to remove blemishes, and books on playing the stock market scattered at the bottom of the bed.

November 19, 2001

Random thoughts on what may yet go down in history as the War Without a Name . . .

Can you remember, off the top of your head, the last thing they came up with? I can't. If the Bushies put it through the sensitivity grinder one more time they'll have to call it the Inoffensive Offensive. They're like a teenage girl experimenting with her name; address the newly minted "Luci" as "Lucy" and she becomes hysterical.

Speaking of word endings, the real epidemic is not anthrax but dropped *g*s. Both Bushes long ago made a point of adopting this speech habit to pass as just-plain-folks, but now it has spread to just about everyone who speaks publicly, from Donald Rumsfeld to Diane Dimond. Their aim is to project jaunty confidence, but the overall effect is that of globetrotting country boys and sleekly coiffed hicks. Dropped *g*s have been weaponized, aerosoled, enspored. Delivered to us in the electronic envelope of television, they waft out and float around us like crumbly mist, fulfilling the ancient prophecy that the English language will end, not with a bang, but with a whoosh.

Also contributing to its death throes is the constant reiteration that we are not making war on a race, religion, nation, or region, but on terrorism. This means we don't dare call the enemy Arabs, Muslims, Afghanis, or Middle Easterners lest we destroy some imaginary coalition, so Bush calls them "the evil ones." Black-and-white thinking is refreshing to a point, but he's beginning to sound like the host of a classic-movie channel introducing Vincent Price Week.

The most curious thing to emerge from the crisis were the descriptions of the 54-year-old Bush as our "young president" that suddenly cropped up in the print media, in columns by Ben Bradlee and Maureen Dowd, to name just two. Combined with regular assurances that Cheney had been whisked off to an undisclosed secret location, it sounded like a coup in the works. Now, though, the infantilization has stopped and the danger is past, thwarted by Bush himself. Whether he realizes it or not, he burnished his own image when he gave Tom Ridge the Javert-like title of Homeland Security Director. The one man in America whose eyes are even more pleading than Bush's own, Ridge looks as lost as a Dickensian orphan, with no trace of the saving pluckiness that goes with the type. His air of helpless abandonment, combined with his incredibly tiny mouth, are a guarantee that Bush will never be called young again.

The War Without a Name is proving that patriotism is the last refuge of the tone-deaf. Just because "God Bless America" is easier to sing than "The Star-Spangled Banner" is no excuse for singing it if you can't carry a tune in a bucket. Emboldened by GBA's un-operatic range, alleged singers with no memory of Kate Smith are murdering it with ululating shrieks and gulpy crooning, or belting it out like the last of the red-hot mamas in the manner of Jessica Simpson, the Las Vegas lounge singer and teenage pop star who performed it at the White House, with something close to bumps and grinds, for a clearly dismayed president.

For once, I liked him. The look on his face was a perfect match for his soulmate, George V, who liked a tune he could whistle, a story with a plot, and a painting that looked like what was written on the little brass plate. Once, when the Grenadier Guards band played a selection from a Richard

Strauss symphonic fantasia, he sent them a note: "His Majesty does not know what the band just played, but it is never to be played again."

I get the distinct feeling that the most important news is consigned to the crawl ribbon at the bottom of the TV screen. While the anchors go on about stress, Afghani pen pals, and buying gas masks, the crawl reports the meaty stuff. In late September it told of Westerners attacked in Saudi Arabia, two Christian churches in Kenya burned to the ground and "We Condemn America" traced in the ashes, an anti-U.S. protest in Athens by 2,000 demonstrators, threats to our ambassador in Indonesia, and the evacuation of the L.A. subway when riders smelled something and their eyes began to water. This last received brief coverage but the rest, including the rumble in the cradle of Western Civ, were never mentioned. Nor was this crawl item from late October: "Sri Lankan terrorists claim responsibility for attack on fuel ship. Seven killed." Where? Whose ship?

I think a lot is happening that they choose to ignore, but to avoid the appearance of censorship they drag it along the bottom of the screen on the assumption that most viewers won't read it. The minority who do read it come in for a more subtle censorship: Because it's impossible to read and listen at the same time, they take in half of the crawl and half of the sound without digesting either one. A handful of beetle-browed eccentrics can be expected to mute the sound and concentrate on the crawl, but there aren't enough of us to matter.

Good news: The War Without a Name is bringing back traditional sexual differences with a vengeance. If sanity is restored, we can thank maps. Men and their maps, men and their pointers, men and their colored tacks and signal flags. The big brass are all over the tube, droning away in the monotone men slip into when they heed the call to fulfill masculinity's solemn duty to be boring. It's like that unbearable stock scene in WWII movies: "Our chaps are here, the Yanks are here, and Jerry is here," says John Loder, slapping the map smartly with his swagger stick. Then comes the synchronizing-of-watches scene, when millions of women refrain from asking how they get the second hand in the same place on every watch for fear that some man will start *explaining*.

Nothing convinces a woman that she is not a man like having her capacity for boredom tested and finding that she comes up short. The war on terrorism has expanded into a war on gender feminism, and an ideal leader has emerged: Rear Adm. John Stufflebeem, who is so boring that he sounds as if somebody had started to embalm him and then stopped.

December 3, 2001

NR's anti-porn issue breathed new life into an old idea I've been mulling over for a long time, so here it is: The Blue Lagoon Syndrome.

Everyone has seen the 1980 movie with Brooke Shields, but few remember the 1949 British version starring Jean Simmons, and hardly anyone has read the 1908 novel on which the movies were based. But taken together, along with the sniggering 1991 spin-off, *Return to the Blue Lagoon*, they offer a case study of our era's defining paradox: Sex isn't sexy.

The novel was written by Henry de Vere Stacpoole (1863–1931), an Anglo-Irishman who sailed the world as a ship's doctor before turning his hand to popular literature.

Essentially a hack, his only bestseller was *The Blue Lagoon*. Set in Victorian times, it's the story of two upper-middle-class cousins, Emmeline and Dick, both eight, who survive a shipwreck and are marooned on a South Sea island with an old salt named Paddy, the ship's carpenter. Knowing himself to be ill, and sensing that rescue will never come, Paddy teaches Dick all he knows about boats and the sea so the children can survive without him if necessary. This is exactly what happens; he dies a couple of years later and they are on their own.

The novel's premise is that two children of their time and class would be utterly ignorant of the facts of life. The advance publicity for the 1949 movie drove this point home, e.g., "They didn't know what passion was until they discovered it together!" The idea of two virgins knowing instinctively what to do hurled my junior high school into a tizzy and guaranteed our identification with the characters. Em and Dick (renamed Michael) were even dumber than we were, yet they managed to figure it all out for themselves without benefit of adults, convincing my best girlfriend and me that it was no longer necessary to ask our mothers questions about wedding nights and such because it was merely a matter of doing what comes naturally.

Our identification did not go beyond fantasies, however, because there was a safety valve at work. We didn't realize it, but our responses were shaped and contained by the unofficial censorship of the times. In 1949, a movie about teenagers coupling on a desert island could not cast teenage actors in the roles, so we were actually identifying with a certified grown-up, 21-year-old Jean Simmons, who had already played opposite Olivier in *Hamlet*. The casting tamped us down in another way: Simmons's beauty had such a grandmother-approved wholesomeness that she always looked as if she had just been scrubbed. It's hard to copy the sexual behavior of someone described as the picture of health.

The restraints on moviemakers forced them to omit one of the most powerful scenes in the book, when Em menstruates for the first time and thinks she is dying. Opponents of censorship cite the artistic power of "reality," but the safety valve of 1949 proved that art's ultimate power is imagination. We had just started menstruating ourselves so the subject was surely on our minds, yet we never wondered about how Em reacted to the event: We were too caught up in the story.

Nor did we expect to see her looking pregnant; nobody "showed" in 1949 movies, even married women. After their first and only kiss on a moonlit beach, the scene fades to black and reopens on Michael searching frantically for Em. He finds her at last in the cave where she has gone to give birth. Their figures are hidden in the shadows and neither of them speaks; then Michael, played by blond Brit hunk Donald Houston, picks up the baby and holds it over his head in triumph as his ringing laugh echoes through the flickering darkness. It was more sensual than the most explicit love scene. The message was unmistakable: He was not a boy, but a man.

In the 1980 Brooke Shields version, the unraveling begins at once. First to go is the sexual innocence—because Leo McKern, who plays the old salt, has salvaged his pornographic photos. We only catch glimpses of them in rapid-fire cut-ins, but it plants the idea that Em and Michael could have picked up some pointers, and it makes the requisite bow to reality: Sailors like dirty pictures.

The principals really are teenagers; she coltish, he callow, both giggly. The more irritating of the pair is Christopher Atkins, who manages to render their purported innocence as grubby tactlessness every time he opens his mouth. "How come all this hair is growing on me?" he wonders, examining his legs. "I never saw anybody bleed like that," he declares, when Em gets her first period. "How come you're getting so fat?" he blurts, when her condition starts to show. It doesn't take him long to transform himself from the castaway-lover of every woman's dreams to the actual male who is seared on every woman's memory, known as The Boy Who Sat Behind Me in Homeroom.

It shouldn't be able to get any worse, but it does. *Return to the Blue Lagoon* is a second-generation orgy about the son of the dead Em and Michael and the daughter of a widow on the ship that rescued him. But alas, this ship goes down also, and the widow with two babies in tow washes up on the same island where Em and Michael once lived. The years pass, and so does the premise of the story, because this is a progressive widow who tells her growing daughter everything she needs to know, including a smarmy disquisition on the menses that sounds just like the Kotex-sponsored film they used to show us in hygiene class, called "That Wonderful Thing That Happens Every Month."

By the time the mother dies, the kids are ready to rock. The gossamer shimmer of sexual awareness is exchanged for that teen favorite, the gross-out. The boy is shown having an erotic dream with a sappy grin on his face. Seeing his erection, the girl has a giggling fit and squeals, "Oooh, does it hurt?" "I know how to get rid of it if I want to." "How?" "Wouldn't you like to know!"

A little later on, a sex-starved lady missionary shows up.

December 17, 2001

D EAR Gentle Readers:
Welcome to the last issue of the year, when I get to write my favorite kind of column: a chatty letter, instead of a logically (more or less) argued, structured (sort of) disquisition on what are grandly known as the Issues of Our Times.

As usual, the first order of business is choosing a suitable quotation for 2001. I came up with several dyspeptic enough to suit my tastes, including one by my soulmate, Schopenhauer, but this time I decided that the clear winner is something that was not said, but would have been if my mother were still with us and could register her opinion on whether we should stop the bombing during Ramadan. I can hear her now. . . .

"That's the best time to get 'em—when they've got their faces in the rug and their asses in the air."

I have big news. Remember my *Passive Suicide Cookbook*? Well, forget it. Around this time last year, I got such an awful pain in my right knee that I had to use a cane. While I was hobbling around, I also found out that my blood pressure was 154/94, so I went on a diet and have so far lost 60 pounds. My blood pressure is now 123/75 and the knee is back to normal. I heard that every excess pound of body weight puts five pounds of pressure on the knees, so no wonder I was practically crippled.

I didn't go on any particular diet, and, needless to say, I didn't join any of those clubs or support groups. I just did commonsense things, plus mild exercises at first, and later, long walks. I even dieted on Christmas last year and Thanksgiving this year—freelance writing is the best training in self-discipline there is, and I have a Southern advantage when it comes to

Thanksgiving. When I was little, my grandmother's aunt was still living at 94, and had vivid memories of what she called "the Woah." She considered Thanksgiving a Yankee holiday and made a point of observing it with soft-boiled eggs and bouillon, so I had the same.

I may feel better physically but my mental outlook is the same as ever, so let's get to my list of what irritated me the most during the past year. Since I'm already on the subject of food, I'll start with noisy TV cooks.

Emeril, who has a band, is the most nerve-wracking. All of them talk too much, kid around, do tricks with utensils, mug for the camera, keep up a steady stream of unfunny patter, and in general show off for the audience, who invariably respond like schoolchildren with a teacher who can't or won't maintain discipline. The din and distractions make it impossible to follow the recipes or study the techniques. Having an audience is part of the problem; it's like trying to cook and converse with your dinner guests at the same time. The kitchen is one place where show biz doesn't work; the sole shining exception being Julia Child —a comic genius without trying.

Not all TV cooks are obstreperous. Martha Stewart is a model of discipline, but that's just the trouble. She reminds me of Fraulein von Frumpel, the villainess in a WWII-era Saturday serial designed to keep us phartlings pumped up for the war effort. Stewart says all the right homemaker things, but I can't help feeling that somewhere in there is an "Achtung!" waiting to come out.

If noisy cooks don't kill me, quiet appliances will. I need white noise; I can't function without it. I have window fans, ceiling fans, and an air purifier going constantly. White noise makes it possible for me to write, to convince myself that there's no world beyond this room. White noise is the sound of silence, the buzz of solitude, so of course America is resolved to stamp it out.

Every machine is now advertised as "quiet" and "soundless." The only way to get a grinding whir is to buy a defective product, but you can't very well demand one without attracting attention to yourself. My latest fruitless search is for a clock that ticks. One ad I saw said, "It doesn't tick! It listens!" Oh, God, I thought, a selfless, compassionate clock. Turns out, what it listens to are signals from the Atomic Clock in Fort Collins, Colorado, which assures its accuracy. Another tickless wonder gives daily moon phases until 2019. I'll probably be a moon phase myself by then. In the meantime, I want loud, tinny TICKING! Is that too much to ask?

I just had an eye exam and don't need new reading glasses, which is lucky because the kind of frames I like—heavy, owlish hornrims that can be put on and removed with a careless sweep of one hand—are completely out of style and unavailable. The latest styles have wire rims and tiny lenses not much bigger than the eye itself. They flatter no one, yet everybody is obediently wearing them. Why do people want to look like Victorian schoolmarms? Sometimes I hate conformists so much that I'd like to sic al-Qaeda on them.

As always, language irritants have abounded this past year. Leading the list is "It's not a matter of *if*, but *when*" in reference to the next terror attack. I don't contest the truth of it; what irks me is the preening that accompanies it—liberals suddenly advertising themselves as realists after spending their entire pre-Sept. 11 lives as total idiots.

Speech habits of the rich and famous have gotten on my nerves so much that I can barely watch the news. Why doesn't John McCain go to the dentist and get that whistling tooth fixed? He sounds like Jack Lemmon in *The Out-of-Towners* when he broke his front teeth on stale Crackerjacks. Worse, Bush's sibilant esses are turning into one long hiss—or as he would say, "hissssss." Somebody must have told him to sharpen his diction to banish the image of the lazy scion and come off as crisp and decisive, but overcompensating always has the opposite effect. Now he sounds as if he doesn't know his asp from third base.

My defining moment of 2001? During the PBS biog of Napoleon, when they gave the dimensions of St. Helena, I thought hungrily, "That's just right for one person."

December 31, 2001

2002

Y OU know what I like about this magazine? I never hear a word
about "the NATIONAL REVIEW family." We must be the only outfit
left that doesn't push the huddle-and-cuddle organizing principle
now rampant in American business, political, and cultural life.

The word "family" has become ubiquitous, right up there with those
automatic ejaculations of "Absolutely!" that have replaced the simple "yes."
At the rate we're going, it threatens to join "aloha" and "ciao" as an every-
thing word that means whatever we need it to mean. Is the phone ringing?
Pick it up and say "Family." Spot an acquaintance on the bus? "Family.
How's things?" Get off before he does? "See you around, Family."

The possibilities are endless. It could become our all-purpose Big Ten
cheer—"Family! Family! Sis boom bah!"—replace "roger" and "ten-four" in
two-way radiospeak, and give Sen. Robert Byrd a golden opportunity to
repeat the ancient history he loves so much. Cato the Elder had such a wild
hair on about Hannibal that he ended every speech, regardless of subject matter, with the words, "Carthage must be destroyed." Byrd, who has never
minded non sequiturs, could wind up his orotund disquisitions on West
Virginia cement with "The family must be preserved."

References to family are getting more and more compulsive, lacking any
direct connection to the subject at hand and frequently clashing with it. On
my last trip to the supermarket, I noticed at the very top of my cash-register
receipt the words: "Spend More Time With Your Family! Hot Rotisserie

Chicken!" That sounds forced, until we realize that the store must have been subconsciously inspired by the excuse that philandering politicians have cooked up to explain sudden early retirements necessitated by their taste for spring chicken.

Even more far-out is the boat-on-a-rope commercial for Eukanuba Dog Food, which is said to contain a teeth strengthener. It tells the tale of a Labrador named Mas who saved "a family in trouble" by pulling a boat containing the whole lot of them to safety through a raging river with the mooring rope clenched in her iron teeth. My, how far we've progressed. Lassie played favorites, reserving her greatest devotion for young Joe; at the end of her trek she dragged herself to his school, not to the family's cottage, but then Lassie was not an American dog.

If all politics is local, all news is family. This is achieved by the widespread practice of tossing in the phrase "and their families," which, as Michael Kinsley has noted, has an immediate cheapening effect.

Read any story about any workplace shooting spree and you will be deep in huddle-and-cuddle by the third paragraph. A recent affray took place at an Indiana factory that makes Nu-Wood, a synthetic used for decorative trimming—i.e., by charming coincidence, a fake substance. One company rep was quoted as saying, "I'm concerned for the people, because they treat me like family." Said another, "It's not like an assembly-line situation. Everyone knows each other, and everyone intermixes with each other." (Is it possible, can it be, that this is why matters erupted into gunfire? Don't ask.)

Even the Health Section—or rather, especially the Health Section—is a clearing house for huddle-and-cuddle, often expressing more concern for "cancer families" than for the cancer patients themselves: How to Tell Your Family you've got whatever it is you've got; How Families Cope with the news; and What If Your Family Is in Denial? A typical recent article told of a man who had a stroke that left him paralyzed and afflicted with double vision and slurred speech for almost a year. "And the worst part, he said, was that he could not interact as he used to with his children and his wife." He couldn't walk, couldn't talk, couldn't see, but the *worst* part was inability to "interact"? Give me a break. (Help Your Family Cope with Your Osteoporosis.)

The most deadly aspect of huddle-and-cuddle is now staring us in the face. Our immigration policy favors family reunification over all other considerations, including national security. Once an immigrant gets in, we let him send for his family members, a policy that favors the very ethnic groups we should be leery of, but neurotic sentiment mitigates against leeriness. Show us a slew of Third World relatives—Eldest Brother, Venerable Aunt,

Honorable Uncle, and two dozen fifth cousins all named Mohammed—and we will show you a visa, because an "extended family" is even more sacrosanct than the immediate kind.

Does it come as any surprise that gays want to marry and adopt? For centuries they celebrated their freedom from the spills and bills of domesticity, but in our relentless obsession with family we have inadvertently activated what was once assumed not to exist: a gay gene for respectability.

Huddle-and-cuddle is an inevitable response to force-fed diversity and political correctness. The instinct to seek out one's own kind is hard-wired into human nature, but we don't dare acknowledge it, so we manufacture artificial ties that bind as we go along. Referring to groups of coworkers, customers, subscribers, and people with the same hobby as the something-or-other "family" imparts a vague sameness in which noble-sounding metaphors such as "the Family of Man" can be personalized and reduced to a manageable size.

I don't usually find a light at the end of the tunnel, but this time I've found two. First, the return of liquor ads to TV means that the word "family" will be verboten for all of 30 seconds.

The other light was shed (no pun intended) by Garfield the Cat. Two Sundays before Christmas, Jon was on the phone with his dreary relatives down on the farm. One by one they came on the line, spouting hearty clichés, exchanging trite sentiments, until we got to his brother, Doc Boy, he of the room-temperature IQ, who was inaudible because he was talking into the wrong end of the phone.

At this, Garfield looked up with his fiendish grin and said: "Happy holidays, all you family members out there."

January 28, 2002

T HANK you for the birthday gifts, including the four low-tech alarm clocks, one of which, as my vigilant post office noted, arrived ticking. We have given "white noise" new meaning and rewritten an old adage: "Be careful what you wish for; NR readers might send it to you."

The arrival of my 66th birthday finds me confronting a hard fact: I'm turning into an odd duck. There are some who would not regard this as a new development, but I refer to the psychological changes said to come with advancing age.

The most surprising change is that I no longer love to read the way I once did. I used to read one book after another—literally—finishing one and immediately starting a second, spending whole days reading books by the yard. Now I pick up a book, read a few pages, see right through the author, and toss it aside in disgust. All I feel like reading now are a few beloved books that I've read over and over, like *Katherine*, by Anya Seton.

I also cancelled all my subscriptions except the *Washington Post* and NR. Most columns and op-eds seem so predictable to me now; I can read the first paragraph and know exactly where it's going, so why pay for that? I've been gleefully adding up my refunds like a miser—something I've never been, in my free-spending, big-tipping life. Chalk up another change.

The subscription I resented the most was that rock quarry of the printed word, the Sunday *New York Times*. I wasn't reading anything in it except Maureen Dowd, who is an "uneven" writer (good when she's good; "off" the rest of the time). I kept remembering the old Peter Arno cartoon of an exhausted dog, feet splayed, tongue hanging out, clearly moribund, being examined by a vet. The caption reads: "I see he's been retrieving the Sunday *New York Times*." I felt like the dog.

I kept telling myself that I needed to subscribe "for professional reasons," but finally admitted that the only thing I enjoyed was the acrostic in the magazine. I tried to subscribe to the magazine only, but was told you can't: They know in their hearts that the puzzle page is all most people want, so to keep from going bankrupt they make you subscribe to the whole paper.

Spending $200 a year on a puzzle was ridiculous, so I cancelled, deciding to xerox the acrostic at the public library. Trouble was, somebody had torn the puzzle page out of the magazine before I got to it. (See what I mean? Nobody in his right mind would steal the op-ed page.) When the librarian saw it, she volunteered to call another branch to see if they had an intact magazine, and have them fax the page to me. They did, and in minutes I had my acrostic.

I tell this story for a reason: to analyze the rush of gratitude—yea, worship—that came over me. It wasn't about getting the acrostic, it was the librarian's attitude. True, it is undeniably heartening in present-day America to find efficiency and promptness amid the purple mountains of human error that dot the fruitcake plain, but that doesn't quite explain it. The fact is, my uncharacteristically plaintive reaction was that of an old person: Someone had very kindly gone out of her way to help me.

Psychologists call this a "breakthrough," others call it an "epiphany." Whatever it's called, I had another one a few days later while cutting my toenails. It's been hard to do lately because my joints are stiff and it hurts to bend my legs into the necessary position, but this time I suffered the added pain of regret.

When I was in college, my grandmother was only a little older than I am now; it must have hurt her to cut her toenails too. Why, instead of running around with boys, didn't I go over to the house and cut her toenails for her? It would have been such a simple favor, but I didn't do it. It never even crossed my mind because I could twist my supple young legs into any position (the '55 T-Bird was a veritable workout salon) and assumed everyone else could too. My sins of commission never weighed on me and still don't, but that one small sin of omission will be on my conscience for the rest of my life.

My new aversion to reading is matched by a literal aversion that has come over my palate: I've lost my taste for booze. I mixed a martini on Christmas but couldn't get it down. I'm now into wine, which I never liked before. Go figure. My physical reaction may have to do with aging, but what interests me more is my new psychological oddity.

I'm saving the corks from my wine bottles. I don't know why, except that cork is expensive, and Marcel Proust lined his walls with it to keep out noise while he wrote. I found myself thinking that when I save enough of them, I can make myself a life preserver. Why I should want a life preserver I can't say, since I don't go near the water. But it just seems a shame to throw away all those perfectly good corks, so I save them in an old duffel bag. I can't wait to see what it will look like when it's full. Go figure.

I have none of the conventional symptoms of geriatric depression, though I did feel sad when Rachel Gurney died. She played Lady Marjorie in *Upstairs, Downstairs*, and was my favorite British actress next to Judi Dench. I don't have any American favorites; they all look alike, sound alike, and expose what I could swear is the same bosom.

If I should ever suffer depression, the most likely cause will be America (make that "Amurrica") itself. I look at it through spread fingers, like a juror looking at gruesome autopsy photos, masochistically fascinated by its coagulated smarminess, mangled syntax, and severed logic: the Black Dahlia of the Western world.

Sometimes I think about spending my final years in France, where I could smoke in peace, or England, where my blood began. I would live in Lincoln because Lady Katherine Swynford, the heroine of my favorite novel, is buried in the cathedral. When the time came, I would want to shoot myself beside her tomb. Unfortunately, there's no way to transport my gun to England, so I shall have to swallow a cork.

February 11, 2002

D ID I ever tell you about the time I was shocked, *shocked*, by unabashed bigotry? It happened when I lived in Seattle. The Arab oil embargo was on, and between that and Seattle's steep hills, I decided it was time to forego the convenience of an automatic and learn how to shift gears.

I called a driving school, made an appointment, and waited outside my building for the instructor. When he pulled up and I started walking toward his car, I noticed that he was staring at me with an expression of curiosity mingled with relief. I found out why when I introduced myself.

"The secretary must have got your name wrong. I've got you down as Miss *Ling*," he laughed, tapping his clipboard. "Whew! I thought you were a slant!"

Having attended racially segregated public schools that classified Asians as white, I was understandably fascinated. Needing no encouragement to expound his views, he explained that all Asians were terrible drivers, but some were more terrible than others. Filipinos were the worst because they were the smallest, and being Catholic, kept taking one hand off the wheel to bless themselves. The Japanese were in the middle ("Ah-so-so. Get it? Ah-so . . . so-so!"). The best, if you could call it that, were the Chinese and Koreans, who were terrible drivers too, but at least they were tall enough to reach the pedals.

"Last slant I had put us both in the hospital," he assured me.

After a couple of lessons I was able to shift gears at quiet residential crossings with no trouble. Encouraged by my progress, the instructor decided to show me how to do something that Seattle drivers took great pride in. I forget what he called it, but it meant holding the car on a hill without touching the brake by alternating gas and clutch in precisely coordinated feedings. It was, he said reverently, the sign of an expert driver.

That was the day I rolled backwards down Queen Anne Hill and plowed into a van that turned out to be the Bloodmobile. The inscrutable F. Ling strikes again.

We've come a long way since 1974. Back then, whites could still assume it was safe to say such things to each other. If you picked the wrong person to sound off to, you were merely diagnosed as "simplistic"—a condition of pre-bigotry something like HIV—and dismissed with an earnest little sermonette or a supercilious sniff. Nowadays, however, my instructor would automatically assume that the white stranger beside him was an avenging angel of diversity tuned to a perpetual frequency of High Snitch. He would know that one little "hate speech" is all it would take to get fired, sued, and condemned to wander through the secular purgatory of community service while the talk shows debated his status as Satan Incarnate.

Actually, the perfect place for him would be radio. Whenever I think of him, I remember those regular stock characters who used to wander in and out of the Jack Benny and Fred Allen shows of the 1940s, saying outrageous things in comical ways, setting up situations, and being so predictable that we listeners could supply the dialogue ourselves. We had only to hear their signature lines ("Pardon me for talking in your face, señorita") to know what was coming next, and millions of us in living rooms across America recited it right on cue. If the golden age of radio could create "Digger O'Dell, the Friendly Undertaker," it could have immortalized a terrified driving teacher. I can hear it now: a wrong turn into Chinatown in the middle of a tong war, somebody saying "Chop-chop" at a bad time, a mix-up involving "Confucius say" and a traffic cop named Cornelius O'Shea. The possibilities were endless back when our Great Diversity really was a gorgeous mosaic, but MultiCulties have crammed comedy into the narrow end of a funnel: When everybody's got a right to be Top Banana, there's no room left for fall guys.

Maybe it's because I remember old-time radio, or maybe it's because I was raised by people who remembered vaudeville, but I relish ethnic humor, the more slapstick the better. One of my favorite parlor games is giving titles to those novelty books the size of sugar cubes: *Who's Who of Irish Libertines . . . Great English Chefs . . . An Unabridged History of the Presbyterian Church of Spain*. Another is answering the question, "How to Avoid Getting Run Over When Crossing the Street in Foreign Countries":

Italy: Take a pregnant woman with you.

Germany: Take a soldier with you.

France: Take an intellectual with you.

England: Take a dog.

I also relish the unconscious ethnic humor of MultiCulties, as when they slip up and say, "Americans of all nationalities." They do their best pratfalls with an ingrained pre-political correctness phrase they can't avoid, which juts out of their rosy scenarios like a blurb for a disaster movie: "white flight." And their best punchline is the knee-jerk commitment made not just by politicians but by everyone with a public role, however minor: PTA presidents, directors of recreation centers, student-exchange guides, and ladies' garden clubs all promise to "end racism."

Their funniest TV spot is the "I Am an American" public-service ad in which a motley crew of citizens vie with each other to claim the greatest degree of motleyness. It opens low with tame statements like "I am half-German and half-Polish, and I am an American." Then they up the ante, and the speed as well, until bevies of earnest people are flashing across the screen finishing sentences for each other: "My parents are from Tasmania and Nigeria, and I am . . . I have a Mexican-Norwegian father and an Irish-Eskimo mother, and I am an . . . My grandfather was half-Turkish and half-Egyptian and my grandmother was a part-Cherokee Portuguese-Canadian, and . . . American!"

If this keeps up, we will soon hear a reprise of the great line from *Forrest Gump*: "I want half of you in front, and half of you in back, and the other half over there."

February 25, 2002

T HE *Washington Post* obituary for columnist Richard Grenier stated that he died of a heart attack while watching the State of the Union address. I was saddened by the news because I liked Grenier's writing, but not at all surprised by the circumstances of his death.

I had an iffy moment myself when Bush referred to "the families I've hugged," but at least it was a line I could have some fun with once I got over the initial jolt. My closest brush with a blood-pressure "event" occurred when he warmed to another theme that circles around our national life like a persistent gnat and insinuates itself through our collective conscience like the fault line of a dropped stitch in a tapestry.

Every president from Jimmy Carter on has parlayed it, each one kicking the intensity up another notch like Emeril Lagasse hurling garlic into his pots. Carter didn't make a lot of speeches about it, choosing instead to hammer the point home by building houses for the poor until we all understood that he was a carpenter with the initials J. C. It was a tough act to follow, but Reagan enshrined Alexis de Tocqueville and told the touring Frenchman's story about the frontier barnraising so many times that he turned "volunteerism" into a buzzword. The elder Bush, propelled by the family tendency to goopiness, coined "a thousand points of light." Then came the Clintons, one creating AmeriCorps and the other talking up The Little Village That Could. Now we have Bush 43 demanding a little chunk of our lives—not much, heck, you won't even miss it—urging us to drop everything to go off somewhere and mentor somebody.

It sounded like nagging to me—when the Bushes aren't being goopy, the family vocal cords tend to slip into the Xanthippe range—but it struck the right note for the times. Americans have always enjoyed being known as the world's most generous people, but something more than generosity is involved when charities have to announce that they don't need any more money, and bloodbanks have to announce that they don't need any more blood, and would we please, please, *stop* donating. That had to hurt, so Bush's presumptuous demand that we sign up for altruistic lost weekends and two compassionate years before the mast must have given millions a new lease on the self-flagellating guilt that fuels the engines of America the Selfless.

Compulsive volunteerism is our new way of pretending to a unity we know we lack. Our old way depended on disasters. From Pearl Harbor to the *Challenger* explosion, we announced "It brought us together," and repeated it until we believed it, but it was rarely heard after Sept. 11. The terrorist attacks made us yearn for something more personal and immediate than the grand sweep of national unity, so we narrowed it down to "We're all New Yorkers now."

The denizens of volunteerism have a word for this sort of parochial yearning. They call it "community"—just that, nothing more, never mind parts of speech; it's noun, verb, adjective, whatever you need it to be. As an all-purpose word it's second only to "family" as a vehicle for American angst, denoting an idyllic unit of humanity made up of kindred spirits with the same needs, all working together for the common good, mentoring each other until everybody rubs off on everybody else, sanding down the rough edges of difference.

A few weeks ago I had a memorable experience when I happened to sit next to a female Community on the bus. It was a new line so I decided to take a ride to see if it stopped at any of the places I need to go. Community was riding for the same reason, so we got to talking about the local bus service. I was clocking the schedule for the Food Lion stop, but instead of going by the direct route, the bus was meandering through leafy, upscale suburban neighborhoods with two-car garages. On and on it went, traversing a sylvan glade dotted with bus stops and nobody waiting at them.

"Why did they put the route out here?" I asked. "These people don't take the bus."

"They're part of the community," said Community.

"But they couldn't have moved out here in the first place if they didn't have cars," I argued.

"The buses have to serve the community."

"Even if they don't need it?"

"You have to think of the community as a whole," said Community.

It was no use. The word squirted out of her like ink from a squid. We were talking past each other; she was intent on gluing everybody together no matter what because she wanted a sense of belonging, but all I wanted was Food Lion.

The pursuit of unity is also behind our memorial jag. It stands to reason that if you build enough memorials, the day eventually will come when there is no one left to leave out: If it moves, carve it in marble. The theme park as a civil right. Symbolism as discrimination. Tom Hanks's truculent plea for a WWII memorial ("It is time") ignores the Iwo Jima statue, but requiring Americans to use their imaginations violates the memorial rights of other members of the military community who aren't Marines.

Hanks will get his memorial, and so, eventually, will such giants of statesmanship as Thomas R. Marshall and William Rufus DeVane King, because if you get enough tourists soaking their feet in the fountain and wondering "Who the hell was he?" you have brought at least some of us together.

Naturally, the line in the State of the Union that upset so many didn't bother me a bit. It never even occurred to me to associate "axis of evil" with Germany, Japan, and Italy. The word is a geometric measurement having to do with arcs; the "Axis" nations of WWII formed an arc across the globe, as do Iran, Iraq, and North Korea.

If that sounds out-of-character, there's a reason. In college I dated a boy who wore a slide rule on his belt and droned on and on about his boring major. At some point in my halcyon days as a captive audience, the word "axis" cropped up in its literal sense and stuck in my mind.

March 11, 2002

T RY this at home: Flip on the TV and check out the first words you hear before the picture comes up. They very likely will be "balsamic vinegar" or "extra-virgin olive oil." The country is obsessed with cooking. Not gourmet cooking—the word is verboten now—just cooking, as in what used to be called slaving over a hot stove.

The hottest stoves around are on the all-cooking-all-the-time Food Network, which has something and someone for every taste. Nostalgic for your sorority days? Watch lovably ditzy Sara Moulton, who takes phone calls while she cooks and gets so gabby that she forgets to give oven times and temperatures. If you're into life-or-death seriousness there's the Samurai of the Spatula, the Iron Chef, grimly presiding over Oriental cooking contests described like horse races ("Number Six is browning on the turn . . . Number Four is starting to show signs of congealing").

Emeril Lagasse has succeeded in making cooking a manly art without wearing a chef's toque. Nobody wears a toque; they're as verboten as "gourmet." Mario Batali wears Bermuda shorts and orange clogs on *Mario Eats Italy*; Jamie Oliver (*The Naked Chef*) ties a tea towel around his waist to protect his ragged jeans; and an Indian girl whose name I forget wears very little of anything: Bib aprons hide cleavages, and she does breast presentations without a chicken.

Nobody is intimidating except the Frenchman who makes life-size swans out of spun sugar. We see them roaring off on their motorcycles to do their own shopping at the farmer's market, or, like the well-named Wolfgang Puck, attempting to drive a Viennese fiacre. The menus usually include travelogues; the Indian girl did a tour of Spain that ended with a ragout of bull testicles, and took us to a utensil-free public mess hall in Calcutta where customers sit on the floor with straw mats for plates while pairs of men lugging huge kettles race up and down the aisles dumping rice on the mats—very much like my mother's presentations.

Adroit frenzy is the order of the day. Nobody except Martha Stewart measures anything, and they all use the homey yet proprietary locution favored by generations of women who really did spend the best years of their lives slaving over a hot stove: "my" instead of "the," as in, "Now I'm going to add my milk." Viewers who need reassurance can tune in to *Food 911*, on which the cook goes to someone's home to repair a disaster. And to make accident-prone viewers feel better about themselves, they all use wadded-up tea towels instead of potholders or oven mitts. It looks awkward and impromptu, and holds out the possibility that the towel will trail in the burner and start a fire.

I confess I've gotten hooked on them despite what I said in an earlier column about noisy cooks. They're still noisy, but they no longer get on my nerves. In fact, I could watch them all day long and occasionally do, which presents some real food-for-thought: If *I* swim with the tide, it must be some tide. What is behind our national cooking fad?

On the simplest level, we need look no further than the current state of the vast wasteland. Newscasters have gotten so repellent, talk shows so superficial, sitcoms so unfunny, dramas so mundane, movies so predictable, that the Food Network offers the best fare on TV in every sense of the word. I can honestly say that I owe much of my improved culinary skills to Fox News. If you have a choice between Shepard Smith and balsamic vinegar, why not opt for the original? If Greta Van Susteren's recently filleted face puts you off, why not look at a real monkfish instead?

On a more complicated level, it may be that America is oversupplied with college graduates who crave a sense of real usefulness. The conflict began generations ago when working-class fathers kept saying, "Don't be like me, earn your living with your brain, not your back." This incessant chant was seconded by she who spent the best years of her life slaving over a hot stove: "Don't be like *him*, make something of yourself!"

Later, as many parents became college graduates themselves, the words changed but the tune did not. We went on marching to it until we created a vast horde of bored and disillusioned victims of dumbed-down curricula and puffed-up jobs who now feel a need to "do something with my hands." They don't want to be factory workers or laborers, but cooking is the perfect compromise: manual work infused with polished elegance, and just enough French to keep you on the right side of the educational divide.

I know all about it. For 40 years I have earned my living with my brain; I never did anything else, and can't do anything else unless you count typing. The downside of American upward mobility is the frustration of the need to feel essential, to provide something that people can't live without—the rueful knowledge that you've never *made* anything that is alleviated when you take up cooking.

Two other possible reasons for the cooking craze occur to me. Back in the '70s, *Cosmopolitan* ran a polemic by a male writer who said the women he knew actually tried to be bad cooks, inviting him to dinner so they could burn something to show him how liberated they were. It may be that women are feeling guilty over feminism, but that doesn't explain why so many men are Food Network junkies.

We might be motivated by the "War on Obesity" declared by the surgeon general. Sensing that the government is getting ready to create a new class of untouchables, we have resolved to stay thin the way the French do, by eating so well that we lose our taste for McFood and non-stop snacking. This also allows us to renew the old war on "our Anglo-Saxon repression," the rationale for the sexual revolution, by cultivating another form of sensuality.

Or maybe we simply like Food Network because we learn from it. It's done wonders for my unfortunate culinary heritage. My English side says, when in doubt, boil it in water; my Southern side, which is also an English side, says, when in doubt, fry it in bacon grease. But now I'm a devotee of balsamic vinegar and extra-virgin olive oil.

March 25, 2002

P LAGIARISM, again. It seems to happen in waves, like high-school shootings. Three or four in a row, then a lull, then another batch, until they all run together in the mind and it becomes hard to tell one from the other.

The latest dustup stars popular historians Stephen Ambrose and Doris Kearns Goodwin. I've never read Ambrose, but Goodwin interests me because I reviewed what may turn out to be the only book she's ever written that she didn't plagiarize: her memoir. I forget the title but it was about growing up as a passionate fan of the old Brooklyn Dodgers. She really is an expert on baseball and I gave her credit for that, but I attacked her on two other counts.

One was her unconscionable padding. She recounts that as a teen she worked behind the soda fountain at the town drugstore, and then proceeds to a detailed description of how to make an ice-cream soda; every squirt, every fizz, every dollop is presented for the edification of the untold millions who have never eaten or seen or heard of an ice-cream soda or set foot in a drugstore.

A good writer simply doesn't do this, even in a featherweight book like this one; rules are rules, and the rule about padding was etched on lit. crit. by Boileau, whom I probably quoted in my review: "All that is needless, carefully avoid/The mind, once satisfied, is quickly cloyed." Especially by chocolate syrup.

The other thing I pounced on was either her hypocrisy or her blindness, I couldn't tell which. Reflecting on her childhood in a provincial Long Island town, she waxed nostalgic over the loss of the tranquility and safety she had known, and tentatively rued the loosening influence of the old monolithic Catholicism in which she had been raised. That did it. "Why," I wrote, "do liberals mourn the loss of the very things that their own politics have destroyed?"

I've read Goodwin's book about the Kennedys and the Fitzgeralds, and the one about FDR during WWII. While they were fairly enjoyable, the thing that struck me about them is that I found nothing whatsoever to underline. Normally, when I get through with a book you couldn't get a quarter for it at a yard sale, but give me a Goodwin and I'll give it back in mint condition; you could use it for a Christmas present with no one the wiser. This may be proof of her innocence: Surely, if she stole from other writers, *something* would stand out. On the other hand, it may be proof of her guilt: Every stolen passage stands out like a sore thumb.

Goodwin is a classic example of mediocrity: There's nothing really wrong with her literary style, but there's nothing really right with it either; its natural home is the term paper, or the "kit" and "materials" that come with "programs" like Hooked on Phonics. Her penchant for stating the obvious with an air of perky pride gives her work the flavor of a dumbed-down version of the Book of Revelation, but she achieves full twit-hood in her ubiquitous television appearances, where it's hard to distinguish her banalities from those of the call-in viewers. This establishes her as "unthreatening," which is the whole point of American life. A typical Goodwinism—"The role of the First Lady was ceremonial and Eleanor really shocked people"—lowers the goalposts enough so that she emerges on the other side as the historian next door, a friendly academic cook making napoleons on Food Network while talking on the phone.

The latest plagiarism controversy is hot news right now, but only because it's a scandal involving celebrities. Nobody, including the media, gives a damn about plagiarism per se. That America regards it as a joke is evident from the cute headlines: "Tripping Over Their Own Footnotes," "Twice-Told Tales," "History Repeats Itself." Ambrose and Goodwin will lie low for a while, then reappear wrapped in mantles of modest triumph like the pill-poppers who shuffle off to the Betty Ford Clinic and live to tell the tale—eagerly, all over the tube.

The errant historians will appear before Larry King, who has forgiven more people than Jesus Christ, and talk about what they've learned and how they've grown. As a final fillip, somebody, somewhere will announce that plagiarism is an "addiction" and we will get six months' worth of talk shows about "PA Syndrome." Americans would never dream of excluding children when inventing new crippling disorders, so expect a spin-off debate about "Copycat Syndrome" and endless checklists on "How to Tell If Your Child Is . . ."

Once plagiarism becomes an officially designated addiction, its sufferers will not only be forgiven, but admired. This is the way America works. We cherish and reward mediocrity, cultivate it like the rarest of orchids. We don't want brilliant original historians because we don't want brilliant original anybodys. If you don't believe it, go to the movies. *I Am Sam* extols the mentally retarded (as did *A Child Is Waiting* way back in 1963), and *A Beautiful Mind*, for all its inspirational façade, warns of the dangers of genius.

Do I think Goodwin is guilty? Let's put it this way. The AP story about what she told the *Boston Globe* states: "She said she had copied from her notes rather than going back to the sources, sometimes losing track of which passages were hers and which were written by others."

I say this is impossible. Sentences are a writer's children; we can pick them out anywhere. Like children, they squirm and wriggle, hop up and down, scream at us, and in general make themselves instantly conspicuous. Blood is thicker than ink.

An interesting offshoot of the grand plagiarism that makes the news is the petit plagiarism that doesn't. In one of my books I coined—I thought—"If at first you don't secede, try, try again." Not long after, it turned up on Southern T-shirts and bumper stickers. Was I plagiarized? No. Anybody with half an ear could come up with that one.

Harder to pull off is the delicious phrase in a letter I just got from a fellow writer: "He has as much sense of play as a geriatric moose." Oh, God, I wish I had said it!

April 8, 2002

I 'M in a nostalgic mood. I just put in for Medicare and Social Security, so we're talking milestones big time. Since I feel like reminiscing, I've decided to tell you about my Aunt Ellen.

She wasn't really my aunt. I don't know what to call her; she wasn't legally adopted, and foster-care programs didn't exist when she came into our family. I suppose she was the ward of my grandparents and they were her guardians, but if so, they were merely courtesy titles because there was never any legal arrangement.

It happened in 1919. The now-sprawling D.C. suburb of Arlington, Virginia, was then a little country town with dirt roads. Ellen was two months old, the youngest of four in a family who lived nearby. They were having a bad time; the father, who drank, had run off, and the mother's epilepsy had worsened since the birth of the new baby, so my grandmother and the other townswomen did what they could to help.

One day, Granny sent my mother over with something for them. The kitchen door was open and the woman was standing at the stove with the baby in one arm, stirring a pot. Just as Mama walked in, she gave a high-pitched shriek and fell into a fit, dropping the baby on the hot surface of the old wood stove. The blanket started smoldering.

Mama grabbed the baby, tore off the burning blanket, put the baby on the floor, and grabbed the wooden spoon from the pot and put it between the woman's teeth. Quick thinking for a ten-year-old, but so typical of the mother I was to know: She never read a book in her life, including mine, but she had the sharpest brain I've ever encountered.

Picking up the baby, she ran down the road to get the sheriff (nobody had a telephone). The upshot of the situation was grim; the mother had to be institutionalized and the four children had to be what was then called "taken in." The sheriff handled it very simply by parceling them out on the spot. The older children were easier to care for and could make themselves useful doing chores, but nobody wanted the two-month-old baby. Since Mama had simply taken her home and Granny had been caring for her, it was a fait accompli. No forms to fill out, no charges of abuse and kidnapping, no armies of social workers bearing anatomically correct dolls, no petitions to recall the sheriff: They just kept her.

Whenever I think of Ellen I always recall Queen Victoria's wish that her pale blond family could import "some olive skin and dark hair." Ellen was our import, a Celtic brunette with jet-black eyes, a dead ringer for Jane Russell. My first memory of her is when Gerry, who was stationed in Hawaii and whom she later married, sent her a grass skirt and she did the hula. Though she looked like a sensuous island girl, her outward femininity and glamour concealed an essential remoteness: She was a hula dancer who kept herself to herself. To say "she loved to read" is inadequate. She read voraciously, as though using books as literal shields to keep the world at bay. Maybe it was her knowledge that she was "adopted," but she refused to let herself *need*.

She proved that at her wedding. Various male relatives offered to give her away, including my father, but she chose to go up the aisle alone. She was the only solitary bride I've ever seen and I was enchanted, even though I had an ear infection and a fever of 102. It was February and they tried to make me stay home, but I set up such an outcry that they relented. I ended up in the hospital but seeing dark Ellen all in white was worth it.

Whenever Ellen was physically demonstrative it made family news. One such occasion was after the war when we visited her and Gerry in upstate New York. When they met our train, she hugged Mama. It was the first thing we told Granny when we got back home, and she promptly got on the phone and spread it around. She didn't hug me, but she belonged to the Doubleday Dollar Book Club and I read all of her historical novels that summer, so we talked a lot. That fall, I showed the kids at school our vacation snapshots of myself with Ellen and told them she was my mother.

I was the official family letter-writer, so Ellen's were always addressed to me. It went on like this, letters and summer visits, until Gerry decided, rather late in life, to go to college on the GI Bill. They moved with the children to a cramped university apartment and we couldn't visit anymore. Since I was in college myself by then, I bombarded Gerry with advice on tricks of the student trade— e.g., you don't need to buy all the textbooks, especially the Samuelson for Econ I, etc. I turned into a compulsive tipster. Not for him, though I liked him, but for Ellen; the move was rough on her, so I wanted to get Gerry through college as quickly and cheaply as possible.

Much later, I dedicated my second book to her, and when I started reviewing and blurbing, I sometimes did it with her in mind. I took historical novels I didn't really want to read because I knew she liked them, so I could send them to her with a copy of my review. I also blurbed a novel about the WWII homefront because it reminded me of her hula period; I didn't particularly like it, but I wanted Ellen to see my blurb on the cover, so I raved it.

She and Gerry, the gregarious joiner, were divorced after 35 years. It was the only time I've ever been affected by "the crisis in modern marriage." She went to live with her son. I phoned her regularly, but something was wrong: She had trouble remembering who I was. "Hi, it's Flo." "Who?" "Flo." " . . . Flo?" Not long after, she was diagnosed with Alzheimer's and had to be put in a nursing home.

I didn't visit her. I wanted to remember her in her grass skirt, doing the hula, and that cape of black hair under the white veil. It would have been too sad trying to reach her—and besides, I already had. After she died, her daughter-in-law told me, "She was so happy and touched when you dedicated that book to her— she didn't say much, but I could tell."

April 22, 2002

NOBODY talks about "Yankee ingenuity" anymore but it used to be a proud catchphrase. Americans were the people who could invent anything, from machines to ourselves.

We used the same technique for both. First, we discerned what was needed and produced it, then we identified the kinks and tinkered with them until we came up with a new, improved model. On the personal level we spoke unabashedly of "reinventing ourselves," celebrating the practice as an essential part of the American Dream.

As long as we confined our ingenuity to machines and self-improvement we had the advantage of dealing with physical matter. You might lose an arm in a machine or a spouse in a quest for a new image, but at least these things are tangible.

The same cannot be said for our latest venture. We're tinkering with concepts now, and the one we have decided to improve upon is so abstract that we don't even realize we're tinkering with it: Freud's theory of Ego, Superego, and Id.

The Ego is a nice young man with rosy cheeks and good prospects. The commonsense realm of the psyche, the Ego urges us to act out of self-interest; to do things that grease our path through life and make us look good, such as deferring to the boss, being neat and clean, and telling white lies. This Freudian Ego, once the American beau ideal, was derailed when the Sixties enshrined "authenticity" and demanded unconditional acceptance. We granted it, carefully refraining from finding fault with anybody for anything, until the new, improved American Ego brought about the collapse of civility that the best and the brightest bemoan and ponder on every op-ed page.

Freud's Superego is a teacher's pet in a Roman toga. The idealistic realm of the psyche, the Superego governs abstractions like duty, honor, nobility of spirit, and making decisions on "a matter of principle." But duty, honor, noble spirits, and matters of principle are lofty stuff, and we can't have that: Somebody might feel "threatened."

There is something Roman about lofty abstractions, but there is nothing Roman about easily threatened Americans unless you count the gelatinous blob that washes ashore at the end of *La Dolce Vita*. Give them a choice between acting on principle and following the bumper-sticker injunction to commit a random act of kindness, and they will take the bumper sticker every time. No country that has declared war on elitism can tolerate a Freudian Superego, so we have produced an American model, the Make-Nice PDQ. It runs on empty.

Thanks to Yankee ingenuity, the Id is but a shadow of its former self. The classic Id is the primitive member of the psychical triumvirate that horrifies the civilized Ego and the idealistic Superego by bringing us face to face with our unspeakable urges—murder, rape, incest, and so forth. Americans have a plentiful supply of these, but we shunt them aside so that our Id can concentrate on more serious unspeakable urges such as racism, sexism, and homophobia. This is clearly not your father's Id: The Freudian Id is Mr. Hyde, but the American Id is Dr. Jekyll in a snit.

Freud reasoned that an Ego governed by social convention and a Superego governed by moral values would successfully "censor" the Id, leading to mental health and public safety. We, on the other hand, give the Ego free rein, censor the Superego, and let the Id censor us, and then wonder why mental health and public safety keep eluding us.

We are the world's most reluctant psychologists, craving the answers that insight alone can provide, yet loath to delve too deeply into human nature for fear of finding something we can't deal with. Shunning insight while noisily proclaiming that we "care about people" is awkward, however, so we have developed a compromise technique that might be called, with the usual American straight face, "unreflective insight." It is insight reduced to shallow, mawkish efforts to "understand" the suffering of the victim du jour by asking dumb questions ("What went through your mind when . . . ?") or by airing superficial documentaries on venerated neurotics like Marilyn Monroe and Judy Garland, featuring a bathrobe-clad Hugh Hefner gassing about "the quality of vulnerability."

Being a writer has made me a lifelong practitioner of no-holds-barred insight, driven by an irresistible impulse to shovel through mountains of received bull to get to the bottom of things. My research tool is the unshock-able member of the psychical triumvirate, the classic Id. Freud said we were supposed to censor it, but I release mine on its own recognizance to see what it can find out.

Take, for example, Andrea Yates. How did such an undesirable woman conceive all those kids in the first place? She looks like Olive Oyl crossed with Susan Sontag. What man would want to sleep with her?

Rusty Yates, that's who. When an unusually handsome man marries an unusually homely woman, all the sentimental slobs curl their toes and sigh, "Love is blind," but there's more to it than that. He may be a narcissist who needs to be the beautiful half of the couple. He may be an S.O.B. taking out kindness insurance to cover his true nature. Or he may be so insecure that he subconsciously picks a wife that other men won't try to take away from him.

Rusty displays aspects of all three. He has maintained his slickly perfect grooming, including that expensive haircut, throughout an ordeal that would find most men disheveled. He can't quite hide the flat coldness—like a wet suit with nobody in it—detectable beneath his cliché-perfect effusions of grief and sympathy. And most revealing of all, he is said to have expressed regret that he now has no children "to carry on my name." He strikes me as a man who is so unsure of himself that he fathers children to prove that he exists; without them, he isn't really "there." If Andrea sensed this too, she may have murdered his children as a way of murdering him.

"Nothing human is alien to me," said Terence. Me neither.

May 6, 2002

L AST year I examined the trend toward nationwide stupidity in two columns about the people I called "Ignos" and "Duhs." Now I ask you to turn your attention to yet another group of American folk heroes: the "Ughs."

We live in stomach-turning times. Dial soap's "You're not as clean as you think you are" commercial shows a dog drinking from a toilet and then lick-ing its owner's face.

Folger's coffee has taken Maxwell House's "good to the last drop" pitch and rendered it literally: The Folger's drinker accidentally spills a drop of his coffee on the diner counter, then bends over and licks it up with a loud slurp.

DiGiorno pizza's sloppy bachelor roommates smack their lips and talk with full mouths as they argue over whether it's delivery or DiGiorno.

Nyquil's man-with-a-cold gets out of bed and goes to the kitchen for a glass of warm milk. On his way back upstairs he snorts, drips, gags, hacks, and has a loud, phlegmy sneezing fit that spills the milk all over his bathrobe.

Tropicana orange juice, striving for a calcium statement, shows us a child patting the belly of his extremely pregnant mother, who is clad in a wet swimsuit.

PermaTreat exterminators announces, "That's a real cockroach problem," and then shows us an actual swarm.

Kodak (I believe it is) features a young man trying to win back his girl-friend by taking a picture of his tattooed pelvis.

A magazine ad for a toilet-bowl cleaner (I can't find the clipping and don't remember the brand) showed a smiling woman in her bathroom. The caption read: "It really works! If you don't believe it, smell my toilet!"

A grocery coupon that turned up in a Sunday paper last December offered $1.00 off on two boxes of the product, which, thanks be to God, I no longer need, because it would be impossible to boycott. The accompanying ad read:

"Guess who's joining you under the mistletoe? Go ahead—kiss your crush. KOTEX has you covered. Stock up for seasonal surprises. (Like your period.) Happy Holidays from Kotex. Kotex fits. Period. Check out Kotex.com."

They used to be called "sanitary napkins" and sold already wrapped in plain brown paper so that women would not be embarrassed to buy them from a male drug clerk, or to be seen buying them by strange men. That was back when toilets could not be photographed; in old movies, bathroom scenes of a man shaving or a woman in a bubbly tub never showed the toilet. The first to be filmed was the one in *Psycho*, and it caused audible gasps and nervous laughter.

Sweatiness was limited to characters who worked hard or engaged in physical struggle. Hairiness was considered feral; armpits could not be shown in deodorant ads and actors like William Holden had to have their chests shaved. As for sloppy table manners, they were second only to black hats as signposts of the bad guys.

These standards were abandoned as relics of hypocrisy and repression, but they are starting to look a lot like civilization as the Ughs tighten their grip on the culture. "Gross-out" movies are now an actual genre, like sci-fi and Westerns, and we can't avoid watching them. Rubrics like "Just switch channels" are useless. Between promos aired repeatedly during station breaks and film clips featured on entertainment news, we get a Best Of sampling of green snot and half- eaten worms without leaving the privacy of our homes.

Of course we miss some scenes, like the pharting contest, but not really. Anyone who has ever had any contact with pubescent males hasn't missed a thing; if you have an eighth-grade diploma you have what amounts to a life-time movie pass. Pubescent males are charter members of Ugh, and the eighth grade is the high noon of their compulsion to exercise the only power they have: the power to disgust. Being disgusting, especially in the eyes of those scary creatures called girls, is their greatest delight.

Since arrested development is as American as apple pie, it is easy to identify the subconscious motivation of the adult male Ughs who produce all these revolting movies and commercials. They are our tassel-loafered Taliban, engaged in a last, desperate striving for male domination under the tacit battle cry, "If you can't beat 'em, disgust 'em."

Unfortunately, it's getting harder and harder to disgust women these days, so the Ugh content of American life must keep expanding to fill the vacuum left by female modesty and delicacy. Consequently, our entire population now has a median age of 14, and a sense of proportion that never gets past the eighth grade.

To see what the Ughs are doing to us, consider the sensation caused by the English leading lady, Mrs. Patrick Campbell, who became the first actress to blow her nose onstage during a crying scene in the 1893 play, *The Second Mrs. Tanqueray*. The realistic touch won the hearts of the audience because they were too far away to see and hear the physical effects of tears, but the blubbery, smeary weeping on daily display in news close-ups has a very different effect on us.

Familiarity doesn't breed contempt, it *is* contempt. We are drowning in the bodily fluids of total strangers. If we add up all the sights and sounds that are forced on us—all the ear wax, armpits, gags, belches, pharts, mouth-slapping, tooth-sucking, nose-picking, and the butt cleavage exposed by wearers of low-slung jeans—it becomes instantly clear what has happened: Everybody is married to everybody else. The Ughs have given us *E Pluribus Unum* in spades; America is one big couple, suffering from the kind of frayed nerves and quotidian strains for which marriage has ever been famous.

Our various "rages"—road, air, subway, whatever—are directed at strangers, yet there is something oddly intimate about them. They seem more like the continuation of an old fight, possessing that sudden bubbling-up quality that invariably precedes domesticity's timeless signature line:

"If you do that one more time I'll scream!"

May 20, 2002

TWENTY years ago when I published a book with Viking, somebody got the fan mail mixed up and sent me Stephen King's by mistake. That has to be my most memorable experience with what the trade calls "reader response," but the Gentle Readers of NR are not far behind. Coming in a very close second is the letter I got the other day:

"I loved your piece about your Aunt Ellen, I really did. It was sweet and tender and loving, and it scared the hell out of me. It sounded like you were getting nice. Please, I beg of you, don't get nice. That's all I need at this point. It would be the end of me, I couldn't go on if you turned nice on us, so please let us know that you're still your old self."

Okey-dokey. I aim to please, so here is a roundup of what keeps me in a rolling boil.

George W. Bush: I don't care if this is a conservative magazine, I can't stand the sight or the sound of him. It's visceral, not political. Everything he does and says—slinging his arms around people, slouching on lecterns, his "strong personal bonds," his hearty-har nicknaming—affects me like sulfuric acid trickling down my spine. He reminds me of every boy in school who ever called me "brain" and "curve-breaker." We also differ on favorite philosophers. Mine is Schopenhauer: "To forgive and forget is to surrender dearly bought experience."

The Anniversary Waltz: Americans are mired in a showy morbidity the likes of which have not been seen since ancient Egypt. The only difference between Ground Zero and Giza is that workmen are hauling building materials down the ramps instead of up. After we pulled out all the stops in the ceremonies marking the six-month anniversary of the attacks, what is there left to do for the first year? We are perilously close to worshiping a hole in the ground.

The obsessive commemorations growing out of 9/11 can only encourage the ones that were already up and running before the terrorists struck. August threatens to turn into one giant wake. It contains the 40th anniversary of Marilyn Monroe's death, the 25th anniversary of Elvis's, and the 5th anniversary of Princess Di's on the last day of the month, which will take us into September, when my quarterly Estimated Taxes are due on the 15th.

All News Is Created Equal: I remember when a news bulletin was just that: "Japanese attack Pearl Harbor. . . . FDR dead." Later, I worked on a newspaper when the wire machines still rang a bulletin bell when something important happened. But nowadays, if you discriminate between this news and that, somebody might call you a "newsist," so the cable shows crank up their ruffles-and-flourishes bulletin music, zoom-flash "Breaking News" across the screen, and announce that a Greyhound bus has overturned in Ogallala, Neb. Don't bother to switch channels; you'll just get "Fox News Alert" with the latest on the boiler that exploded in Toledo.

Offhand, I'd say there are more false alarms on Fox than on MSNBC, but it's hard to be sure now that my mind has started to go. I can state that Fox's early-morning crew is more repulsive than any other early-morning crew. I especially detest the blond clod because he reminds me of the boy in school who put a comforting arm around my shoulders and said, "You'd be a great gal if only you had a sense of humor." (At the risk of driving my Gentle Reader to suicide, I'll make a quick foray into Nice and name the one TV newsman I adore: Roger Mudd on the History Channel.)

The Marriage "Initiative": The Bush plan to end the culture of poverty by leading the proletariat to the altar is doomed to backfire in the manner of the "Togetherness" craze of the '50s, which dinned the buzzwords of marriage propaganda without surcease. I know, I was there. "Marking time" meant waiting to get married; "saving ourselves for marriage" meant staying technically virginal (we were the Keystone Kops of heavy petting); "drifting" meant despairing of getting married; "on solid ground" meant engaged to be married; "something to fall back on" meant getting a college degree in case you didn't get married; and "starting my life" meant finally being married—i.e., not having to read another excerpt from *Modern Woman: The Lost Sex* in the *Ladies' Home Journal* and worrying about what it said.

Result? The feminist movement. I don't know how the Marriage Initiative will end, but I know how it won't. One of the conservative think tanks has argued that the example of family life set by Queen Victoria and Prince Albert changed the English from gin-swilling, cockfighting Regency rakes and doxies into contented monogamous couples, but this is too facile. Victorian morality was adopted by the middle class only; the aristocracy and the poor did not change—they never do.

The All-American Freak-Out: There's a war on against the unhalt, the unlame, and the unstupid. You're nobody unless there's something wrong with you. It's only a matter of time before E.Q., or "emotional intelligence," replaces I.Q. so that the people who ought to be in an institution learning how to make brooms can feel good about themselves.

Our perverse preferences started with handicapped parking spaces, but they are fast approaching the truly bizarre. This was brought home to me one recent night when I was looking for a late movie to watch. I had just seen a public-service announcement for Restless Leg Syndrome, so I was in the mood for escapism.

As I flipped through the TV schedule, a movie called *Twin Falls Idaho* caught my eye. Back in 1959 while in grad school at Ole Miss, I was offered, via letter, a job teaching English in Twin Falls. I accepted, but reneged a month later when my plans changed, so I never set foot in the place. The movie listing triggered my "what if" curiosity. What if I had gone to Twin Falls? How would my life be different? What did I miss? Eagerly, I read the plot description.

It said: "(1999) Drama. Michael Polish, Mark Polish. A kindhearted hooker falls for a man who is physically joined to his dying identical twin brother."

June 3, 2002

' K ILLING two birds with one stone" has been the guiding princi-ple of the well-organized person from time immemorial, but, as with so much else dating from time immemorial, it is now more or less unconstitutional.

Merely using the expression can get you in big trouble with People for the Ethical Treatment of Animals, but I'll have to take the chance. I'm prun-ing my Idea Files, but meanwhile I have a column due, so I decided to kill two birds with one stone and write about what I find so I can throw it out.

When ordinary people make notes on ragged scraps of paper or clip newspaper articles and decorate them with necklaces of frantically scrawled marginalia, it's called "paranoia." When writers do it, it's called "research" and it's tax-deductible. These advantages lend an air of sanity but it's bogus. Idea Files are crazymaking by definition because a writer must constantly ask himself where something "goes." Paranoid amateurs don't have to make bricks out of their straw collection, but we do, so we keep re-filing some tat-tered clip in the hope that it will "go" with other tattered clips and be enough for a column.

Take, for example, the Dec. 26, 1997, clip from the *Washington Times* headlined "Geneticist Says Lesbianism is Cultural, 'Not Inherited,'" about the further findings of geneticist Dean Hamer, proponent of the theory that male homosexuality is inborn. Reluctant to get tangled up in a column that would expose my scientific ignorance, I moved this one from Gay to Women to Feminists to Men and back to Gay again without ever figuring out a way to write about it, adding new marginalia each time I re-filed it. The resulting necklace of notes reads:

"Flash from NR: Men are cradle gays, lesbians are converts. . . . Scientific chivalry lets lesbians off the homophobic hook. . . . At last the Breeding-Heart Right will have to blame something on the environment. . . . Why there is no lesbian equivalent of the female impersonator: Because there's nothing to do. If you want to impersonate a man, all you have to do is sit still, stick to the subject, and say things once instead of three times. This lacks entertainment value."

Sometimes a new clip will segue flawlessly with a quotation from a book that I copied out years earlier. It's still not enough for a column, but the satisfaction is so great that I can almost hear a click as the two snap together in my mind.

This happened with a colloquy by Bonnie Erbe and Josette Shiner in the Oct. 31, 1999, *Washington Times*. Erbe, the liberal half of the team, deplored the behavior of Bob Dole during his wife's campaign for the GOP presidential nomination, claiming it was "purposefully designed" to sink her. Erbe cites his Viagra pitches on national TV while Liddy was trying to be sweet 'n' nice on the hustings, his public statement that Bush's lead was "insurmountable," and, most damaging of all, his announcement that he was thinking of contributing to one of her rivals (John McCain).

Shiner's response was a study in nervous evasion and denial, but novelist Katherine Anne Porter, who was just as conservative, nailed her flag to the mast: "I know that when a woman loves a man, she builds him up and supports him. I never knew a man who loved a woman enough for this. He cannot help it, it is his deepest instinct to destroy, quite often subtly, insidiously, but constantly and endlessly, her very center of being, her confidence in herself as a woman."

I copied out this quotation on the back of a rent receipt for $125, so you know how long I've had it. Now I've finally used it!

Sometimes writers clip articles we know we won't use because we have developed an itchy scissors finger and can't help ourselves. I long ago stopped writing about political correctness; the topic had been done to death and there was nothing more to say, but I went on clipping P.C., like the gem from the *Milwaukee Journal Sentinel* that said Wisconsin was renaming

Squaw Bay because "some" Native Americans find the word offensive; it doesn't just mean woman or wife, but is "a French corruption of an Indian epithet for vagina." What? The gentle, peaceful, ecological, communal, sharing, cooperating, egalitarian Indians used hate speech? How can this be? The article doesn't say.

An Ideas File is a useful weapon for discouraging the kind of people who drop in unannounced. Just leave a note to yourself lying around and you'll never see them again. Crime novelists who deal in unequivocal plots usually get rid of them fast—*Set fire to house on Christmas Eve*—but cultural commentators who interpret the American scene have the added fun of inflicting slow mental torture with notes couched in the cryptic language of free association.

When an idea for a column pops into my head I have to get the gist of it down fast or it's gone forever, so I grab a pen and scratch paper and scrawl *Herc foot, dogcatcher, undertaker.* How'd you like to be sitting here and find that on the coffee table, hmm?

It's my take on American foreign policy. The classical principle *Ex Pede Herculem*—"From the foot alone we may infer Hercules"—gives common sense a much-needed boost by permitting us to infer that if an individual is *this*, chances are he's *that*. Since Arabs and Europeans are eager to infer things about us, we should discard our dread of stereotyping and employ inference to find the kind of people who can handle troublesome foreigners.

A dogcatcher is unlikely to obsess over "Why do they hate us?" He knows why. He's used to it. He's the man everybody hates, the man who enrages "the street" every day merely by driving down it in his truck, unfazed by the tears, ululating shrieks, and muttered threats he leaves in his wake. Send him to the Middle East at once.

An undertaker is used to ridicule and bad jokes at his expense. He expects people to give him the cold shoulder, peer at him with suspicion, shrink from him in disgust, and, at the very least, to put up with him with as bad a grace as possible. Make him ambassador to France.

June 17, 2002

I HAVEN'T checked what are laughably called college curricula lately, but it's a sure bet that English departments, if they still exist, do not require students to read the works of William Hazlitt. Not only is he white, male, and dead, but he wrote an essay that could prove fatal to the

American balancing act our colleges are sworn to uphold. It's called "On the Pleasure of Hating."

Hazlitt (1778–1830) was an intense, eternally irritable intellectual who lived in an age that clashed with his sour temperament. The early 19th century was sunk in the tender emotions of the Romantic era. Writers like Wordsworth had come to regret their earlier enthusiasm for the French Revolution ("Bliss was it in that dawn to be alive . . .") and its violence. Reaction set in, and ideology was replaced by a gauzy veneration of nature and beauty, love and nostalgia, as well as a major switch in the body fluid of record: Blood was out; tears were in.

It was enough to make a cultural commentator gag, and Hazlitt did just that. He decided that his contemporaries on the British literary scene were not mean enough, and, like the Michael Douglas character in *Wall Street* who declared that greed is good, he gave the nod to hatred.

"Without something to hate," he wrote in his notorious essay, "we should lose the very spring of thought and action." By this yardstick, Americans have already passed our use-by date, because we keep draining the spring. Show us a perfectly good, satisfying hatred and we immediately shoot it down.

Should we hate Middle Eastern terrorists? No, because if we allow ourselves to hate them we might start hating people who look like them, and then people who look *something* like them, and before you know it, we will be taken over by blue-eyed, blond-haired Aryan Supermen who hate everybody.

Should we hate pedophile priests? No, because that might activate dormant hatred of Catholics, which might revive Know-Nothingism, which might end in an auto-da-fé, which might set a precedent for hatred of other religions, which might in turn lead to hatred of Islam, which would make it okay to hate Middle Eastern terrorists. This is America's most popular board game; every throw of the dice takes you back to square one.

What about hating John Walker Lindh? Hating traitors has a long and honorable history, but whenever a member of a traditionally hate-able category comes along we stick an "alleged" in front of him; it covers him from head to foot like those ancient Greek shields used in phalanx formations, so that anyone who hates him before he is proven guilty is accused of hating Our Way of Life. If you think you can hate him after he's been proven guilty, guess again: Hating after "closure" time makes you a hate-aholic.

Hazlitt believed that hatred is therapeutic, and that humanity instinctively seeks out antidotes to the enervating effects of too much amity. This natural urge to keep hate alive was responsible for the immense popularity of Sir Walter Scott's swashbuckling novels about medieval Scotland:

They carry us back to the feuds, the heart-burnings, the havoc, the dismay, the wrongs, and the revenge of a barbarous age and people—to the rooted prejudices and deadly animosities of sects and parties in politics and religion, and of contending chiefs and clans in war and intrigue. We feel the full force of the spirit of hatred with all of them in turn.

Englishmen of Hazlitt's time who read these tales derived what he called the comfort of "sorting out ancient hatreds," but no such comfort is available to us because we can't even sort out the ones that have cropped up in the past year.

Literal-minded individuals are quick to accuse Hazlitt of "preaching hate," but he did no such thing. "On the Pleasure of Hating" is a plea for fullness—of outlook, of understanding, of character, of maturity. The pleasures of hating are actually the pleasures of realism, sophistication, and—ready?—self-esteem.

Americans are short on all of the above, for reasons that Hazlitt would readily discern. Hard as it may be to accept, there is such a thing as being hate-deprived. Our latest *cri de coeur*, "Where's the outrage?," is an unconscious rebuke of our own incomplete selves. Where the hell do we think the outrage is? It can't emerge without the kind of hatred that used to be called "righteous wrath."

We also fail to realize that if we reject one towering emotion, we likely will reject others as well. This is why "love" scenes in today's novels and movies, no matter how explicit, give off no yearning, no passion, no electricity. Check out any great love story and you will find that it is really about hate (e.g., *GWTW* is pure Social Darwinism), and Hazlitt understood why this has to be: "Pure good soon grows insipid . . . Love turns . . . to indifference or disgust: Hatred alone is immortal."

He could put his finger on "America's vital interest": We go to war to "stop the hatred." He also would have no trouble spotting the twisted logic behind "hate crimes": It's the hatred we want to punish, not the crime. He might be puzzled by some of our more exotic contortions, such as "harmless little fuzzball," the self-description popular with accused haters like Rush Limbaugh, and "mellowing," the de-hating procedure that transformed former Southern firebrands like Strom Thurmond and James J. Kilpatrick into color-blind integrationists so they could keep their jobs.

Of course, a few things would throw him for a loop: anger-management workshops, "I HATE Hate" bumper stickers, smokers as scapegoats, and moviegoers who think William Wallace wanted to make Scotland safe for democracy. But once he digested it all, he would realize that he had written the perfect description of the 21st-century American mindset: Those who are "dupes of friendship and fools of love" invariably hate themselves "for not having hated and despised the world enough."

You're a good man, Bill Hazlitt. How about a hug?

July 1, 2002

HAVING at last disposed of the avalanche of newspaper clippings known as my Idea Files, I am now sorting out the stack of spiral notebooks that constitute my Journal. All writers are supposed to keep a journal and include it in our literary papers, so that's where mine is going as soon as I kill two birds with one stone and get a column out of it.

The word "journal" calls to mind small, elegant books bound in hand-tooled Moroccan leather, not drugstore school tablets with Garfield on the cover, but that's posterity's problem. My very first spiral volume goes back so far that the faded price sticker says 39 cents. This is the one I'm tempted to toss because it's full of old chestnuts like Socrates' *"The unexamined life is not worth living."* I was still in the stage of writing "How true!" in margins so I come off as positively giddy throughout.

I start to sound more like me in the notebook whose cover proclaims "N.C. State University, Home of 1974 NCAA Basketball Championship" (89 cents). The first entry is about Phyllis Schlafly's *A Choice, Not an Echo*, in which she attacked the writer Edmund Wilson for deprecating America and living abroad. She failed to mention that a Founding Father had felt substantially the same way, so I recorded his two pertinent statements, plus a remark of my own:

"Every day proves to me more and more that this American world was not made for me."

"Am I a fool—a romantic Quixote—or is there a constitutional defect in the American mind?"

"No, Alex, you aren't; yes, Alex, there is."

Many of my journal notations fall into the category of miscellaneous pedantry, things I happen to come across while reading that I simply enjoy knowing. These tend to be Latin one-liners, e.g., *"Scribendo disces scribere"*—one learns to write by writing—and Gore Vidal's deliciously apt reversal of our national motto, *"Ex Uno Plures"*: from one, many.

In the past, many writers used their journals for detailed accounts of dinner parties and long, tortured lucubrations, but keeping a diary has never appealed to me, and whenever I've felt tortured my response has been drink now, write later. I like to make entries that are short and quick, which is why my journals resemble a flea market: a jumble of trash 'n' treasures that are impossible to find again unless I page through each notebook. This is why you've never seen them; I've been meaning to use them for years but they just now turned up: "If the soul is immortal as Christianity claims, it must have existed before our birth. In that case, Christians are believers in reincarnation."

"It takes a woman a long time to figure out that she's being sexually used, but a man who is put to stud grasps the truth at once."

"People should never try to hide their true selves from a writer. That's like trying to hide earth from a mole. We were the original interpreters of the human mind and heart, before the shrinks pulled the rug out from under us. Shakespeare never read Freud, but Freud read Shakespeare."

"I can't listen to Rush anymore. Those hokey populist conservatives drive me up the wall. They think saying 'God' and 'family' every three seconds makes you a conservative. I'm an agnostic old maid but I'm more conservative than any of them."

My longest journal entry takes up a whole page, but not the same page. It's three quotations that I copied into three different notebooks over a period of time. One day, I heard a click in my head and everything fell into place, so I hauled it all together and drew my own conclusion:

Tacitus: "*A woman who has lost her chastity will shrink from no crime.*"

Philippe de Navarre: "*Women have one great advantage: It is sufficient for them to cultivate a single virtue if they wish to be well thought of. . . . If a woman keeps her body intact, all her other defects are hidden and she can hold her head high.*"

Louise d'Epinay: "*The virtues that people wish to give to women in general are almost all virtues against nature, which produce only small artificial virtues and some very real vices.*"

Florence King: "*Be good, fair maid, and you can slit all the throats you want.*"

Usually I never can find the entry I want when I need it, but one time I did, and lived to regret it. I was reviewing a biography of Pete Rose, whose taste, it seemed, was all in his mouth. To point up his penchant for trashy friends in an interesting way, I decided to use a quotation from Graham Greene's *The End of the Affair* that makes reference to Cophetua, the mythical African king who shrank from women of his own rank because only slave girls turned him on.

Miraculously, I turned right to it: "*Beautiful women, especially if they are intelligent also, stir some deep feeling of inferiority in me. I don't know whether psychologists have yet named the Cophetua complex, but I have always found it hard to feel sexual desire without some sense of superiority, mental or physical.*"

Book reviews usually don't draw much reader mail, but I was inundated with letters, all from men: "Could you tell me more about the Cophetua complex? I've got a friend who might have it" . . . "I'm worried about my brother because I think he has a Cophetua complex" . . . "Of course, I don't have any problems that way, but there's a guy in my office" . . .

Normally, I don't care much for poetry unless I spot a good title in it. I spotted two that fairly leapt out at me, so I copied them down. One is in Edna St. Vincent Millay's "Sonnet XXXV": "*Though summer's rife and the warm rose in season/Rebuke me not, I have a winter reason.*" (Probably because men have a Cophetua complex.) The other is in "The Man with the Blue Guitar" by Wallace Stevens: "*It is the sun that shares our works/The moon shares nothing. It is a sea.*" Unfortunately, however, I can't write fiction, so if anyone wants *A Winter Reason* or *The Moon Shares Nothing*, be my guest.

I've tried to break the journal habit but I can't; I made my latest entry today: "The Salt Lake City kidnapping news is so full of hosannas to wholesome happy families that I had to drop everything and re-read *Wuthering Heights*."

July 15, 2002

SLIPPING in under the wire seems to be a specialty of mine. I graduated from public schools in 1953; "under God" was not inserted into the Pledge of Allegiance until 1954, so I am a member of the last class to recite the old version. It's still seared on my brain; now, whenever I have occasion to pledge allegiance, I always finish ahead of my juniors because I automatically leave out "under God."

Having slipped in under the wire, I will now fall between the slats. I am on both sides of the Ninth Circuit's ruling, and for all the wrong reasons.

My main impetus for siding with the court is contained in the statement by House Democratic leader Dick Gephardt, who said he saw "no reason to change the time-tested, venerable pledge." This was only to be expected from a middle-aged liberal who doesn't look a day over 14, but it goes to the heart of the issue. I might be able to work up the requisite conservative fury if "under God" had been in the Pledge all along, but where is the conservatism in defending something that new when it was not even carefully thought through in the first place?

"Under God" was stuck into the Pledge on the spur of the moment at the height of the McCarthy era as a tool to fight Communism, a Republican brainstorm propelled by the same kind of bipartisan mawkish naivete that makes liberals go dewy-eyed over "people-to-people" student-exchange programs as a force for peace. That our penchant for mawkishness remains undiminished was evident when a bevy of congressmen trooped out to the Capitol steps the other day and recited the Pledge, careful to shout out "under God!" like defiant pupils in a rehearsed plan to annoy the teacher.

Americans are suckers for empty gestures. Our doltish leadership is helpless to stop terrorism and the country is facing economic ruin from the corporate banditry of our neo-Robber Barons, so it's time to distract us with one of those all-absorbing hokey crusades that we do so well. It won't be long now before oil tankers start exploding, banks start failing, goldbugs start fleeing, and computer hackers figure out how to open the floodgates of Hoover Dam, but, as our grandstanding leaders well know, we will be too busy shouting "under God!" to notice.

The phrase suggests yet another kind of mawkishness to me: clutter. I dislike manger scenes on public property for the same reason. I don't care who is spiritually offended by them; I am aesthetically offended by their whatnot-shelf "too-muchness." The first time I lived up North, in Bayonne, N.J., I kept recoiling from the life-sized manger scenes in people's yards, six-foot saints in magenta and vermilion robes, with gilt halos affixed to coat hangers coming out of the backs of their necks. My reaction sprang from more than run-of-the-mill tidiness; I have a compulsion to create empty spaces. Call it agoraphilia if you wish—it's my only chance to be a phile instead of a phobe or a thrope—but I'm happiest when I'm getting rid of something. To my way of thinking, "under God" is no different from a pile of old magazines or the accumulated detritus in a desk drawer—out it goes.

Adding "under God" in the Pledge cluttered up the unequivocal spartan simplicity of the original language and made it go "off," so that it just doesn't flow right anymore. There's a rhythm to good prose, which is why I oppose the use of too much punctuation and textual enhancements. If you write a sentence with the proper attention to rhythm, you don't need to add emphasis. You can pick the reader up and carry him along with you—dance with him, as it were—so that he catches your rhythm and supplies the italics and commas in his own mind. No argument by me would be complete without an off-the-wall point that has nothing to do with anything, so here it is: If you danced to the Pledge, "under God" would make you miss a step.

So much for why I side with the court's decision. Now I'll tell you why I'm against it. First, I am sick of all this individualism. Americans bray incessantly about what individuals they are, but the fact is, individuals are the rarest of breeds. Most people aren't even unusual, but an increasingly popular way to banish this hard truth is to file a crazy lawsuit and acquire a one-of-a-kind moniker such as "the woman who got $4 million for spilling coffee on her t**t."

One way to restore legal sanity is to make Mary McCarthy's novel, *A Charmed Life*, required reading for all judges and the would-be rugged individuals who come before them. It's about a moral crisis in a place completely unaccustomed to dealing with such: a bohemian artists' colony. One sentence in particular would make a useful guideline for atheists trapped in a worship service, as well as an inscription for a bronze plaque to hang on courtroom walls: "The true individualist has the courage to wear a mask."

Truth be told, I've had it with the First Amendment because I am a Royalist, and the biggest stumbling block to an American monarchy is our fear of an Established church. We can't have a monarchy without one because we can't have a coronation without one. It's a question of holy oils. An unanointed monarch is a *roi manqué*, but only three faiths—Roman Catholic, Orthodox, and Anglican—have holy oils.

What to do? A greasy king being better than no king at all, the American royalist is tempted to suggest that all three faiths conduct a tripartite coronation, but this is fraught with danger. Americans are so terrified of leaving any religion out of the running that we would have to have an ecumenical coronation by representatives from every creed, oleaginous or not.

There is no telling where it would end, or if it would end except in the death of the monarch. By the time he was Born Again, Circumcised Again, held underwater, plunked down on a bed of nails, and forced to play with rattlesnakes, we would find that we had once again snatched self-defeat from the jaws of compromise.

July 29, 2002

M Y "Ugh" column really struck a nerve. So many of you sent me examples of offensive ads and clippings that I must now be in possession of the largest collection of pictures of toilets outside the ranks of the National Association for the Advancement of Coprophilia.

I have enough for the sequel some of you requested, but rather than labor the point I decided to turn the tables on you and write about the kind of explicitness that doesn't bother me a bit—that, in fact, I enjoy.

Father Flanagan said, "There's no such thing as a bad boy"; adoption pioneer Edna Gladney said, "There are no illegitimate children, only illegitimate parents"; and I say that earthy subjects are offensive only when they are badly presented.

Take laxative commercials. They usually feature a construction worker on a high building or a sports fan trapped in the uppermost stadium tier, praying that the harsh laxative they took won't "kick in" then and there.

"Kick in" is an updated version of "hit the fan" and is intended to trigger the same mental picture. But after the sufferer switches to the advertised brand, the Vesuvian imagery is replaced by the drumbeat of "gentle," "regular," "relaxed," and "natural," prompting our mind's eye to visualize a parade horse effortlessly producing huge curls of manure and dropping them along the route with that equine nonchalance that never fails to make children and other oafs smirk and snicker. These ads run the gamut of bathroom humor from spew to plop in 30 seconds, yet the industry considers them inoffensive, and worse, "creative."

Madison Avenue must have a treasonous mole burrowing in its midst because there is one series of laxative ads that departs from the formula. I always enjoy watching them because they follow the rules for high comedy and succeed as clever entertainment: the Phillips Milk of Magnesia couple, Lucille and Raymond.

Lucille constantly embarrasses her husband with her eerie talent for turning any conversation around to his constipation. She apparently carries a bottle of Phillips in her purse at all times, and whips it out at parties, merrily rattling on about Raymond's "problem," ignoring his hisses and frantic signals to shut up. The spots are funny because Lucille is utterly lacking in insight and self-knowledge. If she smirked, if she noticed Raymond's mortification, if she ever once exhibited even a shred of self-consciousness, the ad would be offensive. But because she's incapable of realizing that anything is amiss, her obtuseness rescues the ad from bathroom humor and turns it into comic material worthy of Burns and Allen.

Lucille is a classic example of that staple of wit, the "Candide character," the innocent and/or dense person who has no idea what is going on. Virtually any subject can be funny as long as a Candide is present to provide the salvaging innocence, but if everyone is in the know, it becomes vulgar.

The absence of the Candide figure is what makes American sit-coms so raunchy. It's not so much what the characters do or say, but rather that they all snicker and smirk. By contrast, British sit-coms turn unawareness into pure gold.

In *Keeping Up Appearances*, the eternally thwarted social climber Hyacinth Bucket (she insists on pronouncing it "Bouquet") has been so successful in steeling herself against unpleasant realities that she is no longer capable of placing a correct interpretation on anything.

She has no idea that her son, Sheridan, is gay. He never appears as a live character, but the audience doesn't need to see him to catch on—Hyacinth's end of their phone calls tells us all we need to know: "You and your friend Tarquin are doing the ironing? Oh, that's nice, dear. . . . You and Tarquin aren't interested in girls? Oh, Sheridan, you don't know how much that warms a mother's heart! . . . You're wearing a knee bandage? Oh, you must look like Mummy's little soldier! What, dear? Oh, well, then, Mummy's little poet or interior designer."

Just as *Jaws* was scarier before we saw the shark, keeping Sheridan off-camera enlists the innocence of the audience for greater comedic effect. If the scriptwriters permitted Sheridan to appear and be as campy as he obviously is, the Candide device would be dismantled and the comedy would turn into broad farce.

I have often said that movies could be censored without attention to religious or family values. All you need is a knowledge of the rules of literary structure, but sadly, the wrong people tend to be censors.

In 1953 the Maryland Board of Motion Picture Censors banned *The Captain's Paradise*, starring Alec Guinness as the bigamous captain of a ferry boat running between Gibraltar and Tangiers, with Celia Johnson as his prim English wife and Yvonne De Carlo as his sultry Moroccan wife.

All goes smoothly until the unfortunate Christmas when he gets their presents mixed up. He gives the Brit a bikini and the sex kitten an apron, but both are overjoyed because Celia has always longed to be sexy and Yvonne has always longed to be domestic. The humor springs not from the bigamy but from an innocent mistake. If he had mixed the gifts up on purpose it would be a movie about a bigamist playing sex games, but the accidental element underscores the theme of human contrariness and gives the story a valuable moral: Don't take people for granted because there is more to them than meets the eye; everyone has a secret life.

As for nudity, it's okay if it's female, but one skin shot I would censor purely for aesthetic reasons is the rear view of the male. Is there anything more depressing than a man's behind? Narrow and shrunken, a stunted little thing, a nether afterthought, the behind that Nature forgot. I've often wondered how men can sit comfortably; it's a wonder the bones don't break through. Why do moviemakers think we want to look at such a study in pathos? Visual pleasure demands an hourglass; a tiny waist that suddenly blossoms into undulating curves to form the most comfortable seat a backyard swing set ever had—now *that's* a behind.

August 12, 2002

T O say that someone "keeps up with current events" is inherently flattering, a compliment denoting seriousness, civic responsibility, and all the other right stuff. An honor student enclosed in a good citizen wrapped in a home owner, you might say.

I used to keep up with current events but now I "follow the news," which, I have begun to sense, denotes qualities of a very different sort. We could play around with various descriptive adjectives—"furtive" and "hunched" come to mind—but the best way to define it is to restate what it is that I now follow: the Nooze.

What, exactly, is the Nooze? Well, for starters there's the now-ubiquitous crawl, the ribbon at the bottom of the screen that enables us to follow still more Nooze while we are following the Nooze. The crawl came into being with 9/11, when terrorism took up so much airtime that they had to find some other way of reporting everything else. After a month or so the crawl was no longer necessary, but by then it had become one of America's "instant traditions," like the public hand-holding of presidents and first ladies begun by Jimmy and Rosalynn Carter. Every news show had a crawl, and none dared be the first to stop.

The crawl is now a repetitive, ungrammatical mélange of eccentric doings that is impossible to ignore. If terrorists took down another landmark building nobody would notice because we are too busy reading the crawl.

Since becoming a Noozehound, I have been dominated by the crawl in two ways. One is my neverending quest for the Ultimate Crawl. It's my Golden Fleece, my Holy Grail, my El Dorado, and I think I've found it. It sailed across the bottom of the screen a few months ago and there hasn't been anything to match it since.

It said: "A survey of Ukrainian prostitutes found that most took to the streets to avoid office work."

The obvious question here is why anyone would take a survey of Ukrainian prostitutes, and the answer is even more obvious: to have something to put on the crawl. CNN probably sends teams of crawl-fillers to remote corners of the globe to research whether riding bareback on wild ponies affects the testicular-cancer rate in Mongolia. The crawlspace is full of Nooze You Can Use, but it came too late for me. As a college graduate in the sexist '50s, I was consigned to boring office work, and I can testify that nothing makes a woman more desperate than being surrounded by typewriters and calculators when she knows what *deus ex machina* means. It's a wonder all female liberal-arts majors didn't become tarts.

The other offshoot of my crawl-reading is unbearable suspense. This happens when I glance away from the screen and then look back just in time to see an incomplete crawl. Such as: ". . . one person's caged bird for breakfast." Somebody ate it! Who? Why? I had to find out, and the only way to do it was to sit through the whole crawl again.

I almost made it, but then the phone rang, and by the time I got back to the TV, guess what I saw? ". . . one person's caged bird for breakfast." Dirty bombs were about to go off, the stock market was about to collapse, and my e-mail provider was about to go out of business, but all I cared about was that effin' bird. The mystery was finally cleared up in my third go at the crawl: A bear in some national park ate a camper's pet canary. What they didn't explain is why anyone would take a birdcage on a camping trip.

Once the Nooze people got us hooked on the crawl, they were faced with the problem of how to drag us away from it and make us watch the "real" Nooze. The situation demanded a controversy to make even the most dedicated crawlhead look up at the screen, and the Elizabeth Smart case supplied one: Has kidnapping been sullied by racial profiling?

Why the rich white girl was lionized while countless inner-city abductees are ignored was debated ad nauseam but nobody nailed the real reason. It goes back to the earliest form of entertainment. To ancient Greek playwrights, it was a given that "tragedy" is what happens to kings and nobles. Such class profiling remained a literary convention until the 19th century; protagonists had to be people of substance because they were the only ones whose problems were substantial enough to interest an audience.

In today's egalitarian climate we are quick to proclaim a universal right to tragedy, but we give ourselves away when we blithely refer to the whodunit we just read as "a good murder." We mean exactly what the ancient Greeks meant: mayhem in the VIP set, a corpse who was Somebody, the juxtaposition of violence and respectability that produces the psychic tension found in every "classic" crime. Lizzie Borden was a well-off churchgoer. The Ripper's victims were prostitutes but the backdrop of a puritanical Victorian society provided the respectability. The Black Dahlia was a tramp but her stunning beauty elevated her above the common herd in the public mind. For a crime to grab us, some element of social superiority must be present.

The Smart family has money and status but their real superiority lies in their innocence. Not just Elizabeth, but the whole clan. Their earnest trust, naïve goodness, and mindboggling optimism personify a lost national purity that we observe with a kind of dumbfounded awe. The Smarts represent the Old America when no Nooze was good Nooze, and we can't get enough of them. Until they came along, the only altar of lost innocence available to us was documentaries about wild animals. No matter what violence feral creatures inflict on their prey, there is no hate, no evil intent, no crime. Lions are not bigoted, piranha are not alienated, vultures are not bipolar, and there is no such thing as a pedophilic cobra.

Meanwhile, the crawl marches on. Trying to read from left to right while words are moving from right to left got me off the rails during the Amtrak crisis. The crawlspace is a cramped, narrow world, so it was only to be expected that as soon as I saw "ARAFAT MUST GO, BUSH SAYS," I yelled "You train-hating twit!"

September 2, 2002

I'VE given you a peek into the files I've been throwing out, but there's still one left: my NOT file. It's where I've kept notes for what I initially thought would make good columns, but which, for one reason or another, did not work out. You're better off not knowing about some of them, but I found a few that are suitable for polite company, so here they are, along with my reasons for spiking them.

1. *Ayn Rand*. I abandoned this one for the simple reason that she exhausts me. That unrelenting intensity and repetitive bludgeoning, that preference for the battle ax over the rapier, that disdain for grace notes and the occasional jeu d'esprit. She's even worse than Alan Keyes—either one of them could kill you. Just thinking about doing a column on her was like thinking about defrosting the fridge or cleaning the oven; I kept taking my notes out and putting them back, telling myself "next time," all the while knowing that next time would never come if I could help it.

It's an odd way to feel about a writer with whom I thoroughly agree, but it's merely a clash of temperaments, not philosophy. One of the bones I have always picked with conservatism is its total rejection of Ayn Rand because of her atheism. To me, there is much more to conservatism than religion, so I cherish a passage from *The Fountainhead* that speaks to one such issue.

Everyone who shares my revulsion against the touchy-feely, emotion-drenched, low-class, womanish mush that America calls "compassion" will appreciate Rand's description of Howard Roark's office:

> He did not smile at his employees, he did not take them out for drinks, he never inquired about their families, their love lives or their church attendance. He responded only to the essence of a man: to his creative capacity. In this office one had to be competent. There were no alternatives, no mitigating considerations. But if a man worked well, he needed nothing else to win his employer's benevolence: it was granted, not as a gift, but as a debt. It was granted, not as affection, but as recognition. It bred an immense feeling of self-respect within every man in that office.

2. *Elliot Richardson*. Now you know my secret crush: a Northeastern liberal Republican, almost as bad as having a secret crush on Nelson Rockefeller or Christie Todd Whitman. I knew a lot of readers would take umbrage if I praised him, but what really kept me from writing about him was that I didn't have enough material—just my memory of his refusal to fire Archibald Cox and his subsequent resignation as Nixon's attorney general, plus one column by Mary McGrory, of all people, who evidently had a secret crush on him too.

She called him "the ultimate public servant" and said he had "an exalted sense of office and duty," but it was her description of him as "incurably high-minded" that really struck home. She knew him well, while I had only seen him on TV, but it was love at first sight. I sensed a reassuring stuffiness in him, an old-money, George Apley quality reminiscent of threadbare Aubussons.

It was also love at first sound. Maybe it's because I was a Roosevelt baby, but I am forever listening for a voice with the power to reassure me. Richardson had it; something about the "r" and the "a". . . . I don't know, but it was the voice of a man with a code, like the old-world aristocrat who paid his gambling debts promptly but let his tailor wait. It might not have been fair, or made sense, but it was his code, and he followed it.

3. *Civility*. I didn't write this one for two reasons: Everybody and his brother was already writing about it and I didn't want to join the crowd; and it contained disparate elements—movies and personal experiences—that I couldn't get to segue as seamlessly as I like.

Two movies express my ideal of civility, both of them, ironically, about savages. *The Naked Prey*, starring Cornel Wilde, is about a white man tested in a deadly trial by African warriors, who strip him of weapons and all clothes except a loincloth, and force him onto a survival course with themselves in hot pursuit. It's a game of "May the best man win," and he does, by outwitting his pursuers, killing revolting food with his bare hands, and fashioning weapons out of nothing. At last, as the colonial fort comes into view, his pursuers stop. Looking back at them, he sees the admiring chief raise his hand in a brusque salute, which he returns in the same spirit.

The other movie is *Zulu*, starring Michael Caine, the true story of a vastly outnumbered British force who successfully defended their remote outpost against endless swarming hordes of South African tribesmen. At the end, the Zulus serenade their triumphant enemy with a song of congratulation, and the Welsh Guards respond with an equally respectful rendition of "Men of Harlech." If you need antidotes to the Enron era, watch these two movies.

My most memorable personal experiences with civility involve my parents. Once, my father needed a dime for something and asked my mother, who said, "Look in my pocketbook." But he wouldn't. Instead he picked it up and brought it to her. That's all that happened, but it was enough for me.

The other incident occurred when I was nine. My aunt was having her first baby and my uncle promised he would send us a telegram as soon as it came. Since I had never even seen a telegram, I begged him to address it to me, and he promised he would. He did. It came while I was at school and my mother signed for it. It lay on the table untouched until I got home. She was dying to know about the baby but she would not open it because it had my name on it.

4. *Queen Mary*. The present Queen's grandmother, she was a fixture of my childhood whose remembered stateliness fills me with such a sense of loss that I couldn't bring myself to write about her. Suffice to say she was so regal that at the Princess Royal's wedding in 1922, nearsighted E. M. Forster bowed to the elaborate towering cake in the belief that it was Queen Mary.

September 16, 2002

D EAR Gentle Readers: I've resolved to write this column without using the word "last" because nowadays it is tied up with that insufferable cliché, "I want to spend more time with my family." The only way to avoid it is to say what I have to say the NR way: This is my l**t column.

It shouldn't come as a complete surprise. I've been dropping hints about discarding my files and sorting my notebooks and journals. When writers start fiddling with their "literary papers," you know something is up. Another hint was my recent tribute to Aunt Ellen. I've long meant to write it and wanted to be sure to get it in before I left.

As to why I'm leaving, the simplest reason has to do with those "clicks" we hear in our heads: Ten years is enough. I've written this column for so long that you know everything I think about everything under the sun; there isn't an opinion of mine you don't already know, except perhaps the ones I have sense enough to keep to myself, but even there you can probably guess. If I were to continue, it would just be overkill.

Moreover, I'm tired. Count it up: I've been writing for 43 years, full time for 35. I started with true confessions at three-to-five cents a word. I've lost track of how many I wrote but it was enough to support myself off and on in the late '50s, with temp jobs at Manpower to get me over the dry spots. At first I was thrilled because it was *writing* and I was getting paid for it, but it soon paled: one dreary, guilt-ridden heroine after another, and having to dream up plots to go with titles like "I Stripped for My Husband's Bowling Team."

I put myself on automatic pilot and kept going for three years solely for the money, but eventually even that paled. Confessions were published anonymously, so I still hadn't experienced the thrill known as "seeing your name in print." One day in 1961 while perusing *The Writer's Market*, I decided to try the small religious mags. They paid peanuts but at least I would get a byline, so I put myself on a different automatic pilot and wrote a sweet, virtuous short story. I forget the title, but the name and address of the mag I sent it to are engraved on my mind: *The Christian*, P.O. Box 179, St. Louis, Mo. (There were as yet no zip codes.)

They bought it for $10. I wanted to frame the check but I needed the $10—that was a big bag of groceries then. I sold more stories to the religious market, including one to *St. Joseph's Magazine* called "After the Ball." The priest-editor had one problem with it initially: I had a scene in which a secular song is sung at a Requiem Mass, not allowed at the time, so I moved the scene to a funeral parlor and they bought it for $75.

How many automatic pilots can you go on before you qualify as a schizophrenic? My third one was the men's market. There were a lot of little mags—*Sir, Escapade, Dude, Gent*—that pre-dated *Playboy*, so I tried them all under my male pen name, Ruding Upton King, from my mother's and grandmother's maiden names. I hit at two (*Escapade* and *Dude*; $150 each), and got my first flattering rejection slips from the others ("Dear Mr. King: You write well, with an individual way of saying things").

I finally got a real job on the Woman's Page of the Raleigh *News & Observer*. It put me off real jobs for the rest of my life, but at least I had a regular salary coming in, so I stopped hacking and wrote the first of my utter failures known as "serious novels." It took me a while, but I finally realized that I am incapable of writing fiction because I am more interested in what people think than in what they do. Translation: I can't plot.

Formula fiction is another matter. My fourth excursion on automatic pilot was the genre known in the late '60s as "soft-core porn," i.e., 200-page paperback novels about sex. Typical title: *Box Lunch.* I wrote 48 in four years, composing them directly on the typewriter—first drafts be damned—finishing a book in a week. My top pay was $1,600 per manuscript; good money then, and the first real money I ever made, even if it did drive me nuts. One night I got an obscene phone call and snapped, "Oh, don't talk shop!"

When I couldn't take it anymore, I contacted an agent who suggested I write an article called *Confessions of a Lady Pornographer.* He sold it to *Penthouse.* Then *Harper's* bought my profile of the Good Ole Boy, which a hardback publisher asked me to expand into my first book, *Southern Ladies and Gentlemen.* It hit big, and I was launched. The publisher bought my second book, *Wasp, Where Is Thy Sting?* on the strength of the title alone; the big mags started asking me for articles, and I was hired as a ghostwriter for a famous lady. I went from tired to exhausted, working on my own book, the ghost job, and articles for *Cosmo,* all at the same time. One night I took a break to watch the news and heard Walter Cronkite say, "And that's the way it is, Monday, January 5, 1976." That's when I remembered it was my fortieth birthday.

You know the rest of the story. I've had many successes, but the one I'm proudest of is this column. I started it in 1992 and I've never missed a deadline or taken any time off. I've written some 230,000 words for NR, and not one of them on automatic pilot.

Many of you have expressed a wish for a bound collection of the complete "Misanthrope's Corner." It wasn't possible before because it couldn't be "complete" until I stopped writing it. Now I've stopped, so I am happy to announce that NR will publish a paperback edition of the whole enchilada sometime next year. The title, which sums up my contribution to editorial discussions, is *STET, Damnit!* Watch for the ads.

And so the time has come to say goodbye. I want to thank you for the delightful letters and thoughtful gifts you've sent me over the years. I've always said that NR readers are the crème de la crème, and you've proved me right time and time again. Here's looking at *you,* kids.

September 30, 2002

ACKNOWLEDGMENTS

THANKS are extended to *National Review* Art Director Luba Myts, who designed the book and its cover, to Associate Editor Sarah Maserati, who proofread the galleys, and to Publisher Edward Capano, with whom Miss King hashed out the details of this collection, and who then oversaw the project to its completion.

Thanks also, of course, to Miss King, without whose prose this collection would not exist. As an extra treat to her readers, Miss King has assembled and provided a delightful sampling of reviews of her books, which follows these acknowledgements. We are gratefiul for such. Enjoy, as you no doubt will.

Like death, taxes, and the sun rising in the East, it is a certainty that Florence King shall be sorely missed. Unmatched writer, loyal correspondent, fixture of *National Review*'s back page, and—whether or not she sought such—beloved literary institution, I'll speak for all here: we are in awe as to how but one, especially one so solitary and curmudgeonly, brought so much pleasure and laughter to so many.

To Florence King and to all that she has meant to *National Review* and its readers—*her* readers—which has been very much indeed, we raise our glasses and toast our dear Misanthrope, uttering her simple and favored sign-off . . .

Dewars.

Jack Fowler
Associate Publisher
National Review

EXTRACTED COMMENTS FROM REVIEWS

REFLECTIONS IN A JAUNDICED EYE

Publishers Weekly—"King expresses her opinions with the subtlety—and effectiveness—of a flamethrower . . . savagely funny."

Kirkus—"Wicked and witty, keeping alive the tradition of Dorothy Parker."

Washington Times (William F. Gavin)—"Judging by the acerbity of her manner and the lean, mean strength of her writing, she is obviously the love child of a union between H. L. Mencken and Dorothy Parker, abandoned in early childhood and raised by Westbrook Pegler. . . . Florence King is the real thing, a Southern spinster (her word) who does not suffer fools and likes to see fools suffer."

Booklist—"The author's acerbic humor runs wild. . . . King is way beyond irreverent and definitely a tonic for too many 'Have a nice day's'. . . . witty, opinionated, and occasionally scurrilous. . . ."

Washington Post (Jonathan Yardley)—". . . one of the few contemporary American essayists of sufficient pungency and wit as to be almost always worth reading. . . . if what she has is jaundice, would that everyone else could catch it."

New York Times (Frank Gannon)—"She's not real pleased with things. And she's honest about it."

Fredericksburg (Va.) *Free Lance-Star* (Robert P. Hilldrup)—"Miss King will never be found guilty of not having an opinion, and when her opinion is a negative one—as is most frequently the case—then she states her case with a rapier wit that leaves the skin peeled from her subject in a manner few have done so delightfully since Ambrose Bierce."

Richmond News Leader (Jay Strafford)—"Miss King writes with the kind of verve and wit (yes, wit, not mere humor) that few people manage these days. . . . Her candor and brilliance, as usual, make delightful reading."

Tulsa World (Ken Jackson)—"This small volume of essays—of urgent and sardonically violent opinion—is a dandy. It's a bludgeon and a stiletto, a cutting edge that also pounds and punctures clichés, modern society's morals and mores, self-satisfied egos and pompous fatheads. . . . she has the wonderful irreverence of truth—and the sharp-penned ability to make the most of it."

Danbury (Conn.) *News-Times* (Max MacNamee)—"When the good lord dished out sugar and spice and everything nice to little girls, Florence King was in the wrong line. Her constituent components are hellfire, brimstone, high-test vitriol, eye of newt and toe of frog—and one hell of a lot of talent. . . . Her writing sings, but it is a Viking's war chant. She displays the energy and devotion to convention of Lizzie Borden."

Raleigh News And Observer (Michael Skube)—". . . brassy, sassy and just a little too smart for the bland burghers of the middle class to feel entirely comfortable around. . . . She is also the one writer I would think twice about before crossing. Miss King observes no pieties, and turns positively viperish at the scent of a do-gooder. . . . Miss King does not hesitate to turn vicious when something clicks inside her. . . . Florence King could join them on Nightline and make breakfast links of all of them."

Richmond Times-Dispatch (Joy Winstead)—". . . filled with quotable lines to amuse and irritate readers in classic Florence King tradition."

Los Angeles Times (Pratapaditya Pal)—". . . insoucient wit. Although King appears on the surface to be a humorist, it would be a mistake to consider her social commentary lightweight. More than any of her male competitors, she is the Will Rogers of our day."

People Magazine (Joanne Kaufman)—"To say that Florence King doesn't suffer fools gladly is an understatement akin to suggesting that Fred Astaire could maneuver quite nicely on the dance floor."

Chattanooga Times (Travis Wolfe)—"Florence King, the thinking person's humorist, has put together another collection of snippety, mirth-making essays that will please her many devotees. . . . Miss King may be too smart for the masses. Ordinary people aren't likely to truly appreciate her talent for combining refinement with vulgarity, but some of us out here in readerland are madly in love with her. Kiss, kiss, Florence."

St. Louis Post-Dispatch (Colleen Kelly Warren)—"Florence King's vision may be jaundiced but it is sharp. . . . Readers, be forewarned. Florence King does not soften her opinions. She hones them razor-sharp, the better to offend you with, my dear."

Miami Herald (William Robertson, Book Editor)—"All week long I have been walking about, reading selected passages to friends. . . . Florence King's eye sure-ly is jaundiced, and I say we need more eyes like hers."

Palo Alto (Calif.) *Times Tribune* (Angela M. Owen)—"The quiet of a Sunday afternoon is disrupted by a giggle which soon turns to laughter, uncontrolled guf-faws and howls of glee while reading Florence King's latest book. . . . King does-n't mince words—even four-letter words, and nothing escapes her sharp tongue and wit."

Houston Chronicle (Mary Lins Shetler)—"Florence King is the queen of the 'old Southern lady humor'. . . . sometimes her wit is so rapier-sharp that the reader almost winces. No one, however, will be able to read this book without laughing aloud at least once. . . . King, peerless when it comes to astringent wit, speaks to many issues in this book—all worth our attention."

Memphis Commercial Appeal (Debbie Gilbert)—"If Dorothy Parker were alive and living in the South, her name would be Florence King. . . . Razor wit leaves few unnicked. . . . Penned with an X-Acto knife. . . . Unconcerned with alienating her audience, Ms. King insults just about every special interest group in America. She presents her case so effectively, however, that the reader is forced to agree. . . . Classically educated and impressively well-read, she's one of the few people in this country who could pass Bloom and Hirsch's cultural literacy test."

Roanoke (Va.) *Times & World News* (Mike Mayo, Book Editor)—"Florence King of Fredericksburg, Va., may well be the funniest writer in America. . . . filled with savage, bawdy humor. . . . dazzling. . . . genuine wit."

Greenville (Pa.) *Record-Argus* (unsigned)—"This woman can write. And think. And express herself."

Fort Lauderdale Sun-Sentinel (Monica Strand)—"Perhaps it would be more appro-priate to compare King to H. L. Mencken. . . . essential and not to be missed."

Charlotte (N.C.) *News & Observer* (William Porter)—"King, who delights in thrusting her stiletto into vulnerable underbellies, is in the first rank of American wits."

The American Spectator (Andrew Ferguson)—"Florence King is a 14-carat, top-of-the-chop, fully developed, salted-in-the-shell curmudgeon. She is also one of the most exhilarating essayists alive: occasionally raunchy but always full of high humor, casually erudite, animated by an original and constantly surprising turn of mind given shape in a prose style as clean and fresh as mountain air. . . . as a satirist and polemicist Florence King has few equals. . . . [Hers] is anti-Americanism of a distinctly American kind. After all, any country that can produce a critic like Florence King can't be half bad."

LUMP IT OR LEAVE IT

Kirkus—"The queen of the wicked-witty school of essayists, southern division . . . makes the likes of Mencken resemble namby-pamby pussycats. . . . King carries on, bitching with giddy, insolent wit, a troublesome polemicist with a ribald sense of humor."

Publishers Weekly—"Opinionated and entertaining. . . . Little escapes her stiletto wit. . . . These scattershot essays reach their targets."

Fredericksburg (Va.) *Free Lance-Star* (Dan Dervin)—"She is unfailingly humorous: a sort of Will Rogers with a hard-hat instead of a Stetson and a whip instead of a lariat. Her whiplash prose crackles with the carefree rigor of a true stylist."

Richmond News Leader (Jay Strafford)—"Florence King, with each successive hilarious and thoughtful book, has become a most worthy successor to the incomparable Miss Parker."

Washington Times (Wesley Pruden)—"Scourge of bloviators, pricker of the pompous and tormentor of the vainglorious. . . . Miss King's arguments [are] largely unanswerable because no one has ever made arguments quite like these. . . ."

Lambda Book Report (Susan Branch Smith)—"Yet, crotchety as she may be on some topics, Florence King is still one of our nimblest and most humorous storytellers. Her honesty—even on the lesbianism she now abdicates—has been unflinching, and no matter what we think of her current views on lesbianism we owe her a debt of gratitude for her outspokenness on all fronts. . . . Whatever Florence King writes I'll read."

Chicago Outlines (gay newspaper; by Allen Smalling)—"Look out, America, Florence King, the pistol-packin' Southern writer with the fastest aphorisms in town, has got a new book and she's mad as hell. In *Lump It or Leave It*, Fearless Flossie puts her pet peeves on display in a series of essays that are as witty and enlightening as they are—let's face it—infuriating. . . . But while King is a curmudgeon, and a politically conservative one at that, you'll find serious aspects to her writing that you won't get from the usual Andy Whiney fluffheads. King treats important topics like education and ethics with passion and wit, but without flippancy. . . . Readers who know King from her memoir *Confessions of a Failed Southern Lady* and last year's collection of essays *Reflections in a Jaundiced Eye* have another treat in store. For the rest of you, *Lump It or Leave It* is a fine introduction to the talents of this remarkable woman."

Booklist (Denise Perry)—"King sees the darndest things through her jaudiced eyes, but most astounding of all is her outrageous prose. . . . Irresistible reading."

Houston Chronicle (J. F. Peirce)—"King is a funny lady with a bawdy sense of humor. . . . She's an accomplished satirist. . . . She's an interesting and abrasive character. She admits to misanthropy and proudly proclaims, 'The liberals don't call me Ku Klux King for nothing.' Read at your own risk!"

Chattanooga Times (Travis Wolfe)—". . . clever and funny. . . . She is an astute observer of society."

The State (Columbia, SC; by William W. Starr)—"She is never less than interesting, often more than annoying and frequently outrageously amusing. Could anyone ask for more?"

Atlanta Constitution (Joyce Slater)—"Ms. King has made a personal and professional life out of violating a sacred tenet of Southern womanhood: she doesn't give a flying flip what other folks think of her. . . . Ms. King has an uncanny knack of hitting a nerve without half trying. . . . Mean she may be, but she sure is fun to read."

Chicago Sun-Times (Rita Mae Brown)—"Venom on a par with Dorothy Parker's literary bite. . . . Whether you put the book down or throw it down, you will have to admit that Florence King is an Equal Opportunity Offender."

Chronicles Magazine (Katherine Dalton)—"She is the kind of eccentric that Southern writers have made careers out of describing, the kind of person you could not possibly make up, and among the few American humorists who are actually funny. . . . you've got to hand it to the woman: her brand of she-devilry is consistent, which is more than most feminists can boast. . . . She is worth reading because she is funny. But what is best about her is that she will say what she thinks, and in a country in which free speech does not really exist, fewer and fewer people, especially writers, have the simple guts to indulge themselves in the luxury of speaking their mind. In the richest country in the world plain-spokenness is the one thing we cannot afford. Florence King's grit is her best quality."

The Columbus Dispatch (George Myers Jr.)—"Florence King's opinions usually are hair-raising without benefit of Nair or razor, but the razor cuts close. . . . she gargles neutron bombs for fun, can spit the eye out of a snake. . . . Don't ask for whom the mad hen scolds; the pen scolds for thee. . . . packs a wallop as large as her tolerance level is small. . . . King does not go gently into the malaise. . . . Readers shouldn't expect special-interest sympathy from this musketeer. She's all-for-none and none-for-all. No joke: She'd skewer anybody for a nickel."

Hartford Press (Kathy O'Connell)—"She is that rarest of creatures, a woman who is undeniably feminine in a distinctively, delightfully Southern way, and undeniably tough, frank, and sensible in a way entirely too many women are afraid to be. She's refreshingly independent, but without the whiny stridency of so many glum feminists; she sometimes sounds downright reactionary, but common sense oiled

with deadly wit is for her what a stiletto was for a member of the Black Hand. . . .
She writes so well it makes my toes curl."

Minneapolis Star-Tribune (Dave Wood)—"Florence King is the sort of writer
whose work you want to carry around with you to read from as you grab folks by
their lapels on street corners. For breathless razzmatazz you can't beat her. . . .
Florence King has strong opinions and is not afraid to state them strongly.
Sometimes excruciatingly conservative, at other times unclassifiable, King is consistent in one thing: When she makes up her mind on a subject and sits down to
write, she doesn't place her mug on one side of the fence and her wump on the
other. . . . Here's a book to cut through the syrup on your snow cone next Saturday
at Lake Nokomis."

Lincoln (Neb.) *Sunday Journal-Star* (Herb Hyde)—"She is irreverent and extremely funny yet serious when she needs to be. Hers are the sort of essays this country
needs more of; there is an overabundance of the stuffy kind."

Memphis Commercial Appeal (Perre Magness)—"She gores every sacred cow and
splatters blood all over the pages. . . . a rip-roaring jeremiad. There is something to
offend everybody here. And something that you wish you'd said."

Anderson (S.C.) *Independent-Mail* (Kathryn Smith)—"I'd hate to wind up as fod-
der for Miss King's misanthropic ruminations. But it sure is fun to read about the
people who have already fallen into her trough. . . . If being fiftysomething means
Miss King can produce a book as good as this one every year, I'm all for it."

San Diego Tribune (Arthur Salm)—"The world would be an awful place indeed
were it full of people like Florence King, but it would be a terribly dull one were
there none whatsoever. . . . King's essays are so well-written that they can be disconcerting and profoundly annoying. It's difficult to concentrate on exactly why
you disagree with something she says when you're busy admiring her style, and her
ear is so precise, her feel for the language so unerring that sometimes you have to
wonder—if you can remember to do so—whether she means what she says or she
just couldn't resist saying it. . . . Okay, so Florence King isn't a team player, and a
lot of people wouldn't want to hang out with her after the game. But you can't keep
that bat out of the lineup."

The Coast Book Review Service—"Profane, opinionated, perverse, preachy, ticked-
off, abused and more than a little hot and bothered, Florence King is a genuine
scream, a lady with a lot on her mind. . . . The essays are wonderful to read, the
outrageous outpourings from a woman's heart and soul, a person who has taken a
long look around and doesn't like what she sees. The humor is of the scalding variety and this woman's targets very often deserve the assault and battery they receive.
Lump It or Leave It, not a book for the faint of heart, is a biting, lacerating bit of
usiness from a talented, tyrannical writer who takes no prisoners. Whewww!"

St. Louis Post-Dispatch (Colleen Kelly Warren)—"I would read Florence King's books for no other reason than that they make me laugh out loud. Her essays resist categorization but all fall solidly in the realm of wit and excellence. . . . King minces no words but makes mincemeat of her targets. . . . Sooner or later, Florence King gets around to offending everyone. She brings an egalitarian approach to the hatchet job that is truly heartwarming to cranks and curmudgeons, regardless of their other alliances."

Jackson (Miss.) *Sun* (Jacque Hillman)—"Florence King has taken it upon herself in recent years to serve as the nation's Southern razor that shaves close. In *Lump It or Leave It* she holds her well-stropped wit ever ready and dumps the foibles of human nature from the tumbril onto her guillotine. . . . The reward is biting one-liners that nick, slice, and have no mercy in the kill. . . . She thoroughly alienates after a paragraph or two, only to have laughter rolling forth following the next one-liner. . . . Only the strong survive King."

Albemarle (N.C.) *News* (Ruth Moose)—"I laughed. I groaned. I slapped my sides and moaned. I think King is today's Dorothy Parker—but better. Bravo!"

Amarillo (Tex.) *News*—"You're likely to laugh out loud while being offended. . . . a writer who puts spleen back in style."

Chattanooga News-Free Press (Louise Rothe)—"She is an unconventional satirist, funny, unpredictable, sometimes raunchy. Nothing, however trite, escapes her wit."

Miami Herald (Marilyn Willison)—"King is one of the few nonfiction writers today blessed with the timing and the acerbity to make readers laugh out loud. . . . [she] brings to mind the aging and outspoken independent maiden aunt who figured so powerfully in many of our childhoods as a woman who could deflate pompous adults and entertain rambunctious youngsters with just a few well chosen words. . . . Visiting her in these pages is a stimulating foray into the mind of a fascinating con temporary observer of modern-day American life—one who, blessedly, has a unique and bitingly wicked sense of humor."

Grand Rapids Press (Nell Frisch)—"The lady can write. . . . She takes on the top-ics most people are taught to avoid discussing at dinner parties. . . . Even if you don't agree with her (and she is opinionated) you will enjoy her fearless and witty attacks."

Chicago Sun (Donna M. Farrell)—"There are no sacred cows left unscathed. . . . I managed to disturb the family and the cats with late night laughter and groans of dismay over her turn of phrase and misanthropic perspectives. The woman is such a witch—and I mean that in the very best sense of the word!"

Newport News (Va.) *Press* (Connie Granger)—"Florence King is out again! Out as in outspoken, outrageous and outlandish! . . . . *Lump It or Leave It* is the latest of the slim volumes that have brought laughter and tears to so many so unexpectedly in recent years. Righteous liberals will once again get all red in the face and sputter while square traditionalists gasp and guffaw. . . . The most circumspect citizens have been reduced to helpless (audible) chuckles by her commentary. Some read King's books in secret because they are embarrassed by her sometimes salty style. Others are unable to resist reading whole passages to anyone they can corner. There are rumors of otherwise respectable persons who have scribbled some of King's succinct prose in their ubiquitous pocket calendars and trot it out on occasion as their own wit and/or wisdom."

Milwaukee Journal (Roger Miller)—"Viciously witty, hilariously iconoclastic. . . . It is purely a howl. . . . It's clear she can turn a phrase. And the knife. . . . She's a mean lady, all right. With the pen."

AUSTRALIAN REVIEWS

The Melbourne Advertiser (Derek Whitelock)—"Ring the bells! Florence King is extra special. This delicious duo of paperbacks [*Reflections in a Jaundiced Eye* and *Confessions of a Failed Southern Lady*] flames like a shooting star across the insipid night sky of current reads.

"Here is a wicked, indignant wit, carapace to a wincing sensitivity and a hatred of humbug. Add high intelligence enriched by wide reading, and honesty to scalding point, about everything, including her own shortcomings, but notably about the human body and her sexual encounters.

"Sprinkle the brew thickly with blistering one-liners, something of an American literary art form, and never better demonstrated. Top it with a glittering prose style, a fierce love of the English language, which she can make strike like a snake or glimmer like a peacock (and a determination to defend it from trendy gobblydegook and computerese), and that's the Florence King dish, gourmet fare for quality starved readers.

"We need more damn-your-eyes humor like this in an increasingly solemn, conformist society. How to categorise Florence King? Touches of the young Dickens, the young Evelyn Waugh, of Dorothy Parker—but really she's unique, a one-off, to use a latinism—because like all lovers of language, she loves her Latin—Florence King is sui generis."

The Canberra Times (Herb Hild)—"Florence King's *Confessions of a Failed Southern Lady* is good fun indeed. Not always clean fun, mind, but that's even better."

The Canberra Times (Herb Hild)—"She does a terrific job of dismantling the myth. . . . The 15 essays in [*Southern Ladies and Gentlemen*] are social anthropology minus the jargon."